CENTRAL AMERICA GUIDE

YOUR PASSPORT TO GREAT TRAVEL!

CRITICAL ACCLAIM FOR OPEN ROAD PUBLISHING'S CENTRAL AMERICA TRAVEL GUIDES

"These guides are packed with reviews of moderately priced accommodations and eateries ... Glassman's reporting is highly opinionated, meticulous, and amazingly descriptive ... Useful for a first-time visitor or veteran traveler, **Open Road Guides** equip the reader with countless tips and personal, valuable advice."
Travel Books & Language Center

"If you have to choose one guidebook, Paul Glassman's **Costa Rica Guide** provides a wealth of practical information, with a sharp eye and a sense of humor."
Travel and Leisure

"**Belize Guide** is *the* book you need. Don't leave home without it. Invaluable."
International Travel News

Guatemala Guide is "filled with useful information ... thoroughly explores the territory and subject."
Booklist

ABOUT THE AUTHOR

Paul Glassman is the leading authority on Central American travel. He has been writing the classic travel guides to the region since 1975. His other books include *Costa Rica Guide, Belize Guide, Honduras & Bay Islands Guide,* and *Guatemala Guide* – all published by Open Road Publishing and available at your local bookstore.

HIT THE OPEN ROAD – WITH OPEN ROAD PUBLISHING!

Open Road Publishing now has guide books to exciting, fun destinations on four continents, but, oddly enough, some people out there still don't know who we are! We're old college pals and veteran travelers who decided to join forces to bring you the best travel guides available anywhere!

No small task, but here's what we offer:

• All Open Road publications are written by authors, authors with a distinct, opinionated point of view – not some sterile committee or team of writers. Our authors are experts in the areas covered and are polished writers.

• Our guides are geared to people who want great vacations, great value, and great tips for both standard tourist sites and fun, unique alternatives.

• We're strong on the basics, but we also provide terrific choices for those looking to get off the beaten path and experience the country or city – not just see it or pass through it.

• We give you the best, but we also tell you about the worst and what to avoid. Nobody should waste their time and money on their hard-earned vacation because of bad or inadequate travel advice.

• Our guides assume nothing. We tell you everything you need to know to have the trip of a lifetime – presented in a fun, literate, no-nonsense style.

• And, above all, we welcome your input, ideas, and suggestions to help us put out the best travel guides possible.

CENTRAL AMERICA GUIDE

YOUR PASSPORT TO GREAT TRAVEL!

PAUL GLASSMAN

OPEN ROAD PUBLISHING

Chapters 2–5, Copyright©1995 by Paul Glassman
Maps & Chapters 1, 6–8, Copyright©1995 by Open Road Publishing*
ISBN 1-883323-17-7
Library of Congress Catalog Card No. 94-69848

Front cover photo courtesy of Guatemala Tourist Commission. Top back cover photo by Mark W. Russell; bottom back cover photo courtesy of Belize Tourist Board.

*The chapters on Panama, Nicaragua, and El Salvador were prepared by the staff of Open Road Publishing.

Every effort has been made to be as accurate and up-to-date as possible, but neither the author nor publisher assume responsibility for the services provided by any business listed in this guide, for any errors or omissions, or for any loss, damage, or disruptions in your travel for any reason.

TABLE OF CONTENTS

APPENDIX A: FOOD & DRINK IN CENTRAL AMERICA

APPENDIX B: WHAT TO PACK

INDEX

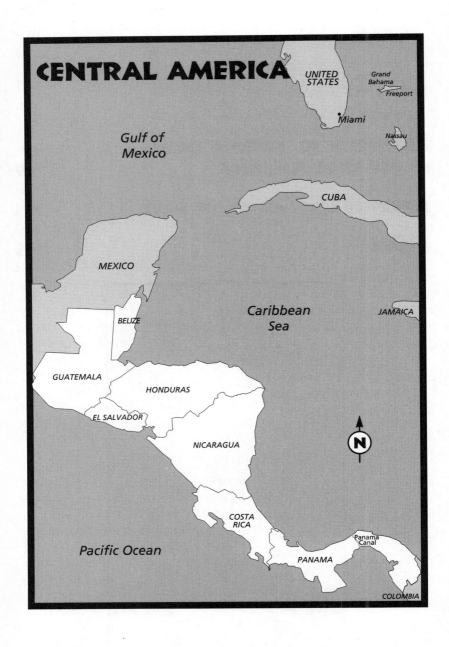

1. INTRODUCTION

Not far away from our busy lives and workaday world is one of the most beautiful regions in the world, an exciting place called Central America. With good reason – as you'll learn from the pages that follow – Central America has become one of the world's leading travel destinations.

Travel with Open Road and discover a world of pristine beaches, mysterious cloud forest reserves, picture-perfect lakes and volcanoes, and exotic wildlife from the elusive quetzal to the majestic jaguar. We'll lead you to the best diving in this hemisphere, unparalleled sports fishing, and exciting rafting and sailing adventures. And when it's time to unwind, we'll show you some of the most terrific beaches in the world – or perhaps a secluded mountain hot spring is more your speed?

Interested in Mayan ruins? We'll take you to Tikal in Guatemala, Copán in Honduras, Altun Ha in Belize. Fascinated by the unique Indian cultures? We'll show you how to stay with a Mayan family, and make it possible for you to travel along a remote jungle river by dugout canoe. Is shopping your thing? We'll guide you to the many colorful markets and bazaars in big cities and small towns.

When it comes to lodging and restaurants, the countries of Central America offer great choices. Stay in a beachside cabina, relax in a rainforest lodge, check out a small bed-and-breakfast, live it up in an all-inclusive resort; it's all here. And you'll be treated to great food and restaurant choices, from elegant waterview dining to wonderful roadside eateries. Feast on *carne asada*, fried plantains, the fruits of the sea – and top it off with the region's fantastic coffee.

In this book you'll find all the travel information you'll need to have the trip of a lifetime to Costa Rica, Belize, Honduras, Guatemala, Panama, Nicaragua, and El Salvador. We present extensive travel planning advice, showing you how to get there, how to get around, what to see – and most of all, how to *experience* the countries of Central America. Read on!

2. COSTA RICA

HISTORY

Even before the first Spaniards arrived, what was to become **Costa Rica** differed from neighboring lands. To the north, in what are now Mexico, Belize, Guatemala, Honduras and El Salvador, and to the south, in mainland South America, civilizations arose based on the cultivation and harvest of bountiful crops of corn by large groups of settled people. Some societies were so powerful and complex that they altered the landscape with great cities, subjugated peoples for hundreds of miles around, traded regularly with distant lands, wrote histories, and made complex astronomical calculations.

Archaeologists have been able to trace a shadowy cultural history of the first peoples of Costa Rica, using the objects they left behind. Pottery from Nicoya from before the time of Christ shows similarities to Mesoamerican styles of the period, with red coloring on a buff background. Elsewhere in Costa Rica, pottery was made in a single color, as in South America. A few hundred years later, jade appeared in Nicoya and central Costa Rica, probably imported from Guatemala.

The northern influence is evident also in the appearance at the same time of the Mexican god Tlaloc on pottery in Guanacaste, in the northwest. In the sixth century, gold from South America began to appear in southern Costa Rica, possibly following the fall of the empire of Teotihuacán in Mexico, and the disruption of maritime trade routes.

By 1000 A.D., multicolored pottery was the norm in Guanacaste and Nicoya, and houses were built in rectangular shapes, all attributes of cultures to the north. Elsewhere in Costa Rica, houses were circular, while pottery featured appliquéd decoration, both characteristics of areas to the south. But while some of the influences of north and south are evident, the dividing line between the two in Costa Rica was generally faint and meandering.

In Costa Rica, there was no empire to be subdued, and usually no surrender. Riches were elusive, and few slaves were imported. Soldiers and fortune-hunters gave way to subsistence farmers. With the passage of time, the settlement came to have more in common with English and French colonies in North America than with other Spanish dominions.

It was **Christopher Columbus** himself who discovered Costa Rica, and whose sailors were the first Europeans to be discovered by the natives of Costa Rica. The encounter took place on or soon after September 18, 1502, when Columbus, on his fourth voyage to the New World, took shelter from a storm at what is now Uvita Island, just off the port of Limón.

Short-lived settlements were established on both coasts, but for more than half a century from the arrival of Columbus, there was no permanent Spanish foothold. Finally, in 1561, **Juan de Cavallón**, with a party of Spaniards and domestic animals, founded the successful settlement of Garcimuñoz in the Pacific lowlands. For lack of finding gold, however, Cavallón himself withdrew.

It was under **Juan Vásquez de Coronado**, Cavallón's successor as governor, that Costa Rica's course began to differ from that of the other Spanish provinces. The search for gold was abandoned, and Vásquez attempted to deal with the natives in friendship. Spaniards cultivated crops for their own consumption, lived mostly in peace, but achieved no great prosperity.

Despite the initial peaceful settlement of the valley, conflict with the natives was inevitable, and the Spaniards dealt with them in characteristically harsh fashion. A few were subjected, and came to live peacefully alongside the Spaniards, to serve them and eventually to intermarry with them. Others were conquered and removed to areas where they could be easily watched over. By far the largest numbers refused to submit.

Without native labor to exploit, without crops to grow for export on a large scale, restricted in trade by Spanish mercantile policy, hemmed into a small valley by hostile environments, Costa Rica stagnated, and the very name of the colony (*Rich Coast*) must at times have seemed a cruel hoax. No great public buildings were erected. Little moved out of the province but small amounts of meat, cacao, honey and potatoes. Traders faced a journey to port made hazardous by Indians. Sea traffic was ravaged by pirates.

Independence, when it came, had little initial effect on Costa Rica. Spain had administered the five Central American provinces from Guatemala; toward the end of the colonial period, Costa Rica was reduced to the status of a dependency of Nicaragua. In practice, however, Costa Rica had long gone its own way. Without the ambitions and class conflicts of the other colonies, living at subsistence, Costa Rica required only minimal government.

News of the independence of Central America, declared in Guatemala on September 15, 1821, reached Costa Rica at the end of the year. A provincial government was hastily formed, and soon acceded to annexation to Mexico. Opinion on the association was divided, however, and a short civil war was fought. The forces of the town of San José, rejecting Mexico, gained the upper hand. In the end, the Mexican empire collapsed in 1823, and Costa Rica joined the **United Provinces of Central America**, with full autonomy in its internal affairs. The most important result of independence was the elimination of Spanish trading restrictions, but since the world was not beating a path to Costa Rica's door, even this freedom was of limited value.

In 1848, all connections with the moribund Central American federation were severed. A strong leader emerged once again in 1849 with the election to the presidency of **Juan Rafael Mora**, a representative of the new coffee aristocracy.

The topsy-turvy politics of Costa Rica in the nineteenth century were only a sideshow to the economic changes that were taking place. Costa Rica was transformed, as coffee came to be cultivated on a large scale.

Inevitably, the rewards of coffee cultivation were not distributed evenly. Some families acquired large expanses of land, transformed their wealth into political power, and developed tastes for culture and the finer things in life that the nation had done without for so long. But despite the emergence of a class structure, there appeared to be land and profit enough for all, and no sector of society failed to advance.

Although he was autocratic, **Tomás Guardia** saw himself as a benefactor of his people. Under his government and those of his two successors, roads were built and improved, public buildings erected, capital punishment abolished, and primary education made free and compulsory, and independent of the church. Coffee earnings, and borrowings against future earnings, financed the expenditures.

The problems of shipping coffee led indirectly to the development of a second major export crop. Coffee was sent by oxcart to the Pacific port of Puntarenas, then on a long voyage around South America to markets in the eastern United States and Europe. To shorten the journey, President Guardia ordered the construction of a railroad line to the Atlantic. Bananas were planted as a stop-gap measure to provide revenue for the financially troubled project.The new crop proved immensely profitable, and large areas were soon planted in the fruit.

Costa Rica's modern, democratic tradition started with the election of 1889, the first that was honest, open, and direct. Peaceful transitions of power, and more active participation in politics by all sectors of the population, characterized the years that followed.

Under **Rafael Angel Calderón Guardia**, a physician who became president in 1940, the measured pace of reform continued as the first social security legislation was enacted. Calderón was to be one of the more controversial figures in modern Costa Rica. His social programs — including paid vacations, unemployment compensation and an income tax — and his early declaration of war on Germany, offended many of his original conservative supporters.

In 1948, Calderón ran again for the presidency, and lost to Otilio Ulate. But the government claimed fraud, and the legislature annulled the results. Tensions rose, and finally broke out into an open rebellion led by **José Figueres**. Armed by the governments of Guatemala and Cuba, the rebels prevailed in a few weeks over the army. The short civil war was the bloodiest in Costa Rica's history, with more than 2000 killed.

José Figueres led an interim administration that attempted to restore order to a disrupted nation. Banks were nationalized and taxes restructured. Most curiously following a civil war, and amid threats from domestic plotters and opponents in exile, Figueres and his allies chose not to purge and restructure the army, but to abolish it altogether, retaining only those elements of the old security forces that they considered appropriate in the Costa Rican context: a national police force, and the military bands.

A constituent assembly proceeded to write a constitution that rejected some of Figueres' proposals, but extended social welfare programs, gave the vote to women, ended discrimination against blacks, and established an electoral tribunal with broad powers to ensure the honesty of elections. Following the legislative elections of 1949, Figueres stepped aside, and **Otilio Ulate**, the victor of the disputed 1948 vote, assumed office as president.

Despite the bitterness of the civil war, politics in Costa Rica since 1948 have been remarkably peaceful and democratic. Exiles have threatened invasions on two occasions, but have found no internal support, and their movements have fizzled. José Figueres himself twice served as president, from 1953 to 1957 and from 1970 to 1974, and his National Liberation Party has dominated electoral politics. But it has only twice held the presidency for more than a single term.

Through the 1980s, unstable coffee prices, oil bills, disruptions of trade in the Central American Common Market, the arrival of refugees from Nicaragua, the shutdown of banana plantations in the face of higher taxes and labor strife, and the costs of social programs all gave the society and economy a jolt. The government has at times been hard-pressed to meet payments on loans from abroad, which take up most export earnings, and the currency has been regularly devalued. National income has fallen in some years, and unemployment has risen.

Elsewhere in the region, economic crises have led to turmoil and bloodshed. In Costa Rica, administrations that have failed to stabilize the economy have been turned out of office democratically. But while Costa Ricans are proud of their stability, it has provided little consolation when they have had to make do with less.

Internationally, Costa Rica has continued to exert a strong moral influence as a nation that has officially renounced the use of arms. Administrations have generally been pro-Western, and some have given more than passive support to armed movements in neighboring countries.

Most recently, reconciliation between all parties in conflict in Central America has been actively promoted. For his key role in putting together a regional peace plan, **President Oscar Arias** was awarded the 1987 Nobel Peace Prize.

The successor to Arias is **Rafael Angel Calderón Fournier**, son of former president Rafael Angel Calderón Guardia. Calderón took office in 1990 with strong business support, coming back after a string of electoral defeats. He has promised to streamline Costa Rica's bureaucracy and pay more attention to domestic problems than his predecessor. But under heavy pressure from the International Monetary Fund, his first actions included unpopular increases in sales taxes and fees for government services.

LAND & PEOPLE

Costa Rica stretches from sea to sea. Sandy beaches fringed by palms, grassy savannahs, warm inland valleys, temperate plateaus, smoking volcanoes, frosty peaks, forested slopes and steamy jungles succeed each other across the landscape. Twice as many species of tree are native to the many regions of the country as to the continental United States. More than a thousand types of orchids flourish. The national wildlife treasures are still being discovered and inventoried.

Yet, by most standards, Costa Rica is small. From north to south or east to west, the country runs only 200 miles. The shortest distance between oceans is only 75 miles.

Costa Rica drapes itself upon a jagged, mountainous spine that runs from northwest to southeast, part of the great intercontinental Sierra Madre-Andes chain. The volcanic **Guanacaste**, **Tilarán**, and **Central** ranges, separated from each other by relatively low passes and valleys, rise successively higher down the northern two-thirds of the country. Traversing the south of Costa Rica and continuing into Panama is the **Talamanca** range, which encompasses the highest points in the country. Cool and even frigid, the mountain slopes remain in part in their natural, breathtaking condition, but are more and more being deforested and exploited as pasture.

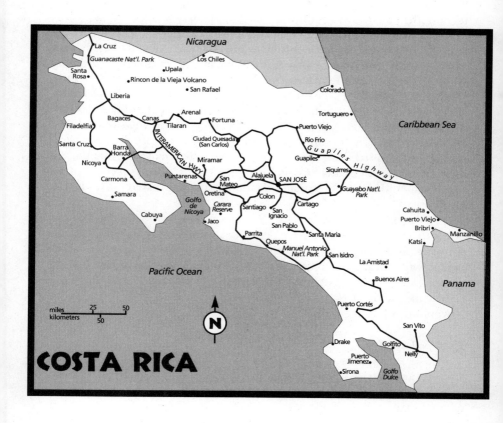

South of the volcanoes of the Central Range is the **Meseta Central**, or **Valle Central** — the Central Plateau, or Central Valley — in every sense the heart of Costa Rica. Measuring only about 20 by 50 miles, the Central Valley covers an area roughly equivalent to that of metropolitan Los Angeles. Yet packed into it are not only the capital city and most of the major population centers, but the richest farmland. Ranging from about 3,000 to 5,000 feet above sea level, with rolling, forested, and farmed terrain, the valley also abounds in natural beauty.

East of the Central Valley, between the Talamanca Range and the Pacific, is the valley of the **General River**, which was isolated from the rest of the country until the construction of the Pan American Highway in the 1950s. Here, at elevations lower and warmer than those of the Central Valley, is Costa Rica's fastest-growing concentration of family farms, many operated by migrants from the more crowded core of the country.

Toward the Pacific, Costa Rica tilts precipitously down a slope broken by fast-flowing rivers, some of them harnessed to provide electrical power. In the northwest, on the edge of the hilly **Nicoya Peninsula**, are miles of sandy beach where Costa Rica's new resort industry is concentrating. Just inland are the savannahs of Guanacaste, populated mostly by fat, grazing cattle.

To the northeast of Costa Rica's mountainous spine, the land slopes down to a broad, low-lying triangle of hardwood forest and jungle, with two sides formed by the Caribbean Sea and the 300-kilometer (186-mile) border with Nicaragua. This is the land of eternal rainfall, where coastal storms can blow in at any time of the year. Elsewhere in Costa Rica, the central mountains block Caribbean storms, and it rains only from May to November, when the winds are from the Pacific.

Flora & Fauna

Costa Rican flora and fauna, and tropical flora and fauna in general, are too varied to be treated justly in a small section of this book, or even in a few books devoted exclusively to the subject. Botanists refer to the natural exuberance of the tropics as "species richness." An area that supports two or three types of trees in the temperate zones might lodge dozens or even hundreds of plant species from ground level to forest canopy in the tropics.

Some dimensions of this natural abundance in Costa Rica: more than 2,000 species of tree have so far been catalogued, twice as many as in the continental United States. Two-thirds of all known seed plants are found in Costa Rica. And there are over 1,000 orchids, ranging from the *guaria morada*, the purple national flower, down to those with blossoms too tiny to be casually noticed; more than 800 species of fern; and so on.

As a bridge between two continents, Costa Rica is home to animal forms both familiar and exotic. More than 750 species of bird inhabit Costa Rica, as many as in all of the United States. These range from common jays and orioles to large-beaked toucans and macaws, and the exquisite and elusive long-tailed quetzals of the trogon family. The national list includes 50 species of hummingbird, 45 tanagers and 72 flycatchers. A checklist of birds of Costa Rica is available for $2 from *Natural History Tours, Box 1089, Lake Helen, FL 32744.*

As for mammals, monkeys abound, among them howler, spider, white-faced, and the tiny marmoset. White-tailed deer, raccoons, and rattlesnakes, all common in North America, live alongside their South American cousins, the brocket deer, coatimundi, and bushmaster. Sea turtles — six of the world's eight species — nest on Costa Rica's shores. Alligators, peccaries (hatchback versions of the domestic pig), tepezcuintles (pacas), jaguars, ocelots, pumas and many other "exotic" species are still not uncommon in parts of the country.

Paradoxically, many of these species are difficult to sight. In settled areas, native animals and plants have been wiped out by hunting, land-clearing and poaching. In less-settled areas, the lack of roads and trails keeps out the interested visitor. Fortunately, however, many species can be seen in Costa Rica's national parks.

People

To themselves, and to those who know them, Costa Ricans are **Ticos**. The nickname derives from the way they speak. Diminutives are common in the language of Latin America. A moment becomes a "little moment," a *momentito*, to indicate "in a little while." But in Costa Rica, the word is *momentico*, and the peculiar ending is applied to the people who use it.

Like their Spanish language, which was locked away for centuries from the outside world by mountains, jungles, and seas, Costa Ricans are gracious, courteous, traditional, even a bit archaic. The *retreta* — that circling of boys and girls in the central square on weekend evenings, with shy glances that could, just could, lead to romance — hung on in Costa Rica even as it was disappearing from elsewhere in Latin America and Spain. Now, dating is the norm. But old-fashioned prudishness survives in public. Movies, for one, are heavily censored.

Blacks were present in early colonial Costa Rica in small numbers as slaves, but those who survived the harsh conditions and ill treatment of that era merged into the general population. A later generation of blacks arrived in Costa Rica at the close of the nineteenth century, from Jamaica and elsewhere in the West Indies, to construct the railroad from San José to the Atlantic, and remained to labor on the banana plantations established by Minor Keith.

The 30,000 blacks in the country today more and more consider themselves Costa Ricans. All legal discrimination ended with the constitution of 1949. Most blacks who attended school since that time learned Spanish as well as English. Bilingualism has earned some good jobs in commerce and the travel industry in the Central Valley, though, as Protestants, they stand apart from other Costa Ricans.

Indians, or native Americans, are Costa Rica's forgotten minority. Their numbers are few — 20,000, perhaps even less — and they live in small groups away from the centers of population.

The Indians of the Talamanca group live in the forested valleys north of the Talamanca mountain range, and in the adjacent Caribbean lowlands. Their ancestors were forced into the area from central Costa Rica and from the Caribbean coast, and there they have remained, except for some who have migrated to the Pacific region. Two tribes survive, the **Cabécar** and the **Bribri**, composed of the remnants of a number of pre-Conquest tribes.

The **Borucas** of the southern Pacific coastal area, near Panama, still live largely where they did before the Conquest. Aside from working their land communally, they live like other rural Costa Ricans. But by their racial heritage, their particular devotion to the celebration of the Immaculate Conception, and through pre-Columbian ritual that survives as superstition, the Borucas maintain a separate identity.

Other Indian groups are the **Chorotegas** of the Nicoya peninsula, who lost the use of their separate language years ago, and are almost indistinguishable from the mestizo, or mixed-blood, Costa Ricans of the area; and a few **Guatusos**, who live in the northern border lowlands east of the Guanacaste mountains.

PLANNING YOUR TRIP

As Latin American countries go, Costa Rica can be rated a relatively carefree destination. Clean hotels are available almost everywhere, the food is generally safe to eat and sometimes of gourmet quality, and service is competent, even gracious. Transportation is well-developed and comfortable in many parts of the country. Officials generally do not expect to be bribed.

Climate & Weather

Most visitors arrive in Costa Rica during the northern winter and spring, and for obvious reasons. This is when it's best to get away from the cold, of course. But it also coincides with the dry season, from about November through April, when the western side of Costa Rica receives hardly any rain, and when temperatures are usually most pleasant.

But there are a few good words to be said for the rainy times, which promoters have taken to calling the "green season" — and not without reason. On the western side of the country, the annual drought is broken in May, and the fields turn green and exuberant. Facing the Caribbean, where the rains take no annual vacation, the downpours are heavier and last longer. For rafters, the rivers are full of water. And for wise travelers, hotel occupancy drops, and so do rates.

And, though it's the rainy season, it never (well, hardly ever), rains all day. That's because weather forms in a different way than in the temperate latitudes, where a mass of clouds could stay in one place for days. In Costa Rica, a rainstorm is usually a daily phenomenon in season, blowing up from the coast on winds that follow the warming of the day, and dispersing after a few hours.

Highland Weather

The highland climate of the major cities — San José, Cartago, Heredia and Alajuela — is often called "eternal spring," a term that is not used merely to attract tourists. Temperatures are in the low seventies Fahrenheit (about 22 Centigrade) during the day throughout the year. High mountains and volcanoes to the north of San José block the clouds that blow in from the Atlantic, and it rains only from April to November or December, when winds are from the Pacific. But a long rainy day is a rarity in the Central Valley.

Mornings are generally clear, followed by a few hours of heavy downpour in the afternoon, sometimes lasting into the night. Clouds hold in the heat of the day; nights are warm. The rainy season is called *invierno* (winter), even though Costa Rica is in the northern hemisphere. In the dry times, or *verano* (summer), not even the thought of rain occurs. Days are uniformly warm and sunny. Nights are clear, and the temperature can sometimes drop into the fifties (about 10 Centigrade).

Pacific Coast Weather

Down toward the Pacific coast, the climate is hotter. In Puntarenas, daytime temperatures are in the nineties (above 32 degrees Centigrade) throughout the year. But at the beaches, refreshing breezes moderate the heat. The rainy season is the same as in the Central Valley, but precipitation is heavier. The exceptions are the extreme north and extreme south. The Guanacaste plain suffers periodic droughts, which bother farmers more than visitors. And around Golfito, near Panama, peculiarities in the mountains and winds bring rains throughout the year.

Atlantic Coast Weather

On the Atlantic slope of Costa Rica, storms may blow in at any time, though rainfall is lightest from February through April and in September. Precipitation is over ten feet at Limón in most years, and even higher to the north. Storms appear suddenly and with a frightening fury, but they are usually quickly gone. Temperatures are generally as hot on the Caribbean as on the Pacific, and the humidity is more enervating.

Higher Altitude Weather

The higher altitudes are cooler. Frosts occur above 2,150 meters (7,000 feet) during the dry season. And atop volcanoes and in the Talamanca mountains, temperatures can plunge from warm to below freezing in a few hours.

National Holidays

Take a quick look at the list of public holidays below. If any occur while you're in Costa Rica, don't plan to get anything done on that day except relaxing.

January 1	*New Year's Day*
March 19	*Day of St. Joseph (San José)*
Moveable	*Holy Thursday*
Moveable	*Good Friday*
	(Many businesses close all Holy Week)
April 11	*Battle of Rivas*
May 1	*Labor Day*
Moveable	*Corpus Christi*
June 29	*Day of Saints Peter and Paul*
July 25	*Annexation of Guanacaste*
August 2	*Day of Our Lady of the Angels*
	(specially celebrated in Cartago)
August 15	*Assumption Day*
September 15	*Independence Day*
October 12	*Columbus Day (Día de la Raza)*
December 8	*Immaculate Conception*
December 24, 25	*Christmas Eve and Christmas*
December 31	*New Year's Eve*

On Good Friday, processions reenact the Passion of Christ, in San José and in villages throughout the country, often with scores of participants in full Roman regalia.

TRAVEL SPECIALISTS

Outdoor Excursions

Mariah Wilderness Expeditions, *P.O. Box 248, Point Richmond, CA 94807, tel. 800-4-MARIAH or 510-233-2303, fax 510-233-0956.* This is a white-water rafting company that grew to become a comprehensive travel planner for Costa Rica, with trips including, but not limited to, sea kayaking, mountain biking, and environment-oriented excursions.

Nature Tours

- **Voyagers International**, *P. O. Box 915, Ithaca, NY 14851, tel. 800-633-0299 or 607-257-3091, fax 607-257-3699.* Voyagers' programs, emphasizing natural history, are run by a Costa Rican travel planner who is also a biologist. Group departures are scheduled throughout the year, and include Monteverde, the Osa Peninsula, river trips, and can include rafting, all accompanied by a naturalist.
- **Adventures Costa Rica**, *16 North 9th St., Bozeman, MT 59715, tel. 406-586-9942, fax 586-0995*
- **McTravel Services Inc.**, *20378 Fraser Hwy., Langley, BC V3A 4G1, Canada, tel. 604-530-5855* (operated by a Canadian and a Costa Rican)
- **Go Travel**, *4930 Côte des Neiges, Montreal, Quebec H3V 1H2*
- **Multicentre Costa Rica**, *4571 St-Denis, Montréal, Québec H2J 2L4, tel. 514-847-9279, fax 847-9280. Specialité: services en francais.*
- **Journeys**, *4011 Jackson Rd, Ann Arbor, MI 48103*
- **Pioneer Tours**, *Box 22063, Carmel, CA 93922*
- **Blyth & Co.**, *68 Scollart St., Toronto, Ontario M5R 1G2*
- **Costa Rica Experts**, *3540 N W 13th St., Gainesville, FL 32609*
- **Ocean Connection**, *16728 El Camino Real, Houston, TX 77062*
- **Mountain Travel**, *6420 Fairmount Ave., El Cerrito, CA 94530*
- **Overseas Adventure Travel**, *349 Broadway, Cambridge, MA 02139*
- **Preferred Adventures**, *One West Water St., St. Paul, MN 55107, tel. 612-222-8131, fax 612-222-4221*
- **Quest Nature Tours**, *920 Yonge St., Toronto, Ontario, M4W 9Z9, tel. 800-387-1483, specializes in birding trips*
- **Quester's Tours and Travel**, *257 Park Ave. So., New York, NY 10010*
- **Sierra Club Outings**, *730 Polk St., San Francisco, CA 94109*
- **Special Expeditions**, *720 Fifth Avenue, New York, NY 10019*
- **UET Travel**, *8619 Reseda Blvd., Northridge, CA 91324, tel. 818-886-0633, fax 818-993-5243*
- **Wilderness Travel**, *801 Allston Way, Berkeley, CA 94710*
- **Worldwide Adventures**, *920 Yonge St., Toronto, Ontario M4W 9Z9*

SOURCES FOR MORE INFORMATION ABOUT COSTA RICA

Tourist Board

- **Costa Rica Tourist Board** (*Instituto Costarricense de Turismo*)*Tel. 800-327-7033.* Use this number to request a mailing that includes some basic flyers about Costa Rica. Or write to:
- **Instituto Costarricense de Turismo**, *Apartado Postal 777-1000, San José, Costa Rica. Tel. 800-343-6332.* Allow a month for a response to a written or telephone inquiry. This is the number for information for

travel agents. It is answered in San José. *Call [2]231733 from within Costa Rica.*
- In the U.S., write or call **Costa Rica Tourist Board**, *1101 Brickell Avenue, ground floor, Miami, Florida 33131; Tel. 305-358-2150.*

Embassies
- **Costa Rican Embassy**, *1825 Connecticut Ave. NW, Washington, DC 20009,* tel. *202-234-2945*
- **Costa Rican Embassy**, *150 Argyle St., Ottawa, Ontario, Canada, K2P 1B7,* tel. *613-234-5762*
- **Costa Rican Embassy**, *14 Lancaster Gate, London W2 3LH, tel. 71-723-1772*

Consulates in the U.S.
- *8 South Michigan Ave., Chicago, IL 60603*
- *4200 Republic Bank Tower, Dallas, TX 75201*
- *2616 South Loop West, Houston, TX 77054*
- *1343 West Olympic Blvd., Los Angeles, CA 90015*
- *28 West Flagler St., Miami, FL 33130*
- *2 Canal St., New Orleans, LA 70130*
- *80 Wall St., New York, NY 10005*

GETTING TO COSTA RICA

It's always a good idea to re-check entry requirements, with either a Costa Rican consulate or a reliable travel agent, before you leave home. Recent regulations:

Citizens of the United States or Canada must have a tourist card or a passport to enter Costa Rica.

Passport holders are issued 90-day visas upon arrival at the international airport. Visas for overland travel to Costa Rica should be obtained in advance at a Costa Rican consulate.

Tourist cards are issued at the check-in counter by airlines serving Costa Rica, upon presentation of a birth certificate or other substantial documentation, accompanied by a photo identification, such as a driver's license. Tourist cards cost $2 and are valid for 30 days. Monthly extensions may be obtained at the immigration department in San José (see below).

By Air

Air traffic to Costa Rica is undergoing a boom, with service available from more and more cities. Major gateways for non-stop travel from the United States to Costa Rica are Miami, Orlando, New Orleans, and Houston. Service is also available, usually with intermediate stops, from Los Angeles, New York, and Dallas.

With a change of plane, you can reach San José via Mexico or Honduras. And direct flights operate between San José and San Juan, Puerto Rico; the Colombian island of San Andrés; and many cities on the South American mainland.

PASSPORTS SI!

Passports are preferable to tourist cards as an entry document for citizens of the United States or Canada. They allow an unquestioned stay of 90 days, and are required by most banks in order to cash a travelers check.

Travelers from countries of Western Europe can also enter Costa Rica with a passport only, as can citizens of Argentina, Australia, Brazil, Colombia, Guatemala, Iceland, Israel, Mexico, New Zealand, Japan, Panama, Romania, South Korea, and Venezuela. Permission is granted initially to stay for 30 to 90 days.

Travelers from most other countries, and all business travelers, must have a passport with a visa issued in advance. Check with your airline or a Costa Rican consulate for requirements.

All tourists may be required to demonstrate their financial resources upon arrival, as well as show a return or onward ticket.

Land borders are officially open from 6:30 a.m. to 10 p.m., with breaks from 11 a.m. to 12:30 p.m. and from 5:30 p.m. to 6:30 p.m.

Fares

As any slightly experienced traveler will tell you, what counts is not what the fares are, but what fare your travel agent can get. An unrestricted round-trip fare between New York and San José can be as high as $1,260. Advance-booking and seat sales will cut the price by half or even more. Travel agencies that do a volume business negotiate lower fares. For example, Voyagers International will sell a ticket from New York for as little as $422, when you buy a tour. Cheap packages can be improvised to take advantage of low fares.

Stopovers can add to the value of your ticket. On **Lacsa**, you can stop in Guatemala if you're traveling from New York, or in Mexico City or Guatemala on the way from Los Angeles.

Charter Flights

Charters from Canada are operated throughout the year by **Fiesta Holidays** in Toronto, **Nolitours** in Montreal, and **Fiesta West** in Vancouver, among others. Charters often depart at odd hours, but they save multiple takeoffs and landings, and the price is right. Currently, very few charters operate from the States.

Information on charter flights is available only through local travel agencies, not from the company that organizes the charter. Prices vary according to where and when you make your reservation, so check around before you pay. There are some bargains available — as little as $700 Canadian funds for your ticket plus a week at a hotel.

Most charter flights land at the international airport near San José. Flights are planned for the airport at Liberia, not far from the Pacific beaches of northwest Costa Rica.

AIRLINES WITH DIRECT SERVICE TO SAN JOSÉ

American Airlines	*Miami*
800-433-7300	*Dallas-Fort Worth*
Aero Costa Rica	*Miami*
800-237-6274	*Orlando*
Lacsa Airlines	*Miami*
800-225-2272	*New York (stops en route)*
	New Orleans
	San Francisco (stops en route)
	Los Angeles (stops en route)
Continental	*Houston*
800-525-0280	
United	*Miami*
800-241-6522	*Los Angeles (stops en route)*

AIRLINES WITH THROUGH SERVICE TO SAN JOSÉ

Taca	*New York, Miami, Houston*
800-535-8780	
Mexicana	*New York, Denver, etc.*
800-531-7921	
Aviateca	*Miami, New Orleans, Houston,*
800-327-9832	*Chicago, Los Angeles*

Buy a Round-Trip Ticket

It's usually cheaper and avoids local taxes, and you might have to show an onward or return ticket to satisfy the immigration authorities in San José.

By Bus

The disadvantages of bus travel all the way to Costa Rica are obvious — long hours in a sitting position, inconvenient connections, border delays, and much else. You can, however, see much along the way, and the price is right. Total fare from the U.S. border to Costa Rica is under $100, and this can be reduced by using less comfortable, slower, second-class local buses. Overland travel will require that you pick up visas in advance for all the countries you'll be transiting.

Some specifics: First-class buses, similar to those used by Greyhound, operate from all U.S. border points to Mexico City, a trip of from 10 hours to two days, depending on your crossing point. Buses of the **Cristóbal Colón** line depart Mexico City at least twice daily for the Guatemalan border, sixteen hours away, connecting with buses for Guatemala City.

Buses for Esquipulas leave you near the Honduran border. From there, travel via San Pedro Sula and Tegucigalpa to Managua. Direct buses operate onward to San José. The trip through Mexico may be shortened by following the Gulf coast route from eastern Texas, avoiding Mexico City.

By Private Boat

With a major marina at Playa Flamingo on the Pacific coast, you might well think of sailing down from California, or through the Panama Canal. If you do so, make sure you clear customs and immigration at the first port of entry: Coco or Golfito on the Pacific, Barra del Colorado on the Caribbean.

By Car

The shortest highway distance from Brownsville, Texas, to San José, Costa Rica, is about 2,250 miles. For the vast majority of travelers, who have limited vacation time, it's simply not worthwhile to consider driving, with six borders to cross, difficult mountain roads, and fears of political turmoil and breakdowns en route.

Your major requirement is a vehicle in good shape. Have it checked out, tuned up and greased before you leave home. Replace cracked or withering belts and hoses, bald tires and rusting brake lines. If you're planning extensive travel off the main roads, consider taking a couple of spare tires, a gasoline can, water for you and the radiator, points, plugs, electrical tape, belts, wire, and basic tools. Otherwise, there's no reason to prepare for a safari, and the family sedan will serve you well. Be prepared to disconnect your catalytic converter south of Mexico, where unleaded gasoline is not available.

Avoid extra fees by crossing borders during regular business hours, generally from 8 a.m. to noon and from 2 p.m. to 6 p.m. It's prudent to travel during daylight hours only, to avoid stray animals and inebriated humans. Fill your tank whenever you can — gas stations can be few and far between. Plan your route to avoid transiting El Salvador — a direct crossing from Guatemala to Honduras is possible.

Essential documents for entry to any Central American country are your driver's license, vehicle registration, and passport with visa obtained in advance. Liability insurance is available in each country you cross. Coverage for damage to your own vehicle may not be available.

Vehicle permits for Costa Rica are issued at the border, are valid for 30 days, and may not be renewed. Drivers wishing to stay longer must take their vehicles out of the country for two days.

Maps of Mexico and Central America are available from your local automobile club or at travel bookstores.

CUSTOMS - ENTERING COSTA RICA

You can enter with any used personal possessions that you'll reasonably need, including sporting equipment. Items unfamiliar to customs inspectors, including medical articles, could be taxed heavily. The exemption for new merchandise is $100 of customs duty. New merchandise may include up to three liters of liquor (which you can purchase on arrival at the airport), one pound of tobacco, and six rolls of film.

CUSTOMS - RETURNING HOME

U.S. Customs allows an exemption of $400 per person in goods, including one quart of liquor and 200 cigarettes. Canadian residents may use their once-yearly $300 exemption, or their $100 quarterly exemption for goods brought home, with a limit of 1.1 liters of liquor and 200 cigarettes.

Costa Rica prohibits the export of pre-Columbian artifacts. In practice, there is a black market in these items, and there is limited official concern for pieces of little artistic value. One should be careful, not least because many artifacts are phony. Items made from protected species, such as turtles and alligators, could also get you into hot water, or at least be confiscated when you try to get them through customs at home.

GETTING AROUND COSTA RICA

By Air

Costa Rica's domestic airline, **Sansa** *(tel. [2]333258 in San José),* operates flights to a number of outlying towns from **Juan Santamaría International Airport**. Fares are a bargain: $35 or less to any point with scheduled service. And you only have to check in at Sansa's San José office. The airline takes you out to the airport in its own van.

Sansa's flights save a lot of the wear and tear involved in overland travel. Even if you like to see things at ground level, they provide an easy lift back to San José. The drawbacks are insufficient flights to a limited number of destinations, variations from schedules, lost reservations, and, occasionally, separation of passengers from their luggage.

Latest destinations and flight frequencies are: to Quepos, daily; to Golfito and Coto 47 (near the Panamanian border), six times weekly; to Tamarindo, four times weekly; to Sámara and Palmar Sur, three times weekly. From time to time, flights are scheduled to Barra del Colorado.

Travelair, a newer airline, offers a more reliable service and more destinations — as well as higher prices. Still, no round-trip ticket on Travelair is more than $115 or so. Current destinations on Travelair are Quepos, Limón, Golfito, and Palmar Sur (all daily); and Barra del Colorado, Nosara, Carrillo and Tamarindo (two to three times weekly). *Call Travelair at [2]327883 in San José.*

Charter flights in small planes are also available from **Tobías Bolaños Airport** *(just west of San José)* to places without regularly scheduled service, such as Tortuguero National Park. Arrange such flights through travel agencies, or directly through the companies listed in the yellow pages under *Aviación.*

By Bus

There are several tiers of bus service in Costa Rica. Depending on where you are in the country and how far you're going, getting around by bus can be pleasant and comfortable, tolerable, or — if you're not prepared — an ordeal.

Service between towns in the Central Valley is provided in large buses similar to those used on the city lines in San José. These generally have padded seats, which are closer together than those in comparable American buses, but comfortable enough for the distances involved.

Fares on suburban routes are generally fixed, no matter how far you travel. Fare cards are usually posted near the driver's seat.

Buses in the Central Valley may be boarded either at their terminals, or at bus stops, which are marked by shelters, rectangular signs, or short yellow lines painted along the edge of the road. Pay the driver, choose a seat, and enjoy the sights along the way.

Buses operating on the major highways between San José and the far points of the country are roughly comparable to Greyhound buses in the United States. They may be older, and lack air conditioning and lavatories, but they are generally well-cared-for, and mechanically sound.

Drivers of long-distance buses try to maintain the maximum legal speed, even on winding roads. Bus crews are ready for such side-effects as nausea with plastic bags (comforting). Prepare yourself with motion sickness pills if you're susceptible.

Tickets for long-distance buses may be purchased in advance, and this is recommended for weekend travel. If you try to board a long-distance bus along its route, it might or might not stop — there's no fixed rule. Try to select a waiting place where the driver will see you well in advance and have a chance to slow down. Ask a handy local for advice.

Buses operating in rural areas outside the Central Valley are of an entirely different breed. Most are similar to American school buses. Some in fact *are* old school buses, right down to the yellow paint. (Old school buses never die. They just go to Central America.) Seats are stiff, with minimal padding, designed for small people traveling short distances.

Rural buses stop frequently to let out and pick up passengers, as well as chickens, cardboard boxes full of merchandise, and whatever else has to move. Add poor roads and steep grades, and a trip of fifty kilometers could take a couple of hours. Many a passenger has to stand in a crowded aisle, for there is often no other way to go.

Country people in Costa Rica are used to conditions on buses, and may even doze off, despite the bouncing and shaking and cramped quarters. Without precautions, however, the visitor may find rural bus trips excruciating.

Fares on all buses in Costa Rica are low, generally less than 2¢ (U.S.) per kilometer.

By Taxi

It doesn't occur to most people, but taxis are a very practical way to get around the countryside in Costa Rica. Current official rates are about 70¢ for the first kilometer, 25¢ for each additional kilometer, and $3 per hour of waiting time. For trips over 12 kilometers, the driver is allowed to negotiate the charge. At the official rate, a 120-kilometer round trip from San José to Poás volcano should run less than $30, including a couple of hours of waiting. Even if you're charged more, the cost should compare favorably to that of renting a car. In addition, you'll be able to look around instead of keeping your eyes glued to the road, and can direct the driver to slow down or stop where you please.

Travel by taxi is not without its problems. Many drivers are used to overcharging tourists, sometimes by claiming that their meters don't work. Look for a driver who will agree to charge the legal rates (which your hotel can confirm), or at least not too much more.

For long-distance travel, of course, you'll want to use airplanes or comfortable buses. But taxis are a good bet for going those last few kilometers in rural areas. In the Nicoya Peninsula and other areas with poor roads, taxis are usually Jeeps or similar vehicles well suited to local conditions.

By Train

Costa Rica's world-famous **Jungle Train**, from San José to Limón, is out of operation, due to repeated landslides, though parts of the line operate in the lowlands for banana plantation tours. Currently, there is limited scheduled passenger service from Limón southward, along the Caribbean, and in the San José area at rush hours.

By Bicycle

Bicycle tours within Costa Rica's national parks are offered by travel agencies in San José.

By Car

Driving your own car makes a small country significantly smaller — but not without a price. Gasoline outlays and car rental rates in Costa Rica are higher than those in the United States. Rental cars are easy marks for thieves, as well as for traffic police looking for payoffs.

Road Conditions & Hazards

Though Costa Rica has had no recent wars, some of the main roads through mountainous areas, and many secondary roads, look as if they've been mined. There is generally no warning even for monumental potholes. On and off paved roads, much of your attention is devoted to dodging potholes, or it should be. Conditions are generally worst toward the end of the rainy season. Many unpaved roads are graded but once a year. Consider December 1 as the end of mud season for driving the dirt roads of Costa Rica.

Inquire at every opportunity about road conditions ahead (usually at gasoline stations), especially in the rainy season, and interpret the response with caution. Costa Ricans will usually tell you that a road is passable. Gringos will say that you can't make it after a heavy rain, what with swollen rivers and mud up to your axles. The truth lies somewhere in between, and depends on what you're driving.

On mountain roads, beep your horn at curves and drive at moderate speeds. The driver going up a hill has the right of way, so be prepared to pull over or back up on narrow stretches. Oncoming drivers will sometimes flash their lights to warn of a hazard ahead. Slow down.

It's never wise to drive at night on unfamiliar roads, especially in the Central Valley, where the winding right of way is used by people, some of them unsober, as well as vehicles.

Watch also for herds of cattle in the road, driven by cowboys on horses or bicycles; and slow-moving trucks. Most hazard signs use easily understood symbols, though a few use words that you might not know.

Legal Matters

The speed limit on the open road is 75 kilometers (47 miles) an hour, and it's seriously enforced. I got my first speeding ticket ever in Costa Rica — the radar clocked me at a blazing 91 kilometers per hour on the flat, straight highway from Limón to San José. You can also get a ticket for not using your seat belt. The worst part is waiting in line at a bank to pay the fine — and pay you must, or risk being turned back at the airport.

Your local driver's license is good for 90 days in Costa Rica. Should you stay longer, you'll need a Costa Rican license.

Be sure to stop at roadside checkpoints if you're flagged down. It's usually nothing sinister. The police might be looking for contraband turtle eggs, not firearms.

But some traffic police are corrupt. A dollar or two in *coffee money* will get the cop to overlook your lack of an original registration or some other claimed infraction. It's annoying to pay, of course, but the Cheshire cat grin, seen through the rear-view mirror as you drive off, is priceless.

In the case of higher demands, confiscation of documents, or requests for payment of "fines" on the spot, get the name of the police officer, if you can. You can file a complaint, and you should, even if it's inconvenient. It's time for Costa Rica to clean up.

Repairs

Many auto parts are hard to obtain outside of San José. Try to have your car serviced and repairs made in the capital or nearby. Parts for some cars are simply not stocked in Costa Rica, but drivers of most Japanese and smaller American cars should have no problems in this regard.

BASIC INFORMATION

Here's some basic information matters, in alpabetical order:

ELECTRICITY

Electrical supply is at 110 volts, alternating current, throughout Costa Rica. Sockets are of the American type, usually without provision for a grounding prong. In remote locations, such as fishing camps, generators may operate on a non-standard voltage.

HANDICAPPED ACCESSIBILITY

There is little positive to report on the accessibility front in Costa Rica. Sidewalks in San José are as rutted and potholed as streets and highways. There are no indentations to allow easy street crossing. Hallways in hotels are usually narrow. Even in major public buildings, such as the airport terminal, there are no handicapped-accessible rest room stalls.

Lapa Ríos, the luxurious wilderness lodge in the Osa Peninsula, provides ramp entryways to some units. But an able-bodied companion is a must for any first-time visit to Costa Rica by a handicapped person.

HEALTH CONCERNS

The health worries that usually accompany a trip to Latin America — mad dashes to the bathroom, general malaise as unknown microbes attack your insides, long-forgotten diseases like typhoid turning up in the best hotels — hardly apply to Costa Rica, where sanitary standards are generally high and most people are educated enough to have an idea of how disease spreads. Good sense and normal caution should be enough to see you through Costa Rica in good health.

In most cases, no special inoculations or vaccinations are required or recommended for visitors to Costa Rica. You can check current conditions by calling the **Communicable Disease Center** hotline in Atlanta, *tel. 404-332-4555.*

Water in San José and in most of the towns of the Central Valley is chemically treated and is probably safe to drink, though many experienced travelers avoid tap water anywhere. If you're not confident of water quality, stick to bottled sodas or beer. Suspect water is easily treated with laundry bleach (two drops per quart, let stand 30 minutes).

For extensive travel at the budget level or off the beaten track, a dose of immunoglobulin for protection against hepatitis and a typhoid booster are advisable. If you're heading to the Caribbean lowlands, where there are occasional malaria outbreaks, and will be staying in rural areas or unscreened budget accommodations, take a weekly dosage of a malaria preventative, such as Aralen.

Budget travelers should avoid fleabag hotels. Fleas and similar insects are not only unpleasant in themselves but can carry disease. If both top and bottom sheets are not clean and clean-smelling, move on.

Having an Operation

Plastic surgery is a growing earner of foreign exchange for Costa Rica. Many people fly in to have breasts, wrinkles, or nose renovated at a fraction of the cost in the States or Europe. If you're interested, check the ads in *Guide* magazine, *Costa Rica Today*, and the *Tico Times*.

You'll also find ads for dentists (*travel to Costa Rica and return home with a beautiful smile*), acupuncturists, homeopaths, ophthalmologists, and many other practitioners, both mainstream and alternative. Some have trained at reputable universities in the United States and Latin America. You won't want to select your care strictly from an ad, so ask for references from anyone you contact, and consider consulting your doctor at home before treatment. Credit cards are often accepted for payment.

If your treatment is not covered by medical insurance at home, you might find that the price is right for treatment in Costa Rica, and all or part of your travel expenses could be tax deductible as well!

Medical Care

Short-term medical insurance is available for about $50 per month, less for students, through **International Cultural Exchange Association,**

P. O. Box 687-1011Y, San José, fax [2]227867. The card issued through this program allows treatment at hospitals of the Costa Rican social security system. This card is not a substitute for comprehensive medical insurance from a company in your own country.

Recuperating and Recovering

A growing number of facilities provides counseling, treatment for drug and alcohol abuse, and post-operative convalescence in benign surroundings. The **Forest Clinic** *in Escazú, tel. [2]285438*, associated with a U.S. clinic, has English-language psychiatric services. **Casa de Campo**, *tel. [2]295309*, has similar services. The luxurious **Tara Resort Hotel** discreetly cares for patients recovering from cosmetic surgery.

I am not in a position to recommend any particular service, but you can get leads through health-care professionals in the United States, or from ads in the *Tico Times* and *Costa Rica Today*.

LEARNING SPANISH IN COSTA RICA

Learning Spanish will ease your way in Costa Rica, and enrich your life afterwards. Your whole living environment is your language laboratory, so chances are you'll pick things up more easily than at home.

What's the Cost?

There are other countries where you can go to language school at a lower price than in Costa Rica, but many students prefer San José's low-key atmosphere and level of amenities, and the comprehensiveness of some of the programs. A four-week package of study, room, meals in a private home, and escorted trips around the country, costs $1,200 or more. Instruction in small groups for four hours daily, without excursions, will run about $900 for four weeks.

These are just general guidelines. Write, call or fax the schools listed below for more details, and ask for referrals from recent students. Some travel agencies also offer study-and-flight packages.

Language Schools

Some of the language schools in Costa Rica are:
- **Instituto Universal de Idiomas**, *Apartado 651-2050, Moravia, tel. [2]570441*
- **Instituto Británico**, *P. O. Box 8184-1000 San José, tel. [2]250256, fax [2]531894*. Teaches both English and Spanish as a second language, in San José and in Liberia, in northwestern Costa Rica
- **ICAI** (*Instituto Centroamericano de Asuntos Internacionales*), *Apartado 10302, San José, tel. [2]338571, fax [2]215238*, runs a comprehensive one- to four-week classroom and tour program, and an intensive ten-week course.

- **Centro Lingüístico Conversa**, *Calle 38, Avenidas 3/5 (Apartado 17-1007), San José, tel. [2]217649, fax [2]332418.* Courses are available in San José, and at a farm west of the city.
- **Forester Instituto Internacional**, *Los Yoses (P. O. Box 6945-1000, San José), tel. [2]253155, fax [2]259236.*
- **Lisa Tec**, *P.O. Box 228-4005, San Antonio de Belén*, has a quiet, suburban location.
- **ILISA**, *P.O. Box 1001-2050 San Pedro, tel. [2]252495, fax [2]254665. Direct line from U.S. and Canada: 800-377-2665.*
- **ICADS** *(Instituto de Estudios de Desarrollo Centroamericano), P. O. Box 3-2070, San José, tel. [2]250508, fax [2]341337 or Box 025216-826, Miami FL 33102-5216,* has programs that combine language study with volunteer work in Costa Rica and Nicaragua.
- **Instituto Americano de Lenguaje y Cultura**, *San Pedro (P. O. Box 200-1001 San José), tel. [2]254313, fax [2]244244.*
- **Instituto de la Lengua Española**, *Apartado 100-2350, San José, tel. [2]277355, fax [2]270211.* Fifteen-week courses.
- **Instituto Interamericano de Idiomas Intensa**, *P. O. Box 8110-1000, Calle 33, Avenidas 5/7 (no. 540), Barrio Escalante, San José, tel. [2]256009*
- **Centro Cultural Costarricense-Norteamericano**, *Calle 37, Avenida Central, tel. [2]259433, fax [2]241480. (P.O. Box 1489-1000, San José).* Associated with the U.S. government. Features computer-assisted grammar-tuning, conversation partners, possible college credits. Facilities are rated excellent by readers, fees are slightly lower than elsewhere.
- **Centro Panamericano de Idiomas**, *P. O. Box 151-3007 San Joaquín, Heredia, tel. and fax [2]380561. U.S. tel. 603-469-3610, fax 469-3500.* Small-town setting for study and family stays, airport pickup.
- **Costa Rican Language Academy and Latin Dance School**, *P.O. Box 336-2070, San José, tel. [2]338938, fax [2]338670.* "Learn our language and lifestyle together."
- **Escuela d'Amore**, *Manuel Antonio National Park (P. O. Box 77, Quepos), tel. [6]770543.* Spanish classes in a resort setting.

In addition, assorted colleges and universities in the United States offer credit courses in Spanish in Costa Rica. For more information, look at the postings at the Spanish or Romance Languages department at a large university near wherever you happen to be.

The Universidad Autónoma de Centro América, *tel. [2]255878, fax [2]252907,* pre-arranges college credits in the United States for a number of its Spanish-as-a-second-language courses.

MONEY & BANKING

Costa Rica's unit of currency is the *colón* ("ko-LOHN"), which is named after Christopher Columbus (Colón in Spanish). Each colón is divided into 100 céntimos (which, with inflation, you will rarely see). In slang usage, the colón is sometimes called a peso.

In this book, I've quoted most prices in U.S. dollars, based on the current rate of exchange (about 125 colones to the dollar). Costa Rica's currency has an unstable recent history, and devaluations are now a routine matter. You may even find that some prices are *lower*, in U.S. dollars, than those I've indicated. However, rates for hotel rooms, tours, car rentals, and other services are fixed in dollars, and then converted to colones at the current rate. You won't get a break on these as the value of the currency shrinks.

Changing Money

Unfortunately, changing your foreign currency to colones could turn out to be your most unpleasant experience in Costa Rica. The levels of bureaucracy in Costa Rica's banks are unsurpassed. You might have to wait in line for more than an hour while somebody in front of you cashes in sheet upon sheet of winning lottery tickets, or has his loan payments calculated on antiquated adding machines and then transferred to record sheets by a teller with hunt-and-peck typing skills (and how they insist on using typewriters!)

And after waiting, you still might not get your money changed. I once had my travelers checks refused because I had no permanent address in Costa Rica. I was turned down at other banks because my brand of travelers checks was out of favor (they wouldn't say why). Some visitors are refused because they have no passports, although none is required to enter the country.

Leaving Costa Rica With Local Currency

U.S. funds may be repurchased at the airport bank before leaving Costa Rica, if available. Avoid leaving the country with extra Costa Rican money, which will be exchanged abroad at an unfavorable rate or not at all.

Receiving Money

Money from home may be received by telegraphic or Telex transfer through a bank in San José. Make sure you know through which bank it will be sent — several have similar names. International money orders may also be sent by registered mail, but safety is not assured. The **U.S. State Department**, *tel. 202-647-5225*, can assist with money transfers. Regular money orders and personal checks are nearly impossible to cash.

TIPS FOR CHANGING MONEY

With a few precautions you can avoid problems with the banks and their sadistic methods. Some suggestions:

• *Buy colones at airport exchange counters before you enter the country.*

• *Exchange a substantial amount on arriving at the airport in San José. The airport bank is relatively hassle-free.*

• *Change money at your hotel, if it performs this service. The rate, however, will be slightly less favorable than at the banks.*

• *Use a bank's specialized exchange office, when available. In downtown San José, the most convenient such facility, operated by Banco Mercantil, is opposite the tourist office, on Calle 5 just south of Avenida Central. Watch for pickpockets as you leave!*

• *If you must exchange money at a bank, get there early in the day, and get as much cash as you feel comfortable carrying. Normal banking hours are from 9 a.m. to 3 p.m.*

• *Use credit cards when possible (see below). As a bonus, you'll save the one-percent commission that most banks charge on travellers checks.*

• *Carry a passport for identification.*

• *Take U.S. dollars in cash or travelers checks. Other currencies, such as Canadian dollars and sterling, are difficult if not impossible to exchange. (See below.)*

• *Do as the Costa Ricans do, and use the black market. Actually, a better term would be "gray market," since unofficial currency transactions operate pretty much in the open, and are no longer even illegal. The street rate may not even be any better than what you'll get at a bank, but there are no lineups, and travelers checks are accepted with a minimum of fuss. Dealers generally operate near the post office in San José. How do you find them? Generally, you don't have to look for them; if you walk through the area, they will find you. Try to carry out the exchange off the street (in a hotel lobby, for example). Have some familiarity with Costa Rican currency, and put your cash away immediately in a money belt or inside pocket safe from thieves.*

If this is more than you want to deal with on a vacation, credit cards are a better alternative.

Credit Cards

Visa and Master Card are widely accepted in Costa Rica, American Express to a lesser extent. You may reasonably expect to use your credit card at restaurants where a meal costs $5 or more per person, and at any large hotel that charges $25 or more for a double room. Smaller, family-run hotels and inns generally do not take credit cards, even for $100 rooms. The bank rate of exchange in effect on the date of your purchase will be applied (the card issuer may charge a commission as well).

Local contacts are: **American Express**, *tel. [2]330044 (230116 after business hours)*; **Visa** and **Master Card**, *tel. [2]532155 (Credomatic, Avenida Central, Calles 29/33)*; **Diners Club**, *210078.*

Sterling, Marks, Francs, Canadian Dollars

If you've ignored my advice and brought along these currencies, try the services of **Compañía Financiera Londres**, *on Calle Central near the corner of Avenida Central (next to La Casona), third floor*. Rates will most likely be less than favorable.

Business Transactions

Goods should generally be shipped to Costa Rica against advance payment or irrevocable letter of credit.

POST OFFICE

Wise residents of Costa Rica use the local mail system only when they have to. Letters from abroad are regularly opened, delayed, or lost while dishonest postal employees look for checks and valuables.

Enclosure of money, checks, or anything other than correspondence ensures that your letter will not arrive. Even registered mail provides limited protection — a $20 maximum indemnity if the letter is sent from the United States.

When possible, avoid the mails altogether, and send a fax. The next-best choice is to use a mail drop in Miami, when available (many such addresses are given for hotels and other services in this book). These letters will be forwarded by private courier for pickup in San José. If you have to use the mails to Costa Rica, send a post card, if your message will fit. Otherwise, use a flimsy air-mail envelope and lightweight paper, to make it obvious there's nothing inside. Good luck!

When writing to hotels, businesses or individuals in Costa Rica, use the post-office box, if known, in preference to the street address. The term "P. O. Box" (in English) is well understood, though you may of course use the Spanish equivalent, *apartado*. Letters may be sent to you in Costa Rica in care of *lista de correos* (general delivery), Correo Central, 1000 San José (or any other city where you may be). There is a small charge for each letter picked up. Tell your correspondents to write neatly or type. Illegible foreign handwriting is responsible for many a letter going astray.

You may receive parcels at *lista de correos*, but, except for used books, there isn't much point in having anything sent. The customs duty usually exceeds the value of the merchandise. Tell the folks at home to send a money order instead.

Approximate postal rates are as follows: for light letters, up to 20 grams, via air mail, to the United States or Canada, 30¢; to Europe, 40¢. Post cards by air to the United States or Canada, 25¢; to Europe, 35¢.

PRECAUTIONS

I like to tell my friends in América del Norte that Costa Rica is like a Carmen Miranda movie: Latin America without the downside. The visitor is relatively un-harassed by peddlers and beggars, and doesn't stick out like a sore thumb, as in some neighboring countries.

But beguiled visitors can sometimes paint a picture more paradisaical than that which actually prevails. It's easy to become entranced by the pace of life, the apparent lack of urban ills, the friendliness of most of the populace.

In fact, there is probably no country in the world where novitiate visitors are more likely to throw normal caution to the winds than Costa Rica. And there is probably no country in the hemisphere where visitors so easily fall victims to petty criminals and con men.

So let me take a moment of your time to counsel you that pickpockets lurk in crowded squares, and wherever there are tourists. Visitors' routes are well defined, and the thieves and con men know exactly where to find you.

People who are overfriendly without reason may well be overfriendly for a very bad reason. The candy or cookie shared by the friendly stranger on the bus could well be drugged.

Those barred windows are not just a Spanish tradition, as some real-estate salesmen would have it — they keep out thieves.

It isn't smart to walk in quiet or deserted parts of town at night.

Costa Rica is no cauldron of crime, but there are bad eggs, especially in San José, as in any urban area. If you don't do anything you wouldn't do in any unfamiliar place, you'll probably be safer than in most other cities.

Losing Your Luggage

If you park your car on any street in San José, it will be broken into, at night, and sometimes during the day. (Fortunately, there are few parking spaces downtown.) Hotel parking lots are not secure unless they are enclosed, with a guard on duty (report many, many readers). Even volcanoes are not secure. You can never, ever leave anything in a parked car with the expectation of seeing it again.

If your luggage rides out of sight on a bus, there's a chance you won't get it back. When using public transportation, it's better to carry hand luggage only.

SHOPPING

Costa Rica offers visitors many rewards, but shopping is not near the top of the list. Only a handful of indigenous crafts — pottery, hand-woven textiles and musical instruments made on a small scale for home use — can be found for sale in stores and museums.

Most of what you see at hotel shops and souvenir stores will be non-traditional handicrafts largely intended for the tourist market — things like miniature painted oxcarts, reproductions of pre-Columbian artifacts, painted wooden frogs, gourd mugs, hammocks, hand-blown glass, and items made from unusual and attractive hardwoods such as rosewood (*cocobolo*), teak, lignum vitae (*guayacán*), and heart of amaranth (*nazarena*). There's also the usual run of straw hats, t-shirts, macramé, ashtrays and the like. Local production is supplemented by more interesting imports of textiles and basketry from Guatemala, El Salvador, and Panama. You should have no trouble finding these, but just in case, I've given the names and locations of some stores in the shopping section of the San José chapter of this book.

If local crafts aren't overwhelming, don't overlook some of the non-souvenir items that are cheaper in Costa Rica than at home. Utilitarian luggage and other leatherwork can, in some cases, be a good buy. Stop into a supermarket and pick up a pound or two or three of coffee. Most brands are ground too finely for your own coffeemaker, and don't travel well in their cellophane packaging. *Volio* is one brand available as whole beans to grind at home, Britt is another, at a much higher price.

TAXES

Almost all goods and services in Costa Rica are subject to a value-added tax (*i.v.a.*), currently 11% and rising. Hotel rooms are subject to an additional tourism tax, bringing the total bite to 14.3 %. At the airport, the exit tax is approximately $8.

TAXIS

In San José, you pay about 70¢ for the first kilometer, 25¢ for each additional kilometer — a bargain! In rural areas, additional kilometers cost slightly more. Waiting time is charged at about $3 per hour. If your trip is over 12 kilometers, you'll have to negotiate the rate with the driver.

TELEGRAMS

International telegrams are handled by **Radiográfica Costarricense**, *Calle 1, Avenida 5, San José*. Telegrams may be dictated by dialing 123, or transmitted through your hotel operator. In all cases, the rates are quite high — usually 50¢ per word or more. Domestic telegrams cost only a few cents per word.

TELEPHONES

Costa Rica has a modern, direct-dial telephone system, with more lines per inhabitant than almost any other nation in Latin America.

Dialing Direct to Costa Rica

From the U.S. or Canada, dial 011-506, followed by the local number in Costa Rica. There are no area codes.

Using Operator Assistance

For collect or person-to-person calls, dial 01-506, followed by the local number; or call your operator.

Dialing 1-800

Some of the toll-free numbers listed in this book will connect you directly to Costa Rica from the United States, and in some cases from Canada as well.

Be cautious! When you use this service, you'll be dealing with an overseas company. Complaints about service, or billings to your credit card, will be more difficult to resolve than if you deal with a company at home. Also, the costs of 800 service to Costa Rica are not inconsiderable, and the person at the other end may not be patient with a long-winded inquiry.

I recommend that you first try a domestic toll-free service when planning your trip.

Dialing Costa Rica Direct

1-800-252-5114 will get you in touch with a Costa Rican operator from the United States, 1-800-463-0116 from Canada. Use this service if you speak Spanish and wish to call collect or need additional local information.

Calling Home Using Your Regular Service

To reach an operator from your home telephone company, or use its credit card, dial 114 for AT&T, 162 for MCI, 163 for Sprint, 161 for Telecom Canada, 167 for British Telecom, from any private or public phone in Costa Rica. From a hotel, you'll have to ask for an outside line.

Dialing Direct for Home

From a private phone, dial 00-1 (for North America), followed by the area code and local number.

Operator Assistance

Dial 09-1 (for North America), followed by the local number. An operator will ask for your instructions (person-to-person, collect, credit card, etc.).

Or dial 116 and give your instructions to the operator, in English, at a slightly higher charge.

Telephone Credit Cards

Telephone credit carsa from the United States, Canada, the U.K., France and Japan are accepted by the Costa Rican telephone system.

Calling From the Phone Company's Offices

In San José, go to **Radiográfica Costarricense**, *Avenida 5, Calle 1.* Visa, Master Card and American Express are accepted at this location.

Calling Your Hotel Operator

This will usually cost far more than any of the above.

SERVICE NUMBERS IN COSTA RICA	
110	*Collect calls within Costa Rica and operator assistance.*
112	*Time of day*
113	*Telephone number information*
114	*AT&T USA Direct (deposit coin at public phone)*
161	*Canada Direct*
162	*MCI to U.S.A.*
163	*Sprint to U.S.A.*
167	*British Telecom U.K. Direct*
116	*International long distance (operators speak English)*
117	*San José police*
118	*Fire department (bomberos)*
127	*Rural police*
128	*Emergency Red Cross assistance*
[2]27-7150	*Traffic police*

Rates

An operator-assisted call to New York costs about $9 for three minutes, or $7 after 7 p.m. A direct-dialed call to New York costs $2 per minute, $1.60 after 7 p.m., 80¢ from 10 p.m. to 7 a.m., and on weekends.

Calling in Costa Rica

Public telephones are available in most towns, most conveniently on the main square – but many are out of order.

The easiest coin phones to understand are those that require you to place your coins (5, 10 and 20 colones) on a rack, to be swallowed as needed. With others, you deposit a coin when signalled to do so. If you're slow about it, your call is cut off. Magnetic-card phones are slowly coming into use.

Rates from public phones are quite cheap — even less than from private homes. Many stores and hotels will allow you to use their phones for a charge of about 25¢ (U.S.) for a local call.

Calling from Hotels

Hotels impose hefty surcharges on phone calls. It will usually be far cheaper to call home collect or charge the call to a telephone credit card, or to call a local number from a pay phone.

Dialing a Wrong Number

Watch your fingers! An extra digit [indicated in brackets in this book] was added in mid-1994 to every phone number in Costa Rica. Verify problem numbers in the telephone directory, or dial 113 for assistance.

If calling from outside Costa Rica, ask your operator to connect you with directory assistance in San José.

TIME

Costa Rica is on Central Standard Time, equivalent to Greenwich Mean Time less six hours.

WEIGHTS & MEASURES

Costa Rica is firmly on the metric system. Gasoline, juice and milk are sold by the liter, fabrics by the meter, tomatoes by the kilo. Gone are the days when visitors were confused by a hodgepodge of yards, *varas*, *manzanas*, *fanegas*, *caballerías*, gallons, and assorted other English and old Spanish measures.

Old usages survive mainly in giving directions. People will usually say 100 *metros* (meters) to indicate a city block, but you'll sometimes hear 100 *varas*. In fact, a block is closer to 100 varas, a vara being an old Spanish yard, equivalent to 33 inches or .835 meters.

SPORTS & RECREATION

The variety of sports and recreational activities in Costa Rica is enormous. Read on!

FISHING

There's great sport fishing in Costa Rica, not only along both coasts, but in mountain streams and lakes as well.

Plenty of world records have been broken, but some fishermen have gone home disappointed. You have to know when the fish are running, and where stocks have been depleted by runoffs and pesticides.

Caribbean Fishing

On the Caribbean side of Costa Rica, the most notorious species is the pesky and finicky tarpon. Tarpon are caught between January and June in rivers, lagoons and estuaries, and weigh as much as 100 pounds. Other species common to the Caribbean are snook, usually weighing over 25 pounds; the related and smaller calba, or fat snook; the bass-like machaca and guapote; mojarra, which resembles a bluegill; and shark, mackerel, mullet and jack crevalle. All are found in inland waters, even shark, though stocks are said to have declined in recent years, due to sedimentation and contamination by pesticides.

Deep-sea fishing in the Caribbean is limited by the unpredictability of storms and heavy surf at river mouths, but some lodges have large boats to get fishermen safely out during calm periods. Species found not too far from shore may include barracuda, jacks, sawfish, tuna and wahoo.

Pacific Fishing

On the Pacific side, black and blue marlins of up to 1,000 pounds are the big attractions, especially up north in the Gulf of Papagayo; along with sailfish, roosterfish, wahoo, rainbow runner, barracuda, a variety of snappers, jacks, pompano, shark, swordfish, yellowfin tuna, bonito, dorado (mahi-mahi), grouper and corvina, or sea bass. The smaller fish are found in river mouths and estuaries, the larger species out in blue water.

Inland Fishing

Inland, some mountain and lowland streams and lakes hold trout (generally on the small side), guapote, machaca and bobo (related to mullet), as well as smaller fish. Inland fishing is permitted all year in Lake Arenal and the Reventazón River; December through August elsewhere.

The most accessible fishing for trout of any size is along the Savegre River at the cabins of the Chacón family (tel. [7]711732. To find a good inland fishing spot, hang out at the bus station of a lowland town at the base of the sierra, such as Villa Neilly. Look for a guy with a fishing rod and discreetly follow him aboard his bus. Stay on for the ascent from the steaming plain, winding back and forth up the face of the mountains, splashing through rushing streams. Take note of where the fisherman gets off, then backtrack and return the next day.

Fishing equipment is in short supply, so serious anglers should bring their own gear, unless availability is confirmed in advance. Your fishing camp or resort will recommend specific types of rods, reels and line when you reserve. For tarpon fishing — the big attraction on the Caribbean coast — six- to-seven-foot rods with 12- to 20-pound line are used. Reels should hold 200 yards of line. For snook and fly fishing, 10- to 12-pound line is enough. Lighter gear is sufficient for guapote and trout in fresh water. For deep-sea fishing, everything is usually provided by the fishing camp or boat operator.

Catch and Release

Most responsible fishing operators in Costa Rica encourage you to return your catch to the sea, and bring home photos, not trophies.

Permits

A permit is required for fishing. If you book a week at a fishing camp, the management will probably take care of this detail. Otherwise, you'll have to buy a permit at the **Dirección de Pesca**, *Calle 24, Avenida 2, tel. [2]552170.* This may have to be further validated at other offices for either river or offshore fishing.

San José-based Fishing Specialists

In San   José, contact:

- **Sportfishing Costa Rica**, *P.O. Box 115-1150 La Uruca, San José, tel. [2]333892, fax [2]236728; or 800-374-4474 U.S.-Costa Rica.* This outfit sponsors an annual two-ocean fishing tournament, and operates boats at Quepos and Drake Bay.
- **Costa Rica Dreams**, *P. O. Box 79-4005, San Antonio de Belén, tel. [2]393387, fax [2]393383.* Fishing off Quepos and Caño Island.
- **Flamingo Bay Pacific Charters**, *tel. [2]314055*

In-Country Fishing Services and Lodges Specializing in Fishing

Outside San José, contact:

- **Hotel Flor de Itabo**, *Playas del Coco, tel. 67[0]0011*
- **Hotel El Ocotal**, *Ocotal, tel. 67[0]0230*
- **Bahía Pez Vela**, *Ocotal, tel. 67[0]0129 (U.S. reservations, tel. 800-327-2880)*
- **Blue Marlin Fishing**, *Flamingo Beach, tel. 67[4]4043, fax 674165*
- **Pesca Bahía Garza**, based at Villagio La Guaria Morada, Playa Garza *(U.S. reservations: P. O. Box 1269, Marathon, FL 33050, tel. 305-289-1900, fax 289-1195*
- **Guanamar**, *Puerto Carrillo, tel. [6]536133 (P. O. Box 7-1880, San José, tel. [2]394544. U.S. reservations: tel. 800-245-8420)*
- **Hotel Tango Mar**, *Tambor, tel. 61[2]2798 (tel. [2]231864 in San José)*
- **Hotel Oasis del Pacífico**, *Playa Naranjo, tel. 61[1]1555*
- **Fred Wagner**, *Puntarenas, tel. 63[0]0107*

- **North-South Sportfishing**, *Quepos, tel. [2]275498*
- **Treasure Hunt Tours**, *Quepos, tel. 77[0]0345)*
- **Reel 'n Reelease Sportfishing**, *Dominical, tel. [6]711903*
- **Río Sierpe Lodge**, *Sierpe River (tel. [2]201712 in San José)*
- **Sanbar Marina**, *Golfito, tel. [7]750874 or 800-435-3239 from U.S*
- **War Eagle Marina**, *Golfito, tel. [7]750838 or [7]885083*
- **Golfito Sportfishing**, *Zancudo, tel. [7]750353*
- **Golfito Sailfish Rancho**, *Golfito (tel. [2]357766 in San José. U.S. reservations: tel. 800-531-7232*
- **Los Almendros**, *Zancudo, tel. [7]750515*
- **Zancudo Pacific Charters**, *Zancudo, tel. [7]885083*
- **Parismina Tarpon Rancho**, *Parismina (Calle 1, Avenidas 7/9, María José Building, tel. [2]226055; U.S. reservations tel. 800-531-7232 or 512-377-0451, or 800-862-1003 direct to San José)*
- **Río Parismina Lodge**, *Parismina (U.S. reservations: tel. 800-338-5688 or 210-824-4442)*
- **Río Colorado Lodge**, *Barra del Colorado (P. O. Box 5094-1000, San José, tel. [2]324063; U.S. reservations: tel. 800-243-9777)*
- **Isla de Pesca**, *near Barra del Colorado (P. O. Box 7-1880, San José, tel. [2]394544, fax [2]392405. U.S. reservations: tel. 800-245-8420)*
- **Casa Mar Fishing Lodge**, *Barra del Colorado (U.S. reservations: tel. 800-327-2880 or 305-664-4615, fax 305-664-3692*
- **Tortuga Lodge**, *Tortuguero, tel. 71[6]6861 (tel. [2]570766, fax [2]571665 in San José)*
- **Silver King Lodge**, *Barra del Colorado, tel. [7]880849 (U.S. reservations: tel. 800-847-3474)*
- **Aventuras Tilarán**, *Tilarán, tel. 69[5]5008. Lake Arenal fishing.*
- **Finca Zacatales**, *tel. [5]711732. Trout fishing.*

Arranging a Fishing Trip From the US
Agencies that book fishing trips to Costa Rica:
- **Flamingo Bay Pacific Charters**, *1112 East Las Olas Blvd., Fort Lauderdale, FL 33301, tel. 800-654-8006, fax 305-522-2637*
- **World Wide Sportsman**, *P. O. Drawer 787, Islamorada, FL 33036, tel. 800-327-2880 or 305-664-8833, fax 305-664-3692*
- **Flamingo Bay Pacific Charters**, *1112 East Las Olas Blvd., Fort Lauderdale, FL 33301*
- **PanAngling Travel**, *180 N. Michigan Ave., Chicago, IL 60601*
- **Dockside Tours**, *339 Hickory Ave., Harahan, LA 70123*
- **Anglers Travel Connections**, *3220 W. Sepulveda Blvd., Suite B, Torrance, CA 90505*
- **Pesca Bahía Garza**, *P. O. Box 1269, Marathon, FL 33050, tel. 305-289-1900, fax 289-1195*

CRUISING THE GULF OF NICOYA

The yacht *Calypso* makes a daily cruise from the yacht club in Puntarenas to seven islands in the Gulf of Nicoya. This is a well-planned excursion that has been improved and refined and copied over the years. A stop is made at a deserted, palm-shaded beach for swimming, snorkeling, beachcombing, and a gourmet picnic lunch that includes fresh gulf fish. They even take a portable toilet ashore.

Fare is about $70, including overland transportation from San José, or slightly less if you're already in Puntarenas. Book the cruise through any hotel in Puntarenas, *or call tel. [2]333617, fax [2]330401 in San José, or 61[0]0585 in Puntarenas.* Longer runs are also available.

Several other companies offer variations on the original Calypso excursion:

- **Sea Ventures**, *tel. [2]327412, fax [2]327510*, operates day trips from Puntarenas into the Gulf of Nicoya, with live music on board, a buffet, and snorkeling. Scuba diving can be arranged.
- **Fantasía Islands Adventures**, *P. O. Box 123-5550 Puntarenas, tel. [2]550791, fax [2]231013*
- The *Costa Sol*, operated by **Grupo Costa Sol** *(tel. [2]200722, fax [2]202095, tel. 800-245-8420 in the United States)*, may well be the largest tour boat in the gulf, a 100-foot yacht with two decks, two bars, and room for 125 passengers. Live music is provided throughout a day excursion, which includes a landing at Bahía Ballena.
- **Blue Seas First Class Cruise**, *tel. [2]337274*, tries to top the others with an open bar.

CRUISING THE COASTAL WATERS

The ship *Temptress* regularly carries up to 62 passengers along the Pacific coast of Costa Rica from Puntarenas. That's too small a load to offer casinos and dance bands; instead, you get the services of a biologist, video movies, board games, open-air bar and film-processing lab. All cabins are on the outside, with large rectangular windows.

Nights are spent underway, days at anchor off national parks and in secluded bays. Two shore excursions, one strenuous and one less so, are offered daily. Both are softly educational, and emphasize wildlife and Costa Rica's natural diversity.

Several routes are available: a six-night southern cruise that takes in Manuel Antonio National Park and the Osa Peninsula; a three-night southern cruise; and a four-night cruise along the Nicoya Peninsula and Tempisque River estuary. The price of $250 to $300 per person per day includes travel from San José to port, water skiing, snorkeling, kayaking, shore excursions, laundry service, and local brands of liquor and beer. There are extra charges to arrange fishing, and for diving.

Contact **Temptress Cruises**, *1600 N.W. Le Jeune Rd., Miami, FL 33126, tel. 800-336-8423, 305-871-2663z; or Cruceros del Sur, P. O. Box 5452-1000, San José, Costa Rica, tel. [2]201679, fax [2]202103.*

CRUISING A TROPICAL RIVER SYSTEM

In colonial times, the San Juan River along the border of Nicaragua was a highway between the interior and the coast. In the nineteenth century, it was an invasion route, the back door to the heart of Central America, used during the conflicts between William Walker, Nicaragua, Costa Rica, and Commodore Vanderbilt. And until a couple of years ago, it was off limits to outsiders, a sometime theater of war in the Sandinista-Contra struggles.

Now you can board a bus in San José, drive past the La Paz falls between Barva and Poás volcanoes, and embark on a river boat at Puerto Viejo on the Sarapiquí. Downriver, past stands of bananas and still-uncut forest, the craft navigates the San Juan, along the northern limit of the Barra del Colorado Wildlife Refuge. Joining you at various times are toucans, crocodiles, sloths, monkeys and butterflies. The delta branch of the San Juan called the Colorado leads into Costa Rican territory, through palms and a network of man-made and jungle canals, to the Caribbean at the village of Barra del Colorado.

From this point, you can fly back to San José after a night along the beach, stay to fish for tarpon, or continue along the canal system to Tortuguero National Park.

River excursions to the Caribbean are offered by:
- **Costa Sol** *(tel. [2]234560 in San José, 800-245-8420 in the United States)*
- **Costa Rica Adventure Tours**, *Hotel Corobicí (P. O. Box 5094-1000), tel. [2]328610, 800-243-9777 in the United States.*
- **Ríos Tropicales**, *tel. [2]336455;* and **Costa Rica Expeditions**, *tel. [2]220333*

RIDING BIKES

Ascend to the top of a volcano, look around, and start down! Or set out from San José . . . it's all downhill, to the east and west. Take your bike along from home, with proper precautions for packing, or rent one when you get to San José.

Costa Rica is a mountainous country, but that doesn't make it a tough go for mountain biking. Distances between overnight stopping points need never be more than 50 kilometers, unless you want a longer day. Roadside refreshment is available at shops and eateries everywhere. Buses will pick up you and your bike when you don't want to re-trace your steps, or when the ascent back to San José looks a *little* too strenuous.

Mountain bike rentals are available from **Costa Rica Sun Tours**,

Avenida 4, Calle 36, tel. [2]553418, for $20 or so per day. (Panet recommends taking your own bike, with the saddle that you're accustomed to).

Geoventuras, *P. O. Box 554-2150 Moravia, tel. [2]828590,, fax [2]828333*, arranges cycling tours for groups of up to 20 persons. These trips are generally non-strenuous: a mostly downhill ride through the Orosi Valley, with hikes in the Tapantí forest reserve, and descents of volcanoes. Vans take the bikes from San José, and lunch is included. Multiple-day tours are also available.

Dos Montañas de Pacuare, *Paseo Colón, Calles 22/24, tel. [2]336455*, organizes one day trips in Tapantí National Park for about $70 from San José.

SLEEPING OUT UNDER THE STARS

Camping is not a traditional outdoors activity in Costa Rica, not least because the outdoors are often viewed as dangerous. And imported equipment, from tents to sleeping bags to good backpacks, can be expensive.

The most obvious places in which to camp are national parks, which usually have sleeping spaces supplied with outhouses and showers.

Organized private campsites are found at Jacó. These have more in common with trailer parks than with getting back to nature.

When camping on a beach or in the countryside, always ask permission if there's anybody around, and offer to pay. You might find some unexpected hospitality. And I won't lecture you about packing out your garbage.

If you don't bring your own equipment, rental gear is available locally at **Alquileres y Toldos Fiesta** *in San Pedro (one block north of Banco Anglo)*, *tel. [2]249155*. Prices are about $35 per week for a two-person tent. Other supplies are available at **Aro**, *Avenida 8, Calles 11/13. Or try calling [2]338090* for an outfit that rents a package of tent, two sleeping bags and water bottle for about $10 per day.

Centro de Aventuras, *Paseo Colón, Avenidas 22/24, next to the Ríos Tropicales travel agency*, runs an exchange of camping equipment. Stop by, *or call [2]550618*. If you're on your way home, consider lightening your luggage and making your tent available to a local camper or other visitors.

GETTING A BIRD'S EYE VIEW

Flightseeing, that staple of scenic viewing in Alaska, has come to Costa Rica. And in a country where so many vistas and topographies are packed into a small area, viewing it all from above is both practical and priceworthy.

But this kind of excursion is not for the faint of heart. Small aircraft, turbulence, and pilot capabilities make for more sudden free falls, dips, and unprogrammed bumps and tilts, and a, uh, more interesting trip, than you're likely to experience elsewhere. Fellow-passengers stare at each other, too cool to verbalize their impressions. Is the pilot really heading into that ridge? Are we going to make it over? Those trees look awfully close. Yes, it's breathtaking.

Providers of airborne sightseeing:
- **Helicopters of Costa Rica**, *south of the main post office next to Banco Lyon, tel. [2]313269, fax [2]333225*
- **Saeta Taxi Aéreo**, *at Tobías Bolaños Airport (P. O. Box 9-163 Pavas, tel. [2]321474, fax [2]329514)* runs a point-to-point service, and offers a menu of day outings from San José, including: View of Poás volcano, one hour, $250; Overflight of Lake Arenal, 90 minutes, $380; the banana zone, two hours, $620; the Talamanca Mountains, 90 minutes, $370. These rates are for four or five passengers.
- **Aeronaves**, *Tobías Bolaños Airport, tel. [2]321413, fax [2]321176*
- **Aerolíneas Turísticas de América**, *Tobías Bolaños Airport, tel. [2]321125, fax [2]325802*
- **Taxi Aéreo Centroamericano**, *Tobías Bolaños Airport, tel. [2]321317*

HORSEBACK RIDING

Horses are available almost anywhere in Costa Rica. Knowledgeable folk are not put off by the small, local animals, known as *criollos* (which are bred to get a job done without consuming excess feed), though larger, more well known breeds — Arabians, Morgans — will also be found. Costa Rican horses can have problems with persons of weight, so if you're over 200 pounds, make sure you advise the agency or operator.

Riding rates can range from $5 per hour to $75 for a day outing to $150 for an overnight trip.

Among regions and lodges that offer equestrian excursions:
- **Guanacaste**: most hotels, and private operators in Monteverde; Hacienda La Pacífica, Cañas; Albergue de Tilarán and Puerto San Luis, Tilarán; Hotel Las Espuelas, Liberia; Hacienda Guachipelín; Hacienda Los Inocentes; Hotel Flor de Itabo, Playas del Coco
- **Nicoya**: Villa Serena, Junquillal; Hotel Rancho Suizo, Nosara; Hotel Oasis del Pacífico, Playa Naranjo; Hotel La Hacienda, Tambor; Hotel Tango Mar

Horseback excursions in the San José area are available from:
- **Hacienda San Miguel**, *tel. [2]291094, at Rancho Redondo in the shadow of Irazú volcano*. Day trips from San José through cloud forest. Beginners are accommodated. About $65 per person.
- **Irazú Horse Trekking**, *tel. [2]232811*. Takes riders right to the top of Irazú volcano, and to other destinations, for a price of about $80.
- **Tipical Tours**, *tel. [2]338486*, arranges rides through cloud forest near

Cerro de la Muerte, with guaranteed quetzal sightings. About $90.
- **Rainbow Tours**, *tel. [2]338228*, has riding near Carara Biological Reserve, about $75.
- **L. A. Tours**, *Avenida Central, Calles 5/7, tel. [2]214501*, has a day outing to a farm near Orotina, on the Pacific slope, about $75.
- **Robles Tours**, *tel. [2]372116, fax [2]371976*, rides to Barva volcano;
- **Magic Trails**, *tel. [2]538146, fax [2]539937*, rides through Prusia Forest Reserve, on the slopes of Irazú.
- **Saragundí Specialty Tours**, *Avenida 7, Calles Central/1 (P. O. Box 7126), San José, tel. [2]550011, fax [2]552155*, has a one-day horseback and hiking tour for about $75.
- **Hotel El Tirol**, *tel. [2]397371, Hotel El Cypresal, tel. [2]374466*, and the other mountain hotels above Heredia also arrange riding.

Horseback excursions in the Caribbean area are available from:
- **Chimuri Lodge** and **Hotel Punta Cocles**, *Puerto Viejo*; various hotels in Cahuita.

SCUBA DIVING

When you think of spectacular diving in Central America, you usually think of Belize or the Bay Islands of Honduras. But — surprise of surprises — Costa Rica holds its own in undersea as well as on-shore natural attractions.

Diving resorts — or resorts with diving facilities — are clustered around Playa del Coco in the northwest (Condovac, Hotel El Ocotal) and at Drake Bay in the southern Pacific coastal area. Cahuita National Park, on the Caribbean, has some coral spots, and there are wrecks to explore just to the south, near Puerto Viejo.

Northwest diving trips generally include islets a couple of miles from the mainland, and sometimes the Murciélago (*Bat*) Islands, 30 miles out. Most diving is at 30 to 40 feet, and mostly what you see is fish, but not just any fish. There are morays, jewfish, octopus, manta rays, grunts, snappers, occasionally sharks, in schools that number in the hundreds. And there are also rock formations, rather than intricate coral reef, though there are some undersea caves and coral clusters.

Water temperatures are generally from 75 to 85 degrees, somewhat lower when winds are from the north during the dry season. Wet suits are sometimes required. Visibility runs up to 80 feet, but can be limited by the same marine microorganisms that make fish so abundant, and by river runoff and silt during the rainiest times. The waters are generally clearest in the Gulf of Papagayo, where there are no river mouths.

Wall and limited reef diving are available off Caño Island, accessible from Drake Bay on the Osa Peninsula, and from Quepos. Some of the densest schools of fish will be seen in this area, among them snapper, grouper, barracuda, eels and rays, along with bright tropical species. Visibility tops out at about 70 feet. Up on the surface, sea turtles, dolphins, and whales are common sights.

Coco Island, farther out in the Pacific, has recently opened as a diving area, offering clear views of sperm whales, sting rays, eels, and the large game fish of the area, along with undersea pinnacles. But the real attraction is the chance to view sharks — hammerhead and white-tip, among others. Visibility is usually between 50 and 75 feet, and currents are strong.

A ten-night excursion to Coco Island on the 120-foot *Okeanos Aggressor* (a floating resort with a capacity of 18 divers), including seven dive days, costs $2,600 or more — and this does *not* include air fare to Costa Rica or any accommodations on land.

Dive Operators

Diving operators in Costa Rica include:

- **Diving Safaris**, *Apartado 121-5019, Playas del Coco, tel. 67[0]0012. Based at Hotel El Ocotal*, one of the most experienced diving services in Costa Rica, with new diesel-powered boats. Courses and certification upgrades, and package trips based at the hotel are available.
- **Virgin Diving**, *Hotel La Costa, Playa Hermosa, Guanacaste (tel. 67[0]0472 or [2]218949)* offers regular diving trips to Bat Island at $115 per person, and daily half-day dives at $55, or $75 with all equipment.
- **Mario Vargas Expeditions**, *Playas del Coco, tel. 67[0]0351*
- **Rich Coast Diving**, *Playas del Coco, tel. 67[0]0176, fax 67[0]0164).* Offers somewhat lower rates than others in the Coco area: $45 for a two-tank dive ($65 with full equipment), $70 for a resort course.
- **Tango Mar**, *near Tambor, in southern Nicoya, tel. [2]231864*
- **Río Sierpe Lodge** *near Drake Bay (P. O. Box 818-1200, Pavas, tel. [2]202121, fax [2]323321)* has packages priced from about $160 per day of diving. Diving is also available at the **Caballito del Mar Hotel** at Drake Bay, *tel. and fax [2]315028.*
- **Flamingo Divers**, *Flamingo Beach, tel. 67[4]4021*, offers two-tank dives for $70 plus equipment rental, full open-water certification for about $400.
- **Viajes Tropicales Laura**, *Limón, tel. [7]582410*, arranges diving along the Caribbean, including wreck diving, as does **Hotel Las Palmas**, *near Puerto Viejo, tel. [2]553939.*

San José Dive Shops

- **Tropical Sceneries**, *Calle 29, Avenidas Central/8 (P. O. Box 2047-1000, San José), tel. [2]242555, fax [2]339524.* Offers one-day dive trips from

San José to Herradura, near Jacó, at $125 per person, plus equipment charges; diving packages based at Río Sierpe Lodge, near Drake Bay; and longer trips to Coco Island.

• **Cruceros del Sur**, *Sabana Norte, San José, tel. [2]326672*. Represents *Okeanos Aggressor* to Coco Island.

• **Deep Sea Scuba**, *Centro Comercial El Cruce, San Rafael de Escazú, tel. [2]326324 and [2]898191,   fax [2]312145*. A diving service operated by a Costa Rican with extensive experience in the States. Excursions are available on both coasts, as well as equipment rentals and service.

• **Mundo Acuático**, *San Pedro, tel. [2]249729*, is a dive shop that operates trips to both coasts.

Agencies that arrange diving in Costa Rica include:

• **Go Diving**, *5610 Rowland Rd., Minnetonka, MN 55343*.

• **See and Sea Travel**, *50 Francisco St., San Francisco, CA 94133*. Books trips on *Undersea Hunter* to Coco Island

• **Aggressor Fleet**, *P. O. Drawer K, Morgan City, LA 70381 Tel. 800-348-2628 or 504-385-2628, fax 384-0817*. Operates *Okeanos Aggressor* to Coco Island.

• The cruise ship *Temptress*, mentioned above, offers diving excursions in its water sports programs.

The **Divers Alert Network**, an association of medical doctors based *at Duke University (P. O. Box 3823, Duke University Medical Center, Durham, NC 27710*, provides emergency medical referral. *Call 919-684-8111*.

Insurance tailored for divers is available from **P.B.A.**, *P. O. Box 907, Minneapolis, MN 55440, tel. 800-446-2671 or 612-588-2731*.

ECOTOURISM

No doubt about it, Costa Rica is the world's ecotourism mecca. There are hundreds of bird species, thousands of plants, and insects numbering in the tens of thousands, in habitats ranging from steaming lowland jungle to cloud forest to frosty peaks. Several worlds are crowded into a land of modest size, and visitors can appreciate them all, with not a few aches and mud puddles in the process.

But is this ecotourism?

You might well ask — and you might well think things are a bit out of kilter — when a local company can call itself Ecological Rent-a-Car.

At its best, eco-tourism is an effort to acquaint visitors with tropical life systems, while doing as little damage to them as possible, and perhaps even protecting and enhancing them. It doesn't necessarily put the whims of the visitor first.

But for most visitors, eco-tourism is a theme, the modern folklore of travel to Costa Rica that corresponds to Mayan culture in Guatemala and schnitzel in Vienna. It involves rafting trips and hikes to hot springs, but largely, it is pattering guides, bus rides, and hotels with good and bad restaurants (with or without cable television), and friendly management.

Ecotourism can be like tourism anywhere. And it can even leave nature in a sadder state than before. But we're dealing with the real world here, and the inescapable fact is that outsiders want to see a part of the world still relatively unaffected by population pressures and human alterations. And Costa Rica would like to see some economic benefit from letting outsiders in.

Ecotour Possibilities

1. Spend several days in a tent near a national park. You fly in by chartered plane, burning fossil fuels. The plane also brings in beer, liquor, and tinned food. A diesel generator provides power. Garbage disappears mysteriously. Birding and turtle-watching excursions are taken in motorized vehicles. After a hard day getting to know nature, iced drinks are always available.

2. Fly to a luxury eco-lodge in the jungle. Locally available jungle materials — hardwoods and palm thatch — were used to construct the guest cottages, along with cement and reinforcing rods brought from San José and abroad. The kitchen serves the finest aged beef fattened in pastures that once were rain forest, the bar has an assortment of domestic and imported liquors. The lodge stands on a huge tract of formerly logged land that is being allowed and encouraged to return to forest. Elsewhere, similar large parcels have been subdivided into smallholdings.

3. You take a bus from San José, are met in a lowland village beyond Braulio Carrillo National Park, and hike for a couple of hours to a clearing, carrying all your food, cooking equipment and sleeping gear. You spend a weekend camping, birding, hiking, spotting snakes and small mammals, listening to branches crack and trees fall, and watching bromeliads and ferns renew life from the decay of the old. Mostly, you try to keep dry or get used to being rained on. Muddy and exhausted, you finally emerge from the rain forest, enlightened about the interactions of natural systems. You are one of the last to take the trip to the clearing. The land has changed hands, and will soon be planted in bananas.

4. You've been looking forward for months to visiting a national park along the southwestern Pacific coast of Costa Rica. Its pristine tropical forest, extending right to the water's edge, alive with tapirs, coatimundis, marmosets, howler monkeys and sloths, was rescued from developers who wanted to cut down the trees, shoo away the animals, and erect concrete resorts on exposed hillsides.

You arrive to find that the forest canopy is, indeed, magnificent, and alive with birds. But the park's horseshoe bays and stunning headlands and views of the glittering water and its cachet as a protected area have made it even more of a destination that the quondam developers ever intended.

Hotels and resorts and restaurants and tour agencies crowd the access road. Foul-smelling liquids seep onto the adjacent beach. Out of season, when the numbers of foreign visitors fall, area hotels boost occupancy with rock concerts, surfing competitions, and other "events" peculiar to any resort area with a marketing team. Park trails, churned to mud by incessant footsteps, are littered with cans and "disposable" diapers. The campsite has long been closed, and there is serious talk of placing the park off-limits for one or several days a week in a desperate hope that some sort of recovery might take place.

A Few Simple Rules

So what can you do to keep your depredations to a minimum?
- Leave things as you found them. Take your garbage out with you when you visit a reserve.
- Buy nothing made from endangered species of plant or animal. This can mean turning your back on coral jewelry and woodware. Ironwood (*guayacán*), purpleheart (*nazareno*), and rosewood (*cocobolo*) are endangered, among others.
- Keep nothing that you catch from the sea, unless you plan to cook it.
- Accept no "eco-tourism" label at face value.
- Ask questions about any excursion, any product, that claims to be ecological: Are local people employed? Are they being displaced from traditional ways? Are local resources used in a sustainable manner?

Sometimes, eco-tourism can also mean staying out of (or being barred from) overcrowded reserves. I could go on and on, but you get my point. When we visit new places, what results is not always what we anticipate, or what we want. Let's recognize the problem, and try to keep things under control.

Can you be an eco-tourist in Costa Rica? It depends on you, and on the choices you make.

SAN JOSÉ

San José, the capital of Costa Rica, is many towns. At its center are steel-and-concrete towers, shops with plate-glass windows displaying the latest fashions and consumer electronic gadgetry, thoroughfares busy with traffic, and sidewalks crowded with neatly dressed businessmen and office workers. All might have been transplanted from a medium-sized Spanish city.

Just west of the main square is the bustling market area, much more Central American in character, where tinkerers, wholesalers, and vendors of food and every necessity of daily life eke out their livings from tiny shops and market stalls and street stands, where buses and delivery trucks and taxis battle to advance through the throngs and commerce overflowing the sidewalks. Here, the buildings are one- and two-story, relatively dingy, and mostly unseen by the casual observer for all the activity around them.

Farther west of downtown San José, and in some of the surrounding suburbs, are the areas of gracious living, where huddled constructions give way to spacious, ranch-style houses with green lawns, always surrounded by substantial fences. This is where California- and Florida-style living — all the amenities in a benign climate — has grafted itself onto the local scene.

And there are the working-class neighborhoods as well, once-independent villages that lodge in simple, neat and non-unpleasant tin-roofed houses, among clusters of coffee and banana trees, the thousands of people who make San José run.

ARRIVALS & DEPARTURES
Airlines Servicing Costa Rica
Scheduled service to San José is currently provided by:
- **Lacsa**, *Costa Rica's international airline, Calle 1, Avenida 5, tel. [2]310033; airport, tel. [2]416244*
- **Aero Costa Rica**, *San Pedro, tel. [2]534753*
- **Sansa**, the domestic airline, *Calle 24, Avenidas Central/1, tel. [2]333258, fax [2]552176*
- **Travelair**, the *other* domestic airline, *Tobías Bolaños Airport, tel. [2]327883, fax [2]203054*
- **American Airlines**, *Paseo Colón, Calles 26/28, tel. [2]571266*
- **Aviateca**, *Calle 1, Avenida 3, tel. [2]554949*
- **Continental Airlines**, *Calle 19, Avenida 2, tel. [2]330266*
- **Taca**, *Calle 1, Avenida 3, tel. [2]221790*
- **SAM** (Colombia), *Avenida 7, Calles 5/7, tel. [2]333066*
- **COPA** (Panama), *Calle 1, Avenida 5, tel. [2]237033*
- **Iberia**, *Paseo Colón, Calle 40, tel. [2]213311*
- **United Airlines**, *Sabana Sur, tel. [2]204844*

Air service to Tortuguero and other places not served by Sansa or Travelair is provided by a number of companies listed in the phone book under *Taxis Aéreos* and *Aviación*.

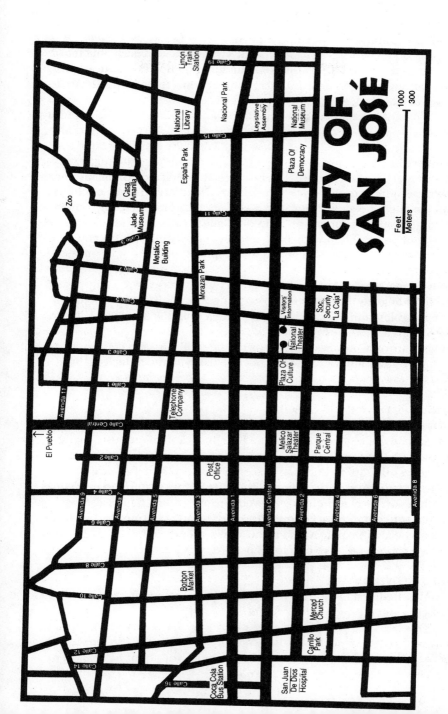

ARRIVING BY AIR

Juan Santamaría International Airport is *located on the outskirts of Alajuela, 17 kilometers west of San José*. It's a small and manageable facility serving both domestic and foreign scheduled flights. Costa Rica's other international airport, near Liberia in the northwest, will handle charter flights of vacationers heading for the beaches.

Local charter flights use the smaller **Tobías Bolaños** airfield *at Pavas, just west of San José*.

Immigration & Customs

Immigration lineups are generally speedy, but if several planes touch down one after another, or a large charter load arrives, you could well stand in line for over an hour. Nex t— before the cursory customs check— comes the tourist information counter. Make reservations here for a hotel in town if you don't already have one arranged, and pick up any other information you need — they're quite helpful.

Exchanging Money

To change money, look for an exchange booth. If it's not open, you'll have to go left and back inside the terminal building after you leave the customs area. *Banking hours are Monday to Friday from 8 a.m. to 4 p.m.* There are also informal money-changers on the sidewalk outside. It's a good idea to change a fair amount at the airport in order to avoid the long lines at banks in town.

Getting to Town By Taxi or Bus

Transport from the airport to San José is available by taxi for about $12; and on the regular Alajuela-San José buses and microbuses that stop in front of the terminal. These run every ten to fifteen minutes, and charge less than 50¢. Luggage space on buses is limited, but the driver might let you put your bags in an otherwise empty seat for an extra fare.

Buses arrive at terminals scattered through central San José. Most are in areas with either no accommodations or less-than-attractive digs. Taxis in San José are inexpensive, so if you arrive after dark and are not sure of your surroundings, take one to your hotel.

DEPARTING BY AIR

All scheduled flights use **Juan Santamaría International Airport**, *17 kilometers west of San José, near Alajuela*.

Getting To the Airport

Any hotel can arrange a taxi to the airport, for about $12, *or you can call the airport taxi company at [2]216865*.

If you can handle your luggage (you might have to pay for an extra seat), *take the Alajuela microbus from Avenida 2, Calles 12/14, San José. These run almost continuously during the day.*

Airport Procedures
First check in with your airline and pay the exit tax, which is currently about $8. You can re-purchase U.S. dollars at the airport bank — if the bank is open and if the currency is available.

Airport Shops & Services
The usual assortment of overpriced airport shops solicits your last Costa Rican coins. *The post office branch is open until 5 p.m.* The duty-free shops, in the departure area, have good assortments of liquor, cigarettes and perfumes, and some odds and ends of other luxury goods. You can carry your purchases with you.

DEPARTING BY TRAIN AND TRAIN EXCURSIONS
Regular service to the coasts, including the **Jungle Train** to Limón, has been discontinued.

Some travel agencies organize train excursions through the Caribbean banana plantations. And if you see a passenger train rumbling through San José, it's the commuter service that runs weekdays between Heredia, the Atlantic Station in San José, and the University of Costa Rica in San Pedro; or the local train from the western suburb of Pavas.

DEPARTING BY CAR
Just follow the signs! Arrows along the main thoroughfares point the way to Limón, Puntarenas, Cartago and other major towns.

DEPARTING BY BUS
Buses to various points in Costa Rica are mentioned in the coverage of towns, parks and beaches in this book. Many leave from the area of the Coca-Cola market, *16 Calle, Avenidas 1/3.* For buses to other points, and to re-check schedules, inquire at the tourist office.

Service to Panama and to all Central American capitals, with connections to Mexico, is provided by **Tica Bus**, *Avenida 4, Calle 9, tel. [2]218954.* Currently there are departures for Panama City on daily at 8 a.m., and for Managua on Monday, Wednesday, Friday and Saturday at 7 a.m. **Sirca**, *Calle 7, Avenidas 6/8, tel. [2]231464*, has service to Managua on Wednesday, Friday and Sunday. Other buses from the Coca-Cola terminal go as far as the Nicaraguan border at Peñas Blancas. **Tracopa**, *Avenida 18, Calles 2/4*, has three daily buses to the border of Panama at Canoas, another to David, in northern Panama.

GETTING AROUND TOWN

Avenidas in San José run from east to west, with odd-numbered avenidas north of Avenida Central, or Central Avenue, and even-numbered avenidas to the south. *Calles*, or streets, run north-south, with odd-numbered calles east of the Calle Central, even-numbered streets to the west. You'll quickly get used to this scheme as you go around the city, though you'll probably confuse your avenidas and calles at first.

The two main areas of interest are the **central business district**, around the intersection of Avenida Central and Calle Central; and the high-toned **Paseo Colón district**, to the west. Paseo Colón is a continuation of Avenida Central. From the western end of Paseo Colón to the center of the city is just over a mile, a distance easily negotiated on foot or on the many city buses that run along Colón.

North, east, west and south of the central area are the *barrios*, or neighborhoods, of the capital — Los Yoses, Sabana Sur, Bellavista, and several dozen others. Adjoining suburban municipalities, such as Guadalupe and San Pedro, comprise the *Area Metropolitana* (Metropolitan Area) with San José, and are, for practical purposes, part of a single city.

By Bus

City buses and those running to nearby suburbs provide a service roughly comparable to that in large North American cities, at a fraction of the price. The fare is usually posted near the door, and on most routes is about 10¢.

Many bus routes start at or near the Central Park. All are identified by both a number and the name of the neighborhood or suburb they serve. These are clearly posted at the stops. In addition, 20-passenger microbuses serve some of the same areas.

Buses and their stops are given for most places of interest mentioned in this chapter. For others, ask at the tourist office.

By Car

This is something you should avoid in San José, if possible. Costa Ricans are aggressive at the wheel, and their lane-changing, honking horns and screeching tires can get on your nerves. Almost all streets are one-way, making for circuitous routings through downtown—when you can move.

Renting a Car

Among car-rental companies operating in San José are:
• **Avis**, *Sabana Norte, tel. [2]329922*
• **Budge**t, *Paseo Colón, Calle 30, tel. [2]233284; also at airport*

- **Dollar**, *Calle 38, Avenida 9, Calle Central, tel. [2]333339; and airport*
- **Hertz**, *Paseo Colón, Calle 38, tel. [2]235959*
- **National**, *Calle 36, Avenida 7, tel. [2]334044*
- **Toyota Rent A Car**, *Paseo Colón, Calles 30/32, tel. [2]232250*
- **U-Haul**, *Paseo Colón, tel. [2]221110*

There are many others listed in the phone book under *Alquiler de Automóviles*, but none offer bargains.

By Taxi

Taxis are a downright cheap way to get around San José. Most trips around the city will cost less than two dollars, or less than a dollar within a neighborhood. Fares are fixed by the government, currently at 70¢ for the first kilometer, 25¢ for each additional kilometer, and $3 per hour of waiting. The tariff rises slightly at night.

What's In An Address?

Josefinos navigate around their city by inertial displacement from known landmarks. An ad for a certain restaurant might say that it is 200 meters west of and 150 meters north of Edificio Chile Picante. "100 meters" is another way of saying "one block" in Costa Rica (though a block is, in fact, somewhat shorter). The translation, then, is: From the Chile Picante building, go two blocks west, then one-and-a-half blocks north.

Believe it or not, buildings also have numbers, but they're rarely posted, so an address giving a house number is of little use. For obvious reasons, I will not always give addresses and directions in the local manner.

WHERE TO STAY

Better Hotels – West End

HOTEL CARIARI, *Ciudad Cariari (P. O. Box 737-1007, Centro Colón, San José), tel. [2]390022, fax [2]392803. 220 rooms. $125 single/$135 double/ $190 poolside/$200 and up for suites. Rates discounted approximately 20% May to October. U. S. reservations: tel. 800-847-2568 (to Costa Rica) or 3501 W. Rolling Hills Circle, Fort Lauderdale, FL, tel. 305-476-5848. American Express, Visa, Master Card.*

The Cariari is not in San José at all, but eight kilometers west of the city, along the Cañas expressway, halfway to the airport. This is a tasteful, modern resort and country-club complex, with a pool, sauna, whirlpool, and casino, and shops. For a fee, guests can use an 18-hole golf course, tennis courts, Olympic-size swimming pool, basketball courts, and gym.

Restaurants include the formal **Vitrales**, open evenings only, and **Las Tejas**, serving all meals. The **Las Maracas** bar has live music on weekends.

HOTEL HERRADURA, *Ciudad Cariari (P.O. Box 7-1880, San José), tel. [2]390033, fax [2]392292. 234 rooms. $124-$150 single/$135-$161 double. U.S. reservations: tel. 800-245-8420.*

The Herradura is another large and modern hotel, constructed in Spanish-colonial style, comparable in facilities to the Cariari. Rooms are among the nicest in or near San José, and have television and air conditioning. There are two pools.

The **Bon Vivant** restaurant, open evenings, serves French cuisine, and is quite expensive; **Tiffany's** serves steaks, chops, and shrimp during the day, and has a daily complete dinner special for about $10; and the **Sakura** has Japanese-style food. And there are a casino, conference facilities, and even a chapel.

HOTEL SAN JOSÉ PALACIO, *La Uruca (P. O. Box 458-1150), tel. [2]202034, fax [2]202036. 154 rooms. $126 to $138 single/$132 to $143 double, $180 and up in suites. Visa, Master Card, American Express. U.S. reservations tel. 800-858-0606.*

Just west of San José, towering on a hill above the Cañas expressway, the new Palacio has the nicest modern-style accommodations in the city. The pool is huge, free-form, with a planted island. There are also exercise rooms, racquetball and tennis courts, sauna, whirlpool, numerous shops, conference rooms, and, of course, a casino. One of the many nice features is that towering trees were preserved on the site, lending a tropical forest atmosphere to the grounds. Access to the hotel is only from the westbound lanes of the expressway.

Cuisine at the Palacio is Spanish, which reflects ownership by the Barceló chain. The main restaurant serves paella, steak and fish at $10 to $15 per main course. The **Anfora** coffee shop has a $10 dinner buffet, and assorted lighter fare.

HOTEL IRAZÚ, *Autopista Gen. Cañas, tel. [2]324811, fax [2]324549. 350 rooms. $88 single/$100 double, less without air conditioning. Mailing address: P. O. Box 962-1000, San José. U.S. reservations, tel. 305-871-6631 or 800-272-6654; Canada, tel. 800-463-6654.*

The largest hotel in San José, always lively with tour groups, the Irazú is located four kilometers west of downtown, in the municipality of La Uruca. The immediate area holds no attraction or views, but the landscaping and a U-shaped building shield guests from passing trucks.

Rooms are air-conditioned, and there are two restaurants, lighted tennis courts, pool, sauna, massage service, and numerous shops and real-estate salesmen in the bustling lobby. An hourly shuttle bus to downtown is available. Lower room rates are sometimes offered on site.

HOTEL COROBICÍ, *Calle 42, Avenida 5 (P.O. Box 8-5480) tel. [2]328122, fax [2]315834. 275 rooms. $115 single/$125 double. U.S. reservations: 7955 N.W. 12th St., Miami, FL 33126, tel. 800-227-4274.*

A modern, cream-colored structure that towers over western San José, the Corobicí is under the same management as the Cariari. The facilities here are very attractive, and include a large pool area, health spa, air conditioning and television, a 24-hour coffee shop as well as the **Fuji**, a Japanese restaurant, and a courtesy bus to downtown. Though the climate doesn't demand it, there's a huge and impressive Hyatt-style towering indoor lobby.

HOTEL EJECUTIVO NAPOLEÓN, *Calle 40, Avenida 5 (P. O. Box 86340-1000 San José), tel. [2]233252, fax [2]229487. 26 units. $86 single/$97 double. Visa, American Express.*

A smaller hotel of executive suites, newly remodeled, catering to business travellers, with highly personalized service. Good location near Paseo Colón. Rooms have TV and air conditioning, and there's a pool and coffee shop. Rate includes a buffet breakfast.

HOTEL PARQUE DEL LAGO, *Avenida 2, Calle 40 (P. O. Box 624-1007), tel. [2]221577, fax [2]231617. 39 rooms. $108 to $132 single/$126 to $148 double, $150 to $228 in suites, $228 to $342 on V.I.P. level. U.S. reservationsw: 800-363-8869.*

A brand-new hotel oriented to business travellers, with assorted small in-room comforts provided: coffee maker, television, hair dryer, mini-bar, room safe, air conditioning, fax-modem connections. Buffet breakfast included in the rate, comprehensive business services (use included at V.I.P. level). No bar or restaurant.

HOTEL GRANO DE ORO, *Calle 30, Avenidas 2/4 (P. O. Box 1157-1007 Centro Colón, San José or P.O. Box 025216-36, Miami, FL 33102-5216), tel. [2]553322, fax [2]212782. 21 rooms. $66 single/$78 double standard room, $80/$90 deluxe, $122/$133 suite.*

A smaller hotel, this is a charming, impeccably restored and updated Victorian house and extensions, with lots of plants and shiny woodwork, courtyard with exuberant vegetation and falls, rooms with cheery floral bedspreads and modern bathrooms with gleaming brass fixtures. House-keeping is impeccable.

Better Hotels - Downtown

HOTEL AUROLA, *Calle 5, Avenida 5 (P.O. Box 7802-1000), tel. [2]337233, fax [2]551036. 200 rooms. $122 single, $133 double. U.S. reservations: 800-465-4329. Master Card, Visa, American Express.*

The Aurola is a San José landmark, a 17-floor aluminum-and-glass tower that mirrors the cityscape and sky. Inside are standard Holiday Inn rooms, pool, casino, underground parking, and shops. The street outside is the focal point for purse-snatching and pickpocketing in San José.

HOTEL VILLA TOURNÓN, *Barrio Tournón, P.O. Box 6606-1000, tel. [2]336622, fax [2]225211. 77 rooms. $50-70 single/$65-$75 double.*

This is an attractive hotel, in the style of an Arizona country resort, with soaring beamed ceilings, fireplaces and huge plants in public areas, and wood floors, carpets and generally soothing furnishings in the rooms. Solar-heated pool, whirlpool, protected parking, shops, air conditioning.

HOTEL BALMORAL, *Calle 7, Avenida Central (P. O. Box 3344-1000), tel. [2]225022, fax [2]217826. 121 rooms. $75 single/$80 double. U.S. reservations tel. 800-448-8355. American Express, Visa, Master Card.*

Rooms at this downtown hotel are good-sized, with air-conditioning and television; and there are a large lobby with ample seating, a shopping arcade, and a casino. The light, garden-style **Altamira** restaurant on the ground floor is easy on the senses.

HOTEL EUROPA, *Calle Central, Avenida 5 (P.O. Box 72-1000), tel. [2]221222, fax [2]213976. 72 rooms. $45-$63 single/$57-$75 double. Visa, American Express. U.S. reservations: tel. 800-223-6764, 212-714-2323.*

An early sixties hotel, with air-conditioned rooms, television, and the advantage of a small outdoor pool. Not a terrific building, the food is ordinary, and I have received some complaints about the housekeeping.

GRAN HOTEL COSTA RICA, *Avenida Central, Calle 3 (P. O. Box 527-1000), tel. [2]214000, fax [2]213501. 104 rooms. $60 single/$80 double. Visa, Master Card. U.S. reservations: tel. 800-327-3573.*

Most Central American capitals have a once-elegant old hotel, and this is San José's. Across from the National Theater and fronting on a small park, the Hotel Costa Rica has a chandeliered rooftop dining room that still exudes some class. The tasteful public areas from a bygone era are now lively with a casino, services, and people scurrying about, but the rooms are downright threadbare and shabby.

HOTEL PRESIDENTE, *Avenida Central, Calles 7/9 (P.O. Box 2922-1000), tel. [2]223022, fax [2]211205. 51 rooms. $63 single/$75 double. U.S. reservations: tel. 800-972-0515.*

The Presidente has especially good service among downtown hotels, and is in the process of expanding, with a 100-room section under construction. Some rooms are air-conditioned, and there are a basic restaurant, bar, a few suites, and the ever-present casino.

Smaller Luxury Hotels

HOTEL L'AMBIANCE, *Calle 13 no. 949, tel. [2]236702 fax [2]230481. U.S. Address: Interlink 179, Box 526770, Miami, FL 33152. 7 rooms. $80 single/$100 double, more in the suite.*

This is a classy hotel in a lovingly restored mansion just north of downtown — the manager describes it, quite accurately, as "a small *grand luxe* hotel with a commitment to excellence." All rooms are off a traditional central courtyard with fountain and miniature tropical garden, and all are individually decorated with antiques. A suite has a large living room, and all units have cable television. Maintenance is impeccable, but just as important is the level of personal, concierge-type service. The restaurant is intimate, excellent, and open to the public (see restaurant section, below).

LA CASA VERDE DE AMÓN, *Calle 7, Avenida 9, tel. and fax [2]230969. U.S. address: Box 025216, Dept. 1701, Miami, FL 33102-5216. 8 rooms. $65 to $80, single or double.*

A restored Victorian house, with huge rooms and public areas, including an upstairs piano salon. Rooms have hardwood floors, wardrobes, wainscoting, area rugs, and new tiled baths. Breakfast, served in the garden, is included in the rate. Sauna available.

D'RAYA VIDA, *north end of Calle 17 (P. O. Box 495-1000 San José, or P. O. Box 025216-1638, Miami, FL 33102), tel. [2]234168, fax [2]234157. 4 rooms. $70 single/$95 double. Credit cards accepted.*

This impeccably kept mansion is a surprise, tucked away behind gates on a dead end just northeast of downtown San José. The neighborhood is far from upper class, but security is good. Airport pickup and return are included in the rate.

Moderate Hotels - West End

COSTA RICA TENNIS CLUB, *Sabana Sur (opposite Metropolitan Park), P.O. Box 4964-1000, tel. [2]321266, fax [2]323867. 27 rooms. $51 single or double. Visa, Master Card, American Express.*

This is a fun place in which to stay, a lively country club with many of the features of the Cariari and Herradura, but in more modest quarters. Guests have use of tennis courts, pools, sauna, bowling alley, and billiard tables, with some restrictions. The restaurant has a limited but reasonably priced menu. No shops or travel services here.

HOTEL AMBASSADOR, *Paseo Colón, Calle 28 (P. O. Box 10186), tel. [2]218155, fax [2]553396. 73 rooms. $62 to $75 single/$75 to $87 double, higher in suites. Master Card, Visa, American Express. U.S. reservations, tel. 800-344-1212.*

Plain, good-sized rooms with minibar and television, public areas in passé peninsular taste (heavy on brooding varnished wood).

APARTOTEL LA SABANA, *La Sabana (P. O. Box 8446-1000, San José), tel. [2]202422, fax [2]317386. 32 apartments and rooms. $42 double room, $54 to $90 for apartments. Visa, American Express, Master Card.*

A newly completed colonial-style structure, conveniently located near the Corobicí Hotel in San José's west end ("150 meters north, 50 meters west of Burger King"). All rooms have air conditioning and cable television, and on-site facilities include a pool, sauna, and washing machines. Good value for San José.

HOTEL BOULEVARD EJECUTIVO, *P. O. Box 3258-1000, San José. $52 single/$64 double ($85/$95 in suites).*

A modern suburban villa in Rohrmoser, the flat area west of La Sabana Park.

APARTOTEL RAMGO, *Sabana Sur, one block south of Metropolitan Park (P. O. Box 1441), tel. [2]323823, fax [2]323111. 16 units. From $50 single to $75 for four persons. Visa, Master Card, American Express.*

Plain but large apartments, each with two bedrooms, kitchen, dining room, laundry area, terrace, and cable TV, in a stark building in a residential area on the western edge of San José. Near shopping and bus to downtown. A good value for families or compatible groups.

Smaller Moderate Hotels - West End

HOTEL PETIT VICTORIA, *Calle 28, Avenida 2, tel. [2]330766. 11 rooms. $55 single or double with breakfast.*

This is a charming (if overpriced) little hotel, a wooden house in the best old San José style, renovated with care. Rooms have double beds with frilly spread, painted woodwork, and private bath with hot water. Outside, a wrought-iron fence surrounds the gardens. The name does not deceive.

Moderate Hotels - Downtown

I'm sorry to say that most downtown hotels in this category are more modest in their facilities than in their prices.

HOTEL ROYAL GARDEN, *Calle Central, Avenida Central, P. O. Box 3493-1000, tel. [2]570022, fax [2]571517. 54 rooms. $51 single/$57 double. U. S. reservations: tel. 800-223-6764 or 212-758-4375.*

Exit San José, and enter the mysterious Orient through the front door of the Royal Garden. An elevator takes you to the second floor, where, at 9 a.m., Chinese music tinkles, curtains keep out all but thin shafts of daylight, and smoke floats over the blackjack tables. An unexpected milieu in Central America. Well-managed.

HOTEL PLAZA, *Av. Central, Calle 2/4 (P.O. Box 2019-1000), tel. [2]571896, fax [2]222641. 40 rooms. $40 single/$52 double.*

Central location, restaurant and bar, carpeted rooms with television, some with balconies, others on air shafts with little light. Good closet space, and perfectly adequate, if anonymous.

HOTEL DIPLOMAT, *Calle 6, Avenidas Central/2, tel. [2]218133. 25 rooms. $27 single/$38 double.*

A small, modern hotel. Rooms have phones, no other extras. Good value for downtown.

HOTEL DON CARLOS, *Calle 9, Avenidas 7/9 (P. O. Box 1593-1000 San José or Box 025216-1686, Miami FL 33102-5216), tel. [2]216707, fax [2]550828. 25 rooms. $46-$57 single/$57-$68 double.*

A remodeled mansion on a quiet street, decorated with pre-Columbian art pieces, modern sculptures, plants and knick-knacks in the patios and on the sun porch. Rates include light breakfast, and other meals are available. Reservations are essential.

GRAN HOTEL DOÑA INÉS, *Calle 11, Avenidas 2/6 (P. O. Box 1754-1002), tel. [2]227443, fax [2]227553. 20 rooms. $60 single/$73 double.*

A very nicely restored large home. Rooms have hardwood furniture, ceiling fan, television, and textured wallpaper, but are just a bit musty. Bar, meals available. There is no particular action for tourists in this fringe commercial area, but if more centrally located hotels are full, you need not hesitate to stay here.

HOTEL ALAMEDA, *Avenida Central, Calle 12 (P.O. Box 680-1000), tel. [2]236333, fax [2]229673. 52 rooms. $43 single/$52 double. Visa, Master Card, American Express.*

If you have to be near the noisy bus station and market area, this hotel is probably your best choice, though it's expensive for where it is, and a renovation has meticulously removed all traces of the Alameda's faded fifties charm. Facilities include a full-service restaurant with a few quite reasonably priced items.

HOTEL DORAL, *Avenida 4, Calles 6/8 (P. O. Box 5530-1000), tel. [2]330665, fax [2]334827. 42 rooms. $29 single/$42 double. American Express, Visa, Master Card.*

A recently renovated hotel on a busy street, quite nice inside, with clean, light, cheery rooms, all with television, phone and tiled bathroom.

HOTEL TALAMANCA, *Avenida 2, Calles 8/10 (P.O. Box 449-1002), tel. [2]335033, fax [2]335420. 56 rooms. $25 single/$33 double. U.S. reservations: tel. 305-925-2700.*

Located in the noisy bus terminal and market area. Some rooms have TV, 24-hour restaurant, bar, casino.

Smaller Moderate Hotels - Downtown

HOTEL SANTO TOMÁS, *Avenida 7, Calles 3/5, tel. [2]550488, fax [2]223950. 20 rooms, all with private bath. $42.50 and $55 single/$47.50 to $65 double, including breakfast.*

The Santo Tomás has matured in just a few years into one of San José's finer small hotels, impeccably kept, with a well-trained staff.

HEMINGWAY INN, *Calle 9, Avenida 9 (P. O. Box 1711-1002 San José), tel. and fax [2]225741. 9 rooms. $35 single/$55 double/$70 triple/$75 in suite, including breakfast.*

Guest rooms in this updated house are on the smallish side, but tastefully furnished and quite comfortable, with narrow beds, television, ceiling fan, wood floors, room safe, and a modern tiled bathroom with electrically heated shower behind a pocket door.

LA AMISTAD INN, *Avenida 11, Calle 15, tel. [2]211597, fax [2]211409. $25 to $35 single/$35 to $45 double.*

A German-operated bed-and-breakfast, in yet another restored house. Good mattresses.

HOTEL REY, *Avenida 7, Calle 9 (P. O. Box 7145-1000 San José), tel. and fax [2]331769. 13 rooms. $40 single/$58 double, including breakfast. Credit cards accepted.*

Next to the National Insurance Institute office tower, this is a freshened-up large house. The lobby is a large, glassed-over patio, light and cheery. Carpeted rooms have two single or one large bed, television, tiled bathroom with shower, and good closet space. Free parking is provided, and the price is fair for what you get.

DOÑA MERCE BED AND BREAKFAST, *14 Avenida, Calles 13/15 (P. O. Box 3660-1000), tel. [2]231582, fax [2]331909. $35 single/$60 double.*

Small bed-and-breakfast operated by a retired Costa Rican couple, on a quiet street not far from downtown.

Budget Hotels

HOTEL CACTS, *Avenida 3 Bis, Calles 28/30 (P. O. Box 379-1005), tel. and fax [2]218616. 38 rooms. $31 single/$35 double, $50 in the newer section, with breakfast.*

It's hard to call this a budget hotel when you get so much for your money: quiet location just a few blocks from Paseo Colón, cable and satelliteTV in the lobby, buffet breakfast of tropical fruits and breads included in the rate, beverage service, congeniality, even secretarial services if you need them.

HOTEL RITZ and **PENSIÓN CONTINENTAL**, *Calle Central, Av. 8/ 10 (P. O. Box 6783-1000), tel. [2]224103, fax [2]228849. 26 rooms. $10 to $23 single/$15 to $25 double.*

A modest, clean, Swiss-run establishment, created by joining and renovating and brightening two formerly separate establishments.

HOTEL GALILEA, *Av. Central, Calles 11/13, tel. [2]336925, tel. [2]231689. 23 rooms. $28 single/$35 double.*

Modern and plain, a few blocks from the center of town, not an attractive area, but a good value if you get a room that doesn't face the street.

PENSIÓN DE LA CUESTA, *Avenida 1, Calles 11/15 (No. 1332), tel. 552896. $25 single/$35 double.*

You'll find a comfortable, homey atmosphere in the rooms in this venerable wooden house.

HOTEL FORTUNA, *Avenida 6, Calles 2/4 (P. O. Box 7-1570), tel. [2]235344, fax [2]232743. 24 rooms. $27 single/$30 double. Visa, Master Card.*

Newer than most hotels in this area (c. 1958), with hot water, private bath, phones in rooms.

HOTEL BIENVENIDO, *Calle 10, Avenidas 1/3 (P. O. Box 389-2000), tel. [2]211872. 44 rooms. $15 single/$19 double/$24 triple.*

This hotel is good news for budget travelers. A former movie theater has been renovated and recycled, with skylights and light wells making a massive building surprisingly cheery. A serious drawback is a location in the Central Market area. Get a room that does not face the street, or look elsewhere.

PETIT HOTEL, *Calle 24 no. 39, tel. [2]330766. 12 rooms. $22 to $24 single, $24 to $40 double.*

A converted private home, with no-frills rooms far more ample and light and airy than at budget hotels downtown. Excellent location one-half block south of Paseo Colón, within walking distance of most intercity buses.

POSADA TROPICAL, *located across Colón from the Petit, the hotel is found behind the Mordisco restaurant and upstairs.*

Sleeps 34 persons in lockable louvered cabinets. No kidding. (34 times $13 per head equals $442, less cost of included breakfast. Not a bad take.)

CASA RIDGWAY, *Calle 15, Avenidas 6/8, tel. [2]336168. $7 to $10 per person.*

Affiliated with a Quaker organization, this lodging house bills itself as "more than just a place to stay." It seeks to attract the ecologically minded, peace advocates, and those generally interested in social issues. Cooking facilities are available.

Eastern San José Hotels

Eastern San José is carbon monoxide alley, where, for a good part of the day, buses, trucks and cars back up as they try to get into or out of town along Avenida Central. Nevertheless, there are some attractive accommodations in the middle- and upper-class residential districts out this way. Hotels away from Avenida Central are preferable.

TORUMA YOUTH HOSTEL, *Avenida Central, Calles 31/33 (P. O. Box 1355-1002), tel. and fax [2]244085.*

A neoclassic tin-roofed mansion, right on Avenida Central. You stay in dormitories. Front door open from 6 a.m. to 11 p.m. Call before you go out to check on available space. If you have an IYHF card, you'll get a discount at affiliated private accommodations throughout the country.

APARTOTEL LOS YOSES, *Avenida Central, Calle 43 (P.O. Box 1597-1000), tel. [2]250033, fax [2]255595. 23 units. $46-$51 single/$54-$59 double. Visa, Master Card, American Express.*

Apartments in three sizes for up to six persons, with kitchen and utensils, protected parking, pool, sun area. Breakfast available. Also conference area.

HOTEL DON PACO INN, *Avenida 11, Calle 33, tel. [2]349088, fax [2]349588 (800-288-2107 in U.S.). 10 rooms. $51 single/$56 double with breakfast.*

A small Spanish-Mediterranean style hotel in a quieter area of San José.

Hotels West of San José

HOTEL MIRADOR PICO BLANCO, *P.O. Box 900-1250, Escazú, tel. [2]281908, [2]283197 (local), fax [2]395189. 25 rooms. $40 single/$46 double. U.S. reservations, tel. 916-862-1170 (Mr. Alcock). Visa, Master Card.*

The Pico Blanco, several white-walled buildings along a cobbled drive, is a hilltop village in itself. Flocks of scarlet macaws flutter from tree to tree. The views of the Central Valley, available from all rooms and public areas, are strictly skyscraper-quality.

POSADA PEGASUS, *P.O. Box 370-1250 Escazú, tel. [2]284196, $40 double)* is more lodge-like, a large private house with porch, and a slice of the same view available from the Pico Blanco.

TARA RESORT HOTEL, *P. O. Box 1459-1250 Escazú, tel. [2]286992, fax [2]289651. 30 rooms and suites. $100 single/$155 double, more in suites. Credit cards accepted.*

Y'all can't miss this white antebellum mansion on a slope above San Antonio de Escazú. Drive through the white gates to the portico, and make your entrance. Beyond the high ceilings, polished hardwood and tile floors, cupola, tropical wood detailing, and chandeliers (all elegant, graceful, and impeccably maintained), are porches with million-dollar views to San José and the Central Valley.

Each suite is individually named ("Lady Ashley Suite," "Scarlet Suite," etc.) Out on the grounds are another 18 rooms in nine hexagonal cottages, and pool and tennis court. Amenities and services include courtesy airport transportation, continental breakfast, champagne on arrival, exercise room, sauna, whirlpool, satellite television, meeting facilities. Children under 12 not accepted.

Luxurious suburban garden apartments are available at **APARTOTEL MARÍA ALEXANDRA**, *Calle 3, Avenida 23, San Rafael de Escazú (P. O. Box 3756-1000 San José, tel. [2]281507, fax [2]285192, 14 units, $135 triple), a block off Escazú's main street in a pleasant residential neighborhood.*

Units have washing machines, air conditioning, and cable television, and the complex includes a pool and sauna, bar, an excellent restaurant, and travel agency. The bus to Escazú leaves from Calle 1, Avenidas 16/18, San José.

HOTEL BOUGAINVILLEA, *Santo Tomás de Santo Domingo, (P. O.*

Box 69-2120, San José), tel. [2]408822, fax [2]408484. 44 rooms. $70 single/ $80 double.

This hotel is out of the downtown core, with all comforts and impeccable service. The site is a large, elongated lot fronting on the cottage-lined main road of a suburban village set amid coffee plantations and orchards. At the street end is the three-story hotel building.

HOTEL AMSTEL ESCAZÚ, (P. O. Box 4192-1000), tel. [2]224622, fax [2]333329. 14 rooms, 2 suites. $63 and up double, with breakfast. U.S./Canada reservations: tel. 800-327-3573, 407-367-9306. Visa, Master Card.

A smallish hotel converted from a luxury private house, with pool, television lounge, bar. Air-conditioned, extensive gardens, facing one of the busiest streets in Escazú.

Bed & Breakfasts

THE VICTORIA INN, Moravia,tel. [2]402320, fax [2]211514 (P.O. Box 6280-1000, San José). $20 single/$30 double, suite $40 with breakfast.

You can stay at this B & B without hesitation. It's a large residence, three blocks east of the town hall in Moravia, a middle-class suburb (opposite the Rincón Europeo restaurant). Two of the five guest rooms, in a separate apartment, have private baths, kitchen, a little garden and washing machine. In the main part of the house, with its huge greenhouse-style sitting area, wicker furniture, and plentiful plants and books, are additional guest rooms (two sharing baths), light and cheery, with lace spreads on the beds. Owners are helpful Tico-Americans. Essential to reserve.

PARK PLACE, P. O. Box 1012, Escazú, tel. and fax [2]289200. $35 double with breakfast.

This is a modern bungalow with brick floors, basketry as decoration, wood panelling, and a high-ceilinged living room with huge glass windows. Views from the second floor are superb. There is some green space around the house, and there are trails through the forest reserve above.

The four guest rooms (two upstairs and two downstairs) each have one large bed, and a single bed may be added. Breakfast is self-serve, and other meals may be prepared by guests. Bus service right to the door is frequent from San José (sometimes a problem in the suburbs). The owner (none other than the personable Pat Bliss, one of the guiding lights of the bed-and-breakfast association) does not live on site, an arrangement that some visitors might prefer. Taxi directions: 1.5 kilometers south of Escazú church.

POSADA DEL BOSQUE, P. O. Box 669-1250 Escazú, tel. [2]281164, fax [2]286381. $49 double.

This is a former plantation house in Bello Horizonte, a pretty area of old farms, pine and oak forest, and ponds, where you'll find some of the wealthiest residents of Costa Rica. The owners of Posada del Bosque, Mr. and Mrs. Gilbert Aubert, aside from being Costa Rican (unusual in the B&B trade), can make their guests feel comfortable in English, Spanish, German and French.

The grounds are grassy and manicured, covered with citrus trees and Norfolk pines. There are two play structure for kids. Inside, the seven guest rooms, more formally furnished than in most guest houses, each bear the name of a local bird species (in English and Spanish), and most have pleasing garden views. Each has a single and a double bed, huge bath, skylight, and wrought-iron sconces. The public area has a fireplace, clay tile floors, and cane ceiling. Breakfast includes mandarin juice from the garden, and yes, you can have *gallo pinto* and *tortillas* in the morning. A rowing machine and exercise bike are available to guests, and a mountain bike can be rented. Beverages are provided on a self-serve, honor bar basis.

Signs at all entrances to Bello Horizonte indicate the way to the Posada.

CASA DE FINCA 1926, *Tres Ríos (P. O. Box 29-1000 San José), tel. and fax [2]256169. $75 double.*

As the name indicates, this was the great house of a coffee plantation, until urbanization replaced the coffee bushes with pleasant suburban bungalows on wide streets. But enter the compound of the house, stand in the formal front garden with its fountain and large trees, and you're back in those gracious days.

The 11 rooms are all different, not as elegant as the public areas, but quite comfortable, with wicker furniture, and large bathrooms — some quite modern — with a shower or tub.

VILLA ESCAZÚ, *P. O. Box 1401-1250 Escazú, tel. and fax [2]289566. $35 single, $45 double, $60 triple.*

Here's a shiny house that might have been transferred from the alps, complete with panelling, stone fireplace, and cathedral ceiling. (In Escazú, the houses are *not* all alike.) Extensive gardens on the surrounding hillside, terraced down to a stream, contain flowers, pines, and 50 varieties of fruit trees — all indicators of good birding — as well as a croquet pitch. Four guest rooms each have twin or queen beds.

Full breakfast is served on a terrace, a barbecue is available, and dinners can be prepared on request. Three blocks from town church and bus stop of San Antonio de Escazú.

The Bed & Breakfast Association

The Bed and Breakfast Association operates a central clearing house and referral system, based at **Park Place B&B**. *Call or fax them at 289200 or 234157 between 10 a.m. and 2 p.m., daily except Sunday, or write to P. O. Box*

1012, Escazú, Costa Rica. They'll try to place you in a suitable home-away-from-home for the duration of your visit, or for part of it.

HOMESTAYS

Arrangements can also be made to stay in spare rooms in private homes, where families are living working and workaday lives, by
- *consulting newspaper ads,*
- *by making living arrangements through a language school (in which case nobody will speak much English). This is one of the more inexpensive routes to take. See language-school listings, pages 76-77.*
- *by using specialized agencies. One such is **Bells' Home Hospitality**, P. O. Box 185-1000, San José, tel. [2]254752, fax [2]245884 (in the U.S., Dept. 1432, P.O. Box 025216, Miami, FL 33102-5216). Rooms are available through Bells' in over 50 private homes in the San José area, at a rate of $35 single or $50 double, including breakfast. The agency provides detailed directions, and can arrange airport pickup. Plans are afoot to make rooms available throughout the country. Write or call for a pamphlet describing the homes and the families with which you can stay. Another agency with higher rates and add-on "booking fees" is **Costa Rica Home and Host**, 2445 Park Ave., Minneapolis, MN 55404, tel. 612-871-0596, fax 871-8853.*

Once you enter the bed-and-breakfast network, you can pretty well be taken care of for your entire stay in the country, with referrals to lodging places and compatible people along your route.

WHERE TO EAT

Downtown

CHALET SUIZO, *Avenida 1, Calles 5/7.* The Swiss Chalet is nicely atmospheric, with wainscotted walls, wooden beams, brick hearth and costumed waiters. Most main courses run $5 to $7, the inclusive lunch $5.

ISLE DE FRANCE, *Calle 7, Avenidas Central/2.* An excellent little French restaurant. Not at all cheap for San José, but moderate as French restaurants go. A daily complete lunch goes for about $10. Open weekdays for lunch and dinner, Saturday for dinner only, closed Sundays.

CASINO ESPAÑOL, *Calle 9, Avenidas Central/2.* The gastronomic tour continues with fine Spanish cuisine. Specialties are quail in wine, tripe, Asturian fabada (stew), and *paella*. Elegant atmosphere and service. Entrees $6 to $10, fixed-price lunch for $5.

For more formal but still friendly Spanish food, turn the corner to **GOYA**, *Calle 1, Avenidas 5/7.* Rabbit in wine, beef with mushrooms, paella, $6 to $9 for a main course.

West End

LA MASIA DE TRIQUELL, *Avenida 2, Calle 40*. Spanish and Continental cuisine in a large old house with plenty of arches and stuccoed walls. *Paella*, sea bass in bearnaise sauce and steak in garlic sauce starting at about $10.

LA BASTILLE, *Paseo Colón at Calle 22*, is a fine French restaurant, the oldest in San José, where food preparation is painstaking. Assorted soups such as consommé with sherry, appetizers like caviar, and classic beef preparations as a main course: stroganoff, filet mignon, tenderloin provenáal in Café de Paris sauce; also sea bass in an interesting wine sauce with apples, grapes and peaches. $15 and up.

LA PIAZZETTA, *Paseo Colón, Calle 40*, features a long list of specialties from the regions of Italy. From about $12, closed Sundays.

Also serving elegant Italian cuisine, but with more familiar fare, such as lasagne and fettucine, is **EMILIA ROMAGNA**, *Paseo Colón, Calle 32/34, tel. [2]332843*. The setting is one of brick arches and plants, and the elegant sustenance is accompanied by breads and flavored butters (salmon and garlic-coriander, among others) prepared on-site. About $20 and up for a meal. Jazz is played every night from 8 p.m. (minimum two drinks).

BEIRUT, *Avenida 1, Calle 32*. Your classic neighborhood Lebanese eatery, anything but elegant, but clean and pleasant. You eat in one of several rooms in an old wooden house. Kibbeh, kabba, schawarma, kebabs and combinations thereof, for $5 and up. Closed Monday, lunch only on Sunday.

MACHU PICCHU, *32 Calle, Avenidas 1/3*, opposite the Beirut, emphasizes Peruvian staples: seafood, potatoes, and corn. Main courses, such as sea bass in wine or with garlic sauce, picante de mariscos (a sort of seafood casserole with garlic, onion, cheese and olives — excellent!) cost $3 to $6 The atmosphere is more home-style than elegant.

The **GRANO DE ORO**, *the hotel in a restored mansion at Calle 30, Avenidas 2/4*, serves light items on a glassed-in porch and out on the patio, from noon to 10 p.m., among them chicken, lasagne, quiche, "enchilada pie," and attractive salads. This is a good place to decompress from any urban hassles.

ANTOJITOS CANCUN, *Paseo Colón, Calles 24/26*, next to Pizza Hut, downstairs, has Tex-Mex tacos, enchiladas and burritos in assorted combinations for $2 to $6, and all the beer you need to wash it down. Kiddy seats available.

LOBSTER'S INN, *Paseo Colón at Calle 24*. Good seafood. Lobster and shrimp are expensive — $20 — but sea bass (*corvina*) is reasonable at under $10, served in a variety of ways, and there are continental main courses — beef in sauces, veal cordon bleu, chicken chasseur.

ANA, *Paseo Colón, Calles 24/26*. An unpretentious and inexpensive

Italian restaurant serving lasagna, spaghetti, veal and non-Italian dishes for $4 and up. Pleasant surroundings, especially in the upstairs dining room.

A few blocks away, *at the corner of Avenida 2 and Calle 24*, **PIZZERIA DA PINO** serves all kinds of pizzas starting at $3, along with lasagna.

BEMBEC, *just south of Colón on Calle 40*, is an informal terrace-and-garden eatery and pastry shop. You sit at terrarium tables (literally - you'll see what I mean), and select from an unusually creative menu of fruit plates, salads, burritos, tacos, and items unique to the establishment. As little as $4 for a light meal, more for the substantial daily specials, or with a large dessert, such as peach cake.

MORDISCO, *Paseo Colón, Calles 22/24 (next to the Ríos Tropicales travel agency)* specializes in food that is good for you. A light meal costs about $5, and the open setting is attractive, but can be noisy.

ARIRANG, *at Paseo Colón and Calle 38, in the Centro Colón building*, is your standard Korean family restaurant. It's very good, and at $4 or so for a main course, the price is right. *Open 11:30 a.m. to 2:30 p.m., and 5:30 to 9:30 p.m.*

SODA PINTICO, *in the same building as Arirang, on the ground floor*, is a rare eatery in this neighborhood that serves Costa Rican-style food, in this case in luncheonette surroundings. It will be hard to spend more than $3. Just make sure you arrive by 4 p.m.

Chinese eateries are less plentiful in the west end than elsewhere in San José, but you'll find a couple *on Calle 32 just north of Colón*. **JARDIN FELIZ** has a Szechuan-style menu, with the likes of spicy chicken and vegetables for $4 to $6.

LOS RANCHOS, *near the east end of Sabana Norte (just behind Burger King – go around the block)* is currently the top-rated steak house in San José. Tender beef comes in assorted cuts with jalapeño or less exotic sauces, and a salad bar; and grilled chicken and seafood are available as well. $10 and up, set lunch about $6. *Open for lunch, and from 7 p.m. for dinner, continuously on Saturday, to 9 p.m. on Sunday.*

SODA TAPIA, *Calle 42, Avenida 2, opposite Metropolitan Park.* More a café than a soda, good for sandwiches and fruit salad at the outdoor tables.

West End Self-Service Joints

AUTO SERVICIO COLÓN, *Calle 34, Avenidas Central/1*, is a bar with a self-service food counter.

SAN JOSÉ 2000 is not a restaurant, but a shopping center in suburban Uruca. If you're staying at the Hotel Irazú next door, you'll find some good alternative eating here. **LA FUENTE DE LOS MARISCOS** offers seafood at prices much lower than elsewhere in the city: shrimp from $3 to $10, depending on the size, a combination dish for $4.

EL TAPATÍO, a Mexican restaurant and bar, serves several kinds of *mole*, tacos and burritos for about $5, accompanied by beer and recorded jazz. And there are a Chinese restaurant and a steak house. *From the Paseo Colón area, it's a short hop by taxi or the Alajuela bus to San José 2000 along the Cañas expressway.*

Hotel Dining

L'AMBIANCE, *Calle 13 no. 949,* in a restored mansion, has the most elegant dining room of any downtown hotel, in a garden-style setting. The service is attentive. About $15 or $20 per full meal. *Phone 226702 to reserve.*

The **HOTEL DON CARLOS,** *Calle 9, Avenidas 7/9,* serves a daily lunch amid the plants in its pleasant courtyard patio. Choose from lasagne, pasta, or a Tico-style rice-and-beans-with-something for about $5, sometimes to the accompaniment of guitar music.

At the **HOTEL LA GRAN VÍA,** *Avenida Central, Calles 1/3,* the restaurant is a quiet, light corner up on the third floor. The lunch of the day goes for about $4, and there are assorted complete breakfasts for $3. This is a good place to eavesdrop on long-term foreign residents as they plot their projects.

Among other hotels, the **AMSTEL** *(Avenida 1, Calle 7)* is notable for quality preparation and presentation, though not originality. A complete dinner goes for about $12. Lunch, for $7 or so, can include such main courses as sea bass meuniäre or a Tico-style combination plate or chicken in fruit sauce. The **HOTEL VILLA TOURNÓN,** off the downtown beaten track, also has some fans.

Probably no city in the hemisphere has as many **Chinese** eateries for its size as San José. Chinese food generally runs in the medium price range. You pay extra for rice.

One of the better Chinese restaurants is the **NUEVA CHINA,** another is **EL AVE FÉNIX,** *both in San Pedro (see below).*

In the downtown area, a good choice is **FULUSU,** *Calle 7, Avenidas Central/2.* Any main course is large enough to share among two persons. As little as $6 for a meal.

LUNG MUN, *Calle 1, Avenidas 5/7,* serves Tico-style food at its lunch buffet, for about $3. A la carte American and Cantonese food runs $4 to $6 for a main course. If you have a hankering for shrimp, you can get it in your chow mein here for much less than elsewhere.

Another good downtown choice, with both western and oriental choices (including Szechuan plates), and an extended *dim sum* breakfast, is the restaurant of the **HOTEL ROYAL GARDEN,** *Calle Central and Avenida Central.* Lunch costs just $5.

Two good Chinese restaurants are located *on Calle 11, between Avenidas 6 and 8.* **TIN JO** offers Gen. Hon's chicken (with cashews, served in bird's nest), sweet and sour pork and seafood dishes, as well as more ordinary Cantonese dishes, at $5 and up for a main course, $10 and up for large shrimp. *Down the street,* **DON WANG**'s specialties, such as diced chicken with peanuts and hot peppers, are spicier, and prices are reasonable.

LA HACIENDA, *Calle 7, Avenidas Central/2*, is one of many restaurants in San José specializing in charcoal-broiled steaks and chops. Mixed grills, steaks or luncheon specials for $8 and up. **KAMAKIRI** steak house, *Calle 3, Avenidas Central/1*, upstairs in the arcade, is more lively, with music. **LA ESMERALDA**, *Avenida 2, Calles 5/7*, is a lively, clean, cathedral-like, open-to-the-street establishment with strolling Mexican musicians. Steaks from $5, set lunches for $3 or less, including a beverage.

BALCÓN DE EUROPA, *Avenida 9, Calles Central/1*, is more than a restaurant, it's a tradition, recently moved to this location. The establishment, extremely popular, serves Italian-style meat main courses. For the price, the food is more attractively served than you might expect, and you get real vegetables, not just rice.

A charming hole-in-the-wall that also serves Italian food is **SAN REMO**, *Calle 2, Avenidas 3/5*, with house spaghetti, lasagne, and standard Costa Rican fare, with nothing over $5, including some shrimp dishes. Capuccino, pastries and breakfast are served as well.

You could spend weeks in San José and think that native-style food didn't exist. **LA COCINA DE LEÑA** (The Wood Stove), *in the El Pueblo shopping center north of downtown*, is one of a few places where you can enjoy home cooking. Tiny tables, piles of firewood, whitewashed walls, subdued lighting, and decorations of colorful enamelware and gourd beakers all re-create the atmosphere of a dark, smoky country kitchen. The menu — printed on a paper bag — is a lesson in traditional Costa Rican cooking. Most entrees are served with tortillas and beans, and run $4 to $6, or you can get the complete lunch special for $5. *To get here, take the Calle Blancos bus from Calle 3, Avenidas 5/7.*

Also in El Pueblo are **LANCER'S STEAK HOUSE,** which offers complete, low-priced lunches; and numerous other eating and drinking spots.**PAPRIKA**, *Avenida Central, Calle 31*, in the back of a commercial building, with Swiss and Italian specialties. Meals will run you $12 and up, about $8 for the inclusive weekday lunch.

Cafés

There aren't many of these, but two are reminiscent of Europe. The **PARISIEN CAFÉ** of the **Gran Hotel Costa Rica**, *Calle 3 at Avenida 2*, provides sidewalk seating with a view to the national theater, the Plaza de la Cultura, and the continuing activity of vendors and buskers in the adjacent small park. A fine place for extended sitting, reading, or people-watching at any hour — it's open through the night.

More elegant is the café across the street in the **National Theater** itself where, at marble-topped tables, surrounded by works of art and bathed in recorded chamber music, you can enjoy a sandwich and coffee for less than $3, or a luncheon special for slightly more.

Sodas

Sodas are San José's all-purpose coffee shops and diners, where in simple, soda-shop surroundings you can enjoy anything from a cup of coffee or a drink to a sandwich or a steak. The blue-plate luncheon special usually runs $4 or less with tax and service. Similar fare and clean surroundings are available at almost any soda in San José. Among them are:

SODA CENTRAL, *Avenida 1, Calles 3/5*. A hole in the wall with cheap sandwiches and drinks.

SODA PALACE, *Avenida 2, Calle 2, on Parque Central*. Good seats for watching the main square. Mainly drinks and sandwiches. A block to the east, the soda of the Melico Salazar theater, **La Perla**, *at Avenida 2, Calle Central*, offers Spanish items such as paella, as well as set lunches, and is open through the night for drinks and bocas.

RISAS, *Calle 1, Avenidas Central/1*, is somewhere between a soda and a restaurant/bar. *Ceviche* (marinated-fish cocktail), stews and steaks for $5 and up, fishburgers and American-style (large) hamburgers in several decorations for $2.50, and even meatball heroes are served. Open 11 a.m. to midnight.

Also somewhere in-between is **SPOON**, *on Avenida Central, Calles 5/7*, with light lunches and heavy desserts. About $5 for lunch with lasagna, a salad or the plat du jour, or $2 for something gooey with coffee.

CONFETTI'S, *Avenida Central, Calle 15*, is a modern and clean restaurant-bar along soda lines, good for a drink and a rest after a tour of the National Museum.

POLLO CAMPESINO, *Calle 7, Avenidas 2/4*, serves chicken roasted on a spit over a coffee-wood fire, and many a resident swears by the result. This is a cozy, informal, crowded hole-in-the-wall with a beer-barrel bar, and you'll probably think I've sent you to the wrong place. If somebody in your party doesn't like chicken, ask for the Chinese menu.

MANOLO'S, *Avenida Central, Calles Central/2*, a favorite of many long-time San José residents, is open 24 hours to serve whatever you like in whatever atmosphere you choose. Proceed no further than the open-to-the-street snack joint at ground level for greasy, finger-shaped Mexican donuts (*churros*) and a cup of coffee, then hurry on your way. Or stop for more than a few minutes on the balcony one flight up, for the lunch of the day ($3), Manolo's club-like special sandwich, croissants with orange cream, breakfast combinations, or something else from the extensive but not expensive menu (even a filet mignon weighs in at under $6), with quick, coffee-shop service.

For finer tastes, ascend a short staircase to yet another dining area, large and formal and overlooking the street through large windows, where sirloin tips and other formally prepared steaks and chops go for about $10 and up.

Vegetarian

This is not an easily achieved style of eating in Costa Rica. Even your beans and rice are likely to contain generous amounts of lard.

SODA VISHNU, *Avenida 1, Calles 1/3*, is vegetarian, with fruit and vegetable cocktails, and an Indian-flavored lunch special for $2.

NUTRISODA, *Avenida 2, Calle 3*, downstairs in the arcade next to the Gran Hotel Costa Rica, is vegetable-oriented.

East of downtown is **DON SOL**, *7 Avenida B, no. 1347 (go up the east side of the Casa Amarilla, then a half-block east)*, with a complete lunch for a couple of dollars, and a la carte salads, fruit drinks, vegetable stews and pastries.

EL EDÉN, *Avenida 5, Calles Central/1*, has a daily lunch for $3, including soup and dessert, more bland than the fare at its counterparts.

Inexpensive Food

There are cheap eateries all around San José, including the sodas mentioned above. Almost any modern office building has a ground-floor luncheonette where clerical workers take a quick and affordable lunch.

Additional choices:

RESTAURANT POÁS, *Avenida 7, Calles 3/5*, is a jungle of palms, bromeliads, ferns, begonias, corkscrew vines, and parrots, with more natural life than you'll see on a bad-luck or rainy day in the wild. Blue-plate lunch specials go for $3 or less. Some, like *casado* (meat with cabbage and rice and beans) and *olla de carne* (stew) are home-style Costa Rican classics. Breakfast and dinner are served as well.

CANDILEJAS, *Avenida 4, Calles 1/3*, a cut above a soda, is usually crowded with secretaries having a budget meal at café-sized tables. Choose from native-style steak, casado, and the like for $3 and up, or the daily blue-plate special for only $2. Food is simple, but tasty.

PATTIE SUPREME, *on Calle 9, Avenidas 6/8*, opposite the Soledad Church, serves the Afro-Caribbean counterpart of the empanada, with a filling of meat, chicken or lobster, for as little as 50 cents.

For a whole array of cheap, inelegant eateries, hasten to the **CENTRAL MARKET**, *Calle 6, Avenida 1*, where you can fill your stomach with cabbage, rice, beans, eggs, and/or stew for $2.

Self-Service

The point-and-shoot method of ordering is useful if you're in a hurry, or if your Spanish produces unpredictable results.

CHIPS, *on Calle 5 opposite the Plaza of Culture*, is a step up from most fast-food joints, with lasagna, chicken, omelettes, salads, a changing assortment of specialties, and pizza; $4 and up for lunch, less for the daily special.

GOYA, *Calle 1, Avenidas 5/7*, **LUNG MUN**, *Calle 1, Avenidas 5/7*, both mentioned above, and sometimes other restaurants, have cafeteria set-ups at lunchtime where you can fill your plate for $3 or less.

KING'S, *Avenida 1, Calle 3*, has chop suey and Tico-style food, at $3 for a full meal.

Snacks

POPS, *Avenida Central, Calles 1/3* (and just about everywhere else in San José) has the best ice cream in Costa Rica. From 5¢ for a cone.

PASTELERÍA SCHMIDT, *Avenida 2 at Calle 4*, sells excellent breads and pastries, which may be eaten in, with a cup of coffee, or carried out. *Another location (among many) is at Avenida Central and Calle 11.*

San José's ubiquitous fruit carts sell bananas and pineapple and papaya at almost every corner. At Christmas, they offer apples and grapes, which are great and expensive delicacies. And there are many hamburger and hot dog vendors as well.

Escazú Restaurants

Farther west, and south, in suburban Escazú, is the **EL CHURRASCO** steak house *(tel. [2]289332, (150 metros al sur del Centro Comercial Blvd. Rosa).* Look for a sign pointing the way from Escazú's main street. Here you get brick surroundings and pottery decorations. Steak comes in assorted cuts and sizes, draft beer is served, and there are salads and appetizers — and music on Friday and Saturday evenings. $10 and up. *Drive, or take the Escazú bus from Avenida 1, Calles 16/18, San José.*

The **MARÍA ALEXANDRA** restaurant, *in the "apartotel" of the same name*, nearby, is also excellent. Chef Hans, of durable fame, cooked for John F. Kennedy when he came to Costa Rica. The establishment is known for its fine sauces, and if you like shrimp, this is your best bet in the area.

ABACUS, *on the main street into Escazú*, serves cràpes of both the main course and dessert variety, the former with anything from roast beef to vegetables; and there are Tex-Mex items and desserts. About $6 and up.

LUCAS, an informal eatery in the same part of town, has Costa Rican-style items (tacos, casado combination plates), as well as more elegantly prepared steaks and fish, and also gets a crowd for beer, wine and elaborate desserts. About $9, less for the lunch special.

San Pedro/East End

This is not an area that most visitors get to on their first trip. But you'll go out this way to be near a university crowd, or if you visit the insect museum. If you're not already planning to be in the immediate area, call first to check if the restaurant is open.

LE CHANDELIER offers the finest continental dining in San José. Meats and poultry are served in delicate sauces, vegetables are crisp, and service and presentation are faultless. Le Chandelier's exterior is unpretentious, but the beamed ceilings, fireplace and rough-stuccoed walls inside suggest the *campagne*; additional seating is on the terrace. You'll spend at least $20 for dinner — it's worth it— but the tab can run much, much higher. *From the traffic circle in San Pedro (Calle Central at the bypass highway), go south two blocks past Burger King, then west, then take the first turn south. Call [2]253980 to reserve.*

The **NUEVA CHINA**, *Calle 11, Avenida Central, San Pedro,* is everybody's recommended Chinese restaurant. The decor and ambience are authentically oriental, right down to the imported tile. The menu has two sections, Chinese and "international" (if you want it). *To reach the Nueva China, take the San Pedro bus from Avenida 2, Calles 3/5.* A bit nearer to downtown, **EL AVE FÉNIX**, *on Avenida Central on the way into San Pedro, a block east of the traffic circle,* gets high marks from many connoisseurs of Chinese cuisine.

TEQUILA WILLY'S (tel. [2]251014) serves Tex-Mex nachos, fajitas, enchiladas and the like in a wild decor. *The locale is a large blue-and-white house, about two blocks east of La Nueva China.*

Food With A View

About five kilometers past San Antonio de Escazú, on a winch-class road that loses its pavement, is **TIQUICIA**, an adobe, peasant-style house with terrace, where meats are cooked over wood and charcoal. For less than $10 you can have a combination plate or chicken and rice, with beer (not too much!). If you're driving, turn right at the Miramontes restaurant on the way up to San Antonio, then inquire for "Tee-KEE-sya" at every turn.

Above Aserrí, on the road to Santa María de Dota, is **MIRADOR RAM LUNA**, a somewhat more formal establishment with the appearance, at first glance, of a small hilltop estate. Inside, the large dining area is glassed-in, with ferns and broadleaf plants providing a greenhouse air. A fireplace serves to burn off any chill at the 1825-meter altitude. Here you enjoy yet another slice of Central Valley view, along with excellent steak-house fare, reasonably priced at $5 and up for a main course. The Mexican-style sirloin, and steak stuffed with cheese and ham, are both good choices. Open for lunch and dinner every day. If you're not driving, Ram Luna is easiest to reach by taking a bus to Aserrí, then a taxi.

BARS & CLUBS

Drinking is a pastime that most Costa Ricans feel comfortable with, and the visitor, in turn, will feel comfortable in any halfway-decent-looking bar. All are reasonably priced, with domestic drinks for $1 or less. Bocas (snacks) are served on the side, sometimes at a price in the fancier establishments. Many of the downtown bars are good places to rendez-vous with other foreigners. Among them:

ESMERALDA, *Avenida 2, Calles 5/7*, mentioned above as a restaurant, is popular at night for drinking to a background of mariachi music.

MARLEY'S, *Avenida 1, Calles 5/7*, serves chili con carne and chili dogs, Virginia ham sandwiches, and good steaks, and keeps the television tuned to crucial games. Bocas are free from 4 to 6 p.m.

TROPICAL TINY'S, *Avenida 2, Calles C9/11*, heavy with red brick, is also screen-oriented.

NASHVILLE SOUTH, *Calle 5, Avenidas 1/3* is your light-wood, down-home bar where serious music is played, and chili con carne and fried chicken are served.

DISCO TÚNEL DEL TIEMPO, *Avenida Central, Calles 7/9*, is a discotheque, not a bar, probably more to local tastes than yours, but centrally located.

Around the corner, the **BIKINI CLUB**, *Calle 7, Avenidas Central/1*, has pretty waitresses. There are some gay bars in this area.

RESTAURANT-TABERNA POÁS, *Avenida 7, Calles 3/5*, a budget eatery during the day, does double duty as a dance hall at night, a perfect locale for a jungle fantasy out of *El Grande de Coca Cola*. Venture among the palms, bromeliads, ferns, begonias, corkscrew vines, and parrots, and wiggle it.

CHARLESTON BAR, *Calle 9, Avenidas 2/4 (opposite the church and around the corner from the gas station)*, is loaded with memorabilia of bygone days in another country. The bar at the **PARK HOTEL**, *Av. 4, Calles 2/4*, is a gathering spot for Americans and other foreigners on extended stays. The neighborhood is just a little bit seedy, but not in a dangerous way.

DISCO SALSA 54, *Calle 3, Avenidas 1/3*, is just what it sounds like.

TABERNA CAYUCO, *Calle 11, Avenidas 1/3*, is said to show videos of X-rated movies, a genre banned from cinemas.

KEY LARGO *is at Calle 7, Avenida 3, on Morazán Park* is a nice, old house, and also San José's most notable prostitute pickup point. The ladies and taxis line up outside.

BAR MÉXICO, *Avenida 13, Calle 16*, is a bright spot in a run-down neighborhood, painted on the outside in red, white and green, well-kept with polished wood tables in the arched interior. Marinated fish and snacks are served with the drinks, but the attraction is mariachi music. *Open from 3 p.m., from 11 a.m. Saturday, closed Sunday. Walk from the Coca-*

Cola bus terminal area, or take the Barrio México bus from Avenida 2, Calles 6/ 8.

Boobs are the subject at **JOSEPHINE'S**, *Avenida 9, Calles 2/4, tel. [2]572269*, one of the few non-hotel clubs that put on a live dance show for dining guests. If bouncing breasts under diaphanous disguise are what you seek, you'll find them, along with steaks, chicken, and lighter snacks. Drinks are not overpriced, and putas are not visibly on the prowl, which makes for a wholesome and relaxed air at San José's premier nightclub presentation.

EL CUARTEL DE LA BOCA DEL MONTE, *tucked away on Avenida 1 between Calles 21 and 23, east of downtown*, is a lively, late-hours bar and native-style eatery. There are full meals of steak, tripe, and fish, with salad, bean soup, fried plantains and yuca, for $6 on *down*; but you'll mostly come for the difficult task of keeping up with the locals at drinking. There's live music on some evenings. The name recalls an early appelation of San José.

BROMELIAS, *a couple of blocks away at Avenida 3, Calle 23*, is a bar in a recycled and modernized section of the huge customs shed that handled cargo coming in on the now-defunct railroad.

EL YUGO DE ORO *in Cinco Esquinas, just north of downtown San José*, is a favorite late-hours place for many Ticos, who enjoy the *bocas* (snacks). But what snacks! — cannelloni gratinée, beef cordon bleu, assorted seafood, barbecued tidbits, all served free with drinks or available as menu choices for $7 and up. A mariachi band often plays till midnight, and there are luncheon specials. Any taxi driver can take you for $2 or less. *Call [2]572088 to check if they're open.*

In the west end, **GALLERY Y BAR SHAKESPEARE**, *Avenida 2, Calle 28 (next to the Teatro Olivier)*, usually has guitar music or some other low-key entertainment in the evening. Cover charge of a couple of dollars.

For drinking and dancing, **EL PUEBLO** shopping center, mentioned above under restaurants, has numerous bars and *boâtes*, ranging from intimate to multi-level, as well as trinket shops for an evening of browsing in a pleasant mock-colonial environment. *Take the Calle Blancos bus from Avenida 3, Calles 5/7, or a taxi.* Head east to San Pedro to find a university crowd near the University of Costa Rica.

CLUB COCODRILO, *on Calle Central in San Pedro*, is a popular hangout, with continuous movies, flashing lights, videos, and a namesake over the huge bar.

TX, *several blocks to the west on the same street*, shows music videos and serves original near-lethal drinks.

The **BAR BALEARES**, *a block west of the Mas x Menos supermarket*, sometimes has reggae music, and provides chess boards and darts on demand.

LA VILLA, *just over a block south of Banco Anglo*, attracts a more serious crowd to enjoy movement music of the hemisphere, and inexpensive food and snacks.

HORA ZERO, *a block in the opposite direction from Banco Anglo*, serves inexpensive food to the accompaniment of sixties rock.

Men will feel comfortable at **CLUB MADRID**, a pool hall with cheap drinks, *a block east and almost two blocks north of the San Pedro church*. And women will feel comfortable nearby at **LA TERTULIA**, a feminist gathering point. Don't confuse your gender.

SEEING THE SIGHTS

San José does not have all that much in the way of obligatory sights to see. If your time is short, limit your rounds to the high points: the **National Theater** and **Plaza of Culture**, the **National Museum**, and the **Jade Museum**. These can be seen in a half-day, or between excursions to the volcanoes and countryside around San José.

At a more leisurely pace, you can cover the itinerary below, and get to know the city better, in a couple of days or more. Most of the places mentioned are within a half-mile or so of the Central Park.

Downtown & Vicinity
The Main Square

Any walking tour of San José starts at the **Parque Central** (the Central Park, or main square), *bounded by Calles Central and 2, and Avenidas 2 and 4*. Bus after city bus stops and accepts the long queues of commuters along all four edges.

The park is an oasis in all this, a neat, gardened square where workers on their breaks and anyone with a few moments to spare will sit on benches and pass the time of day. Public concerts are offered on most Sunday mornings in this musically concerned city.

Across Calle Central from the park is the **Catedral Metropolitana** (**Metropolitan Cathedral**), one of the many undistinguished urban churches of relatively recent vintage in Costa Rica. Cream-colored, blocky on the outside, with neo-classical pediment and columns at the entry, the Cathedral has a massive, barrel-arched interior. Much more interesting is the ecclesiastical administration building attached to the rear of the Cathedral, done in the charming and disappearing nineteenth-century San José style, with a European face — in this instance stone-cased windows and pediments straight out of Renaissance Italy — and a red tin roof.

On the north side of the square, at the corner of Calle Central, is the restored **Melico Salazar theater**, a period piece of pre-depression tropical urban architecture, with fluted Corinthian columns, balconies, and stuccoed relief sculptures in the pediments.

National Theater

A *couple of blocks down Avenida 2, at the corner of Calle 3*, stands the **Teatro Nacional** (**National Theater**), which over the years has come to embody San José and its self-image as a cultural center. And with good reason, for a more impressive public structure is to be found in no city for a thousand miles to the north or south.

Though sometimes advertised as a replica of the Paris or Milan opera, the block-long National Theater is neither, and stands on its own. Columns and pediment and window arches are carved into the massive stone blocks of its majestic Italianate neo-classical facade, which is crowned with allegorical statues of Dance, Music, and Fame (copies of the originals, which are protected from pollution elsewhere). The sides of the building are less elegant, faced with cement plaster, and the tin roofing is purely San José.

Especially impressive inside the theater building are the foyer, upstairs, with its three-part ceiling painting representing Dawn, Day, and Night; the interior marble staircases; the gilt decorations throughout; and, of course, the multitiered great hall.

The National Theater is the locale of regular concerts by the national orchestra, which was transformed into a full-time professional and teaching organization in 1971, with the acquisition of a number of foreign musicians; and of performances by the youth orchestra, and native and foreign drama companies and artists. Tickets are sold in advance at the kiosk alongside the theater, for as little as $2. Admission for sightseeing costs about $1.

Opposite the entrance to the National Theater is a little park where vendors of handicrafts — model oxcarts, dolls, jewelry and leather— display their wares. Adjacent is the stately **Gran Hotel Costa Rica**, with its pleasant ground-floor café. There's another café in the theater itself.

Central Avenue

North of the theater, the stretch of **Avenida Central** for several blocks in each direction is a **pedestrian mall**, where vehicles are restricted or banned for part of the day. In place of cars, the avenue fills up with shoppers, along with buskers, and merchants of a hundred products and services that you weren't looking for, but which you will no doubt find useful. A great press mounted on a truck squeezes sugarcane for juice.

Vendors peddle ices, and roast sweet corn, and flowers and toys and sunglasses and lottery tickets and shoe laces and fruit. Lamination of identification cards and engraving of jewelry and valuables are performed on the spot, for minimal fees.

Plaza of Culture

Along Avenida Central between Calles 3 and 5 is the **Plaza de la Cultura** (**Plaza of Culture**). The commercial buildings that once occupied the site were razed to create an open expanse with flowers, benches, and platforms, where outdoor performances are sometimes given.

To preserve the broad vista to the adjacent National Theater, a complex of exhibit halls has been constructed *below* ground level. Foremost of the displays is the exquisite gold collection of the Banco Central de Costa Rica, with over a thousand pre-Columbian decorations, mostly from burial sites in the southern Pacific coastal region of Costa Rica. Also included are jade ornaments from Costa Rica and other countries. And there are pre-Columbian ceramics, modern art, and numismatic items as well. *Currently open only from 10 a.m. to 5 p.m. Friday through Sunday.*

Near the entrance to the exhibit area, at the corner of Avenida Central and Calle 5, is the **information center** of the Costa Rican Tourist Board (Instituto Costarricense de Turismo), where the personnel are quite helpful in answering questions, providing maps, schedules and brochures, and generally orienting the visitor. *Hours are 9 a.m. to 5 p.m., Monday through Friday.*

National Museum

Six blocks east of the Plaza of Culture, and up the hill known as the Cuesta de Moras, is the **National Museum** (**Museo Nacional**), housed in the old Bellavista Fortress, once the headquarters of the now-defunct army.

Of major interest in the museum is the pre-Columbian collection, one of the largest of its kind. All of the materials are shown quite logically, divided into the three major cultural zones of the country, and arranged chronologically for each. Many but not all of the exhibits are labelled in both English and Spanish, and a map helps to explain Costa Rica's importance as a meeting point of three cultural traditions.

The National Museum has an extensive collection of colonial furniture; printing presses and historical imprints from the era of independence; period costumes; portraits of presidents and politicians; and a cellar of religious art, including saints in wood and plaster, vestments, and paintings executed over the period from colonial times to the present. An ethnohistory exhibit bespeaks a growing awareness by modern Costa Rica of multicultural contributions to national life. A geology exhibit illustrates tectonic plates, and explains the tremors you may feel from time to time.

Bellavista fortress itself is one of the few colonial-style structures in San José, dominating the central part of the city, massive, towered, gray and brusque on the outside, pocked by bullet holes from the 1948 civil war, but quite lovely from the inner gardened courtyard, with tile roofs, whitewashed walls, and covered passageways. All of the exhibit rooms have high, beamed ceilings. On sale at the museum shop are examples of Talamanca Indian weaving, bows and arrows, and gourd crafts, which are some of the best souvenirs available in San José. Inquire as well about museum-sponsored excursions to sight quetzals or sparking volcanoes.

The National Museum is open every day except Monday from 8:30 a.m. to 4:30 p.m. (Sunday from 9 a.m.) There is a small admission charge.

Plaza of Democracy

Across Calle 15 from the National Museum is the **Plaza of Democracy**, dedicated in 1989 to mark 100 years of popularly elected governments. Like the Plaza of Culture, this open area was created by demolishing houses and offices, replacing them with terraces and amphitheater climbing the hill, suitable for cultural activities, and, with the Legislative Assembly nearby, for political demonstrations as well.

Just to the north across Avenida Central, the **legislature** is a cream-colored, Moorish-style building. You may go in the side door and look around, but it's all quite unprepossessing and uninteresting, except, perhaps, as an artifact of Costa Rica's rather un-Latin non-aggrandizement of its political institutions.

National Park

North of the legislature is **Parque Nacional** (**National Park**), one of San José's nicely landscaped shady squares. The city planners have gone in for tall trees that make for a wonderful cool shade in the middle of the day. The park's centerpiece is an allegorical statue depicting the five Central American nations in arms, driving out the American adventurer William Walker, who had installed himself as ruler of Nicaragua in 1856.

Across from the north side of the park is the **National Library** (*Biblioteca Nacional*), a modern and not particularly attractive airline-terminal sort of building, decorated with a splotchy mosaic of the sun. There are exhibit areas inside.

A block east of the library, at Avenida 3, Calle 21, is the old, Victorian-style Limón train station, now a national monument and open to the public as the **Railroad Museum**.

Stop by to admire the impressive steam engine of the Northern Railway (as the line was called before nationalization) on a spur in front, and the collection of memorabilia inside. There are photos of old San José, as well. *Hours are 9 a.m. to 3:30 p.m., 10 a.m. to 3 p.m. on weekends, with a small admission fee.*

Northwest of National Park is the block-square compound that formerly housed the **National Liquor Factory**. Liquor is a big business in Costa Rica, in terms of the size of the country, and most of it is the business of a government-owned company. The site is being converted into a cultural center.

España Park

West of the liquor factory, between Avenidas 5 and 7, at 11 Calle, is **Parque España (Park of Spain)**, also known as **Parque de la Expresión**, an enchanting little enclave of towering tropical trees transplanted from around the country. On Sundays, many of San José's artists display and sell their work here.

On the north side of Parque España, at Avenida 7 and Calle 11, is the modern office tower of the Instituto Nacional de Seguros, the government insurance monopoly. On the eleventh floor is the **Museum of Pre-Columbian Jade (Museo de Jade)**, *open Monday through Friday from 9 a.m. to 3 p.m.* The name of the museum is somewhat misleading, for the collection is comprehensive, with contemporary pottery, tools, weapons and dress of the surviving native peoples of Costa Rica.

The jade museum also offers from its high perch some excellent views of San José and environs — to the north and the volcanoes from the lounge, and to the south and the city center from the vestibule. The first building visible to the south is the **Edificio Metálico (Metal Building)**, an unusual structure designed in France by Victor Baltard, architect of Les Halles. Incongruous and green-painted, with rusting roof panels, the Edificio Metálico was one of the first of the pre-fabs, shipped in pieces from Europe. It's now used as a school.

Across Calle 11 from the insurance building is the attractive, Spanish-style **Casa Amarilla**, which houses Costa Rica's foreign ministry.

North of Parque España is **Barrio Amón**, one of the more traditional neighborhoods of San José. Here are large, older homes in wood, decorated with fretwork and crowned with steep tin roofs; and stuccoed brick homes with Renaissance and baroque elements, sometimes painted in pastel colors. See this tropical wedding-cake architecture while you can. Construction in San José has slowed down with the economic problems of recent years, but these buildings are sure to disappear.

The Zoo

At the northern edge of downtown is **Parque Zoológico Simón Bolívar (Simón Bolívar Zoological Park)**. *Follow Calle 7 north, then Avenida 11 east to the entrance.* Here are turtles, monkeys, macaws, peccaries, vultures, jaguars, alligators, ducks, and much else brought from all parts of Costa Rica to a rain forest planted in the middle of the city, complete with palms, bromeliads and aromatic plants. The zoo is well worth a visit if you have even a mild interest in the wildlife of Costa Rica. Also here is an information center for the national parks where publications are on sale. *Bolívar Park is open Tuesday through Friday from 8:30 a.m. to 3:30 p.m., weekends and holidays from 9 a.m. to 4:30 p.m., with a small admission charge.*

South of the zoo, back in the central part of the city, is **Parque Morazán**, *divided by heavily trafficked Calle 7 and Avenida 3 into four separate gardens.* The nicest is the Japanese-style northeast section, with ponds, a temple-like gazebo, little bridges, and a kids' playground. The structure at the center of the park is the **Temple of Music**, another of San José's tributes to the finer things.

Watch your wallet or your purse in this area — pickpockets abound.

Snake Museum & Other Points of Interest

On Avenida 1, between Calles 9 and 11, is the **Serpentario (Serpentarium)**, another of San José's manageable mini-museums, or collections. Here you can encounter several dozen snakes, (among them a copperhead, jumping viper, bushmaster, boa constrictor, black cobra, parrot snake, and the star of the show, a python 5.3 meters long), in circumstances benign rather than frightening, fully labelled in Spanish (with some signs in English as well) as to species and habits, and well-lit. Some are not from Costa Rica, you will be pleased to know. If you wish to contemplate and identify dangerous species before an excursion into the wild, this is the place. You'll also find frogs, toads, iguanas, and lizards, all to be viewed for one small fee. Hours are 9 a.m. to 6 p.m. every day. Look for the Fuji Film sign and take the stairs up.

Turning west, on Calle 7, Avenidas Central/1, with a $2 admission charge, is a collection of old photos of San José, which you may want to skip if your interest in local history is limited.

Farther west, on Calle 2, facing a pleasant mini-park, is the baroque palace that houses the **Central Post Office** (**Correos y Telégrafos**, or **Cortel**).

Central Market

The **Central Market (Mercado Central)**, *at Calle 6 and Avenida 1,* is a block-long area housing vendors of flowers, baskets, vegetables, shoes, spices, and a few souvenirs. It's small and sedate by Central American standards, but worth a walk-through. Other markets nearby are the **Borbón**, *a block north, at Calle 8 between Avenidas 3 and 5,* and the **Coca-Cola bus terminal and market** (named for an old bottling plant), *Calle 16 between Avenidas 1 and 3.* Just as interesting as the markets is the thriving general commerce of the area, where stores, stalls and street hustlers hawk fruit, firecrackers, flypaper, firearms, and countless other articles, many of which you'd have trouble finding at home.

Carrillo Park

One last downtown reference point, *bounded by Avenidas 2 and 4, and Calles 12 and 14*, is **Parque Carrillo** (**Carrillo Park**), also known as **Parque Merced**, after the church nearby. The park is typically treed and nicely landscaped, though the neighborhood is heavily trafficked and noisy.

One interesting feature, though, is the park's centerpiece, a four-foot-diameter pre-Columbian stone sphere from Palmar Sur, in the southern Diquis region. Other examples of these near-perfect forms are to be seen at the National Museum and, as originals or reproductions, on many a lawn in San José, where they are popular decorations.

Centro Commercial

North of downtown, and of interest to visitors with time to browse and shop, is the **El Pueblo Shopping Center** (**Centro Comercial**). This is a tasteful, charming collection of shops, offices and restaurants, constructed in a style reminiscent of a colonial village, with narrow lanes, wrought-iron lamps, tile roofs, whitewashed brick and stuccoed walls, and beamed ceilings. It's almost better than the real thing. Most of the action at El Pueblo takes place after dark. *Take the Calle Blancos bus from Avenida 5, Calles 1/3, or a taxi.*

Paseo Colón & Sabana Park

Less than a mile to the west of downtown, at the opposite end of the upscale **Paseo Colón** district, is **Parque Metropolitano** (**Metropolitan Park**), or **La Sabana**, once the airport for San José. A drained lake has been restored, trees have grown back, and extensive sport facilities have been erected, including a pool, gymnasium, and stadium.

On the east side of the park, facing Paseo Colón, is the former airport control tower, a Spanish-style structure now converted to the **Museo de Arte Costarricense** (**Museum of Costa Rican Art**). Most of the paintings reflect an appreciation of the bucolic and the archaic that contrasts with modern Costa Rican life. Of the works displayed, Francisco Amighetti's woodcuts have earned the most fame outside of Costa Rica. *The museum is open every day except Monday from 10 a.m. to 5 p.m., and there is a small admission charge. Any Sabana bus from Avenida 3, Calles Central/2, or from the Central Park, will stop near the entrance.*

The **Museo de Ciencias Naturales** (**Natural Sciences Museum**), *is located near the southwest corner of La Sabana park, at Colegio La Salle*, a secondary school. The collection includes thousands of stuffed birds, monkeys, and other denizens of the wild, many in mock-ups of their natural habitats. *The museum is open Monday through Friday from 7 a.m. to 3 p.m., Saturday until noon, with a small admission charge. Buses from the Central Park marked "Sabana Cementerio" stop nearby.*

Outside Downtown
Insects & Fish

The high point of San José for visitors interested in insects will be the **Entomology Museum** (**Museo de Insectos**), *housed in the basement of the Escuela de Artes Musicales on the north side of the University of Costa Rica, in San Pedro. Take the outside steps down, on the east side of the main entry. Hours are from 1 p.m. to 5 p.m. Monday through Friday, and there is a small admission fee. Take a San Pedro bus near the Social Security building (La Caja), Avenida 2 between Calles 3 and 5.*

Most of the collection, which you can examine to the accompaniment of music filtering through the ceiling, is housed in one large room. The specialty is butterflies.

As long as you're out here, you might want to look in on the university's own nature reserve, in the middle of the ring of classroom buildings, and its botanical gardens. *For more information, call [2]535323, extension 5318.*

(For those who are *really* into insects, there is another **Museo de Insectos y Mariposas** [**Insect and Butterfly Museum**] *in suburban Santo Domingo de Heredia, 300 meters west of the bridge on the River Virilla, open daily except Monday from 9 a.m. to 5 p.m., admission $5.* This includes the private Whitten Collection, which the curators claim is one of the largest of its kind.)

Further west, in San Francisco de Dos Ríos, is **Mundo Sumergido** (**Submerged World**), an exhibition of tropical fish, featuring Caribbean fish in a re-creation of their coral reef habitat, as well as Atlantic and Pacific species. *The fish are on display in the back of an aquarium shop, four blocks east and two blocks north of the Y-junction on the road into town. Call [2]275491 for information.*

Butterflies

Spirogyra is an urban butterfly garden northeast of downtown San José *(Calle 46 at Avenida Central, Guadalupe, "50 meters west, 150 meters south of San Francisco church")*. On display are a couple of dozen of the 4000 resident Costa Rican species, in an environment of flowering plants that provide nourishment, and fruit species that butterflies call home. *Hours are 8 a.m. to 4 p.m., admission about $4. Take the Guadalupe bus from Avenida 3, Calles 3/5.*

Oxcart Museum

South of central San José, in the working-class suburb of Desamparados, is the **Oxcart Museum**, in a venerable house that contains as well artifacts of the old rural life-style on which Costa Ricans look so fondly. *Open daily except Monday from 8 a.m. to noon and 2 to 6 p.m.*

MOVIES, THEATER, & OTHER ENTERTAINMENT

Admission to first-run American and other foreign films runs about $1.50 in San José — a bargain. Most have subtitles, so you'll be able to hear the original sound track. A few are dubbed into Spanish (*hablado en español*, the ad will say). Newspapers give current attractions and sometimes the show times. Rarely, however, do they reveal the address of the theater, so look it up in the phone book under "*Cines,*" or ask at your hotel desk.

Check the billboard at the **National Theater**, once repairs are finished, for concerts, plays and recitals, some featuring internationally known artists. Tickets are bargain-priced, starting at $2. San José has a number of active theater groups, and their performances, including some open-air theater, are advertised in the newspapers. Performances are given at the restored 1920s **Teatro Melico Salazar**, and **Teatro Laurence Olivier** *at Avenida 2, Calle 28, near Paseo Colón*, among others. Next to the Olivier theater, **Sala Garbo** exhibits art movies and classics.

On the raunchy side, supposedly staid San José has more than its share of strip joints and raunchy bars. Massage parlors advertise in various publications. Be protective of your pockets and your health.

Non-striptease musical acts are featured at the bars and night clubs of some hotels, especially the **Irazú**, **Corobicí**, and **Cariari**. The major downtown hotels usually have bands on weekends.

SHOPPING

There are wise and worthwhile purchases to be made in San José, but they won't necessarily be items intended for tourists. The limited selection of domestic handicrafts includes leatherware and items made from wood, and crocheted and macramé articles. T-shirts and similar universal souvenirs help fill the shops, along with handicrafts from neighboring countries.

Various leather stores have shoes, attaché cases and handbags that are similar in quality to what you would find in the United States. Prices are slightly lower than at home (if the stuff at home isn't on sale). Among such shops are **Galería del Cuero**, *Avenida 1, Calle 5; and Del Río, Calle 3, Avenida 5.*

La Galería, *at Calle 1, Avenida Central/1*, exhibits and sells paintings, painted wood articles, and bowls of rosewood and other tropical hardwoods. The grains and fineness are exquisite, but do you really want to spend up to $100 for a portion-sized salad bowl? Assorted woodware is also available at **Magia**, *Calle 5, Avenidas 1/3*, and **Suraska**, *Calle 5, Avenidas 1/3*. And there's a good selection in the shop at *Calle 5, Avenida 5.*

The **National Handicrafts Market** (**Mercado Nacional de Artesanías**), *Calle 11, Avenidas 2/4*, is a store with handicrafts similar to what you'll find in hotel gift shops — woodware, small cotton hats, macramé, and t-shirts. A few blocks away, **CANAPI**, an artisans' guild, *Calle 11, Avenida 1*, has a similar, larger store, lately with attractive bamboo furniture. Down the block, the **Souvenir Shop**, *at Calle 11, Avenidas Central/1*, has relatively inexpensive wood carvings and Guatemalan handicrafts. More centrally located is **ANDA**, *Calles 5/7, Avenida Central*, another artisans' outlet, with mostly wood and leather crafts.

You'll sometimes find examples of weaving by Costa Rica's indigenous population on sale at the shop of the National Museum. The shop of the **Neotrópica Foundation**, *Calle 20, Avenidas 3/5*, has handicrafts made from traditional materials.

At the public markets, such as the **Central Market**, you'll find a fair selection of what crafts there are in Costa Rica, along with fruits and groceries. The ornamental plants are beautiful, and cheap, but you can't take them home. (Well, you *can*, but you better get the right procedures from your department of agriculture before you even think about doing so.) Tidbits of pottery, hammocks, and paintings are hawked in the little park in front of the Gran Hotel Costa Rica, adjacent to the Plaza of Culture.

The largest collection I've seen of wood items, dolls, leather, t-shirts, embroidered blouses, ashtrays, pots, straw hats, jewelry, and other items ranging from silly to superb is in the gallery of stalls called **La Casona** *on the east side of Calle Central, just north of Avenida Central*. Some of the leather is quite nice, and there are many items from Panama (*molas*), Guatemala (weaving), and El Salvador (cloth birds) to supplement local production.

Antiques will also be found in the Central Market area, and at some hotels. Pre-Columbian pottery cannot be bought legally, and reproductions are getting scarce. But if you're interested, one place where you can look at pre-Columbian effigy mortars, pottery, and colonial antiques is through the window and inside **Familiar La Viña**, a family eatery and imbibing spot *at Avenida 7, Calles 4/6*. You might even go in for a bite and a glass of something.

PRACTICAL INFORMATION FOR SAN JOSÉ
Banks

You'll have no trouble finding a bank in downtown San José. *Most are open from 9 a.m. to 4 p.m., Monday through Friday.* The **Banco de Costa Rica** branch *at Calle 7 and Avenida 1 is open until 6 p.m.*, and is convenient to some of the larger hotels. **Banco Mercantil** has an exchange boutique downtown with quick service, *at Calle 5 near Avenida Central, opposite the* *tourist office on the Plaza of Culture, open weekdays from 9 a.m. to 5:30 p.m.* Watch for pickpockets outside.

For D-marks, Canadian dollars and French francs (if you've ignored my advice and brought along these currencies), try the services of **Compañía Financiera Londres**, *on Calle Central near the corner of Avenida Central (next to La Casona), third floor.*

Black-market money-changers, during periods when they are tolerated, *congregate along Avenida Central between Calles 2 and 4, near the post office.* There's usually only a small spread between the official and free market rates.

Doctors

Emergency medical attention for visitors is available at any public hospital. The most centrally located is **Hospital San Juan de Dios**, *Avenida Central and Calle 16, tel. [2]220166.* For a Red Cross ambulance, *call [2]215818.*

For treatment on a non-emergency basis, try the **Clínica Bíblica**, a church-related organization, *at Calle 1, Avenidas 14/16, tel. [2]236422*; the **Clínica Americana**, *Avenida 14, Calles Central/1, tel. [2]221010*; or the **Clínica Católica** *in Guadalupe, tel. [2]255055.* They have English-speaking doctors available, and provide service 24 hours.

Embassies & Consulates

Most of the addresses below are for consulates. For those not listed, look in the phone book under *Embajadas y Consulados.* Most are open mornings only.

- **Belgium**, *Los Yoses (east of downtown), tel. [2]256255*
- **Belize**, *Guadalupe, tel. [2]539626*
- **Canada**, *Calle 3, Avenidas Central/1, ground level (P. O. Box 10303-1000 San José), tel. [2]553522*
- **Denmark**, *Paseo Colón, Calles 38/40, tel. [2]572695*
- **El Salvador**, *Los Yoses, tel. [2]253861*
- **France**, *Curridabat, tel. [2]250733*
- **Germany**, *Rohrmoser, tel. [2]325533*
- **Guatemala**, *Barrio California, tel. [2]335283*
- **Honduras**, *Los Yoses, tel. [2]340949*
- **Italy**, *Avenida 10, Calles 33/35, tel. [2]342326*
- **Japan**, *Rohrmoser, tel. [2]321255*
- **Mexico**, *Av. 7 no. 1371, tel. [2]338874*
- **Netherlands**, *Los Yoses, tel. [2]340949*
- **Nicaragua**, *Avenida Central, Calles 25/27, tel. [2]333479*
- **Panama**, *San Pedro, tel. [2]253401*
- **Switzerland**, *Centro Colón (Paseo Colón/Calle 38), tel. [2]214829*

- **United Kingdom**, *Paseo Colón, Calles 38/40, tel. [2]215566*
- **U.S.A.**, *Pavas (western suburbs), tel. [2]203939 (8 a.m. to 4:30 p.m.), 203127 (evenings and weekends). Send mail to P. O. Box 10053-1000, San José.* The bus for Pavas leaves from Avenida 1, Calles 16/18, San José. A train departs from the old Pacific station for Pavas at 6:30 a.m. and 12:45 and 5:45 p.m.

Laundry

You'll probably entrust your cleaning to your hotel or a neighborhood laundry. One of the few self-service laundries is **Lavamatic**, *in the Cocorí shopping center (Centro Comercial) east of downtown.* Take a San Pedro bus from Avenida 2, Calle 5, laundry in hand. Or try **Burbujas** *in San Pedro, half a block west, the 25 meters south of the Más x Menos supermarket.*

National Parks

The **National Park Service** has an information center *in the Bolívar Park zoo.* A booklet on the parks in English, with descriptions and travel advice, is on sale, though some of the information is outdated, and you should ask for current details about any park you intend to visit. Inquire also about seasonal conditions in the more remote parks. Some of the personnel speak English.

Post Office

The main post office is **Correos y Telégrafos** (or **Cortel**) *is at Avenida 1, Calle 2.* A rate sheet is available at the counter to the left, inside the main entrance on Calle 2. Line up at the bank of windows to weigh your letters and buy stamps. *Hours are 7 a.m. to 9 p.m. weekdays, Saturday from 8 a.m. to noon.* General-delivery mail (*lista de correos*) is kept in the first large hall toward Avenida 1, at window 17 — there's a separate entrance. The philatelic department is through a separate door off the main lobby, and upstairs.

Supermarkets

Supermarkets are not hard to find anywhere in San José. A huge one is **Yaohan**, *at the end of Paseo Colón on Calle 42, opposite the Corobicí Hotel.* Like many other supermarkets, Yaohan has a selection of general merchandise — pots and pans, towels, plastic goods — in addition to food items. Inside parking is available. One centrally located general department store is **Galerías Plaza de la Cultura**, *Avenida Central, Calles 5/7.* There are others to the west along Avenida Central. Browse through any of these, and you'll soon find that the selection of locally made items is quite limited, while imported goods are expensive.

And, if you happen to be looking for an item of hardware, you can always stop in at **Ferretería Glazman**, *Avenida 3, Calles 12/14.*

Telegrams

Radiográfica Costarricense handles domestic and international telegrams. If you have access to a private phone, you can send your telegram by dialing 123. Otherwise, take your message to the telegraph office *at Avenida 5, Calle 1,* or send it through your hotel operator. Domestic telegrams are inexpensive — about 3¢ (U.S.) per word, 6¢ in a foreign language. Overseas telegrams are frightfully expensive.

Telephones

Public coin telephones are plentiful in San José, but they are not kept in good repair, nor are the appropriate coins — 5, 10 and 20 colones — always abundant. *A good place to find working coin phones is outside the ICE building at Calle 1, Avenida 2.* Some hotels have public phones in their lobbies. In addition to other options, overseas calls can be made from the offices of **Radiográfica Costarricense**, *Avenida 5, Calle 1.* Visa, Master Card and American Express are accepted at this location.

Tourist Office

The visitors' information center of the **Instituto Costarricense de Turismo** (**Costa Rican Tourist Board**) *is located at Avenida Central and Calle 5, at the entry to the underground exhibit area in the Plaza de la Cultura.* Maps, hotel brochures and a sheet of bus and train schedules are available, and extensive files are maintained on special-interest areas — cultural attractions, camping, and business services, to name a few.The personnel will usually try hard to obtain information they don't have. All speak English. *Hours are 9 a.m. to 5 p.m., Monday through Friday, Saturday to 1 p.m. For information by telephone, call [2]221090 or [2]216127.*

Water

Tap water in San José (and in most larger towns of Costa Rica as well) is safe to drink. But if you're wary of it, for reasons of taste or chemical difference from what you're accustomed to, or are just plain cautious, stick to bottled soda water (*soda*, or *agua mineral*). Water pressure in much of San José is quite low. The better hotels have pressure tanks and pumps, but in more modest accommodations, you may get no more than a dribble from the tap.

Walking

Being a pedestrian in San José is at times a risky business. At some intersections, traffic lights are arranged so that it is technically impossible to cross in the clear. And even where the signals appear to be with you, many a driver will slip into gear and bear down on you the moment the light changes. Be cautious and fleet of foot.

Weather

The average daily high for San José varies hardly at all from month to month — it's almost always in the mid-seventies Fahrenheit (22 to 25 Centigrade). Average nighttime lows are about 60 (15 degrees Centigrade), excellent for sleeping. Even the recorded extremes are moderate — 92 is the highest temperature ever recorded in San José, 49 the lowest (33 and 9 degrees Centigrade).

Precipitation, however, is quite variable. It rains almost every day from May to October (Costa Rica's "winter"), with monthly totals of about 10 inches, and the air gets to be uncomfortably sticky toward the middle of the day. The rains slacken off in November, and from January until the end of April, precipitation is a freakish event.

Aside from rain, there are a number of seasonal signs in lieu of sharp differences in temperature: variation in length and clarity of daylight; the flowering of poinsettia, erythrina trees, coffee plants and other species throughout the year; and alterations in the richness of the green of surrounding hills.

EXCURSIONS FROM SAN JOSÉ

Costa Rica is small enough, and travel facilities are well enough developed, that you can reach many far points of the country by public transportation and return to your hotel in San José by nightfall. In order to actually *see* anything, however, you'll probably want to confine your one-day trips to the environs of San José and the Central Valley, e.g., Ojo de Agua springs, Poás and Irazú volcanoes, Cartago and the Orosi valley, and Alajuela and towns on the way to Sarchí.

By taking a tour or renting a car, you can extend your one-day travel range to the Pacific beaches near Puntarenas and at Jacó, and, perhaps, the port of Limón on the Atlantic. By chartered plane, you can also make a one-day trip out of a visit to the Tortuguero reserve on the Caribbean.

Day outings are also arranged through travel agencies for white-water rafting, volcano climbing or volcano watching, diving, horseback riding, jungle exploration, cruises in the Gulf of Nicoya, kayaking, and mountain biking; and the list keeps expanding. Numerous companies offer one-day rafting excursions from San José, mostly on the Reventazón River.

Major Travel Agencies
• **American Express/TAM**, *Calle 1, Avenidas Central/1, P. O. Box 1864-1000), tel. [2]330044, fax [2]228092 (night/weekends, tel. [2]230116)*

- **Blanco Travel Service**, *Avenida Central, Calles 7/9, tel. [2]221792*
- **Costa Rican Trails**, *P. O. Box 2907-1000, San José, tel. [2]224547, fax [2]213011*
- **Henchoz Tours**, *Calle 5, Avenidas 3/5, (P. O. Box 883-1002), tel. [2]339658, fax [2]339357*
- **Intertur**, *Avenida 1, Calles 3/5, tel. [2]331400. Advertises discount tours.*
- **Infotur**, *on Avenida 2 opposite the rear of the National Theater (P.O. Box 93-6150 San José), tel. [2]234481, fax [2]234476*, makes reservations at most hotels and for rafting, car rentals, etc. They also have a garbled on-line database.
- **Tropical Pioneer**, *P. O. Box 29-2070 Sabanilla, tel. [2]539132, fax [2]534687*. Rafting.
- **Turismo Creativo**, *7 Calle, Avenidas Central/1 (P. O. Box 1178-1011), tel. [2]331374, fax [2]330368*
- **Tursa**, *lobby of Gran Hotel, tel. [2]336194*
- **Swiss Travel Service**, *Hotel Irazú, tel. [2]326039*
- **Tikal Tours**, *Avenida 2, Calle 7 (P.O. Box 6398-1000), San José, tel. [2]571480, fax [2]231916*

You'll probably book where it's most convenient, generally at your hotel. Bear in mind that agencies work on commissions, and will sometimes try to sell you the most expensive trip, no matter what your interest, e.g., a flying tour to Tortuguero, instead of a more leisurely canal-boat excursion (if that's what you're after). If you have trouble getting what you want, do not hesitate to contact a trip operator directly. You can even consider calling from abroad — most have personnel who speak English.

Specialty Tour Companies
- **Ríos Tropicales**, *Paseo Colón, Calles 22/24 (P. O. Box 472-1200, Pavas), tel. [2]336455, fax [2]554354*. Rafting and kayaking excursions.
- **Costa Rica Adventure Tours** (*Río Colorado Lodge*), *Hotel Corobicí (P. O. Box 5094-1000), tel. [2]328610, fax [2]315987*, has packages that include jungle cruises along the Tortuguero Canal and Sarapiquí and San Juan rivers, and tarpon fishing in the Caribbean region.
- **Costa Rica Rainbow Connection**, *P. O. Box 7323-1000, tel. and fax [2]407325*, is a holistic network and alternative travel service, "using the tremendous potential of Costa Rica as a high-energy healing land." Workshops and power-center visits are planned, and a recent tour was on the theme "Journey through wonders and wisdom of magical Costa Rica."
- **CIPTR**, *Calle 40, Avenida 4, tel. [2]552693*, takes groups to Carara reserve, among other destinations, and employs local people to provide food and horses to participants.
- **Parismina Tarpon Rancho**, *Calle 1, Avenidas 7/9 (María José Building, tel.*

[2]226055 or 800-862-1003 (U.S.-C.R.), fax *[2]221760*, offers sport fishing trips on both coasts, as well as tours to Tortuguero.

- **Costa Rica Expeditions**, *Calle Central, Avenida 3 (P. O. Box 6941-1000), tel. [2]220333, fax [2]571665*. Rafting; coastal and river. Fishing; birding and national park tours. Mainly a wholesaler.
- **Aventuras Naturales**, *Avenida Central, Calles 33/35, tel. [2]253939, fax [2]536934*. Rafting, mountain biking.
- **Geotours**, *P. O. Box 469Y-1011 San José, tel. [2]341867, fax [2]536338*. Specializing in tours to Braulio Carrillo, Santa Rosa, Guanacaste and Cahuita national parks, and Carara Biological Reserve.
- **Geoventuras**, *P. O. Box 554-2150 Moravia, tel. [2]828590, fax [2]828333*. Specializing in natural history, language study, mountain biking, volcano trips, birding. An unusual tour includes old and functioning gold mines, as well as the Monteverde reserve.
- **Horizontes**, *Calle 28, Avenidas 1/3 (P. O. Box 1780-1002), tel. [2]222022, fax [2]554513*. Bus and cycling trips to national parks.
- **Costa Rica Dreams**, *P. O. Box 79-4005, San Antonio de Belén, tel. [2]393387, fax [2]393383*. Fishing off Quepos and Caño Island.
- **Sportfishing Costa Rica**, *P. O. Box 115-1150 La Uruca, tel. [2]339135, fax [2]236728, 800-374-4474 direct from U.S.* Fishing along the west coast.
- **OTEC Tours** (**Organización de Turismo Estudiantil Costarricense**), *Calle 3, Avenidas 3/5, Calles tel. [2]220866, fax[2]332321*, specializes in travel for Costa Rican students. You can use their services if you're a student, a teacher, or are under 26 years of age, and provide two photos, though their prices are only marginally lower than elsewhere. Their offerings include one-day diving and equestrian trips.
- **Sertur**, *Avenida 5, Calles 1/3, tel. [2]572363*. In addition to the usual run of excursions, Sertur has day river trips, birding excursions to Caño Negro Wildlife Refuge (a little-visited wetlands area in the San Carlos plain), and a multi-day beach and marsh tour along the Pacific coast.
- **Cotur**, *Calle 36, Paseo Colón/Avenida 1 (P. O. Box 1818-1002, San   José), tel. [2]330155, fax [2]330778*. Three-day, two-night tours on the Miss Caribe to Tortuguero National Park by bus and canal boat. They also have mountain and coastal fishing programs. Make sure you get a written confirmation.
- **Cruceros Mawamba**, *P. O. Box 10050, tel. [2]339964, and Mitur   (Hotel Ilan-Ilan), Paseo Colón, Calles 20/22 (P. O. Box 91-1150), tel. [2]552262, fax [2]551946*, have Tortuguero packages similar to Cotur's. Mitur also has an overnight trip to Lake Arenal, including a boat trip.
- **Rancho Leona**, *tel. 71[6]6312, in the village of La Virgen on the Sarapiquí river*, sponsors jungle kayaking excursions.
- **Jungle Trails** (*Los Caminos de la Selva*), *Calle 38, Avenidas 5/7 (P.O. Box 5941-1000, San José, tel. [2]553486, fax [2]552782)*, organizes rain-

forest and mountain hikes, rafting, and tree-planting excursions.
- **Saragundí Specialty Tours**, *Avenida 7, Calles Central/1 (P. O. Box 7126), San José, tel. [2]550011, fax [2]552155*, has a one-day horseback and hiking tour for about $75. They also arrange bungee-jumping, which they claim carries a German certification (as if you could verify this).
- **Tropical Sceneries**, *P. O. Box 2047-1000, San José, tel. [2]242555, fax [2]339524*, offers one-day dive trips from San José to Herradura, near Jacó, at $125 per person; diving packages based at Río Sierpe Lodge, near Drake Bay; and longer trips to Coco Island.
- **Tipical Tours**, *tel. [2]338486*, arranges horseback tours.
- **Robles Tours**, *tel. [2]372116, fax [2]371976*, rides to Barva volcano; **Magic Trails**, *tel. [2]538146, fax [2]539937*, rides through Prusia Forest Reserve, on the slopes of Irazú.
- **Rainbow Tours**, *tel. [2]338228*, has riding near Carara Biological Reserve, about $75; **L. A. Tours**, *Avenida Central, Calles 5/7 (P. O. Box 492-1007), tel. [2]214501*, has a day horseback outing to a farm near Orotina, on the Pacific slope, about $75.
- **Calypso Tours**, *Arcadas building by the Gran Hotel (P. O. Box 6941-1000 San José), tel. [2]333617, fax [2]330401*. Cruises to islands in Gulf of Nicoya and to Cocos Island; diving, and trips to Monteverde. The gulf cruise is perhaps the most highly rated day trip in Costa Rica. **Seaventures**, an associated company, takes participants sailing across the Gulf of Nicoya, and offers sail charters.
- Day trips in the Gulf of Nicoya are also offered by **Bay Island Cruises**, *P. O. Box 145-1007, tel. [2]312898, fax [2]394404*; and **Fantasía Island Cruise**, *P. O. Box 123-5400 Puntarenas, tel. [2]550791, fax [2]231013*.
- **Costa Rica Sun Tours**, *Avenida 7, Calles 3/5, San José (P. O. Box 1195-1250 Escazú), tel. [2]552011, fax [2]553529*. Specialties are river fishing, and stays at Tiskita Lodge near Panama and the Arenal volcano observatory.

NEARBY TOWNS
MORAVIA & CORONADO

Moravia is a handicraft center *seven kilometers northeast of downtown San José*. The best-known shop is the **Caballo Blanco**, *located on one corner of the main square*, where thick leather belts and furniture and finely manufactured items of luggage are on display. There are other souvenir and wicker furniture shops and stands on the road into town, and a craft shopping mall, **Mercado de Artesanías Las Garzas**, *a block south and a block east of city hall*, with stocks of items from all over Latin America.

The crafts alone are not enough to draw a visitor to Moravia. One also comes here to sit on the large square and watch a slower, smaller-town life than that of San José. You'll note far fewer cars on the streets than in the capital, knots of people in conversation, and an indescribable something that turns out on closer examination to be an unaccustomed quiet.

The bus for Moravia leaves from Avenida 3, Calles 3/5, San José. Get off at the stop in Moravia where most other passengers debark. This is two blocks from the square. To continue your tour, walk back to the bus stop and wait for a bus marked "Coronado."

Beyond Moravia, the Coronado road rises through an area of lower-middle-class suburbs, where small and well-cared-for wood and concrete-block homes stand in clusters among coffee groves and pasture. *About one kilometer before Coronado, in Dulce Nombre*, is the **Instituto Clodomiro Picado** of the University of Costa Rica, where snakes are studied. Ask the bus driver to let you off nearby if you wish to visit. A few rattlers, *fer de lance* and coral snakes are on display. *Hours are 8 a.m. to noon and 1 to 4 p.m., Monday through Friday.* On Friday afternoons, you can witness the "milking" of snakes for their venom, from which antivenin is made.

After a visit to the Institute, walk or drive up the hill to **Coronado**, a sleepy, pleasant farming center with a surprisingly large and impressive tropical cement-clad, tin-roofed Gothic church. Some points in town offer good views to San José, and the direct road back to the capital is lined with substantial houses that take advantage of the vistas.

The direct bus for Coronado leaves from Calle 3, Avenidas 5/7, San José. You can walk down to Moravia in less than an hour, and be rewarded with sights more interesting than those in the two towns themselves.

SAN ANTONIO DE ESCAZÚ

The hill village of **San Antonio de Escazú** features a fine Ravenna-style church, and good views down to San José and across to the hump-shaped volcano Barva. Brightly painted oxcarts are in use as a practical means of moving goods in an era of expensive gasoline, and not merely to please the eye of visitors. Oxcarts and drivers (*boyeros*) are honored in a celebration in San Antonio on the second weekend in March.

On the peak above town is the **Reserva Forestal Pico Blanco** (**Pico Blanco Forest Reserve**). In fact, the reserve has been so successful in returning farms and pastures to forest, that the white rock that gives the mountain its name is no longer visible from San José. The variety of birds up here, including the motmot, is somewhat different from what you'll be led to find on most tropical birding trips.

Several hotels and guest houses in San Antonio de Escazú, and below in San Rafael de Escazú, provide more tranquil surroundings than you'll find in San José.

Buses for San Antonio leave from Calle 16, Avenidas Central/1.

THE CENTRAL VALLEY

In almost every way, the Central Valley is the heart and soul of Costa Rica. Most of the population lives on this twenty-by-fifty mile plateau, bordered to the north by the Poás, Barva, Irazú and Turrialba volcanoes, and to the south by an older mountain ridge. Almost all of Costa Rica's industry, most of the all-important coffee crop, and much produce for home consumption come from here. Public administration, education and power generation are centered in this mini-state.

And as if all the facts about industry and agriculture and human resources were not sufficient for one small region, the Central Valley is blessed as well with more than its share of natural beauty: great slopes carpeted with coffee trees, and broken by waterfalls, rippling streams, and rivers of rapids; pine groves and pastures on rolling hills; rocky canyons and lakes; a climate as benign and temperate as any on earth, where almost anything will grow; slumbering volcanoes, their slopes carved into farms of neat squares; and small, well-built houses everywhere. It is as close to one's idealized vision of the "country" as one is likely to get.

The Coffee Basin

Pine forests dominated these basins for centuries. The Spaniards found the climate at altitudes of 900 to 1,500 meters ideal for subsistence agriculture, if not for wealth-producing plantation crops, and began to cut back the natural cover. Coffee trees, of course, came eventually to be the main vegetation in the valley, complemented, according to slight differences in altitude, by sugarcane, corn, and pasture. Coffee is now to Costa Rica what citrus fruit is to Israel. Yields per acre and caffeine content are among the highest in the world.

The relatively advanced development of the Central Valley makes it easy for the visitor to explore. Roads go everywhere, and on most of them, buses are both comfortable and frequent. Good hotels and restaurants are not part of the valley's blessings, though there are some good establishments; and no place is far from the haven of San José.

CARTAGO

Costa Rica's old capital is today not at all colonial in flavor. Virtually all structures of the pre-independence period were damaged or destroyed by a string of natural disasters: earthquakes in 1841 and 1910, and intermittent rains of ash and debris from the always-threatening volcano Irazú that looms over the city to the north.

ARRIVALS & DEPARTURES
Arriving By Bus

Buses for Cartago leave from Avenida 18, Calle 5, San José, about every ten minutes from 5 a.m. to 11 p.m. These proceed northward to Avenida 6, where you can catch them on the corner.

Aside from its religious structures, Cartago is on the routes to the **Irazú volcano** and the **Orosi Valley**, and many day tours make a brief stop in town.

WHERE TO STAY & WHERE TO EAT

Do not try to stay overnight in Cartago! All the hotels, clustered a block up from the market, across the railroad tracks, are fleabag, noisy dives of the worst sort. (I know!)

The food situation is mildly brighter. There are numerous modest *sodas* and restaurants around, including one behind the basilica, and fast-food outlets in the center of town.

SEEING THE SIGHTS

But despite its political decline, Cartago remains a religious capital. *Ten blocks east of the main square* is the **Basílica de Nuestra Señora de Los Angeles** (Basilica of Our Lady of the Angels), with its six-inch-high black statue of the Virgin, the object of special devotion on August 2, and of pilgrimages throughout the year.

According to tradition, the little statue was discovered on the out-skirts of Cartago on August 2, 1635, by a girl named Juana Pereira. It was twice removed and placed in a box, and each time miraculously reap-peared in its original location. Yielding to divine will so clearly expressed, the ecclesiastical authorities decided to build a church where the Virgin had been found. The statuette twice was stolen from its shrine, in 1824 and 1950, but each time was returned. The original church was damaged in the 1920 earthquake, and the present basilica dates from 1926.

That is the religious background, which is considerably more impres-sive than the structure itself. The basilica stands out as an agglomeration of confused styles, roughly Byzantine at the front, with a motley collection of angels grafted on, domes bubbling overhead, barren, gray stone blocks forming the sides and rear. It is as if the officials of the Church realized that they had to do something for their Virgin, but, having abandoned colonial and native artistic traditions, found themselves at a loss as to how to go about it.

The interior of the basilica is no better. Vaults and columns painted in splotches of green and brown and glittering silver defocus one's attention from the altar.

The shrine of **La Negrita**, as the statue is familiarly called, is below ground level. Nearby is a room full of discarded crutches, and miniature gold and silver hands, legs, arms, and assorted other parts of the body, all testifying to the healing powers of the Virgin and of the waters that flow from the spring under her shrine.

Back at the center of Cartago are the more esthetically pleasing ruins of the **Church of the Convent** (**Iglesia del Convento**, or, more simply, **Las Ruinas**). Only the massive, moss-encrusted stone-block walls remain of this colonial structure, with their simple, pleasing, Moorish-Spanish contours. The roof fell in during the 1910 earthquake, after the structure had been damaged in previous tremors, and the church was abandoned. The walls now enclose a gardened space, where bougainvillea, pines and a lovely pond attract a variety of birds. The cobbled section of street in front of the church adds to the atmosphere.

IRAZÚ VOLCANO

At 3,432 meters (11,260 feet), **Irazú** is the highest volcano in Costa Rica. It is also one of the most active, and certainly the most feared, a rumbling presence, continually steaming, boiling and fuming, that has practically destroyed the city of Cartago on more than one occasion, and played continuing havoc with the lives of farmers who till the soil and raise livestock on its slopes. But paradoxically, the volcano is also a benefactor. Its ash renews the richness of the soil, even while it blocks water pipes and roads.

The distinction of Irazú among volcanoes in the modern world is that is one of the few semi-active ones that can easily be viewed up close. A paved highway climbs right to the peak, which is protected as a national park. If you happen to ascend when the peak is free of clouds — a near impossibility during the rainy season, and an uncertain condition even in dry times — you'll be rewarded with views to both oceans, or at least to a good part of the country.

ARRIVALS & DEPARTURES

Get an early start! Aside from the unique experience of ascending a volcano, you'll want to beat the clouds to the peak in order to get an ocean-to-ocean view.

By Bus

Public buses for Irazú leave on Saturday and Sunday at 7:30 a.m. from Avenida 2, Calles 1/3, San José (near the Gran Hotel); they make a stop in front of the ruined church in Cartago a half hour later. Fare is about $4. Call [2]519795 to check the schedule.

On other days, you can catch a bus in Cartago along side the Ruinas church for Tierra Blanca, on the volcano's slopes and hike the rest of the way — a strenuous effort in the thin air — or else look for a taxi at the end of the line.

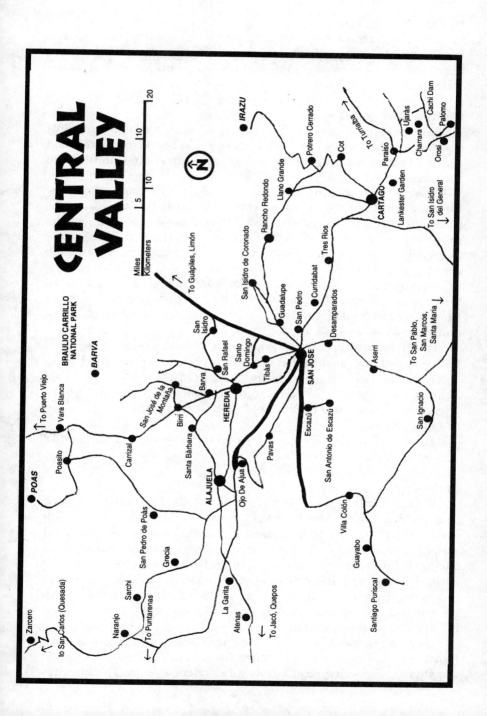

By Car, Taxi, or Tour

Otherwise, go in a rented car, on a tour, or in a taxi from Cartago. The crater is 32 kilometers from Cartago, or 54 kilometers from San José, and the route is well marked. There's a nominal admission charge to the volcano, usually collected only at busy times.

SEEING THE SIGHTS

Visitors to Irazú should be prepared with warm clothing. A couple of sweaters will do, though a down ski jacket would not be too much. Rain gear will help even during the dry season, when wind-borne moisture will sting the skin.

The ride up Irazú proceeds slowly, through pastures and corn fields. Past the town of **Cot**, the air becomes increasingly windy and cold, and the trees more twisted. On the cool, ash-fertilized slopes, potatoes are the main crop, along with carrots and onions. And there are many dairy farms, all now recovered from the 1963-65 calamities, and awaiting the next ones.

Sites on the way up Irazú include the neat farming villages of **Potrero Cerrado** and **Tierra Blanca**, each dominated by a church; a pair of *miradores*, or lookout points, furnished with concrete picnic stools, and a rambling old white, tile-roofed sanatorium.

Past the sanatorium, a trail leads to the **Prusia Forestry Reserve** on the western slopes, an area that was replanted after it was turned into a desert in the 1963 eruption. Hiking trails, campsites, and picnicking facilities are available. Common trees are pine, alder and eucalyptus. There is also an unusual mushroom forest, where some species grow up to a foot across.

You'll find a run-down hotel about 20 kilometers out of Cartago, 12 kilometers from the crater.

At the Top

Over the last few kilometers of the ascent, the face of the mountain changes dramatically, from green pasture to oak forest laden with epiphytes at the park boundary, then to a seared, boulder-strewn primeval surface of ash and bare soil where wind-beaten ferns and shrubs maintain a tenuous hold. Around the next turn, one half expects to encounter a herd of dinosaurs poking their heads through the mist. Charred tree trunks stand as monuments to the last period of intense activity, while a few younger saplings take root for what will probably be an abbreviated life in the severe surroundings.

Once atop Irazú, you can examine a small exhibit on geysers, fumaroles, mudpots, ash, and other forms and evidence of volcanic activity. Slog through the ash and view the craters — slowly. The air at this altitude is short of oxygen, and you will be short of breath, as well as buffeted by wind and mist. The **Diego de la Haya** crater contains a lake, tinted to a rusty hue by dissolved minerals. The main, western crater, which swallowed up several earlier craters, currently shows virtually no activity or gas emissions.

There are active fumaroles on the northwestern slope. Much of this, it bears emphasizing, will not be visible because of the clouds that shroud the peak even during much of the dry season. But even when the top of Irazú is clouded over, a few minutes of exposure to the nasty environment and a glimpse of the fantasy-world landscape will be long remembered.

Avoid the area on the side of the main crater opposite the parking lot.

THE OROSI CIRCUIT

East of Cartago is the well-traveled scenic circuit through the **Orosi Valley**. The route covers only about 55 kilometers from Cartago, easily driven at a leisurely pace in a couple of hours. Bus travel requires some backtracking, but a trip to the halfway point will give you more than half the available pleasure.

SEEING THE SIGHTS
Orchids

About seven kilometers east of Cartago is the **Lankester Botanical Garden** (Jardín Lankester) of the University of Costa Rica. Take the Paraíso from Cartago's main square, or drive, from Cartago to the Ricalit roofing factory (on the left), then continue one-half kilometer down the side road to the south, to the entrance.

The Lankester Garden is most famed for its orchid collection (said to be showiest in March and April), the largest of its kind in the world, begun as a private effort by Charles (Carlos) Lankester, a native of England. But there is much, much more in this well-planned wonderland: bromeliads and other epiphytes, acres and acres of transplanted hardwoods, fruit trees, bamboo groves, cacti, medicinal aloe plants, dreamy and deadly nightshade, and many others. Species are identified only by Latin tags, but you'll recognize some as house plants, especially in the more jungly areas, where ponds are crossed with the aid of bridges made from vines. One large section has been left untended to grow back to native forest.

Guided walks through the gardens are offered on the half hour from 8:30 a.m. to about 2:30 p.m. daily. You can wander through at other times, but you'll be assigned an employee as a tail to make sure that you stick to the brick path and don't pick anything. *Admission is about $1.*

To continue your trip without a car, go back to the highway and pick up a bus marked *Orosi.*

Views

A couple of kilometers past Paraíso on the road to the south is a *mirador*, or lookout point. Take advantage of it if you can for 20-mile views down into the great Orosi valley, carpeted with pasture, sugarcane, and, of course, dark green coffee forest. The **Río Grande de Orosi** snakes along at the bottom and joins lesser streams to form the **Río Reventazón** — the Foaming River. The town of **Orosi** can be picked out, along with smaller clusters of houses and ranches and coffee plantation centers on hillsides and in the lesser valleys spreading out in all directions, as clearly as if you were flying overhead. In the distance is the very end of **Lake Cachí**. This is surely one of the most spectacular views in a country of spectacular views, superior in clarity to any road map.

The lookout point is a garden with manicured pines, hedge cedars, bougainvilleas, and picnicking and play areas and shelters. Even if you're traveling by bus, it's a good place to stop with a box lunch. Or you can pick up snacks at the adjacent stand.

WHERE TO STAY

Just before the lookout point, modest accommodations are available, all affording outstanding vistas down into the Orosi valley.

The bed-and-breakfast of the Teutol family, *tel. [5]747632*, has three rooms with warm quilts, at about $15 per person. English, Spanish and German are all spoken fluently.

SANCHIRÍ LODGE, *tel. and fax [5]733068, 800 meters off the road*, charges $40 with breakfast for up to three persons in rustic woodsy cabins, each with a balcony on the edge of a precipice, and a bathroom below lined with sheet stone quarried on the site. The restaurant serves olla de carne, picadillo, mondongo, and other country specialties for about $5.

OROSI

After the lookout point, the road twists and descends into the valley, and finally straightens and runs flat along the river, through coffee groves to the garden town of **Orosi**, in colonial times a village where Indians were forcibly settled. Here is a lovely restored church dating from the mid-eighteenth century, with brightly whitewashed walls and red tile roof. In violation of all tradition, the main door faces eastward, rather than to the west. The church houses a small collection of religious art. There are hot springs at the edge of town, but you can safely save your swimming for later.

ARRIVALS & DEPARTURES

Most buses to Orosi end their run near the Motel Río (see next page).

Without a car, you can walk or hitch a ride toward the Cachí Dam, or backtrack to Cartago to pick up a bus to Cachí, through Ujarrás.

COFFEE TOURS

Orosi Coffee Adventure offers daily tours at the **Renex plantation** and mill tours (on the main road, past the village), at 10 a.m. and 2 p.m. The fee is $16 with lunch, $12 with a snack only, and, according to when you visit during the year, you can see the picking, washing, repeated peeling, fermenting, washing, drying, and sorting of the famous bean before packing for export.

For information, contact **Aventuras Turísticas de Orosi**, *tel. [5]733030.*

TAPANTÍ NATIONAL PARK

A branch road two kilometers from Orosi passes the Río Macho hydroelectric works, and winds ten kilometers up yet another beautiful valley to **Tapantí National Park**, accessible only in your own vehicle or on foot. There are nature trails a kilometer past the entry point (you pay a small fee), with plants well marked with their names, and explanations of their roles in forest life. Signs point the way to a bouldery wading area in the rushing Río Macho, which is known as a good trout stream.

Three kilometers past the hiking area is a lookout point, which offers prime views to a chute of water, and down the valley, but as vistas go in Costa Rica, this one is not of national standing.

WHERE TO STAY

A youth-hostel-type shelter, with mattresses only, is available to visitors for a small fee. *Call [2]334160* and ask for a radio patch to Tapantí if you wish to reserve a space.

CABINAS KIRI, *just before the entry to the park and 300 meters off the access road*, has four guest rooms in two cabins, at about $39 per person with three meals. You can also stop here just for a meal or drink.

THE UJARRÁS MISSION

Past the dam, a kilometer and a half to the west down a side road, at **Ujarrás**, are the remains of a Spanish mission, one of the first churches in colonial Costa Rica. According to tradition, a humble Huetar Indian fished a box from the river and carried it to Ujarrás, from where it could not be budged. When opened, it was found to contain an image of the Virgin. A church was built on the site, in about 1560.

A few years later, when the British pirates Mansfield and Morgan landed at Portete, a force was hastily organized to expel the invaders. After a prayer stop at Ujarrás, the defenders marched to the Caribbean, where they defeated the superior English force. The victory was attributed to the Virgin of Ujarrás. The church was later abandoned after a series of earthquakes and floods, and the image, now less recalcitrant, was taken to Paraíso. But the ruins, in a manicured park, remain a pleasing sight. They are the locale of an annual tribute to the Virgin in mid-March.

WEST & NORTH OF SAN JOSÉ
BRAULIO CARRILLO NATIONAL PARK

North from the town of Heredia is **Braulio Carrillo National Park**, which takes in the extinct **Barva** and **Cacho Negro** volcanoes. The park was established to protect the flora and fauna along the highway to Guápiles and Limón, in the Caribbean region.

Carrillo Park, which varies in altitude from 500 to 2,906 meters (9,534 feet, the peak of Barva volcano), encompasses tropical wet forest, premontane wet forest, and montane wet forest, or cloud forest. All that "wet" means that branches are laden with orchids, bromeliads and mosses, while ferns, shrubs and much else compete with trees for floor space. On the Atlantic slope are numerous waterfalls and pools. Strong winds blow through, between the Irazú and Barva volcanoes.

Common animals in Carrillo Park include foxes, coyotes, white-faced, spider and howler monkeys, ocelots, sloths and several species of poisonous snakes. More than 500 bird species have been catalogued, including the uncommon quetzal, the long-tailed symbol of liberty whose feathers were treasured in ancient Mesoamerica. Spottings of the quetzal are usually made in the forest atop Barva.

ARRIVALS & DEPARTURES
By Car

One entry point is 20 kilometers from Heredia, reached via a road through San José de la Montaña, and the horse country and oak forest beyond. This route will take you to the crater lake atop **Barva Volcano** (see below).

The toll road to the lowlands (*Autopista a Limón*) runs right through the saddle between the Barva and Irazú volcanoes, roughly following a historic cart road that connected San José with the railhead at Carrillo, before the line from Limón to San José was completed. The eerie roadside vegetation is untouched by farmers, in contrast to readily accessible terrain everywhere else in the country. The winding highway, fog, and heavy traffic make it unwise to stop just anywhere along this route, though there are some sections of the park partially developed for visitors.

The Alto de la Palma entrance, north of Moravia, has been closed to visitors because of landslides and preservation work on the old cart road. Inquire at the park service as to current conditions.

By Bus

Buses for Guápiles will drop you at the ranger station near the entrance to the Zurquí tunnel. Departures are about every half hour from Calle 12, Avenidas 7/9, San José.

WARNING ABOUT BRAULIO CARRILLO PARK

Braulio Carrillo Park along the toll highway is a muggers' paradise. Visitors alone or in small groups are easily cornered on secluded trails. Perpetrators disappear easily into San José, not far away. Numerous visitors have been robbed at gunpoint, and their cars vandalized or stolen.

The trail from the ranger station, on the south side of the Zurquí tunnel, is relatively frequented, and probably safe (I make no guarantees). Farther on, the Botarrama trail, beyond the River Sucio, should be avoided, unless you are advised by a reliable source, or are with a fair-sized tour group.

BARVA VOLCANO

Barva (2,906 meters) presents a different aspect from the other major volcanoes of the Central Valley, Irazú and Poás. Its peak is lower than that of its neighbors, and forested. The top is reached by a trail, so it doesn't constitute an "attraction" for groups on tour buses. Views from the top are limited. But the cloud forest is fascinating, and with a start by car or by public transportation, Barva can be visited on a day outing from San José.

The narrow road through San José de la Montaña, winding up Barva's flanks through horse-grazing pastures and oak forest, is paved as far as Sacramento, and passable beyond with four-wheel drive. If you've come by car, park and lock at this point, or as far beyond Sacramento as you can go. Three kilometers beyond the end of the pavement is a ranger station, at the boundary of Braulio Carrillo Park. *Official hours here are from 8 a.m. to 4 p.m.*

Ascending Barva

A muddy jeep trail (used only by official vehicles) ascends from the ranger post through dense, moss-laden high cloud forest, then narrows and descends to the lake in Barva's crater. Once you reach the shore, you can continue for another 200 meters or so, via a more difficult and squishy trail, to a lookout point at a higher elevation, though it is usually fogged in. At a steady pace, you can reach the lake from the ranger station in under an hour, and return — mostly downhill — in about a half-hour.

By public transportation, take a Paso Llano bus from Heredia (5 , 6:30 or 11:30 a.m.), get off as far as it goes toward Sacramento, and start walking. From here, it's about two hours or more to the peak. Later buses go only as far as San José de la Montaña, adding still another hour to your walk, through beautiful forest and past small dairy farms, but along a paved road, and not very adventurous. Confirm bus hours, and current rules concerning camping, with the park service at the zoo in San José before you go.

The **Jungle Trails** travel agency, *near the Hotel Torremolinos (tel. [2]553486)*, regularly organizes trips to the top of Barva.

ALAJUELA

Located just a short ride west of the capital, **Alajuela** ("a-la-HWEH-la") is Costa Rica's second city, founded late in the colonial period, in 1790. Bustling, with a climate warmer than San José's, Alajuela is an important cattle marketing and sugar-processing center, and, increasingly, a site for small manufacturing industries. The denizens of the town are famously good humored, and well they might be, for Alajuela is the most pleasant of the provincial capitals, a place where lingering around the square is the chief diversion, and a recommended one.

Alajuela's main claim to fame is as the birthplace of **Juan Santamaría**, the drummer boy who set fire to the headquarters of the American adventurer William Walker in 1857, thus helping to bring about the defeat of the filibuster forces that had taken control of Nicaragua.

ARRIVALS & DEPARTURES

By Car

The city is just a short hop from San José. If you're driving, take the Cañas highway (Autopista General Cañas, or simply *la pista*). The turnoff for Alajuela is near the airport.

By Bus

Buses leave from Avenida 2, Calles 12/14, San José, every 15 minutes or so until about midnight, then every hour on the hour. The bus terminal in Alajuela is at Calle 8, Avenidas Central/1, three blocks west of the square. Microbuses leave as well from Avenida 4, Calles 2/4 for San José.

WHERE TO STAY

HOTEL ALAJUELA, *Calle 2, Avenidas Central/2 (P.O. Box 110, tel. 41[1]1241), a half-block from the square, $27 single/$34 double*, is a fairly clean, homey, and relatively modern establishment, with 32 modest rooms.

On the edge of town, **APARTOTEL EL ERIZO** (*P. O. Box 61-4050 Alajuela, tel. and fax 41[2]2840), ten blocks west of the square along Avenida 1, at the Lucky Strike sign*, has 11 harshly furnished garden apartments in a stuccoed block, with cooking and laundry facilities, as well as phones and televisions. The gardens are pleasant, anyway. The rate is $60 daily, and each sleeps three or four persons.

HOSTAL VILLA REAL, *tel. 41[4]4856, two blocks north and one block east of the church*, is a bare-bones traditional wooden house, clean and adequate, operated as a lodging place by enthusiastic young people. There are five rooms sharing bath at $12 single/$22 double/$30 triple. Tell Flavio that I sent you.

WHERE TO EAT

There are a few enjoyable restaurants in Alajuela.

JOEY'S, *a drinking and eating spot open to the square.* About $6 to $8 for a meal. Joey's doubles as a travel agency and home-away-from-home for wanderers.

MARISQUERÍA LA SIRENITA, *on the south side of the main square near the church*, serves inexpensive seafood. With harsh fluorescent lighting and minor nautical decor, you won't come for the atmosphere. But the sea bass in a tomato-and-herb sauce is excellent for a couple of dollars or so, and you can order shrimp by size without breaking your budget.

The **CENCERRO** (the cowbell), *upstairs on Avenida Central, facing the park*, serves charcoal-broiled steaks and fish and chicken dishes. $8 and up.

For more home-style cooking, try **LA JARRA**, *at Calle 2 and Avenida 2, a block south from the square and upstairs*, with many windows to catch the breeze. About $6 for a full meal, $3 for the daily luncheon special, sandwiches for less.

LAS COCINAS DE LEÑA, *Calle 2, Avenida 6 (three blocks from the square along the same street as the Hotel Alajuela)* is an unpretentious Tico-style bar and grill. Mexican and Tico snacks — *nachos, chalupas* — and grilled steaks and fish go for $4 and $5. Live music on weekends.

SEEING THE SIGHTS

The **main square** of Alajuela is a shady forest-garden, with mango and palm trees, where locals and not a small number of resident foreigners observe the passing of the day from stone benches. Also hanging out in the park, more literally, are a few two-toed sloths, those snail-slow creatures that look slug-ugly in photos but are cute and furry in the flesh.

A statue of the **Erizo** (the Hedgehog, as local hero Juan Santamaría is affectionately known, for his bristly hair) may be seen *a block south of the main square, on Calle 2.* Torch in hand, rifle at his side, he stands ready to repeat his deed.

Facing the east side of the central park is the city's **main church**, an uninteresting neo-classical structure with simple lines. (For orientation purposes, Calle Central runs along the east side of the park, by the church, Avenida Central along the south.)

About five blocks east of the central park is a more attractive church, built in a Costa Rican simplified baroque style, with angels popping up around the edge of the faáade.

A block north of the square is the **Juan Santamaría Historical Museum**, *housed in the solid building at the corner of Calle 2 and Avenida 3*. Costa Ricans and Yanqui-bashers will examine the artifacts and battle paintings of the Walker war. Others will admire the building itself, with its wide archways, massive beams, whitewashed walls and tile roof. *Hours at the museum are 2 p.m. to 9 p.m., daily except Monday.*

POÁS VOLCANO

Poás has several distinctions. It has one of the largest geyser-type craters in the world — 1.5 kilometers across and 300 meters deep. It contains two lakes, one in an extinct crater, one in the fuming main crater. It is in continuing activity, in the form of seeping gases and steam, as well as occasional geysers and the larger eruptions of every few years (the last in 1978). Most practically for the visitor, it is easily reached by a paved road to the peak (2,704 meters — 8,871 feet— above sea level), and the facilities atop the mountain are the best in the national park system.

Get an early start! Aside from the unique experience of ascending a volcano, you'll want to beat the clouds to the peak in order to get an ocean-to-ocean view. Take a good look at the volcano before you start your ascent. If the cloud cap is dense and widespread, it might be better to wait for another day.

Poás is open to visitors from 8 a.m. to 3:30 p.m. Rain gear will come in handy even in the dry season, when heavy winds whip clouds across the peak. Take a sweater or jacket as well. Temperatures can dip sharply in minutes.

ARRIVALS & DEPARTURES

Two routes are available, through Alajuela or Heredia. These converge at the little village of Poasito, high on the volcano's slopes.

By Car

If you're driving, take the Cañas expressway to Alajuela, then follow the clearly marked road via San Pedro de Poás and Poasito. The peak is 37 kilometers from Alajuela, 59 kilometers from San José. An alternative route from San José goes through Heredia and Barva, and up to Los Cartagos and Poasito, through equally dramatic and windy landscapes as those along the Poasito road. Try both routes.

By Bus

A public bus to Poás (Tuasa, *tel. [2]337477*) leaves on Sundays only from 12 Calle, Avenidas 2/4, San José. Be there by 8 a.m. Fare is less than $5. This is an all-day excursion — bring a snack. The ride up takes two hours, with a twenty-minute rest stop at a café high on the volcano, near Poasito. Three hours are allowed on top before departure, more than ample time to see both accessible craters and the cloud forest.

On other days, buses are available from Alajuela to Poasito (lately at 5 a.m. and 1:30 p.m.). This still leaves you ten kilometers from the peak. You'll have to walk, hitch, or hire a taxi to finish the ascent.

By Tour or Taxi

Tours operate to Poás most days from San José, or you can hire a taxi to take you all the way at a reasonable cost.

ORIENTATION

The climate atop Poás is less severe than that on Irazú; the peak is several hundred meters lower, and the steam and gases burn out a smaller area. Vegetation is therefore more abundant. But on a windy day, or when the peak is enshrouded in a dripping pea soup, the visitor will find nothing benign about the environment. Nighttime temperatures well below freezing are not uncommon.

Much of the upper part of Poás is cloud forest, the enchanted, cool, moist environment where orchids and bromeliads and vines thrive at every level, along with humble ferns and mosses on the ground. The Poás cloud forest is especially rich in mushrooms and lichens. Parts of the national park are former pastures that are being allowed to return to their natural states; these contain many oak trees. Other sections near the peak are meadow-like, or are characterized by low shrubs and gnarled and twisted trees.

Wildlife in the Poás forest is not abundant, possibly because nearby slopes are farmed intensively. Among the inhabitants are brocket deer, coatis, sloths, cougars, and the Poás squirrel, which has been found only in this vicinity. Birds include several types of hummingbirds, trogons, and the emerald toucanet among more than 70 recorded species.

With increasing volcanic activity in recent years, rains of gases, acids and ash have damaged crops in the surrounding area, and caused authorities to limit access to the park. Currently, visitors may spend no more than 30 minutes at the main crater. They are warned to leave immediately if they feel any irritation of the throat or eyes, not to picnic near the lookout, and not to drink from the park's acidic water system.

SEEING THE VOLCANO

The substantial **Visitors Center** includes an auditorium where a half-hour slide show about the national parks is sometimes given. Orient yourself at the exhibit area before walking around, since you'll be covering a lot of territory. Aside from a model of the volcano and its craters, there are some wonderful peek-a-boo contraptions where you can try to identify animals by their tracks, samples of volcanic products, volcanic cross-sections, and descriptions of flora.

The Craters of Poás

From the visitors' center, you'll probably head first to the **main crater**. Along the walkway you'll notice the plant called the *sombrilla del pobre* (poor man's parasol), which is characteristic of the open areas of Poás. The leaves grow up to two meters across, which explains the name and occasional use of the plant.

Visitors are not allowed to descend into the fuming main crater, but the views from its rim are impressive. At the bottom is a sometime lake formed by rain water, its shade of green changing according to the amount of sulfur it contains at any given time. Water level varies according to the whims and fury and fractures of the earth underneath. Intermittent geyser activity results from water seeping into fissures along the bottom of the lake, then boiling and exploding upward. More likely, you'll see gas and steam escaping from fumaroles along the lake's edge. The rim of the crater is burned and strewn with rock and ash, and only a few shrubs struggle for survival in the noxious environment.

After a visit to the active crater, climb to **Laguna Botos**, the water-filled extinct crater near the highest point on the volcano. The lake is named for an Indian tribe that once inhabited the area.

The last major attraction atop Poás is the **nature trail**, a run of about half a kilometer through a relatively undisturbed stretch of cloud forest, providing a more interesting route to the crater than the road. The signs in Spanish along the way are more poetic than informative, and some specific labels of trees and plants would be useful (says the gringo). This is the most accessible area of forest of this type in Costa Rica.

Vistas & Fog

Unfortunately, it's easier to describe many of the features of Poás than actually to see them. The top of the mountain is often clouded over, at least partially. However, the clouds shift frequently. If the main crater is obscured at first, take another look before you leave. The shroud might have lifted. The view to either coast, and northward into Nicaragua, might also open up from time to time, so keep an eye peeled.

OJO DE AGUA & ENVIRONS

A few kilometers south of Alajuela, just southeast of the international airport, are the **Ojo de Agua** springs and recreation area (not to be confused with the town of the same name, which is west of the airport). Water gushes from the earth at a rate of 200 liters per second, and most of the flow is directed into an aqueduct that supplies the city of Puntarenas, on the Pacific.

Much of the remainder is used for the amusement of the citizenry. In the tree-shaded park surrounding the springs are three pools, tennis courts, and a lake with rowboats. On weekends, this is a great place to rub elbows and much else with the locals. Go during the week if you prefer solitude, or serious swimming (or pass it up altogether if the pool at your hotel is more to your taste). Entry costs about 50¢, and changing rooms are available. There are cheap eateries both inside and outside the gates. Through no particular logic, the recreational facilities are managed by the national railroad company.

Buses operate to Ojo de Agua from Avenida 2, Calle 22, San José, hourly on the half hour during the week, and every fifteen minutes or so on weekends. There are also buses from Alajuela and Heredia.

West of Ojo de Agua, at **Guácima**, is the **Butterfly Farm**, where several dozen species of the insect are raised for live export to European exhibitions. The part open to the public is a hillside rain forest under protective netting. A dammed stream tumbles into a pond, ferns and fronds and violets and impatiens step up and around the boulders, trees tower above. And, of course, there are butterflies, several dozen species or more, according to the season, along with ants and spiders and lizards that the netting doesn't keep out, and displays of leaf-cutter ants under glass.

The butterfly exhibit opens every day at 9 a.m. Tours operate continuously (the last starts at 3:30 p.m.), terminating at a stand where t-shirts and mounted butterflies may be acquired. The earliest hours are best for watching butterflies emerge from their cocoons.

The farm also offers a "bee tour" aboard a traditional oxcart, a two-hour excursion that includes a look at hives, explanations of bee life cycles, and insights into Mayan apiculture in ancient America.

The farm is about half a kilometer south of Guácima, southwest of the international airport. Take the road around the airport, or the road westward from the Cañas expressway through San Antonio de Belén. Signs are posted at every junction. A direct bus runs intermittently from San José (currently Monday, Tuesday, Thursday).

The Butterfly Farm is open daily from 9 a.m. to 3:30 p.m. Admission is a steep $9 for the butterfly tour, $8 for the bee tour and oxcart ride, or $16 for both (this is not a misprint). Rates are lower for students and children, but most families can find better values elsewhere. *Phone 48[0]0115 for information or bus directions from Alajuela.* The owners speak English.

LA GARITA/DULCE NOMBRE

West of Alajuela, along the highway to Atenas, at **Dulce Nombre**, is the **Zoológico de Aves Tropicales** (Tropical Bird Zoo, "ZOH-oh AH-veh"), which holds an outstanding collection in a lovely landscaped setting. (In fact, the area around Dulce Nombre and La Garita is replete with beautiful gardens and plant nurseries.) Species represented include owls, honeycreepers, toucans, hawks, parrots and macaws.

Usual hours are 9 a.m. to 5 p.m. daily, admission is a couple of dollars. Stop this way if you're passing through the area, or have a special interest in tropical fauna.

ARRIVALS & DEPARTURES
By Bus

The Atenas or La Garita bus from Alajuela passes the entrance (on the north side of the road), or you can look for a Dulce Nombre bus from the Coca-Cola terminal in San José.

By Car

By car, drive eastward for three kilometers from the Atenas exit of the expressway.

WHERE TO STAY

Several bed-and-breakfasts, largely owned by retired Americans, are located in the area around Atenas. These are described at the end of this chapter.

WHERE TO EAT

The road onward to Atenas is popular for weekend excursions. Various roadside restaurants specialize in chicken roasted over coffee wood, and barbecued meats. The **FIESTA DE MAÍZ** eatery serves *pozole*, *tamales*, *tortillas*, and everything else fashioned in whole or part from corn, the traditional staff of life of Central America — corn on the cob, corn fritters, tamales, corn soup, corn stew, corn bread. *Open Fridays through Sundays only.*

About four kilometers up the road from the Fiesta de Maíz toward Turrúcares is **LAS CAMPANAS**, a charming indoor/outdoor roadhouse illuminated by fixtures with macramé lamp shades, where the likes of *paté de foie*, chili con carne, sirloin in sauce, and quail are served, along with rabbit, which is not on the menu. You can be served in English, French (*Ö la canadienne*) or Spanish.

Country Lodging Near San José

Attractive alternatives to city hotels are to be found in the villages and valleys and on the mountain and volcanic slopes around San José. Despite surroundings of orchards and forests, the inns and lodges of the Central Valley are only minutes from downtown San José, and a short ride from the international airport.

The valley hotels are most suitable if you have a car at your disposal; or are a repeat visitor, and know exactly what you are getting. But anyone can consider them as a base for all or part of a stay in Costa Rica. And, should you change your mind about your preferred style of accommodation, you needn't feel isolated and locked in. These hostelries will also give you a rough idea of country living in the Central Valley, in case you're considering a move. For approximate locations, see the map at the beginning of this chapter.

FINCA ROSA BLANCA COUNTRY INN, *P. O. Box 37-3009, Santa Bárbara de Heredia, tel. [2]399392, fax [2]399555. Six suites, one master suite. $85 to $170 single, $115 to $200 double, $29 per additional person, plus tax. U.S. reservations: tel. 800-327-9854.*

I was uncertain whether to list the Rosa Blanca as an accommodation or a point of interest. The main house, set amid orchards of citrus, macadamia and cashew trees, is a fantasy made real, a combination of Gaudiésque and Pueblo Indian elements, along with personal whimsy.

Stuccoed walls curve around a central, 40-foot chimney, pre-Columbian ceramics in its niches. Nooks abound, bedecked with collectibles and treasures from around the world. A staircase climbs skyward to the master suite with its crows-nest bedroom and terrace, and pool/tub filled by a stream coursing through a rock garden. In another suite, a scene painted in a niche continues the view through an adjacent window. The Black-and-White room has an art nouveau theme. And this is just the start.

The plantings around Rosa Blanca attract birds, which can be spotted in the foliage right outside the various levels of the main house. Views, according to cloud patterns, are variously to mountains and valleys and near and distant hamlets.Breakfast is included in the rate, and other meals will be prepared on request. Also for rent is a cottage (*casita*) built in the style of a traditional Costa Rican country house, with three bedrooms, for $100 to $150 per day, less by the week or month.

To get to Rosa Blanca, from the airport or Alajuela, drive through Santa Bárbara, turning north at the sign before Barrio Jesús.

POSADA DE LA MONTAÑA, *P. O. Box 1-3017, San Isidro de Heredia, tel. and fax [2]398096. U.S. reservations, P. O. Box 308, Greenfield, MO 65661, tel. 417-637-2066. $30-40 single/$35-45 double, including breakfast, $70 and up for units with kitchenettes, lower rates for rooms sharing bath. Visa, Master Card, American Express.*

On a cool, wind-swept slope, the **Mountain Inn** is an American-owned bed-and-breakfast on several acres affording long views of San José, the Central Valley, and the forests stretching toward Limón between the volcanoes Irazú and Barva. The property includes coffee and fruit plantings and a huge vegetable garden, all of which attract birds. Six rooms in the main house, each with two beds, are off a huge *sala* with fireplace. Six more concrete "cabina"-style units, with outside entry and parking at the door, can be combined with kitchenettes for families or groups. Washing machines are available to guests, and horses can be hired nearby. Beverages and airport pickup available. Children and pets welcome. English, Spanish, Russian and French spoken. This is the closest accommodation to Braulio Carrillo National Park.

If driving, take the Limón Highway to the San Isidro de Heredia exit (left side), continue four kilometers to the bridge, then 1.5 kilometers north. Signs point the way. Call for bus instructions.

The hotels below are along the road between Birrí and San José de la Montaña, north of Heredia. Buses run from Heredia to San José de la Montaña. Continue by taxi, if you're not driving.

HOTEL DE MONTAÑA EL PÓRTICO, *P. O. Box 289-3000, Heredia, tel. [2]276022. 16 units. $65 double, $12 per additional person. The best of the country lodges in the immediate area, with brick-and-wood units clustered around a pond, a restaurant, sauna and pool. Phone 212039 in San José to arrange transportation.*

HOTEL CYPRESAL, *P. O. Box 7891-1000, San José, tel. [2]374466, [2]231717 in San José, fax [2]216244. 24 rooms. $57 single/$63 double. Credit cards accepted. Also with pool, whirlpool, sauna, large restaurant.*

Units have kitchenettes, TV, television, some have fireplace. Horses available, also meeting facilities, along with package trips with excursions to several national parks, using the hotel as a base.

CABINAS LAS ARDILLAS, *tel. [2]228134. Adjacent to the Cypresal in a pine-and-cedar park.*

Units, built of logs and brick, have long valley views, and there are a restaurant and play area. The rate is about $40 for a unit that will sleep a couple and two children, $75 for a much larger unit into which up to eight persons can be crowded.

Higher up, near the park at **Monte de la Cruz**, is:

HOTEL EL TIROL, *P.O. Box 7812-1000, San José, tel. [2]397371, fax [2]397050. 23 units. $90 double in chalets, up to $175 double in suites, breakfast included. Visa, Master Card, American Express.*

The main building here is genuinely Tyrolean, in a suitable mountain landscape of conifers and meadows, and the cottages are dollhouse versions, with cutout wood trim. Each guest unit has a bedroom upstairs and a sitting area with convertible bed downstairs, and welcome electric heaters. Adjacent is a section of private forest, with hiking trails and waterfalls.Riding horses are available. Dinner is served in front of a fireplace in the main building, and is attraction enough for many visitors. Steak and seafood and rabbit main courses are offered on a French menu. A complete meal costs about $20, and is usually excellent. El Tirol reminds me of the original Trapp Family Lodge in Stowe, Vermont.

ORQUÍDEAS INN, *San José de Alajuela (P. O. Box 394, Alajuela), tel. 43[9]9346, fax 43[9]9740. 18 rooms. $57 single/$68 double with breakfast. Visa, Master Card.*

This is a colonial-style hotel in a little estate just past the junction for Grecia on the road from Alajuela to Poás volcano. Rooms have arched openings, and furniture throughout is of white wicker. The higher rate is for a suite with hardwood floor, and a huge terrace overlooking the pool. The location is good if you'll be ascending Poás by car; road noise could be a problem. Airport pickup available.

LA PROVIDENCIA ECO-LODGE, tel. *[2]317884*, has four rustic no-frills cabins behind the restaurant of the same name, almost at the top of Poás volcano, for $60 double. Horseback riding is available.

TUETAL LODGE, *Tuetal (P. O. Box 1346-Alajuela), tel. and fax 421804. 7 rooms. $28-$35 single/$35-$40 double.*

In the village of Tuetal Norte, about a $2 taxi ride from Alajuela, four blocks west and one-and-a-half blocks south of the church. Some units have a kitchen. Breakfast available at $3, and beverages. English-speaking owner.

POÁS VOLCANO LODGE, *Vara Blanca (P. O. Box 5723-1000 San José), tel. and fax 41[9]9102. 8 rooms. $70 double, $110 in suite.*

A lodge with a British country flavor, built of stone, concrete, and hewn beams, surrounded by pasture, forest, and Central Valley views.

VILLA BLANCA HOTEL, *San Ramón (tel. [2]284603, fax [2]284004 in San José). 36 units. $95 double in cottages, $68 in lodge rooms.*

This is an attractive cloud-forest country lodge on a huge cattle farm 20 kilometers northwest of San Ramón (which is along the highway to Puntarenas), including a forest reserve and trails. The main building has the flavor of a traditional hacienda great house, with open kitchen and a central fountain. Cottages are unusually attractive, with exposed beams Call for information about package stays. Day trips to the property from San José cost about $70.

Near La Garita

LA CHATELLE. *P. O. Box 755-1007, tel. 48[7]7781, fax 48[7]7271. $99 in luxury unit, $80 double in standard unit, with breakfast and airport transfer. Rates lower May, June, and August through November.*

Here's an idiosyncratic collection of one-unit cottages, all named for volcanoes. The "luxury" units (their term), with cone-shaped roofs reminiscent of Africa, have a queen-sized and single bed in a loft, another bed downstairs, and full kitchen; the Presidential Suite, with woody decor, has a vaulted ceiling. Standard units have brick walls, and are probably damp on rainy days. Facilities include a pool. The grounds are lush and rolling, and there is a steak-house restaurant that gets a weekend clientele. The rate includes breakfast and transfer from the airport; but a rented car would be helpful, as the owners, who include an American, are not always around to see to the needs of guests. The hotel is one kilometer south of the Fiesta del Maíz restaurant on the road to Atenas.

LA PIÑA DORADA *bed-and-breakfast, Turrúcares, tel. and fax 48[7]7220. 5 rooms, $55 to $75 double.*

If you follow directions (take the first left after the Fiesta de Maíz restaurant in La Garita and continue 2.8 kilometers) and show up here under your own steam, you'll think you've wandered out of your way. La Piña Dorada is just your standard Spanish-Mediterranean country estate, with vaulted central ceiling in the great house, formal library, huge *sala* with arched picture windows, hand-carved chairs, projection TV, and all the other bare necessities. The grounds, covering two acres, include citrus, banana and mango trees, a goldfish pond with falls and a palm isle, parking under cover, and a large illuminated pool squarely in front of the house.

Guest units vary in size — the largest has a huge sitting room. Comfortable furnishings include wicker chairs, and double or king-plus custom beds. Local art hangs everywhere. Despite the overwhelming facility, hospitality afforded by Mr. and Mrs. Bill Coffey is home-style and friendly. Wine is served at cost, breakfast is huge, with sausage or bacon. Here's your chance to live like the rich and famous for a few days, or for a few weeks, while you see Costa Rica.

By taxi, it's just 15 minutes from the airport to La Piña Dorada.

THE WILD EAST

North and east of the mountainous backbone of Costa Rica is the triangle-shaped Caribbean coastal region, a vast area of dense tropical forest. No time of year, no remote corner of the Atlantic slope, is ever dry. Clouds blow in from the sea throughout the year. Those that don't drench the area directly shed their water against the central mountains, from where it flows back to the Caribbean in numerous rivers, and often overflows onto the low-lying, poorly drained land. Rainfall at Limón, in the center of the coastal strip, reaches 150 inches in many years, and near the Nicaraguan border, approaches 200 inches.

The trip to Limón is an interesting descent from highlands to jungle through varied zones of vegetation. The Caribbean coastline is one nearly continuous sweep of white beach, most of it deserted. Wildlife treasures abound, including green turtles in their protected nesting area at Tortuguero. Fishing, especially for tarpon, is world-class. The blacks who form a large part of the lowland population are a fascinating culture, quite different from other Costa Ricans. And also, there is nothing menacing in those parts of the Caribbean lowlands where the visitor is likely to tread.

TAKE THE OLD TRAIN

Inquire at the tourist office or a travel agency about the availability of excursions along the old Jungle Train line. Currently, **TAM Tours** *(tel. [2]222642) operates a train on a lowland portion of the line, with a stop at a banana warehouse.*

GUAYABO NATIONAL MONUMENT

About 20 kilometers north of Turrialba, on the slopes of the Turrialba volcano, is **Guayabo National Monument**. Although Costa Rica is especially rich in pre-Columbian antiquities, its early inhabitants lived nomadic existences, or concentrated in villages and towns built of highly perishable materials.

There are no great native ceremonial centers that survive to this day, as they do in Honduras, Guatemala, El Salvador, and Mexico, or at least they have not yet been discovered. Which is why the Guayabo complex, with its constructions of natural and hewn stone, is considered important by Costa Ricans.

The Guayabo site includes paved walkways, walls, and circular stone constructions, or mounds, that might have been foundations for conical houses of a South American sort, with sides of saplings covered with palm thatch. The largest mound has a stairway oriented to the volcano Turrialba, and volcanic ash found in pottery here indicates that the mountain might have figured in ceremonies or cures. Subterranean and surface aqueducts, terminating in rectangular stone storage tanks (also signs of South American cultural influence), are still serviceable. These run from some of the hundred or so springs (which first drew people to settle here), and were stepped to slow the flow of water.

ARRIVALS & DEPARTURES

By Bus

Buses that pass not far from the site currently leave Turrialba Monday and Friday at 11 a.m., and return on the same days at 1 p.m.

By Car or Taxi

Access to Guayabo is by a winding road in poor condition. The last few kilometers are unpaved. Your best bet, if you're not driving, is to hire a taxi in Turrialba for the round trip.

SEEING THE SIGHTS

In addition to the 20-hectare archeological site, Guayabo comprises a 217-hectare natural zone of premontane rain forest dense with vines and epiphytes, and alive with birds and animals. About 160 bird species have been recorded. Residents include sloths, raccoons, coatis, and many others. The astounding aspect is that most of this life has regenerated or been attracted in just the 25 years that the former pasture has been protected. The natural attractions will be for many the main reason for visiting.

Guayabo is open daily from 8 a.m. to 3 p.m. In order to protect the site from foot traffic in delicate areas, as well as from looters, visitors may enter the archeological zone only on a guided walk, which is arranged on demand. *The fee is about $2.* Guides speak only Spanish, but are good communicators, and will show an English fact sheet, as required, to get across the main points.

WHERE TO STAY

HOTEL LA CALZADA, *almost adjacent to Guayabo, has five double rooms, sharing bathroom, for about $21 double, Visa accepted. Call 560465 or fax 560427 to leave a message, or write P. O. Box 260-7150 Turrialba.*

This is a pretty spot with a pond (where you can fish for tilapia), long-distance views over pastures, and trees and plants identified by signs and tags. Tico-style meals are available as well if you're just visiting Guayabo for the day.

LIMÓN

Limón, Costa Rica's main Caribbean port, opened to banana traffic in 1880, but its place in national history is more venerable. Christopher Columbus landed offshore, at Uvita Island, in 1502. The first Spanish attempts at settlement were made in the area. Intermittently through the colonial period, encounters with the British and Dutch, both commercial and bellicose, took place at Portete, just a few kilometers to the north.

The port city of Limón that grew with the railway was as much a part of the British West Indies as of Costa Rica. Blacks from Jamaica and other islands constituted most of the population, and English was the only language that mattered in business. Immigrant workers kept their British passports, sent their children to school in English, read Jamaican newspapers, and went to the movies to see British films. Limón and the banana lands were separated from Costa Rica not only by language and culture, but also by a law that forbade blacks from crossing the Central Valley or overnighting there.

Limón today is a mixed Hispanic and Afro-Caribbean city, but more and more, the Hispanic predominates. The local Creole patois, permeated with Spanish words, is the language of the older generation. Blacks are discouraged from using what Hispanic Costa Ricans consider "bad" English, though many can still speak a rather elegant and formal Caribbean dialect. English has no official status, and is studied only in secondary school.

Compared to the towns of the Central Valley, Limón is shabby. Compared to other ports on this coast — Belize City, Puerto Barrios in Guatemala, La Ceiba in Honduras — Limón is pristine with its paved streets, functioning sewers, a clean market. Of teeming tropical ports, it is a good choice for the outsider to sample. But if people-watching in a throbbing, hot town is not your cup of tea, move on to the beaches and parks to the north or south.

ARRIVALS & DEPARTURES
Arriving By Air
The airstrip is three kilometers south of town, along the sea. **Travelair** (*tel. [7]327883*) has a flight on Mondays, Wednesdays and Fridays from San José, fare $88 round trip.

Arriving By Bus
Buses for Limón leave every hour from 5 a.m. to 7 p.m. from Avenida 3, Calles 19/21, San José.

Departing By Bus
Cahuita and Puerto Vargas can be reached on day excursions from Limón, though they're more fun if you stay for a day or two.

From Limón, rickety, usually crowded buses leave from Avenida 4, Calles 3/4 at 5 a.m., 10 a.m., 1 p.m. and 4 p.m., arriving at Cahuita in about an hour, and at the junction for Puerto Viejo about 30 minutes later. There are buses at 6 a.m. and 2 p.m. that go right into Puerto Viejo and on to Manzanillo. Get to the station early to find a seat.

The public bus for Playa Bonita, Portete and Moín runs every hour from Calle 4, Avenidas 3/4 in Limón.

Return buses for San José leave every hour from 5 a.m. to 7 p.m. from Avenida 2, Calle 2.

Departing By Taxi
A taxi from Limón to Cahuita costs about $25.

Departing By Train

The train to the banana-producing Estrella Valley, south of Limón, leaves Monday through Friday at 4 a.m. and 3 p.m. Return trains from the end of the line at Ley River are at 5:50 a.m. and 4:50 p.m. This train will get you close to the Hitoy Cerere Biological Reserve. Or, you could ride only as far as Penshurst, and continue southward to Cahuita by bus on the coastal highway.

Departing By Air

Travelair *(tel. [2]327883)* has a flight to San José on Mondays, Wednesdays and Fridays, fare $88 round trip.

GETTING AROUND TOWN

Avenida 2 is Limón's main street, running east from the railway passenger station to Vargas Park, near the waterfront. There is no odd-even segregation of *avenidas* and *calles*, as in San José. The freight line of the railroad, running to the docks, bounds Limón to the south, along Avenida 1. Street numbers are posted, but some of the signs are in the wrong place. Locals use their own tags — Avenida 2 is the Market Street.

WHERE TO STAY

It isn't a good idea to arrive in Limón on a weekend without a reservation. The best hotels are on the northern edge of town, or farther out at Portete.

HOTEL MARIBU CARIBE, *Portete road, tel. [7]584010. 24 units. $68 single/$85 double.*

The newest hotel near Limón, on a rise along the water, with commanding views. Guest rooms, relatively small, are in unusual round cottages with high thatched roofs. All are air conditioned. Amenities include a double pool, air conditioning, and television. Restaurant and bar, tour service.

HOTEL MATAMA, *Portete (P. O. Box 686-7300 Limón), tel. [7]581123, fax [7]584499. 16 units. $52 single/$70 double/$17 additional person.*

These are attractive bungalows sleeping up to eight, well finished with details in tropical woods, in a nicely lush hillside setting. Some units have little interior gardens in the bathrooms. There are kids' and adults' pools, and an attractive open restaurant.

More inexpensive accommodations near the above hotels are mentioned below, under Playa Bonita and Portete.

HOTEL ACÓN, *Calle 3, Avenida 3, P. O. Box 528-7300, tel. [7]581010. 39 rooms. $27 single/$36 double.*

Best in the center of town, despite plain, bare rooms and washbasins that drain into the showers. Clean and air-conditioned.

HOTEL INTERNACIONAL, *Avenida 5, Calles 2/3 (P. O. Box 288), tel. [7]580423. 25 rooms. $15 single/$20 double with fan, $18/$30 with air conditioning.* New and cheery, replacing a hotel that collapsed in the 1991 earthquake. Try to get a room with outside windows, rather than one of the cubicles toward the center of the building. Protected parking is included in the rate.

HOTEL MIAMI, *Avenida 2, Calles 4/5, tel. [7]580490. 32 rooms. $16 single/$25 double, less with fan only.* Bare rooms right on the main street, but, with air conditioning, one of the better buys in Limón.

HOTEL PARK, *Avenida 3, Calles 1/2, tel. [7]580476. 14 rooms. $15 to $19 single/$20 to $23 double.*

Once Limón's grande dame, with restaurant, bar, good view of the port, and an aura of faded glory. Adequate, if you can do without air conditioning. Rooms without sea view cost less. Not too clean.

HOTEL TETE, *Calle 4, Avenida 3, tel. [7]581122. 14 rooms. $15 single/ $25 double.*

In the center of the action, opposite Limón's market, but clean.

WHERE TO EAT

With the sea nearby, lobster and shrimp cost slightly less in Limón than in San José. Another specialty is Jamaican-style cooking, but unfortunately, it's a home phenomenon that only rarely makes its way to restaurant menus.

In general, you can eat wholesomely and heartily in Limón, but not always exquisitely.

LIFEBUOY (yes, that's the name), *Avenida 3, Calles 2/3, opposite the Hotel Acón,* is a McDonald's-style walk-up-and-order place with not only cheeseburgers and fried chicken, but also Caribbean-style rice and beans, and fresh fruit drinks. $4 and less for a meal.

MARES, a bar and restaurant, is sort of pleasant, *opposite the market on Avenida 2, Calles/3/4,* and open to the sidewalk on one side — and to a supermarket on the other. Sit on wicker chairs, watch the street action or the shoppers (depending on which way you're facing), and consume standard Tico fare of burgers, spaghetti, or beef. About $6 for a full meal.

LA FUENTE, *Calle 3, Avenidas 3/4,* is cleaner than the run of restaurants here. About $6 for a meal.

If none of these places attracts you, you can get roast chicken to take out, with a stack of tortillas, at Avenida 2, Calles 6/7. For the cheapest meals, try rubbing elbows with the locals at the eateries inside the market buildings.

The **AMERICAN BAR** is an open-to-the-street place *at Calle 1 and Avenida 2, opposite Vargas Park.*

SEEING THE SIGHTS

The favorite place for sitting down in Limón is **Vargas Park**, *a square of jungle at Avenida 2 and Calle 1, facing the sea*. Giant hardwoods struggle against the odds with strangler figs, huge palms shoot toward the sky, vines and bromeliads compete for space and moisture, birds dart and flit through the tangle.

Across from the park is Limón's perfect tropical-port **city hall**, with its cream-colored stucco, open arcades and breezeways, balconies, and louvered windows. Limón's older architecture is well suited to the climate. Thick walls moderate the extremes of temperature, concrete overhangs block the sun and keep people dry when it rains, as it does drenchingly often.

The **market**, *on Avenida 2 between Calles 3 and 4*, is ever lively, set back in a large building in its own little park. Stop in and admire the papaya and passionfruit, as well as the more mundane but no less impressive one-pound carrots. The streets around the market are Limón's social center, where purveyors of food and games of chance set up shop during the Columbus Day celebrations and for the month preceding Christmas. The Columbus Day "carnival" season features floats, street bands, dancing and masquerades, and everything else that one expects to find in the islands at Mardi Gras.

Limón is located on a rocky point, and is one of the few places along Costa Rica's Caribbean coast without a beach. There's a government-sponsored pool in town, but most visitors will prefer the nearby beaches.

EXCURSION TO TORTUGUERO NATIONAL PARK

You can also get to **Tortuguero National Park** and back in a day, though, again, an overnight stay is preferable. Package visits to Tortuguero are most easily arranged from San José. See page 182 for more details on your options. In Limón, **Tortuguero Odysseys** *(tel. [7]581940 or [7]580824)*, **Caribbean Magic** *(tel. [7]581210)*, **Mawamba tours** *(tel. [7]584915)*, **Viajes Tropicales Laura** *(tel. [7]582410)* and the **Hotel Maribu** all offer excursions to Tortuguero, ranging upward from $60 for a day trip.

Tortuguero Canal

The **Canal de Tortuguero**, a 160-kilometer stretch of natural rivers, lagoons and estuaries, and connecting man-made waterways, runs from Moín almost to the Nicaraguan border. The canal is the main "highway" of the northern coastal region. Cargo and passengers move on narrow, tuglike, 30-foot-long launches.

TORTUGUERO NATIONAL PARK

Several hours and 55 kilometers out of Moín (*80 kilometers north of*

Limón), the cleared fields suddenly give way to what first appear to be green cliffs towering above the canal and lining the rivers that stretch inland. A closer examination reveals that they are unbroken stands of trees, many over 100 feet tall. A sign and checkpoint announce that you have entered **Tortuguero National Park**.

Trees canopy the waterway, and trail vines. Pastel-colored toucans and macaws, monkeys swinging through the trees, sloths hanging from branches, alligators taking the sun, turtles lounging on logs, and, perhaps, some of the coatis, jaguars and ocelots that roam the forest will come into view, if the frequent, heavy rainfalls do not inhibit your sightings. The screams of monkeys and whistles of birds pierce the air.

ARRIVALS & DEPARTURES

Getting to Tortuguero and staying in the park are not easy unless you arrange a package trip through a tour company. There is no regularly scheduled air or boat service.

By Air

The landing strip, four kilometers north of the village, is currently served by chartered flights operated in conjunction with lodging-and-tour packages. On your own, you can have an air taxi service drop you at the park and pick you up a few days later.

By Boat

Traffic on the canal is sparse and irregular, and without advance arrangements through a travel agency, you can't count on anything. When locals can't find a boat, they simply walk along the beach – six hours to Parismina, twelve or more to Tortuguero — and count on friendly dugout owners to take them across intervening estuaries.

The traditional route to the park, by canal boat from Moín, just north of Limón, has been choked with vegetation, and is impassable from time to time. When the Caribbean is calm, boat operators take open water as far as Matina, but this can be dangerous, as storms blow in without warning. Another way is to take a car or taxi along the canal-side road as far as Matina and hire a boat there.

Operators of trips from Moín include the reliable Mr. Alfred Brown-Robinson of **Tortuguero Odysseys** *(tel. [7]581940 or [7]580824)*, who runs a round trip in twelve-passenger boats. Departure from Moín is at 8 a.m., travel time is about three hours. Cost is $60, not including tours in the park.

The riverboat *Francesca*, *tel. [2]260986 in San José*, operates a 26-foot fiber glass boat with 150 horses of power from Moín to Tortuguero, zipping through the least interesting parts of the canal, and slowing down for troops of monkeys and other canalside inhabitants. The boat is narrow enough to permit easy viewing by all passengers. Trips are booked with a minimum of four passengers, at $60 each.

Caribbean Magic, *P. O. Box 2482-1000, San José, tel. [2]581210,* has a $60 one-day trip to Tortuguero from Moín. Or make arrangements for a day trip through the **Hotel Maribu Caribe** or one of the other hotels north of Limón.

Some boat owners offer cheaper service from the Moín canal terminal (they congregate by the signs that read *Se hacen viajes a los canales*), but be cautious about using their services. I've received complaints from visitors who wasted their time stuck in the lilies. *To inquire about government boat service (unreliable and recently suspended), phone [7]581106.*

Booking a Tour

In the case of Tortuguero, it's worth it to book travel and sleeping in a single package. But beware! Overbooking and trip cancellations can be a problem, and the cheapest service is not always your best choice.

Cotur, *Calle 36, Paseo Colón/Avenida 1 (P. O. Box 1818-1002, San José), tel. [2]330155, fax [2]330778,* has a three-day, two-night package trip from San José that includes a bus ride, travel to Tortuguero on a canal boat, all meals, accommodations at the Jungle Lodge, and a half-day tour of the park. The price is about $200 per person. Departures are usually on Tuesday and Friday, but there are extra trips when demand warrants.

Similar trips are offered aboard the *Mawamba* (highly rated by readers), a larger, more enclosed boat. The price is lower on the Mawamba tour if you stay at the basic Sabina's Cabinas instead of Mawamba Lodge. *Call [2]339964 in San José to arrange your travel, or [7]581564 in Limón.* **Mitur**, *P. O. Box 91-1150, San José, tel. [2]552262, fax [2]551946,* has a virtually identical program, based at the Hotel Ilan Ilan. Parismina Tarpon Rancho, near the southern end of the park, is also a base for some turtle-watching trips.

Costa Rica Expeditions *(tel. [2]570766, fax [2]571665)* charges more than other companies, but its trips are generally more reliable. A one-night visit to Tortuguero (no park tour included) costs $200 per person, or $300 per person if there are only two passengers, with air transportation one way and return by boat and bus; a trip with air transportation both ways, and a tour through the park, costs $240 per person (or $360 with only two passengers); a two-night trip with air travel one way costs $300 per person or more, again with extra charges for park tours.

The riverboat *Francesca, tel. [2]260986 in San José* (see above) offers a $160 two-night package trip, using the Manatí Lodge.

The tour boat ride along the canal is usually slow, deliberately so, to allow and encourage you to spy and hear howler monkeys, sloths, and birds that frolic and lurk along the way. One attractive alternative is a package offered by the **Río Colorado Lodge** (*Box 5094, San José, tel. [2]324063, 800-243-9777 in the United States*) that includes bus transportation to Moín, a cruise through the canal to Barra del Colorado with a stop at Tortuguero National Park, a night's lodging, and return by a different route along the San Juan and Sarapiquí rivers. (Note that this tour does not allow nighttime observation of turtle nesting in season).

WHERE TO STAY

The village of **Tortuguero** (population about 300) *is near the northern limit of the national park, on the bar between the canal and the Caribbean,* a hodgepodge of one- and two-story clapboard houses and shacks scattered along muddy paths through unkempt grass. Tortuguero was a fishing settlement long before the park was established, and largely remains so.

The village has a remote and unconcerned air, but it's also one friendly place, where the Creole and Tico inhabitants welcome visitors with open arms, as well as flowing liquor and music at nightly parties in the dance hall.

Canal-Side Lodges

The **TORTUGA LODGE** (*25 rooms, all with private bath*), *operated by Costa Rica Expeditions, is more than three kilometers north of Tortuguero village, just across the canal from the airstrip.* The few second-story rooms, with balconies trimmed with bamboo and cane, are the most desirable. All rooms have passageways outside, and plenty of chairs and rockers where you can sit and chat with fellow jungle club members, while you regard the gardenias and ferns and parrots on the grassy grounds.

The dining room is a thatched pavilion with reed mats on the ceiling and rough-hewn trees as pillars, and, with dart board, it doubles as a bar outside meal hours.

Motor boats with guides are available for fishing or exploring the waterways of the park, at $30 per hour and up, and excursion to Tortuguero Hill and to see turtle nesting in season (June to October) are available for $11 per person and up. To get to Tortuguero village on your own, have one of the hotel's launches take you across to the airstrip. It's then a one-hour walk along the beach.

The rate for a room and fixed-menu meals at Tortuga Lodge, if you're not on a package, is about $100 single/$147 double, about half-price for children under ten. Contact **Costa Rica Expeditions**, *San José, tel. [2]570766, fax [2]571665 for information, or tel. 71[6]6861 direct to the lodge.*

MAWAMBA LODGE, *one kilometer north of the village of Tortuguero, has about 16 rooms in basic screened cement and wooden cottages.* The compound is less tidy and attractive than that of other canal-side lodges. The principal advantage here is that Tortuguero village and park headquarters are accessible via the beach, about a 15-minute walk, which liberates you somewhat from depending on the hotel for transport and optional excursions. *Call [2]339964 in San José for details.*

The **JUNGLE LODGE**, *one kilometer from the park*, is a neat complex of red-roofed elevated buildings on the bank opposite the village — look for the windmill. The waterlogged clearing is planted with tough grass, broken by coconut palms, tropical plants and fronds, and provided with dry walkways and rough-hewn log benches. The 14 rooms are good-sized, comfortable but not luxurious. All are panelled with dark wood, hold three beds, and have fans and private showers. Everything is kept quite clean. *Contact Cotur (see Miss Caribe, above) if you would like to stay here without a tour. The rate is about $45 single, $60 double.*

The **HOTEL ILAN-ILAN**, *operated in conjunction with the Mitur excursion*, has comparable canal-side facilities to those at the Jungle Lodge, but in rather plain concrete block units.

MANATÍ LODGE, *tel. [7]881828, north of the village near the turtle research station*, is smaller than most other canal-side lodges, with a thatch-roofed wharf, attractive grounds, and rooms in three wooden structures. *A two-night stay, in conjunction with the riverboat Francesca, costs about $200 per person.*

In the Village

There are also rooms for rent in the village of Tortuguero. At **SABINA'S CABINAS** *(tel. 71[8]8099)*, clapboard units spread out on a trim and tidy grassy seafront property, with ginger plants and palms, the rate is about $5 per person, or $20 double with private toilet facilities, or more if the traffic will bear it.

BRISAS DEL MAR has less attractive cabinas at a lower price, and a bar and dance floor. The no-frills **CABINAS MERYSCAR**, along a lane that leads from the information kiosk south toward the beach, has cubicles going for $6 per person or less, and serves cheap meals. And there are other, similar establishments facing the waves.

The advantage in staying at Sabina's or one of the nearby spots is that you can hike to the beach or through part of the park on your own, or more easily hire a local guide or dugout. At the canal lodges, you are a captive of your tour program.

It's also possible to camp in the park, but the best rain protection is essential.

WHERE TO EAT

Food, if you're not on a package, is available at several places around the village. The attractive no-frills **PANCANÁ** restaurant, currently Canadian-run and the best alternative to hotel food, serves lasagne, chili con carne, and rice and beans with fish for about $6, and good sandwiches. Most tables are on a patio. *From the park information kiosk, head south and take a turn from the lane that leads toward the beach.*

MISS JUNIE, *north of the village center*, will serve home-style rice and beans with fish or meat and salad for about $5, on two hours' notice.

SEEING THE SIGHTS
Turtle Haven

Tortuguero National Park is most famed for the nesting sea turtles that give their name to both the park and the adjacent town. Every year from June to November, turtles waddle ashore at night, climb past the high-tide line, excavate cavities in the sand and lay their eggs, then crawl off, exhausted. Only fifty years ago, the waves of turtles were so dense that one turtle would often dig out the eggs of another in the process of making its nest. The eggs were gathered by locals almost as soon as they were deposited, and enjoyed great popularity not only as a food, but because of their alleged aphrodisiac powers. The turtles, too, were often overturned and disemboweled for their meat and shell.

Tortuguero is one of the few remaining nesting places of the green Atlantic turtle, a species that reaches a meter in length and 200 kilograms in weight. Other species that nest at the beach are the hawksbill, loggerhead, and the huge leatherback, which weighs up to 700 kilograms. Each turtle comes home to Tortuguero every two to four years, and returns several times in the season, usually at intervals of twelve days, to nest again.

TURTLE TIMETABLES	
Peak Nesting Seasons at Tortuguero	
Green:	*July -September*
Leatherback:	*May and June*

Turtle Hazards

Even with human enemies partially under control in the park, the turtle eggs, slightly smaller than those of hens, face numerous perils. Raccoons, coatis and coyotes dig them out and eat them up. The hatchlings that emerge two months after laying face a run for the sea made perilous by crabs and lizards, and birds that swoop down and pluck off tasty morsels of leg or head. Only a small fraction of hatchlings reaches the sea, and fewer still make it to adulthood. The odds are being improved somewhat by programs that see to the safe transfer of hatchlings to the water.

But protection of the eggs is only a partial solution to the multiple threats to turtles, and to their survival as a species. Fibropapilloma, a cancer that attacks green, Ridley and loggerhead turtles, is on the increase worldwide. (The Turtle Hospital in Marathon, Florida, is making important advances in understanding the disease and how it is transmitted.) Pollution of the seas kills turtles slowly and horribly. Heavy oil glues jaws shut, and plastic blocks digestive systems. Turtles that ingest junk starve over a period of six or seven months, as their fat layer is consumed.

Protected Fauna & Flora

The park is also an important conservation area for other plant and animal species, as much of the tropical forest nearby is cut down. Freshwater turtles, manatees and alligators are found in canals, as well as sport fish, and sharks that reach up to three meters in length.

Forest animals include the jaguar, tapir, anteater, ocelot, white-faced, howler and spider monkeys, kinkajou, cougar, collared peccary, white-lipped peccary and coatimundi. You'll probably hear these rather than see them in the dense vegetation. Over 300 bird species have been reported, including the endangered green macaw, Central American curassow, and yellowtailed oriole. Most easily sighted are the large birds that frequent the waterways, such as anhingas, flamingos and kingfishers.

All of Tortuguero is wet — rainfall averages 5,000 millimeters (200 inches) per year — but there are several vegetation zones. Morning glory vines, coconut palms and shrubs characterize the sandy beach area, while other sectors are covered with swampy forest that bridges the waterways. In the forest on higher, less saturated ground, orchids and bromeliads live at all levels and take their nourishment from the air, and "exotic" house plant species, such as dieffenbachia, flourish. **Tortuga Hill**, a 390-foot rise, is the highest point all along the Caribbean coast of Costa Rica.

TORTUGUERO DO'S & DONT'S

If you can arrange it, you'll come to Tortuguero during nesting season, June to November. Strict rules are enforced to protect turtles from poachers and over-curious visitors. Among them:

1. Walk on the beach only when allowed. Inquire of park rangers or at your hotel.

2. Do not shine flashlights on turtles. Lights distract and disorient them. (Lights are usually not needed to see turtle tracks.)

3. Do not touch an overturned turtle. Some have been flipped by researchers.

4. Do not take any action on your own if something appears untoward. Report the problem to a researcher or ranger.

Hiking

Two **trails** lead through the rain forest from park headquarters. The longer, **Gavilán**, takes about 40 minutes to cover, slopping through puddles and mudholes. Guides will point out little poisonous snakes darting past, and tree snakes that you might mistake for leaves. Look, but don't touch. Some of the plants are irritating or poisonous.

Cruising the Canals

Birders and observers of wildlife in general will perhaps appreciate more a cruise through the park's canals. (A half-day excursion is included with most packages.) From the water, you'll have a better chance of spotting cormorants, egrets, herons, anhingas, sandpipers, and man-of-war, as well as roaring howler monkeys, white-faced monkeys, fresh-water otters, assorted trees, and those wonderful, iridescent blue morpho butterflies. Most guides employed by the lodges are familiar with nomenclature in English as well as standard Spanish and local usage.

Local guides with non-powered canoe-like boats (some are modified Colemans) may be hired in the village, near park headquarters, at a rate of about $3 per person per hour, or $2 per person per hour if you paddle yourself. Rates may be slightly negotiable, but most village guides are *not* adept at spotting or naming animals.

Consider going out on your own, after taking the excursion included in your package. Head inland to the smaller canals, where the vegetation bridges overhead, and the motors of fishing boats are too faint to be heard above the rustlings of coatis on the forest floor and the whistlings of birds at every level above.

Stay out of the water when you take out a boat, and don't swim along the beach. The sand is great for walking and beachcombing, but sharks are sighted regularly. The black sand is also well littered with plastic and glass, a reflection more of the currents (the same ones that help the turtles to shore) than of anyone's sloppiness. Posts along the beach indicate distance from a point just north of the turtle research station and airstrip, in increments of one-eighth mile.

BARRA DEL COLORADO

The Tortuguero Canal terminates at the settlement of **Barra del Colorado**, *which sits astride the mouth of the Colorado River, a delta branch of the San Juan River that borders Nicaragua.* Barra prospered in the forties as a lumber center and depot for cargo coming downriver from Nicaragua. But as woodcutting and river trade declined, so did Barra's fortunes. The population is now down to a few hundred, many of Nicaraguan descent.

Barra serves today as a sport fishing center. But it also has its attractions as an out-of-the-way place with a friendly populace, where one can stay on the edge of the wild in relative comfort. Flora and fauna in the surrounding area are protected, at least nominally, in the **Barra del Colorado National Wildlife Refuge**.

The wide San Juan lies entirely in Nicaragua, but Costa Rica enjoys full rights to use the river. More than a hundred years ago, Cornelius Vanderbilt established a combination riverboat-ferry-stage coach service that used the San Juan as part of a passenger route across Nicaragua, connecting with steamers from both coasts of the States. The service was disrupted during William Walker's takeover in Nicaragua, and as part of the post-war settlement, Costa Rica pushed its border north to the banks of the river. Panama thereafter dominated interoceanic transport, though the San Juan has been proposed from time to time as part of a new canal.

The most famous navigators hereabouts nowadays are the sharks that move between Lake Nicaragua, upstream on the San Juan, and the Caribbean. Sharks frequent the coast down to Tortuguero as well, feeding on the abundant fish and making swimming one of the less peaceful diversions available.

ARRIVALS & DEPARTURES
By Air
Travelair *(tel. [2]327883)* has a daily flight from San José, fare $88 round trip.

By Boat
Small cargo boats operate up the San Juan and Sarapiquí rivers to Puerto Viejo, which is tied by road with San José. Or you can travel this route with more certainty on the package boat trip operated by the **Río Colorado Lodge** through Tortuguero.

Private boats may be hired for jungle cruises in the vicinity, or for trips to Tortuguero Park.

WHERE TO STAY
RÍO COLORADO LODGE, *12 rooms. Package price $300 per person daily minimum per day of fishing with meals, use of boats, and guides; or $75 single/$100 double without fishing. San José office: Hotel Corobicí, P. O. Box 5094-1000, tel. [2]324063. U.S. reservations: 12301 N. Oregon Av., Tampa, FL 33612, tel. 800-243-9777 or 813-931-4849. Simple but comfortable screened cabins, whirlpool, satellite TV.*

This is mainly a fishing lodge, but the management also organizes excursions through the Tortuguero Canal and welcomes non-sportsmen to beachcomb and relax on the edge of the jungle. A mini-zoo on the grounds hold animals from the area. Open all year, within walking distance of the airstrip.

SPORTS & RECREATION ALONG THE CARIBBEAN

Caribbean Fishing

Although remote, the Caribbean coast of Costa Rica is world famous for sport fishing. Tarpon, or *sábalo*, is the most notable (or notorious) species, most easily found in rivers and lagoons from January to June, with March and April the best months (though tarpon habits are unpredictable, and some claim June and July are best). Tarpon generally weigh from 60 to 100 pounds. A world-record 182-pound tarpon was caught from the Tortuga Lodge in 1987.

Second to the tarpon as a sport fish is snook *(róbalo)*, generally caught from mid-August to mid-October, and averaging over 25 pounds. Other species are snapper *(pargo)*, machaca, guapote, bass, mojarra, king mackerel, grouper, catfish, sawfish, and jacks, which generally run under five pounds.

Almost all the fishing along the coast is in fresh-water river estuaries and lagoons, which at times are converted into furious cauldrons of spawning fish. At the right times, not having a good catch is virtually impossible. However, fishing is said to have declined in recent years in inland waterways, due to sedimentation and contamination by pesticides.

Fishing in the open waters of the Caribbean is a risky business, due to the unpredictability of winds and storms, and heavy surf at estuaries, but some lodges have large boats to get fishermen out, or will fish in open water during the limited calm periods.

Fishing Camps

In addition to the Río Colorado Lodge, the following fishing camps are located along the Caribbean:

PARISMINA TARPON RANCHO, *near Parismina (40 kilometers north of Limón), tel. 71[2]2583. 10 rooms, from approximately $250 per person per day of fishing. San José address: P.O. Box 5712, tel. [2]357766; U.S. reservations: P. O. Box 290190, San Antonio, TX 78280, tel. 800-531-7232 or 512-377-0451, fax 377-0454, 800-862-1003 direct to San José.*

Rebuilt after the 1991 hurricane, Tarpon Rancho will soon "split" into a nature-oriented lodge at the current location, and a newer fishing lodge between the Parismina River and the Caribbean. Rooms are in wooden cottages. Fishing is from 16-foot aluminum skiffs. An unusual feature here is *King Kong*, a mother ship that carries skiffs through dangerous surf at estuary outlets to safer waters beyond. Open January through November. Rate includes open bar, accommodations in San José, and transport to and from lodge.

Lodge policy is: "We have a tremendous record for catch and release, and we are very proud that our guests are participating with us in this program."

RÍO PARISMINA LODGE, *From $285 per day of fishing, including transfer from San José. U.S. reservations: P.O. Box 46009, San Antonio, TX 78246, tel. 800-338-5688 or 210-824-4442, fax 210-824-0151.*

One of the newest of the Caribbean fishing lodges, located opposite Parismina village. You'll find a few more amenities here than at other coastal fishing camps, including a pool and Jacuzzi. Wood-panelled rooms, clustered four to a building, have ceiling fans, are on a jungle estate. Fishing craft here are 21 feet long with 125-hp outboards, which the operators claim reduces the danger of crossing rough surf at river mouths. Food is said to be good, equipment is well maintained, and most drinks are included in the package price. *Closed July and part of December.*

ISLA DE PESCA, *near Barra del Colorado. 12 units, approximately $250 per day, all-inclusive. In San José: P. O. Box 7-1880, tel. [2]394544, fax [2]392405. U.S. reservations: tel. 800-245-8420. Simple A-frame cottages, with full bathrooms. Fishing is from 16-foot skiffs. Rates include the flight from San José to Barra, as well as use of boat and guides, and meals.*

Isla de Pesca is also the jungle base for a river safari along the Tortuguero Canal, and the San Juan and Colorado rivers. Rates range from $150 to $300 per person for a one- or two-day trip.

TORTUGA LODGE, mentioned above under Tortuguero. Packages with fishing from a skiff run $350 for the first day, $189 each additional day, with room, meals, guide, basic fishing equipment, and transport from San José. Add $160 per day if you're alone. *Call Costa Rica Expeditions, tel. [2]570766, for information.*

CASA MAR FISHING LODGE, *Barra del Colorado. 12 rooms. $300 per day and up. U.S. reservations: P. O. Drawer 787, Islamorada, FL 33036, tel. 800-327-2880 or 305-664-4615, fax 305-664-3692.*

Unlike some other fishing lodges, Casa Mar has full-time electricity. Guests stay in screened wooden cottages, each with two rooms. Package rate includes meals, boat, guide service, transport from San José, and bar consumption. Open January through mid-May and September through October.

SILVER KING LODGE, *tel. [7]880849, fax [7]881403, 800-847-3474 in U.S. From $350 per day of fishing inclusive.*

One of the newest fishing operations, Silver King has about 20 nineteen-foot boats equipped with depth finders and fish locators. They're authorized to take anglers over to lakes and rivers in nearby Nicaragua, which, for obvious reasons, have been little exploited in recent years. Facilities are a bit more finished than at other lodges, with ceiling fans, tiled bathrooms, and large beds. One-upmanship report: rates at Silver King Lodge include not only meals and boats and guides, *and* open bar, *but also* laundry service, *and* if you call their 800 number, they'll send you an excellent video of lodge facilities and on-site fishing action.

Contact any of the fishing lodges, or their U.S. representatives, for a fat packet of information that will give you ample details about the quality of cooking, guides, boats, camp furnishings, and fishing grounds, along with ample endorsements, all of which will demonstrate, beyond reasonable doubt, why it is the premier fishing resort on the Caribbean.

CAHUITA NATIONAL PARK

Cahuita National Park has beaches as beautiful as any on the Caribbean. Just offshore is a living coral reef, the most accessible in Costa Rica, where brightly colored fish feed and breed. In the marshes and forests of the park, animal and bird life are abundant.

The coral reef, which consists of the remains of small animals called polyps, lies up to half a kilometer from shore, and from one to seven meters under the surface. With diving equipment, you can see the formations — brain, elkhorn, star and dozens of other corals — as well as the fish, sponges, crabs and snails that are attracted to feed and live on the reef. At two points on the reef's western side, cannonballs, anchors, cannon and bricks have been found, giving evidence that a Spanish galleon (or more than one) sank in these waters.

In the reef-protected shallows of Cahuita, sargasso and other grasses flourish, along with conch and ghost crabs. Dead trunks of trees lie just under the water, penetrated by seawood borers, the termites of the sea.

Beyond the reef at the south end of the park, Cahuita's lovely beach, beaten by huge waves, backed by coconut palms, is a nesting site for green, Hawksbill and leatherback turtles. The gentle sweep of the bay is quite unusual on this coast. In some sections, little pools form at low tide, temporarily isolating fish.

Inland, Cahuita's protected area includes extensive areas of marsh. The **Perezoso** (Sloth) **River** that flows to the sea in the park is dark brown in color, said to be an effect of the high tannin concentration, which also reputedly keeps a cap on the local mosquito population. The forests are alive with howler monkeys, white-faced monkeys, three-toed sloths, anteaters, and collared peccaries. Raccoons and coatis are often seen along the nature trail, which penetrates the damp world of ferns and bromeliads and huge jungle trees.

The town of **Cahuita**, *45 kilometers from Limón, at the northern end of the park*, has sandy streets, widely separated houses, a friendly assortment of people, and a range of hotels and eating places.

The southern entrance to the park is about six kilometers farther on, at **Puerto Vargas** (Vargas Harbor), which is a bay, not a village. Here the park administration, nature trail and camping facilities are located. There are no banks, no car-rental agencies, no fishing lodges (as yet), no significant action.

ARRIVALS & DEPARTURES

Arriving By Bus

From San José, comfortable, direct buses for Sixaola (without a stop in Limón) depart from Avenida 11, Calles Central/1 *(tel. [2]210524)*, at 6 a.m., 2:30 p.m. and 4 p.m., passing both entrances to Cahuita Park. The trip through Braulio Carrillo National Park and the humid coastal plain takes about four hours.

From Limón, rickety, usually crowded buses leave from Avenida 4, Calles 3/4 at 5 a.m., 10 a.m., 1 p.m. and 4 p.m., arriving at Cahuita in about an hour. Get to the station early to find a seat.

Arriving By Taxi

A taxi from Limón to Cahuita costs under $25.

Departing By Bus

Departures from Sixaola for Limón are at 5 a.m., 8 a.m., 10 a.m., and 3 p.m.; from Sixaola for San José at 5 a.m., 8 a.m. and 2:30 p.m. These buses pass Cahuita about 25 minutes out of Sixaola.

Buses for San José pass Cahuita at approximately 7 and 10 a.m. and 4 p.m. For Limón, buses pass at approximately 6:30 and 10 a.m. and 1:30 and 3 p.m. Buses southward, to Puerto Viejo, pass at about 7 a.m., 3:30 p.m. and 5 p.m.

WHERE TO STAY

Most hotels can be reached by dialing *[7]581515* and asking for the appropriate extension. Or, ask the operator for the hotel by name. Reservations can also be made by faxing **Cahuita Tours**, *[7]580652.*

HOTEL JAGUAR, *tel. [7]581515, ext. 238 (P. O. Box 7046-1000 San José, tel. [2]263775, fax [2]264693). 45 rooms. $30 single/$55 double with breakfast and dinner, $75 double in deluxe rooms. Visa, Master Card.*

The Jaguar sets the standard for Cahuita. Guest rooms, in several buildings well-spaced on informal grounds, are extraordinarily large. Covered passageways are punctuated with squares of garden. A number of the design features effectively aid passive cooling without air conditioning. Unusually for this area, hot water supply is ample. There are trails through the property, 17 acres with fruit trees and exuberant and unruly vegetation. Cuisine is excellent, and with two meals included in the rate, the Jaguar is a bargain. Located at Black Beach.

Central Cahuita

HOTEL CAHUITA, *tel. [7]581515, extension 201. 10 units. $17 per person.*

Best of a few small hotels in the center of the village (a relative matter).

Harsh, motel-style rooms are off a pleasant courtyard, and most can sleep up to six persons. Small pool. A section of hotel rooms is currently being renovated.

CABINAS VAZ, *tel. [7]581515, extension 218. $18 single/$22 double.*
Similar to the Hotel Cahuita, without the arches in the dining area.

SURFSIDE CABINAS, *tel. [7]581515, extension 246 (P. O. Box 360, Limón). 15 units. $18 single/$22 double with breakfast.*
Substantial concrete row units, a few blocks from the park entrance, on the way to Black Beach (Playa Negra). Protected parking.

CABINAS JENNY, *tel. [7]581515, extension 15. 10 rooms. $26 to $35.*
A two-story, cream stuccoed building in an excellent location overlooking the sea. The higher rate is for the upstairs rooms with balcony over the ocean, and cross ventilation.

Black Beach

Black Beach, *a kilometer from the center of Cahuita*, where the following accommodations are located, is more isolated, not that any part of Cahuita is urban.

ATLÁNTIDA LODGE, *extension 213 (fax [2]289467 in San José). 30 units. $40 single/$45 double/$50 triple with breakfast. Visa, Master Card, American Express.*
Atlántida Lodge is a compound that has steadily expanded and improved its facilities over the years, without losing the informality characteristic of Cahuita. Pale yellow stuccoed bungalows with thatched roofs are set among the palms and grass and fruit trees of spacious grounds. Hammocks hang from the trees, quiet pets roam the length of their chains, and toucans reside in their own screened enclosure. A buffet breakfast of fruits and breads is included in the rate. Other meals can be prepared on request, and nothing could be more enchanting than dining in the gazebo as subdued lights sparkle on the grounds and mysterious noises filter out of the forest.

CABINAS TITO, *ext. 286. 10 units. $30 double.*
Of accommodations that are operated by local people, these are the most attractive. Separate wood-panelled cabins with porch are in a quiet area.

COLIBRÍ PARADISE, *tel. extension 263. 3 units. $40 each.*
Comfortable little one-room cottages, each sleeping up to four, painted a cheery white and blue, with stove, refrigerator and hot shower. Take the path from the beach road, or enter by car from the highway. A good buy.

CABINAS Y CHALET HIBISCUS, *one of the few lodging places in Cahuita fronting directly on the sea*, has two attractive but small bungalows for $45 double, and two houses that sleep up to six persons for $80 and

$100 respectively. The beach is coral rock, but there's a pool on-site and the grounds are attractive.

Other Places to Stay

And there are many, many, many other cabinas available past Moray's along the lanes that lead back from Black Beach, some with owners from your own hometown, most with just two or three rental units. If you plan to stay a while — and why not? — check in anywhere, drop your luggage, and spend a pleasant few hours walking around, exploring the lanes and nooks and crannies of Black Beach, inspecting accommodations, and striking a deal.

Camping is currently available at Vishnu, on one of the lanes leading up from Black Beach; and in Cahuita National Park at the southern entry point, Puerto Vargas.

Roadside stopping-places on the way to Cahuita:

CLUB CAMPESTRE CAHUITA, *tel. [7]551676 ([2]234254 in San José, fax [2]215005, P. O. Box 214-1150 La Uruca). 24 kilometers south of Limón. 20 rooms. $50 for a unit that sleeps up to six. Visa, MasterCard.*

A Tico family-style resort and campground on a palm-shaded lot, recently rebuilt, with kids' and adult pools. Rooms have fans. The thatched-roof restaurant is pleasant, serves a variety of seafood at moderate prices, and even has a surprising list of imported wines.

where to eat & Drink

The cuisine of the **HOTEL JAGUAR** would get high ratings in San José, so you will be surprised to find such excellent fare in this little place. The style is continental, with an emphasis on elaborate sauces made with local spices and the best meats, and inclusive of native vegetables. The menu changes daily, and features such items as sirloin in peanut sauce; medallions of beef in two sauces; shrimp in herb sauce; fish steamed in banana leaf with chutney; dorado (mahi-mahi) in herbs; lobster; moussaka; and even, at times, chile con carne.

LAS ROCAS, *at Black Beach, not far past Moray's*, has the most pleasant atmosphere of any dining spot in Cahuita, in a glassed-in room looking out to palms, the beach and the sea. It's also the most formal place, with tile floor, panelled bar and ceiling fans. You won't spend more than $8 for steak or fish.

CABINAS BLACK BEACH serves lasagna, among other items, in a pleasant bar and restaurant. The restaurant at the **HOTEL CAHUITA** is popular, with lunch and dinner for $6 and up. Right next to the entrance to the park, the restaurant under the great thatched roof (behind the concrete building) serves good *casados* (meat or fish or chicken with rice, beans and cabbage) for $5, and assorted steaks, fish, Italian items, and sandwiches; and there is another restaurant under the concrete rotunda across the way, with a basic menu of fish and steak, from about $5.

Of drinking spots, **LLOYD'S BAR** is the one with the fewest hassles (if you don't want hassles), and the only one that reserves the right of admission.

SPORTS & RECREATION

Moray's, *near the rural guard post (at the turn to Black Beach), tel. [7]581515, ext. 216*, is one of several places that arrange boat trips, snorkeling, horseback rides, and jungle and mountain walks, with most trips running about $25 for a half-day. The slopes of the Talamanca range begin just a kilometer inland. One little house on the main street has souvenirs, of a sort.

The **Hotel Cahuita**, the **Cahuita Jaguar**, and several others rent out bikes, snorkeling equipment, and boogie boards.

Mr. Alan Foley, who operates out of a window at the Hotel Jaguar, can arrange an outing to the **Bri-Bri Indian reserve**, south of Cahuita and inland. For $25 a person, it's something like spending an afternoon visiting relatives, except that the family that takes you in and provides lunch lives in a compound of thatch-roofed houses and makes baskets and carved gourd jugs. Mr. Foley also can arrange a tour of a banana plantation, snorkeling at various points along the coast, and canoeing on the Sixaola River through Bri-Bri lands. Ask him as well about low-cost fishing from small boats with hand lines – not elegant, but at about $60 for two persons, it beats by far what you'd pay at one of the fishing lodges north of Limón.

Viajes Tropicales Laura, *tel. 581515, extension 244*, can arrange trips up to **Tortuguero** and back, without the necessity of your going to Limón to organize things.

Brigitte's Cabinas, *up the lane before the Jaguar Hotel*, has half-day horseback trips to the mountains behind Cahuita, for about $30.

If you plan to snorkel, you'll find the water clearest from February through April, when it rains the least. The park is usually nearly deserted (where do all these people go?), except on weekends and at holiday periods, which should be avoided.

ECO-EXCURSIONS

Fifteen kilometers south of Cahuita is **Puerto Viejo** (Old Harbor), where you'll find **ATEC**, the local eco-tourism association based at an office opposite **Soda Tamara** a block back from the water, which is a general store and eatery with a few tables inside. They can fill you in on where you'll find trails and mangroves and coral in places like the **Gandoca-Manzanillo Wildlife Refuge**, and where you won't; and where an overgrown cacao farm will make for a rewarding flora-hunting excursion.

ATEC will also set you up with local guides for snorkeling, fishing for snapper from a dugout, trekking up through the rain forest of Rest-and-Be-Thankful Hill, herb- and bush medicine-hunting, expeditions into the Kekîldi Indian reservation, monkey- and toucan-spotting, meals in village homes, and a horseback ride to the hill settlement of San Rafael (among other adventures);, but be prepared to wait for up to two days to get your trip organized — communication is quite poor, and messages usually have to be hand-carried.

Half-day trips generally run about $15 per person, full-day trips $25, boat trips $80. Students get a discount. More difficult overnight trips can also be arranged, if you have camping equipment.

And if you're indecisive about where to stay, a map outside the ATEC office indicates all the small, mostly locally owned lodging places in town and stretching toward Manzanillo (which should make you even more indecisive).

ATEC is a non-profit organization, and a model of what low-impact tourism can be. *You can write to ATEC, Pto. Viejo de Talamanca, Limón, or fax them at [7]537524. Be patient in waiting for a reply.*

Jungle walks and horseback rides can be arranged through some hotels, most notably **Cabinas Chimuri** in Puerto Viejo, the owner of which is authorized to take visitors into the Kekoldi indigenous reserve to the south.

THE PACIFIC NORTH

Pacific Costa Rica covers a vast sweep of territory along the wide side of the country, from Nicaragua down to the Panamanian border. Overlooking a complicated, varied terrain are the volcanoes and mountain peaks of the Guanacaste, Tilarán, and Talamanca mountain ranges, which largely block the rains that blow across Costa Rica from the Caribbean. Winds from the Pacific blow rain clouds ashore from May through October, while the rest of the year is dry.

But there are exceptions to this general picture. The Guanacaste lowlands of the northeast, hemmed in by coastal mountains, are subject to periodic droughts. In the south, on the other hand, near Golfito, the coastal mountains act as a watershed, and it rains throughout the year. In general, rainfall, humidity and discomfort increase toward the south. The daytime temperature throughout the area is generally in the nineties Fahrenheit (32 to 37 Centigrade).

PUNTARENAS

Puntarenas is a one mile-long sandspit (which is what its name means), sticking out into the Gulf of Nicoya, a narrow, muddy estuary on one side, clear water on the other. Opened to shipping in 1814, the port was for many years Costa Rica's only outlet to world commerce. The coffee crop moved down to the coast from the highlands on oxcarts with a legendary breed of driver, rough and ready, but scrupulously honest.

The location of Puntarenas would appear strategic for the visitor. Ferries provide the easiest access to some of the nicer beaches on the Nicoya peninsula. Cruises touch the many islands in the Gulf of Nicoya. Puntarenas is the nearest Pacific point to San José.

Unfortunately, though, some of the city is a dump. I don't mean only that the beach is contaminated for its whole great length along the south side of town. The central part of the city is composed of dismal, rotting and rusting, ramshackle structures, cheap flophouses, and bar after bar oozing drunks. A stench often permeates the humid, dense air.

Beyond the commercial center, the sights are more pleasant. There are some nice residences and hotels near the western tip of town and back toward the mainland, and a substantial yacht club. The headquarters of the port, at the main pier, are in a lovely old building. On Calle 7, there is a marvelous tan, crazy-stone church, looking quite English. Eating in the open-air diners along the beach and mixing with the crowds that come down for the day from San José can be pleasant. But you didn't come all the way from home to linger here. Costa Rica has much nicer seaside places to offer.

ARRIVALS & DEPARTURES

Arriving By Bus

Buses for Puntarenas leave from Calle 12, Avenida 9, San José, every hour from 6 a.m. to 6 p.m. The trip takes about two hours.

Arriving By Car

The main automobile route to the coast from San José is via the Cañas Expressway, past the airport, funnelling onto a winding, narrow road past San Ramón. Total driving time is about two hours. An improved highway through Santa Ana and Orotina to the coast is planned.

Departing By Boat or Ferry

The main reason for a foreign visitor to go to Puntarenas is to leave promptly for one of the nicer places along the coast. Many are accessible by boat, either directly or in combination with car or bus travel.

A passenger-and-automobile ferry operates daily between Puntarenas and Playa Naranjo, on the Nicoya Peninsula. Sailings from Puntarenas are at 4, 7 and 10:30 a.m. and 1:30 and 4:30 p.m.; from Playa Naranjo at 5:15 and 8:30 a.m., noon, and 3 and 6 p.m. *Phone 61[1]1069 to check schedules.* Arrive well before scheduled departure time, park, and line up for your ticket. The crossing takes a little over an hour. Buses for Nicoya meet the ferry.

The Playa Naranjo ferry provides a shortcut to the southern part of the Nicoya peninsula. Buses going to the town of Nicoya meet the ferry, but public transport to other places is hard to find. Playa Naranjo is a dock and little else, but lodging is available just down the road.

A passenger-and-car ferry also leaves for Paquera, also in the Nicoya Peninsula and south of Playa Naranjo, daily at 6 a.m. and 3 p.m. This is a newly upgraded service, so check at the tourist office in San José or hotels in Puntarenas for departure point and recent schedules. Buses and taxis provide onward connecting transportation from Paquera toward Tambor, Cóbano, and Montezuma.

Departing By Bus

Buses for San José leave from Calle 2 and Avenida 4, Puntarenas, one block east (toward the mainland) from the main pier.

Buses depart for various nearby and distant towns from a shelter along the sea opposite the bus station for San José. Schedules are posted. The bus for Santa Elena, near Monteverde, leaves at 2:15 p.m., for Quepos at 5 a.m., 11 a.m., and 2:30 p.m. There are five daily buses for Liberia. The bus for Barranca, at the armpit of the peninsula, leaves from the market in Puntarenas.

GETTING AROUND TOWN & EXCURSIONS

Though Puntarenas is not a usual long-term stopping point for visitors from afar, **Cata Tours** has an office in town *(tel. 613948)*, and can place you on day trips to Miravalles volcano, Palo Verde Park, along rivers, and to Monteverde. Prices range from $65 to $90.

Elegante Rent A Car has a local office, *tel. 611958.*

WHERE TO STAY

HOTEL TIOGA, *Paseo de los Turistas (Avenida 4, beach side), Calle 17, ten blocks west of the large pier), P. O. Box 96-5400, tel. 61[0]0271. 46 rooms. $32 to $47 single/$40 to $60 double.*

Nice rooms, many with views to the sea, well-maintained, air-conditioned. Best of the downtown lodgings. There's a pool, and a moderately priced restaurant. Rates include full breakfast in the fourth-floor dining-room-with-a-view. Higher rates are for rooms with hot water and balconies.

HOTEL CAYUGA, *Calle 4, Avenidas Central/1 (one block north of the* *microwave tower), P. O. Box 306-5400, tel. 61[0]0344, fax 61[1]1280. 31 rooms. $12 to $20 single/$15 to $28 double.*

Located near the center of town, which is unfortunate, because this is the best hotel buy in Puntarenas, clean, modern, with a fair restaurant and air conditioning.

HOTEL RÍO, *P. O. Box 54-5400, tel. 61[0]0331. 15 rooms. $10 single/ $14 double, more with private bath.*

A modern hotel a half-block west of the market, downtown. The new rooms here have fans and private baths. Boat services available. Best deal for budget travelers.

Various *cabinas* (simple rooms with few facilities) are also available at locations along the beach, at prices of about $8 per person and up:

OASIS DEL PACÍFICO *(tel. 61[0]0209), at 7 Calle on the sea, has 17 basic rooms going for $26 to $44 double,* a pool which is available for day use, fast food, dancing, and an owner from France. Cooking facilities are available in some units. A half block from the bus station, the **HOTEL IMPERIAL** is a clean old wooden building that faces the water and offers rooms with shared baths for under $10 per person. And there are loads of other cheap hotels.

La Punta

HOTEL LA PUNTA, *P.O. Box 228, tel. 61[0]0696. 20 rooms, 1 suite. $16 single/$27 double. Visa, Master Card.*

A tan, two-story plantation-style building, unpretentious, clean, and cheery, just one block from the ferry for Playa Naranjo. Tiled pool, whirlpool, table tennis, bicycles for rent, communal TV. The open-air restaurant with juice bar is reasonably priced, at $4 or so for breakfast, $6 for lunch with fish. Look for the south-seas style second-floor veranda. English spoken.

HOTEL LAS BRISAS, *Calle 31, tel. 61[2]2120. 20 rooms, $33-$45 single/$57-$67 double.*

Of recent construction, clean and airy. The higher rates are for larger rooms with tubs, and balconies with views away from the city, to the mountains of the Nicoya Peninsula and the hilly islands of the gulf. All units are air-conditioned, with plain decor, cement-tile floors, and Formica table. There's a pool and basic restaurant.

COMPLEJO TURÍSTICO YADRÁN, *Paseo de los Turistas (P.O. Box 14-5000), tel. 61[2]2662, fax 61[1]1944. 43 rooms. $83 single/$100 double. Visa, Master Card, American Express.*

This hotel occupies the best piece of real estate in Puntarenas, at the tip of the main boulevard. All rooms are carpeted, with air conditioning and color television. Some have balconies, with stunning views of the gulf. Facilities include a third-floor restaurant (relatively pricey), bar, children's and adult pools, bicycles for rent, and conference rooms. Very quiet, usually empty.

WHERE TO EAT

The best food, like the best lodging, is toward the tip of the peninsula. **LA CARAVELLE**, *on Paseo de los Turistas between Calles 19 and 21*, is a French restaurant, with nautical displays and wood panelling inside, and a *terrasse* for outdoor eating. As formal a place as you'll find in Puntarenas, it offers the expected pepper steak, steak-frites and sea bass for $10 or so per person, shrimp and lobster for more, and Chilean wine by the glass for only $2. Open for lunch and dinner, closed Monday and Tuesday.

Next door, the **BIERSTUBE**, with high ceilings and heavy beams, accommodates up to 200 would-be Bavarians, inside and at sidewalk tables.

Elsewhere, the restaurants of the **HOTEL LA PUNTA** and the **HOTEL LAS BRISAS**, *near the car ferry for Playa Naranjo*, offer good value and pleasant outdoor eating areas.

Downtown, you'll find the most fun, and the freshest fish, at the open-air eating places along the beach, near the main pier.

SPORTS & RECREATION

Being a place where the sea and boats have always been important, Puntarenas celebrates with particular enthusiasm the **Festival of the Virgin of the Sea**, on the Saturday before or after July 16. Boats are festooned with decorations and pass in review. Dances, parades, beauty contests, fireworks and drunkenness are part of the goings on.

Swimming

Since the beach at Puntarenas isn't inviting, you might want to look for other swimming opportunities. The boats mentioned below will take you to some nice beaches on the Nicoya Peninsula for overnight stays. Nearer to Puntarenas, the best swimming is at **Doña Ana beach**, a public park with ample jungly shade and picnic areas and a restaurant, on a rocky inlet along the road to Caldera and points south. The Mata Limón bus from Puntarenas passes the entrance.

Cruises

The yacht *Calypso* makes a daily cruise from the yacht club to seven islands in the Gulf of Nicoya. Fare is about $70, including overland transportation from San José, or slightly less if you're already in Puntarenas. This is a well-planned excursion that has been improved and refined and copied over the years. A stop is made at a deserted, palm-shaded beach for swimming, snorkeling, beachcombing, and a gourmet picnic lunch that includes fresh gulf fish. They even take a portable toilet ashore. *Book the cruise through any hotel in Puntarenas, or call tel. [2]333617, fax [2]330401 in San José, or [6]610585 in Puntarenas. Longer cruises are also available.*

Cruises along similar lines are offered by **Fantasía Island Cruise**, *tel.* [2]550791, **Bay Island Cruises**, *tel.* [2]312898; **Blue Seas First Class Cruise**, *tel. [2]337274*; and **Sea Ventures**, *tel. [2]329832, fax [2]327510.*

Arrangements can also be made to visit the islands in the Gulf of Nicoya. On **Chira**, the largest, near the northern end of the gulf, cattle are raised and salt is extracted from sea water. **Guayabo**, **Negritos** and **Los Pájaros** islands are biological reserves, noted for their abundance of seabirds. **Guayabo** is an important nesting site for brown pelicans, and peregrine falcons are known to hibernate there. **Cedros** and several smaller islands have no restaurants, hotels or any other facilities, and few inhabitants, but are excellent locales for birding. **San Lucas** island, halfway across the gulf, was formerly a prison colony, and is now being developed as a tourist destination. A regular boat service has sometimes operated on Sunday mornings.

Fishing and Water Skiing

To hire a boat for touring, or for fishing or water skiing, try Fred Wagner at **Casa Alberta**, *tel. 63[0]0107*; or **Taximar**, with an office at the *Hotel Río, tel. 61[1]1143 and 61[0]0331.*

MONTEVERDE CLOUD FOREST RESERVE/SANTA ELENA

High on the ridge above the coastal plain are the town of **Santa Elena**, and the adjacent farming colony and cloud-forest reserve of **Monteverde**. Costa Rica is rich in montane tropical rain forest of the type included in the Monteverde reserve — the forest atop the volcano Poás is one example, and is much more accessible.

The slow ascent to Monteverde offers spectacular views, the rolling, pastured countryside is idyllic and even spiritually uplifting, and the reserve is large. The inns in the area invite the visitor to linger and explore the forest, or relax in the fresh mountain air.

The Monteverde farming colony was founded on April 19, 1951, by Quakers from Alabama, some of whom had been imprisoned for refusing to serve in the U.S. armed forces. There were only oxcart trails into the area at the time, and the trucks and tractors of the settlers had to be winched up the mountains.

Land was laboriously cleared, and the colony eventually found some prosperity in dairy farming. Monteverde cheeses now have a solid share of the Costa Rican market. Over the years, some of the original families moved on, while non-Quakers bought land in the area. Monteverde is now a mixed, largely English-speaking community.

Conservation Pioneers

The original settlers set aside 2,500 hectares of land to protect native plant life, even as it was being destroyed by clearing in other parts of the colony. A private foundation, the **Tropical Science Center**, now administers the **Monteverde Cloud Forest Reserve**. Government protection has been afforded to the rare species found at Monteverde, including the golden toad (*sapo dorado*), which is known to live only in rain pools in the vicinity.

The area of the reserve has been expanded to 10,000 hectares (22,000 acres) by the purchase of adjacent lands, some of which had been farmed but are now being allowed to return to their natural state. Another 5,000 hectares comprise the **Children's Tropical Forest** (*Bosque Eterno de los Niños*). These protected areas now form the core of the 110,000-hectare **Arenal Regional Conservation Unit**, stretching along the Pacific backbone of Costa Rica.

ARRIVALS & DEPARTURES

Arriving By Bus

A bus operates to Monteverde from Calle 14 (extension of Calle 12), Avenidas 9/11, San José, departing Monday through Thursday at 2:30 p.m., Saturday and Sunday at 6:30 a.m. *Telephone 61[1]1152 in Monteverde, [2]223854 in San José to check the schedule.* Currently, the Sunday departure from San José is omitted in the rainy season. The trip takes about five hours.

Pacific Transfer runs a bus called the *Silver Bullet Express* with reserved seats and snacks, with seats for $40 one way, $70 round trip from San José. *Call [2]272180 (fax [2]281015) for schedules and pickup points.*

From Puntarenas, a bus departs daily for Santa Elena, six kilometers from the reserve, at 2:15 p.m. (from Calle 2, along the beach). Buses are of the uncomfortable school-bus type that serve the back roads of Costa Rica. If you miss the direct bus from San José, connect with this bus in Puntarenas (leave San José no later than 11 a.m.) or at the Lagarto junction, kilometer post 149 on the Pan American highway. (Take a bus from the Coca-Cola terminal area, 16 Calle, Avenidas 1/3, heading toward Cañas or Liberia, leaving no later than 11:30 a.m. The Santa Elena bus passes Lagarto at about 3 p.m.)

From Tilarán, near Lake Arenal, one daily bus departs for Santa Elena is at noon.

From the junction on the Pan American Highway, it's a two-hour ascent by bus on a bumpy, unpaved road to Santa Elena, with spectacular views, on a clear evening, of the sunset and orange-tinged sky over the Nicoya Peninsula, below and in the distance. When visibility is limited, you'll have to settle for views of the nearby landscape, as it changes from rolling hills covered with citrus and mango trees to steep grazing lands on the slopes of the mountain ridge, patches of oak and evergreen forest, and many a cool, misty valley with scattered clusters of farmhouses.

Arriving By Car

Travel by car will cut as much as a day from a round trip to Monteverde, and facilitate getting back and forth between the reserve and scattered hotels and restaurants. Follow the Pan American Highway (Route 1) to the junction at kilometer 149. The last 32 kilometers of dirt road will usually take at least an hour and a half to cover, and in the rainy season may be passable only with four-wheel-drive. There is currently a controversial plan to pave the route.

You can also reach the reserve by the little-travelled route that follows the crest of the mountain range from Tilarán, near Lake Arenal.

Arriving By Tour

Most travel agencies in San José offer tours to Monteverde. Transportation can be arranged as well through some of the hotels mentioned below.

Departing By Bus

The bus for San José departs from the cheese plant Monday through Thursday at 6:30 a.m., Friday through Sunday at 3 p.m. *Telephone 61[1]1152 in Monteverde to check the schedule.* Currently, the Saturday departure is omitted in the rainy season. Passengers are picked up at hotels along the way, and at the bank in Santa Elena. Tickets can be purchased in advance at the San José bus station or at El Bosque restaurant and at some hotels in Monteverde.

The bus for Puntarenas departs at 6 a.m. from Santa Elena; for Tilarán, near Lake Arenal, at 7 a.m.

A bus leaves from Santa Elena for Tilarán at 7 a.m.

From Tilarán, near Lake Arenal, one daily bus departs for Santa Elena is at noon.

WHERE TO STAY

PENSIÓN EL SUEÑO *(tel. 61[3]3656)*, charges about $5 per person with shared bath, or $9 with private bath, serves meals, and can procure horses.

PENSIÓN EL TUCÁN *(tel. 61[1]1007)* charges about $7 per person with shared bath in second-floor rooms that are better than others in town, or about $9 with private bath. There's an eatery downstairs.

And there are various other *cabinas* in the area with similar low rate.

HOTEL-FINCA VALVERDE'S *(tel. and fax 62[2]2557, 10 rooms, $30 single/$38 double, $8 per additional person, credit cards accepted)* is a guest ranch, just off the road and not far from Santa Elena, but with a remote air, as the installations are set well back on a large property of forest and pasture. Woody rooms are in cabins elevated on stilts. All come with a balcony, tubs and a loft, and can sleep up to four persons. There's also a restaurant. Horses can be hired for riding on the trails here, at about $5 per hour. And with all the foot traffic in the Monteverde reserve, you chances of seeing sloths and armadillos and quetzals and toucans just might be better on a private property such as this.

PENSIÓN A DIFFERENT PLACE is a plain block structure with economy rooms at about $5 per person — and that includes breakfast!

PENSIÓN MONTEVERDE (MONTEVERDE INN), *(10 rooms, about $10 per person, or $25 with three meals)*.

Million-dollar views at guest-house prices. The large, rustic and clean if Spartan bedrooms are in several farm buildings off the main visitors' route. Most have private bath, the showers are hot. One kilometer past Santa Elena, go right for 400 meters, then left another 500 meters. You'll need your own vehicle, or a willingness to settle in, and then hike out when necessary. Horses are available for rent at about $5 per hour.

HOTEL HELICONIA, *tel. 61[1]1009, fax 61[3]3507. 22 rooms. $55 and up double.* A rustic, chalet-style building, a kilometer up from Santa Elena. Downstairs rooms have tile floors. Upstairs rooms, with more panelling, are pleasanter, but walls are thin and some bathrooms have large un-curtained windows. Add about $6 for each meal taken at the hotel. Horses and boots are available.

HOTEL EL ESTABLO, *tel. 61[2]2854 ([2]250569 in San José), fax 61[3]3855. 20 rooms. $40 single/$50 double.*

One of the nicer of the new hotels in Monteverde, a collection of several small tiers of rooms with balconies and walkways and public lounge areas with fireplace, all enclosed by walls of windows, lending an outdoor ambience to the indoors. Rooms are wood-panelled, with carpeting, good mattresses, and nicely finished detailing. Large family rooms are available. The restaurant serves only beer and wine to accompany meals (about $20 for breakfast, lunch and dinner) in keeping with the family atmosphere. Transport from San José can be arranged.

CABAÑAS LOS PINOS *(tel. 61[0]0905, 6 units)* is a set of cabins spaced amid pines (obviously). The tariff is $45 double/$70 for four persons/$100 for six.

HOTEL DE MONTAÑA MONTEVERDE, *tel. 61[1]1846. 30 rooms. $40 single/$55 double/$62 in family room. In San José: P. O. Box 70, tel. [2]333890, fax [2]226184. American Express, Visa, Master Card.*

Located about 1.5 kilometers from Santa Elena, the Hotel de Montaña is cozy and rustic, with hardwood-panelled rooms, and beds covered with thick woolen blankets. There are acres of adjoining farm and woods available to guests for exploration, and spectacular views down toward the Pacific. Horses are available for rent, and boots are lent for hiking through the reserve. Amenities include Jacuzzi and sauna (at an extra fee). Transportation to the hotel can be arranged through the San José telephone number.

HOTEL BELMAR, *tel. 61[1]1001, fax 61[3]3551. 32 rooms. $45 single/ $55 double.*

The Belmar consists of towering three-story chalet-style buildings which, though not in an indigenous contemporary architectural idiom, suits the high forest surroundings. Rooms are not as large as elsewhere, but beautiful panoramas are afforded from the private balconies, all the way to the Gulf of Nicoya. Attentive service by the owners. Boots, horseback trips and transportation to the reserve are available. They'll also pick you up in San José on request. Set meals cost about $8 each, $5 for breakfast. Turn left off the road to the reserve about 1.6 kilometers out of Santa Elena, then continue 300 meters to the hotel.

HOTEL EL BOSQUE, *tel. and fax 61[2]2559. 21 rooms. $20 single/$28 double/$34 triple.*

The rooms here are well off the road from the restaurant of the same name, in seven lowland-ranch-style buildings of stuccoed block and timber, set in a wide semicircle on attractive grounds with pines and gardens. All rooms have private bathroom with hot shower, cathedral ceilings, and good mattresses. They're not only a good buy, but if you stay here you get a 15 percent discount in the restaurant.

The hotel property includes nine hectares with trails, some through primary forest. Camping area available. About three-and-a-half kilometers from the reserve.

MONTEVERDE LODGE , *tel. 61[1]1157 (P. O. Box 6941, San José, tel. [2]570766, fax [2]571665). 27 rooms. $76 single/$89 double/$103 triple. Visa, American Express, Master Card.*

This is one of the most substantial hotels in Santa Elena, a jumble of clapboard siding, Plexiglas bubbles, triangular mini-pediments, humdrum brick-and-reinforced concrete interior, and high-tech steel-and-glass greenhouse that would suit the Musée Pompidou — altogether an architectural stomach ache.

But the rooms are the best-equipped in the area, wood-panelled, with terrazzo floors, desk, good mattresses, full tiled bathroom, and outset windows. Features include a whirlpool in view of the lobby. And, whatever the esthetics, the design is intended to bring the outdoors indoors while keeping out the elements, which purpose is accomplished; and the operator, Costa Rica Expeditions, is environmentally conscientious.

Inclusive packages are offered. Example: two nights, three days with meals, transportation from San José and one day in the reserve, about $300 per person. Fixed-menu meals are served (add $35 daily), cribs available at no charge. Children under ten pay half or less for meals, room.

SUNSET HOTEL, *tel. 61[3]3558, off the road leading to the Santa Elena Reserve, has three rooms with heavy wooden furniture at $18 per person with breakfast.*

The price is right, and the location is good if you have a car and want to be in a quiet spot. German is spoken, as well as English, and the cooking is good.

WHERE TO EAT

If you find good food at your hotel, don't look any farther! Most visitors flop back to their rooms and showers after a day of trudging, and outside eateries have not developed to the same degree as hotels, though there are a few choices.

The **SAPO DORADO** *tavern and lodge is on a rise about a kilometer toward the reserve from Santa Elena*, affording views to the Gulf of Nicoya from its terrace. Pizzas, soups, beef, tuna steak, pastas, and cheesecake are the fare, subject to daily rotation and announcement on the chalkboard. They always have a vegetarian offering, and try to limit fat content.

EL BOSQUE (The Forest), *a restaurant 2.2 kilometers out of Santa Elena*, charges lower prices than you'll pay in most of the hotels of the area, in a large room with many windows to afford a view of the greenery and mist all around. Casados and similar standard Tico fare goes for about $6. If you order anything with a fancy name, you're asking for trouble.

The **FONDA VELA HOTEL** has a pleasant candle-lit dining room set with cloth napkins and wine glasses, and with good food. Breakfast or lunch $5 to $6, dinner about $10. And there are various diners in Santa Elena, and a couple of unpretentious coffee shops along the road to the reserve, none particularly distinguished. **LA CASCADA**, *on a rise above the road*, has glass walls for forest viewing while you eat, and a menu of steaks served with loud music (just what you came to Monteverde for).

WAITING TO ENTER MONTEVERDE

From time to time, the number of visitors allowed into the reserve may be limited, in order to protect the fragile trails. Current policy is to admit no more than 100 persons into the reserve at any time. Since the hotels in the area can accommodate many times this number of persons, it is almost inevitable that you will have to wait to enter during the dry season.

SEEING THE SIGHTS

The Monteverde cloud forest is created by winds, particular temperature and moisture conditions, and mountainous topography, which combine during the dry season to hold a steady cloud cover along the continental divide.

During the rainy season, of course, the forest receives its full share of precipitation from storms blowing up from the coast. The rains, and the moisture in the air, nourish trees and plants rooted in the ground, as well as many plants that live at the upper levels of the forest, and take their nutrients directly from the mist and dust that pass through the air.

The result is an enchanted, fairy-tale environment, where trees are laden with orchids, bromeliads, mosses and ferns that obscure their branches, where the moisture and mild temperatures and sunlight filtered by the forest canopy encourage the exuberance of begonias, heliconias, philodendron and many other tropical plants in every available space on the ground.

Of over 400 bird species, the most notable is the *quetzal*, with its long arc of tail feathers. It nests in the trunks of dead trees. Other visually spectacular species include the three-wattled bellbird, the great green macaw, the bare-necked umbrellabird, and the ornate hawk-eagle. Assorted trogons in addition to the quetzal inhabit the reserve, along with more than 30 varieties of hummingbird. About 500 kinds of butterfly are found. Among the more than 100 mammalian species are howler, white-faced and spider monkeys; coatis and their cousins, raccoons; and pumas, ocelots, jaguars, tapirs, and kinkajous. Some of these may be seen scurrying for cover as you walk through their territory.

Hours & Facilities

The reserve is open to the public from 7 a.m. to 4 p.m. every day. Sign in, and pay your entry fee (currently about $10, less for students). Give the person at the reception desk an idea of your route so that somebody can look for you if you don't return.

Currently, no tent camping is permitted in the reserve. Fewer than a dozen beds are available in a couple of basic rooms for about $5 per person, and these are often quickly taken. *Call 61[2]2655 to try to reserve a space.*

Guided walks in English or Spanish can be arranged at the reserve entry. These last about three hours, and cost $25 per person. Currently, scheduled departures are at 7, 7:30, 8, 8:30 and 9 a.m. The earlier the better, before the arrival of large numbers of visitors chases off the animals. Slide shows are also given in a building in the reception area, at 4:30 p.m. daily, and there is a small gift shop.

CAÑAS

At kilometer 188 is the farming center of **Cañas** (altitude 90 meters). Good accommodations are available, along with easy access to Tilarán and Lake Arenal (see below), Palo Verde National Park, and the lazy lowland rivers of the vicinity.

ARRIVALS & DEPARTURES
Arriving By Bus

Buses for Cañas depart five times daily from Calle 16, Avenidas 1/3, San José.

WHERE TO STAY

HACIENDA LA PACÍFICA, *P.O. Box 8-5700 Cañas, tel. 69[0]0050. 28 rooms and cottages. $45 single/$68 double. Visa, Master Card, American Express.*

Five kilometers north of Cañas, along the highway, the attractive La Pacífica offers three different types of units, ranging from modest to quite comfortable (though without air conditioning) in cottages widely spaced on shady lawns.

La Pacífica is a self-styled *Centro Ecológico* (Ecological Center), a model farm where environmentally sound methods are used to raise cattle and crops. All of the hacienda, covering about 16 square kilometers of cultivated fields, pasture and windbreaks, is open to visitors for exploration, along roads, trails, on foot or on horseback (for a modest fee with guide).

HOTEL EL CORRAL, *tel. 69[0]0222. 12 rooms. $15 single/$28 double. Visa, Master Card.*

Right on the highway, a plain, two-story tan building with clean, adequate rooms, air-conditioned. Inexpensive restaurant with odd decor.

Also in Cañas, **CABINAS COROBICÍ** *(tel. 69[0]0241)*, six blocks east of the highway, is basic but friendly, with rooms for about $5 per person.

WHERE TO EAT

LA PACÍFICA presents a good table (see above), and is worth a stop. Nearby on the highway, and *adjacent to the rapids of the Corobicí River*, are two roadside restaurants: the **RINCÓN COROBICÍ**, with steaks, fish and souvenirs; and the less formal **EL GUAPINOL**.

SPORTS & RECREATION
Float Trips

Safaris Corobicí, *tel. and fax 69[0]0544, located next to La Pacífica on the highway*, runs float trips on the Corobicí, a tropical river that lazes through marsh, mangrove and pasture to Palo Verde National Park. No paddling is required; you sit back and watch for egrets, toucans, monkeys, herons and alligators from your privileged perch. Prices range from $35 for a two-hour trip to $60 for a half-day motorized trip to the Tempisque River, with lunch. If you wish, you can also take part in reforestation by planting a tree on any trip.

Motor Boat Trips

Transportes Palo Verde, *at Hotel El Corral, tel. 69[1]1091*, operates motorized river trips through Palo Verde park and the salt-water estuary to the Tempisque River, at similar prices. Children under 14 go half price on all these trips, which are, in fact, eminently suited for kids, in contrast to white-water excursions on other rivers in Costa Rica.

Bicycle Trips

Bicycle trips down from Lake Arenal are also available from **Safaris Corobicí**, *tel. and fax 69[0]0544*.

The Zoo

Just down a side road from Safaris Corobicí is a **mini-zoo** with peccaries and other small forest mammals in a barnyard setting.

TILARAN, LAKE ARENAL

Tilarán (altitude 564 meters), *22 kilometers from Cañas* through foothills of the Tilarán range dotted with cylindrical hydroelectric stations, is picturesque, warm, slow-paced, clean, and lightly trafficked, a ringer for a hill town in the Portuguese Algarve. Tilarán is developing as a center for adventures on and around Lake Arenal.

Four kilometers beyond Tilarán, the branch road approaches fjord-like, man-made **Lake Arenal**, the perfect Arenal volcano at its south end, islands sprinkling its waters. Much of the land surrounding the lake comprises **Arenal National Park**, currently in a state of development and expansion.

The lake is said to be good for sport fishing: guapote, a bass-like fish, and machaca populate its waters. And a constant breeze makes it a world-class windsurfing destination. Volcano-watching, hiking and general "ecotourism" are also attracting more and more Costa Ricans and foreigners to Lake Arenal, and some new accommodations have appeared in Tilarán and above the lake to serve them.

Under Arenal's surface are the remains of twelve pre-Columbian settlements, which were encountered with the aid of American satellite photographs and radar tracking. They appear to have been incinerated during an eruption of Arenal several thousand years ago, in the manner of Pompei. This archaeological curiosity was submerged during the construction of the Arenal hydroelectric project and the filling of the lake.

ARRIVALS & DEPARTURES

Arriving By Bus

Buses for Tilarán leave from Calle 14, Avenidas 9/11, San José, at 7:30 a.m., 12:45, 3:45 and 6:30 p.m. The trip takes about three hours. From Ciudad Quesada (San Carlos), buses depart for Tilarán at 6:30 and 9:30 a.m., and 1 and 3 p.m., passing through Fortuna.

Arriving By Tour

The Mitur travel agency in San José *(tel. [2]552031)* has a two-day, one-night trip to Lake Arenal, via San Carlos, that includes time on the lake in a boat; and other agencies offer comparable outings.

Departing By Bus

From Tilarán, buses depart for San José at 7 and 7:45 a.m. and 2 and 5 p.m.; for Arenal, across the lake, at 10 a.m. and 4 p.m. and 10 p.m.; for Cañas at 5, 6:20, 7:30 and 10 a.m. and 3:30 p.m.; for Monteverde at noon; for Puntarenas at 6 a.m. and 1 p.m.; and for San Carlos (Ciudad Quesada) at 7 a.m. and 12:30 p.m.

Departing By Car

By car, you can attempt the road past Nuevo Arenal toward Arenal volcano, but unless you have four-wheel drive, you might have to turn back. A typically rutted Costa Rican country road winds along the crest of the Tilarán mountain range toward Santa Elena and Monteverde. With a sturdy vehicle, it takes two hours or less to negotiate the 50 kilometers to the reserve.

The first seven kilometers are paved, to Quebrada Grande. Beyond, the road climbs to La Florida, and deteriorates to a rock bed running through windblown, pastured hills, and little family farms. Old-style milk cans are left for collection at the gates. Various side roads lead off to dead ends, or down to Las Juntas de Abangares. If you're at the wheel, ask directions at every fork, for Nubes, and then for Santa Elena.

GETTING AROUND THE LAKE

The right fork at the lake approach takes you six kilometers to **Tronadora**, where there are some basic cabinas with lake access. The main road runs northwest, then circles the waters through the highlands above. There are no shoulders on which to pull off to admire the view, and few access points to the tempting water below.

The town of **Arenal** (or Nuevo Arenal), altitude 620 meters, *29 kilometers beyond the junction at the lake approach, at the end of the pavement,* is a neat assemblage of concrete bungalows. "Old" Arenal lies somewhere below, in the lake. **Fortuna**, with a stretch of poor road in between, is 73 kilometers distant, past Arenal volcano.

A few buses a day ply this route all the way to Ciudad Quesada (San Carlos).

WHERE TO STAY

CABINAS EL SUEÑO, *tel. 69[5]5347. 12 rooms. $15 single/$25 double. Visa, Master Card.*

A block from the square, and pleasant enough, with carpeted rooms, upstairs courtyard and fountain. **Soda El Parque**, underneath, serves basic meals at low prices.

CABINAS LAGO LINDO, *tel. 69[5]5977, near El Sueño*, are the bargain place in which to stay in Tilarán, six airy rooms with linoleum floors and slim beds, at $7 per person, or $20 double with private bath.

CABINAS MARY, *tel. 69[5]5479, on the square*, has rooms with bath for $7 per person, or $5 per person sharing toilet facilities.

And there are other lodging places with rooms for about $5 per person.

THE SPOT/EL LUGAR tourist center, *tel. 69[5]5711*, makes arrangements for fishing and water sports, and has mountain bikes to rent. They have 16 rooms for $25 single/$45 double with hot water and fan. The lobby opens up to a pleasant garden behind a commercial building; the adjacent **CATALA** restaurant is the most formal dining area in town.

THE ART OF FUN/AVENTURAS TILARÁN *(tel. and fax 69[5]5008)* is a sports shop that arranges windsurfing, horseback rides, cave tours, river tubing, lake fishing, and boat rides. These mostly cost $50 or under for the day. Overnight biking and camping trips can also be ordered up. Windsurfers and mountain bikes are available by the hour or day, and lessons can be arranged in several languages. They can have rooms to rent in several houses around Lake Arenal at about $15 per person, bed and breakfast.

Lodges and Sport Centers Around Lake Arenal

These facilities, along or (more usually) above the lake, can be reached most easily from Tilarán if you have a car.

PUERTO SAN LUIS *(P. O. Box 02-5710, Tilarán), tel. 69[5]5750, fax 69[5]5950. 20 units. $34 single/$62 double. Master Card, Visa.*

This is an informal recreational resort, on a rolling lakeside plot, one of the few accommodations with direct access to the water. Cabina rooms are well-equipped, if not well-decorated, with carpeting, television, double bed, mini-refrigerator, and tiled bath. To reach Puerto San Luis, take the right fork as you approach the lake from Tilarán, and continue for about two kilometers through the village.

HOTEL TILAWA VIENTO SURF, *P. O. Box 92, Tilarán, tel. 69[5]5050 or 800-851-8929 direct to Costa Rica, fax 69[5]5766. 28 rooms. $52 single/$66 double/$81 triple with breakfast.*

The Tilawa, modeled after the Palace of Knossos on Crete, caters to windsurfers and others who don't mind staying in a setting of splendor. Comfortable guest rooms are decorated with Guatemalan spreads, and have orthopedic beds. Bathrooms have both tubs and showers. Junior suites at a slight higher rate have cooking facilities. All rooms overlook the lake, and afford splendid views to your choice of four volcanoes, gardens and fountains.

The specialty at Tilawa is outfitting guests for riding the wind on Lake Arenal. Rigs are ready at a separate lakeside launching area (and access to the lake is difficult except at the few spots with permits), and lessons are available. Just specify your board length when you reserve, and bring along your favorite helmet and shorty wet suit. Daily rates are $35 to $40 for a board. Canoes are available for similar rates, there are mountain bikes and Hobie Cats, and fishing can be arranged.

ROCK RIVER LODGE *(P. O. Box 2907-1000 San José, tel. [2]224547, fax [2]213011). 11 units. $40 double, $12 per additional person.* The six bedrooms here each come with a double bed and upper and lower bunks, in a woody building on a hill overlooking Lake Arenal from the north, about 18 kilometers from Tilarán. Another five individual bungalows with kitchenettes rent for about $50 double.

MIRADOR LOS LAGOS, *tel. 695484 (P. O. Box 31, Tilarán). 7 units. $40 for up to four persons.*

What a pretty spot this is . . . cottage units on a slope looking down to a fishing pond, rolling farmland and pasture, and the winding waters of Lake Arenal. Rooms are country-plain and neat, with double beds and hot water. In the wooden main house, a pool table is available to guests.

CHALET NICHOLAS *(P. O. Box 72-5710 Tilarán, tel. and fax 69[5]5387 in Tilarán for messages)*

An American-owned cozy "first-class guest house" (as the sign says) at kilometer post 48, two kilometers west of Nuevo Arenal, a chalet with magnificent views from the front porch down to Lake Arenal. And when the clouds lift, Arenal volcano comes into view. Two bedrooms sharing a bathroom, and an upstairs loft with private bath, are available for $39 double.

The **SWISS BED AND BREAKFAST**, *just east of Nuevo Arenal*, is open intermittently when the gate is not chained.

LA CEIBA BOAT, BED AND BREAKFAST *(P. O. Box 9, Tilarán, fax. 69[5]5387)*, up a steep side road from the unpaved lakeside road, has four clean, comfortable guest rooms with hot water in a bungalow with lake view, renting at $20 per person. The giant ceiba tree that gives the place its name towers over the garden, and there is adjacent primary forest with trails. This is a restful spot, cool and pleasant. There's a Ping Pong table, sailboat for up to four persons available for rent, beach access; lunch and dinner cooked on request. English, Spanish, German spoken.

SIGHTS TO SEE

Arenal Botanical Garden, *on a hillside about 4 kilometers east of Nuevo Arenal*, has about 1200 species of plants on permanent display, most prominent among them cloud-forest plants such as bromeliads and heliconias. And, of course, butterflies and birds are attracted to such surroundings. *Admission is about $4 per person when the gate is unlocked. For information, call 69[5]5266, extension 273, in English.*

WHERE TO EAT

For fine dining in Tilarán, you better bring along your own food. Otherwise, the **CATALA RESTAURANT** in The Spot Hotel has a formal atmosphere and standard menu. **CABINAS MARY** and **CABINAS EL SUEÑO** also have plain dining rooms.

But if you have a car and want pleasant views with your food, by all means continue to one of the hotels around the lake, mentioned above.

NORTHWARD FROM CAÑAS

Back on the Inter-American Highway, at **Bagaces** (kilometer 215), is the junction for the Miravalles thermoelectric generating project, 27 kilometers to the northeast on the Miravalles volcano.

MIRAVALLES VOLCANO LODGE, 30 kilometers from Bagaces at the end of a road onto the volcano, is a ranch house on a farm where heart of palm is produced. Package ranch vacations run about $300 for two nights and three days, including walks to fumaroles. Call **Natural Expeditions**, *tel. [2]272920*, if you're interested in visiting.

PALO VERDE

Southwest of Cañas, near the mouth of the Tempisque River, is **Palo Verde National Park**, a reserve of seasonally dry tropical forest of the type which once covered much of this area. Birds flock to Palo Verde, and so do birders: the leafless state of the trees during the dry season makes it easy for the latter to view the former. At least 300 species have been recorded at Palo Verde. There are hiking trails and observation points.

ARRIVALS & DEPARTURES

Uno, an agency that specializes in trips to Palo Verde, can be reached *at tel. [6]537589, fax [6]536713.* Cost of a day outing is about $100.

Palo Verde is best reached by way of the Lomas Barbudal Reserve. Other access routes cross private property. Inquire at the National Parks Service in San José before visiting.

AREA RESERVES

Less developed for visitors is the adjacent wetland **Lomas Barbudal Biological Reserve**, a refuge for migrating waterfowl, including herons, egrets, ducks and grebes. The station for the reserve is reached by taking an unpaved road from the kilometer 221 marker on the Pan American Highway, negotiable in a sedan in the dry season. Six kilometers out, the terrain drops off sharply, from bare flatlands with scattered trees to a river bottom that remains moist throughout the year, alive with bird songs and dense with trees and bushes. If you arrive by car, continue to the second parking area, adjacent to the station, if road conditions look promising. Here bird lists and t-shirts are on sale, and there are exhibits of butterflies and other fauna. There are trails from this point, and a picnic area nearby.

At the mouth of the Tempisque River is the **Rafael Lucas Rodríguez Caballero Wildlife Refuge** (**Refugio de Vida Silvestre**), which encompasses a variety of habitats ranging from dry forest to marsh to lagoons to pasture and evergreen groves, where peccaries, deer, white-faced monkeys, waterfowl and crocodiles can be observed, among others. The Rodríguez Caballero Refuge may be reached by raft and motorboat from the La Pacífica ranch and hotel along the Pan American Highway. *For information about the wildlife refuge, contact the Wildlife Department (Departamento de Vida Silvestre) of the Ministry of Natural Resources, Energy and Mines, Calle 9, Avenidas 11/13, San José, tel. 338112, or the national parks information center in the San José zoo.*

In the refuge is the **Palo Verde Biological Station** of the Organization for Tropical Studies, where research facilities are available and outside visitors may stay for about $50 daily, with meals provided, if space is available. The fee for a day visit is $15. *Contact the Organization for Tropical Studies, P. O. Box 676, 2050 San Pedro, tel. 406696, fax 406783; or P. O. Box DM, Durham, NC 27706 U.S.A., tel. 919-684-5774.*

LIBERIA

Liberia, the major city of northwestern Costa Rica, is a bustling place with wide, clean streets, relatively good accommodations, and a pleasant, dry climate. All lowland towns should be like Liberia. Strangely, modern Liberia is one of the oldest cities of Costa Rica, founded in 1769, when the area was part of Nicaragua, then a more prosperous and populated colony than Costa Rica. **La Agonía**, dating from the last century, is one of the senior churches of the country.

Liberia is the capital of **Guanacaste**, a province with a separate tradition and a separate history from the rest of Costa Rica. The province takes its name from the *guanacaste* (earpod) tree that provides shade on vast, flat grasslands. In a country short on folklore, Guanacaste provides tradition and color for all of Costa Rica. The *punto guanacasteco* is the national dance. Music played on the *marimba*, a xylophone-type instrument used by pre-Columbian Indians of Guanacaste, with sounding boxes made from wood or gourds, arouses nostalgic feelings in San José, though it has no roots there.

For most Costa Ricans, Guanacaste signifies vast herds of cattle munching away on the grasslands. The folkloric figures par excellence of the area are *bramaderos*, Costa Rica's poor man's cowboys, mounted on horses with elaborately decorated saddles, and *boyeros*, tenders of oxen.

ARRIVALS & DEPARTURES
Arriving By Bus
Buses for Liberia leave from Calle 14, Avenidas 1/3, San José, every day at 7, 9 and 11:30 a.m., and 1, 4, 6 and 8 p.m. Most are modern units, and cover the route in about four hours. There are additional buses from Avenida 3, Calles 18/20.

Departing By Bus
Liberia is the transportation crossroads of northwestern Costa Rica.

From the bus terminal, a block from the highway, and three blocks north and four blocks west of the square, buses leave for San José about every two hours from 4:30 a.m. to 8 p.m. Other buses for San José depart from the Pulmitán terminal a block away.

For La Cruz, passing the entry to Santa Rosa National Park, about every two hours from 5:30 a.m. to 8 p.m. (some of these buses continue to the Nicaraguan border at Peñas Blancas); for El Coco beach at 5:30 and 8:15 a.m., and 12:30, 2, 4:30 and 6:15 p.m.; for Playa Hermosa and Playa Panamá at 11:30 a.m. and 7 p.m.; to Santa Cruz and Nicoya, every hour throughout the day; for Cañas Dulces, 6 a.m., noon and 4:30 p.m.; for Puntarenas, five daily buses.

Current schedules are clearly posted.

WHERE TO STAY
HOTEL EL BRAMADERO, *P. O. Box 70-5000, tel. 66[0]0371. 24 rooms. $27 single/$39 double with air conditioning, $19/$28 with fan.*

A modest motel with rooms arranged around a courtyard and pool, and a large pavilion restaurant, the Bramadero has seen better days. Located at the turn from the highway into town. Travel services and car rental available.

NUEVO HOTEL BOYEROS, *P.O. Box 85, tel. 66[0]0722, fax 66[2]2529. 62 rooms. $41 single/$57 double. Visa, Master Card, American Express.*

Also located at the turn into town. Modern, with air conditioning, pools for kids and adults, and attractive leafy landscaping. Bands sometimes perform on weekends — inquire beforehand if you need a good night's sleep.

HOTEL LAS ESPUELAS, *tel. 66[0]0144 (P. O. Box 1056-1007 Centro Colón, San José, tel. [2]339955, fax [2]331787). 40 rooms. $47 single/$60 double. Visa, American Express, Master Card.*

Best in the area, a hacienda-style building with palm-shaded grounds, courtyard filled with birds and flowers, a good, reasonably priced restaurant with kids' menu, quiet central air conditioning (highly unusual), pool, and meeting facilities. Located on the highway, about a kilometer south of the turn into town.

Las Espuelas has several package trips from San José that include excursions to beaches, to a cattle ranch (with horseback riding, $150 overnight), and to Santa Rosa National Park.

Budget Lodging

For cheaper, no-frills lodging, the **HOTEL GUANACASTE** *(tel. 66[0]0085), half a block in from the highway, near the Hotel Bramadero*, will do in a pinch. Cubicles in assorted sizes go for $20 or less double, most with private toilet.

HOTEL LIBERIA *(tel. 66[0]0161)*, **PENSIÓN MARGARITA** *(tel. 66[0]0468)*, and **PENSIÓN GOLFITO** *(tel. 66[0]0963)* all have rooms for $6 per person or less.

WHERE TO EAT

Most of the above have hotels have restaurants and bars.

The **POKOPÍ** restaurant, *opposite the Hotel El Sitio on the Nicoya road*, is a small steak and seafood house. *Open from 11 a.m. to 10 p.m., later on weekdays.* Attached is the Kuru disco.

SODA GABI, *on Avenida Central about two blocks past the square (opposite the highway)* serves breakfast and lunch. **LAS TINAJAS**, *on the square*, has hamburgers, milk shakes and fried chicken.

HOTEL LA SIESTA, *two blocks south of the square*, has an inexpensive no-frills no-hassle restaurant, with beef and fish main courses for $5 or less, and even shrimp for under $10.

SEEING THE SIGHTS

The **museum/visitors' center** is located in one of the oldest houses in Liberia, three blocks south and one block east from the square. Stop in, and ask any questions you might have. On display are saddles, brands, and other implements and artifacts of the ranching life. If you're interested, ask for directions to some of the other old houses in town. *For phone inquiries, dial 66[1]1606. Hours are 9 a.m. to noon and 1 to 6 p.m., Sunday to 1 p.m., closed Monday, open holidays.*

The major point of interest in Liberia is **La Agonía**, the church *at the end of Avenida Central* that provides a taste of the old Costa Rica. It's a simple, low-slung building of stuccoed adobe and rubble, with just six amphora providing decorative elements along the pediment — altogether colonial in style, though records show that construction of the church started well after independence, in 1852, when Liberia was a remote outpost known as the town of Guanacaste. *The front door is usually open from 3 to 4 p.m.*

Not too far away is the house of a local character who, in manner of fellows in rural New England, collects glorious junk and exhibits it on his porch — saw blades, oxcart wheels, great wooden mortars and pestles, a Detroit Tigers batting helmet. Don't even think about buying. And on Avenida 4, a giant guanacaste tree has been left to live out its natural life nearly in the middle of a not-so-busy intersection. Three cheers!

EXCURSIONS

Several travel agencies arrange excursions from Liberia. The **Hotel Las Espuelas** (see above) has inclusive tours from San José. **Guanacaste Tours** (*P.O. Box 55-5000 Liberia, tel. 66[0]0306, fax 660307*) runs day trips to beaches and parks. **Punto Norte** (*tel. 66[1]1313, fax 66[1]1736, P. O. Box 26-5000 Liberia*) is based at **Hotel El Sitio**. They run trips to national parks and coastal wildlife reserves, ranch trips, and arrange boat trips, diving and fishing; and an investment tour that gives you partial reimbursement if you take the plunge.

SANTA ROSA NATIONAL PARK

Located 36 kilometers north of Liberia, **Santa Rosa National Park** was established in 1971 as a historical monument. The natural treasures of the park, which were originally included only incidentally, are now the main attraction for the foreign visitor.

The Santa Rosa hacienda was the scene of one of Costa Rica's most glorious military episodes — an episode that lasted the approximately fourteen minutes it took for a Costa Rican force to defeat the invading army of William Walker on March 20, 1856. Walker's army — and much of the opposing Costa Rican army as well — was finished off not long afterward in a cholera epidemic. The original great house of the Santa Rosa hacienda still stands as a monument to the victory.

Among the many natural features of the park are an extensive protected area of deciduous dry tropical forest; and **Nancite beach**, where hundreds of thousands of Pacific Ridley turtles nest from August until December every year.

ARRIVALS & DEPARTURES

The junction for the access road to Santa Rosa is at kilometer 269 on the Pan American (Inter-American) Highway. If you're not driving, you'll have to hitch or, more likely, walk the seven kilometers from the highway to the hacienda building and administration center.

Arriving By Bus

Buses leave Liberia for La Cruz and/or Peñas Blancas about every two hours from 5:30 a.m. to 8 p.m., passing the junction. From San José, buses for La Cruz depart from Calle 14, Avenidas 3/5 *(tel. [2]231968)* at 5 a.m. and 7:45 a.m. and 4:15 p.m. Time to the junction is about five hours.

Departing By Bus

Return departures from Peñas Blancas are at 11 a.m. and 3:30 p.m. From Liberia, buses leave for La Cruz and Peñas Blancas about every two hours.

SEEING THE SIGHTS

Partly because of its historical importance, the park is quite well run, and is one of the most visited in the national park system. Best time to visit Santa Rosa is in the dry season, when thirsty animals congregate around the permanent water holes and streams, making for easy viewing. During the rainy season, when few visitors appear, markers along the nature trail may be down.

Facilities at or near the park center include a historical museum in the old great house of the hacienda, seven kilometers from the Pan American Highway, and a nature trail nearby. The campsite, about a kilometer away, back toward the park entry, then down a side road, near the administration building, is basic, with showers and latrines, as well as many picnic tables. There's a small fee to camp, in addition to the admission fee to the park.

The *casona*, or great house of the Santa Rosa hacienda, is a large, whitewashed building with aged tile roof and wooden verandas. Part of the casona might date from the colonial period, though the age of the building is indeterminate. Houses of this sort were continually repaired, remodeled and expanded during their useful lives. The stone corrals around the house are almost certainly a few hundred years old, and were in use until the hacienda was nationalized. Great wooden mortars and pestles lie in the shade of the eaves. In the clearing in front of the casona is a huge guanacaste tree, witness to past battles.

Beaches, Turtles, & Canyons

Nancite Beach is one of two known nesting areas in Central America for the **Pacific Ridley Sea Turtle**. During the rainy season, the turtles crawl up onto the beach, first by the dozens, then the hundreds, then the thousands, to shove each other aside like so many commuters fighting for space, dig nests, and lay eggs before departing for the open sea. Green and leatherback turtles nest at the beach as well, but in smaller numbers than the Ridleys. With humans and other predators scooping up eggs when park employees aren't looking, and vultures and frigate birds diving down for bits of hatchlings, less than one percent of the eggs make it to the sea as young turtles. Crabs and sharks lie in wait to further deplete their numbers.

Access to Nancite is controlled, in order to protect the turtle eggs. Inquire at park headquarters before heading for the beach, by trail or in a four-wheel-drive vehicle.

Naranjo, a larger beach than Nancite, is an excellent locale for bird watching. You can camp here along the shifting estuary. The **Mirador Valle de Naranjo** trail affords a view of Naranjo Beach, as well as of the **Peña Bruja** outcrop.

Cuajiniquil ("kwa-hih-nih-KIHL") **Canyon**, at the northern edge of the park, contains a series of waterfalls, as well as numerous palms and ferns in its moist environment. **Platanar Lake**, covering a hectare, is four kilometers north of the great house and administrative area, and attracts varied waterfowl as well as mammals during the dry season.

North of the main section of Santa Rosa Park is the **Murciélago Annex**, a rugged, seaside strip of scrub forest and rocky outcrops where jaguars and mountain lions roam. Notable in this section of the park is **Poza El General**, a year-round waterhole, which can be reached by trail.

The Murciélago section was expropriated by the Costa Rican government from former Nicaraguan president Anastasio Somoza. Access is via the Pan American Highway to the turnoff for Cuajiniquil village, 30 kilometers north of the junction for the main section of Santa Rosa Park. The entrance to the park annex is eight kilometers past Cuajiniquil.

There are also several isolated beaches near Cuajiniquil, both within and without the park. **Playa Blanca** is especially pretty. You can sometimes hire boats to poke around the inlets or to take you to the Murciélago ("bat") Islands, about 25 minutes out to sea.

Junquillal Bay Recreation Area (Area Recreativa Bahía Junquillal) including turtle nesting sites, dry forest and mangroves, is currently being developed for visitors, with campsites and trails.

Access to the Park Annex

Roads lead to various bays and Playa Blanca. You'll need a four-wheel-drive vehicle to penetrate very far into the park annex, otherwise you can rent horses in Cuajiniquil, or hike.

Buses operate at 5 a.m. and noon from La Cruz, 20 kilometers south from the Nicaraguan border on the Pan American Highway (see below), to Cuajiniquil (you can board one of these at the highway junction), and sometimes directly from Liberia (recently at 3 p.m.; inquire at the tourist office there, or the bus station).

There are a couple of inexpensive rooms available for rent above the **CUAJINIQUIL** restaurant. *Call the public phone, 669030, to inquire about availability.* Farther on, the **COOPEJUSA** ("Ko-o-peh-HOO-sah") restaurant serves meals and offers horseback rides on a cattle ranch, as well as beach access.

THE NICOYA PENINSULA

The **Nicoya Peninsula** is separated from the rest of Costa Rica by the Gulf of Nicoya, as well as by Indian heritage, and a colonial past as part of Nicaragua. Sparsely populated, with poor roads, Nicoya enjoys a relatively dry climate, due to the barrier of hills and low mountains along the coast. Those same mountains create a series of sun-drenched beaches with rugged, dramatic backdrops.

BARRA HONDA NATIONAL PARK

About 14 kilometers northeast of Nicoya, off the road that leads to the Tempisque River and the Pan American Highway, is **Barra Honda National Park**, with its extensive limestone caverns, and peaks offering long-distance views out over the Gulf of Nicoya.

Barra Honda mountain, once thought to be a volcano, rises 300 meters above the surrounding plain, and is pocked by holes where the roofs of underlying caves have collapsed. The caves were formed — and are still being formed — by the rapid erosion and chemical decomposition of layers of limestone sediment that once lay on the bed of a prehistoric sea. A geological fault line runs roughly along the nearby Tempisque River; the former seabed was steadily lifted as the Nicoya Peninsula slid alongside the mainland.

There are more than two dozen caves in Barra Honda, some of them still hardly explored.

Facilities in Barra Honda Park include trails, latrines, drinking water, and a campsite. The bluffs are high, and will require quite a lot of exertion to ascend. Park headquarters are in the town of Barra Honda, four kilometers west of the highway from Nicoya to the Tempisque River. It's another six kilometers to the center of the park.

ARRIVALS & DEPARTURES

By Tour

If you're interested in descending into the caves, contact the National Park Service at the Bolívar Park Zoo in San José. A park ranger must accompany you. Tours with descents into the caves are operated by Turinsa, Avenida 3, Calles 3/5, San José, *tel. [2]219185.*

Departing By Bus

Alfaro buses depart at 2:30 p.m. from Calle 14, Avenidas 3/5, San José, for Hojancha, passing the turn for Barra Honda at dusk in the dry season. More feasibly, travel first to the town of Nicoya, then take a morning bus heading by the turnoff for the park, 15 kilometers from Nicoya. A bus at 10:30 a.m. goes to the town of Barra Honda; other buses reach Santa Ana, about two kilometers from the park.

Departing By Ferry

Vehicles cross the Tempisque River on the direct road from Nicoya to San José on a ferry. Service is continuous, from 6 a.m. to 7 p.m. (to 9 p.m. on Sunday, Monday and Friday). At busy times, the ferry might make several trips until you get aboard. Fare is about $3 for a car and driver. Snack stands will feed you while you wait.

NEARBY SIGHTS & LODGING

Near the caves, **LAS DELICIAS** (*Delights*) is a cooperative project to involve local people with tourists, and vice-versa. Three cottages are available at about $15 per person per day, campsites for just a few dollars, and meals are served. *Call 68[5]5580, a public phone nearby, to reserve.*

NICOYA COAST BEACH RESORTS
PLAYAS DEL COCO

The beach here is in a dramatic setting on a large horseshoe bay with great rocks offshore, sailboats gliding around, and dozens of fishing boats tied up or on their way in to or out from shore. But this is one of the Pacific points most easily reached from San José, and it shows. The little town and the central part of the beach are dirty, though there's less litter the farther you walk from the center.

ARRIVALS & DEPARTURES

Playas del Coco (or simply **Coco**) is the center of a mega-beach area that includes **Ocotal**, to the south, and **Playa Hermosa** and **Playa Panamá**, to the north. Public transport to nearby beaches is limited, so many passengers arrive to Coco by public transportation and are picked up, or continue by taxi.

Arriving By Bus

Buses leave Liberia for Coco approximately at for El Coco beach at 5:30 and 8:15 a.m., and 12:30, 2, 4:30 and 6:15 p.m. Service may be curtailed in the rainy season.

One bus a day leaves from Calle 14, Avenidas 1/3, San José, at 10 a.m. for El Coco; the trip takes just under five hours.

Arriving By Car

To drive to Playa Hermosa or Playa del Coco, take the main Nicoya highway and turn off at the Tamarindo restaurant, 20 kilometers from Liberia. El Coco is 15 kilometers onward.

Departing By Taxi or Foot

To reach the nearby beaches of Ocotal or Playa Hermosa, if your hotel isn't arranging transport, it's easiest to take a taxi or hitch.

Departing By Bus

A bus leaves for San José at about 8:30 a.m., and there are six daily buses for Liberia in the dry season.

To continue by bus to beach towns to the south, take the Liberia bus as far as the junction at the Tamarindo restaurant, and flag down a bus going your way.

WHERE TO STAY

HOTEL FLOR DE ITABO, *P. O. Box 32, tel. 67[0]0292, fax 67[0]0003. 22 rooms, 5 suites. $60 single/$65 double, $45 in bungalows slightly less in low season. American Express, Visa, Master Card.*

This attractive hotel, well managed by European owners, is not on the beach — in this case an advantage. The large, beamed, tile-floored restaurant (reasonably priced) looks out through archways to the huge adults' pool and children's pool, lawns shaded by coconut palms, and jungly gardens beyond. Rooms are comfortable, with carved hardwood bedsteads, air conditioning, and satellite television. Suites, at $95 daily, have cooking facilities.

Boats are available for deep-sea fishing at $450 to $560 per day, or $30 per hour on a 21-footer; and, unusually for Pacific coastal hotels, river fishing as well. And horseback riding and trips to Rincón de la Vieja are offered. Private transportation from San José can be arranged, along with car rental. But if you have to go a kilometer from the beach to find pleasant surroundings, is this where you want to be? English, German, Italian and French are spoken.

HOTEL COCO PALMS, *P. O. Box 188-5019, tel. 67[0]0367, fax 67[0]0117. Twenty rooms. $60 to $70 double. Visa, Master Card.*

This hotel, one block from the beach next to the soccer field, has just been totally renovated under its new German management. All rooms are air conditioned, with attractive wicker furniture. Facilities include a central thatched roundhouse restaurant, pool, and casino. Unfortunately, some rooms have only views of parked cars outside picture windows.

At the beach, accommodations are of the popular sort, without hot water, and with neighbors close on. The **HOTEL CASINO PLAYAS DEL COCO** offers the best of the available *cabina*-type rooms with sea view and private bath for $25 double, or $40 in a unit that will sleep a family. If you're stuck in back, the rate is slightly lower. The price drops from July through November.

There are similar places to stay, such as **CABINAS EL COCO** next door, which also has a few better rooms, and **CABINAS LUNA TICA**, to the left as you face the beach.

WHERE TO EAT

The **DON HUMO ("MR. SMOKE") ROTISSERIE** restaurant, *where the road leads off toward Ocotal,* is the most modern and formal eating place in town. There is excellent chicken roasted over a wood fire, as well as fish and kebabs. The operators, who speak English, can also arrange for deep-sea fishing.

PIZZERIA PRONTO, *on the entry road a couple of blocks from the beach*, is one of several pizza joints.

Assorted stands sell fried fish, and there are several bars. Or try the **HOTEL FLOR DE ITABO** for a sit-down meal away from the crowds.

SPORTS & RECREATION

Diving

• **Diving Safaris**, *at the Hotel Ocotal (see below)* is the oldest operation of its kind in the area.

• **Virgin Diving** *(tel. 670472) at La Costa Hotel and Villas*, up the coast at Playa Hermosa, offers half-day, two tank dives for $55, or $75 with equipment. They also give open-water courses for $300 and an introduction to scuba for $95.

• **Rich Coast Diving** *(tel. 670176, fax 670164)*, on the main road into Playas del Coco, near the beach, offers somewhat lower rates than others in the area: $45 for a two-tank dive ($65 with full equipment), $70 for a resort course.

Fishing

Various hotels and shops rent fishing gear and boats. The **Mareas** shop organizes fishing at under $40 an hour — not bad.

PLAYA OCOTAL

Three kilometers south of El Coco, **Ocotal** is reached by an unpaved road, rutted and difficult to negotiate in the rainy season. But there are rewards, if you're interested in a secluded hotel, deep-sea fishing, or diving.

ARRIVALS & DEPARTURES

Access to Ocotal is by car or taxi from Playas del Coco.

WHERE TO STAY

HOTEL EL OCOTAL, *tel. 67[0]0230, fax 67[0]0083 (P.O. Box 1, Playa del Coco). 43 units. $100 single/$125 double/$240 in suite. Slightly lower April through November. American Express, Visa, Master Card.*

This hotel is in a bare but dramatic clifftop setting colored with frangipani and bougainvillea, overlooking multiple coves and inlets with black-sand beaches and rocky islets offshore. Some rooms are in a row looking seaward, with walls of glass. More attractive are individual villas with two larger rooms in each, parquet floors, and a better bathroom. Ten new units are at beach level, next to the diving shop and the third swimming pool. (Management will not confirm the type of room you will have.) All rooms are air-conditioned, with television, coffee-maker, and mini-refrigerator.

Facilities include tennis courts, pool, riding horses, and equipment for fishing and water skiing. Deep-sea fishing programs, using 32- and 42-foot boats, are available at $600 to $750 daily per boat. Despite its isolation, the hotel's restaurant is reasonably priced. Security measures are quite evident.

VILLA CASA BLANCA, *P. O. Box 176-5019, Playas del Coco, tel. and fax 67[0]0448. 12 units. $51 single/$57 double with breakfast.*

This inn is a welcome ray among the anonymous lodging places of the vicinity, a Mediterranean villa set back from and overlooking the sea. The interior is open and lofty, with varnished wood ceilings and warm tile floors; the management is North American and friendly; and the rooms, all with private baths and wood trim, have individually selected furnishings and decorations, including canopy beds in some. All rooms have overhead fans, and some are air-conditioned. Two condominium units are also available at about $100 daily.

VISTAS DEL OCOTAL *(tel. [2]553284 in San José, 514-381-3382 in Montreal)* are row condominium units consisting of a bedroom, sleeping loft and cooking area, located in the flat terrain below the Ocotal Hotel. The property has a pool. The rate is $96 for up to three persons, $110 for six. These would be cramped with six, and maybe even with three persons.

BAHÍA PEZ VELA, *tel. 67[0]0129, P. O. Box 7758 San José; or c/o World Wide Sportsman, P. O. Drawer 787, Islamorada, FL 33036, tel. 800-327-2880 or 305-664-4615. Fishing packages from about $325 per day.*

Located at Playa Negra, another beautiful little black sand cove about two kilometers past Ocotal via a concrete road, Bahía Pez Vela was the first of the west-coast fishing resorts in Costa Rica. Specialties are sailfish, roosterfish and dorado.

SPORTS & RECREATION
Diving

Diving Safaris, *based at Ocotal,* schedules a scuba dive every day of the year at 9 a.m. The staff includes PADI instructors and divemasters. With two new diesel-powered boats and a pontoon boat, Diving Safaris regularly takes visitors out to the Bat and Catalina islands. Courses and certification upgrades are available, as well as week-long packages. *Make arrangements at the Hotel Ocotal; or write to Diving Safaris, Apartado 121-5019, Playas del Coco, Costa Rica, tel. 67[0]0012.*

PLAYA FLAMINGO

Four kilometers onward from the turn for Villas Pacífica is **Flamingo Beach**, a stunning horseshoe of white sand in the web of a hand-shaped promontory, bordered by cliffs and a large hill.

What distinguishes Flamingo is what man has added to nature: a marina which, though small, is the most complete in the region. For all the money that has been poured into the attractive facilities at Flamingo, there's no town, and little shade. If you're not into fishing, sunbathing and real-estate pitches, and don't have a car to circulate to other locales, Flamingo can get old rather quickly. Flamingo has the air of a town looking for the next rich sucker to come along.

ARRIVALS & DEPARTURES
Arriving By Bus

From San José, buses depart daily at 8 a.m. (direct) and 10:30 a.m. (connecting) from Avenida 3, Calles 18/20; return trip at 2 p.m. *Phone [2]217202 to reserve.* Buses for Brasilito, Flamingo and Potrero leave daily from Santa Cruz at 4 a.m., 10:30 a.m., and 2:30 p.m. The run to Potrero takes about two hours. Verify this schedule at the tourist office before leaving San José.

Express bus service is provided three times weekly from San José, fare $30 each way (about five times the fare on the public bus). Departure is in the morning from the Herradura and Cariari hotels, returning in the evening. *Call [2]391584 or [2]392921 to reserve.*

Arriving By Air

By air, charter a seaplane to take you right to the marina from Pavas airport outside San José. The fare is about $450 each way for five passengers. Call the Flamingo marina, tel. 67[4]4203, to make arrangements. Otherwise, fly to Tamarindo (see page 331), then take a taxi, if you haven't arranged to be picked up by your hotel.

Arriving By Boat

I'm told that the approach to the slips at Flamingo is through water that is quite shallow for sailboats. If you plan to dock at Flamingo, clear customs and immigration first at Playas del Coco (if approaching from the north), otherwise you'll be sent back.

Departing by Bus or Air from Flamingo, Brasilito, and Potrero

Buses for Santa Cruz depart from Potrero depart at 5 a.m., 2 p.m. and 4 p.m., passing through Flamingo and Brasilito. The run to Potrero takes about two hours. Verify this schedule at the tourist office before leaving San José. The return bus to San José leaves at 2 p.m. Or, you can book the express bus back from Flamingo (see above), or a flight from Tamarindo.

WHERE TO STAY

HOTEL PLAYA FLAMINGO *(90 rooms)* and **PRESIDENTIAL SUITES** *(23 condos, 120 rooms), tel. 67[4]4010, fax 67[4]4060 (P. O. Box 692-4050 Alajuela, tel. [2]391584, fax [2]390257). $110 single/$120 double. Suites from $180 double, $205 for four persons. Visa, American Express, Master Card.*

The sprawling main hotel here, at water level, is all first-class, except for the need to cross a road to reach the beach. Rooms are large and comfortable, air-conditioned, with televisions, and most have terraces.

FLAMINGO MARINA RESORT, *tel. 67[4]4141, fax 67[4]4035 (tel. [2]218093 in San José). 35 rooms. $110 double/$185 in suite. Visa, Master Card, American Express.* This low-slung tan concrete building overlooks the Flamingo marina. All rooms have sea-view terraces, and the standard rooms are nice enough.

VILLAS FLAMINGO, *tel. 67[4]4215, [2]390737 in San José. 24 units. $115 double to $171 for six.*

This is the first accommodation along the road into Flamingo, where the road bends along the sea, and currently the best value. Two rows of two-level apartments are set back across a grassy and treed area from the beach. Each modern unit has two bedrooms, three bathrooms, several sleep sofas, fans (no air-conditioning), and upstairs terrace. There is a pool on the property, but no hotel services are available. Rates are slightly lower by the week, and the monthly rate is about $1,800.

WHERE TO EAT

Just down the road from the Hotel Playa Flamingo is **MARIE'S RESTAU-RANT**, an attractive, informal, open-air bistro. Complete breakfasts are served for $5, as well as lasagne, cordon bleu, Mexican combinations, and seafood items for $7 and up, tacos and sandwiches for less.

Up at the pinnacle of Flamingo, **MAR Y SOL** offers a continental menu with sea view. About $15 and up, *call 67[4]4151 to reserve.*

TIO'S BAR, *on the way into Flamingo*, is also a restaurant, recreation center and general hangout, with golf driving range, tennis court and pickup softball games.

Over on the mainland, two kilometers from the center of Flamingo, **HAL'S AMERICAN** serves roast chicken, pizza and pasta with sea view under a thatched roof. You can play mini-golf before, while, or after you eat. *Call 67[4]4057 for delivery to your room.*

A few basic food items are available at the **MARINA TRADING POST**.

SPORTS & RECREATION

The **Quicksilver Dive Shop** *at Flamingo, tel. 67[4]4010*, offers windsurfers, mountain bikes and boogie boards for rent. They'll take you diving.

Flamingo Divers, *tel. 67[4]4021*, offers two-tank dives for $70 plus equipment rental, full open-water certification for about $400.

The **Marina Trading Post** has information about privately owned beach and hillside houses available for rent, at up to $300 per night. Catamaran rentals can be arranged as well.

Deep-sea fishing in the Flamingo area, at $250 to over $1000 per day, is available from:

• **Flamingo Bay Pacific Charters** (*tel. [2]314055 in San José; or 1112 East Las Olas Blvd., Fort Lauderdale, FL 33301, tel. 800-654-8006, fax 305-522-2637*), with packages from $300 per day of fishing, including room, meals, and transport from San José.

• **Blue Marlin Fishing**. Stop in at their office in Flamingo, *or call 67[4]4043, fax 67[4]4165.*

• **Sportfishing Costa Rica** (*P.O. Box 115-1150 La Uruca, tel. [2]333892 in San José, 800-374-4474 U.S.-Costa Rica direct*).

NIGHTLIFE

Restaurants and shops of interest to visitors are sparse in the Flamingo area. A rental car is almost a necessity for any variety in dining, food shopping, beaches, etc.

Amberes is a bar-casino-disco up the hill in the Presidential suites where you can while away your time as your colones trickle away.

PLAYA PAN DE AZÚCAR (SUGAR BEACH)

A dirt road winds up into the hills beyond the village of Playa Potrero and down to solitary **Playa Pan de Azúcar**.

WHERE TO STAY

HOTEL SUGAR BEACH, *tel. 680959 (P. O. Box 66-5150 Santa Cruz). 10 rooms. $68 double with fan, $90 double with air conditioning.*

This hotel's brochure calls its beach the most beautiful in Costa Rica. With a gentle hillside and gray sand, trees growing down almost to the water, and streams meandering through, I can't take issue with the claim. Four rooms are in an elevated round house, the others in ranch units with front porches facing the bay and offshore islands.

Food is served under a great rotunda. Breakfast $3 to $4, main courses at lunch and dinner from $6. A pet iguana scurries around the grounds, and monkeys and macaws share the hillside with guests. Horses are available, and a dive shop is planned. There's nobody out here but you and the people at the hotel. With advance notice, you can arrange a pickup at Tamarindo airstrip, or at Perla's Cantina in Playa Potrero, where the bus from Santa Cruz ends its run.

PLAYA TAMARINDO

Tamarindo is a wide, mostly empty beach curving around a miles-long bay, with rocks and little sandy islands offshore. Pelicans float overhead and dive into the waters, skiffs bob up and down in the gentle surf. The setting is nearly perfect. And yet, many who know the Nicoya beaches say that Tamarindo is spoiled. Which is a measure of what some of the other beaches are like.

The village is fairly peaceful and low-key. The tamarinds that give the beach its name are the trees with the dangling seed pods and brush-like leaves. Birding is excellent in the nearby mangroves and tidal pools.

ARRIVALS AND DEPARTURES

Arriving By Bus

A direct bus for Tamarindo leaves from Calle 14, Avenidas 3/5, San José, daily at 3:30 p.m.; *phone [2]217202 to reserve*. Another bus leaves from Avenida 3, Calles 18/20 at 4 p.m. The trip takes about five hours. From Santa Cruz, a bus for Tamarindo leaves the main square at 3:30 p.m. The **Hotel Tamarindo Diriá** has a direct air-conditioned bus three times a week for $50 round trip (versus $10 for the public bus).

Arriving By Air

There is daily air service from San José as well, on **Sansa** airlines, *tel. [2]335330*. Fare is under $40 each way, and inexpensive packages with hotel are available. **Travelair** *(tel. [2]327883)* flies most days of the week to Tamarindo from San José, fare $114 round trip.

Arriving By Car

If you're driving from San José, the preferred route to Tamarindo is the road that forks from the main Nicoya highway at Belén. Continue through Huacas (instead of turning for Flamingo) to the junction for the dirt road to Tamarindo. Total distance is 38 kilometers from Belén. Tamarindo can also be reached by road from Santa Cruz, unpaved for part of the way.

Departing By Bus

A return bus for San José leaves at about 5:45 a.m., and there is usually another bus at about noon. Or inquire at the Tamarindo Diriá for the express bus.

Departing By Air

Some Travelair and Sansa flights touch down in Nosara or Sámara on the way back to San José.

WHERE TO STAY

HOTEL EL JARDÍN DEL EDÉN, *tel. 67[4]4111 direct to hotel; tel. [2]202096, fax [2]249763in San José. 18 rooms and 2 apartments. $80 to $100 single/$97 to $125 double ($140 in apartment); $15 per additional adult, $10 per child. Rates include breakfast.*

This is the nicest small hotel to have opened recently along the Pacific, a hilltop Mediterranean villa that is pleasant both to regard and to inhabit. Each room is different in size and shape. Most have terraces, some have private flower-bordered sandy gardens, all have ocean and sunset views, some are reached through winding passages that suggest medieval intrigue. Bedspreads are cheery, showers are oversized and lined with Talavera tile, lighting is dazzling or subdued according to your requirements, there are both air conditioning and ceiling fan, and a minibar-refrigerator stocks beverages at unusually fair prices. Apartments have a separate bedroom and a Mexican-tiled kitchen, and built-in wardrobes. Even the service sinks in the corridors are disguised to fit the decor.

There are fountains, terraces and gardens, a pool with bar and Jacuzzi and larger free-form pool in succession down the hillside, and stone-flagged walkways. The included buffet breakfast consists of fresh breads, fruits, juices, eggs prepared to order, and lots more. The restaurant changes its offerings daily to take advantage of available fresh ingredients.

The Jardín del Edén –Garden of Eden – is about 400 meters back from the main road in Tamarindo.

HOTEL PUEBLO DORADO, *tel. and fax [2]225741. (P. O. Box 1711-1002, San José). 22 rooms. $75 single/$89 double. American Express, Visa, Master Card.*

Across the road from the beach, a sleek *art modern* concrete hotel with all the essentials: air-conditioning, medium-sized pool, bar and restaurant, t-shirt-and-tanning-lotion shop, and guest rooms on two levels with tile floors and minimal but attractive furnishings. English and French spoken, limited but reasonably priced menu.

HOTEL PASATIEMPO, *fax 68[0]0776. 10 bungalows. $80 double.*

On the way into the Tamarindo Bay development, the new Pasatiempo consists of attractive cottages surrounding a pool. Each has tile floor, high ceiling, overhead fan, one or two beds, and bathroom with vanity and large shower. A short walk from the beach. The restaurant is currently frequented by the owners of other hotels in Tamarindo.

CABINAS ZULLYMAR, *tel. [2]264732. 27 rooms. $26 to $50 double/$32 to $57 triple.*

At the end of the road, rooms with private bath, around a shady courtyard. Curiosities in an otherwise simple place are the hardwood doors on the older rooms, carved with pre-Columbian motifs. All rooms have fans, and newer units have hot water and refrigerators, the higher-priced ones with very high ceilings, better bathrooms and refrigerators. Across the road from the Zullymar is its former Bar, El Tercer Mundo (Third-World Bar). Why they changed that wonderful name, I'll never know. Good, plain food is served, mostly beef and fish, at $4 to $5 for a main course.

CABINAS POZO AZUL, *tel. 68[0]0147. 27 units. $30 to $40 per cabina, $20 to $32 in the low season (June, and August through November).*

Despite the "cabina" tag, these are housekeeping units, with refrigerator and stove, on a hillock at the entry to town. They're relatively new, most are air-conditioned, and there's a large pool. Standard units have two beds, larger ones have three beds and a separate kitchen. A good buy. A few units with fan only go for lower rates.

HOTEL TAMARINDO DIRIÁ, *tel. 68[0]0474 (P. O. Box 4211-1000, tel. [2]330530, fax [2]553355 in San José). 60 rooms. $80 to $114 single/$90 to $114 double, higher in suites. American Express, Visa, Master Card.*

The senior hotel at Tamarindo has attractive, mature grounds landscaped with lush tropical trees and colorful shrubs, and a pool. The air-conditioned rooms are on the small side, with televisions (with satellite programming), and worn Spanish-colonial furniture and flamingo bedspreads that could bear updating. Attractive restaurant. Water skiing and fishing are available.

WHERE TO EAT

With a resident French-speaking population that requires gratifying food, Tamarindo is the culinary capital of Pacific Costa Rica. Lucky you.

JOHAN'S BELGIAN BAKERY is a surprise eating spot, with no pretense at all, serving fresh croissants, rye bread, waffles piled with fruit, sandwiches, cookies, and gourmet pizza to eat in or take out. For about $3, you can have a light meal, accompanied with fresh juice, in the shady compound in back, overlooking a tidal inlet, while you watch the sea birds, and ducks and roosters wandering about. *Hours are 6 a.m. to 5:30 p.m.*

LOCO RANCHO, *next to Johan's*, is an informal open-air bar and eatery with rock music, bamboo dividers, and assorted sandwiches, pastas, pizzas and salads. $8 and under for everything.

At the opposite end of the spectrum is **EL MILAGRO**, where the dining is formal inside and on the terrace of a tan bungalow, to the accompaniment of light music, with views through archways to the sea. Red snapper, dorado and steak-and shrimp combinations are served at $10 and up, less at lunch.

Check out the restaurant of the **JARDÍN DEL EDÉN**, the hotel on the hill above town. One of the owners is a French chef by training, with a commitment to using only fresh ingredients.

The **COCONUT CAFÉ**, owned by the people from Johan's, is perfect for a long fantasy evening, an open bar under a thatched roof, with palms, and cushioned rattan furniture in seemingly random groupings. The menu is creative and changes daily. Recently included were couscous, pepper steak, Thai chicken and red chicken curry. Figure $15 as a minimum. Open at 6 p.m.

The **FIESTA DEL MAR** restaurant, under the huge thatched roof where the road ends in the village, is where, for $6 to $20, you can get a whole fish or lobster, casado, steak, chicken, or, sometimes, *talluza*, a Guanacastecan specialty made with ground corn, ham, fish, lobster, cheese, chicken, and whatever else is around the kitchen.

Near the end of town, the restaurant of the **HOTEL PASATIEMPO** currently has a very good chef, and is a favorite after-hours gathering spot for proprietors of *other* hotels. $10 and up for the day's fish or filet in sauce.

SPORTS & RECREATION

Fishing at Tamarindo, and windsurfing and water skiing and swamp trips, are available from **Papagayo Excursions**, *tel. 68[0]0859*. Their trips can be booked at the Hotel Tamarindo Diriá gift shop.

A less expensive fishing alternative is to look for the fellow who sells burgers and snacks out of a trailer at the end of the road (if he's still around). He can take up to five people fishing in an outboard for about

$40 per hour, with extra charges to rent rods and reels.

Iguana Surf, under the thatched cupola right after the Tamarindo Bay Resort, rents out surfboards, kayaks and boats, and there are also rentals at the Pueblo Dorado hotel.

Flamingo Divers offers its services from a shop opposite the Coconut Café.

Several other tour shops around town can arrange for boat trips through the estuary to spot birds in the mangroves, or to Tamarindo National Wildlife Refuge (see below) or Playa Grande, just up the coast, to spot nesting turtles.

Tamarindo National Wildlife Refuge, south of the village of Tamarindo, is a turtle nesting area that also includes a variety of mangrove types. Birding trips through the waterways of the reserve and turtle-watching trips in the nesting season (November through April) are available from local operators. Typical species are egrets, frigatebirds, pelicans, gulls, spoonbills, and Muscovy ducks.

SOUTHERN NICOYA

Opposite Puntarenas are the dramatic bays and inlets and sandy and rocky beaches of the very end of the Nicoya Peninsula.

Despite the proximity of San José in a straight line, limited ferry service, poor public transportation, unpaved roads and the fact that this is a dead end have, until recently, made the area relatively little-traveled. Of course, these are ideal conditions for those who wish to make discoveries away from the crowd at their own pace.

The two gateways to this area, from Puntarenas, are the ferry ports of Playa Naranjo and Paquera.

PAQUERA

Paquera, *24 kilometers from Playa Naranjo*, is a beach town and ferry terminal.

ARRIVALS & DEPARTURES
By Car/Ferry

The dock for the new car-and-passenger ferry from Puntarenas is at Puerto Paquera, a couple of kilometers from the center of the village. For schedules from Puntarenas, check with the tourist office in San José. There should be at least two daily sailings in each direction.

By Bus

Buses take passengers onward to Tambor, Cóbano, and Montezuma. For other destinations, you'll have to drive, take a country taxi, or walk.

WHERE TO STAY

RESTAURANT-BAR-CABINAS GINAMA *(tel. 61[1]1444, ext. 119)* has basic rooms at about $12 double, and a restaurant with tablecloths.

Farther on, **CABINAS ROSITA** *(tel. 61[1]1444, ext. 206)*, just off the road, has rooms for about $18 double.

ZORBA'S PLACE, *400 meters off the main road at Playa Pochote, right on the sea,* is a bare-bones beachfront compound with a few rooms for rent at $25 double, and Greek salad, keftedakia and fried fish. If you want to get away from the development that affects southern Nicoya beaches, stop here.

SEEING THE SIGHTS

Curú National Wildlife Reserve takes in a section of sea and shore north of Tambor, including both forest and beach. White-tailed deer, snakes, and small forest animals such as pacas, opossum and raccoons populate the woods; hawks, egrets, motmots and woodpeckers are common; and sea turtles occasionally nest on the beach. As with most other reserves (as opposed to parks), the land is private property. *Phone 61[2]2392 in advance for permission to enter.*

Bahía Ballena

At kilometer 41, you reach **Bahía Ballena** (*Whale Bay*).

WHERE TO STAY

PLAYA TAMBOR BEACH RESORT. *402 rooms. U.S. reservations, tel. 800-858-0606, or through travel agents. $100 to $120 per person daily (children $35) inclusive.*

Playa Tambor is Costa Rica's world-class all-inclusive beach resort, a village of low-lying thatched and concrete buildings that stretch over just part of a property that covers thousands of hectares. There are vast, open lawns, but also many trees and flowers and shrubs.

Rooms are in several garden-style clapboard-sided wings, entered from outside terraces and stairways. Each is air-conditioned, has a cheery pastel decor, and comes with two large beds with good mattresses, television, phone, mini-bar, louvered closet, safe-deposit box, muted textured wallpaper, a marble bathroom with tub, and private balcony or terrace bordered by a trellis.

Most common facilities are roofed over and open to the air, from the vast, cathedral-like lobby, to the main restaurant with its soaring thatch; and when the wind is up, everything roars! The pool, in the form of an overgrown amoeba, meanders on and on, under a water polo net to two bars. The beach is long and shaded by almond trees. Facilities also include more intimate bars, a theater, and tennis and basketball courts, as well as windsurfers, sailboats, and ocean kayaks, most of which can be used at no extra charge.

Optional activities are scheduled daily, including aerobics, water gymnastics, volleyball games, tropical dance lessons, and limbo parties. There are also a kids' club, beauty salon, infirmary, gift shop and newsstand, and travel agency.

All meals, snacks, local brands of drinks and wine with meals and a nightly show are also included. Most food is served buffet-style, with a nightly theme, though a la carte dining in the Rancho (a pueblo-style structure with a mismatched thatched roof) is an option. Only tours (half-day fishing, $250), horseback rides, laundry and transport from San José carry a surcharge.

THE PACIFIC SOUTH

The southern Pacific beaches of Costa Rica are every bit as inviting and pleasing to the eye as those along the Nicoya Peninsula, though they differ in character. Most are more open, sweeping, and exposed, with fewer bordering outcrops of rocks. The farther south you go, the more humid and rainy is the climate, and the more lush and exuberant the vegetation that runs up to the sand. The mugginess is always relieved and attenuated, however, by breezes blowing off the water.

There is one fact about the southern beaches that is often not mentioned in polite company: they are dangerous for swimming. Large volumes of water flow toward shore across a deceptively smooth, broad front of waves, then recede in fast-flowing, unpredictable streams. If you are not a good swimmer, stay close to shore.

Beach hotels are concentrated at **Jacó** and at **Manuel Antonio** (near Quepos), but there are numerous little-frequented beaches as well where cabinas and similar basic accommodations are available. You can poke around and explore for some of these paradisaical hideaways if you decide to rent a car in San José.

PLAYA JACÓ

Jacó ("ha-KO") has what other beach places in Costa Rica are missing: streets, and life. It is a pleasant community, where you can stroll and look in stores, shop for groceries, choose from a selection of restaurants and snack bars, and buy a souvenir at some place other than the captive boutique of your hotel. Vacation houses are scattered on coconut-palm-shaded lots, surrounded by wild grass and carefully manicured gardens. Accommodations range from basic to expensive, and there are definitely places in between.

Jacó is the nearest of the beach resorts to San José (if you don't count Puntarenas), three hours away by public bus, less by car, or a half-hour hop by chartered plane. The beach at Jacó is typical of this section of coast — wide, long, curving to promontories, littered with driftwood, palm-fringed in parts, vegetation creeping over some small dunes. There is also a certain accumulation of trash — diapers, bottles, juice cartons — in the most frequented sections, but the beach is large enough that most of it is inoffensive. Surfers have made Jacó their home away from home.

And there are natural attractions, as well. Sea turtles lay their eggs most nights from July to December at Playa Hermosa, three kilometers to the south.

ARRIVALS & DEPARTURES
By Bus
Bus departures from the Coca-Cola station, Calle 16, Avenidas 1/3, San José, are at 7:15 and 10:30 a.m., and 3:30 p.m. *Call Transportes Jacó, 41[5]5890, to confirm the schedule.* The **Jacó Beach Hotel** runs its own bus for groups. **Pacific Transfer** runs a bus called the *Silver Bullet Express* with reserved seats and snacks for $23 one way, $35 round trip from San José. *Call [2]272180 (fax [2]281015) for schedules and pickup points.*

By Air
Chartered small planes use the airstrip alongside the entry road.

Departing By Bus
Bus departures from Jacó for San José are at 5 and 11 a.m. and 3 p.m. Or take the **Pacific Transfer** express bus, *tel. [2]272180.*

The San José bus can drop you at Carara Reserve, or at the highway junction for Herradura and other smaller beachside villages nearby. Southbound buses generally do not enter Jacó — you'll have to head out to the highway and flag one down.

WHERE TO STAY
EL JARDÍN, *tel. 64[3]3050, fax 64[3]3010. 7 rooms. $54 single/$61 double. Visa, Master Card.*

Rooms — small but attractive, with varnished woodwork, desks, stuccoed walls and tiled floors, and fans — are set in a compact, nicely landscaped compound with a pool. French-speaking owners. Continue along the entry road to Jacó, without turning onto the main street, and you'll end up at El Jardín.

HOTEL POCHOTE GRANDE, *P. O. Box 42, tel. 64[3]3236 (fax [2]204979 in San José). 24 rooms. $61 single/$90 double.*

An attractive Spanish-style, two-story hotel in a quiet garden compound. Rooms have plain furnishings, high ceilings, tiled bathroom, mini-refrigerator, and terrace. Pool. Usually booked solid in the dry season. German spoken.

HOTEL JACÓ BEACH, *tel. 64[3]3032. (P. O. Box 962-1000 San José, tel. [2]201441). 130 rooms and suites. $88 single/$100 double. U.S. reservations, tel. 305-871-6631 or 800-272-6654; Canada, tel. 800-463-6654.*

The main hotel building, a newer building and cottages are spread out on extensive grounds — kids have lots of space to run around. Rooms are large, and all are air-conditioned, some have refrigerator and TV. Amenities include a pool for adults and one for kids, tennis courts, casino, travel service, pool tables, and other games. The disco can be noisy. Most of the facilities are showing signs of wear, and food choices are quite limited for a large resort hotel. Transportation arrangements can be made through the Hotel Irazú in San José.

HOTEL COPACABANA, *P. O. Box 150, tel. and fax 64[3]3131. 28 rooms $50 single/$62 double, $85 in suite, lower from May to November. Reservations in British Columbia: tel. 604-731-2665, fax 604-682-2766.*

A new, two-story hotel Canadian-operated, with the advantage of a beachside location and pool. Caters mainly to charter groups. Some units have air-conditioning or cooking facilities.

HOTEL COCAL, *tel. 64[3]3067. 26 rooms. $33 to $39 single/$49 to $56 double.*

Low-slung, Spanish-style, with most rooms off arched passageways around the two pools in the courtyard. A few rooms face the water, at the higher rates. The architecture, and the use of fans even in outdoor areas, keep this hotel much cooler than most others. Very attractive dining area overlooking the beach. Reserve through Hotel Galilea in San José.

VILLAS ESTRELLAMAR, *P. O. Box 33, tel. 64[3]3102, fax 64[3]3453. 20 units. $57 double, less in low season. Visa, Master Card.*

Large and attractive stuccoed bungalows in a park-like setting around an 18-meter pool. Each unit has two double beds, a terrace, a kitchen with refrigerator, tiled bathroom, laundry area, and terrace. Thatched-roof bar, French spoken, good value.

HOTEL JACOFIESTA, *P. O. Box 38, tel. 64[3]3147, fax 64[3]3148. 84 rooms. $80 for one to four persons in housekeeping units, $66 in standard rooms.*

This is a well-thought-out and well-run establishment, of recent construction. One U-shaped section of cabina (studio) units, with pantile roof, blue-and-white painted stucco and rough wooden posts supporting an outside passageway, mimics the style of old-fashioned Costa Rican country houses. The section of hotel rooms, in three two-story buildings set around the pool, carries similar themes more subtly. Facilities include several pools, tennis court, pedal boats, and restaurant. Off-season rates may be available. All in all a very good value.

CHALET SANTA ANA, *tel. 64[3]3233. 8 units. $33 to $44, less out of season.*

Studio units in a stucco and brick building on a well-tended lot, across from the Jacofiesta. Lower-priced units sleep three, higher-priced units sleep up to five and have cooking facilities.

VILLAS MIRAMAR, tel. 64[3]3003. 9 units. $40 double/$56 for four/$70 for six. Master Card, Visa. Colonial-style cottages with kitchenettes on extensive grounds. Good value.

CABINAS EL BOHÍO. There are about ten nice, newer units here with kitchen, *in a good location near the water*. The official rate is about $45, but they'll discount them except at the busiest times. There's a pool on the somewhat overgrown grounds.

Cheap Lodging

The run of *cabinas* is generally better than elsewhere along the coast. **CABINAS ALICE**, $30 double, with front terrace and near the beach, are good for the price. **CABINAS CLARITA**, *next to El Jardín*, has rooms for $20 double with private bath, and also lockers and showers available for day trippers.

TROPICAL CAMPING is an extensive, coconut-palm-shaded area (watch where you pitch your tent), with basic sanitary facilities. Dry season only, $2 per person.

Nearby

TERRAZA DEL PACÍFICO, *P. O. Box 168, tel. 643222, fax 643424. 43 rooms. $68 single/$85 double. Five kilometers south of Jacó, along a beach.*

A standard white resort, Italian-managed, with grassy grounds, pool, casino, restaurant. Rooms are attractive, with red tile floors, and television, air-conditioning, safe-deposit box, telephone. This is a charter-class hotel, booked by tour groups. Guests can only easily use the services made available by the management.

WHERE TO EAT

LAS FRAGATAS, *right at the first intersection in Jacó*, has open-air dining with tablecloths, on a terrace surrounded by potted plants and ferns. About $6 and up for fish and beef variously prepared, and beverages made from fresh fruits. The house fish (sea bass stuffed with ham, cheese and shrimp) is good.

Just across from Las Fragatas is **LOS FAROLES**, another open-air eatery, Canadian-run, with pizza and pasta.

Modest and pleasant is **LE CAFÉ DE PARIS**, *a storefront-and-terrasse facing the main street*, with patisserie, salads, fresh-squeezed juices, croque monsieur, and burger and frites. About $4 to $6 for a light meal, or you can just have a coffee and pastry and hang out.

The **ZABAMAR** has a menu of continental fare that changes daily, but includes the like of chicken in wine or fish cooked to order. $8 to $12, open at 6 p.m.

The **GRILLE FLAMBOYANT** is currently the spot in Jacó for those who want a formal evening. Tables are available both inside, looking through windowed archways, and on a terrace. The fare is continental — steak in sauce mâitre d'hotel, fish meuniére — at $8 and up.

The **GRAN PALENQUE**, a large thatched enclosure near the Hotel Jacó Beach, has seafood and *paella*, and, mostly, sunset views. The **OYSTER** is a large, thatch-roofed pavilion along the main street, serving seafood at $10 to $25 per meal.

PANCHO VILLA'S Mexican eatery serves enchiladas and tacos, and steaks and lobster and a castle of shrimp, for $6 to $20.

And there are many, many other eateries, mostly burger and snack joints, and seafood restaurants, as well as a Chinese restaurant, which are inexpensive for fish, not so for shrimp.

SPORTS & RECREATION

The folks at Los Faroles restaurant will help make arrangements for fishing. Bicycles are rented at the hardware store and various other locations for about $1 an hour . . . not a bad idea in this spread-out town.

PRACTICAL INFORMATION

A bank is available for changing travelers checks.

Stores include a "supermarket" (a large convenience store), and a bakery. The gas station is at the south end of town.

Manglar Rent A Car, **Elegante Rent A Car**, **Budget**, and assorted other car-rental outfits have agencies at Jacó, mostly on the main street.

You'll find a self-service laundry on the main street near Villas Miramar.

QUEPOS/MANUEL ANTONIO NATIONAL PARK

Once a banana shipping center, **Quepos** ("KEH-pos") saw its fortunes decline with those of the plantations nearby. The town is now languid and shabby, with a strip of dingy sand. Who would guess that the nicest beaches in Costa Rica are just over the ridge? Read on.

Seven kilometers beyond Quepos are the perfect beaches of **Manuel Antonio National Park**, each an arc of sand curving around a bay strewn with islands of rock, and shaded by green bordering forests. All are backdropped by dramatic cliffs. **Manuel Antonio beach** is one of the few places in Costa Rica where unspoiled primary forest grows right to the high-tide mark, allowing visitors to bathe at times in the shade.

South Espadilla is the northernmost of the park's beaches, followed by calmer Manuel Antonio beach, offshore of which are some coral spots. **Third Beach** has tidal pools where brightly colored fish and eels are intermittently stranded. Last is **Puerto Escondido**, access to which is made difficult by the bordering rocky promontory.

Some of the most frequently observed animals at Manuel Antonio are marmosets — the smallest of Costa Rican monkeys — white-faced and howler monkeys, raccoons, pacas, opossums, and two-and three-toed sloths. Easily sighted seabirds includes frigate birds, pelicans, terns, and brown boobies. A network of trails winds along the sea, and all through the forest.

ARRIVALS & DEPARTURES

By Bus

Direct buses for Manuel Antonio depart from the Coca-Cola terminal in San José (Calle 16, Avenidas 1/3) at 6 a.m., noon and 6 p.m. Slower buses that terminate in Quepos depart at 7 and 10 a.m. and 2 and 4 p.m. The trip on the direct bus takes more than four hours, and can be nausea-inducing on the run down to the coast. On weekends, it's best to buy your ticket in advance at the bus company office inside the Coca-Cola market.

Pacific Transfer runs a bus called the *Silver Bullet Express* with reserved seats and snacks for $35 one way, $60 round trip from San José. *Call [2]272180 (fax [2]281015) for schedules and pickup points.*

Buses also operate along the coast to Quepos from Puntarenas, to the north; and from San Isidro de El General and Dominical, to the south.

A local bus for Manuel Antonio National Park departs about every two hours from the south end of Quepos, next to the cinema along the seafront. On weekends in the busy season, service is continuous.

By Air

Sansa, the domestic airline *(tel. [2]335330)*, usually has at least two daily flights from San José to Quepos. Fare is about $35 round trip, and inexpensive packages with hotel room are sometimes available. **Travelair** *(tel. [2]327883)* has two flights on most days of the week to Quepos from San José, fare $60 round trip.

Departing By Bus

Direct buses leave Manuel Antonio for San José at 6 a.m., noon and 5 p.m.; slower buses from Quepos at 5 and 8 a.m., and 2 and 4 p.m. For the **Pacific Transfer** express bus, *call [2]272180 in San José.*

Buses leave for Puntarenas at 4:30 a.m. and 3 p.m.; for Puriscal at 5 a.m. and noon; for Dominical and San Isidro de El General at 5:30 a.m. and 1:30 p.m.

Departing By Air

Sansa *(tel. [2]335330)* and **Travelair** *(tel. [2]327883)* usually have at least two daily flights to San José. With advance notice, Sansa will pick you up and take you to the airport in Quepos for a nominal charge. Reconfirmation of your return flight is essential.

WHERE TO STAY

HOTEL PLINIO, *P. O. Box 71, Quepos, tel. 77[0]0055. 6 rooms, 1 cabin. $50 single/$68 double, lower May through June and August through November. Visa, Master Card, American Express with surcharge.*

The Plinio is a roadhouse built into a hillside, with extensive woodwork, high thatched roof, and great balconies hung with hammocks — it looks like a big tree dwelling. Friendly owners, and good food. Rooms are near the popular bar and restaurant, but this is not a raucous all-night place. The rate includes a buffet breakfast. One kilometer out of Quepos.

HOTEL MIRADOR DEL PACÍFICO, *P. O. Box 164-6350, tel. and fax 77[0]0119. 20 rooms. $63 single/$74 double with breakfast.*

This hotel runs everywhere up a hillside, in three two-story buildings with porches, some reached with the aid of a funicular, or by bridges that fly across declivities in treehouse manner. There are two restaurants, one at the very top of the hotel's private mountain, with sea view, and steak and fish for about $15 for a full meal. German spoken.

MIMO'S HOTEL, *tel. and fax 77[0]0054. Six rooms. $74 double with fan, $91 with air conditioning.*

A cheery pink two-story roadside hotel. Rooms are huge, with large bed and sofa bed, and kitchenette, and lots of light.

HOTEL BAHÍAS, *P. O. Box 186-6350, tel. 77[0]0350, fax 77[0]0171. 10 rooms. $57 single/$75 double/$85 triple with breakfast. Visa, Master Card, American Express.*

A charming small hotel in Costa Rican country style. All rooms are air-conditioned, attractive with tile floors and rattan furniture. The larger ones, at a slightly higher price, have both a tub in the bathroom and a Jacuzzi right in the bedroom, under a skylight, with a garden hanging overhead. Informal grounds, small pool.

LA COLINA, *P. O. Box 191, Quepos, tel. 77[0]0231. Fiv e rooms. $35 single/$45 double including continental breakfast.*

A modest, homey hillside bungalow. Good value, French spoken. If you were me, you'd head here first.

COMPLEJO TURÍSTICO EL SALTO, *P. O. Box 119, Quepos, tel. 77[0]0130. Six rooms. $58 single/$75 double.*

This is one of several "private reserves" that have materialized near Manuel Antonio National Park, as at Monteverde. At El Salto, aside from the undeveloped lots that comprise the protected area, there are hilltop rooms with private bath and ceiling fans, and majestic views to Quepos and the inland mountains, but not to seaward. The entry road is quite poor.

HOTEL EL LIRIO, *P. O. Box 123, Quepos, tel. 77[0]0403. 9 rooms. $75 double ($40 May through September).*

An intimate lodging place. The rooms here are in a two-story concrete bungalow and extension, on grounds shaded by huge trees (which lodge a collection of 150 orchids). Each room has fans, tiled bath, sea views, and such nice touches as dhurries on the floor and mosquito canopy over the bed (more for decoration than from necessity). Pool and light meals.

HOTEL LA MARIPOSA, *tel. 77[0]0355, fax 77[0]0050, P.O. Box 4, Quepos. 10 rooms. $140 single/$208 double/$345 for four including two meals and service charge. U.S. reservations: tel. 800-223-6510.*

The nearly legendary Mariposa is one of the more tasteful hotels in Costa Rica, an intimate, luxury establishment in a dramatic clifftop setting. Each Mediterranean-style cottage is on two levels, with separate bedroom, beamed ceilings, deck, and unusual bathroom with interior garden. The views to the horseshoe beaches below and islets offshore are spectacular, from both the terraces and the small pool. Rates include light breakfast and full dinner with fixed menu (occasionally held up, according to reader reports, while the waiter tries to sell a horseback or boat tour). Children and credit cards are not accepted, reservations are essential. Three-and-a-half kilometers out of Quepos.

EL DORADO MOJADO, *P. O. Box 238-6350, tel. and fax 77[0]0368. 8 units. $125 with breakfast in villas, $75 in rooms; $75 and $50 in rainy season.*

This is an attractive hillside complex, modern in style and unusually well designed. The villas have large windows, like greenhouses, but with generous overhang to shade the interiors. All units are air-conditioned, the villas sleep three or four persons, smaller rooms two persons.

VILLAS NICOLAS, *tel. and fax 77[0]0538, P. O. Box 26, Quepos. 12 units/19 rooms. $81 single/$93 double, to $175 for four, lower from May through November. No credit cards.*

These are ocean-view, Mediterranean-style condominium units in the semi-manicured hillside jungly setting common to hotels at Manuel Antonio. Water cascades down from the whirlpool into a large swimming pool, with a stone and wooden deck. Each unit has one or two bedrooms rented individually or in combination, Spanish-style furnishings, kitchen, tiled floors, archways, and white walls with generous wood trim. The larger "villas" are on two levels, and most have ample terraces, and cooking facilities.

EL COLIBRÍ, *P. O. Box 94, Quepos, tel. 77[0]0432. 10 units. $75 double, less in rainy season.*

Gilles and Pierre offer good taste in their compound — rooms with tiled floors, varnished beams, louvered doors, and cooking facilities. The hilltop Mediterranean-style units, back from the road, across the gardens (where something is always in bloom) are the nicest, with porches and hammocks. 4.2 kilometers from Quepos.

LA QUINTA, *P.O. Box 76, Quepos, tel. 77[0]0434. 5 units. $65 to $75 double.*

This is an intimate hilltop hotel, with extensive grounds and magnificent sea views, a somewhat less pretentious version of the Mariposa. Mediterranean-style cottages all have three beds, tiled showers, terra cotta floors, and small refrigerator and hot plate. An "overflow" unit is less desirable. The personable owners, a French-Hungarian couple, are on-site to see to guests' needs. Pool. Breakfast and beverages available. 4.5 kilometers from Quepos. (The owners and I buy our sheets at the same store. They can explain.)

At the Beach

CABINAS ESPADILLA has 20 units with cooking areas for $28 single/$35 double, more with a separate kitchen. The rate drops substantially during the rainy season, except in July.

The **VELA BAR** (*P. O. Box 13, Quepos, tel. 77[0]0413*) has seven attractive rooms for $28 single/$40 double, $10 additional with air conditioning.

Next door is **VILLA BOSQUE** (*tel. 77[0]0463, fax 77[0]0401*), a new hotel with 13 frilly rooms, the nicest in this less-than-top-notch area. The rate is $80 double with air conditioning, $70 with fan. They have a restaurant and parking with 24-hour guard, and the service is friendly.

HOTEL KAMUK, *P. O. Box 18, tel. 77[0]0379, fax 77[0]0171. 28 rooms. $57 single or double.*

If you stay right in town, either by choice or because everything on the way to the park is taken, this brand-new three-story seafront hotel is several cuts above everything else. The halls are bright and airy with skylights and light wells, and the rooms are better than those in most of the resorts, with carpeting, two large beds, air conditioning, wallpaper and generally pleasing decor, phone, television, and terrace. No pool or spectacular views, unfortunately, but a good value for this area.

Aside from the Kamuk, there are several modest hotels where you can get a reasonably priced room if everything on the way to the park is filled, or too expensive for your budget. The **HOTEL VIÑA DEL MAR** looks out on the muddy beach, which is the best view downtown. The seafront grounds are pleasant, but the rooms are just cubicles with attached toilet and shower. $15 and up for a double. The places back toward the bus station all charge less, and give you less.

On the edge of town toward the road to Manuel Antonio, the **HOTEL QUEPOS**, *tel. 77[0]0274*, has cubicles and a family atmosphere for $20 double, or $25 with private bath. The **HOTEL CECILIANO**, *tel. 77[0]0192*, at $35 double with private bath, is somewhat better, and can provide parking in the courtyard. **CABINAS EL TAURO** and **CABINAS DOLLAR** charge somewhat less, and are adequate.

WHERE TO EAT

Read the menu carefully if you stop into any restaurant on the road to Manuel Antonio. Despite modest appearances and even more modest offerings in a few cases, some of the prices are shockers.

EL BYBLOS, the French hostelry, easily has the most dramatic dining environment south of San José, a tremendous porch with towering roof, hung with basket lamps, entered by a hardwood stairway over the fountain and pool, looking out over a jungle valley. This is a formal restaurant.

The **HOTEL PLINIO**, *one kilometer out of Quepos*, has a bar and restaurant with good German and Italian food. The bread is home-baked, the salads are crisp, and I can recommend the lasagne. There are also pizzas and steaks. $7 and up for a main course. If you're not staying at the Plinio, it's worthwhile to go over for a drink and a meal.

The **BARBA ROJA** bar, *opposite the Divisamar*, commands the same magnificent sea and cliff views available from the Hotel Mariposa. There are assorted daily specials for $8 and up, burgers for a couple of dollars, and rock music.

The **URUGUAYAN STEAK HOUSE** is a large indoor-outdoor eating area with *fogata* where the meat is genuinely charred in pampa fashion. Steaks and kebabs go for $10 to $14, and some unusual items like red (*sic*) salmon are on the menu at a higher price.

Various other eateries offer pricey French or continental food. **LA BRISE**, *near the entry to La Quinta*, has a light, white, gardeny, all-windows decor, and such fare as pepper steak, suprâme de poulet and fettucine pistou at $10 and up for the main course alone. **LA ARCADA**, Italian-style and one of the first restaurants on the road to the park, is another relatively pricey joint, at $8 for ravioli, $15 for a fish-and-beef kebab.

KAROLA'S RESTAURANT, *down in a valley off the main road*, is an open-air but intimate bar and dining area, overlooking a forest. $10 and up. Locals rave about the food.

Of several eateries at beach level, the most popular is the large, open-air **MAR Y SOMBRA**, *located where the road from Quepos meets the beach*. A whole fried fish goes for $4 and up, depending on the size, and there are huge tropical fruit plates, breakfasts (from 6 a.m.), the usual rice-and-bean combos, and beef and pork main courses for $4 to $6.

In Quepos itself, you'll find numerous places in which to eat inexpensively in clean surroundings. **EL GRAN ESCAPE**, *on the main street*, serves Tico food in a large room with lamps dangling from the ceiling and posters decorating the walls. Breakfast or a full meal of casado can cost under $5. Wine available. Popular with visitors looking for food without pretense. **MAR BLUES**, *on a side street by the Hotel Kamuk*, has large hamburger platters with fries, daily specials, breakfasts, and drinks of all sorts.

GEORGE'S AMERICAN, *on the way toward Manuel Antonio*, is on a corner and open to the street, serving burgers, Mexican *antijotos*, and seafood in preparations that change daily. At the **NAHOMI** pool (see below), along the water south of town, the terrace restaurant serves sandwiches, fish, and Costa Rican specialties in pleasant surroundings at surprisingly low prices — as little as $7 for a meal with a small steak.

VISITING MANUEL ANTONIO PARK

Despite the sometimes frenzied activity at Espadilla beach, things turn peaceful as soon as you cross a stream (wading in the rainy season) and enter the park. Check the depth by watching others cross. If you plan to swim, leave your camera and valuables at your hotel desk.

Visiting hours are from 8 a.m. to 4 p.m.

Take a good look at the map posted at the entrance, and plan your route — trails are not well-marked. Take note of the illustrated signs warning of the *manzanillo de playa*, a tree with poisonous, apple-like fruits, and sap that irritates the skin.

Caution is advisable when swimming here. Red Cross personnel are on hand at busy times, but otherwise, there are no provisions for beach safety, and the currents are notoriously tricky. Stay out of water deeper than your waist.

SIGHTS AROUND QUEPOS

If you continue straight after entering Quepos, past the left turn for Manuel Antonio, and go down toward the docks, then take a half left, you can climb the hill to the old **banana company** residential compound, a suburb of pleasant, uniform, tan clapboard bungalows with red tin roofs, set behind fences on well-manicured grounds shaded by huge palms. There are sport and community centers, including one of the largest swimming pools around, and views that rival those available from the resort hotels of the area.

The houses are owned by Standard Fruit, and populated by Costa Rican managers, not gringos. It's all quite a contrast to the town below. By the way, the roads are private, and you're not supposed to enter the compound, but foreigners who can't read the signs are not chased away.

Down below the fruit company homes, if you continue along the shore and around the bend about a half-kilometer from town, you'll come to **Paradero Turístico Nahomi**, which is a sort of public-resort-complex-without-hotel, a series of concrete-and-stone terraces on a rocky point of land almost surrounded by water. Here you'll find an inexpensive and pleasant shaded outdoor restaurant, open from 11 a.m.; and two **pools** and dressing rooms, which you can use from 9 a.m. on for a small fee. The surroundings are palms and plants, and except for some nearby warehouses, the scene is as pleasant as you'll find in the area.

Slightly off the tourist track is foggy **Londres** ("London"), a farming village which you can reach on a driving or mountain-bike excursion through scenery more hilly and interesting than what you see as you travel down the coastal highway. To head to London, take the turn north, about four kilometers past the first entry to Quepos, near the airstrip. A dirt road meanders through palms, pastured hills, and sugar-cane plantings. About ten kilometers on is a steel suspension bridge, more impressive than those right on the highway, over a river that rushes over boulders even in the dry season. And just beyond is Londres proper, an out-of-the-old-days hamlet populated by barefoot peasants of no pretense, with whom, if you choose, you can raise elbows with a refreshment at the Club Social Londinense.

SPORTS & RECREATION AROUND QUEPOS
Rafting

Ríos Tropicales, the rafting-and-kayaking travel agency, has a local office on the road to the park, *tel. 77[0]0574.*

Amigos del Mar (tel. 77[0]0082), with an office in Quepos, runs full-day white-water rafting trips for $60-$70, as well as more restful float trips.

Diving

Amigos del Mar operates dive trips at about $65, and an introductory course for $100, full certification for $300. The Quepos area, however, is not particularly noted for diving.

Fishing

Sportfishing Costa Rica *(P.O. Box 115-1150 La Uruca, tel. [2]339135 in San José, 77[0]0505 in Quepos, 800-374-4474 U.S.-Costa Rica direct)*, on the road that runs along the water south of town, and **Costa Rica Dreams** *(P. O. Box 79-4005 San Antonio de Belén, tel. 77[0]0593 in Quepos)*, offer deep sea fishing at $450 to $650 per day for up to four persons.

Longer fishing or naturalist trips are available to Drake Bay on the Osa Peninsula, Corcovado National Park, and Caño Island. Sportfishing Costa Rica has its own hotel, the **DORADO MOJADO**, with kitchenette units and clubhouse, and shuttle to Quepos. **Treasure Hunt Tours** *(P. O. Box 187, Quepos, tel. 77[0]0345)* has boats for inshore fishing. Inquire at La Buena Nota or at your hotel.

All sportfishing operations counsel you to release your catch. In any case, there's no easy way to bring your trophy home.

Sightseeing from a Boat

One goal of day-trippers from Manuel Antonio is **Isla de Damas**, which, despite the name, is no island, but a peninsula, ten kilometers up the coast from Quepos. The floating restaurant-bar **Tortuga** serves meals of fresh fish at about $6. To get aboard, turn off the coastal highway at the Pepsi-Tortuga sign. The estuary is one kilometer onward. Little motorboats will take you out to the Tortuga, or you can hire them by the hour to cruise through jungle-lined channels.

This is a beautiful, fascinating area, off the usual visitors' track, with secluded vacation homes and fishermen's shacks along the water. You can get here by taxi, or Erick at the Hotel Divisamar will put a group together for a trip in his van. Several tour operators charge about $65 for a boat ride through the Damas estuary, with lunch at the floating restaurant, but you can do it yourself for about a fourth (or maybe a fifth) of that price.

Costa Rica Dreams *(tel. 77[0]0593)* operates a half-day tour that might be a better value. For $200, up to four passengers are carried to various coastal points, including rookeries of frigatebirds and boobies. Departures are at 8 a.m. and 1 p.m., and beverages and fruit are included.

Horseback Riding

Stable Eqqus *(tel. 77[0]0355)*, among others, has riding horses available. Inquire at the Hotel La Mariposa.

Gambling

The casino is at the **Hotel Kamuk** in Quepos.

PRACTICAL INFORMATION

Some of Manuel Antonio's touristic development has spilled down into Quepos, in the form of a few shops and services for tourists. One beachwear outlet, **La Buena Nota** *(tel. 77[0]0345)*, at the entrance to Quepos, has used books, and owners who are said to be helpful to disoriented tourists. Among other facilities are a bank, and, at the highway junction, a gas station. **Elegante Rent A Car** has an agency, tel. *77[0]0115*.

Various small businesses have horses for hire, scuba and snorkeling equipment; beach chairs, surfboards and umbrellas to rent, and offer boat tours of Damas Island, or dinner cruises.

CHIRRIPO NATIONAL PARK

Northeast of San Isidro, in the Talamanca mountains, is **Chirripó National Park**, which includes Cerro Chirripó, at 3,820 meters (12,530 feet) the highest mountain peak in Costa Rica. The habitat of the park ranges from rocky, frigid heights and glacial lakes to the stunted, windblown *páramo* of the harsh altitudes of the tropics, to oak and evergreen forest, highland meadows, and cloud forest. Wildlife at Chirripó is not as varied as at some of the lowland reserves, but includes pumas, mountain goats, rabbits, and tapirs, among others. *Quetzals* can be sighted at lower altitudes.

There are several trails to Chirripó peak. The ascent generally takes two days. The usual route is through **El Termómetro** (The Thermometer), a climb where the visitor measures if he has what it takes to continue; then up cliffs and across valleys and plains to **Valle de los Crestones**, where shelters are available, with wood stoves and basic washing facilities.

With an early start on the second day, a climber can beat the clouds to the peak of Chirripó, four kilometers distant. Those who make it to the top are rewarded with views not only of two oceans, but of the chain of mountain and volcanic peaks marching to the northwest toward San José, and valleys and lakes along the way. An alternate way down, on the third day, is by way of **Sabana de los Leones**, with its concentration of birds and cold streams.

Before going to the park, verify current conditions and bus schedules with the National Park Service at the zoo in San José, *or call [2]334070.* February, March and April are the best months for a visit, with the least rainfall. December and January are also relatively dry, but colder. Water, warm clothing, and hiking boots are requisites — this is not a park for casual drop-ins. Horses are available to assist hikers with their gear.

ARRIVALS & DEPARTURES

By Bus or Car

Access to Chirripó Park is via bus at 5 a.m. or 2 p.m. from San Isidro to the village of San Gerardo de Rivas, where park headquarters are located, or by four-wheel-drive vehicle through San Gerardo de Rivas to the park entrance, which is 15 kilometers from San Isidro.

WHERE TO STAY

Accommodations in San Gerardo are available at the *cabinas* of the **ELIZONDO FAMILY** *(public phone [7]710433, extension 106)*, with private bathrooms, and meals can be prepared.

CORCOVADO NATIONAL PARK

Corcovado National Park, *in the southern part of the Osa Peninsula*, includes vast stretches of the only virgin lowland rain forest in Central America. Among the natural treasures of Corcovado are trees of 500 species (including one kapok, or silk-cotton, that is said to be the largest tree in Costa Rica); numerous endangered mammals, among them cougars, jaguars, ocelots, margays, jaguarundis and brocket deer; eagles and macaws; assorted monkeys; snakes; tapirs; and peccaries, which may be the most destructive and dangerous species in the park.

Vegetation zones range from mountain rain forest down to beach, and fresh-water and mangrove swamps. At **La Llorona**, a river empties in a waterfall directly into the ocean.

SEEING THE SIGHTS

You don't just drop into Corcovado. With its remote location, Corcovado attracts mainly scientific researchers, and visitors on all-inclusive packages with boats, buses and oxcarts organized beforehand. There are extensive trails along the beach and in the forested interior, however, as well as campsites. You can do Corcovado on your own if you're prepared with camping equipment, rain protection, high boots, snakebite kit, food, water containers and purification means, and repellent against the sandflies that infest the beaches. For walking along the beaches and up the beds of rivers, old sneakers, rafting sandals or surf shoes will come in handy.

Check with the park service in San José before any visit to Corcovado, or at least with the park office in Puerto Jiménez *(tel. [7]785036)*. Allow for contretemps — chartered planes that don't show up to airlift you out, never-ending downpours, bogged-down buses, etc.

Admission to the park costs about $2. Meals are currently available at ranger stations at $4 for breakfast, $6 for lunch or dinner; though there is no guarantee that vittles will be available if you just drop in. Advise park headquarters in Puerto Jiménez of your scheduled whereabouts, when possible.

There are no sheltered bays along this stretch of coast, and the breakers are often over ten feet high. Sharks frequent the waters off the entire face of the peninsula (in case you doubt it, look at the skulls that decorate lodges and the general store in Carate). Swimming should be ruled out, except for a wade near shore. Sharks also swim into the rivers of Corcovado when the water is over a meter deep.

Ridges of high jungle run parallel to the beach of pebbles and black sand, split from each other by meandering rivers. Birding is excellent from any vantage point along the beach, (viewing along interior trails in the park may be limited by the close foliage and lack of windows). The **Madrigal River**, about two kilometers from La Leona station, is marked by a boulder beach, where broad waves crash against the gentle curve of coast.

Carate, about a kilometer past the eastern edge of Corcovado Park, is a *pulpería* (general store), a dirt landing strip, and a rusting sluice that remains from the days when gold panning was legal. This is the end of the dirt road around the edge of Osa from Puerto Jiménez, and some camper vehicles make it this far and use the beach as a base for exploring the park.

If you're coming out of the park here, you can currently find a ride on Mondays, Wednesdays and Saturdays at 11 a.m. in a car operated by **Transportes Carate-Jiménez**. From Puerto Jiménez, departures are at 7:30 a.m. on the same days.

CORCOVADO PARK TIPS

Walkers regularly transit the park on their own, and most make it through without incident. This doesn't mean that a solo trip is absolutely safe. Do you know what to do if you encounter a group of peccaries? Are they more dangerous if they're moving or if they're stationary and feeding? Are you equipped to deal with snake bites? How about sharks in rivers? You are probably okay if you stick to the beach, but a walk through the interior of the park is best attempted with a qualified guide.

WHERE TO STAY IN CARATE

CORCOVADO LODGE TENT CAMP. *Reservations: **Costa Rica Expeditions**, P.O. Box 6941, San José, tel. [2]570766, fax [2]571665. Package rate from $225 with air travel from San José and meals, one night's lodging. Additional nights $50 single/$80 double with meals.*

A more formal lodge will eventually be built on the site of Corcovado Lodge Tent Camp, but I don't think it could ever come close to the sense of adventure and romance of the current facility.

This is modern adventure tourism. Guests walk from the Carate airstrip, while luggage and Cokes and beer are transported on a donkey cart with pneumatic tires, led by a teenaged, nature-boy native guide in muscle shirt, shorts and mud boots, who is as much a part of the scenery as the green cliffs overhead, where scarlet macaws flit in and out of the palms and a huge wild fig engages in life-and-death struggle with a strangler fig — except that the *arriero* maintains contact with base via the VHF radio strapped to his waist. A major mishap in this neck of the country is a collision of the donkey cart with a rock, sending a case of beer over the side, to pop and foam into the sand.

The custom-built tents at Corcovado Lodge, screened and with rain flaps, are erected close to each other on a ledge about fifteen feet above the beach. Each is on a platform at sitting height above an individual porch, oriented toward the beach and sunset, and no furniture is provided other than two beds of foam on boards and sapling legs. In front, hammocks are set in the palms. The surf roars below into the night, fades as if turned down, then pounds again. Electrical lighting is limited; the sun plummets after 6 p.m., and reappears at about 5:45 a.m.

Set, plentiful meals are served in a hillside dining pavilion, and there are a couple of toilet-shower houses on the way up. Behind the lodge, a trail leads up the hillside. Spottings may include scarlet macaws, spider monkeys, and the tiny green poison-arrow frog, among others.

Horseback excursions are available from Corcovado Lodge at an extra charge. Several excursions into the park are recommended, but most packages do not include any guided walks or hikes.

SOUTH OF PUERTO JIMÉNEZ

The lush, rolling landscape south of Puerto Jiménez is cattle country, sprinkled with surviving and second-growth forest, ponds where ducks and geese putter about, and plots of fast-growing pulp trees where cleared and burned-off forest produced luxuriant pasture and abundant crops only until the ashes and humus were exhausted and the hard clay below had nothing more to yield. The bumpy road south fords assorted rivers and streams; bridges are being installed, in some cases by the U.S. Army Corps of Engineers, and National Guard units. The farms and pastures soon diminish in numbers and extent, for there are only limited accessible markets.

WHERE TO STAY SOUTH OF PUERTO JIMÉNEZ

LAPA RÍOS, *P. O. Box 100, Puerto Jiménez, tel. [7]785130. 14 bunga-lows. $115 per person with meals and transfers.*

In the jungle near the southern tip of the Osa Peninsula, atop a hill that commands the vicinity, a thatched roof of epic proportions marks Lapa Ríos, the most luxurious tropical-forest lodge in Costa Rica.

Within rises another remarkable structure, a great interior treehouse, its several platforms, attained by a handcrafted cantilevered circular staircase, affording vistas through breaches in the thatch to dense forest stands, cliffs, beaches, and Punta Banco on the far side of the gulf. Below, awed diners converse in whispers, over the finest cuisine in a remote area, and perhaps some of the best anywhere outside San José.

All this, and much more, is Lapa Ríos, a personal dream — and devil — of John and Karen Lewis. Both ex-Peace Corps volunteers, they have given it all up and bet the bank on regenerating several hundred hectares of rain forest, with which the hotel is legally and permanently intertwined.

Guest units at Lapa Ríos — each a suite — have huge view decks, thatched roofs, screens and bamboo shades, and private garden with shower. One has a ramp for disabled accessibility. They are built on several parts of the property, some close to the sea, some high up, all within hearing and viewing range of squirrel monkeys, toucans, and the macaws that lend their name to the resort. The pool is cleaned by an ion filter, rather than chlorine.

Beyond the magnificence and comfort of the site, with its trails through forests to falls, natural pools and beaches, there are tours in and around the peninsula on offer, along with boat trips to Caño Island.

Transport to the lodge is arranged when booking.

BOSQUE DEL CABO WILDERNESS LODGE, *6 cottages. $80 single/ $120 double with meals. Reserve through Costa Rican Trails, P. O. Box 2907-1000, San José, tel. [2]224547, fax [2]213011. In Puerto Jiménez, inquire at Mini Mercado El Tigre.*

Bosque del Cabo is a comfortable lodge *in* the wilderness, near Cape Matapalo, 1.5 kilometers off the track that twists and meanders around the Osa Peninsula. Ample bungalows set on the cliff edge beyond manicured lawns and gardens offer stunning views to window rocks and deserted beaches. Varnished local woods are used entirely in construction and panelling. There are louvers on all sides, an outdoor shower in a private garden, more than sufficient shelving, mosquito netting over the beds, sapling posts to support the porches. One cottage is divided for use by families. Dining is in a central open thatched-roof structure, and, befitting the Italian-Costa Rican heritage of the lady of the manor, includes home-made pasta.

Activities here include hikes, including one to a falls with three pools; a walk down to the beach, birding, and horseback riding (about $20); though this is a superb site for reading, meditating, and being left alone.

Much of the lodge property is regenerating forest, with some plantings by the owners, Phil and Barbara Spiers. They are also making practical arrangements to stop the smuggling of fledgling macaws out of the peninsula.

ZANCUDO

Think of **Zancudo** as a tropic isle. A beach village south of Golfito, Zancudo can be reached overland if you have a sturdy vehicle and no schedule, or if the bus is running on the day you go. But most of the connections are by water.

"Zancudo" (san-KU-do) is the Spanish word for a particularly vexatious mosquito; though you will usually not be bothered if there is any kind of breeze. The settlement sprawls along five kilometers or so of beach, and at most of the lodging places, you'll see sand, breakers, mangrove, coconut palms, and maybe another building down the way a bit, if at all. Surfers have come here for years, and now there is just enough in the way of amenities to make Zancudo the right place for anyone who requires a beach without Big Tourism.

ARRIVALS & DEPARTURES
Arriving By Bus or Taxi
A bus sometimes leaves for Zancudo and Pavones from Golfito daily at 2 p.m. Check first if it's going all the way or will terminate ten kilometers from the beaches. A taxi costs about $50.

Arriving By Car and Ferry
If you're driving to Playa Zancudo from Golfito, take the road back toward the Pan American Highway, then turn right onto the unpaved road about halfway along, at the El Rodeo saloon. About 18 kilometers from the junction is a flat-bottom jungle cable ferry over the Coto River (great photo opportunity). Operating hours are from 5 a.m. to 8 p.m., the fare under $2. Beyond the ferry, the road is unpaved, and in parts is best negotiated with four-wheel-drive and high clearance, or not at all. Take every right turn through the jungle and scrub farms, and you'll get to Zancudo in under two hours when conditions are good.

Arriving By Boat
To reach Zancudo by boat (or to arrange fishing), inquire at the docks or Luis Brenes' restaurant in Golfito. Since Zancudo sprawls for several kilometers along the gulf, and traffic is sparse, you should tell your boat driver where you want to land: at the center of the village, or farther south along the beach near Cabinas Los Cocos or the Hotel Sol y Mar.

At low tide, passenger boats swing out into the open waters of the gulf, past deserted beaches, run past rain forest and cliffs that reach to the water's edge, and circle around sand bars at the mouth of the Coto Colorado River to the beach. At high tide, a shorter routing is available via "La Trocha," the old banana-shipping canals that cut through the peninsula opposite Golfito. This is a more reassuring route.

Departing By Boat
From the village, you can often get aboard a return boat for Golfito at the dock on the inland side; or ask for Mauricio nearby at the general store with the sign for a public phone, or at your hotel.

WHERE TO STAY/WHERE TO EAT
From south to north, the accommodations and facilities at Zancudo are these:
Four kilometers from Zancudo Point and the Coto Colorado River

are various accommodations operated by Rainer Kremer, who speaks in a patois of German, English and Spanish, never stands still, and appears to have stepped out of the movie *"Fitzcarraldo."* His informal **TRANQUILO RESTAURANT**, ever expanding, *sits across the road from the beach*, amid pens of turtles and ducks, facing a private mangrove jungle. Expect to find the unexpected: chicken in walnut sauce, garlic fish, Linzensuppe, at $5 to $10 for a meal. Upstairs is **FIN DEL MUNDO**, four guest rooms mit verandah und hammock, about to be enveloped by strangler figs, at $10 per person.

 HOTEL SOL Y MAR *(P. O. Box 88, Golfito), tel. [7]750353*, has four designer units in the palms, geodesic domes with tin roofs. Owners are Bob and Monika Hara, who speak English and German. The restaurant here serves Tico and American food—eggs, sandwiches, steamed vegetable, chef's salad — at $4 per item or less.

 CABINAS LOS COCOS, run by long-time beach resident Susan England and Andrew Robertson, has two cheery doll-house clapboard cottages (another architectural story, being relocated United Fruit Company houses), in an informal tropical garden with friendly parrots. Each unit has a refrigerator and stove, mosquito netting over the beds, and decks with table and chairs, and can sleep three, at $30 per day. The owners also have a silkscreen printing operation, and arrange boat excursions to the orchid gardens and to other beaches. They can be reached through the phone at the Hotel Sol y Mar, which is about 100 meters away.

 North of Cabinas Los Cocos, the two kilometers to the point are slightly more densely built. The Hotel-Restaurant-Bar **PITIER**, also known as **FROYLAN'S**, *tel. [7]773006*, is a Tico family-style compound. $10 per person gets a room with fan and private bathroom. Nearby, **EL COQUITO** is a similar place with a big thatch-roofed bar, subject to weekend invasions of loud music. Plain family-size rooms with bath and fan go for about $15 each.

 Roy's **LOS ALMENDROS** *(P. O. Box 41, Golfito, 10 rooms, $15 single/ $25 double, tel. [7]750515)* is a neat, fishing-camp kind of establishment, of substantial, cement-board, motel-style rooms facing seaward on palm-shaded lawns. Each has a bath and overhead fans. Meals and beverages are served to residents and walk-ins. You can also rent a 22-foot fishing boat at $250 for the day, with radio, sonar, meals and the rest.

 CABINAS RÍO MAR, *down near the point*, consists of an old yellow-painted railroad work car, and a set of six plain railroad-style guest units with bath and fan. About $8 per person, and more basic than other places.

AROUND THE VOLCANOES - OR ALL OF COSTA RICA IN ONE DAY!

North of San José, over and beyond the volcanoes Irazú and Poás, is an area that includes gently rolling pastured hillsides often shrouded in fog; high montane tropical forest barely touched by human settlement and exploitation; hot springs gurgling up from the interior of the earth; jungle dripping with heat and wet; homesteads hacked out of the forest by modern pioneers; and banana lands that have been cultivated for more than 100 years. All this is within just 60 kilometers of San José in a straight line.

But until recently, mountains, rivers, jungle, and traditional trade routes that ran elsewhere, kept most of this triangle off the beaten track for visitors and Costa Ricans alike. Now, with the completion of a few strategic stretches of highway, it's possible to make a circular trip through this varied area in a matter of hours, even by bus. But for the lack of beaches, it's almost like seeing all of Costa Rica, and every era of its development, in just one day.

The route described below takes you clockwise from San José. But this is just one possible itinerary. You can spin off from San Carlos toward the northwest, past the sparking volcano Arenal, and down to the Pacific coastal lowlands; take a shortcut northward over the saddle between Poás and Irazú volcanoes; or continue to Limón and the Caribbean instead of returning to your starting point.

By bus or car from San José, head to the west, along the Cañas and Soto expressways, in the direction of Puntarenas. The old Pan American Highway, parallel to the newer road, passes through the towns of Alajuela, Grecia and Sarchí. At Naranjo, a sinuous branch road turns northward, up and out of the Central Valley, across the relatively low stretch of hills between the Tilarán and Central volcanic mountain ranges.

SAN CARLOS

About 48 kilometers north of Naranjo, and 95 kilometers from San José, is **Ciudad Quesada**, which most Costa Ricans call **San Carlos**, a bustling trading center for the surrounding prosperous area of meat and dairy production. San Carlos in itself does not count as a tourist attraction. But it's on the way to everywhere, and getting here, on a winding road through fog-shrouded, pastured hills, is a scenic meander.

ARRIVALS & DEPARTURES
Arriving By Bus

Buses for Zarcero and San Carlos leave hourly, or more frequently, from the Coca-Cola station, Calle 16, Avenidas 1/3, San José.

Departing By Bus

From San Carlos, you can go on by bus toward Arenal volcano, and around Lake Arenal; deep into the low-lying tropical forest north of Poás and Irazú volcanoes, and back to San José through Braulio Carrillo National Park; or even to remote Los Chiles, near the Nicaraguan border at the eastern end of Lake Nicaragua.

Some schedules, as recently posted:
- to Fortuna, 6 a.m., 6:30, and 9:30 a.m., 1, 3, 3:30 and 6 p.m.
- to Arenal and Tilarán, near the Pan American Highway, via Lake Arenal and Fortuna, at 6:30 and 9:30 a.m., 1 and 3 p.m..
- to Puerto Viejo and Río Frío, north of the volcanoes of the Central Valley, about every two hours from 5 a.m. to 5:30 p.m.
- to Los Chiles, about every two hours from 5 a.m. to 5 p.m.
- to San José, buses depart every hour from 5 a.m. to 5 p.m.

WHERE TO STAY

HOTEL CONQUISTADOR, *tel. 46[0]0546. 30 rooms. $14 single; $20 double.*

A pleasant, colonial-style building. Rooms are plain, with private bath, good for the price. Protected parking. On the edge of town, along the street that leads toward San José.

The **HOTEL CENTRAL** *(tel. 46[0]0766, 49 rooms, $16 to $24 single/ $30 to $33 double)*

On the square, a concrete, unadorned building with plain rooms that will do for the night. And there are other, lesser hostelries.

Southwest of San Carlos

VALLE ESCONDIDO LODGE *(P. O. Box 452-1150 La Uruca, tel. [2]310906, fax [2]329591).*

This new lodge is situated in a stand of primary forest, off the road that leads from San Ramón to La Tigra. Riding horses, mountain bikes and hiking trails are on-site. Most visits are arranged as a two-night package from San José, including hikes, talks, and a viewing of Arenal volcano, at about $400 per person.

North & West of San Carlos

A paved branch road runs northward through mostly flat, hot, sugarcane and citrus country, to **Los Chiles**, near Caño Negro Wildlife Reserve and the border with Nicaragua. You need not stop at the border. You can keep going all the way to the shores of Lake Nicaragua, and across it toward Managua.

LA QUINTA LODGE, *18 kilometers from Ciudad Quesada on the road to Los Chiles*, is a roadside family-style stopping place with pool, snack bar open weekends, hammocks, basketball court, and guest facilities in a large house and cottages. The rate in bunks in the cottages is about $14 per person up to eight persons accommodated in each. In the house, a large family room goes for about $40. The River San Carlos, alive with tarpon, runs alongside the property, and you're welcome to drop a line down the steep bank (strictly catch-and-release). Caimans sometimes stop and sun themselves on the rocks. *Call 46[4]0731 in Ciudad Quesada to reserve.*

TILAJARI RESORT, *Muelle de San Carlos (P. O. Box 81, Ciudad Quesada), tel. and fax 46[1]1083. 54 rooms. $70 single/$80 double. Visa, Master Card.*

Amid the sugarcane fields, along the San Carlos River, Tilajari is a full-fledged country club in facilities and appearance, except that the golf links haven't yet been installed on the acres of lawn. But you will find racquet ball, lighted tennis courts, a large pool and kids' pool, sauna, and a restaurant with a shaded terrace overlooking the River San Carlos.

Rooms are in pantile-roofed villas, and are on the plain side, with quiet central air conditioning. Suites, for only slightly more than the regular room rate, have a loft, separate bedroom, and television and refrigerator. These are more substantial facilities than anywhere else in the area, but the nicest part is the river that winds through the property, along which you might chance upon a crocodile taking a break. Riding horses are available, and trips to Arenal volcano and Caño Negro reserve, jungle walks and boating are arranged. About 21 kilometers from Ciudad Quesada.

RÍO SAN CARLOS LODGE, *P. O. Box 354-4400 Boca de Arenal (tel. 46[0]0766, fax 46[0]0391, $63 single/$80 double with breakfast).*

A lovely country house with wood-panelled rooms (one with tub inset in the floor), arched windows overlooking the San Carlos River, swimming pool, and views of Arenal volcano. The grounds are covered by trees and cultivated flowering plants. An attractive stopping point, indeed, 9 kilometers north of the junction at Muelle, but the sugar mill across the road could be a distraction at harvest times.

TOWARD NICARAGUA

To the north, the lands that roll on toward Nicaragua are being opened to settlement by new roads, constructed as part of development schemes that have led to the destruction of forests and animal life.

CAÑO NEGRO NATIONAL WILDLIFE REFUGE

Caño Negro National Wildlife Refuge was set aside to save some of the native bird species. **Lake Caño Negro**, frequented by migratory birds, covers 800 hectares in the rainy season, but dries up to a fraction of that size from February through May. Rare species here include the Nicaraguan grackle. There are also anhingas, ibis, northern jacana, roseate spoonbills, rare jabiru storks, and cormorants. Puma, jaguar, ocelots, and monkeys (spider, white-faced and howler) are found in the dry parts of the reserve.

ARRIVALS & DEPARTURES

By Car or Boat

Caño Negro is located southeast of the village of Los Chiles, which can be reached by paved road. A dirt road continues southwest past the lake, and onward toward Upala. In rainy times, the lake may be accessible only by boating up the Río Frío and Patos River from Los Chiles.

By Tour

Sertur, in San José, is one of the travel agencies that operates excursions to Caño Negro. Basic camping facilities are available.

By Bus

Buses run from Ciudad Quesada (San Carlos) to Los Chiles about every two hours from 5 a.m. to 5 p.m. One or two buses a day run between Los Chiles and Upala, passing the refuge; or, it's a walk or taxi ride of about 15 kilometers.

TOWARD SAN RAFAEL DE GUATUSO

At a remote cattle farm on the slopes of Tenorio Volcano, is **MAGIL FOREST LODGE**, with ten rooms sleeping three or four persons each, private bathrooms, and bar. Getting here is a tropical adventure, off the paved road and over a cable bridge. The rate is about $120 double with meals. A typical package trip, about $500 for three nights from San José, includes meals and lodging, a visit to caves, birding and orchid-hunting walks, horseback trips to mountain lookouts, a boat ride on the Celeste River and one through the Caño Negro reserve, and a visit to an Indian reserve. Currently, departures are Mondays and Saturdays at 8 a.m. *For information, write to P. O. Box 3404-1000, San José (Avenida 10, Calle 14), or call [2]212825, fax [2]336837.*

Contact the lodge to arrange transport by helicopter or by four-wheel-drive vehicle from San José or from an airstrip in the region.

TO ARENAL VOLCANO

The main route from San Carlos for visitors is to the northwest. A good paved road winds and curves downward, then runs through humid, cattle-grazing lowlands, toward Arenal volcano, the Tilarán mountain range, and Arenal lake and dam.

Currently, a section of road after the dam is unpaved, and passable during the rainy season only by bus or in a four-wheel-drive vehicle.

Beyond this difficult stretch are several water sports facilities on Lake Arenal, the town of Tilarán, and the Pan American Highway at Cañas.

FORTUNA

Fortuna, *45 kilometers from San Carlos*, is a pleasant and neatly laid out farming center. But its attractions lie in what is nearby: Arenal volcano; the hot springs at Tabacón; an impressive falls on the Fortuna River; caves; and fishing in Lake Arenal.

ARRIVALS & DEPARTURES

By Air

Mr. César Romero, former crop duster and proprietor of Hotel Rancho Corcovado, will shortly inaugurate an air service to Fortuna (to an airstrip adjacent to his hotel, naturally), taking passengers from San José in just fifteen minutes or so. Call 47[9]9090 for information.

By Bus

The alternative is a winding bus ride of several hours from the capital. Take one of the Ciudad Quesada (San Carlos) buses that leave the Coca-Cola terminal (Avenida 1, Calle 16) in San José every hour. In Ciudad Quesada, connect with buses that leave for Fortuna at 6, 6:30, and 9:30 a.m., and 1, 3, 3:30 and 6 p.m.

By Tour

Arenal is full of tour shops, both attached to the various lodging places and freestanding. One guide to whom I've received several recommendations by satisfied clients is Gabino, who operates from an office on the main road near the church.

Currently, the rates for excursions look to me to be a bargain: at the **Hotel Fortuna**, a volcano night tour, or a day trip to the volcano with a stop at hot springs, goes for $10 per person.

You can go on your own, of course. But prices are so reasonable, that you should probably take your first trip with somebody who knows the terrain.

WHERE TO STAY

HOTEL RANCHO CORCOVADO, *tel. and fax 47[9]9090. 30 rooms. $45 double, $15 per extra person. Weekly packages available.*

Located about eight kilometers east of Fortuna at a hamlet called Tanque (TAN-keh), Rancho Corcovado is a modern roadside lodging place with clean, tile-floored rooms, each with two or three beds with good mattresses, bedside lamps, and overhead fans, and, as they say here, a very good attention from the family headed by César Romero. There are two small TV lounges, and childrens' and adult pools. The veranda restaurant and bar at the rear overlook a river and pond where caimans pass the day, and howler monkeys and assorted other small mammals frequent the site. A tennis court is under construction.

LAS CABAÑITAS, *tel. 47[9]9091*, recently under construction on the eastern outskirts of Fortuna, will have 30 Swiss-appearing cottages of wood and stone with tile roofs, a restaurant, pool, and second-story lookout for volcano observation.

CABINAS EL TUCÁN, *tel. 47[9]9048*, is a great value for no-frills lodging if you're travelling by car: six plain, neat, clean rooms in two cottages, at about $10 per person, sharing bath. From the eastern entry to town, turn right, right again, and go 300 meters through a cow pasture, to where you can lodge just as if you were in the middle of the *campo*.

HOTEL SAN BOSCO (*27 rooms, tel. 47[9]9050, fax 47[9]9178*), *two blocks off the main street*, is the most substantial lodging place right in town. The newer section has large rooms with accoutrements such as shower doors, which raise the price, if not the comfort, to $30 single/$40 double; while the older part is good enough, with little extras like headboards on the beds, at $14 single/$24 double. And there is a third-floor observation platform for viewing Arenal's fireworks on clear nights.

HOTEL FORTUNA (*13 rooms, tel. 47[9]9197*), to the left side entering town from the east, has new, clean rooms with tile floors at $10 per person with private bath, $5 per person sharing bath. Good value.

ALBERGUE BURÍO (*Burío Inn, P. O. Box 1234-1250 Escazú, tel. 47[9]9076, or [2]280267 in San José, 8 rooms, $18 per person*) enfolds a gardened alleyway opposite the plaza. That's a modest situation, indeed, but management counts for everything here. The owners know *everything* about the area and can arrange cave and volcano trips and fishing ($30 per hour on Lake Arenal, $300 for a group on the Río San Juan in Nicaragua). Rooms have private bath and are clean and modestly attractive, with stuccoed and panelled walls and overhead fan, and a single and a bunk bed. Breakfast is included in the rate.

And there at least half a dozen other hotels and cabinas in town. **CABINAS CARMELA**, *on the main road opposite the church (tel. 47[9]9010)*, has an enclosed parking area, and rooms for $15 single/$20 double.

WHERE TO EAT

LA CHOZA DEL LAUREL (Hut of the Bay Tree), *west of the church on the main road*, is a folksy eating spot with long wooden tables set up under a rough-shingled roof, set with home-style pottery ware. You'll be ushered into the kitchen to serve yourself from pots of rice and beans, chicken and rice, tamales, and other simmering country specialties, and charged according to what you consume, from $3 to $6. Fruit drinks and herbal beverages are also served. You won't do better for wholesome fare, and you can arrive as early as you wish for breakfast.

Elsewhere, **RANCHO LA CASCADA**, *on one corner of the square*, serves a standard assortment of "international" chicken, steak and fish main courses for $5 to $7 under a high thatched roof. **EL JARDÍN**, *on the main street opposite the square*, also offers plain food in soda-shop surroundings.

SEEING THE SIGHTS

You will probably have come to Fortuna to get a closer look at Arenal volcano (see below), but while you're here, numerous other adventures are available within easy reach of your hotel base. The most distant is Caño Negro Reserve, about an hour's drive north. Other easily reached destinations are the Venado caves, just north of Lake Arenal; Lake Arenal itself, for fishing (but there are few points where you can get right down to the water); and the surrounding countryside for horseback riding and walking and birding. With some guidance, you can set out by foot for Monteverde, about 20 kilometers and several mountain ridges away.

The **Fortuna River Falls** (Catarata Río Fortuna) *are about 5.5 kilometers from town*, from a turn from the main road by the church. Follow the washboard road for 1.4 kilometers through rolling pastures, then turn right and continue another 4 kilometers. If you reach a bridge on the first road, you've gone too far. A short path leads to a viewpoint from which you can appreciate a narrow chute that plunges from the forest into the valley below. It would be a long walk out this way, but it makes for a pleasant horseback excursion or motoring detour.

Tabacón, *12 kilometers past Fortuna*, where the road drops into a lush river valley, is the site of several hot springs gushing out from near the base of Arenal volcano.

TABACÓN RESORT, once a low-priced getaway, has been rebuilt into a colonial-style country club and spa with a fee of about $12 for day use of the pool, water slides and restaurant. A hotel is under construction. Across the road and down a short path, you can enjoy no-frills bathing in steaming pools along the river for about $2.

ARENAL VOLCANO

Mount Arenal (1,633 meters), which overlooks much of the San Carlos plain and the northern Pacific lowlands, has the distinction of being the volcano in Costa Rica that most *looks* like a volcano, with its characteristic conical shape. It also acts like one, having erupted spectacularly in 1968 and spewed ashes over a wide area.

And it hasn't stopped since. On most nights, clouds of iridescent gas cling to the summit. The earth rumbles, and boulders the size of a house explode a thousand feet into the air, to a resounding orchestral accompaniment of pops and crackles and booms, and arc and fall a thousand feet back to the crater, to bounce and shatter their way down. Lava in red and orange and yellow spews and slithers along the slopes.

Nobody in his right mind climbs Arenal. Several people who have attempted to do so in recent years, including at least one tourist, have been killed. But there is no peril in observing the fireworks from a safe vantage point in the valley below, or even hiking on the *lower* part of the slopes.

Several lodges in Fortuna or closer to Arenal offer safe ringside seats, with a view from the porch of your room and across an intervening river valley to the nighttime show; others sponsor day or night excursions to favorite lookout points, and almost every travel agency in San José organizes volcano-watching excursions — just make sure before you go that recent activity has been reported, and that the weather has been clear.

Several travel agencies in San José operate day-long volcano-watching excursions to Arenal, with stops in Sarchí and at hot springs, at about $85.

About 60 kilometers from San Carlos, the road drops to beautiful, mountain-girt Lake Arenal, crossing the earthen dam that separates the lake from its natural drainage, the Arenal River.

WHERE TO STAY

ARENAL OBSERVATORY (*tel. [2]552011, fax [2]553529, $60 per person, book through travel agencies*) is a research station and set of cabins that offer ringside views of the fireworks on the volcano — at a safe distance of about two-and-a-half kilometers, separated by the valley of the Agua Caliente river. Canoes available, fishing arranged. This facility may be closed at times to the public; or inaccessible except with four-wheel-drive vehicle. Taxi fare from Fortuna is $25 or more.

At kilometer 61, a rough branch road leads over hills for two kilometers to **POSADA ARENAL** (**ARENAL LODGE**), *tel. 46[1]1881 (P. O. Box 1139-1250, Escazú), tel. [2]282588, fax [2]282798). 11 rooms. $63 to $86 single/$74 to $97 double, $97/$114 in suite. Visa, Master Card, American Express.*

Arenal Lodge is a ringer for a white summer cottage that you might find near a lake in New England. Mostly, it's a fishing lodge, and boats with guides for lake fishing are available at $150 per day for two. They'll also arrange tarpon fishing near the Nicaraguan border, and lake, hot springs and volcano-watching expeditions, and horseback riding. The suite is a huge room with dark wood panelling, large tub, and a privileged view of Arenal volcano from its private balcony.

Though it can be continuously rainy in this area, there is a large patio hung with plants and birds in cages, sheltered by translucent roofing, and with a fireplace to chase away chills. Geese run around on the grassy hills, under the palms. Billiard table available. December and January are the rainiest times here, when Caribbean clouds reach this area. Call the lodge before you visit for current fishing and volcano-viewing conditions (in English).

HOTEL LOS HÉROES *(P. O. Box 6083-1000 San José). 12 rooms. $80 to $110 double.*

This is not an imitation of a Swiss chalet, it *is* a Swiss chalet (or several of them, actually), perched on a hillside farm above Lake Arenal, about 10 kilometers past the dam, dedicated to Juan Santamaría and Arnold von Winkelried. Rooms have wall-to-wall carpeting, and plenty of hot water. The restaurant at Los Héroes serves fondue, of course (about $10), and has the most extensive wine list in the area.

Continuing Around the Volcanoes

EL TUCANO COUNTRY CLUB, *Agua Caliente de San Carlos, tel. [4]461822, fax 461692 (P. O. Box 114-1017, San José 2000, office at Paseo Colón, Calles 24/26, tel. and fax 219095). 40 rooms. $64 single/$77 double/ $89 triple.*

El Tucano is a tropical spa and rain-forest country club, on an absolutely lovely estate of colonial-style buildings, with tennis and volley-ball courts and carefully tended gardens, at an elevation of 950 meters. There is no other place like it in Costa Rica. The grounds are traversed by a river of warm mineral water (said to be curative for arthritis and degenerative diseases), which feeds the medicinal Jacuzzi. There are also saunas, three swimming pools (including one for children), a miniature golf course, horses ($5 per hour), nature trails, and a casino, which guests are encouraged to patronize.

Meals are served in a huge dining room, decorated with woven mats and paintings of toucans, to the soothing accompaniment of the rushing stream just beyond the lattice. Food is largely Italian-style, and well prepared, and prices are moderate, at about $7 for most main courses.

Anybody can dine at El Tucano, and non-guests may use the facilities for a small fee. Round-trip transportation from San José costs $120 for up to six persons. If you're driving, look for the large white gate on the north side of the road to Puerto Viejo.

Beyond La Virgen, near the farthest point that you can go from San José on this road, is:

SELVA VERDE LODGE, *Chilamate, tel. 71[6]6459. 50 rooms. $80 single/$130 double in River Lodge; $130 double to $184 for four persons in* *bungalows, including meals and taxes. U.S. reservations: 3540 NW 13 St., Gainesville, FL 32609, tel. 800-858-0999, fax 904-371-3710.*

Located on a 500-acre farm and private reserve, with both well-manicured gardens and wild areas. Buildings are joined by a long, thatch-covered passage. The River Lodge, with most guest rooms, consists of several buildings on posts, connected by elevated walkways, projecting guests *into* the forest canopy. Rooms in this section have private bathrooms. A new combination dining room and bar overlooks the river. Across the road from the check-in area, and up a hillside, are five secluded bungalows, with space for up to four persons.

Aside from birding and jungle walks and horseback rides on the lodge properties and in nearby reserves, Selva Verde is a good base for river fishing and rafting. All kinds of trekking, cycling and rafting excursions can be arranged through the Florida office. Reservations are essential. You can also drop in and use the trails as a day visitor for a fee of about $5. A facility with shared baths accommodates groups, and conference facilities are available.

PUERTO VIEJO DE SARAPIQUI

Seventy kilometers from San Carlos or Heredia, **Puerto Viejo** was, until a few years ago, the end of the road, whence one traveled onward only by light cargo boat on the Sarapiquí River, toward the San Juan River and Barra del Colorado on the Caribbean. Before peace broke out in Nicaragua, much of this area was effectively off limits to outsiders; but it has a colorful history as the fluvial highway to the interior used by William Walker and other adventurers and filibusterers of the last century.

A road extension now provides a way through to the south and east, though you might still be able to negotiate your way aboard a river boat, and make a round trip back to San José via the Tortuguero reserve and Limón. Patience and a flexible schedule would be absolute requirements for such a journey, as floods and fancy play havoc with promised departures. A surer way to float the river is on a rafting excursion organized in San José, or an inclusive trip along the Sarapiquí to Tortuguero.

ARRIVALS & DEPARTURES
Arriving By Bus

Buses operate to Puerto Viejo from Avenida 11, Calles Central/1, San José, daily at 6:30, 9, 10 (express) and 11 a.m. and 1, 3:30 (express), 4 and 5:30 p.m. Other buses taking the longer route via Heredia depart at 6 a.m., noon and 3 p.m.

Departing By Bus

Buses depart for San José at 4:30, 6:30, 8 (express) and 10:30 a.m., and 2, 3 (express) and 4:30 p.m. Slower buses via Heredia depart at 7:30 a.m. and 4:30 p.m.

Departing By Boat

Be at the dock (next to the car-repair lot) to catch the 11:30 a.m. boat down the Sarapiquí to the San Juan River on the border with Nicaragua, calling on the way at jungle river outposts. Fare is about $4 per person,

You can sleep at the basic **ORO VERDE STATION** *(call [2]349507 in San José for information)* and catch the boat at dawn to return upriver.

To keep moving in one direction, you can also charter a boat here. The fare for four people to Barra del Colorado is about $200, and for slightly more, you can get to Tortuguero National Park.

WHERE TO STAY

Here at what was a short time ago the end of the line (unless you planned to continue downriver to fight in Nicaragua), visitors' accommodations are sprouting, and by the time you pass through, travel shops should be in place to provide excursions on the Sarapiquí River from town, in addition to those offered by nearby hotels.

HOTEL MI LINDO SARAPIQUÍ, *tel. [7]766074. 6 rooms. $13 per person.*

On the entry street into Puerto Viejo, small, new rooms with over-head fans, perfectly adequate.

HOTEL EL BAMBÚ, *tel. 76[6]6005. 9 rooms. $45 single or double with breakfast, credit cards accepted.*

A substantial white concrete building across the street from Mi Lindo Sarapiquí, more attractive in the lobby (wicker furniture, plants) than in the rooms, but you get large windows, television and fan.

Lesser accommodations for under $10 per person include **CABINAS MONTEVERDE**, *next to El Bambú*; and **HOTEL GONAR**, *near the dock.*

Near Puerto Viejo

EL GAVILÁN LODGE *(P. O. Box 445-2010 San José, tel. [2]349507, fax [2]536556). Twelve rooms. $46 single/$57 double.*

El Gavilán is just north of Puerto Viejo on a turn from the road to Guápiles, between the Sarapiquí and Sucio rivers. Eight of the rooms are adjacent to the farmhouse, crowded with three beds, with basic bathrooms. Four better rooms are in an outbuilding. Bathing is available in river and whirlpool. Guests should bring their own alcoholic beverages.

El Gavilán operates day trips from San José in its own van. Birding, boating, horseback riding, jungle walks, and fishing and kayaking are either included, with transportation and meals, in the fee of about $85, or can be arranged. The owner-operators are a German and a Costa Rican.

PAST PUERTO VIEJO

A good road heads southeast around Barva volcano. Much of the land to both sides is already cleared in a rather untidy fashion. Cattle are grazing, and corn is growing. You see signs at intermittent mud tracks that lead to clusters of shacks, announcing that so-and-so many farmers have benefitted from a distribution of land. At one point along the road, there is an outpost of the *Comando Atlántico del Batallón Relámpago* (Atlantic Commando of the Lightning Battalion), in helmets and camouflage fatigues, ready to control any subversive activities in this strategic area. Pinch yourself, and remember that these are not soldiers — more blur of the distinction between army and civil guard.

Near Las Horquetas

RARA AVIS, *P. O. Box 8105, 1000 San José, tel. and fax [2]530844. The rate for accommodations is about $50 per person with meals, or $85 single/$155 double/$185 triple in rooms with private bath. From San José, add about $50 for a taxi to Las Horquetas (from where the tractor leaves at 9 a.m.), or take the 7 a.m. Río Frío bus. Reserve through travel agencies in the United States or by phone in Costa Rica, and verify that qualified guides will be on-site.*

This 1,500-acre reserve, on the site of a former prison colony, is oriented toward visitors who want to experience the rain forest with all its rough and muddy edges. Arrival from Las Horquetas, 15 kilometers distant, is by a jarring tractor cart ride over a barely passable track paved in part with rough logs. Mud boots are required for walking the trails, and formidable rain gear. Sleeping facilities are bunkrooms, though rooms with private bath are also available at a facility a sloppy hike away from the dropoff point. Numerous visitors are enthusiastic about the experience, but some complain that it's Devil's Island.

Activities at Rara Avis are birding, swimming in jungle streams and at the base of a towering waterfall, and guided hikes to learn about the complex interactions of plants and animals. Scientific investigations are sometimes in progress and there are programs to raise butterflies and export decorative plants.

3. BELIZE

HISTORY

Long before white men came to the New World, Belize was inhabited by a people called the **Maya**. Dozens of ruined cities in fertile river valleys and throughout the northern plain show that in Mayan times, Belize was far more densely populated than it is today. The Mayan way of life was a stable one: at least one settlement, Cuello, was continuously inhabited for more than 2,500 years. And the Maya were in some ways more advanced than the Europeans of the Middle Ages, for they practiced mathematics and astronomy with astonishing facility.

The more important Mayan cities, such as **Xunantunich**, in western Belize, and **Lubaantun**, in the south, consisted of a main plaza and several lesser plazas, each surrounded by temples set atop mounds, or pyramids, and such smaller structures as palaces with interconnecting rooms, ball courts, and sweat baths. Massive as they sometimes were, these structures were built by the most rudimentary, labor-intensive techniques. Not having the true arch, the Maya used a primitive version, called the *corbel*. Successive stones on each side of a doorway or hall projected inward, until they could be capped by a single stone. The corbelled arch, with its limited span, resulted in interior spaces that now seem claustrophobically small.

In the cities, carved stones (or *stelae*) and altars, were set in paved plazas, carved with glyphs that recorded dates, names of rulers, births, deaths, and other significant events. As well, the Maya sculpted the landscape. When a hilltop got in the way of a city plan, it was leveled. When water supply was undependable, plazas were sloped to catch runoff in reservoirs. Throughout the Mayan area, cities were built and rebuilt, reaching their greatest development during the Classic period, from about 300 to 800 A.D.

While much of the way of life of the Maya remains mysterious, their mathematical and calendrical system is fairly well understood. The Maya

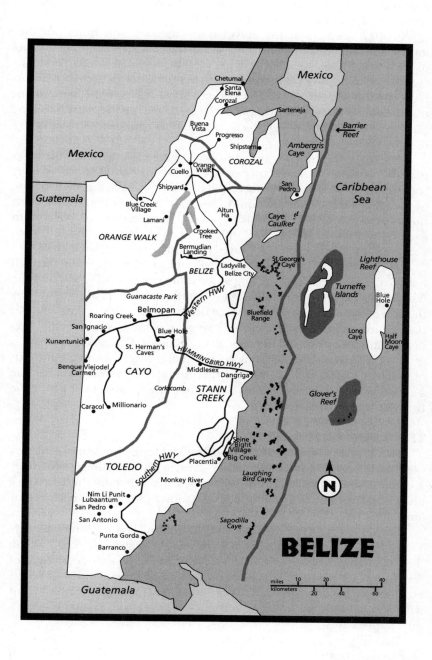

used a zero long before the Europeans, and a system of dots and bars to represent the digits from zero to nineteen.

It often seems that the Maya were obsessed with time, but that impression could result from a hazy understanding of most other aspects of their way of life. As a farming people, they needed a reliable way to measure time, though they refined their system to an accuracy unsurpassed in the ancient world. The Yucatán Maya, for example, figured out that the planet Venus passes between the earth and the sun every 584 days. Modern astronomers, using precise instruments, put the figure at 583.92 days.

The basic Mayan year, sometimes called the *vague year*, was made up of 360 days, along with an extra period of five days. A shorter, sacred year, sometimes called the *tzolkin*, consisted of 260 days, each tagged with one of the 260 possible combinations of twenty day names and thirteen day numbers. Any one day would have a name composed of its position in each of the two years (for example, *4 Ahau 2 Cumku*), and any such compound name would be repeated only once every 52 solar years.

Despite its grandeur, the Classic civilization of the Maya went through a sudden and swift decay, starting in the ninth century A.D., when all city building in Belize and the adjacent lowlands came to a halt, to judge by the lack of later inscribed dates. What disaster took place at that time can only be imagined, but speculation brings up war, revolt, drought, epidemic, and exhaustion of the land as possibilities. Reduced populations lived in and around the decaying ceremonial centers for some hundreds of years, as Mayan civilization moved northward to the Yucatan. But the settled existence of large groups had all but disappeared by the time the first Europeans came to Belize.

THE EUROPEANS ARRIVE

From the arrival of the Europeans almost to the present, the history of Belize is one of neglect and plunder. This, of course, is the story of many a colony. But in Belize, the neglect was made worse by the territory's uncertain legal status. The plunder of resources went on unbalanced by any concern for the future of the land.

Belize was at first under Spanish dominion. The explorers Vicente Yáñez Pinzón and Juan Díaz de Solís passed through in 1506 or 1508 on their way from Honduras to Yucatan, which gave Spain title by right of discovery, at least in European eyes. But in the subjugations of native empires, Belize was bypassed. There were few inhabitants, no obvious treasures, and no harbors, and a treacherous reef obstructed the maritime approach.

Britain's reluctant acquisition of Belize traces back to the early seventeenth century, when Puritan settlers from Providence Island, off

Nicaragua, set up trading outposts along the coast of Central America. The Spanish chased away the Puritans in 1641, but other, less peaceful Britishers were more difficult to uproot.

These were the English and Scottish buccaneers who preyed upon the Spanish ships that carried gold and the raw materials whose trade Spain sought to monopolize. Many a Spanish cargo of logwood, a source of dyes, was brought to market by buccaneer capitalists. Belize, with many rivers along which to shelter, and a barrier reef to snag the larger ships of the Spaniards, became a buccaneer haven. A Scottish captain, Peter Wallace, set up a camp at the mouth of one of the rivers, and some say that his name was corrupted into "Belize," the name of the river and country.

By the latter half of the eighteenth century, the British government became more amenable to helping out the woodcutters in what came to be called the **Bay Settlement**. Britain's presence in the Caribbean was increasing. A protectorate was established along a part of the Central American coast called the **Mosquito Shore**, where the Indian population remained unconquered by the Spanish.

Laborers in the Settlement were black slaves, brought over from Jamaica. Slavery in Belize, however, was not the harsh system that it was in other locales. Slave and master worked side by side, ate the same food, slept in the same rude huts in forest camps. Few slaves took up the Spanish offer of freedom for runaways, and many joined in the defense of the settlement against the Spanish in 1798.

Over the years, the status of the settlement was regularized. Spain stopped protesting the British presence after losing her American colonies. An 1859 treaty confirmed the boundaries that still exist between Belize and Guatemala. Meanwhile, the United States recognized British claims in Belize in return for the termination of the British protectorate over the Mosquito Shore and the Bay Islands, off Honduras. In 1862, British Honduras formally became a colony at the request of its inhabitants, although Britain did not take over administration until 1871.

Throughout the nineteenth century, the population of Belize was transformed. The original British and blacks intermarried and formed the **Creole** class that still dominates Belize. On the fringes of the colony, immigrants appeared in what had been unpopulated territory.

Efforts to diversify the economy of Belize started and stopped over the years. Bananas and sugar cane were planted in the Stann Creek valley of central Belize, and *chicle* (gum) was bled from sapodilla trees in the forests. But high costs, transportation difficulties and disease brought these and other developments to grief. British Honduras stumbled along, seeing only occasional prosperity when the price of mahogany temporarily recovered, or when war created work opportunities abroad. The introduction of mechanical equipment cut forest employment even in the good times, and a series of hurricanes in the 1930s and 1940s caused severe damage and left the colony increasingly dependent on British subsidies.

It was the continuing economic crisis that spurred Belize's independence movement. The colonial administration devalued the currency in 1949, bringing on a sudden increase in the cost of living. Belizeans protested vehemently and without effect, but the People's Committee formed at that time turned into a political party that agitated for independence. Gradually, a democratic system took shape, and by 1965, Belize had full internal self-government.

The only obstacle to complete independence was Guatemala. When the boundaries between Belize and Guatemala were set in 1859, Britain promised to help construct a road from Guatemala City to the Caribbean. Britain helped plan the road, but it was never completed, and a renegotiated treaty that defined British obligations more clearly was never ratified by Guatemala.

The matter was largely forgotten until the 1930s, when Guatemala claimed compensation from Britain to dispose of the road issue. Later, Guatemala demanded that Britain hand over Belize.

As Belizeans began to demand independence, Guatemala became at times histrionic about its claims, and threatened to invade. The matter was negotiated, and even conditionally settled, with Britain offering Guatemala at various times money, a veto over Belizean foreign policy, and chunks of Belizean territory and seabed that might contain oil. Belizeans, wary of a traditionally anti-black Guatemalan government, rejected all agreements.

In the end, Belizean independence was proclaimed on September 21, 1981. Despite some trepidation and a closed border, no Guatemalan invasion took place. British troops remained in Belize to defend the new nation for as long as necessary. In 1988, Belize and Guatemala reached a tentative agreement to normalize relations, but distrust between the two countries continues.

LAND & PEOPLE

With an area of only 8,866 square miles (22,700 square kilometers), Belize is slightly larger than Massachusetts. From the western land border with Guatemala to the Caribbean edge is never a distance of more than 75 miles. From the Rio Hondo at the Mexican frontier to the short southern border with Guatemala along the Sarstoon River, Belize stretches a total of 180 miles. These are the dimensions of a mini-state, and yet Belize is a land of physical variety, from humid coastal swamp to coral islets to pleasant upland plateaus.

In the north, the coastal area is neither land nor sea, but a sodden, swampy transition between the two, thick with mangrove and grasses, and bordered by tussock grasses, cypress, and sycamore where the land truly separates from water, more than ten miles inland. Toward the center of Belize, the landscape gradually wrinkles. Great inland stretches are covered by sandy soil. Barrens of southern pine —"pine ridge" in local parlance — alternate with stretches of savanna. Throughout the central region run river valleys, carpeted with soil washed down in floods from higher elevations to the south and west.

In southwestern Belize, the land rises dramatically to the granite plateaus and peaks of the Maya Mountains. **Victoria Peak**, in the Cockscomb range, is Belize's highest point, at 3,800 feet. Abundant rainfall runs off to the northwest from the highlands in a number of streams that eventually join the Belize River. To the southeast, short rivers rush through a slope combed with overhanging ledges and caves, carrying sand, clay, and silt that over the years have enriched the coastal belt and created beaches.

Southern Belize is a true tropical rain forest, low-lying and wet, with a dense cover of palms, ferns, lianas, and tropical cedar. It rains through most of the year in the south.

Offshore of mainland Belize, a shallow submarine valley and ridge run parallel to the coast. The visible peaks of the ridge, ranging from ephemeral pinpricks to substantial stretches of sand, coral, and swamp, are the islets that Belizeans call the **cayes**. Parallel to them, and just beyond, is the 200-mile-long coral barrier reef, second in extent only to Australia's, with its abundant marine life. Together, the cayes and barrier reef are what attracts most visitors to Belize.

Birds

Over 500 bird species in Belize include ducks, geese, kites, kingfishers, quail, pheasant, partridge, turkey, crane, pigeon, the great curassow, crested guan, curlew, snipe, ibis, stork (including the rare jabiru, illustrated on paper currency), heron, pelican, grampus, frigate bird, seagull, grackle, egrets, buzzards, nightjar, hawks, osprey, spoonbill, vultures, hummingbirds, owls (spectacled, great-horned and others), toucans (billbirds), macaws, and many other members of the parrot family. Birdwatching areas abound in the many habitats of Belize, but one of the most notable is the **Crooked Tree Wildlife Sanctuary**.

People

Belize is small, but its population of less than 200,000 is minuscule, even for a country of its size. With all the available elbow room, and the lack of roads and other communications, several ethnic groups have been able to maintain their separate identities. The different peoples of Belize eat and think and dress in their own ways. Even the houses of one group differ from those of another.

About 40% of Belizeans are Creoles, 33% are Mestizos, about 10% are American Indian, or Mayan, 8% are Garifuna, and 4% are white. The remainder are of some other descent, including East Indian, Lebanese, and Chinese. But cultural groups in Belize transcend racial lines, and with intermarriage, and occasional crossovers in cultural identity, the picture is even more complicated than the figures indicate.

Creoles are the dominant ethnic group in Belize. They are the people who most think of themselves as Belizean. Though predominantly African in origin, Creoles come in all shades, and it's perfectly possible to be a blond, blue-eyed Creole, for the term also denotes a way of life.

The Creole language is mellifluous, picturesque, and hardly intelligible to outsiders who speak English. Archaic usages and phrases abound. A *backra* is a white man, the term deriving from the raw backs of whites who stayed in the sun too long. A meal is *tea*, as it still is in Ireland. Syllables are stressed as if to maximize rhythm. No social stigma attaches to speaking Creole, as it does in some of the former British islands; all classes converse in the lingua franca. Fortunately for outsiders, Creole Belizeans are also adept at a more standard and equally charming form of English.

In central and southern Belize live the **Black Caribs**, also known as **Garífunas**, or **Garinagu**, a people unique to the eastern shore of Central America. To outsiders, a Black Carib may be indistinguishable from a Creole Belizean. But Caribs jealously guard their separate identity and language. Though less than eight percent of the population, they play an important part in national life.

Mestizos are the second-largest cultural group in Belize. Most are descended from refugees from the Caste War in Yucatan in the nineteenth century. Others migrated to the western Cayo district from Guatemala, and more recently, refugees from El Salvador have made their way to Belize. Mestizos speak English in commerce and when dealing with outsiders, but Spanish is their language at home. Spanish has official status in Belize, and many non-Hispanic Belizeans can get along in the language, which is becoming increasingly important as trade links with Mexico and Central America develop. In the north and in Belize City, the accent is Mexican; in the west and south, Guatemalan.

All of the indigenous people of Belize today are called **Maya**, though they belong to three distinct ethnic groups, and are only partly descended from the original inhabitants. Their languages are related, but different enough from each other that members of one group cannot understand those of another. Though they live mostly apart from each other, they have come to share a common identity as Indians.

Some of the most visible of the recent immigrants are Mennonites, members of an Anabaptist religious sect who trace their origin to sixteenth-century Switzerland. Most Mennonite sects reject mechanization, and employ only human and animal labor. Mennonite men and women, in denim coveralls and simple print frocks, are now seen not only near their settlements in the Orange Walk district and in the west, but wherever in Belize their business takes them.

PLANNING YOUR TRIP
Climate & Weather
Dry Season

The record is clear. Most visitors arrive in Belize during the dry season, the northern winter and spring. It coincides with the driest, coolest, most pleasant time in Belize, generally from late November to April. And for divers, the waters offshore are clearest in March and April.

The dry season in the extreme south lasts only from February to April, and is punctuated by storms.

Wet Season

There are also a few good words to be said for what's known as the wet season, which in northern Belize runs from May or June to October, with light rains into December or January. But it never (well, hardly ever), rains all day, because weather forms in a different way than in the temperate latitudes, where a mass of clouds could stay in one place for days.

Temperatures

Temperatures are highest from March to September, and the air is often uncomfortably humid on the mainland, though sea breezes provide some relief along the coast. The temperature in Belize City is usually in the 80s or 90s Fahrenheit (27 to 35 Centigrade), dropping to the 60s or 70s (18 to 24 Centigrade) at night. It's cooler from November to March, with highs in the 70s or 80s, and lows generally in the 60s (15 Centigrade).

In the highlands, nighttime temperatures can even drop to near freezing. Average annual temperature at Belize City is about 80 degrees (27 Centigrade).

ENTRANCE REQUIREMENTS

All visitors need a passport and onward or round-trip ticket in order to enter Belize. No visa is required for visitors from the United States, Canada, or the United Kingdom, nor for citizens of most countries of Western Europe, the Commonwealth, Central and South America, and U.S. dependencies.

THE BELIZEAN CALENDAR

It's annoying to find that businesses are closed down when you were planning to change money, go shopping, and arrange for your flight home. Take a quick look at the list of public holidays below. If any occur while you'll be in Belize, don't plan on getting anything done on that day except relaxing.

January 1	*New Year's Day*
March 9	*Baron Bliss Day*
(Moveable)	*Good Friday*
	Holy Saturday
	Easter Monday
April 21	*Queen's Birthday*
May 1	*Labour Day*
May 24	*Commonwealth Day*
September 10	*National Day*
September 21	*Independence Day*
October 12	*Columbus Day*
November 19	*Garifuna Settlement Day*
December 25	*Christmas*
December 26	*Boxing Day*

Note also that Sunday is still observed quite seriously as a day of rest in Belize. Bus and air service are curtailed. No businesses are open. The churches are full, the bars are empty. Go back to the beach.

A visa *is* required to be issued before arrival for citizens of China, Colombia, Cuba, India, Libya, Pakistan, Peru, South Africa, and Taiwan. Contact the **Immigration and Nationality Service**, Belmopan, Belize, for issuance.

A visitor's permit will be stamped into your passport at your point of entry. Permits are usually valid for thirty days. However, if your funds are short, or if your appearance is unsavory, you could be allowed a shorter stay, or turned away altogether. Be prepared to show about $50 for each day you plan to stay in Belize, if asked. And try to look presentable, even if it's not your normal style.

For an extension of your permit to stay in Belize, apply at a police station in one of the major towns, or to the immigration department in Belize City, 115 Barrack Rd, and pay the fee of about $15.

Land borders are open around the clock. The exit tax is $12 at the airport (about $2 for children).

MAKING RESERVATIONS

It's always best to try to call at least a day before your intended arrival, in order to make sure that your room is clean and ready. Use toll-free numbers, when available, to contact a hotel's agent in the States, or call Belize direct. Some resorts will request a follow-up check or a credit-card authorization to hold your space when you call well in advance.

When in Belize, call ahead to the next place where you'll be stopping. (Yes, the phones work!) While you're on the line, or when you get to the front desk, *ask for a discount*. Many hotels will give you credit for the 20 percent that would normally go to a travel agent or wholesaler, especially during the rainy season.

USING TRAVEL SPECIALISTS

Specialized Tour Agencies

- **Great Trips**, *P. O. Box 1320, Detroit Lakes, MN 56501, tel. 800-552-3419 or 218-847-4441, 218-847-4442*. The folks at Great Trips know as much as anyone about Belize. A strong point is that they sell Belize as it is, with no illusions about what you'll be getting. Great Trips also issues a number of comprehensive brochures and booklets with information about travel services in Belize, as well as general background.
- **Magnum Americas**, *P. O. Box 1560, Detroit Lakes, MN 56502, tel. 218-847-3012, 800-447-2931, fax 218-847-0334*. Experienced agency representing several major resort properties in Belize, as well as smaller hotels.
- **Triton Tours**, *1111 Veterans Blvd., Suite 5, Kenner, LA 70062-4103, tel. 800-426-0226 or 504-464-7964, fax 504-44-7965*. Long-standing Belize specialists.
- **Belize Tradewinds**, *8715 West North Avenue, Wauwatosa, WI 53226, tel. 800-451-7776 or 414-258-6687*.
- **Best of Belize**, *672 Las Gallinas Ave., San Rafael, CA 94903, tel. 800-735-9520 or 479-2378, fax 800-758-2378*.
- **Travel Belize Ltd.**, *637-B South Broadway, Boulder, CO 80303, tel. 303-494-7797, 800-626-3483*.
- **Belize Resorts**, *c/o J. C. Travel, 10127 Sunset Dr., Miami, FL 33173, tel. or 305-595-3459, fax 305-595-2003*.
- **Le Grand Travel**, *211 Pearl St., Monterey, CA 93940, tel. 408-646-1621*.
- **Island Expeditions Co.**, *368 - 916 W. Broadway, Vancouver, B.C., Canada V5Z 1K7, tel. 604-687-2428*.
- **Sea Belize & Land Tours**, *10051 S. W. 48 St., Miami, FL 33165-6379, tel. 800-322-1202 or 305-559-0439, fax 305-551-9154*.
- **Vacation Representatives**, *3355 W. Alabama, Suite 750, Houston, TX 77098, tel. 713-526-2262 or 800-444-2992*.
- **Ocean Connection**, *16734 El Camino Real, Houston, TX 77062, tel. 800-365-6232*.

- **Sea & Explore**, *1809 Carol Sue Ave., Gretna, LA 70056, tel. 800-345-9786 or 504-366-9985, fax 504-366-9986.*
- **Toucan Travel**, *32 Traminer Dr., Kenner, LA 70065, tel. 800-747-1381, 504-465-0769, fax 504-464-0325.*
- **Voyagers International**, *P. O. Box 915, Ithaca, NY 14851, tel. 607- 257-3091 or 800-633-0299, fax 607-257-3699.*Wildlife, eco-tourism.
- **International Zoological Expeditions**, *210 Washington St., Sherburn, MA 01770, tel. 800-548-5843, fax 508-655-4445.* Fred Dodd arranges great trips to the smaller cayes, especially South Water Caye. Highly recommended.

Nature Tours

Some of these agencies have space reserved at remote lodges, which are difficult to book on your own:
- **Victor Emmanuel Nature Tours**, *P. O. Box 33008, Austin, TX 78764, tel. 800-328-VENT, 512-328-5221.*
- **Worldwide Adventures/Quest Nature Tours**, *920 Yonge St., Toronto, Ontario, M4W 9Z9, tel. 800-387-1483,* specializes in birding trips.

GETTING TO BELIZE

By Air From North America

Most visitors will reach Belize by connecting with daily flights from Miami, Houston, or New Orleans. From one of these gateways, the regular one-way fare to Belize City is usually between $150 and $200.

Major airlines serving Belize City from the United States are **TACA**, from Miami, New Orleans and Houston, *tel. 800-535-8780*; **Continental** *(tel. 800-231-0856 or 800-525-0280)*, from New Orleans via Houston and Honduras; and **American Airlines** *(tel. 800-624-6262).* All of these airlines can quote through fares from most U.S. and Canadian cities, even those that they don't service directly.

Since many flights leave from U.S. gateways early in the afternoon, you might not be able to make it all the way to Belize in one day.

By Other Air Routes

Aerovías and **Aviateca** *(tel. 800-327-9832)* fly several times a week from Belize City to Flores and Guatemala City, Guatemala. Taca flights continue to San Salvador. **Tropic Air** *(tel. 800-422-3435)* operates a tour flight from Belize City to Flores, Guatemala, for bus connections to the Mayan ruins at Tikal.

By Charter Flights

Charters direct to Belize are currently operated only from Canadian cities — twice a week from Toronto, and once weekly from Vancouver and sometimes Winnipeg. Operators are **Adventure Tours**, a Toronto whole-sale travel agency, **Fiesta West**, and **P. S. Holidays**.

Information on charter flights is available only through local travel agencies, not from the company that organizes the charter. Prices vary according to where and when you make your reservation, so check around before you pay. There are some bargains available — as little as $700 for your ticket plus a week at a hotel in Belize City (if a week in Belize City is what you want).

By Way of Cancún

A charter flight to Cancún will eliminate several landings and takeoffs and changes of plane from most departure points in the United States and Canada, not to mention slashing your costs. Buses to Chetumal, on the border with Belize, run about every hour from Cancún, a trip of five to six hours, connecting with hourly buses for Belize City.

By Driving

The 1,350 miles from Brownsville, Texas, through Mexico to the border of Belize can be covered in as little as three days. The shortest route on paved, all-weather highways through Mexico is by way of Tampico, Veracruz, Villahermosa, Escarcega and Chetumal. Burros and pedestri-ans in the roadway may slow you down at times, but the route is eminently driveable.

By Bus and Train

Bus travel to Belize is easy and cheap. Fast, comfortable, first-class coaches operate from all U.S. border points to Mexico City. Buses for Chetumal, near the Belize border, leave several times a day from the southern inter-city bus terminal in Mexico City. Seats are reserved, so buy tickets as early as possible.

It costs less than $75 to go from Laredo, Texas, to the border of Belize. Travel time is 35 hours, or less by the Gulf Coast route via Veracruz (which might involve midnight bus changes). Buses leave Chetumal hourly for Belize City, from 4 a.m. to 6:30 p.m., passing through Corozal.

Express trains with sleeper cars operate through Mexico as far as Merida, where connections may be made for buses to Chetumal on the Belize border. First-class fares are as economical as those on buses, and second-class Mexican train travel is quite cheap.

By Private Boat & Plane

Maritime ports of entry are Belize City, Corozal, Dangriga, San Pedro (Ambergris Caye), Barranco and Punta Gorda. Report your presence to the police or immigration authorities at one of these ports as soon as possible after entering Belizean territory. No special advance permits are required. You'll need to present the documents of the vessel, a clearance from the last port of call, three copies of the crew and passenger manifest, and three copies of a list of stores or cargo.

Philip Goldson International Airport at Belize City is the only authorized entry point for private planes. Permission to land must be obtained if arriving from Colombia. Belizean airspace is open during daylight hours only. Landing fees are about $5 plus $1.60 per ton of aircraft weight above three tons.

Radio frequencies are: airport control tower, *121 MHz*; aerodrome, *118 MHz*; VOR-DME, *114.3 MHz*.

CUSTOMS ALLOWANCES - ENTERING BELIZE

Visitors are allowed to bring anything they will reasonably need, including fishing and diving equipment. Twenty imperial ounces of liquor (57 cl), 200 cigarettes, and one bottle of perfume may be entered duty-free. Don't bring any firearms for hunting unless you've arranged for clearance in advance.

Pets can be brought to Belize only with written permission obtained in advance from the Ministry of Agriculture. Proof of inoculation against rabies, and a veterinarian's certification of good health, are required. *For information, call 02-45230 in Belize City.*

Citizens' band radios will be held by customs until a license is obtained from the Belize Telecommunications Authority.

CUSTOMS ALLOWANCES - RETURNING HOME

U.S. customs allows an exemption of $400 in goods for each U.S. resident, including one quart of liquor and 200 cigarettes.

Canadian residents may use their once-yearly $300 exemption, or their $100 quarterly exemption for goods brought home, with a limit of 1.1 liters for liquor, and 200 cigarettes.

These specifics are academic, since you probably won't buy much in Belize. Whatever you take home, don't include pre-Columbian artifacts, coral, fish, or shells, including anything made from turtles. These could be confiscated on your way out of Belize, in your home country, and/or land you in jail or delayed with a court case.

GETTING AROUND BELIZE

By Air

Scheduled flights in small planes provide the most convenient way to get around coastal and offshore Belize. Caye Caulker, Caye Chapel, and Corozal, in the north, and Dangriga, Big Creek (Independence) and Punta Gorda, in the south, are served several times daily by **Maya Airways** and **Tropic Air** from Belize City. A virtual air bridge connects Belize City to San Pedro, on Ambergris Caye. Charter service to all points is available from both the municipal airstrip and the international airport. The frequency of service makes it easy to connect with international flights and avoid having to spend a night in Belize City.

Fares are quite reasonable. It currently costs about $20 to fly from Belize City to Ambergris Caye. To Punta Gorda, otherwise an all-day trip by road, the fare is $50.

Small planes afford an unsurpassable sightseeing opportunity. The sparkling tranquility of Caribbean waters, the scattered dots and irregular masses of land that are the cayes, the barrier reef evidenced by a long line of breaking waves and a sudden change from deep to pale-blue waters, can be no better appreciated than from a plane flying at low altitude.

By Bus

Buses run hourly between Belize City and the major towns to the north and west, as well as to Chetumal in Mexico. Service to Dangriga, south of Belize City, is limited to four runs in each direction daily, and on most days, there are only two buses all the way to Punta Gorda. Service is curtailed on Sundays on most routes. Fares are low: the longest bus trip, from Belize City to Punta Gorda, costs about $10.

All bus companies sell reserved seats in advance. It's not a bad idea to show up early and try to get a seat toward the front, which is generally more comfortable.

By Boat

Caye Caulker, Caye Chapel, and Ambergris Caye are served by scheduled passenger boats from Belize City. The fare is about $10 per person or less. Boat operators can drop passengers at other islands on the way, such as Long Caye and St. George's Caye, but pickup will be chancy. There is also fairly reliable daily service between Dangriga and Tobacco Caye, and weekly to Glover's Reef.

Otherwise, getting to an island offshore will be arranged as part of a fishing and diving package; or you'll have to charter a boat to fit your own schedule. Figure $100 as a bare minimum from a coastal town to a nearby caye by the barrier reef; more to distant cayes; and up to several hundred dollars to one of the atolls, such as the Turneffe Islands or Lighthouse Reef.

Boat service between Belize City and coastal towns has all but disappeared in favor of road transport.

Cruising on a Houseboat

Weigh anchor and set off for your cruise on inland waters where few visitors penetrate. Enter the Burdon Canal, constructed long ago to connect Belize City with the south, in response to the plaints of Sibun farmers whose produce boats were swamped at sea, since bypassed by the newer roads running inland. Onward, through the Northern and Southern lagoons, the majestic Maya Mountains to the west, howler monkeys and toucans and jabirus in the scrub and forest along the way. Drop anchor at whimsy and jump over the side, or troll for fish as you explore.

But pay attention, first, at your obligatory captain's training course where you'll learn the ins and outs of being a jungle pilot.

River Haven proposes this unique adventure from its river port at Freetown Sibun, southwest of Belize City. The houseboats are not luxurious in Kashmiri style, but trim 10- by 15-foot floating cottages, with accommodations for four in two separate sleeping areas, full bathroom, 12-volt lighting system, CB and AM/FM radio, kitchenette, fresh-water tank, and four-foot-deep rear deck.

The rate is $600 by the week, or you can get a day cruise with pilot and lunch for $200 for up to eight persons (with stops for fishing, snorkeling, swimming, birding, crocodile-watching) and shorter mid-week and weekend rentals.

Follow the signs to River Haven's port, three miles from the junction at Mile 16 on the Western Highway. *For information, write to River Haven, P. O. Box 78, Belize City, fax 02-32742. Visa, Master Card accepted.*

By Car - The Roads

There are two driving experiences in Belize; the Northern and Western highways, along with improved sections of the Hummingbird and Southern highways - and everywhere else.

The main roads running from Belize City to the Mexican and Guatemalan borders are two lanes wide, and paved in their entirety. The Northern Highway is almost totally flat, while the Western Highway has some gentle grades and ascents in the rolling countryside past Belmopan. If you stick to these roads — which will get you to or near much of what there is to see in Belize — you need have no worries about driving down in the family car. Elsewhere, roads in Belize are generally narrow, bumpy, and a challenge to vehicle and driver.

Liability insurance coverage, required in Belize, is available at booths just inside the borders from Mexico and Guatemala. It is not advisable to enter Belize on Saturday or Sunday, when the insurance agencies are closed. You'll need your driver's license and registration to get your vehicle into Belize. You'll be required to obtain a temporary 90-day driver's license unless you show an international license.

Automobile Rental

Four-wheel-drive Land Rovers, Suzukis and Jeeps are available for rent, and are highly recommended for visits to some of the Mayan ruins, or the Mountain Pine Ridge forest reserve.

The prices, however, can be astounding. National Car Rental quotes a rate of $80 daily for a Jeep Cherokee *plus* 55 cents a mile after the first 75 miles. For that price, you don't get insurance or a drop of gas, or even a firm reservation. Avis quotes a rate of $500 for a small, four-wheel drive Suzuki Samurai, $650 per week for an Isuzu Trooper.

These prices, hard as it is to believe, are *lower* than they were a couple of years ago, and with increasing competition, there is every chance that they will approach the affordable at some future date. You can sometimes find older vehicles for rent at reduced rates, though the mechanical condition will be chancy. You will be substantially responsible for any damage to a rented vehicle.

It's also possible to rent a car in Mexico and drive it into Belize, if you don't tell the agency where you're going. But don't blame me if you have a breakdown or accident, and the car has to be towed back to Mexico for lack of parts. Pay the high cost of a Belizean car rental, or take a taxi, or use public transport.

BASIC INFORMATION

Listed below, in alphabetical order by topic, is practical information and recommendations for your trip to Belize.

BUSINESS HOURS

Most stores are open from 8 a.m. to noon and from 1 to 4 p.m. Many stores are open during morning hours only on Wednesday and Saturday. Some businesses are open from 7 to 9 p.m. as well. Banks are generally open from 8 a.m. to 1 p.m. with afternoon hours on Friday.

ELECTRICITY

Electricity is supplied at 110 volts, alternating current. American and Canadian appliances should work without any adapters, but ask about the voltage in your hotel before you plug anything in. Some hotels at remote locations have electricity furnished by generators at 12 volts.

HEALTH CONCERNS

Public health standards in Belize are generally higher than elsewhere in the region. If you're traveling to the cayes to sun, swim, fish and dive, there are few health precautions to take. Your food will be safe to eat, you'll have bottled beverages or treated water to drink, and your accommodations will probably be screened to keep out troublesome mosquitoes and other insects. Your biggest problem could be overexposure to the sun. Take it in small doses at first. And remember to wear a shirt when you go snorkeling, so your back doesn't get fried.

Good sense, of course, will tell you to get your health affairs in order before you travel. Catch up on immunizations, such as those for tetanus and polio, and consult your doctor if any condition or suspected condition, such as an ear infection, might trouble you during air travel or when diving. Take along the medicines that you use regularly, and an extra pair of prescription glasses.

For extensive travel in mainland Belize, a malaria preventative, such as Aralen, is advisable. Adult dosage of Aralen is two tablets per week, preferably starting two weeks before leaving home. If you exercise normal cautions about what you eat and drink, no other special shots are needed. But if you're really roughing it, say, on an archaeological dig, your local health department or tropical disease clinic might advise a dose of immunoglobulin for protection against hepatitis, and a typhoid booster. Also, watch what you eat when you're off the beaten track, and try to avoid spreading your own germs to rustic eateries when you're ill.

Despite the well-promoted image of Belize as the "Adventure Coast," resist the urge to carry or use hunting knives, harpoons, spears, and other pointed objects. Wounds heal slowly in the topics, and if you do hurt yourself in some remote location, you might find medication unavailable.

Public water supplies in the major towns are generally chlorinated. In some rural areas, water for domestic use is runoff from roofs, stored in cisterns, or "catchments." It's not always safe to drink. An easy treatment is to add a couple of drops of laundry bleach (easily carried in a dropper bottle) to a quart of water. Shake and let stand a half-hour.

MONEY & BANKING

Belize's currency, the dollar, is worth about 50¢ in U.S. funds. Prices for tourists are sometimes quoted in American dollars, so always make sure which currency you're talking about. *In this book, all prices are quoted in U.S. dollars, unless Belizean (Bz) dollars are specified.*

Belizean paper currency comes in denominations of 1, 2, 5, 10, 20, 50 and 100 dollars, coins in units of 1, 5, 10, 25 ("shilling") and 50 cents, and one dollar.

U.S. dollars in cash are accepted everywhere in Belize, though, technically, you are supposed to change all foreign money at banks. U.S.-dollar travelers checks are accepted at most hotels, often with no commission deducted (banks make a small charge). Canadian dollars and sterling may be exchanged at banks. Other currencies will be turned down. Normal banking hours are generally from 8 a.m. to 1 p.m. weekdays, with afternoon hours on Friday, with some variation.

Personal checks are not accepted by hotels, except from repeat visitors. However, you may send a personal check as a deposit when reserving a room.

Credit Cards

American Express, Visa, and Master Card are now widely accepted at hotels and shops, though a surcharge of at least five percent will be added to your bill at smaller hotels, and at most shops and restaurants. The issuing company's exchange rate costs you another one or two percent.

The service agency for both Visa and Master Card is **Credomatic**, *Hutson St. at Eyre St., Belize City, tel. 32911, fax 32912.* Cash advances are available, with a service charge deducted from the proceeds, in addition to the charge imposed by your bank.

Make sure to re-convert your Belizean money to U.S. dollars before leaving the country. The airport bank will exchange Belizean currency to U.S. dollars, with a tax of 2 percent on anything over U.S. $50.

POST OFFICE

Belize's stamps, with their exquisite depictions of the nation's tropical flora and fauna, are among the most beautiful of any country's. Send plenty of cards and letters, even to friends who are not philatelists.

Post offices are located in all towns, and most hotels will accept letters. Hours are 8 a.m. to noon and 1 to 5 p.m. The air mail rate for a post card or half-ounce letter to the United States or Canada is 60¢ Belizean.

Letters may be received at the post office in Belize City or other towns if addressed to your name in care of General Delivery; or you may have your mail sent to your hotel. Documents of value should be sent by registered mail. Gifts should not be sent, except books, which pass duty-free. The Belizean mails are generally quick and reliable.

SHOPPING

Nobody comes to Belize for the shopping. The selection of handicrafts pales in comparison to what Mexico and the rest of Central America have to offer. There are, however, a few purchaseables, along with some items to avoid.

Black coral jewelry is supposed to be sold only by authorized persons, though you'll find it everywhere. In the interests of conservation, avoid articles made from coral or turtle shell. Among the other odds and ends for the tourist trade are jewelry made from ziricote (a hardwood) and mahogany carvings, straw hats, and t-shirts advertising the country, the cayes, the Belizean ski team, and Belikin beer. Clothing and handicrafts from Guatemala are widely sold, and the prices are reasonable, though of course somewhat higher than in Guatemala itself.

STAYING OUT OF TROUBLE

There are only a few possible sore points for visitors to keep in mind. Theft is a serious problem in Belize City, best dealt with by staying at a secure hotel and by not carrying valuables. Use of controlled substances is a touchy matter anywhere. Exercise caution, even if it appears that the locals smoke up with abandon. Native standards will not necessarily be applied to you, and the police might not be polite if they even suspect you of having smoked dope.

The Belize Tourist Board issues this advisory:

In an effort to preserve our resources and amenities for the enjoyment of others, the following is prohibited by law:

• Removing and exporting of coral.
• Hunting without a license.
• Picking orchids in forest reserves.
• Removing archaeological artifacts.
• Spear-fishing (while scuba diving).
• Overnight camping in any public place, including forest reserve
   (except with police permission).

Sorry campers, if you discover the most beautiful spot in the world and pitch your tent, you could be arrested. Always get permission first. *For permission to stay on public land, call the Ministry of Natural Resources, Belmopan, tel. 08-22037 or 72232.*

Export of turtle parts is also prohibited.

TAXES

Your hotel bill for room and meals is subject to an 8-percent tax. The departure tax at the international airport is $12, $2 for children. There are no local add-on sales taxes, which mitigates somewhat the impact of high prices for imported goods.

TELEPHONES & TELECOMMUNICATIONS

A modern, automatic telephone system serves Belize City and the major towns. In fact, **BTL** (Belize Telecommunications Ltd.) is very much like any phone company in North America or Europe, which makes it much the exception in this part of the world.

Calling Belize

From the United States, dial 011-501, followed by the abbreviated Belizean area code (2 for Belize City, 4 for Corozal, etc.) and the local number. Rates are less than $2 for the first minute from the States during the day, and just under $1 for each additional minute. From Canada, the tab is much heftier, $3 Canadian for the first minute and $2 thereafter.

Call 800-235-1154 to place a collect call to Belize from the United

States (800-578-1154 from US Sprint phones). From Canada, the number is 800-463-1154.

For telephone numbers not listed in this book, ask your local operator to connect you with directory assistance in Belize. There is a charge from the United States, but the service is usually free from Canada.

Calling Home from Belize

A three-minute call to the States costs about $5, or $7 person-to-person from a private phone or a BTL office. To Europe, the direct-dial rate is about $9 for three minutes ($12 person-to-person); to other countries, $12 ($16 person-to-person). For service, dial:
- 114 Calls to Central America and certain other Latin American countries
- 115 Other international calls
- 555 AT&T USADirect (for collect and credit-card calls)

AREA CODES IN BELIZE		
	From the U.S.A.	*Within Belize*
Belize City	*011-501-2*	*02*
Caye Caulker	*011-501-22*	*022*
Ladyville	*011-501-25*	*025*
San Pedro	*011-501-26*	*026*
Orange Walk	*011-501-3*	*03*
Corozal	*011-501-4*	*04*
Dangriga	*011-501-5*	*05*
Placencia	*011-501-6*	*06*
Punta Gorda	*011-501-7*	*07*
Belmopan	*011-501-8*	*0*
San Ignacio	*011-501-92*	*092*
Benque Viejo	*011-501-93*	*093*

Calling Within Belize

Public telephones are available in most towns, identifiable by green booths and lineups. They accept 25¢ coins.

Calls can also be made from BTL offices. In Belize City, the telephone office at 1 Church St. is open from 8 a.m. to 9 p.m. every day. At offices in the major towns of each district, hours are 8 a.m. to noon and 1 to 4 p.m., mornings only on Saturday. Services also include telegrams (20¢ per word to the States), telex, and fax transmission and reception.

Within Belize, use the full area code with "zero" prefix for long distance: 02 for Belize City, 04 for Corozal, etc. Long-distance calls cost from 15 to 60 cents U.S. per minute during the day. Rates drop by 50% between 6 p.m. and 6 a.m.

Service numbers in Belize are:
- 90 Fire and Ambulance
- 110/112 Operator
- 113 Directory Assistance
- 121 Time of day ("Talking Clock")

Calling from Hotels

Hotels impose hefty surcharges on phone calls. Local calls in Belize City can cost as much as $1 each, even if nobody answers. In-country long-distance costs as much as $5 if placed from a hotel, against 50 cents from a pay phone. Look for a pay phone, when convenient, or place your call from the BTL office. From a hotel, verify charges first. It will usually be cheaper to call home collect or charge the call to a telephone credit card.

TELEVISION

Television came with a whack to Belize a few years ago. Local broadcasting did not exist. Then, suddenly, dish antennas made it possible to receive and re-broadcast satellite signals, and a whole new world opened. Belizeans became Chicago Cubs fans, watched the news from Atlanta, and followed soap operas from Venezuela. As elsewhere in the remote tropics, television changed small-town ways. People stayed glued to the tube, instead of chatting on the street or patronizing bars. Life suddenly seemed dull, compared to what took place on the screen.

Most hotels, even the most modest ones, have a television, and many have their own satellite dishes.

TIME

Belize is on Central Standard Time, equivalent to Greenwich Mean Time less six hours.

WEIGHTS & MEASURES

You'll find the English system of pounds, ounces, inches, yards and miles in use in Belize, though gasoline is sold by the American gallon. And since so much of what Belizeans use is imported, packages are often labeled in the metric system.

In this book, I follow local usage, and give distances in miles and yards.

WHERE TO FIND INFORMATION ABOUT BELIZE

- **Belize Tourist Board**, *c/o J. Pask Associates, 415 Seventh Ave., New York, NY 10001; Local tel. 212-268-8798; 800-624-0686; Fax 212-695-3018.* Contact the Belize Tourist Board's New York representative for exquisite brochures, and a Vacation Planner with listings of hotels and services.

For specific information about prices, tours, etc., you'll have to contact the travel agency or hotel directly.

- **Belize Tourist Board**, *Box 325, Belize City, Belize.* The Belize Tourist Board will send a packet of information on request, but will not respond to specific inquiries. For a quick answer, you're better off to contact their New York representative.
- **Embassy of Belize**, *2535 Massachusetts Ave. NW, Washington, DC, 20008, Tel. 202-332-9636, fax 202-332-6741*
- **Belize High Commission**, *112 Kent St., Suite 2005, Ottawa, Ontario K1P 5P2*
- **Belize High Commission**, *10 Harcourt House, 19A Cavendish Square, London W1M 9AD*
- **Belize Tourist Industry Association**, *99 Albert St., Belize City, Belize, Tel. 02-75717.* Call or drop in only.
- **Belize Tourist Office**, *Calle 58 No. 488, Mérida, Yucatan, Mexico*
- **Belize Tourist Office**, *Lobby, Hotel Parador, Av. Tulum No. 26, Cancun, Mexico*
- **Chief Information Officer**, *Government Information Service, Belmopan, Belize.* This office distributes a free monthly publication, *Belize Today*, which covers official activities and, to a certain extent, events and places of interest to tourists.
- **Belize Chamber of Commerce and Industry**, *63 Regent St., Belize City, tel. 73148 (tel. 75108 for the chamber's Export and Investment Promotion Unit)*
- **Comptroller of Customs**, *Customs House, Fort St., Belize City, tel. 77405*
- **Central Bank of Belize**, *Treasury Building, Belmopan (or P. O. Box 852, tel. 77216, Belize City)*
- **Economic Development Office**, *P. O. Box 42, Belmopan, tel. 08-22526*
- **Chief Education Officer**, *West Block, Belmopan*
- **Belize Newspaper Association**, *P. O. Box 707, Belize City*
- **Principal Immigration Officer**, *East Block, Belmopan*
- **Investment Promotion Office**, *Investment Centre, Belmopan*

SPORTS & RECREATION

Belize offers a terrific variety of sports and recreational activities. For example:

FISHING

Spectacular variety and quantity of fish, and a relative scarcity of sports fishermen, make the waters of Belize an angler's dream. Fish is so abundant in Belize that hardly anybody bothers to sell certain species — they're given away. On the cayes, hotel menus groan with seafood specialties. Lovers of fish as well as fishermen come away sated.

Flats Fishing

In the flats, bonefish is abundant all year. Average weight is about two to six pounds, but they come larger. Permit are also found throughout the year, while tarpon are usually fished from March to July, and average 40 pounds in weight. Other common species are barracuda, snook, jacks, several types of grouper, and varieties of snapper, including mutton, mangrove, black, yellowtail and red.

Ocean Fishing

On the ocean side of the great reef just off the cayes, fishing is said to be excellent for king mackerel, Spanish mackerel, grouper, barracuda, snapper, bonito, blackfin tuna and wahoo. Farther out, deep sea fish include swordfish and tuna. White and blue marlin and sailfish pass through Belizean waters from February through April and September through November.

River Fishing

Belize's rivers and estuaries are good for snook, tarpon, bonefish, snappers, and jack-crevalles. Catfish abound off Belize City, but they're a garbage fish that thrives on sewage. Other marine life includes dolphins and sharks. Commercial fishermen catch shrimp, conch (sea snail) and spiny lobster (or "crawfish"), most of it exported to the United States. Lobster season is from July 14 to March 15. Conch season is from October 1 through June 30.

Preparation

Hotels in the cayes rent out boats and fishing tackle. Guides will steer you to the best-known fishing grounds. But the waters are still so unexploited that you're likely to find a few good spots on your own.

Many of the offshore resorts mentioned elsewhere in this book have week-long fishing packages at an inclusive rate, or you can book such packages through the travel agencies mentioned above. Live-aboard fishing expeditions are also available on the boats mentioned above, in the diving section.

Fishing tackle and rods and reels available at hotels may be of limited variety. Experienced sportsmen will want to bring their own equipment, including a variety of rods, perhaps one each of a light and medium spinning, or fly rod, and one heavier spinning, fly, or baitcasting rod.

What Will It Cost?

A lot of fishing travel is sold as a package that includes room, meals, travel from Belize City to your hotel, and morning and afternoon fishing on six days from a skiff either along the reef or in the flats. The price generally runs from $1,200 to $1,500 based on double occupancy. And despite Belize's reputation for high prices, this is less than you'll spend at fishing lodges elsewhere in Central America.

To book your fishing on-site for only part of your stay, you'll pay about $175 to $200 for a full-day excursion in the flats or along the reef in a small boat for three people, less (but not much less) for half a day. Deep-sea fishing costs about $400 for a full day, $250 for a half day, or more, depending on the boat.

Some leading specialists in arranging fishing in Belize include:

• **Action Belize**, *c/o Van Every, 425 Pine Lake Dr., Naples, FL 33962, tel. 813-775-2079.* Many satisfied clients.

• **PanAngling Travel**, *180 N. Michigan Ave., Chicago, IL 60601, tel. 800-533-4353 or 312-263-0328, fax 312-263-5246.*

• **World Wide Sportsman**, *Box 787, Islamorada, FL 343036, tel. 800-327-2880, 305-664-3692.*

There are many fishing operators within Belize, mentioned throughout this book.

SPELUNKING - EXPLORE THE NETHERWORLD

Limestone underlies a good part of Belize, and much of it is perforated by caves.

The **Chiquibul** cave system under the Maya Mountains could be the largest system of caverns in the Western Hemisphere. Over 100 miles of passageways have been surveyed, some as much as 100 yards wide. The Belize Chamber is one of the five largest natural caverns in the world. Near the Caves Branch River, south of Belmopan, rivers flow through caves, emerge, and drop back down again. Inland from Punta Gorda, cliffs are combed with smaller caverns.

Adventurous Belize (*Box 233, Belize City, tel. 02-33903, fax 02-33966*), operated by Ian Anderson, offers caving, among many available capers, on a 60,000-acre leased plot near Belmopan, perforated by hundreds of caves. Mr. Anderson is not your typical tour operator. When you accompany him into the jungle and down into caves, you go *his* way, which is to leave sites as if you had never been there. Cigarettes are bagged and removed. Footprints are washed off crystal.

JOURNEY IN THE JUNGLE

Mr. Anderson of the caving trips also offers a subsistence course, a sort of jungle-style Outward Bound, in which participants set off without tents, build shelters of cohune palms, extract water from vines, dig latrines, and live among unexcavated Mayan ruins on breadnuts and whatever game they can track. With global positioning system equipment and cooperation from Her Majesty's Forces in case of urgency, you can't get too lost, but that's the least of potential contretemps. Making it in the wild could well involve clobbering a fer-de-lance that lies in your path. (There's a limit to leaving things as you found them.)

Review your medical insurance before you even think about signing the detailed waiver of liability. If you have your doubts, consider one of the less pure excursions in the wild offered by some of the lodges near San Ignacio-Chaa Creek *(tel. 092-2188),* **duPlooy's** *(tel. 092-3301),* or **Red Rooster Inn**, *tel. 092-3016,* among others.

KAYAKING THE SEA FROM CAYE TO CAYE

- **Slickrock Adventures**, *P. O. Box 1400, Moab, Utah 84532, tel. and fax 801-259-6996.* Oldest operator of kayak trips in Belize, from a base at Glover's Reef, with transfer from the mainland by sailboat.
- **Laughing Heart Adventures**, *P. O. Box 669, Willow Creek, CA 95573, tel. 800-541-1256 or 916-629-3516,* regularly runs kayaking trips.
- **Ecosummer Expeditions**, *1516 Duranleau St., Vancouver B.C., Canada, tel. 604-669-7741, fax 669-3244 or 936 Peace Portal Dr., Blaine WA 98230, tel. 206-332-1000 or 800-688-8605.*
- **Laughing Bird Adventures**, *P. O. Box 131, Olga, WA 98279,* is a new company, operating trips of from five to eleven days from Placencia.
- **Baboon River Canoe Rentals** *in Burrell Boom, Belize, tel. 028-2101,* can set you up with a canoe or kayak for paddling along the Belize River. They're only 20 miles from Belize City, but the area is a jungle, alive with iguanas, toucans, and macaws along the banks.

HORSEBACK RIDING

Horses are available in western Belize, in Mountain Pine Ridge and near San Ignacio, and even in San Pedro out on Ambergris Caye. Rates vary wildly, from about $20 for a day on your own to $75 on a guided ride.

- **Mountain Equestrian Trails**, *at Mile 8 on the road into Mountain Pine Ridge, (Central Farm P.O., tel. 082-3180, fax 092-2060)* pioneered horseback travel in Belize. Their full- and half-day trips take visitors over trails and along rivers to waterfalls and canyons that can't be seen from roads. Cost is $45 to $65 per person, excellent box lunch included. They also have multi-day packages that alternate days of riding with motorized visits to ruins, and caving trips.
- **Guacamallo Treks**, *Mile 4-1/2, Pine Ridge Rd. (P. O. Box 198, Belmopan), tel. 092-2188, fax 2060, at Maya Ranch.* Guacamallo offers rides to the vast Caracol archaeological site, a shorter ride to Pacbitun, and a wagon trip to the Barton Creek Mennonite community. Costs range from $35 for a short ride with breakfast to $280 for the Caracol ride with a night's lodging before and after.
- **Banana Bank Ranch**, *near Belmopan, (P. O. Box 48, Belmopan, tel. 08-*

23180, fax 22366), is an American-owned beef farm where 25 saddle horses are kept.

Other lodges and establishments that keep horses or regularly arrange riding are:

- **Warrie Head Lodge**, *Mile 56.5, Western Highway, Teakettle Village. Information through Belize Global Travel Services, 41 Albert St. (P. O. Box 244), Belize City, tel. 02-77363, fax 75213.*
- **Maya Mountain Lodge, duPlooy's, The Grove, Chaa Creek, Nabitunich**, and **Easy Rider Stables**, *all in or near San Ignacio.*
- **Isla Equestrian**, *in San Pedro, Ambergris Caye.*
- **FITS Equestrian Tours**, *2011 Alamo Pintado Rd., Solvang, CA 93463, tel. 800-666-FITS, 805-688-9494, fax 805-688-2943*, arranges horseback trips in west-central Belize.

RIDING THE RAPIDS, CANOEING, FLOATING THE LAZY RIVER

You can arrange canoe trips and rafting, at the **Red Rooster Inn**, *2 Far West St., San Ignacio, tel. 092-3016, fax 2057.* A full-day float trip on the Mopan River (Class I and II rapids) costs from $30 to $50 per person, depending on the number in the group. Included are lunch, snacks and equipment. Half-day biking/rafting tours cost the same or slightly more, again depending on numbers. For more adventure, Red Rooster also has river trips extending over two, three and four days, at about $40 per day.

Unaccompanied float and canoeing trips down the Macal, Mopan and Belize rivers are offered by the Red Rooster Inn, Float Belize and others in San Ignacio. An all-day trip, unaccompanied by guide, costs $30 and up, depending on where you arrange to be retrieved, and there are hourly and half-day rates.

CRUISING THE COAST

Chartering a Sailboat

To have a sailboat waiting for you, contact a travel agency that specializes in Belize, or one of these sailing services:

- **Associated Mystic Yacht Charters**, *9 Navyaug Rd., Mystic, CT 06355, tel. 800-873-2692, fax 203-536-6081.*
- **Belize Charter Services**, *P. O. Box 743, Belize City, tel. 02-31138.*
- **Belize Marine Enterprises**, *P. O. Box 997, Belize City, tel. 02-45798, fax 30263*, offers sail charters from a base on Moho Caye, less than a mile out from Belize City. Weekly rates range upward from $1,400 "crude" for a 31-foot Irwin, to $7,000 for a boat that sleeps six, with crew and food. Look over the boat *carefully* before you set out and, preferably, before you put down any money.
- **Fanta-Sea Charters**, *Box 768, Belize City, tel. 44396*, operates with a Stingray sailboat out of the Ramada Royal Reef Resort.

• **Caye Caulker Sailboats**, *Caye Caulker, tel. 022-2196.*
• **Seaing is Belizing**, *Caye Caulker, tel. 022-2234.*

Chartering a Motor Boat

Motor vessels without sails can also be secured. **Barothy Belizean Enterprises**, *P. O. Box 1076, Belize City, tel. 025-2017*, operates the 36-foot *M. V. Lucretia B.* for customized cruising.

Taking a cruise

The ship *Caribbean Prince* sails regularly during the winter from Belize City to Ambergris, Chapel, Caulker, Laughing Bird, Sapodilla and Tobacco cayes, as well as Placencia and Punta Gorda, and continues on up the jungle-lined Río Dulce to Lake Izabal in Guatemala. That's a lot of Belize in twelve days. Prices run from $1,700 to $2,300 per person. For information, contact **American Canadian Caribbean Line**, *P. O. Box 368, Warren, RI 02885, tel. 800-556-7450.*

The Ukrainian-registered *Gruziya* sails regularly from St. Petersburg, Florida, to Belize, and onward to Honduras. The five-deck vessel has two restaurants, a casino, pool, disco, and a crew offering an unusual Russian and Ukrainian experience in the Caribbean. Contact **Odessa America Cruise Company**, *170 Old Country Rd., Mineola, NY 11501, tel. 800-221-3254.*

Special Expeditions, *720 Fifth Ave., New York, NY 10019, tel. 800-762-0003, 212-765-7740*, also regularly runs seaborne adventures through Belizean waters.

SCUBA DIVING

Belize, of course, is the country that was made for diving.

The water is warm, usually about 80 degrees Fahrenheit. A wet suit is needed only as protection against sharp outcroppings. Visibility is superb — often over 100 feet. Waters are calm and practically free of currents in the lee of the reef. Accommodations on the cayes are within a few minutes' ride of major dive sites.

And the diving sites are spectacular.

The barrier reef, alive with coral and resident fish in every color on the artist's palette, runs for 174 miles parallel to the coast, and, mostly, just a few feet under water, making for easy dives and efficient use of oxygen.

Toward the open sea, steep walls drop off a hundred feet or more. Three atolls rise up from the ocean depths, offering shallow lagoons and a ring of submarine ramparts in waters thousands of feet deep. There are patch reefs and caves. And the Blue Hole of the Lighthouse Reef Lagoon, dropping hundreds of feet under the ocean floor, is comparable to no other diving spot anywhere.

Almost all Caribbean corals can be found: brain, elkhorn, lettuce and star coral; pillar coral, several feet long, on patch reefs; undulating sea fans; bouquets of sponges; coral canyons, ledges and caves; orange tube sponges on walls; black coral trees. There are caves with stalactites that once lay underground, but were flooded in prehistoric time. There are canyons and walls and ledges and cracks and clefts.

And there are schools of rainbow-colored fish — parrotfish, grunts, blue chromis, butterfly fish, indigo hamlets, angelfish, and rock hinds that favor the reef, as well as eels, snappers, tarpon, jacks, groupers and stingrays passing through, all glimmering and shimmering in shafts of light. And dozens of manta rays and turtles; dolphins; nurse sharks that you can pet, if you trust your guide; and sharks from which you are best advised to flee.

Visibility is always greater than 50 feet, and well over 100 feet during the driest months, from December to April.

Dive Operators

Typically, a short resort diving course costs about $125; a certification course over four to five days, $400. If you're booking a week-long diving package at an offshore resort, inquire as to whether instruction is included in the price.

Here are some operators or representatives of diving services:

• **Out Island Divers** on Ambergris Caye offers one-day excursions by a combination of plane and dive boat to the Blue Hole of Light House Reef, as well as shorter outings, with guaranteed departures. Two of their boats are live-aboards. *Contact them at P. O. Box 7, San Pedro, tel. 026-2151, fax 2810, or P.O. Box 3455, Estes Park, CO 80517, tel. 800-258-3465 or 303-586-6020)*

• **Indigo Belize**, *P. O. Box 450987, Sunrise, FL 33345, tel. 800-468-0123*, operates the *M/V Manta IV* diving boat, complete with shark cage and video equipment. In San Pedro, inquire at the Belize Yacht Club, or call 026-2130, fax 2834. Their overnight trip to Lighthouse Reef, with five dives and five meals, costs about $230 per person. A three-dive day trip to the Turneffe Islands costs about $110 per person

• **Fantasea Watersports**, *tel. and fax 026-2576*; **Amigos del Mar**, *tel. 026-2706*; **Bottom Time Dive Shop**, *tel. 026-2348*; **The Dive Shop**, *tel. 026-2437*; **Reef Divers**, *tel. 026-2371, fax 2028*; **Hustler Tours**, *tel. 026-2279 (all on Ambergris Caye)*

• **Belize Diving Services**, *Caye Caulker, tel. 022-2175*

• **Blackline Dive Shop**, *P. O. Box 332, Belize City, tel. 33187, fax 31975*

• **Dive In**, *Ramada Royal Reef Resort, Belize City, tel. 30265*

• **Adventure Coast Divers**, *Mile 3, Northern Highway, Belize City, tel. 33185*

• **Belize Diving Service**, *P. O. Box 667, Belize City, tel. 22143*

- **Caribbean Charter Service**, *P. O. Box 752, Belize City, tel. 45814*
- **Maya Landings Marina**, *P. O. Box 997, Belize City, tel. 45798, fax 30263*
- **Placencia Dive Shop**, *Placencia, tel. 06-22017*
- **Boulder Scuba Tours**, *1737 15th St., Boulder, CO 80302, tel. and fax 303-449-8617*
- **A B W Travel**, *2413 N E 53rd St., Kansas City, MO 64118, tel. 800-678-6871.* Representing St. George's Lodge, the most serene diving lodge in Belize, and others
- **Go Diving**, *5610 Rowland Rd., Minnetonka, MN 55343, tel. 800-328-5285, fax 612-931-0209*
- **Hot Dive International**, *P. O. Box 790027, San Antonio, TX 78279, tel. 800-346-8348*
- **Oceanic Society Expeditions**, *Fort Mason Center, Building E, San Francisco, CA 94123*
- **See & Sea Travel Service**, *50 Francisco St., San Francisco, CA 94133, tel. 415-434-3400, 800-DIV-XPRT*
- **Tropical Adventures**, *111 Second North, Seattle, WA 98109, tel. 800-247-3483, 206-441-3483, fax 206-441-5431*

Snorkeling equipment is available for rent on Ambergris Caye and Caye Caulker for just a few dollars.

LIVE-ABOARDS

Terrific diving is within easy reach of almost any hotel on the cayes, and even of those on the mainland. Absolutely superb diving at the Blue Hole of Lighthouse Reef, or where the sea creatures are not yet accustomed to seeing masked humans, is a little farther out. To reach a number of such sites requires dragging your gear to the dock every morning, setting out for a long ride, returning for lunch, setting out again, and returning to your hotel, followed by repeated packing up and unpacking as you move on to your next diving base.

Or, you can live aboard your dive boat, and roll off the dive platform shortly after you roll out of bed.

Live-aboards come at a price. A week-long trip, with six days of diving, runs from $1,200 to $1,500, based on double occupancy. And the diving can be tougher. You'll spend more time in the water, probably at greater depths than if you dive from a shore base, sometimes in uncharted seas. Medical help in an emergency is *not* at hand.

But live-aboards also come with amenities: sundecks, video libraries for evening entertainment, good-sized rooms, and often photo-processing facilities. And since the diving is usually limited only by decompression tables and safety considerations, the cost per dive can turn out to be even more reasonable than from a land base. As many as five daily dives are scheduled.

Here are some of the live-aboards currently operating in Belizean waters:

- The 120-foot *Wave Dancer* carries 20 passengers in ten large suites, and provides hot towels, mints on your pillow, and similar necessities. Week-long diving trips run $1,500 to $1,600 per person. *Contact Peter Hughes Diving, 1390 S. Dixie Highway, Coral Gables, FL 33146, tel. 800-932-6237.*
- The **Belize Aggressor**, 110 feet, also carries 20 passengers in air-conditioned cabins, and has underwater cameras for rent, and slide processing. The rate is about $1,400 per person for a weekly trip with five-and-a-half days of diving at Lighthouse Reef, the Turneffe Islands, and Glover's Reef. Resort and certification courses are available on board. *Contact Aggressor Fleet, P O Drawer K, Morgan City, LA 70381, tel. 800-348-2628 or 504-385-2416, fax 504-384-0817, 45798 in Belize City.*
- **Barothy Belizean Enterprises**, *P. O. Box 1076, Belize City, tel. 025-2017, operates the 36-foot M. V. Lucretia B.* with customized live-aboard diving.
- The *Manta IV* sails to the Blue Hole three times weekly. *Contact Indigo Belize, P. O. Box 450987, Sunrise, FL 33345, tel. 800-468-0123, 305-473-1956, fax 305-473-6011.*
- *Off-Shore Express* operates from Ambergris Caye. *Contact Coral Beach Hotel, San Pedro, Belize, tel. 026-2001.*
- *Reef Roamer II* sails once or twice weekly to diving spots at Lighthouse Reef, including the Blue Hole. Visitors to Ambergris Caye can fly out to Lighthouse Reef to join the ship, or take the smaller *Reef Roamer I. Contact Out Island Divers, P. O. Box 7, San Pedro, Belize, tel. 026-2151, fax 2180, or P.O. Box 3455, Estes Park, CO 80517, tel. 800-258-3465 or 303-586-6020).*

Scuba Safety

A decompression chamber is maintained at the airstrip at San Pedro, Ambergris Caye, supported by a surcharge on all air-tank rentals in Belize. Additional facilities at Cozumel, Mexico, are available. In a pinch, the Royal Air Force has been known to transport divers needing assistance.

Most Belize operators are in touch with the **Divers Alert Network**, an association of medical doctors based at *Duke University (P. O. Box 3823, Duke University Medical Center, Durham, NC 27710). The number for emergency medical referral is 919-684-8111.*

Insurance tailored for divers is available from *P.B.A., P. O. Box 907, Minneapolis, MN 55440, tel. 800-446-2671 or 612-588-2731.*

But these facilities are no substitute for your own precautions. You should:

- Never dive alone

- Tell your guide when you last dived
- Inquire about unusual conditions
- Never dive if you don't feel alert and well
- Never drink and dive
- Never dive where you can't easily get out
- Never dive while on medication, unless you first consult a doctor
- Never feed fish while diving — you could attract sharks and barracudas
- Never dive beyond your physical capabilities
- Avoid diving if you have asthma, diabetes, or are subject to seizures
- Dive with a partner you can trust; your life depends on your buddy
- Do not touch coral or unfamiliar sea plants or fish. You could suffer painful injury
- If confused or unsure, get out of the water
- Inspect your diving equipment carefully
- If unsure of your divemaster, ask for a referral from a recent client. Otherwise, look elsewhere.

ECOTOURISM & TRAVEL ALTERNATIVES

No doubt about it, Belize is one of the world's ecotourism centers. Trouble is, nobody is quite sure what ecotourism is.

For some, eco-tourism means getting close to nature, rather than just getting away. It means learning about natural systems, and how they interact. But it doesn't necessarily have any benefit for nature (a fact I learned when my son's Boy Scout troop raised money to clean up after trekking eco-tourists in Nepal.)

For others, ecotourism is travel that enhances or preserves the natural environment. It applies the visitor's money to good ends.

It can involve:
- composting and recycling of waste generated by tourists;
- employing the resources of local communities without turning them from traditional ways;
- reducing the pillage of native species of plants and animals;
- encouraging sustainable use of resources and respect for local people, rather than cultural change and imposition of foreign ways.

This is tourism that doesn't necessarily put the whims of the visitor first. When you book an ecologically-oriented excursion, consider its impact both on you and your surroundings.

ECOTOUR POSSIBILITIES - THREE ADVENTURES

Here are some typical adventures of the type booked by nature-oriented visitors.

Adventure A: You spend several days in a cabin in the rain forest near a Mayan ruin. You've arrived in a chartered plane that burns fossil fuels, along with beer, liquor, tinned food, and paper products. A diesel generator provides power. Non-compostable garbage disappears mysteriously, either buried or carried to an off-site dump. Animal-watching excursions are taken in Jeeps and motorboats, a generator smashes any hint of bird songs until well after sunset. After a hard day getting to know nature, iced drinks are always available. Were it not for the lodge, the Mayan ruin would surely have been looted, and the forest burned over for farmland.

Adventure B: You take a bus from Belize City, and are met at a roadside marker. You hike to a clearing, carrying all your food, cooking equipment, and sleeping gear. You spend a weekend birding, hiking, spotting snakes and small mammals, listening to branches crack and trees fall, and watching bromeliads and ferns renew life from the decay of the old. Mostly, you try to keep dry or get used to being rained on. Muddy and exhausted, you finally emerge enlightened about the interactions of natural systems. But you are one of the last to take the trip. The land has changed hands, and will soon be cleared and planted in orange trees.

Adventure C: You join a snorkeling trip to an underwater reserve, where fish and coral are protected from commercial exploitation, and visitors are controlled. But you find that vigilance is inadequate to keep the hordes from stepping on and breaking off coral, or feeding the fish. The reserve has attracted the kind of attention and visitor traffic that is likely to do in the coral, rather than save it.

THE REALITY OF ECOTOURISM

What is ecotourism in Belize? At its best, it is the serious effort of a few operators to acquaint visitors with tropical life systems, while doing as little damage to them as possible, and perhaps even protecting and enhancing them.

Ecotourism can also be nothing more than the folklore of travel in Belize, corresponding to handicrafts and colonial monuments in Guatemala, and schnitzel in Vienna. It can be a superficial walk through a zoo, overcrowded reserves where footsteps scare away the animals, squandered resources and new sources of trash, uninformed pattering guides, restaurants with good and bad food and hotels with or without cable television and friendly management. Ecotourism can be like tourism anywhere.

But we're dealing with the real world here, and the inescapable fact is that outsiders want to see a part of the world still relatively unaffected by population pressures and human alterations. And Belize would like to see some economic benefit from letting outsiders in.

PROTECT THE ENVIRONMENT

So what can you do to keep your depredations to a minimum?

• Touch *nothing* if you can possibly avoid it. Touching kills coral. Touching unfamiliar plants in the forest could kill *you*.

• Buy *nothing* that appears to come from the ocean or the forest or ancient cities, unless you are assured by an authority (not the seller) that commerce in the product is legal. This means not buying coral jewelry or tropical birds or Mayan artifacts. Hardwood carvings are all right.

• Eat *nothing* that is out of season. Lobster season is July to March. Forget the beast the rest of the year, no matter the temptation.

• Keep *nothing* that you catch from the sea, unless you plan to eat it.

• Leave *nothing* on the land that wasn't there before you arrived, unless it will decompose.

Can you be an eco-tourist in Belize? It depends on you, and the choices that you make.

EARN COLLEGE CREDITS

Check the listings on the department bulletin boards at local universities for possibilities. Archaeological digs are one way to run up credits, independent studies another.

Maya Mountain Lodge, *P. O. Box 46, San Ignacio, tel. 092-2164, fax 092-2029*, offers a summer workshop in rain forest ceramics and a course on developing rain forest-related curricula for schools. Planned future course offerings include rain forest biology, botany in Belize, tropical cooking, and tropical gardening. Fees are $500 to $750 per week, including course fees, room and board, depending on accommodations. These courses are intended for degree credit, at one unit per week.

The Institute for Central American Development Studies *in San José, Costa Rica*, sponsors internships in Belize and other Central American countries, structured to provide a recommended 15 credits for a semester program, or 8 credits for the summer. Themes are agriculture, women's studies, the environment, public health, and journalism. Fees are hefty — about $6,000! *For information, write to ICADS, P. O. Box 025216-826, Miami, FL 33102-5216, or call their office in Costa Rica, tel. 506-250508, fax 506-341337.*

STAY WITH A MAYAN FAMILY

There's an unusual program afoot in Punta Gorda, in southern Belize, that arranges for visitors to stay with families in the interior, instead of in formal hotels.

It involves spending hundreds of dollars for your ticket, taking time off from work, and ending up somewhere in the bush to sleep on a hard bed or in a hammock in a thatch-roofed hut with a dirt floor, stumble in the dark through the scratching chickens to an outhouse, eat rice and beans, and wash with cold water. If you see it strictly in these terms, skip to the next section.

So what's in it for you?

Meeting local people as people, who go about their daily business and farm and survive and enjoy life on their own, not as servants to outsiders. Learning how corn is soaked in lime water and ground and formed into tortillas; how wild herbs are used in cooking, and to cure illness; how local materials are harvested from the forest to build houses; how crops are grown with a minimum of chemicals; tilling corn and beans along with your hosts; splitting firewood; beating clothes on rocks in a river; hiking to caves.

It's also visiting ancient cities in the company of the descendants of those who built them; seeing how it's possible to live without cars and piped gas and electricity, and also how radios and satellite TV have made their way to some of the more remote places on earth. It's giving indigenous peoples the assurance that they have something to contribute to the rest of the world, as well as allowing them to share the cash that normally flows to more go-getter types in the tourist trade.

If you're interested in staying with a Mayan family, contact **Toledo Visitors Information Center**, *P. O. Box 73, Punta Gorda, tel. 07-22470.* Since this is a shoestring operation, send an international reply coupon, or a check for $2, to cover reply costs.

The price of lodging is under $15 per person per night, meals are less than $5 each, and there is a registration fee of about $10.

More formal guest houses are being organized in participating villages, with western-style toilets.

THE CAYES

Spread out in a 200-mile-long chain parallel to the mainland of Belize are the **cayes**, the little islands that are, for most visitors, the main stopping-points in the country. For divers, the cayes are bases for exploring the wonders of the nearby barrier reef, second in length only to the Great Barrier Reef of Australia. For fishermen, they are the gateway to teeming, barely exploited waters. And for just about everyone, they are idyllic locales for relaxation, where palm trees wave in gentle breezes along barely frequented beaches, people go about their business in tiny settlements with sand streets and small-town ways, and the cares of the world have no place.

The main cayes of interest to visitors are described below, followed by mention of a few mainland resorts with facilities and attractions similar to those found on the cayes.

AMBERGRIS CAYE

Largest of the cayes, **Ambergris** (pronounced by locals with the accent on the second syllable) is 25 miles long, separated from the Yucatan mainland of Mexico only by a narrow channel. The island, in fact, was once claimed by Mexico. On a map, the elongated land mass with its several peninsulas and sea inlets is clear enough, but up close, most of Ambergris is mangrove swamp, that amorphous bordering condition that seems to belong to neither land nor sea. The limited dry land, and most of the coconut trees and people, are concentrated toward the island's narrow southern tip. Ambergris boasts a premier location for exploring the barrier reef, and its hotels, fishing, and diving facilities are the best in the country.

SAN PEDRO

San Pedro is the major settlement on Ambergris, a little town of colorfully painted, mostly wooden, tin-roofed houses, criss-crossed by a half-dozen sandy streets. It is the only place in the cayes that has a number of motor vehicles, but this does not bespeak a bustling air. The island's fleet of pickup trucks carries visitors from the airstrip on the southern end of town to hotels and lodging houses, and odd bits of cargo from the docks. Four-wheel all-terrain vehicles service outlying hotels. But mostly, the streets belong to strollers.

The adjectives usually attached to San Pedro are "delightful" and "charming." The houses are huddled close one upon another, and much of the foot traffic of the place moves through narrow alleys. The same houses in Belize City would constitute just another shanty town, but in San Pedro, they are well maintained, the streets are fairly clean, and a refreshing breeze usually blows through. The effect of the close quarters is one of sociability and friendliness.

Telephone dialing code for San Pedro is *026 from elsewhere in Belize, 011-501-26 from the U.S.*

ARRIVALS & DEPARTURES

Arriving By Air

San Pedro is about 35 miles from Belize City. The airstrip is just south of San Pedro, a walk of a hundred yards or so. A virtual air bridge operates from both the Belize City municipal airstrip (fare $20) and Philip Goldson International Airport (fare $25). Flights are added as needed to accommodate waiting passengers. There is no need to enter Belize City if your destination is San Pedro.

Airlines serving San Pedro are: **Island Air**, *tel. 31140 in Belize City, 2484 in San Pedro.* Eight flights daily, and charters. Call Island Air first —

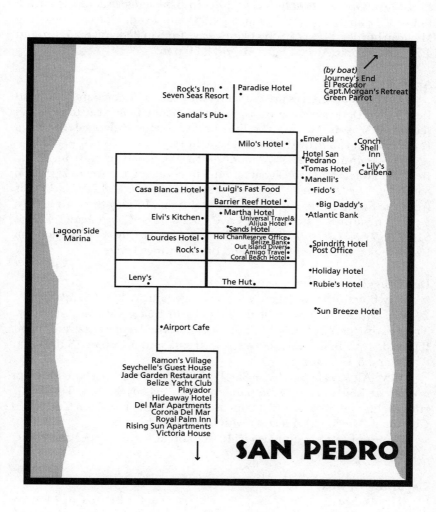

(by boat)
Journey's End
El Pescador
Capt.Morgan's Retreat
Green Parrot

Rock's Inn •
Seven Seas Resort
Paradise Hotel
•

Sandal's Pub•

Milo's Hotel •

•Emerald
Hotel San
Pedrano
•Tomas Hotel
•Manelli's

•Conch
Shell
Inn

• Lily's
Caribena

Casa Blanca Hotel•
• Luigi's Fast Food
Barrier Reef Hotel •

•Fido's

•Big Daddy's

Elvi's Kitchen•
• Martha Hotel
Universal Travel&
Alijua Hotel •
•Sands Hotel

•Atlantic Bank

Lagoon Side
• Marina

Lourdes Hotel •
Rock's •

Hol ChanReserve Office•
•Belize Bank•
Out Island Divers•
Amigo Travel•
Coral Beach Hotel•

•Spindrift Hotel
Post Office

Leny's
•

The Hut.

•Holiday Hotel

•Rubie's Hotel

•Sun Breeze Hotel

•Airport Cafe

Ramon's Village
Seychelle's Guest House
Jade Garden Restaurant
Belize Yacht Club
Playador
Hideaway Hotel
Del Mar Apartments
Corona Del Mar
Royal Palm Inn
Rising Sun Apartments
Victoria House

SAN PEDRO

they sometimes have a special round-trip fare during slow periods; **Tropic Air**, *telephone 45671 in Belize City, 2012 in San Pedro*. Operates 11 flights daily from Belize City. **Maya Airways**, *telephone 77215 or 72312 in Belize City*. Operates eight daily flights in 6-passenger planes from the Belize City airstrip, from 7 a.m. to 4:30 p.m. From Corozal, near the Mexican border, Maya Airways planes leave for San Pedro at 8:25 a.m. and 4:25 p.m, Tropic Air at 8:50 a.m. and 2:50 p.m.

Arriving By Boat

Several boat services are currently available between San Pedro and Belize City. Details of boat transportation change from year to year and season to season, but somebody is always going. **Universal Travel**, *8 Handyside St.*, can provide current schedules.

The *Andrea (tel. 026-2578 or 02-74988)* departs from in front of the Bellevue Hotel in Belize City at about 3 p.m. during the week, 7 p.m. on Saturday. The *Thunderbolt Express*, a speedboat *(tel. 026-2217)*, departs from the Swing Bridge in Belize City at 4 p.m. Monday through Friday, 1 p.m. on Saturday, stopping at Caye Caulker and Caye Chapel. Fare is $10. The *Triple J (02-44375)* leaves for Caye Chapel, Caye Caulker and San Pedro at 9 a.m. from the north end of the Swing Bridge.

Departing By Air

Any hotel or travel agency will arrange your ticket. **Island Air** *(tel. 2484 in San Pedro)* has eight flights daily to Belize City, and charters. **Tropic Air** (tel. 2012) has 11 flights daily. **Maya Airways** operates eight flights daily to Belize City, between 7:30 a.m. and 5:15 p.m. (Sundays at 8 a.m. and 5:15 p.m.)

Maya Airways planes leave San Pedro for Corozal, near the Mexican border, at 7:55 a.m. and 3:55 p.m. every day except Sunday. Tropic Air runs flights at 9:30 a.m. and 3:20 p.m. Hourly buses run from Corozal to Chetumal, Mexico, connecting with buses for Cancun.

Planes of both companies will also stop at Caye Chapel and sometimes Caye Caulker on request.

Departing By Boat

The *Andrea (tel. 026-2578 or 02-74988)* leaves for Belize City Monday through Friday at 7 a.m., Saturday at 8 a.m., from the Texaco wharf by Lily's Hotel.

The *Thunderbolt Express (tel. 026-2217)* leaves from the Lagoon Side Marina (the white house near the soccer field) Monday through Saturday at 7 a.m., stopping at Caye Caulker and Caye Chapel.

The *Triple J (tel. 02-44375)* leaves for Caye Chapel, Caye Caulker and Belize City at 3 p.m.

GETTING AROUND TOWN

Along the seaside in San Pedro, everything is boats, from skiffs to cabin cruisers to rusting fishing boats, tied up to docks in stages of repair from serviceable to caved in. Life for residents and visitors alike focuses on the water, of course, but if you want a change from fishing and diving, turn to bird-watching on the swampy, lagoon side of the island. No expertise is needed to spot flamingoes, pelicans, egrets, and those great diving frigate birds. Other favorite activities are shelling and general beachcombing. But be aware that much of what washes up is plastic containers of one sort or another which, with no use to anyone, remain as permanent eyesores.

As a Hispanic town, San Pedro has its share of traditional fiestas tied to the Catholic faith of most of the inhabitants. Christmas and Easter are celebrated with processions and church services. The town's particular fiesta is June 29, the day of Saint Peter, which coincides with the blessing of the fleet. A more secular celebration takes place on November 27, the anniversary of San Pedro's formal incorporation as a township, in 1985.

WHERE TO STAY

In Town

PARADISE RESORT HOTEL, *tel. 026-2083, fax 2232. 41 rooms. $50 to $100 single/$70 to $150 double (about $20 less May through October) plus 5% service plus tax. $20 for third person, children $10. Visa, Master Card, American Express. U.S. reservations: Paradise Tours, Box 42809-400, Houston, TX 77242 tel. 800-537-1431 or 713-850-1664, fax 713-785-9528.*

Located on the northern fringe of San Pedro, Paradise Resort is an exception among town hotels in that it has an extensive, private sandy beach. One of the original hotels here, it has grown and improved steadily. Facilities include a bar and gift shop, rental of diving and fishing equipment, and travel services. The restaurant (see below) is pleasant, and open to the public, and there is an additional snack bar by the beach.

SAN PEDRO HOLIDAY HOTEL, *tel. 026-2014, fax 2295. 16 rooms. $75 with fan, $85 air-conditioned, single or double, plus 10% service plus tax. Apartments, $120 double. Rates about $20 lower out of season. American Express, Visa, Master Card. Reservations: P. O. Box 1140, tel. 44632 in Belize City.*

The Holiday Hotel is a series of interconnecting, well-maintained wooden and concrete buildings. There's only a small sign, but the entrance is marked by the figure of a seagull swinging overhead. There's more beach here than at most other in-town hotels, an advantage, as is the adjacent Celi's Restaurant, one of the better eating spots in San Pedro. Outboard motorboats are available through local guides, and there's a dive shop and travel service.

CORAL BEACH HOTEL, *P. O. Box 16, tel. 026-2031, fax 026-2834. 11 rooms. $30 single/$45 double with fan, $45/$65 with air conditioning, plus $30 for three meals, plus 10% service plus tax.*

This hotel is a homey little place with its front porch on San Pedro's main street, with no sand, no grounds, no pretense to being other than a base for divers. Food is good and plentiful. The hotel's Tackle Box Bar is detached, located a block away, over the water, attached to a little "sea-quarium", a pen in the sea; and the dive shop is there as well. Fishing boats are available for rent, but the emphasis is on diving for people of all skill levels. Packages available (example: three nights with diving and meals, $350 per person).

SPINDRIFT HOTEL, *tel. 026-2174, fax 2251. 30 rooms. $50 double with fan, $80 to $125 double with air conditioning, no service charge. One- and two-bedroom apartments with kitchenette available. Visa, Master Card, American Express.*

Lower rates may be available in off-season. An attractive new concrete building, and something of a town center, with the post office, pharmacy and travel agency on its ground floor. Seafront rooms are air-conditioned.

HOTEL SAN PEDRANO, *tel. 026-2054. 7 rooms. $18/$28.*

This is one of several smaller, clean hotels in town. Meals are provided for guests on request. Private bath, good for the price.

LILY'S CARIBEÑA, *tel. 026-2059. 11 rooms. $35/$45, lower May-October.*

A bare-bones little place right on the water. The best rooms open onto a veranda with good sea views. All rooms have fans, and have been freshened up recently with new panelling and linoleum and lighting.

BARRIER REEF, *tel. 026-2075, fax 2719. 10 rooms. $48 single/$65 double.*

Located in one of the oldest houses in San Pedro, and an adjacent extension. Rooms in the original building have verandas for watching town life, and the sea nearby. Boat available for guests. Subject to late-night noise — across the street is Big Daddy's disco.

Other lodging places in San Pedro are the **TOMAS HOTEL** ($35 double), **RUBIE'S HOTEL**, and **MILO'S HOTEL**, in both of which the charge is about $15 per person sharing bath, or less. Rubie's has some rooms with private bath at $25 to $35 double, with the higher rates on the upper floor. None have any special features, but all are acceptably clean.

North of San Pedro

ROCK'S INN, *14 units. $95 to $125 double, $10 per additional person, plus 10% service, slightly lower May through October. Phone 026-2336, fax 2349, or 800-331-2458 in the States.*

There are two stories of apartments here in a white building in old

Miami-Cozumel style, with balcony and concrete balustrade facing the sea. It's all fairly new, and each room has a kitchenette with microwave and utensils, a main room and bedroom, tiled shower, air conditioning and ceiling fan. Clients here bubble with satisfaction over the value. Located just past the Paradise Resort and a condominium project.

SEVEN SEAS RESORT, *tel. 2382, fax 2472. 12 units, $95 per night.* About a half-mile north of San Pedro, these apartments with kitchenettes are in a three-story building covered with wood shakes. There are no services or pool.

Hotels Accessible Only By Boat

The following hotels are reached by boat only. Except for Journey's End, which provides a courtesy water taxi, you'll have to pay for every trip to town after your arrival.

EL PESCADOR, *tel. 026-2975, fax 026-2398. 12 rooms, all with private bath. $110 single/$180 double with three meals, plus 15% service plus tax. No credit cards. Weekly fishing package $1,375 with transport from Belize City. Reservations: P. O. Box 793 in Belize City.*

Located three miles north of San Pedro, El Pescador is a self-contained light-tackle fishing camp/resort, specializing in bonefish, tarpon, and permit. Rooms are in a large plantation-style house built by two German brothers, one of whom is the manager. Meals are buffet-style, mostly fish. Airport transfers and diving and fishing packages available on request.

JOURNEY'S END CARIBBEAN CLUB, *P. O. Box 13, San Pedro, tel. 026-2173, fax 2028. 70 units. From $137 single/$184 double, $45 additional for three meals, no service charge. Rates higher at holidays. American Express, Visa, Master Card. U.S. reservations: tel. 800-447-0474 or 305-456-8708.*

Strewn over an expanse four miles north of San Pedro, Journey's End has comprehensive resort facilities: Olympic pool, whirlpool, billiards, lighted tennis courts, sundeck for naturists, basketball, sailboats, windsurfers, multiple bars and restaurants, and even slot and poker machines. Journey's End was featured in an episode of *Lifestyles of the Rich and Famous*. Jimmy Carter and Erma Bombeck slept here. Zack Lewis thought the disorderly site plan and unshaded, baking concrete surfaces could be a drawback, and he didn't use the tennis court or billiards. Take the free boat from San Pedro (just north of Paradise Resort Hotel) at 9 or 11 a.m., 2 or 6 p.m. Trips back are at 8 and 10 a.m., noon and 4 p.m.

CAPTAIN MORGAN'S RETREAT, *tel. 026-2567, fax 2398. 21 units. $130 single/$170 double high season, $95/$120 low season plus 5% service plus tax, $35 for three meals. Rates higher at holidays. Master Card, Visa, American Express. U.S. reservations: Magnum Americas, Box 763, Detroit Lakes, MN 56501, tel. 800-447-2931.*

Captain Morgan's has a comfortable beachcomber's atmosphere. Each thatched-roof cabana, named for a pirate captain, comes with double beds, cross ventilation, porch, fan, and tiled shower. The grounds are well shaded. Facilities include a fresh-water pool and 40-foot-high crow's nest. Fishing, sailing, snorkeling and diving available, as well as diving and fishing packages. One transfer each way from San Pedro is included.

The sand-floored grill serves sandwiches, and the upstairs dining room offers fixed-course meals, with treetop-level views out to sea. Non-guests are welcome to dinner by reservation. Captain Morgan's is about a ten minute walk south of Journey's End.

GREEN PARROT RESORT, *P. O. Box 36, San Pedro, tel. 026-2331. 7 units. $65 single/$80 double; or $100 single/$150 double/$180 triple with three meals. No credit cards. U.S. reservations: Morrison Travel, 2401 N. Federal Highway, Boca Raton, FL 33431, tel. 800-328-1005 or 800-432-2069.*

Green Parrot is a small resort of wooden beachside guest cottages with private facilities, six miles north of San Pedro, and five minutes from the Mexico Rocks snorkeling site. The central three-story tower that houses the restaurant and bar provides excellent views seaward. Boat from San Pedro arranged with reservation. Food is served family- or buffet-style, with a rotating menu that includes Italian, Mexican, and Belizean specialties, as well as lots of seafood. Divers will be picked up at the resorts dock for outings arranged through San Pedro dive shops.

South of San Pedro

RAMON'S VILLAGE, *tel. 026-2071. 61 rooms, including cabanas and suites. $105 to $135 double, up to $225 in suites, extra person $10, plus 10% service plus tax. Meals additional. Summer discounts available. U.S. reservations: P. O. Drawer 4407, Laurel, MS 39441. tel. 800-624-4215, 601-649-1990, fax 649-1996.*

Just outside San Pedro, Ramon's is known among repeat visitors as well-managed and carefree. Recently renovated. The grounds are nicely landscaped, and the salt-water swimming pool is a rare feature on the island. Full fishing and diving facilities, windsurfers, sailboats, bicycles and motor scooters for rent, excellent food, and one of the nicer beaches close to town.

BELIZE YACHT CLUB, *P. O. Box 1, San Pedro, tel. 026-2777, fax 2768. 44 units. $125 to $150 double plus tax and 10% service charge.*

The Yacht Club is a condominium boat-and-apartment complex a quarter-mile south of San Pedro, with some of the most attractive accommodations in Belize. The architecture is Spanish-colonial, with red tile roofs and archways everywhere. On-site are a gym, fresh-water pool, extensive gardens, and artificial reef. All units have a terrace and sea view.

The marina supplies water and fuel, and can take boats with up to a seven-foot draft. All that's missing is a restaurant.

Show this book (and this sentence) and request a 20% discount.

HIDEAWAY HOTEL, *tel. 026-2141. 29 rooms. $50 per person with two meals plus 10% service plus tax. In summer, the rate drops to about $30 double without meals.*

Located about 3/4 mile south of San Pedro, the Hideaway is not directly on the beach, but provides access to facilities for its guests. With a fresh-water pool, this hotel is a very good value. The bar has some relatively inexpensive sandwiches, and breakfast items at a couple of dollars each.

CARIBBEAN VILLAS HOTEL, *P. O. Box 71, San Pedro, tel. 2715, fax 2885. 8 suites, 2 rooms. $85 to $180 ($65 to $120 June through October, higher at holidays), no service charge.*

One of the more attractive lodging places in San Pedro, a Mediterranean-style building with archways and red roof, and comfortable accommodations in an assortment of sizes, with archways, wicker furnishings, tiled floors, large bathroom-dressing room, both ceiling fan and air conditioning, cross ventilation, and full cooking facilities, including microwave oven. Three can sleep in most units, and a deluxe unit has a huge loft with a second bath.

The beach is large, and outdoor facilities include two hot tubs, showers, and a 30-foot "people perch," a tower with one bird-viewing level at treetop level, and a second with a view to the lagoon side and to the sea. Grounds are intentionally kept much as they were when the land was acquired by the friendly owners. The rate includes daily maid service *with dishwashing*, pickup at the airstrip, and use of bikes.

VICTORIA HOUSE, *tel. 026-2067. 31 rooms, all with private bath. $95 single/$110 double in standard rooms, $120/$150 in cottages, $125/$170 in deluxe rooms with air conditioning, plus 10% service plus tax. Low-season rate $68 single/$80 double. Suite and beach house available. Small charge for additional person or children. Add $40 plus 10% service for three meals (children half price). Major credit cards accepted. Reservations: P. O. Box 20785, Houston, TX 77030, tel. 800-247-5159 or 713-529-6800, fax 713-661-4025.*

This classy hotel consists of a lovely old plantation house and thatched-roof Mexican-style cottages, along the nicest beach on the island, about a mile south of San Pedro. The cottage units have tile floors, hardwood vanities and shutters, two large beds with floral bedspreads, art prints on the walls, a desk, mini-refrigerator, shower stall, and high thatched roof, as well as a porch — altogether, several cuts above what you'll find elsewhere in San Pedro. Other rooms, in row units and the main house, are also quite large, with wicker furnishings and pastel decor. Meals are fixed-menu with plain, plentiful fare. Service is top-notch.

The grounds at Victoria House ramble on, with plenty of hammocks on shaded porches and between the palms, expanses of grass, and flower beds — landscaping details which are absent elsewhere on the island. The beach compound includes a volleyball area, and a three-sided bar in a separate pavilion, with free popcorn. Bicycles are provided at no charge for commuting up the sand lane to town, and the hotel van and boat make regular runs at no charge. There are also golf carts ($10 per hour), kayaks and windsurfers for rent. Diving and fishing are available at Fantasea Watersports right on the hotel dock.

Apartments

"Apartment" is a loose term here — sometimes it means a hotel room with a hot plate, sometimes two bedrooms and a separate kitchen and dining room. The **DEL MAR** apartments *(tel. 2695)*, south of the airstrip, are single rooms with a stove and refrigerator stuck in. The rate is about $40 a day. **MAYAN PRINCESS SUITES**, *tel. 2778 (800-346-6116 in the U.S.), fax 2784*, are air-conditioned furnished apartments with one bedroom, kitchenettes, right in the center of San Pedro overlooking the sea, available for $110 single/$125 double, 20% less in off-season.

Smaller apartments are available in town, and attached to several hotels mentioned above. The **TOMAS HOTEL** has one for $30 a day. And real estate agents will be happy to set you up in a condominium unit or private homes when these are available.

WHERE TO EAT

Prices for food in San Pedro are not inconsiderable. When you see the basket of carrots strapped into a seat on the plane, you'll understand something about the cost structure. Nevertheless, some eating places provide good value, and you can choose from a variety of cuisines that includes Creole-Belizean, Mexican, Italian, Chinese, and unadorned American.

ELVI'S KITCHEN is the current trendy eating spot in San Pedro. You can't miss the huge thatched roof. Inside, a tree sprouts in the middle of the sand floor of the main cavern. There is another, step-up level to the side. White walls with dark wood trim are decorated with assorted bottles. And aside from all this island atmosphere, the food is generally better than you'll find elsewhere in San Pedro.

The **PALM** restaurant *of the Paradise Hotel* is a pleasant white-and-pastel room with nautical decor and overhead fans. With soup, beverage, appetizer and dessert, your bill will run to $30 per person, or more; or $6 or so for breakfast.

JADE GARDEN, *about half a mile south of the airstrip*, is one of the better eating places in town, and certainly the most distinguished, setting-wise. It's in an elevated, South Seas-style building with wood siding and cathedral ceiling. You sit on wicker chairs inside, or dine on the porch with sea view. The menu is Cantonese, with chops and American-style seafood as well. $12 and up for a full meal, $5 and up for sandwiches with French fries. If you've reached that point, phone 2126 or 2506, and they'll even deliver to your lodgings. More modest Chinese food is available at the **EMERALD** restaurant *on San Pedro's main street*. The usual chow mein and fried rice are served, along with some house specials, such as chicken with cashew or pineapple. Under $10 for most items, and they have a light lunch special for under $4.

South of town, **MICKEY'S PLACE**, *in the Hotel Playador*, has a mixed menu that includes a Mexican assortment, lobster, Veracruz-style fish. $10 and up for a main course, less for sandwiches or breakfast.

THE HUT, *at the south end of town where you turn from the main street to go to the airport*, serves bar food with a Tex-Mex flavor in a room.

LILY'S RESTAURANT, *snuggled along the passageway right under Lily's Hotel*, is unpretentious but pleasant, dark-wood-panelled, with wicker chairs under fluorescent lights. The owner-cook has a reputation for doing up seafood properly. A meal with broiled fish, fried conch fritters or chicken runs under $14, and breakfast is available.

CELI'S RESTAURANT *is adjacent to the Holiday Hotel* — go through or alongside the hotel, then left along the beach. There are no secrets: the kitchen is open to the dining area with its white walls, dark beams and carved posts and wicker chairs. The regular menu includes hamburger platters, fried fish, shrimp and lobster main courses (Creole, fried, Parmesan, stuffed — you name it) for $6 to $20. They open for breakfast at 7 a.m. (ranchero eggs, waffles, omelettes $3 and up), not for lunch.

One of the better values for light fare is the **COFFEE SHOP** *by the airport*. Breakfasts, waffles, burritos, tostadas, chile con carne, hamburgers and sandwiches go for about $3 to $4. Open from 6:30 a.m. to 3 p.m., and air-conditioned.

NIGHTLIFE

Drinking spots are abundant, in hotels, in restaurants, and as freestanding establishments. **Sandal's** *is near the north end of the main street*, **Fido's** *is in the thatched shopping center in the central part of the seafront*, and **Big Daddy's** *is a block to the south*. Big Daddy's is also a disco, and the action goes on late into the night. The **Tackle Box Bar** *is on a pier over the water*. Butts and crumbs accumulate on the sand floor, which is renewed as necessary. The **Mayan Xtasis** disco and bar, recently inaugurated in the Casa Blanca hotel, brings the noise over to the other side of town.

For a uniquely Belizean entertainment, attend the Wednesday-night chicken drop at the bar of the **Spindrift Hotel**. Patrons bet on where a chicken ends up doing his business on something like an oversized bingo board.

SPORTS & RECREATION

Diving

All hotels offer diving, either with their own boats and equipment, or through local dive shops.

Typically, a short resort diving course costs about $125; a certification course over four to five days, $400; a day's diving, $50 to $75 for each of four persons with two dives, or $35 for a one-tank dive, or $40 for a night dive. Rates may be higher when booked through your hotel rather than in town, or lower, especially between May and October. For example, **Island Adventures** at Fido's, tel. 2697, advertises an excursion with two dives, including tanks and weights, for $40. **Hustler Tours** has a six-dive package for $100, a four-dive package for $65.

Rental rates for equipment vary considerably. Figure a minimum of $7 daily for either a regulator or buoyancy compensator, $5 for mask, snorkel and fins. If you haven't pre-arranged diving, these dive shops are available:

- **Fantasea Watersports** *(Chris Berlin and Rebecca McDonald, PADI instructors), Victoria House, tel. and fax 2576, 2615 evenings.*
- **Amigos del Mar**, *tel. 026-2706*
- **Bottom Time Dive Shop**, *Sun Breeze Hotel, tel. 2348*
- **The Dive Shop**, *tel. -2437*
- **Reef Divers**, *tel. 2371, fax 2028*
- **Hustler Tours**, *Hustler pier (north of San Pedro)tel. 2279, fax 2719*
- **Out Island Divers**, *opposite the Sprindrift Hotel, tel. 2151, fax 2810, (reservations to P.O. Box 3455, Estes Park, CO 80517, tel. 800-258-3465 or 303-586-6020)* has diving boats with live-aboard accommodations. Their star attraction is a Saturday excursion to Lighthouse Reef. Divers fly out to Northern Caye early in the morning and board the *Reef Roamer II* for a brief dive into the singular Blue Hole, followed by a wall dive at Half Moon Caye, a visit to the Booby Bird Sanctuary, and a wall dive on Long Caye. The cost is about $200, or up to $300 for a two-night trip with seven dives. Mid-week trips can be arranged, and they have other multi-dive packages to the Turneffe Islands, as well as a less-expensive Blue Hole trip by water direct from San Pedro. Departures are guaranteed.
- **Indigo Belize** *(P. O. Box 450987, Sunrise, FL 33345, tel. 800-468-0123),* operates the *M/V Manta IV* diving boat, complete with shark cage and video equipment. In San Pedro, inquire at the Belize Yacht Club, or call 2130, fax 2834. Their overnight trip to Lighthouse Reef, with five dives and five meals, costs about $230 per person. A three-dive day

trip to the Turneffe Islands costs about $110 per person; and they have daily diving along the reef as well.

Fishing

Fishing in the flats and along the reef costs $175 to $200 for a full-day excursion in a small boat for three people, less (but not much less) for half a day, while deep-sea fishing costs about $400 for a full day, $250 for a half day, or more, depending on the boat.

If your hotel can't help you with fishing, here are some contacts: **Francis Leslie**, *tel. 2128*; **Roberto Bradly**, *tel. 2116*; **Melanie Paz**, *tel. 2437*, **Romel Gómez**, *tel. 2034*.

Snorkeling

Scuba diving takes some training and some dollars and some time. For the casual visitor, a first acquaintance with the underwater world off San Pedro is often through snorkeling.

A snorkeling trip from San Pedro, if booked through a travel agency, runs $15 to $20, usually to **Hol Chan Marine Reserve** (see below), and including a park admission fee.

All-day snorkeling trips with a stop at Caye Caulker are run by Tony Eiler on his boat, *The Rum Punch*, from the Tackle Box pier. The $35 fee includes drinks, but lunch is $5 extra (such are priorities in Belize). On some days, a beach barbecue-snorkeling trip is operated for $40 per person.

Snorkeling trips are a hotly competitive item from time to time, and some operators are offering discounts on the above. At **Rubie's Hotel**, you can currently book a place on a snorkeling excursion to Hol Chan Marine Reserve for $12.50 ($5 for children); a Caye Caulker trip for $25; or just rent snorkeling gear for $5 for the day and go out on your own. Look around and ask around. There are snorkeling boats everywhere, and you might even find a better rate.

• **Hustler Tours**, *tel. 2279*, at the pier just north of San Pedro, runs a jungle river trip a couple of days a week that takes you across to the Northern River on the mainland, for about $65 per person. They also have morning and afternoon glass-bottom boat rides for about $12, and run the catamaran *Mee Too* on snorkeling trips to Caye Caulker ($40), and a snorkeling-and-barbecue trip to Rocky Point, north of San Pedro, for $45 per person.

• **Fido Badillo**, *tel. 2286*, in Fido's courtyard, also runs a boat trip across the channel to the New River and Altun Ha. **Island Adventures**, *also at Fido's*, has a Caye Caulker trip, and a sunset cruise that calls at Journey's End and then heads through a channel to the lagoon side to watch the orb descend. Pay $15 to get aboard.

Boat Trips

There are also glass-bottomed boat excursions. $15 will get you a ride of a couple of hours with a stop of about a half-hour for snorkeling (if you don't insist on staying dry). Look near the Salty Dog pier.

Charters

Charter trips to Caye Caulker and Belize City are available at the **Lagoon Side Marina** (*the two-story white house adjacent to the soccer field on the lower west side of San Pedro*), *tel. 026-2488*. They also have canoe rentals, and can arrange other water sports. At **Bottom Time Dive Shop**, *tel. 2348*, a 35-foot Bristol is available for $50 per person, minimum three persons.

HOL CHAN RESERVE

At the southern tip of Ambergris is **Hol Chan Marine Reserve**, a national park that includes part of the barrier reef, as well as mangroves, and a stretch of seabed with its own sinkhole and underlying cave – a smaller version of the famed Blue Hole of Lighthouse Reef. The three sections are ecologically related – species spend different parts of their lives in each of the three zones.

Snorkeling tours often stop in the reserve, which is named for a cut in the reef (Hol Chan means "little channel" in Mayan). The walls of the channel are lined with coral, and the cave is home to green moray eels. The channel serves as a throughway for fish commuting to feeding areas.

Hol Chan Reef Rules:
1. Plants and wildlife are not to be touched or disturbed.
2. Fishing and collecting are prohibited.
3. Boats must tie up at buoys.
4. Entry fee of $3 must be paid.
5. Stepping on coral is prohibited. Look for sandy or grassy footings, and only when absolutely necessary.
6. Stay horizontal. Clouds of sand deteriorate coral.

Hol Chan Realities:
1. There is no effective patrol, or supervision of visitors.
2. Snorkelers often step on coral, and intentionally break it off.
3. The establishment of the reserve has served to channel visitors to a small and fragile part of the reef, and threatens the destruction of the very habitat under protection.
4. Boat traffic at the reserve is heavy, and snorkeling and scuba diving are dangerous at peak periods.

Do your part. Follow the rules for visiting Hol Chan (which apply to the coral reef in general), or you could be one of the last visitors.

Sailing

The *Winnie Estelle*, a 66-foot island trader sailboat, is operated from the Paradise Hotel dock most days on a cruise that includes snorkeling stops, lunch, and drinks, for $45, $20 for children. *Call 2394 for information.*

Otherwise, look around the **Tackle Box Bar** for sailboats on day trips from Caye Caulker. They'll take you back for about $10.

Horseback Riding

Isla Equestrian, *by the airstrip*, has horses available for exploration of the byways of Ambergris Caye.

Travel Agencies

Universal Travel *(tel. 2137)* and **Amigo Travel** *(tel.2180)*, opposite the Spindrift Hotel, will sell you airplane tickets, arrange tours, and even rent out bicycles and scooters. **Travel and Tour Belize Limited** *is at the airstrip.*

PRACTICAL INFORMATION

A branch of the **Atlantic Bank** is located on Barrier Reef Drive, not that you'll need it, as travelers checks are accepted at most establishments.

There are several groceries in town with stocks of Pringles, Cheese-Whiz and liquors, most notably **Rock's**, a block west of the Coral Beach Hotel,

For camera rental (video and underwater), try Joe Miller in Fido's courtyard, *tel. 2577.* $25 to $75 per day.

CAYE CAULKER

Located south of Ambergris Caye, about twenty miles from Belize City, **Caye Caulker** has been described as a slightly enlarged version of Gilligan's Island. Like Ambergris, Caulker is partly swamp, and has only a limited settled area. But the island and town are much smaller — it measures a half-mile by about five miles, with fewer than 600 inhabitants. Facilities for visitors are less developed.

Once a pirate lair, Caye Caulker is now a relatively prosperous community of fishermen. Lobsters and conch are the main catch. Some of the residents are also skilled at boat-building. The island is called *Cayo Hicaco* in Spanish — hicaco is a species of palm, the coco plum — whence comes the English name, which is also spelled Corker.

For years, Caye Caulker was *the* place in Belize for hanging out and watching the sea. Times have changed, and with the inauguration of a landing strip and an air shuttle to Belize City, accommodations are in a state of flux. Expect prices to rise, hotels to change hands, restaurants to redecorate and raise pretenses.

Telephone dialing code for Caye Caulker *is 022 from elsewhere in Belize, 011-501-22 from the U.S.A.*

ARRIVALS & DEPARTURES

Arriving By Air

A ticket to Caye Caulker on **Island Air** *(tel. 31140 in Belize City)* or **Sky Bird** *(tel. 32596)* costs about $30 round trip from the Belize City municipal airport, $50 from the international airport.

Arriving By Boat

Most boats for Caye Caulker leave from A&R's Texaco station on the north side of Haulover Creek in Belize City, near the Swing Bridge. Departure is at about 11 a.m., fare about $6 per person, or more if one of the local touts claims a commission for allegedly having brought you (usually the case). Later boats will make the run for a higher price. The hour-long trip out is a tour of the cayes in itself, a zig-zag route following the path of least resistance, zipping through mangrove-lined passages, thwack-thwacking in open water, speeding over a flat surface in the lee of Caye Chapel.

Most boats are double-outboard skiffs, some are tiny single-outboards. Take the largest boat available for a more comfortable passage. Various sources will advise you to take Chocolate's boat, though there must be ten persons of all shades who claim to be Chocolate. The *real* Chocolate is available at Mom's Restaurant, *or you can call him on Caye Caulker at 022-2151.*

Capt. Jim Novelo, like Chocolate, has good reason to understand gringos. His boat, *Sunrise*, can also be booked in advance *(tel. 022-2195, fax 2239)*. If possible, try to share a boat with local people, and pay only upon arrival at Caye Caulker.

Another boat, the *Thunderbolt Express*, leaves from the south side of the Swing Bridge for Caye Caulker and Ambergris Caye Monday through Friday at 3:30 p.m., Saturday at 1 p.m. *Phone San Pedro (026-2488) to confirm that the boat is running and to inquire for additional departures.* The *Triple J* leaves for Caye Chapel, Caye Caulker and San Pedro at 9 a.m. from the north end of the Swing Bridge in Belize City. *Call 02-44375 to verify the latest schedule.*

Departing By Air

You can go back to Belize City, or, on **Island Air**, to Caye Chapel or Ambergris Caye, when volume warrants.

Departing By Boat

Speak to the captain who brought you out (if you were satisfied with the service) to arrange your return to Belize City.

Otherwise, tell somebody at your hotel of your travel plans. Deisy's Hotel can book your trip the day before, and there are others who will make advance arrangements for slightly less than what you paid to get out to Caye Caulker. Or be out by the dock near the Martínez Restaurant at 6:30 a.m. Unusually, departure is prompt, at 7 a.m. One boat usually leaves at 6:45 a.m. from Deisy's, as well.

The *Thunderbolt Express* from Ambergris Caye touches Caye Caulker at about 7:45 a.m.

For Ambergris Caye or Caye Chapel, look for the *Triple J* at 10 a.m. or the Thunderbolt Express at about 4:30 p.m., or arrange a dropoff from a sailboat headed that way.

WHERE TO STAY

Caye Caulker is small enough that you can look over a few places before settling on one that suits you and that has a room available. If you're traveling at an unusually busy period, you can call **Dolphin Bay Travel** *(tel. 022-2214)* from the mainland to book your room.

The **TROPICAL PARADISE HOTEL,** *toward the south end of the village on the reef (east) side, next to the old island cemetery. For reservations, call 022-2124, fax 2225, or write to P. O. Box 1573, Belize City.*

This is the most substantial lodging place in Caye Caulker, a neat compound of golden clapboard buildings. Three new luxury cabanas, with air conditioning, refrigerator and television, go for $60 double, $70 triple, plus tax. Five other cabanas, and the ten clean, light, plain rooms with fan and private bath, go for $37 to $45 for one or two persons. The hotel has a fair-sized sandy compound with lounge chairs, and full-time hot water.

The **SEA BEEZZZ,** *just next to the Tropical Paradise on the far side from the village,* has some high-security rooms. The cost is about $20 per person.

TOM'S HOTEL *(27 rooms, tel. 2102) is a neat, white building about 100 yards south of the Paradise.*

Rooms in the main building go for $12 with two beds and $18 with three beds. They're neat and clean, with shared bath. There are also four small cabanas with one double and one single bed each, and private tiled bath, for $35 per night, a good buy.

SHIRLEY'S GUEST HOUSE *(tel. 2145), next down the coast,* has nice but small rooms, some sharing bath ($20 double), some with private bath ($30 double). It's not your best deal money-wise, unless you take into account the relative privacy, with an extensive sandy area and well-tended plants, and then it starts to look very good indeed.

Near the Water

Clustered near the water on the reef side, in the middle part of the village near where boats dock, are: **DEISY'S HOTEL** *(6 rooms, tel. 2123)*; **LENA'S HOTEL**, *behind Deisy's (11 rooms, tel. 2106)*; and **VEGA'S FAR INN** *(7 rooms, tel. 2142)*.

The **REEF HOTEL**, *just north of the Miramar and looking out to sea*, is more substantial than its neighbors, a concrete structure downstairs and wood-clad on the upper level, painted white with red trim. Rooms have private showers, and the rate is $20 single/$25 double, slightly less during the low season from May through October.

Next door, the **RAINBOW HOTEL**, the light-blue and green building, has 16 rooms with private showers for $25 double downstairs, $30 upstairs.

At the northern end of the village, by the Cut, is **THE SPLIT**, a palm-shaded beach village of nine clapboard cottages and thatched-roof rooms. With ample sand and water on three sides, it is one of the more desirable locations on the island. *The rate is about $25 double, $35 for four persons, less during the rainy period. Telephone 022-2187.*

There are at least a dozen other places where you can rent a room inexpensively by the week or month, either on the beach, or set back in the village.

WHERE TO EAT

Lobster is the best buy on Caye Caulker, when it's in season, from mid-July to mid-March. Boiled or broiled, it costs $5 or less as a main course. By the time lobster gets to Belize City, the price has more than doubled.

The **TROPICAL PARADISE HOTEL** has what comes closest to being a real restaurant. Banks of ceiling fans put out a breeze to lift the roof. Main courses such as curried shrimp or steak with beans, plantain and rice — a good-sized portion — go for $4 to $6, sandwiches and breakfasts for less. **MARÍN'S RESTAURANT**, *in the southwest part of the village*, and the **MARTÍNEZ RESTAURANT**, offer similar fare less attractively, at slightly lower prices.

Follow the crowds to the **SAND BOX** restaurant for one of the most reasonably priced menus in Belize, and the best home cooking on the island. A filling bowl of chili con carne (with chili!) is just $3, and they also have lasagne, snapper filet, barbecued chicken, stroganoff, and other pleasant surprises for $6 and less. Most eateries on the island are dark and dreary, but the Sand Box is light and airy, with high ceiling and plenty of windows, and a sand floor, of course. Take a good look at the menu.

SOBRE LAS OLAS, *located to the north of the cluster of hotels at the long pier*, has a menu of Mexican and seafood items.

SPORTS & RECREATION
Snorkeling & Boat Excursions

Prices for excursions from Caye Caulker are generally lower than elsewhere in Belize. A snorkeling trip out to the reef in a sailboat or a small motorboat, with stops in two or three places with different types of coral formations, will cost under $10.

A run to Ambergris Caye and back, again in either a sailboat or motorboat, or a snorkeling trip to Hol Chan Marine Reserve, will cost under $15 per person.

Talk to the boat owners any morning, in the vicinity of the Martínez Restaurant, where they get groups together, or inquire at **Seahawk Sailing**, *to the north near The Cut,* or try one of these operators with fixed abodes:

Island Sun offers daily sailing trips to the reef for about $10 with rental of snorkeling equipment, $15 for a trip to Hol Chan reserve off Ambergris Caye. **Sunrise Boat Tours** (Jim and Cindy Novelo, *tel. 022-2195, fax 2239*), has a fixed-price menu of trips: $13 to San Pedro and Hol Chan Reserve, $12 to $25 to cayes to the north or south, $35 to the Turneffe Islands. All prices are per person based on ten passengers. Get aboard for a Robinson Crusoe adventure.

Snorkeling equipment can be rented at a number of places — one is next to the police station (which is usually locked up) — for less than $5.

Diving

The island's dive shop, **Belize Diving Services** *(tel. 022-2143), at the northwest corner of the village, by the soccer field,* offers two-tank dives for $35 to $50, night dives, a four-day entry-level course for $300, and full equipment rental. Inspect your equipment carefully before you go out. *Write to P. O. Box 667, Belize City, to make advance arrangements.*

Underwater Photo Adventures

Sea-ing is Belizing is an unpretentious gift shop and photo studio, toward the north end of the village, by the soccer field. Owner James Beveridge offers underwater photo safaris to all offshore areas of interest, and underwater photography courses, as well as books, photos, slides and film for sale. *Call 022-2189, or write to P. O. Box 374, Belize City, for advance arrangements.* Chocolate, the boat operator of local renown, has a gift shop well stocked with t-shirts and post cards, toward the north end of the village, reef side.

Dolphin Bay Travel, *tel. 022-2214, just south of the piers,* arranges air tickets. **CariSearch** *(postal address: 47 Caye Caulker),* run by a marine biologist, offers marine tours and lectures, and also operates Galería Hicaco, an art gallery and gift shop, near the Tropical Paradise Hotel.

PRACTICAL INFORMATION

The **post office** is at **Celi's store and bar,** which is inland from the Tropical Paradise Hotel.

CAYE CHAPEL

Caye Chapel measures only one by three miles. Most of it is covered by coconut plantations and beaches. The island boasts a location just off the barrier reef only fifteen miles from Belize City, and has its own landing strip.

ARRIVALS & DEPARTURES

Arriving By Air

Maya Airways and **Tropic Air** flights between Belize City and Ambergris Caye.

Arriving By Boat

The *Triple J* boat *(tel. 02-44375)* leaves for Caye Chapel, Caye Caulker, and San Pedro at 9 a.m. from the north end of the Swing Bridge in Belize City, from Ambergris Caye at 3 p.m.

The *Thunderbolt Express (tel. 026-2217)* leaves from the Lagoon Side Marina on Ambergris Caye at 7 a.m., stopping at Caye Chapel on the way to Belize City. Departure from the Swing Bridge in Belize City is at 4 p.m. Monday through Friday, 1 p.m. on Saturday. Sometimes, other boats for Ambergris Caye, will stop at Caye Chapel on request.

WHERE TO STAY

PYRAMID ISLAND RESORT, *32 rooms and two beach houses. $60 single/$96 double, plus 10% service plus tax. Add $30 per person for three meals. Low-season rate $40/$60. Master Card, Visa, American Express. Reservations: Box 192, Belize City, tel. 02-44409, fax 32405. U.S. reservations tel. 800-458-8281.*

This resort owns all of Caye Chapel. Accommodations are in a long row of die-of-depression fifties-motel-style plywood rooms with plastic panelling, linoleum, and cheap furniture. But they're slowly being renovated, they all face seaward and are air-conditioned, and the beach is long and sandy and beautiful.

The central bar-common room rises to a pyramid roof, visible by any navigator. In addition to the dive shop, gift shop, and fishing and diving boats found at most of the better hotels on the cayes, Pyramid Island has a fresh-water pond, tennis and volleyball courts (at no charge) and a golf driving range, as well as a full-service marina — and a beach party on the last Sunday of every month.

Fishing in small boats is available at $125 for two persons, diving for $50 per person, snorkeling at $15 per person.

ST. GEORGE'S CAYE

Nine miles out from Belize City, **St. George's Caye** was the site of the major settlement and informal capital of Belize from about 1650 to 1784. A Spanish fleet was driven away just off the island in 1798, an incident that secured Britain's hold on the territory. An old graveyard from the early settlement remains at the southern tip of the island.

St. George's Caye suffered badly in 1961 when Hurricane Hattie washed away a good part of the island, but rebuilding has proceeded over the years. Today, it is a little slice of paradise, with at least two windmills, a venerable cemetery, a dozen private cottages with neat lawns on island-wide lots, several docks, and a rest-and-recreation base for British forces. There are no facilities for the public, and unless you're staying at one of the two lodging places, the island is basically not visitable.

WHERE TO STAY

ST. GEORGE'S LODGE, *10 rooms and 6 cottages. $228 to $257 per day per person, including airport transfers, meals, two dives daily, tanks, and weights. 25% reduction for non-divers, 50% for children. American Express, Master Card. Reservations: Box 625, Belize City, tel. 02-44190 (radio patch to lodge), fax 30461; tel. 800-678-6871 in the U.S.*

St. George's is the most serene of the diving lodges I have encountered in Belize, a state that results from the nature of the island — a non-commercialized getaway — and the seemingly imperturbable personality of the owner, Mr. Fred Goode.

The main building is a shipshape roundhouse, hardwood-panelled, shuttered, and set above the grassy ground on piers. Guest rooms in this part are like cabins aboard ship, each with a full bathroom. Over-water cottage units are larger, with thatched roofs, and air circulation over, under, around and through. Waves lap underneath the clefts in the floorboards. Electricity is provided full-time by windmills and batteries. Meals are mainly seafood, plain but copious, served family style. Bring your own bottle of liquor. Coffee is brought right to your door at 6:30 a.m.

There are a sun deck and a palm-shaded beach, and a solar-heated hot tub, but most guests come to enjoy diving with no distractions, and ratings of St. George's Lodge are consistently high. The reef is a half-mile out, and varied sites for divers of all levels are no more than twenty minutes away. Equipment includes three compressors and four dive boats. Instructors and a divemaster on site can complete dive training started elsewhere, or certify from scratch. Fishing, too, can be arranged, and there have been numerous perfectly contented guests who were out doing not much at all.

COTTAGE COLONY. *(For information, contact the Bellevue Hotel, 5 Southern Foreshore, Belize City, tel. 77051, fax 73253; The rate is about $100 single or double, $1000 for a week-long dive package, $1400 for a fishing package).*

Cottage Colony is a set of cute guest units with porches and cut-out trim, built in rows close to one another. Floors are of polished wood, furniture is wicker, the bathrooms are motel-standard with showers. Two units in front, near the beach, are larger, with kitchens. The arrangement of the cottages across a sandy-gritty compound affords little breeze, and there is no cross-ventilation, but the air conditioning cools things off. Barbecues and picnic tables are provided. There is a dive shop on site.

Cottage Colony affords an opportunity to stay on a pleasant and little-visited island with easy access from Belize City.

SPANISH LOOKOUT CAYE

This 234-acre mangrove island is just ten miles east-southeast of Belize City.

WHERE TO STAY

SPANISH BAY RESORT, *71 North Front St., tel. 72725, fax 72797 in Belize City. 10 units. From $160 daily including meals, diving and tax, from $100 daily non-diving. Credit cards with surcharge. Spanish Bay is a divers' resort, two miles from the barrier reef, affording easy access to a number of southern sites less frequented than those near Ambergris Caye and Caye Caulker, some of them uncharted.*

A powerful dive barge takes groups out in short order to reef, walls, and as far as the Turneffe Islands; and compressors, air tanks, belts and weights are sufficient for as many divers as the lodge can sleep. The central roundhouse bar-dining pavilion sits over the water and is almost encircled by a deck. Inside, it's spacious and airy, hung with maps and charts, and stocked with board games for evening amusement. Guests stay in individual over-water cottages, each with two double beds, with hot water, fans, and hardwood panelling. Price includes transport from Belize City. Only drinks at the bar are extra. And since Spanish Bay is just a jump from Belize City, it can be a base for inland travel as well.

MIDDLE LONG CAYE

This island, southeast of Belize City, is about 45 minutes away by boat.

MOONLIGHT SHADOWS LODGE has just two thatch-roofed cabanas on the island, going for about $50 per day. Fishing can be arranged, but there is no diving equipment, and you'll come out here just to be away from *everything*. Food can be prepared according to your preferences, or you can do your own cooking. *Call 08-23665 to discuss everything.*

BLUEFIELD RANGE

These are small cayes 20 miles south of Belize City, inside the barrier reef. A commercial fishing camp is located here; otherwise, there are no inhabitants.

WHERE TO STAY

RICARDO'S BEACH HUTS, Father and son Eterio and Ricardo Castillo have constructed five simple, over-the-water guest cabanas at their lobster and fishing camp in the Bluefield Range, 21 miles south of Belize City. Visitors may birdwatch, snorkel, or fish from dugout canoes. They also have an unusual opportunity to look in on the lives of the fishermen. There's lots of sand here — more than at many a formal beach resor t— and unspoiled, unlittered mangrove and palms, as well as the usual aquatic attractions.

The minimum charge for a stay at Ricardo's is about $150 for two persons for two nights and three days. This includes meals and transportation, and for additional days, the charge is about $30. For information, speak to Anna Lara at the Mira Río Hotel, 59 North Front St. (P. O. Box 55, tel. 02-44970) in Belize City.

TURNEFFE ISLANDS

Twenty-five miles east of Belize City, the **Turneffe Islands** form a large ring surrounding a shallow lagoon — an atoll. Most of the cayes are swampy, but a few contain enough sand to support coconut trees, and are used as fishing camps.

The main attraction for visitors is the fishing. The flats within the island group are said to contain one of the largest concentrations of bonefish in the world. Permit frequent the deeper waters and, like bonefish, are present all year, while tarpon run in the spring in large numbers.

For divers, there are sharp dropoffs, coral varieties and sponges on the ocean side, while snorkeling is good in the relatively shallow waters of the Central Lagoon and inside the reef. Bird sightings regularly include great numbers of blackbirds, brown pelicans, frigate birds, sandpipers, terns, and cormorants.

WHERE TO STAY

TURNEFFE FLATS, *6 individual cabins. About $1,800 per week of fishing, including transfer from Belize City; $1,300 diving; $950 non-fishing. The fishing rate includes a guide and skiff for every two fishermen. No additional service charge. Reservations: Box 36, Deadwood, SD 57732, tel. 605-578-1304, fax 605-578-7540. Open all year.*

A fishing and diving camp situated on the northeast side of the island group. Despite the remote location, the cabins are wood-panelled and attractively furnished, and provided with private baths. The camp chef serves up meals with seafood, of course, as well as fruit and fresh-baked pastries. The package price includes a stay of one night in Belize City, and a two-hour boat trip to the island on a 31-foot Ocean Master.

TURNEFFE ISLAND LODGE, *9 rooms. U.S. address: 11904 Hidden Hills Dr., Jacksonville FL 32225, tel. 800-338-8149. One-week package $1200 diving, $1600 fishing, $900 relaxing, including meals and transport from Belize City.*

On 12-acre Caye Bokel, this is a village of houses on tall stilts with screened porches, standard-issue catch-the-breeze structures. The lodge has a 38-foot dive boat, and the main attractions are diving where relatively few divers go, and fishing for bonefish and permit in the flats. Diving packages generally include three dives daily.

BLACKBIRD CAYE RESORT, *P. O. Box 888, Belize City, tel. 77670, or 800-537-1431 in the U.S. $1,100 weekly, or $1,350 for diving, or $1,550 for fishing, including boat from Belize City, meals, tax and service charges.*

This is a sports resort with an ecological theme, on mangrove-covered Blackbird Caye, one of the major islands of the Turneffe group. Visitors are invited to swim with bottlenose dolphins (the subjects of ongoing studies) and view alligators, turtles, and manatees from fairly close up. For scientists — and maybe for you — an attraction is that local species live largely without mainland influences, and some of the resident birds have flourished, while becoming virtually extinct on the mainland.

Guests stay in single-room thatch-roofed cottages on stilts, each with private bath. No liquor is available except for what you tote along. Fishing packages include two sorties daily. Diving packages include three dives daily.

LIGHTHOUSE REEF

Sixty miles east of Belize City is the **Lighthouse Reef Lagoon**, its shallow waters surrounded by a reef and the open sea. Lighthouse Reef is barely populated, but not unvisited, for it is home to some rare wildlife, and its waters hold the **Blue Hole**, one of the natural wonders of Belize.

WHERE TO STAY

LIGHTHOUSE REEF RESORT, *tel. 800-423-3114. 9 cabins. $1100 weekly; $1200 weekly with diving; $1500 weekly with fishing, meals and transport included.*

Convenient to the Blue Hole, this resort is a luxury getaway even without the diving. Guest rooms are air-conditioned, and there is lots of lonely beach. Unlike most offshore lodges, Lighthouse Reef Resort has an airstrip, and divers on week-long packages get out here in less than a half-hour from Belize City.

SEEING THE SIGHTS

Half Moon Caye Natural Monument, *near the southern end of the 30-mile-long, 8-mile-wide lagoon*, is Belize's first national park, a bird sanctuary for the nearly extinct red-footed booby. White boobies predominate on Half Moon Caye. Elsewhere, most adult boobies are brown. Other species that make their home on the sandy caye include the magnificent frigate bird, ospreys, mangrove warblers, and white-crowned pigeons, as well as nearly a hundred others. Iguanas also live here, and hawksbill and loggerhead turtles lay their eggs on the beaches. Vegetation is sparse, mostly coconut palms, along with a few ziricote and wild fig trees. The waters off Half Moon Caye are said to be among the clearest in Belize, with visibility of 200 feet. The solar-powered lighthouse on the island, and the one on Sandbore Caye, to the north, give the reef its name.

Camping is permitted on Half Moon Caye. Visitors should check in first at the Audubon Society in Belize City.

The **Half Moon Caye dropoff** is rated unbeatable by many divers, plunging from a coral ridge 25 feet under the surface down, down, down, several thousand feet, broken by caves and canyons, bridges and tunnels.

More than 400 feet across, the **Blue Hole** is a shaft that drops from the ten-foot-deep lagoon, and opens into a series of elaborate, stalactite-filled caverns, starting at a depth of about 90 feet, and continuing down to 400 feet. The caves were formed in another geological age by underground rivers. In a more recent time, the ocean crashed through the ceiling of the cavern, creating the Blue Hole. Locals say it is the lair of a sea monster. Tilting stalactites indicate that earthquakes have shifted the formation from its original alignment.

From the air, the Blue Hole is recognized by a change in the color of waters, from the light blue of the open sea to the darker blue of the Lighthouse Reef Lagoon to the deep blue of the shadowy Blue Hole.

Out Island Divers, *at San Pedro on Ambergris Caye (tel. 026-2151)*, offers a one-day excursion to Lighthouse Reef, with a brief dive into the Blue Hole, followed by two wall dives and a visit to the Booby Bird Sanctuary. **Indigo Belize** *in San Pedro (tel. 026-2130)* operates overnight diving trips to the reef on the *M/V Manta IV*, including five dives.

LAUGHING BIRD CAYE

Laughing Bird is a *faro*, an atoll-like island rising steeply from the sea floor and enclosing a central lagoon, and so unusual in Belize that it is a protected area. Located about 20 miles east-southeast of Placencia, the island is home to the laughing gull, as well as pelicans, green herons, swifts, and melodious blackbirds.

GLOVER'S REEF

Seventy miles southeast of Belize City, **Glover's Reef National Park** is a circular stretch of coral surrounding a lagoon, virtually duplicating a Pacific atoll. The cayes on the southeast side of the reef were in earlier times the base of the pirate John Glover. There are no permanent inhabitants at the reef, though it is visited from time to time by commercial fishermen. Pieces of old pottery indicate that the Maya of Belize frequented the reef in pre-Columbian times.

WHERE TO STAY

MANTA REEF RESORT, *Southwest Caye. U.S. reservations: 14423 S.W. 113 Terrace, Miami, FL 33186, tel. 800-342-0053, fax 305-388-5842. 10 cabanas. About $1200 per person weekly, including meals, diving, and transport out by boat, $1500 fishing, $1000 for R&R.*

Manta Reef gives immediate access to little-explored dive sites: Spaghetti Western, Barrel Head, and Hot Fish Hollow, among others. Whale sharks are common sights, along with the manta rays that lend their name to the establishment. Divers of all skill levels are welcome, and everyone begins with a check-out dive, followed by an optional review course. Two daily boat dives and two night dives per week are included in packages, along with beach dives. Bonefishing is available right at the resort, or from skiffs in the flats of Glover's Reef Atoll. Accommodations are in panelled cabanas with wicker furnishings, more attractive than usually found offshore, and an air-conditioned house is available. Food is ample. Add about $500 single occupancy, children under 12 half price.

FISHING SEASONS AT MANTA REEF

Bonefish and permit	*All year*
Tarpon	*March through June, November*
Grouper	*December and January*
Billfish	*March through May*
Barracuda, snapper, jack, wahoo, mackerel, bonito, tuna	*All year*

GLOVER'S ATOLL "RESORT" AND BIOLOGICAL FIELD STATION is an isolated yet accessible colony of seven rustic cabins *on 15-acre coconut-covered Long Caye, directly on the reef, and nearby North East Caye*. The

Lomont family, who have run things here for years, offer a Sunday trip out to Glover's Reef at 8 a.m. from Sittee River, where they also have a modest guest house (arrive by the 8 a.m. Saturday Z-Line Punta Gorda bus from Belize City, connecting with truck at Sittee River junction, or taxi).

The price is right: less than $100 per person for a week, under $150 for two weeks, including the boat ride (three to six hours, returning Saturday). And — get this — you pay only half as much to camp. Nobody tends to your every wish here, and some aspects are rather basic. But you get cooking facilities (bring, buy or catch the food, or take meals with the caretaker), well water, porch, hammock, lanterns, outhouse, and gravity shower, and can rent boats and canoes. Bring your own towels.

For divers, limited snorkeling and diving gear is available, along with a compressor. You can wade out to the dropoff, or rent a diesel boat for a longer run. Bring equipment to fish for tarpon, snapper, jacks, bonefish and barracuda.

Out at Glover's Reef, rentals and services are usually on a cash basis, to minimize overhead, though Master Card and Visa can be accepted with advance approval (a 10% surcharge will be applied). Sample charges: $50 for half-day sailboat charter, $5 daily dugout rental, $12 for an air tank plus equipment rental for a dive from shore. Scuba instruction and certification are available.

BELIZE CITY

Though roads have been built in the past few decades, and patterns of commerce are slowly changing, Belize City still huddles along the shore, unsturdy, vulnerable to the ravages of nature, largely depending on ships to bring it nourishment and the practical necessities of life from far and wide. Merchants and tradesmen, hawkers and hangers-on predominate on the streets. Though the air and light are different, the city and the texture of its life contain a whiff of early Boston or Newport.

Belize City is mostly a shanty town. Built in a swamp and on sand dunes, allegedly on a foundation of rum bottles, its houses are falling-down affairs of decaying bare wood, propped up on stilts above the dust and dirt of the streets, and the waste that sits in drainage canals until a rainstorm washes it out to sea. The city is known to people from the countryside and remembered by some unfortunate visitors not for its historic buildings or for the bustle of its streets, but for the resourcefulness, daring, and success of its thieves.

Belize City is what the rest of Belize is not. With more than 60,000 inhabitants, it is a churning cauldron of people, while the rest of the land is almost empty. The pace of life in the countryside is relaxed, and the visitor feels inconspicuous. In Belize City, outsiders are constant targets for hucksters.

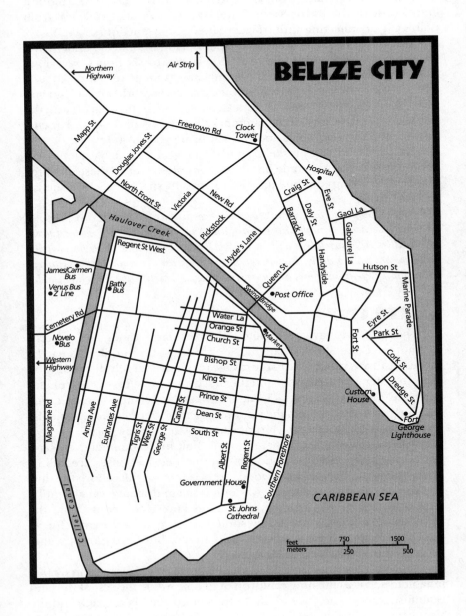

Be Careful!

The street hustles of Belize City are reminiscent of Cairo's. Newfound friends pester visitors for loans to pay for sick relatives' hospital bills. A gentleman who met you last week, though you arrived yesterday, has come up with the controlled substance you requested. A boat owner will take you on a tour of the cayes tomorrow, but needs your money to buy gasoline now. Opportunities for gainful employment are limited, which explains the preponderance of these characters.

Less amusing are the pickpockets and thieves, whose numbers are few, but whose talents are legendary. I have been in Belize City a number of times and haven't lost anything, but a certain proportion of visitors is not so lucky.

Aside from all the hassles, the generally shabby environment is enough to make the place no fun.

Even if Belize City were as tranquil as other parts of the country, the hotel situation could be enough to make those with limited funds move on. Of several dozen lodging places, only a few establishments, mostly newer ones, are comfortable, secure, and pleasant all at once. Older hotels are generally in dismal neighborhoods or housed in dismal buildings — harshly furnished, poorly ventilated and dark. Most distressing of all are the pretensions of some of these dives, expressed through their rates.

In general, avoid the side streets south of the Swing Bridge and west of Albert St., especially at night; though evening strolls are, in general, not recommended. Lightly trafficked areas, such as the environs of the Fort George Hotel, are a hangout of muggers even in the late afternoon. If you arrive by bus after dark, take a taxi to your hotel.

Not that it's impossible to stay happily in Belize City. Startling improvements in accommodations have come about in just a year, and there are even a few budget establishments that provide safe havens amid the hubbub. A number of interesting restaurants serve continental, Creole, Mexican and oriental cuisine for which no excuses need be made, and at a few, the prices are even affordable. A dive shop, travel services, and a central location make the old capital a feasible base for day trips to fishing grounds, diving spots, and inland sights.

And if you're willing to confine yourself to the six blocks or so of the Fort George area, you might consider the city absolutely delightful. You'll be safe enough, as long as you don't do anything that you wouldn't do in New York.

Rates are in US$, subject to change. Dialing code for Belize City phone numbers is *02 from elsewhere in Belize, 011-501-2 from the United States.*

ARRIVALS & DEPARTURES

Arriving By Air

Yes, there are two airports. **Phillip Goldson International Airport** *is about ten miles west of the city, off the Northern Highway.* The modern terminal includes a duty-free shop, bar, banking and postal counters, and telephone office. There are a few rather limited hotels nearby (see hotel listings, below), handy if you'll be flying onward the next day. The pricier hotels in Belize City have courtesy phones, in case you've arrived without a reservation.

Taxi fare from the airport into Belize City is about $15 for up to five people. A local bus leaves for town at 6 and 8 a.m., noon, and 4 and 6 p.m., passing all bus stations in Belize City. The alternative way into town is to flag down a bus on the Northern Highway, just over a mile from the terminal.

Most domestic flights use the **municipal airstrip**, located about a mile north of the city center, along the Caribbean shore. Flights to San Pedro on Ambergris Caye depart from the international airport as well. Charter flights are available from both the international airport and the airstrip. Taxi fare from town to the airstrip is about $3.

International Airlines

Following are the airlines that fly to and within Belize (with their Belize addresses):
• **TACA**, *41 Albert St., tel. 77363*
• **American Airlines**, *New Road at Queen St., tel. 32168*
• **Continental**, *32 Albert St. in the Hindu temple, tel. 78309*
• **Aerovías** *(Guatemala), 55 Regent St., tel. 75445*; service currently Tuesday, Saturday and Sunday to and from Guatemala City via Flores/ Tikal; Wednesday and Friday to Chetumal (Mexico) and Guatemala City.

Local Airlines

• **Island Air**, *tel. 31140*, serves Caye Caulker and San Pedro (Ambergris Caye).
• **Maya Airways**, *6 Fort St., near the Fort George Hotel, tel. 77215, and Tropic Air, tel. 45671*, serve Caye Chapel, San Pedro (Ambergris Caye) and coastal towns.
• **Sky Bird**, *tel. 32596*, serves Caye Caulker.

In most cases, flights can be boarded at either the municipal airstrip, on the edge of downtown, or, for a higher charge, at the international airport.

All destinations are less than an hour away. There are more than a dozen flights daily for San Pedro, on Ambergris Caye, some of which continue to Corozal. The other major route is southward to Dangriga, Big Creek (opposite the Placencia Peninsula) and Punta Gorda. For recent schedules, see coverage of each town in this book, or stop in at any travel agency in Belize City.

Local airlines also offer charter service to any airstrip in the country.

Arriving By Bus

Terminals of intercity buses are along or near Collet Canal, about eight blocks west of Regent St., downtown. There are no attractive accommodations in the immediate area. If you arrive in the late afternoon or at night, take a taxi to your hotel to avoid possible undesirable encounters.

For the latest schedules, stop in at the tourist board. Schedules of buses between Belize City and the major towns, as of publication of this book, are given in individual town coverage.

Departing By Air
From the International Airport

The airport bus departs at 5:30, 7:15, 8:30 and 11:15 a.m. and 3:30 p.m. and 5:30 p.m. Fare is about $1. The route is from Pound Yard Bridge along Cemetery Road and Central American Boulevard to the Northern Highway. *Call 73977 or 77811 to check the latest schedule and routing.*

Departure tax is about $12, $2 for children.

A couple of duty-free shops are open for all departing flights, and their prices are excellent for liquor.

The airport bank, open 8 a.m. to 11 a.m. and noon to 4 p.m., will exchange Belizean currency to U.S. dollars, with a tax of 2 percent on anything over U.S. $50.

From the Municipal Airstrip

Flights depart from the municipal airstrip, located about a mile north of the city center, along the Caribbean shore, for San Pedro on Ambergris Caye, Caye Chapel, and Caye Caulker, and for the coastal towns of Corozal (near Mexico), Big Creek (near Placencia), Dangriga, and Punta Gorda. Taxi fare from town to the airstrip is about $3.

Departing By Bus

Terminals of inter-city buses are mostly along or near Collet Canal, about eight blocks west of Regent St., downtown. Each company has its own station or parking spot, among them:

• **Batty Bus**, *15 Mosul St. at Bagdad, tel. 72025.* Northbound buses to Orange Walk and Corozal, and Chetumal, Mexico; and west to Belmopan, San Ignacio, Benque Viejo.

- **Novelo Bus**, *West Collet Canal, tel. 77372*. Westbound buses to Belmopan, San Ignacio, Benque Viejo.
- **Venus Bus**, *Magazine Rd., tel. 73354*. Northbound buses to Orange Walk and Corozal, and Chetumal, Mexico.
- **Z-Line**, *Magazine Road, tel. 73937*. To Dangriga, Punta Gorda.

ORIENTATION

Most hotels, businesses and points of interest are clustered in an area measuring about a thousand yards square, around the mouth of **Haulover Creek**, which untidily divides the city in two. Your basic reference point is the **Swing Bridge**. Since all streets bear names instead of numbers, a street map or taxi driver will come in handy when you're looking for anything. For streets beyond the central area indicated on the map on page 145, consult the map of Belize available from the Tourist Board.

Note that street numbers on one side of a street have no necessary relationship to those across the way.

Wise residents of Belize City carry umbrellas in the dry times as well as the wet, to shield themselves from the sun. Visitors, as well, should avoid unnecessary exposure. It's easy to forget that you're subject to frying as you go about doing whatever you're doing.

GETTING AROUND TOWN

Car Rentals

Rentals cost a fortune in Belize — usually well over $100 a day — but rates are inching downward as competition increases. In general, you're better off with *name brand* companies, including:

- **National Car Rental**, *126 Freetown Rd. tel. 31587, and at the international airport, tel. 025-2294.*
- **Avis**, *Fort George Hotel, tel. 31987.*
- **Budget**, *on the Northern Highway, tel. 32435.*
- **Hertz**, *Mile 2-1/2, Northern Highway, tel. 32710.*
- **Crystal Rental**, *1-1/2 miles Northern Highway, tel. 31600*, is an exception. Readers have praised their service, and I've used them with no problem. A full-sized used car goes for $50 to $60 daily, and they'll extend discounts during the rainy season.

Other operators have used vehicles at lower rates, but are unreliable, and some, according to readers, are out-and-out con artists. Alternatives to car rental include tours; taxis from Belize City; or taxis from district towns in combination with buses.

Taxis

Check with the tourist board for the latest rates, and verify the price with the driver before you go anywhere. Recent fares are $2 for a short trip (or $1 per person for two or more passengers); by the hour, $5; $15 to the international airport. Fares to out-of-town destinations are by negotiation. Taxis have green license plates.

Taxi operators include **Cinderella Plaza Taxi**, *tel. 33340*; **Caribbean Taxi**, *Albert St., tel. 72888*; **City Garage**, *Queen St., tel. 45833*; **Baldemar Varella**, *73600*.

WHERE TO STAY

Away From Downtown

These hotels are away from downtown hustles, but just a short taxi ride from anything you need.

BELIZE BILTMORE PLAZA, *Mile 3, Northern Highway, tel. 32302, fax 32301, cable 183-BILT-PLAZA-BZ. 90 rooms. $100 single/$110 double, no service charge. U.S. reservations: tel. 800-327-3573.*

Located in a mixed-use suburban area, the Biltmore is plain on the outside, but inside is another matter. In the best Central American tradition, the Biltmore is oriented to a courtyard, and it's past the entry that you'll find the gazebo, gardens with almond and coconut trees and banana plants and aloe (with giant crabs hiding among them), and most public facilities. You don't have to go far to appreciate Belizean wildlife. Resident turtles and even crabs lurk in the gardens. Call the architecture, with its pediments and columns eschewing excess decoration, a sort of post-modern English colonial.

The swim-up bar at the pool is open on weekends and when numbers warrant. Cuisine in the Victorian Room, with its dark wainscotting, is both continental and regional, with items such as broiled chicken, grilled snapper, and tournedos bearnaise, at about $10. The Squires Lounge is inviting. A discount is available on-site on a space-available basis when you show this book — phone first. A taxi from the Biltmore to downtown costs about $4.

RAMADA ROYAL REEF RESORT, *Newtown Barracks (P. O. Box 1248), tel. 32670, fax 32660. 120 rooms. $144 single/$155 double plus 10 percent service, tax. U.S. reservations tel. 800-854-7854.*

Everything about the Ramada has a cool marine feel, from the pastel blue, white and maroon of this Disneyesque multi-story structure rising beside the water, reflecting the sea and the reef, to the tile in the lobby, to the glassed-in, air-conditioned public areas that have the feel of an aquarium. You'll see structures such as this at Disney World or in the Bahamas, but there is nothing else like it in Belize.

Tip: If you make your own reservation through Ramada's toll-free number, keep asking for a lower rate — you can get a third or more off the rack rate at certain times of year.

Fort George Area

This neighborhood is generally lower-key and cleaner than the rest of the city. However, the streets are devoid of life from well before sunset, and late-afternoon and nighttime strolls are out of the question.

THE VILLA, *13 Cork Street (P. O. Box 1240), tel. 32800, fax 30276. 41 rooms, $95 single/$110 double, plus 10% service plus tax. U. S. reservations: tel. 800-333-3333.*

An attractive, modern concrete building near the sea. The new wing, where most of the rooms are located, is in elegant tropical style, with carpeted hallways and pleasing pastel decor. Rooms all have balconies, air conditioning, television, fan, telephone, and a decor comparable to that in a traditional downtown hotel in North America. The higher up, the better the view to sea and town. Beds in various rooms are either king- or queen-sized. And for a price, you can get a suite with a whirlpool, kitchenette with microwave, two baths, and two balconies. The top-floor restaurant is one of the best in the city. Courtyard pool.

FORT GEORGE HOTEL, *2 Marine Parade (P. O. Box 321), tel. 77400, fax 73820. 75 rooms. $100 to $140 single/$115 to $155 double, plus 10% service plus tax. U. S. reservations: Radisson Hotels, tel. 800-333-3333.*

The Fort George has long been an oasis in the city, a British colonial establishment where everything works, and the hustle outside isn't allowed to intrude. With renovation, the hotel's air of tradition has departed, but the facilities are still good: pool, fishing dock, grounds fringed with coconut palms, newsstand, travel desk, gift shop, car-rental service. The Fort George is under the same management as The Villa.

CHATEAU CARIBBEAN, *6 Marine Parade (P. O. Box 947), tel. 72813, fax 30800. 23 rooms. $70 single/$80 double.*

A seafront colonial mansion, with attached new wing, near the Fort George. Some maintenance is due, but there is a terrific atmosphere of faded Caribbean glory, especially in the restaurant. Air-conditioned.

FORT STREET GUEST HOUSE, *4 Fort St. (P. O. Box 3), tel. 30116, fax 78808. 5 rooms, $44 single/$58 double with breakfast, no service charge. Credit cards accepted. U.S. contact: Emerald Reef, P.O. Box 2664, Evergreen, CO 80439, tel. 800-538-6802.*

Bed and breakfast in a picture-perfect old house with porches all around, plenty of wicker, wind chimes, wainscotting, high wood ceilings and fans, inviting sitting area. It's not all perfectly refinished, just nicely worn, and totally charming. Leave your notes for the staff (wake-up time, coffee requests, etc.) in a bottle by your door. Shared bathrooms.

COLTON HOUSE, *9 Cork St., tel. 44666. 4 rooms. $30 single/$35 double, $35/$40 with private bath, $10 per extra person.*

Here's one of the nicer of Belize City's smaller lodging places, an updated and restored gracious merchant's home, dating from 1928.

Colton House is airy, with lots of natural light, high ceilings, overhead fans, area carpets, attractive wallpaper, and many other homey details, such as old-style bankers lamps, built-in wardrobes, and hardwood furniture.

BELIZE GUEST HOUSE, *2 Hutson St. at Marine Parade, tel. 77569. 4 rooms. $33 single/$44 double. Credit cards with surcharge.*

Pleasant, clean, seaside house. All rooms with shared bath and fan. Drinks available, no restaurant. Four-wheel-drive rental vehicle available.

North of the Swing Bridge

DIBÁSEI, *26 Hydes Lane, tel. 33981, fax 32136. 9 rooms. $30 single/$40 double.*

The *guest house with a cultural difference* is a re-habbed, blue-painted wooden house at the corner of New Road, hosted by proud folk from Dangriga. It's all clean and modern, and each large, carpeted, plywood-panelled guest room bears the name of a bird in the Garifuna language. Most are air-conditioned, and all have individual bathroom and shower. Decorations include Garifuna fish nets and John-Canoe masks. Lectures are scheduled, and a craft shop is in the works.

ROYAL ORCHID HOTEL, *New Rd. and Douglas Jones (P.O. Box 279), tel. 32783, fax 32789. 22 rooms. $45 single/$55 double plus tax. Visa, Master Card, American Express.*

A new, four-story, Chinese-run hotel. Unadorned, but modern and comfortable, with big rooms, each with television, air conditioning and fan, telephone, and fully vented bathroom. Secure parking is provided.

EYRE ST GUEST HOUSE, *7 Eyre St., tel 77724. 9 rooms. $10 to $28 per person.*

An older, once-elegant building, quiet, cool, and clean. Most rooms share bathrooms, and only these are a good value. Inexpensive vegetarian meals are served.

BAKADEER INN, *74 Cleghorn St. (off Douglas Jones St.), tel. 31400, fax 31963. 12 rooms. $40 single/$50 double.*

First of all, you've got to give the owners credit for architectural originality, with their post-modern Tudor façade. Inside, facilities are strictly U.S. motel-style. There's nothing of interest in the area, but this will be an attractive lodging place if you're traveling by car, since protected parking is available.

KAHLUA GUEST HOUSE, *120 Eve St., tel. 31130, fax 31185. 12 rooms. $30 to $40 single/$35 to $45 double.*

Good seafront location. All rooms are off an enclosed side porch, and all rooms, though plain, have television, telephone and air conditioning.

GLENTHORNE MANOR, *27 Barrack Rd., tel. 44212. 6 rooms. $25 to $35 single/$35 to $45 double, plus tax and service, including breakfast.*

This historic wooden mansion, designed by a fugitive Italian architect, contains the oddest combinations of hardwood detailing and modern accretions. Every guest room is different. Guests may use the kitchen and, for a fee, the washing machine and dryer. Owner Winil Grant Borg, of the distinguished Belizean family of public servants and artists that named this building after their one-time London residence, will fill you in on historical details, and see that you are well started every morning with Creole bread, Johnnycakes and fried fish. In the sitting room, among the solid mahogany furniture, is the throne used by the Queen of the Bay.

South of the Swing Bridge

BELLEVUE HOTEL, *5 Southern Foreshore, tel. 77051, fax 73253. 37 rooms. $79 single/$83 double plus 10% service plus tax. Full American plan $25 additional. Visa, Master Card, American Express. U.S. reservations tel. 800-223-9815.*

On the seafront, the Bellevue is housed in what was once a fine old seafront home, expanded over the years into the present building. The air conditioned rooms are quite large for Belize City. The dining room menu is certainly more elegant that what you'll generally find in Belize City. The Southern Foreshore neighborhood, in decline for a number of years, is now improving. The hotel also owns cabanas on St. George's Caye, and has an in-house travel agency.

HOTEL MOPAN, *55 Regent St., tel. 77351, fax 75383. 12 rooms. $25 single/$35 double (more with air conditioning, when available).*

Located toward the south end of Regent St., the Mopan is a large old house with screened-in porch. Though run down, it has long been a base for aspiring Indiana Joneses, and some old Belize hands swear by it. Owners Tom and Jean Shaw, distinguished in Belizean society, have as much knowledge as anyone about the country. The neighborhood, less seedy than others in the city, includes a number of historic buildings.

EL CENTRO HOTEL, *4 Bishop St., tel. 72413, fax 74533. 13 rooms. $35 to $50 single or double. No service charge.*

A modern businessman's hotel with comforts available in a minimalist fashion: small, industrial-carpeted, plywood-panelled rooms tucked under stairs, and narrow halls. Very clean, air conditioned, with private baths, in-room phones, televisions, even an ice machine (welcome on sweltering days). Good value for Belize City. A block from the central park. Only a few rooms are available at the lower rates.

Budget Lodging South of Swing Bridge

SEASIDE GUEST HOUSE, *3 Prince St., tel. 78339. 8 rooms. $13 single/$19 double, or $8 per person in bunk room.*

A find for budget travelers — modest, clean, American-run, pleasant, and safe, with an occasional sea breeze and Caribbean view. Inexpensive breakfasts are served. Five blocks south of Swing Bridge, then east. Ask for Phillip.

BELCOVE HOTEL, *9 Regent St. West, tel. 73054, fax 77600. 9 rooms. $20 or less per person.*

Located along Haulover Creek on one side, and a seedy section of Regent St. on the other. Most rooms share bathrooms. The management also runs a resort on Gallows Point Caye and a travel agency specializing in services for boat owners, who are the main and perhaps only clientele.

Northern Edge of Downtown

Other acceptable lodging places are **FREDDY'S GUEST HOUSE**, *86 Eve Street, tel. 33851, on the northern edge of downtown, $20 double,* with just three rooms; and **MARIN'S TRAVELODGE**, *6 Craig St., $10/$14,* clean, small cubicles.

By The Airport

There isn't much in the way of lodging out here, but you can find a place to sleep if you have an early flight and are dead set against spending another night in Belize City. At the **BELIZE INTERNATIONAL AIRPORT HOTEL** *(tel. 025-2049),* just outside the international airport along the Northern Highway, rates in the 60 run-down, musty rooms are about $25 per person with air conditioning. Apartments are available.

If you have a car, you can try the **RIO HAUL MOTEL** *(tel. 44859), at mile 5 on the Northern Highway, near where the Belize River empties into the sea.* There's nothing much out here, but the place has been painted and improved recently, the air conditioners work, and the charge is only about $25 double.

WHERE TO EAT

Except for snack places, you'll be able to eat in Belize City mostly at standard meal hours, typically 6:30 to 10 a.m., noon to 2:30, and 6:30 to 11 p.m. Many restaurants are closed for all or part of Sunday.

Some of the best dining in the city is in the hotels. The fifth-floor, glassed-in dining room of **THE VILLA**, *13 Cork St.,* is a can't-miss experience in Belize City. Air-conditioned, with full city views.

Another good choice is the **REEF RESTAURANT** *of the Ramada Royal Reef Resort on Barrack Road, northeast of the town center.* What can you say about a restaurant that offers Carlo Rossi as the house wine? That it is reliable and consistent, with a genuine hotel chef on staff.

The elegant upstairs dining room of the **CHATEAU CARIBBEAN**, *6 Marine Parade,* affords lovely views to the sea. Service is good.

Across the Swing Bridge, the dining room of the **BELLEVUE**

HOTEL, *5 Southern Foreshore*, has an elegant menu. With a drink, a full dinner will run $20 or more. American Express and Visa accepted.

THE GRILL, *164 Newtown Barrack Rd.*, is away from the downtown hustle past the Ramada, a pleasant, modern, air-conditioned dining room overlooking the sea. Many items are prepared over charcoal, but there are also shrimp creole and pepper steak for more delicate palates. $6 for the lunch special, about $10 to $15 for dinner.

MOM'S, *7145 Slaughter House Rd. (Near Technical College)*, always lively, is a long-time favorite of visitors, and many Belizeans as well.

On a Sunday morning, when Belize City looks like a ghost town, walk into Mom's, and discover where everyone has been. Rice and beans with assorted accompaniments, burritos, roast beef, stew chicken, sandwiches and breakfast combinations with eggs and fry jacks, or French toast and ham, go for $4 to $8, and there are kids' portions; palates with loftier tastes will find lobster or shrimp salad. Wine is served as well as beer. They'll even accept your credit card (Master Card or Visa).

Mom's was started at the south end of the Swing Bridge by a transplanted American grandmother, who brought her favorite recipes from the old country. In its former location on Handyside Street, it was a gathering place and communication point, where you can post a message, meet travelling companions, and read posters advertising new budget hotels and services. *Open from 6 a.m. to 10 p.m., closed Saturday.*

The **FOUR FORT STREET** is a picture-perfect verandaed house hung with lanterns and plants, the tables set with lace tablecloths, fans wafting overhead. Intrigue, romance and adventure lurk.

Queen Street is the site of several popular Chinese restaurants, especially **SHEN'S PEKING PANDA**, *just north of the Swing Bridge*, and upstairs. $8 or so will get you a Szechuan specialty, such as chicken and cashews. Other Chinese restaurants include **CHINA TOWN**, *across the street from Shen's*, and not as good; and the **GOLDEN DRAGON**, *off Queen St. opposite Barrack Rd.*, $2 to $6 for sandwiches and standard Belizean and Chinese fare.

DIT'S, *50 King Street*, light and clean and well-fanned, is popular with locals for Belizean-style rice and beans with chicken or beef, meat pies, and tamales. No main course costs more than $3.

Nearby, the **MEXICAN CORNER**, *29 King Street*, is a favorite hole in the wall of not the slightest pretension, a room of painted boards with a fan overhead. The fare is Yucatecan and Hispanic specialties.

Light Fare

CELEBRATIONS, *16 Queen St. opposite the radio tower*, and the **BLUE BIRD**, *35 Albert St.*, have ice cream, fruit juices, and burgers and sandwiches for less than $2.

Pizza by the slice is sold at the **PIZZA HOUSE**, *King St. west of Albert*. **PETE'S PASTRIES**, *41 Queen St.*, has meat pies, tamales, enchiladas, and pies and tarts made from lemon, raisins, coconut and many other fruits, cow foot soup on Saturday.

SEEING THE SIGHTS

The Fort George Area

A good place to start a tour of Belize City is the **Fort George Hotel**. Originally it was Fort George Island, and was the locale of a barracks until the 1850s. The strait separating the fort from the city was filled in, in the 1920s, and a park was laid out to honor the dead of the first World War. Nearby are the Customhouse, the tomb of the benefactor Baron Bliss, and a lighthouse.

If any neighborhood has class in Belize, it is the one around the Fort George. The streets are quiet. A breeze blows in from the sea. A few large, old, plantation-style residences, hung with balconies, have been restored or otherwise spruced up to serve new functions. One is the **Chateau Caribbean Hotel**, *facing the water on Marine Parade*, another the **U.S. Consulate** *at 29 Gabourel Lane*, one of the few U.S. diplomatic missions without armed guards, originally built in New England, and transported to Belize as ballast and re-erected around 1870. Still another is the **Four Fort Street Guest House**.

Queen & Front Streets

Fort Street leads from the Fort George neighborhood to **Queen Street**, where the offices and showrooms of the major import houses of Belize, as well as the police station and the post office, are located. Most of the buildings are the by-now-familiar one- and two-story clapboard affairs, bare or with peeling paint. Belize's merchant class is not pretentious. Gradually, newer concrete buildings are replacing some of the old structures. At the corner of Front Street, facing Haulover Creek, is the **Paslow Building**, several stories housing the main **post office** downstairs, and government offices upstairs.

Continue left (seaward) along North Front Street. In the modern building at number 83, on the second floor, you'll find the information office of the **Belize Tourist Board**. *Hours are 8 a.m. to noon and 1 to 5 p.m. (to 4:30 p.m. on Friday). For assistance, call 77213 (fax 77490).*

The Swing Bridge

The **Swing Bridge** *crosses Haulover Creek at the center of Belize City*, with vehicles and pedestrians in constant motion throughout the day and into the night over its roadway and narrow walkways. The only breaks in the action come at 5:30 a.m. and 5:30 p.m., when the bridge is opened to allow boats to move up and down the river. Haulover Creek is a delta branch of the Belize River, and a major trade artery. The bridge is at the point where livestock was once "hauled over" from one bank to the other.

South of the Swing Bridge

At the southern end of the bridge is the modern **City Market**, recently rebuilt. Take a walk through for a sampler of tropical fruits and vegetables, some as colorful as the fish along the barrier reef, and equally exotic, with names like soursop and mammey apple. Here's your chance to match the real thing with the strange name.

South of the river is Belize City's Central Park, or **Market Square**, with its municipal buildings and what was once the national administration center. The **Supreme Court** is a grand old edifice, with an ironwork stairway leading up from the street to a long, second-floor veranda. Neoclassical columns and pediments lend an incongruous, pompous air to the building. The town clock looks out from a central tower.

In the vicinity of Market Square are the national headquarters of the major banks, all in solid concrete buildings that contrast with the prevailing architecture. Running on parallel sides of the square are Albert Street and Regent Street, once known as Back Street and Front Street. Along Regent Street are some of the oldest surviving buildings of Belize City, with brick basements where slaves were kept.

A block to the east of the square, facing the water on Southern Foreshore near Bishop Street, is the **Baron Bliss Institute**, a fiftyish building of flowing Frank Lloyd Wright-ish lines, which includes a theater, library, museum, and the National Arts Council. A Mayan stela from Caracol and two altars are on display, well documented. The legacy of Baron Bliss is one of the more curious bits of Belizeana.

Farther down Regent Street is **Government House**, a plantation-style clapboard mansion on spacious, well-tended seafront grounds, with ample shuttered, screened and windowed openings. Locally reputed to have been designed by noted British architect Christopher Wren more than 150 years ago (obviously a posthumous work), the building served as the residence of the superintendent, and later the governor, of British Honduras. The official home of the Queen's representative in Belize, the governor-general, is now Belize House in Belmopan. But this most elegant of Belizean residences still serves for official functions, and as a guest house for visiting royalty. The Prime Minister maintains an office in the compound.

Across from Government House is **St. John's Cathedral**, constructed between 1812 and 1826 of red brick imported from England as ships' ballast. The style is traditionally Anglican, but more on the scale of a country church than a cathedral. *Farther south, at the end of Albert Street*, is

Yarborough Cemetery, burial site of prominent figures from 1781, and of lesser members of the community since 1870.

SHOPPING

This is not a major activity for visitors, but you can try **Cottage Industries**, *26 Albert St.*, for pricey straw baskets, decorated conch shells, hardwood spoons, and necklaces of hardwood beads. The cow-horn carvings are interesting and, in a certain way, attractive. Hotel shops offer mahogany and ziricote carvings, black coral, and straw hats, as does **Burnaby's** art gallery, *9 Regent St.* Admiral Burnaby's also has paintings, t-shirts, and assorted gift items.

The **National Handicraft Center**, *3 Fort St.*, is a big shed with paintings, coral and slate carvings, baskets, bottled Belizean herbs, and t-shirts — altogether a one-stop shopping center for Belizean souvenirs. Among the benefits: it's air-conditioned, they take credit cards, and you can probably buy coral items without worrying about whether they're legal. **Go Tees**, *23 Regent St. at Prince St.*, has many, many t-shirts, many of them works of art. They also have Guatemalan crafts and carvings in rare local hardwood.

At various shops, you'll see coral necklaces, black and otherwise. It is illegal to buy black coral from unauthorized persons, and you probably shouldn't buy it at all, though you'll probably be offered some on the streets.

NIGHTLIFE

For an evening of drinking and/or dancing, head for Queen St., just north of the Swing Bridge.

At the corner of Daly St., is the **Hard Rock Café**. The steak is the best in Belize, and there are also blackened fish and Cajun shrimp, at $10 to $15 for a main course. It's not New York's Hard Rock, but with air conditioning, a third-floor view, and wrought-iron decor, it's as yuppie a place as you'll find in Belize.

The Big Apple is a centrally located dance hall, *at 67 North Front St.* Farther out, *on the Northern Highway*, and reachable by taxi, is the **Lumbaa Yaad**. *Call 31790 to see when they open.* Back in town, budget travelers sit around over drinks and watch the river at **Dimas' Mira Rio**, *59 North Front St.*

For the best strangers' drinking spot, I recommend the **Belize Biltmore Plaza Hotel**, *a couple of miles out on the Northern Highway.* Tucked behind the restaurant is the **Squires Lounge**, a modern, homey, pub sort of place, with tiled, U-shaped bar, polished hardwood surfaces, glasses hanging from overhead racks, and subdued lighting. The *karaoke* (sing-along machine) attracts British soldiers and talented locals, including some of the hotel's own employees. Prices are moderate as things go in Belize.

Caution after Dark

Several other spots downtown have run the cycle of opening, dissolving into violence, and shuttering. Be careful of where you venture after dark, re-check any recommendations to night spots that are not mentioned here, and, in any case, *please take a taxi back to your hotel*. It's a few dollars well spent, even if you're on a budget.

EXCURSIONS FROM BELIZE CITY

Audubon Society

The **Belize Audubon Society**, *12 Cork St., tel. 77369*, manages wildlife reserves in Belize in cooperation with the government and private organizations. It's a good idea to check in with the Audubon Society to inquire about the current state of facilities and seasonal conditions if you're planning a trip to the **Community Baboon Sanctuary** at Bermudian Landing in the Belize District; the **Cockscomb Basin Wildlife Sanctuary** in southern Belize; the **Crooked Tree Wildlife Sanctuary** north of Belize City; and the **Half Moon Caye Natural Monument**. No special arrangements are needed before stopping at **Guanacaste Park**, near Belmopan, or the **Blue Hole National Park**, along the Hummingbird Highway.

The Audubon Society also has a bird checklist, and, especially valuable in the field, a glossary giving "translations" of bird names from Creole to English. *The mailing address is P. O. Box 1001, Belize City.*

Note that two reserves managed by the Audubon Society are strictly for research, and are off-limits to visitors. These are **Bladen Nature Reserve** in the Maya Mountains, and **Society Hall Nature Reserve**, at the northern edge of Mountain Pine Ridge.

Boats

Regularly scheduled boats operate to Caye Caulker, Caye Chapel and Ambergris Caye. Even if you don't have time to linger on one of these islands, the boats make for budget-class tours of offshore Belize. Fare is usually $10 or less. Dropoffs can be arranged at other cayes that are not far off the route.

Most frequent service to Caye Caulker is from **A&R's Texaco** station, on North Front St., at 11 a.m.

• *The Andrea (tel. 026-2578 or 02-74988)* departs for San Pedro, Ambergris Caye, from in front of the Bellevue Hotel at about 3 p.m.during the week, 7 p.m. on Saturday.

- *The Thunderbolt Express*, a speedboat *(tel. 026-2217)*, departs from the Swing Bridge at 4 p.m. Monday through Friday, 1 p.m. on Saturday, for Caye Caulker, Caye Chapel and Ambergris Caye.
- *The Triple J (02-44375)* leaves for Caye Chapel, Caye Caulker and San Pedro at 9 a.m. from the north end of the Swing Bridge.

Let's say you want to take a day trip from Belize City to one or several cayes, and poke around the lagoons to the south. Where do you go?

- **A&R's Texaco station**, *on Front St. along Haulover Creek*, is where boat owners gather to find passengers for Caye Caulker. The operators come without recommendations, and without safety equipment, and drive hard bargains (bargains?).
- **Captain Chocolate** *(tel. 022-2151)* and **Capt. Jim Novelo** *(tel. 022-2195)* on Caye Caulker regularly pick up passengers in Belize City for day trips to outlying cayes, at mostly fixed prices, based on a minimum group size.
- The hotels along the sea — the **Fort George**, **Ramada Royal Reef**, and **the Bellevue** — have their own boats or resident charter operations.
- Belize City marinas will charter skiffs with operator and life jackets. From **Blackline Marina** *(mile 2 on the Northern Highway, tel. 33187)*, a boat for the day for three persons, with stops at two cayes and some snorkeling, will cost about $150. I've been satisfied with their services and safety.

Other boat parks are **Caribbean Charter Service**, *Mile 5, Northern Highway, tel. 45814*; and **Belize Marine Enterprises**, *tel. 45798*.

SPORTS & RECREATION
Diving & Dive Shops
- The **Blackline Dive Shop and Marina**, *at mile 2 on the Northern Highway (P. O. Box 332, tel. 33187, fax 31975)*, runs diving and fishing trips from Belize City, or will outfit and drop you on an offshore caye, or just rent out equipment. Dive trips run $75 per person for the day, reef fishing $250 for a group of three, and there are assorted other river and sea excursions on offer, including a Belize River Safari for $50 per person.
- **Dive In**, t*el. 30265, at the Ramada Royal Reef Resort*, offers two-tank dives at a price of $60 per, and night dives for $50.
- **Adventure Coast Divers**, *Mile 3, Northern Highway, tel. 33185.*
- **Belize Diving Service**, *P. O. Box 667, tel. 22143.*
- **Caribbean Charter Service**, *Mile 5, Northern Highway, P. O. Box 752, tel. 45814.*
- **Maya Landings Marina**, *P. O. Box 997, tel. 45798, fax 30263.*

TOURS/TRAVEL AGENCIES

The agencies listed below will arrange excursions to various parts of the country.

Major agencies/operators:

- **Belize Mesoamerica Tours**, *4 South Park Street (P. O. Box 1248), tel. 73383, fax 30750*. Day tours to inland sights (about $60 to $75 per person) and to Tikal.
- **G & W Carib Holiday**, *International Airport (P. O. Box 820, Belize City), tel. 025-2461, fax 2645*.
- **Gilly's Tours**, *31 Regent St., tel. 45264*, has been recommended by some users. Overnight trips to Lamanai cost about $125 per person, day runs to Xunantunich about $65.
- **Mayaland Tours and Travel**, *67 Eve St., tel. 30515, fax 32242*. You an inquire here about the Belize Aggressor dive boat.
- **Mira Rio Travels**, *at the little river-front Mira Rio Hotel, 59 North Front St., tel. 44970*, arranges stays on some of the smaller offshore cayes.
- **Maya Circuit Tours**, *P. O. Box 428, tel. 77051, fax 73253*. This is the travel agency of the Bellevue Hotel.
- **Native Guide Systems**, *6 Water Lane (near the Bliss Hotel), P. O. Box 1045, tel. 25819, fax 74007*. The owner is one of those knowledgeable gentlefolk who have made the transition from hunting and chicle gathering to guiding birders, divers, and archaeologists.
- **Belcove Yacht and Travel Services**, *9 Regent St. West, tel. 73054, fax 77600*, advertises services for yacht owners, from customs clearance to laundry. Located in the riverside Belcove Hotel, with adjacent docking, on the earthy south side of Haulover Creek, they operate the Gallows Point Resort on Gallows Point Caye, to which day trips are offered for about $35 per person, including snack. Also day diving and river trips.
- **S & L Travel**, *91 North Front St. (P. O. Box 700), tel. 77593, fax 75200*, is run by two of the most experienced guides in Belize. Day trips and custom tours available.
- **Mom's Triangle Inn and Restaurant**, *11 Handyside St., tel. 45073, fax 78163*, serves as agent for several inland lodges, for Blackline Marina on the edge of Belize City (mentioned under Dive Shop, above), and is the leading unofficial place for meeting, and picking up the latest information and unconfirmed rumors. Adventurous Belize, with an office at Mom's *(tel. 33903, fax 33966)* runs day trips to caves and underground rivers.
- **Mayaland Tours**, *64 Bella Vista, tel. 30515 (fax 32242)*, runs day and overnight tours to inland sights. About $60 per person for day trips, $300 per person overnight.
- **Sunrise Yacht Excursions** *at the Ramada Royal Reef Hotel (tel. 30265)* has

daily trips to Goff's Caye ($65) and a sunset cruise ($35) on an air-conditioned boat, and a two-tank dive for a hefty $95 *plus* equipment rentals.

Other general travel agencies are:

- **Universal Travel**, *8 Handyside St. (opposite Mom's Restaurant), tel. 30963, fax 30964*
- **Belize Global Travel Services** *(American Express representatives), 41 Albert St., tel. 77363*
- **Belize Tours**, *115 Albert St., tel. 75443, fax 77681*
- **Belize Travel Adventures**, *168 N. Front St., tel. 33064*
- **Jal's**, *148 North Front St., tel. 45407.*

PRACTICAL INFORMATION

Banks/Money Exchange

Belize City's banks, clustered around Market Square, are: **Atlantic Bank**, *6 Albert St.* (associated with Chase Manhattan); **Bank of Nova Scotia**, *Albert and Orange Streets*; **Barclays Bank**, *on Albert St.*; and **The Belize Bank of Commerce and Industry**, formerly the Royal Bank. Catch them before 1 p.m. on weekdays (extra hours from 3 to 6 p.m. on Friday).

Most hotels and restaurants accept U.S. cash and travelers checks without charging commission, so there's little reason to change money at a bank. Some fellows on the street will offer to pay more than the going exchange rate if you follow them up a dark alley. Hmmm.

Consulates

The major consulates are:

- **United States**, *29 Gabourel Lane (Fort George area), tel. 77162, open 8 a.m. to 5 p.m. Monday through Friday*
- **Canada**, *89 North Front St., tel. 31060 or 44182*
- **Mexico**, *20 North Park St. (Fort George Area), tel. 30193*
- **Costa Rica**, *8 18th St., tel. 44796*
- **Netherlands**, *14 Central American Blvd. at Banak St., tel. 73612*
- **El Salvador**, *120 New Road, tel. 44318*
- **Guatemala**, *Northern Highway*
- **Honduras**, *91 North Front St., upstairs, tel. 45889*
- **Jamaica**, *Hyde's Lane at New Rd., tel. 45446*

The **British High Commission** *is on Embassy Square in Belmopan, el. 08-22146.*

Groceries

Brodie's Supermarket, *at Albert and Church streets, just south of the Central Park,* has a large selection of canned goods, local and imported liquors, wine, drugs, and sundries, mostly imported. Figure about double the American price for anything. If you're tired of eating out, go to the deli counter for sliced cold cuts and salads. They're open in the morning on Sundays, in addition to the more usual hours during the week.

Across Albert St., **Romac's** also has a large selection of packaged foods, as does the **Save-U Supermarket**, *on the north side of Haulover Creek, a mile upriver at the Belcan Bridge.*

Immigration

For an extension of your permission to stay in Belize, or other immigration problems, go to the **Immigration Department** *at 115 Barrack Rd., tel. 77237.*

Post Office

Located on Queen Street, at the north end of the Swing Bridge. Hours are 8 a.m. to noon and 1 to 5 p.m., to 4:30 p.m. on Fridays. Post cards to the States or Canada cost 30¢ Belize (15¢ U.S.), lightweight letters 60¢ Belize (30¢ U.S.).

Telephones

Telephone calls from your hotel are charged at extortionate rates. Look for a pay phone, or call collect, or from the air-conditioned **telephone company** offices *at 1 Church St. (near the Central Park), open every day from 8 a.m. to 9 p.m.* Two USA-Direct phones are available at this location, or you can dial 555 from any phone to reach AT&T in the States.

Pay phones are located in the larger hotels, and in green booths throughout the city.

Tourist Office

The **Belize Tourist Board** (or Bureau) is *located at 83 North Front St. (across the street from the post office, a couple of buildings toward the sea) on the second floor.* You can purchase a map of Belize here, and inquire about buses and current hotel rates. *For assistance by telephone, call 77213 (fax 77490). Hours are 8 a.m. to noon and 1 to 5 p.m. (to 4:30 p.m. on Friday).*

NORTH FROM BELIZE CITY

Not too long ago, the Northern Highway was an insult to vehicle and body. A single-car-width strip running down its center had once been paved, but the accumulated potholes of many years did so much damage to vehicles that wise drivers kept to the unpaved shoulders.

Bad as the Northern Highway used to be, its construction in the 1930s was a major advance for the colony. An alternative was provided to the coastal boats that provided a sometimes shaky link between Belize City and Corozal, and a great impetus was given to the development of the sugar industry. Mayan ruins were raided for surfacing materials, a cultural loss, but a practice in keeping with the methods of the Maya themselves, who often re-used the building materials of their ancestors.

With realignment and reconstruction, the Northern Highway is less of an adventure, though the recherché thrills of extreme discomfort and uncertain arrival time can still be experienced on the southern Humming-bird Highway and such secondary roads as exist in Belize. The Northern Highway is now one of the easier routes for the traveler who wants to visit archaeological sites, experience some of the tropical vegetation zones from coastal swamp to pine barren to limestone scrub to luxuriant semi-rain forest, observe wildlife in the Crooked Tree sanctuary, or look in on the small-town mestizos and rural Mayans and Mennonites of the north. Handily, the road provides a gateway to Mexico as well.

Driving time from Belize City to the Mexican border, a distance of about 90 miles, is under three hours. Buses take four hours or less. The route is almost totally flat, and, now that the road is wide and in good repair, less interesting than it was when traffic was forced to move at a snail's pace.

At **Ladyville**, a community that stretches along the road in the vicinity of Mile 9, is **Phillip Goldson International Airport**. Ladyville is well-built and prosperous, with assorted small industry, British and Belize Defence Force barracks, and a couple of hotels (mentioned under Belize City). It is also home of **Raul's Rose Garden**, pointed out to passing tourists as the most reputed house of ill repute in Belize, though it is not the sole contender for that title.

THE BABOON SANCTUARY

At Mile 18, a branch road leads directly westward to villages with such picturesque names as **Double Head Cabbage**, **Burrell Boom** and **Bermudian Landing**. All are on the Belize River, which once served as a meandering highway to the coast. **Bermudian Landing**, *26 miles from Belize City*, formerly a timber transfer point, is now mainly a farming and ranching center, known for its unique **Community Baboon Sanctuary**.

No, there aren't any baboons in Belize, at least, not as the word is used in other countries. *Baboon* is the local name for the black howler monkey, which flourishes in forests along the Belize River. Similar communities elsewhere are threatened by forest destruction. This sanctuary was established in 1985 to forestall problems, as forest lands are converted to farming.

Unusually, all of the sanctuary consists of private lands. Owners have pledged to preserve food trees, riverside vegetation, and forest corridors in areas of cleared land, in order to give black spider monkeys a sufficient area in which to sustain their population. The payoff for the farmers is reduced erosion.

Trails through the sanctuary allow visitors to look in on — or up to — howler monkey family life. Howlers travel in the treetops, in groups of four to eight, feeding on leaves, flowers, and fruits, especially wild figs. Listen for the howlers' piercing, rasping call — it's more like the roar of a lion than a howl.

The lowland forest of the sanctuary varies from dense riverside tangles of trees and vines to drier pine forest and savanna, and is home to almost 200 species of birds, and many other forms of wildlife.

ARRIVALS & DEPARTURES
By Taxi

The easiest way to reach the sanctuary is to drive or take a taxi or a tour. The road is slippery clay in parts.

By Bus or Car

Buses for Bermudian Landing leave George St. near Orange St., Belize City, at noon, 1 p.m. and 3:30 p.m.; another leaves at 12:30 p.m. from beside the Pacific store on Cemetery Rd., Belize City. Return buses are at 5 a.m. and noon. Inquire for directions and current schedules at the Belize Audubon Society, 12 Cork St., Belize City (tel. 77369), before you visit. (The Audubon Society sponsors the reserve, along with the World Wildlife Fund and the Zoological Society of Milwaukee County.)

The new route of the Northern Highway passes through stunted pines and scrub in sandy soil, gnarled, twisted trees, palmetto and savannah. There is some seasonally dry forest that loses its leaves for part of the year, and large expanses of pasture. Intermittently, a road leads off to some farming venture started up for the export trade. But as in the rest of Belize, the land is mostly empty of people.

Signs identify occasional settlements, such as **Biscayne Village**, population 268. Several miles down the road another sign wishes you a good journey upon leaving the same village — though you haven't seen more than one or two houses. Staggered irregularly along the way are 15-foot steel posts, installed to hinder small dope-smuggling planes from using the wide, straight, smooth road as an airstrip. Most of the poles have been removed, or bent aside. There are few places to stop for a drink, and no gas stations until Orange Walk.

At Sand Hill, the route divides into the New Northern Highway, and the Old Northern Highway. The latter meanders toward Orange Walk just inland from the coastal swamps.

WHERE TO STAY

A couple of bare rooms are available next door to the sanctuary for about $10 a double, and meals can be arranged for a few dollars each. There is also tent space.

LITTLE EDEN GUEST HOUSE *(tel. 028-2052, P. O. Box 1713, Belize City)* is a pottery studio with a couple of guest rooms sharing toilet facilities, on a palm-studded mini-estate. The rate is about $40 double with breakfast, and the location is convenient if you're driving and don't wish to spend the night in Belize City.

SEEING THE SIGHTS

Hours at the sanctuary are 8 a.m. to 5 p.m. A welcome center has maps and exhibits concerning the land-use plan, and answers the question on everybody's mind: why do howler monkeys howl?

In the company of a local guide (fee about $5 per hour), you can walk through the pretty village, with its modest houses scattered under the cashew trees and coco plums, and simply step out of the horse pastures and into dense tropical forest, sprinkled with ramrod mahogany trees, in one of the strips that make up the reserve. Your guide will point out the trumpet tree on which the howlers feed; identify the flora, and maybe a passing gibnut; and on a good day, steer your eyes toward a baboon. But be warned: though you can sometimes see whole families of monkeys crossing the cable that provides passage over the road, on other days they're stay-at-homes.

On the way to the Baboon Sanctuary, the road follows the Belize River. Baboon River Canoe Rentals in Burrell Boom can set you up with a **canoe** or **kayak**. *Call 028-2101 before you set out to set the rate and make sure somebody's there.* It's less than 20 miles from Belize City, but it really is jungle, with iguanas, toucans, and macaws giving you the once-over all along your route.

ALTUN HA

*About 28 miles north of Belize City along the poorly maintained Old Northern Highway is the junction for the access road to **Altun Ha**. Follow the side road for two miles to the west to reach the ruins.* The name of the site is simply a translation into Mayan of **Rockstone Pond**, a nearby settlement.

Mounds covered by trees and vines, the remains of what was once a great city, spread out over an area of more than 25 square miles at Altun Ha. Excavations have been concentrated in the central part of the city, where more than 275 structures have been found in an area about one thousand yards square.

The Altun Ha archaeological zone is open from 9 a.m. to 5 p.m., with a small entrance fee.

Early Altun Ha

Altun Ha was probably first settled long before the Classic Mayan era, perhaps as many as 2000 years ago. For a Mayan city, the site was unusual. The soil is thin and poor, which has led some to speculate that Altun Ha was a trading center rather than a self-contained agricultural community.

Agriculture might also have been important to the inhabitants of Altun Ha, not only for staples — corn, beans and squash — but also to produce export crops, such as cacao. Other possible food sources were wild plants, game, and, unique to the Maya of Belize, seafood.

ARRIVALS & DEPARTURES

By Tour or Taxi

The most practical way to get to Altun Ha is by tour or taxi, or in a rented car. The road is narrow, lined with dense forest, and potholed, but passable at a slow pace.

Passenger-and-cargo trucks come down the old highway in the morning and return from Belize City in the evening — not very practical for a day's round trip. Otherwise, you can try to hitch a ride, though there's little traffic past the junction at Sand Hill.

Keep in mind that almost all the trees have been cut down at Altun Ha, and the site is open and bare and frankly less attractive to a casual visitor than Xunantunich, Caracol, and Cahal Pech in western Belize.

WHERE TO STAY

Past the junction for Altun Ha on the old Northern Highway is:

MARUBA RESORT, *Mile 40.5, Old Northern Highway, tel. 03-22199. 14 rooms. $84 single/$106 double, plus 15% service plus tax. Add $35 in junior suite, $50 for three meals. Visa, Master Card, American Express. Airport pickup, $45. In the United States: Maruba Tours, P. O. Box 300703, Houston, TX 77230, tel. 800-627-8227 or 713-799-2031, fax 713-795-8573.*

Just beyond the ruins of Altun Ha, and off the tracks that most visitors follow, **Maruba** is in a class by itself among the lodging places of Belize, a luxurious fantasy that blends almost seamlessly into the jungle.

Rock-paved paths lined by flowers lead through palm-shaded grounds past parrots and toucans and garden sitting areas with tables tiled in *faux* tablecloths, to a flower-bordered pool where the shower emerges from a waterfall; to a massage room wafting incense; to a central rotunda dining pavilion, where the furnishings seem to sprout from the jungle floor along with the palms and ferns. The creatures of the vicinity, morelet crocodiles and kinkajous, gather at a pond.

The guest rooms are all different, some individual cabanas, some in small outbuildings, others updated Mayan *ranchos*. One has a tub of Mexican tile, stuccoed walls, a platform bed with cane sides, and a futon as an alternative to the mattress. The jungle suite, up on the third level, shares the forest canopy with macaws and monkeys, and comes with video, whirlpool and refrigerator.

The kitchen relies on produce grown on-site — pineapple, grapefruit, limes, mangos and coconuts — and game is usually on the menu. Presentation is excellent, right down to the exotic beverages served in coconut cups.

Beauty is the theme of Maruba. Try on a full body massage; tropical herbal wrap; seaweed body wrap; aromatherapy massage; mineral baths. The ingredients are drawn from petals and leaves and seeds and bark, in consultation with a local herbalist.

Maruba has an a la carte menu for body treatments ($45 to $60), or, if you've been roughing it underwater or on a boat, you can be picked up for lunch, a visit to Altun Ha, and a choice of treatment, at about $150. Assorted packages are available. If you choose the right package for a river trip from San Pedro, on Ambergris Caye, you'll stop here for lunch.

Stop me from going on.

CIRCLE K LODGE, *up the road from Maruba and 14 miles from the junction with the new Northern Highway*, offers basic summer camp-style cottages with linoleum floors and no decoration, on disorderly grounds. The rate is about $25 double. *Call the community phone, 03-22600, to make contact, and inquire if meals are available.*

TOURING THE RUINS

The major structures of Altun Ha, called pyramids and palaces, surround two central plazas, which have been excavated and partially restored. ("Pyramid" is a handy designation for a massive platform of rubble faced with finished limestone blocks, surmounted by a temple. "Palaces" are more rambling structures than pyramids, with less massive bases.)

At Altun Ha, the temple bases are roughly oval in form and terraced, with staircases facing the plaza. The temples atop the bases, where they survive, are multi-roomed limestone structures, with corbelled interior arches. The *corbel*, or false arch, consists of layers of stone on each side of a room, protruding successively inward, until the two sides can be capped by a single block. The corbel can span only a narrow width, so massive Mayan structures contain claustrophobically small amounts of interior space.

Plazas A and B

Plaza A, the more northerly of the two central plazas, is surrounded by five pyramids and one palace. The visible parts of its temples are only the outermost of a series of superimposed buildings. The Maya periodically built new, more elaborate temples right on top of their old ones. The direct ancestor of all the temples was probably a simple thatched hut atop a paved platform. Both elements grew and became more complex and sturdy over the centuries.

Pyramid **A-1**, the **Temple of the Green Tomb**, on the west side of Plaza A, revealed an especially rich funeral chamber in its depths, with human remains and more than 300 jade pieces, including pendants, beads and figures, as well as earrings, obsidian rings, pearls, and the crumbling fragments of a codex, or book. Excavations in structure **A-4**, to the southeast, uncovered beads of a gold-copper alloy, pearls, and seashells from the Pacific, indicating that goods from as far away as southern Central America reached Altun Ha.

Plaza A was apparently the center of Altun Ha until about 550 A.D., when the addition of Plaza B enlarged the ceremonial precinct.

Structure B-4

On the east side of **Plaza B** is structure **B-4**, the **Sun God Temple**, named for the carvings of Kinich Ahau, the sun god, on either side of the first set of steps. At just 59 feet in height, it is the tallest structure at Altun Ha, but its importance has to do with more than its relative prominence. For in a tomb in the rectangular stone-and-mortar mass at the top of the temple was discovered the largest carved-jade piece ever found in Middle America, a squashed-looking representation of Kinich Ahau weighing more than nine pounds.

Other tombs in structure B-4 held offerings of jade pendants and beads. Charred jade fragments found near circular altars suggest that periodic reconstruction of the temple was accompanied by the destruction of valuable objects.

About 500 yards south of Plaza B is a reservoir that was fed by springs and rain runoff. A stable water supply was, of course, essential to any large settlement, and the Maya improved on the original natural pool.

Carbon-14 dating techniques place the first reconstruction of a building at Altun Ha at about 150 A.D. Building went on for several hundred years, and the center probably flourished until about 900 A.D. The desecration of tombs indicates that Altun Ha was not simply abandoned in a migration to some other location, but came to an end amidst civil turmoil and revolt. Finds of trash from about the fourteenth and fifteenth century show that people still lived at Altun Ha, at least intermittently, but it was no longer part of the great Mayan cultural tradition that survived in the Yucatan, to the north.

CROOKED TREE WILDLIFE SANCTUARY

Astride the Northern Highway about halfway between Belize City and Orange Walk is the **Crooked Tree Wildlife Sanctuary**, consisting of several lagoons, and surrounding marshes and swamps. Operated by the Belize Audubon Society, the 3000-acre reserve is currently in a state of development.

Notable at Crooked Tree is the jabiru, a stork that is the largest flying bird in the hemisphere, with a wing span of up to twelve feet. Jabirus nest in the northern lowlands of Belize starting in November, during the dry season. There are also wood storks, and assorted herons, ducks, grebes, kingfishers, vultures, ospreys, kites, hawks, anhingas, egrets, and many other bird species, water-loving and otherwise. The varied habitats and plentiful food sources also attract black howler monkeys, crocodiles, coatimundis, and turtles and iguanas.

ARRIVALS & DEPARTURES

Only the western part of the reserve, taking in the Northern and adjacent lagoons, is open to casual visitors.

Arriving & Departing By Car

Take the Northern Highway to mile 33, where a branch dirt road cuts west onto a causeway over the Northern Lagoon, terminating at the old logging village of **Crooked Tree**, four miles from the highway.

About 50 miles north of Belize City, after the old and new Northern Highways reunite, is the Tower Hill toll bridge over the New River, built in 1967. If you're driving south, the old Northern Highway, following a more easterly route near the coastal wetlands, is the road to take to the Altun Ha archaeological site. Just beyond the river on the west side (going north) is **Jim's Cool Pool**, a spring-fed circle of water, with a roadside refreshment area. Buses, unfortunately, don't stop there.

Arriving & Departing By Bus or Foot

From Belize City, the **Jex** bus departs for Crooked Tree at 11:55 a.m. and 4:30 and 5:30 p.m. from in front of the Habet Store, 34 Regent St.; a Batty bus leaves at 4 p.m. Departures from Crooked Tree for Belize City are usually at 5, 6 and 7 a.m. Verify schedules at the Audubon Society, 12 Cork St., if you plan to travel by bus.

Otherwise, it's a hot and dusty (or wet and muddy) walk from the junction on the Northern Highway, and there isn't enough traffic to count on hitching a ride. Residents of the village might have boats available for exploring the area. Toward the end of the dry season — April and early May — the water could be too low to launch a boat. But much can be seen on foot, from along the causeway lined with lily pads, and the shore of the long, low, lagoons, quiet and deserted except for water birds, and quite lovely.

WHERE TO STAY

CROOKED TREE RESORT *(P O Box 1453, Belize City, tel. 44101, $52 single/$65 double, 10% service).*

In an idyllic lakeside locale, has seven barely furnished, raised sapling cabanas with hot showers, on the edge of Crooked Tree village. The access road can be difficult during rainy periods, but walkways fashioned from tree stumps will keep your feet dry. The cuisine is plentiful rice and beans in the large, thatch-roofed dining room. Attractive dock and deck. Horses, guide service, tours and fishing are available by advance arrangement through **Native Guide Systems**, 1 Water Lane, Belize City, tel. 25819.

BIRD'S EYE VIEW LODGE, *tel. 72304 in Belize City. The rate is $45 single/$55 double with breakfast.*

There are five concrete rooms toward the south end of the village — turn left after you cross the causeway. Look right out from your room to jabirus in the lagoon.

PARADISE INN has four cabanas *to the north of the causeway, beyond Crooked Tree Resort,* at $50 single/$70 double, plus $15 for three meals. Boat tours ($20 per person), horseback riding ($15), fishing and birding are arranged. *Call 025-2535 if you plan to stay here, before you go out.*

Farther south, birders and naturalists will find the more isolated **CHAU HIIX LODGE**, on a large tract of land that includes habitats ranging from riverside forest to pine ridge. Streams and underground springs draw a variety of wildlife, even during dry periods.

SEEING THE SIGHTS

The visitors' center, on the right-hand side at the end of the causeway, has displays that will help you identify birds and plant features, such as the logwood swamp across the water to the southeast. Three trails range from a one-hour loop on the *jacana trail* to a two-hour trek out the *limpkin trail.*

Before visiting the reserve, drop in at the **Belize Audubon Society**, *12 Cork St., tel. 77369, Belize City,* and inquire about the current state of facilities, and to pick up a folder.

LAMANAI

The Orange Walk district abounds in archaeological sites. **Lamanai,** one of the largest Mayan cities in Belize, stretches for several miles on high ground along the west side of the New River Lagoon. Lamanai was occupied from the early formative period of the Maya until well after contact with Europeans — one of the longest continuing spans known for any Mayan site.

Lamanai was probably first inhabited 3,500 years ago. The earliest permanent buildings were erected around 700 B.C. and were continually enveloped by larger, more elaborate structures. The last stage of the major temple at Lamanai, **N10-43**, was completed around 100 B.C., and might well have been the tallest Mayan structure of its day.

Lamanai was excavated by a team of archaeologists from the Royal Ontario Museum, led by David Pendergast. More than 700 buildings were identified in the two-square-mile central section. A ghastly cache of children's bones found under one stela suggests that human sacrifice might have been practiced. A ball court marker dates from around the tenth century A.D., a time when Mayan civilization elsewhere had declined. The city's name might mean "submerged crocodile," reflecting the special esteem held by the Maya for that animal. The crocodile motif shows up on pottery and architectural decorations.

ARRIVALS & DEPARTURES
From Orange Walk & New River
In a four-wheel-drive vehicle, Lamanai is about 35 miles — and two hours — from Orange Walk by a track that takes a wide circle away from the New River. Most visitors, however, arrive on a more interesting adventure excursion up the New River. Guide operators provide ponchos, which also serve as windbreakers on what can be a surprisingly cool ride.

From Belize City
A day tour to Lamanai from Belize City is priced at about $125, but seats may be discounted out of season or on a last-minute basis. One reliable operator with guaranteed departures is **Belize Mesoamerica Tours**. In Orange Walk, inquire of **Jungle River Tours**, *20 Lover's Lane (P. O. Box 95), tel. 03-22293.*

Jim's Lamanai Experience has recently been operating daily trips to Lamanai from Jim's Cool Pool restaurant, just north of the toll bridge over the New River. Departure by boat (the *Lamanai Lady*) is at 8:30 a.m., returning to the highway at 4 p.m., tour price $28. You can also book this trip through the Batty Bus office in Belize City *(Mosul St. at Bagdad, a block from East Collet Canal, tel. 72025)* for $52, including the ride both ways on the bus.

WHERE TO STAY
LAMANAI OUTPOST, *tel. and fax 02-33578 in Belize City, 800-537-1431 in the U.S. $70 single/$90 double.*

This relatively new lodge is, indeed, an outpost of adventure, at Indian Church on the edge of ancient Lamanai, surrounded by dense forest alive with monkeys and macaws. You'll stay here mainly to visit the ruins, but there are additional attractions and activities: canoeing, windsurfing, horseback riding, massages, tarpon fishing, plant hunts in the jungle. Guests are charged an additional $150 for transportation, or stay on a package that costs from $125 to $150 per person per day inclusive.

TOURING THE RUINS

The ruins of Lamanai are unreconstructed and only partially cleared, with limited trails cut by archaeologists and squatters. The footing is slippery in the extreme, and the mosquitos are fearsome, even for Belize. Apply repellent before you enter the site, carry along a recall dose, and cover as much of your body as you comfortably can.

A small visitors' center focuses on wildlife and vegetation in the area, and holds some of the objects discovered at the site. Notable are eccentric flints, tripod vases in various shades of red (some with hollow legs containing pebbles for acoustic effect), and stone sculptures.

Temple of the Masks

Near the boat landing is structure **N9-56**, the **Temple of the Masks**, named for its decorations of large facial medallions, or masks. The underlying structure dates from about 200 B.C., but mostly later, outer layers of construction are visible. Its major sculpture, about nine feet high, is a realistic face, with what might be a jaguar pelt across the top section, and a basketweave motif on the upper surface and down the sides. The walls inside still retain some of the red pigment originally used to decorate the temple. Within, two tombs have been discovered. One contained a body encased in a clay shell, alongside wooden figures with jade jewelry — an odd procedure even according to standard Mayan practice of the time.

A rounded throne-like structure at the base contains curving channels. Could these have drained off the blood of sacrificed captives?

Overturned *stelae*, or inscribed stones, litter the base of the Temple of the Masks, and all of Lamanai. The figure on Stela 9 has been identified from its glyphic inscription as *Lord Smoking Shell*, a ruler of the city.

Most stelae have been left where found, face down. Some are cracked by the heat of fires that once were burned before them, probably after the decline of Lamanai. In parts of Guatemala, natives still burn incense at the ancient sites.

The High Temple

Structure N10-43, the **High Temple**, rising to 112 feet, the largest structure at Lamanai, is dated at 100 B.C. It may be climbed by a steep, intact staircase, to a perch above the jungle, swamps, and lagoon. There is no surviving superstructure, or sanctuary, at the summit, as on Mayan temples of the Classic period, such as those at Xunantunich. Most likely, whatever stood atop the High Temple was built of wood and thatch, and rotted away. Findings here include a large black-on-red bowl dated at 700 A.D., seashells, and a dish containing a bird skeleton.

Beside N10-43 is a rather eroded **Ballcourt**. In the cistern under the large central marker were found traces of mercury, which probably was mined in northern Mexico.

Farther south is **Indian Church**, one of the few remaining outposts of Spanish missionary efforts in Belize. A sixteenth-century church, built of stone from ancient Lamanai, was destroyed by Maya loyal to their traditional ways. Only the lower walls remain. A second church was erected by the persistent Christians, but it too was attacked, though more of it remains standing.

In the immediate area is the modern village of **Indian Church**, its houses of cane and split wood erected on Mayan mounds.

More Than a Ruin . . .

Lamanai is an ancient city, but it is also a botanical reserve and wildlife habitat. Troops of howler monkeys have specific territorial claims in the ruins. Oropendolas are common around the Temple of the Masks, *Aracaris*, a type of toucan, near Temple N10-9. Northern jacanas frequent the edge of the lagoon.

Trees along the trails are labeled for easy identification. The *give-and-take* tree has poisonous spines, but the sap of its roots is curative. The huge tubroose, or *guanacaste*, is often used in boatbuilding. Strangler figs, allspice and copal, with a resin used for incense, jam the jungle floor. And there are silk cottons (or *ceibas*, held sacred by the Maya), rubber trees, cedars and breadnuts (*ramón*, once a Maya staple).

SOUTHWEST OF ORANGE WALK

About 30 miles from Orange Walk are the Mennonite settlements clustered around **Blue Creek Village**. Farther on is an area set aside for conservation and ecological studies by the Programme for Belize.

WHERE TO STAY

CHAN CHICH LODGE, *12 cottages. $75 single/$90 double plus tax, meals $33 per person per day, no obligatory service charge. Master Card, Visa, American Express. Reservations in Belize: P.O. Box 37, Belize City, tel. 02-*

75634, fax 75635. In the United States: P.O. Box 1088, Vineyard Haven, MA 02568, tel. 800-343-8009, fax 508-693-6311.

Almost as far from Orange Walk as Orange Walk is from Belize City, Chan Chich is one of the newest of Belize jungle resorts, one of the most comfortable, and certainly the most controversial. The thatch-roofed cottages and common buildings sit squarely in the plaza of a Mayan ceremonial center, overlooked by another, larger plaza. To some eyes, this is a desecration. To others, it's a practical way to forestall further looting (some of the temples can be entered by looters' slit trenches), while encouraging knowledge of the ancient and modern Maya, and of the tropical forest. Chan Chich (possibly "little bird" in Mayan) is part of a series of related, adjacent projects, that include farming, archaeology, and wildlife preservation and research on large tracts of privately owned former logging and chicle land.

Despite the remote location, the cabins, built largely from locally obtained thatch and hardwood, have electricity, hot showers, and ceiling fans. All have porches. The central building contains the kitchen, dining area and bar. And the surrounding forest is populated by monkeys and assorted cats and the rest of the menagerie for which Belize is famous, as well as orchids and tropical trees.

SHIPSTERN NATURE RESERVE

Butterflies are at home in the lowlands and marshes *near Sarteneja*. The **Shipstern Nature Reserve**, a private operation, breeds and exports the insects for show and sale, on a 22,000-acre tract just southwest of Sarteneja, and seriously interested entomologists will find a visit worthwhile. The area is home to as many as 200 butterfly species, some of which live in the forest canopy, and face extinction when trees are cut.

Sponsored by the International Tropical Conservation Foundation of Switzerland, the Shipstern Reserve includes Belize's only protected seasonally dry forest, as well as mangroves and salt lagoons. The forest is still growing back after being flattened by Hurricane Janet almost 40 years ago. Migrating birds from the north frequent Shipstern Lagoon. Prized visual catches include the black catbird, white-winged dove and Yucatan jay. Tapirs, white-tailed and brocket deer, ocelots and even jaguars wander the savanna.

TOURING THE RESERVE

Best viewing is on sunny days. Trails lead from the reception building through three types of hardwood forest, with trees labeled with Latin and local names. It's easiest to take a day drive out this way from Orange Walk. Hours are 9 a.m. to noon and 1 to 4 p.m., closed on holidays. Tours cost about $5 per person.

SANTA ELENA/MEXICAN BORDER

Santa Elena, *on the Hondo River (Río Hondo)*, is the Belizean customs and immigration post at the international bridge, *95 miles (144 kilometers) from Belize City*. The town across the bridge, in Mexico, is **Subteniente López**. Border posts on both sides of the river are open around the clock.

Mexican tourist cards can usually be obtained on the other side of the bridge upon showing credible identification, preferably a passport.

Money changers give a fair rate at the border for American cash, and a slightly less favorable rate for Belizean currency.

Visitors entering Belize at Santa Elena go through formalities in a matter of minutes. *Caution for drivers:* Vehicle insurance is available across the road from the immigration building on weekdays, and sometimes on Saturday mornings. Liability insurance is required, and officials will allow you to proceed at other times only with reluctance.

Aside from insurance and immigration and customs posts, there are no facilities of any kind except a couple of duty-free shops, and basic rooms and travel-trailer parking on the Mexican side.

Belizean bus companies provide onward service right into **Chetumal, Mexico**, with a stop for immigration formalities.

WEST FROM BELIZE CITY

Traveling west from Belize City usually means going almost all the way to the Guatemalan border. It's not that far away — about 80 miles — but there isn't much in between except the still-developing new capital at **Belmopan**. Out toward the end of the line are the Spanish-speaking towns of **San Ignacio** and **Benque Viejo**, and the major Mayan ruins of **Xunantunich**. A branch road off the Western Highway provides access to **Mountain Pine Ridge**, a beautiful area of pine and hardwood forests in the foothills of the Maya Mountains, much of it held as a government reserve for controlled logging.

The Western Highway is wide and smooth-surfaced and fairly straight to past Belmopan, then paved and gently winding to San Ignacio, and onward to the border of Guatemala. The road roughly follows the course of the Sibun River for about thirty miles. The Sibun, and the Belize River, to the north, were once major trading arteries. Great mahogany logs came floating downriver at the height of the rainy season, when they could clear the rapids, and goods had no other way to move at any other time of year than in shallow-draft boats. Early in the century, before roads were even envisioned, obstructing rock outcrops on the Belize River were dynamited, and Haulover Creek was widened and dredged to allow lumber to pass more easily.

To the west and south, lumpy foothills march into the distance over the flat baseland, toward the Maya Mountains. It's easy to imagine them as cayes, or islands, in the sea that once covered this plain.

THE BELIZE ZOO

At mile 30 on the Western Highway is the turnoff for the **Belize Zoo**, located just off the road to the north. A zoo this is, but one with multiple messages, and like few that you've seen.

Keel-billed toucans and king vultures and crested guans perch on trees draped in wire mesh. Pathways wind through plots of forest inhabited by a jaguar, a tapir ("mountain cow"), a puma and an ocelot, to a bridge over a turtle pond. As much as possible, the animals reside in re-created habitats. There are black howler monkeys ("baboons"), tayras ("bush dogs"), margays and crocodiles, boa constrictors ("wowlas"), tepezcuintles (gibnuts, or pacas), coatimundis ("quash") and gray fox, great curassows and macaws.

Visitors from far away are welcome, but more than anything else, the zoo aims to heighten the awareness of Belizeans about their heritage of natural treasures. A section of a Mayan frieze shows ancient illustrations of the animals that live here. Part of the visitors' center is reserved for work with schoolchildren. Folksy signs and illustrations tell how the king vulture — King John Crow to Belizeans — prevents disease, and put in a plug for habitat preservation:

Animals clearly come first. While there is plenty of water to be pumped into ponds, the only toilet facilities for humans are outhouses, with no provision to wash hands (despite government warnings about cholera). Re-created habitat affords shelter from sun and from prying visitors, who peer from largely unshaded pathways. At midday, your chances of spying a jaguarundi or peccary or puma or ocelot are rather dim.

Hours at the zoo are 10 a.m. to 4:30 p.m. daily. Admission fee is $5 U.S. Any Belize City-San Ignacio bus will drop you at the turnoff. Take a look at the map before you start off! Trails wind seemingly at random. Take refreshments — none are available on-site.

GUANACASTE PARK

Guanacaste Park is a protected section of rain forest replete with orchids, bromeliads and ferns filling the air at every level. Named for the huge guanacaste (earpod or tubroose) tree, the park is a small (52-acre) plot between the Western Highway and the confluence of Roaring Creek and the Belize River. There is a network of nature trails, and birding is excellent. Numerous mammals, including kinkajou, gibnut, agouti and deer, can also be seen. Best of all, Guanacaste Park is readily accessible. The entrance is on the north side of the Western Highway, at the junction with the road to Belmopan. It's a pleasant locale for a picnic if you're traveling through by car or bus.

A word of warning: Guanacaste Park is a mugger's paradise. The predictable appearance of lone visitors on its isolated trails attracts low-lifes who find easy escape along the Belize River or into nearby Roaring Creek and Belmopan. Walk through the forest of Guanacaste Park only in a group — wait for others if you're alone. Consult the guards at the entry.

BELMOPAN - THE CAPITAL CITY

Located about 50 miles from Belize City, **Belmopan** is the young capital of the new nation. Like its larger cousins, Washington, D.C., and Brasilia, the city was planned from scratch.

What a strange place for a Belizean town is Belmopan, arising from the pastures and scrub all around. It sprawls over open green spaces. Block houses are set well apart on curving drives in suburban-style designated residential sections, at least a mile from anything, in a city where many do not have cars. Long sidewalks connect the different sections — a challenge in the hot sun, or the rain. The centerpiece of the capital is a complex of two multi-windowed, low-lying, concrete-and-brick government office blocks that come to an apex at Independence Hill. The buildings are designed in an adapted Mayan style, though they could also be taken for a tropical junior college campus.

The population of Belmopan is only about 4,000, and not growing rapidly toward the projected figure of 40,000. Belmopan is not unattractive, and not unpleasant. It's just, well, bland.

The impetus for the relocation of the capital was the devastation of Belize City by a hurricane in 1961, for the second time in thirty years. The new capital, sited near the country's geographical center, sheltered from coastal storms and free of swampy surroundings, is intended to spur development of the interior. The name of the city derives from the first syllable of Belize, and from Mopan, one of the original Mayan tribes of the country.

ARRIVALS & DEPARTURES
Arriving By Bus

Buses running between Belize City and San Ignacio stop in Belmopan about every hour throughout the day. Three or four buses coming from Dangriga pass through most mornings, and stop again during the afternoon on the return run.

Departing By Car

Past Belmopan, the Western Highway traverses rolling, lush country-side. Vegetation is exuberant where land remains fallow between shifting use as corn plots and pasture and orange groves. The road is narrower, and the going is slower, with curves, and occasional climbs and descents.

At mile 59 is the turnoff for **Spanish Lookout**, a Mennonite center six miles to the north. You'll see horse-drawn carts at the roadside, and straw-haired, straw-hatted kids waiting for their parents to return by bus with supplies from the city.

Three Flags, at mile 61 on the Western Highway, is a gas-station-general store-restaurant, and universal stopping point on the way to San Ignacio. Breakfast and sandwiches, prepared to home-style standards, are available for $3 or so, chicken and fish dinners for $7 to $8, and everything is served on a pleasant shaded terrace. If there's anything you need, from children's books to cheese, check the store.

WHERE TO STAY

It's not inconceivable that you will spend a night in Belmopan, even if you don't have business with the government, as the capital is near the crossroads of the Western and Hummingbird highways.

The most substantial hotel is the relatively new **BELMOPAN CON-VENTION HOTEL**, *near the bus station and market, and within walking distance of the government center. The rate is $50 single/$60 double. Tel. 08-22130, fax 23066, or write to P. O. Box 237, Belmopan.* This hotel, government-owned (but on the market), is modeled after a U.S. motel. All 20 rooms are air-conditioned, with large beds or twin beds, carpeting, fan, bureau, wicker sofa, television, snack table, and full bathroom. There's a good-sized pool as well.

Other hotels are the **BULL FROG INN**, *at 25 Half Moon Avenue (P. O. Box 28, 14 rooms $50 single/$62 double plus tax with air conditioning, tel. 08-22111, fax 23155, Visa and Master Card) with a bar and restaurant*; and the **CIRCLE A LODGE**, *at 37 Half Moon Avenue (P. O. Box 221, tel. 08-22296. 14 rooms, $25 single/$30 double, plus 10% service, Master Card and Visa).* Both are clean and airy bungalows, but they're way on the other side of town from where the bus pulls in — about a mile away. Take a taxi if you have any luggage.

Near Belmopan

BANANA BANK RANCH, *P. O. Box 48, Belmopan, tel. 08-23180, fax 22366. $35 single/$45 double, or $55/$65 with private bath, $65/75 in cabanas, plus 10% service plus tax. Add $28 for three meals. No credit cards.*

Banana Bank is an American-owned beef farm where guests are more than welcome. On-site amusements, activities and attractions include horseback riding on trails through 4000 mostly jungled acres (25 saddle horses are kept), river trips, a Mayan ruin, swimming, canoeing, birding, resident artist (and co-owner), stargazing through an eight-inch telescope, lagoon with crocodile, a pet jaguar, a deer, peccary, kinkajou, coati, and spider monkey (not necessarily in order of interest). The last three are shaded by a huge tree wrapped and felled by a strangler fig. And there are assorted ornamental plantings moved from nearby forest.

A problem with many a Belizean resort is that rooms lack character. At Banana Bank, boy, do they have character. Four cottage (or cabana) units each have two bedrooms, with tile floor, wicker chairs and sofa, curving walls, canopy bed on raised platform (one has a water bed), large screened openings, and high thatched ceiling. Bathrooms in each cottage are shared. Four assorted guest rooms are available in the main ranch house, variously wicker- or wood-panelled, with lace bedspreads, screened loft, bunk or double or single beds, soaring ceilings, verandas, arches, paintings, and furniture that I can only begin to describe as idiosyncratic. Two of these rooms have private baths. Another house on the property, a wooden, domed structure on stilts, resembles a Baha'i temple.

The folks here are positively romantic about their cattle, and barbecued beef, and beef in general, are mainstays on the menu. Beer is stocked, but bring your own booze. For river fishing, bring your own rod.

Access is via a turn eastward from the Valley of Peace road that forks north from the Western Highway near Belmopan — this takes you right onto the ranch — or you can turn in opposite the Belmopan airstrip, proceed a half-mile to the bank of the Belize River, wave and shout, and be taken across in a boat. Pickup in Belmopan can be arranged. The taxi ride costs about $10.

WARRIE HEAD LODGE, *Mile 56.5, Western Highway, Teakettle Village. 8 rooms. $45 single/$55 double, plus 10% service plus tax. Add $27 per person for three meals. Group rates available. Reservations: Belize Global Travel Services, 41 Albert St. (P. O. Box 244), Belize City, tel. 02-77363, fax 75213.*

On the site of an old logging camp, Warrie Head Lodge is a working citrus and vegetable farm. There are, as well, 500 acres of protected riverside forest and bush, with black howler monkeys, coatis, waris, toucans, orchids, and trails to allow you to see it all.

Two of the guest rooms are in the main lodge, with fans, and double beds with good mattresses, sharing a cedar-panelled bathroom. One master bedroom in the same building has a private bath. Five other large, airy rooms in a separate building have private baths, table fans, tile floors, real closets, and good beds. Meals are served on a screened porch on the second floor of the main lodge building. The bar runs on the honor system.

River swimming is available at a shingle beach along an eddy pool on the Belize River, and canoes and horses can be rented. As well, a spring-fed creek with little falls and a rock-lined swimming hole fill up in the dry season, as ground water percolates down from the hills. Excursions are also available to Mountain Pine Ridge and Xunantunich.

Though the lodge property borders the Western Highway, and is easily reached, you should contact the Belize City office if you're interested in staying here — the lodge is often filled with groups, and a cook is sent out only when it is known that there will be guests. The *warrie* (or *wari*) of the name is the white-lipped peccary, which the creek next to the lodge is supposed to resemble.

WHERE TO EAT

The **BULL FROG** is the best eating spot in town. Meals are served in a shady, open pavilion, though the menu is the usual fried chicken, steak, and rice and beans, plus Tandoori fish fillet. Try the limeade ("lime water"). Six dollars and up, $11 for lobster, a couple of bucks for sandwiches.

If you're out on the market square waiting for a bus, you can step into the **CALADIUM** restaurant. Hamburgers and sandwiches go for about $2, steak and chicken meals for $5 to $8, and the fans will help cool you off.

SEEING THE SIGHTS

The Department of Archaeology has a vault of ceramics, stone tools, carved monuments and other antiquities, which may be visited by the public on Mondays, Wednesdays and Fridays from 1:30 to 4:30 p.m, *but only with two days' advance notice. Enter the building that is to your right, as you look up to Independence Hill, and go down to the basement. Call first (tel. 08-22106) to make an appointment, at least two days in advance.*

Back on the Western Highway, just past the junction for the Hummingbird Highway and Belmopan, is the village of **Roaring Creek**. Once a major crossroads, Roaring Creek is now overshadowed by the capital. There are about a thousand residents.

PRACTICAL INFORMATION

The **British High Commission** *is housed on Embassy Square (tel. 08-22146).* The **U. S. embassy** has an office here *(tel. 08-22617),* but most functions are carried out in Belize City. A couple of banks have branches near the market, but otherwise, there is not much in the way of commercial activity.

MOUNTAIN PINE RIDGE

At **Georgeville**, *a wide spot in the road 66 miles from Belize City*, is the junction for the branch road into the **Mountain Pine Ridge Forest Reserve**, a 300-square-mile area of controlled logging, and also a concentration of spectacular scenery.

Here, on the west slope of the Maya Mountains, numerous short streams rush through granite rocks and tumble over falls, eventually to join the Belize River. The sand and gravel of the broken terrain and the cool air make for a relatively sparse growth of pine and grasses at higher altitudes that recalls scenic landscapes of more northerly latitudes.

In fact, this mountainous landscape is as unrelated to its tropical surroundings as it appears. Geologists believe that the granite ridge gradually drifted westward, and rose up over millions of years along with the limestone seabed that underlies lowland Belize. This "suspect terrane" (in the language of geologists) meets the tropical rocks below along a spectacular fault line, marked by an escarpment, creeks, falls, and breakneck changes in vegetation.

At lower altitudes, and in river valleys, are lush, dense, bromeliad- and orchid-laden hardwood forest. Numerous caves perforate the landscape. The plentiful water and lack of people, the variety of birds and butterflies and foliage, the views down warm canyons and up to the high saw-ridge of the Maya Mountains, make the Mountain Pine Ridge area ideal for leisurely exploration in a sturdy vehicle, on foot, or on horseback.

ARRIVALS & DEPARTURES

There's no public transport into Mountain Pine Ridge. You can arrange a tour, or rent a vehicle for an excursion, in Belize City or, more easily, in San Ignacio. A taxi trip for a few hours will cost at least $100, an individual place on a trip, when available, $20 to $40.

The roads are mostly good and graded during the dry season, but there are rocky stretches that will give you and even the sturdiest vehicle a good shaking, and maybe do some damage. Inquire about conditions if it's been raining. Logging roads in the reserve are well marked, and there's little chance of getting lost.

WHERE TO STAY

Though Mountain Pine Ridge is a reserve, it contains several private accommodations:

PINE RIDGE LODGE *is about five miles into the reserve along the main access road; call 092-3310 for a radio patch to the lodge. Or write to: P.O. Box 2079, Belize City, or 2968 Somerton Rd., Cleveland Heights, OH 44118, tel. 216-781-8288 or 932-7342.*

Located on rolling, sandy-grassy grounds dotted with pines and broken by frothing streams. Rates are from about $35 double, more in river-view units, and will probably rise once the six cabins are more finished. These are well spread among the pines, and for now, they only have beds, louvers, screens, and bare cement bathrooms. Lighting is by kerosene lamps and candles. There are river pools for swimming, and an 85-foot waterfall on the property.

Meals are served to guests and drop-ins on a thatch-roofed terrace for $4 to $6. As the sign says, this is the last place to stop for a cold beer, and it also strikes me as a mountain biker's haven. Things are strictly laid-back and low-key. Guided trips into the nooks and crannies of the reserve are available.

HIDDEN VALLEY INN *is on the way to the falls of the same name, 17 miles from the Georgeville turnoff; Rates at Hidden Valley Inn are about $80 single/ $105 double with breakfast, plus 10% service and tax, and another $25 for lunch and dinner. Add about $150 to pick up a small group at the international airport. Contact the Inn at P. O. Box 170, Belmopan, tel. 08-23320, fax 23334, or in the U.S. at C.W. Maryland & Co., 1220 E. Park Ave., Tallahassee, FL 32301, tel. 800-334-7942 or 904-222-2333, fax 904-222-1992.*

Set in the midst of scrub pines on an 18,000-acre estate, Hidden VBalley Inn has twelve rooms in six stuccoed, tin-roofed cottages with tile floors, fireplaces and electric lights, and full bathrooms with tubs. A central lodge room contains the dining area, library and video entertainment. Available activities here are horseback riding, mountain biking and rafting, and tours are available to some of the more remote parts of Mountain Pine Ridge and the ancient city of Caracol. Trails wind through the property, and guests can be given a lift to sites for birding and hiking.

BLANCANEAUX LODGE, *about 15 miles from the Georgeville turnoff, and a few minutes past Pine Ridge Lodge on the main road south; for reservations, 14 Fort St. in Belize City, tel. 45286, fax 31657)*

Recently re-opened after a dormancy of some years. In a country where everything has an unusual background, Blancaneaux stands out as a partnership between a local woman, Martha Williams, and a noted Hollywood director. Construction is native-style, of saplings ("pimento") stuccoed on the inside, with thatched roofs. Six individual cabanas furnished with Guatemalan blankets and decorations rent for $75 single/ $100 double per day with breakfast, six lodge rooms for $65 single/$85 double, sharing bathrooms. Swimming is in river pools. Guests report being more than satisfied, especially with the food. Pizza is prepared in a wood-burning oven, hot espresso is always available, and guests may use the piano.

Mountain Equestrian Trails has thatch-roofed **CASA CIELO COTTAGES** are available for rent here as well. The four units go for $80 double, including breakfast and dinner. *Mountain Equestrian Trails is 3/4 mile off the main road into Mountain Pine Ridge, at mile 8, just before the junction for the San Antonio-Cristo Rey road (Central Farm P.O., tel. 082-3180, fax 092-2060).*

SEEING THE RESERVE
Thousand Foot Falls

The main route leads south from the Western Highway, rising from tropical hilly jungle to sandy pine barrens. Past the entrance checkpoint, the main road traverses an area of pines standing up in red dirt — pure Georgia.

Follow the Baldy Beacon road westward. Out this way are the heights known as Baldy Beacon and Baldy Sibun, with some of the oldest rocks and soils known — anywhere!.

A rock-strewn spur leads back to the north, braking suddenly at the edge of a gaping canyon. Steps lead partway down the escarpment, from which you can look across to the **Hidden Valley** (or **Thousand Foot**) **Falls**, a narrow chute of water spilling a thousand feet over rock. Below, vegetation changes over several thousand feet from pine to leafy jungle. If you had an impression of Belize as all lowlands, you will be suddenly and totally undeceived. The falls are 20 miles into the reserve.

Nature's Water Park

The main road of the reserve continues southward from the Baldy Beacon junction, crossing the Río On 18 miles from the Western Highway. Here the river splashes down over huge boulders and chutes and dashes through granite water slides, to and through and around pools ranging from personal solar-heated Jacuzzis to Olympic-sized. Park at the picnic area, or farther down, and scamper out over the rocks for a delightful swim in lukewarm waters, but take care. Nature's water park comes without lifeguards or first-aid stations, and accidental careens and loose footing result in bruised arms and bashed heads.

Río Frío Cave

Five miles beyond, past the government camp at **Augustine**, signs point the way to several caves. The largest, the **Río Frío Cave**, is at the end of the side road, about a mile from the camp, after a descent through lower rain forest. Trees at the parking area are handily labelled — rubber trees, mahogany, breadnut, and many other species. Walk into the forest, to the huge, arched, 65-foot-high cave mouth, and beyond. There's no need for a flashlight here — plenty of light enters. Observe the bared strata of rock, and stalactites. There are no stalagmites, but rather, a boulder-strewn riverbed with sandy beaches where the Río Frío flows through.

Continue over a rock formation that looks like rice terraces, and another that looks like a waterfall, and you'll come through to daylight again.

There are many other caves in Mountain Pine Ridge, some of them spectacular. Contact a travel agency in Belize City or one of the hotels in San Ignacio to engage a guide for further exploration.

In the area of Mountain Pine Ridge are several private reserves. **Slate Creek Preserve**, near the northern edge, encompasses lands voluntarily protected against clearing by private landowners. The area is habitat for many resident and migratory species. Mountain Equestrian Trails (see below) operates riding trips through the area. **Society Hall Nature Reserve** is closed to the public, and used for research purposes.

SPORTS & RECREATION
Camping
Camping is available for a fee at **Pine Ridge Lodge** (above), and permitted at **Douglas D'Silva Forest Station** (Augustine Village), the administrative center about ten miles to the south of the main reserve entry. Ask permission of the forestry officer there.

To stay elsewhere in the reserve, you have to apply first at the Forestry Department in Belmopan, though permission is usually denied. Several lodges in the Cayo area operate overnight trips to Mountain Pine Ridge and Chiquibul Forest Reserve, to the south (presumably with permission). *Inquire locally, or try calling Neil Rogers, tel. 092-3452.*

Horseback Riding
Horseback trips into Mountain Pine Ridge, are offered from January to September by **Mountain Equestrian Trails**. Full- and half-day trips take visitors over trails and along rivers to waterfalls and canyons that can't be seen from the roads. Cost is $45 to $65 per person, excellent box lunch included. Any travel agent in Belize will book a ride and connecting transportation.

Spelunking
Mountain Equestrian Trails also operates spelunking excursions, some by boat and raft to caves with Mayan remains, to which it has the exclusive rights to bring visitors. *Mountain Equestrian Trails is 3/4 mile off the main road into Mountain Pine Ridge, at mile 8, just before the junction for the San Antonio-Cristo Rey road (Central Farm P.O., tel. 082-3180, fax 092-2060).*

Treks
Guacamallo Treks, *Mile 4-1/2, Pine Ridge Rd. (P. O. Box 198, Belmopan), tel. 092-2188, fax 2060, at Maya Ranch*, has horseback treks to the vast

Caracol archaeological site, a shorter ride to Pacbitun, and a wagon trip to the Barton Creek Mennonite community. Fees range from $35 for a short ride with breakfast to $280 for the Caracol ride with a night's lodging before and after. Call for scheduling.

CARACOL

South of Mountain Pine Ridge, in the Chiquibul Forest, is the **Caracol archaeological site**, a once-densely settled area of ruins and roadbeds that flourished in the Classic Mayan era. One of the pyramids, called **Canaa**, or **Sky Place**, rises 139 feet (42 meters) above the plaza floor, two meters higher than the largest structure at Xunantunich. The ruins cover more than 30 square miles.

The siting of Caracol in a part of the Maya Mountains devoid of reliable water supply is a mystery. Specialized plants might have been harvested there, for trade to other Mayan areas. In any case, Mayan engineering ingenuity overcame natural limitations, with the design and construction of reservoirs and agricultural terraces.

Caracol was settled around 300 B.C., and occupied well into the Late Classic period of Mayan culture. Carved deities date mostly from around 600 A.D., when other Mayan sites were declining. The glyphs on one of the structures at Caracol record a war with Tikal, the major Mayan site 60 miles to the northwest, in present-day Guatemala. The wars might have yielded slaves or other profits, for Caracol went through an active construction period soon after, while Tikal itself experienced a period of stagnation. The population of Caracol and its surrounding city-state might have been as high as that of all modern Belize.

Among unusual features at Caracol is the widespread use of tombs for group burials, possibly of nobles of lower rank, and not only for rulers.

Excavations are being carried out by archaeologists from the University of Central Florida, led by Arlen and Diane Chase.

ARRIVALS & DEPARTURES
By Tour

Caracol has just re-opened to visitors after several years off-limits to the public. All the lodges in Mountain Pine Ridge (see above) and some of the operators in San Ignacio arrange one-day tours, in cooperation with the archaeologists on the site. Expect a long day's round trip.

SPELUNKING EXCURSION
The Chiquibul

The **Chiquibul cave system** that extends to the west into Guatemala underlies much of the Maya Mountains, and could be the largest system of caverns in the Western Hemisphere. Over 100 miles of passageways have been surveyed, some with widths of over 100 yards. The Belize Chamber in the Chiquibul system is one of the five largest natural caverns in the world. Recent explorations have yielded fossils of extinct species of insects and crustaceans previously unknown.

The caves are not yet open to visitors, and permission to enter must be obtained from the Department of Archaeology in Belmopan. The best time to explore is in the dry season — the underground rivers that helped create the caves can flood them during wet periods.

SAN IGNACIO

San Ignacio, also known as **Cayo**, or **El Cayo de San Ignacio**, is the major town in western Belize. *Located about 72 miles from the coast*, it was once a loading point for the chicle and mahogany that came out of the surrounding forests. Both industries have now declined, and San Ignacio has become a bustling agricultural center, serving the cattle, citrus and peanut farms of the area.

ORIENTATION

With good accommodations, ruins and Mayan villages nearby, caves to the south in the Maya Mountains, and the clear, clean waters of the **Macal River** available for recreation, San Ignacio is a lovely place in which to spend a few days, comfortable in the midst of the tropical forest, and far away from the cares of anywhere.

The Hawkesworth Bridge, which connects San Ignacio with the village of Santa Elena on the east bank of the Macal River, is the only suspension bridge in the country, a substantial and unexpected engineering accomplishment in a garden setting. It is the Brooklyn Bridge of Belize, illustrated on, among other places, milk cartons.

Like many a town built on hills, San Ignacio has a certain amount of physical charm, arising in part from changing vistas available from different points, of residential neighborhoods, of the river flowing into the distance, of the hillsides all around carpeted in tropical forest.

San Ignacio has the air of an outpost of the British Empire, of the sort depicted by E. M. Forster, Paul Scott and Eric Blair, remote yet cosmopolitan. British Forces roll through the streets every now and then, along with an occasional Gurkha unit. Members of the Belize Defence Force jog double time. (Guatemala, and intermittent claims to Belize, is not far off). Horse-drawn carts of Mennonites pass by (the clapboard architecture and many second-story porches make a perfect backdrop), as do huge four-wheel-drive pickup trucks of American missionaries. And don't let me fail to mention the Lebanese, the Chinese, the Sri Lankan, the South African, and the Swede who make this their home.

Most of the townspeople of San Ignacio are Mestizos and Mayan; and Spanish, with Guatemalan overtones, is the main language. But there are also storekeepers of Lebanese descent, and assorted settlers from far and wide who have found here just the right combination of pace, economic opportunity, climate, adventure, and rolling, unspoiled landscapes. San Ignacio sits in a valley, and the surrounding rolling hills, furry with vegetation, misty after a rain, are always visible from the declivities of its streets.

Across from San Ignacio is **Santa Elena**. The sister towns are connected by the substantial **Hawkesworth suspension bridge**, spanning the Macal River, a tributary of the Belize River. Together, the two towns have about 7000 inhabitants.

Cayo has the best hotels in western Belize, which makes it a good base for seeing the Mountain Pine Ridge area, the major Mayan center of Xunantunich, and smaller ruins. River trips, jungle walks, and an easy-going air will tempt the visitor to stay on. Accommodations are available both in town, and in unusual cottage resorts in the surrounding country-side.

ARRIVALS & DEPARTURES

Arriving By Bus

Batty Buses leave Belize City (Mosul St. at Bagdad, a block from East Collet Canal, *tel. 72025*) for San Ignacio at 6, 6:30, 7:30, 8, 9 and 10:15 a.m. The schedule varies slightly on Sunday. Most of these buses continue right through to the Guatemalan border. Novelo buses leave Belize City (19 West Collet Canal, *tel. 77372*) about every hour from 11 a.m. to 7 p.m., and at 9 p.m., passing through San Ignacio about two-and-a-half hours later and continuing to Benque Viejo. Sunday departures are from noon to 5 p.m. only. There are additional Shaw buses running between Belmopan and San Ignacio.

Arriving By Air

An improved civilian airstrip off the Western Highway is ready and waiting for scheduled flights. Until these materialize, an air taxi is the quick way back to the international airport and your flight home.

Arriving By Car

Maxima Car Rental, *tel. 092-2265*, has junior-sized pickup trucks available at about $75 per day.

Arriving By Taxi

Taxi trips (including waiting time, prices courtesy of the local taxi cartel) to the Guatemalan border cost about $15; to Xunantunich, $25; to

Belmopan, $30; to Belize City, $75; to the airport, $88; to the Belize Zoo, $50.

To Flores, Guatemala, the fare is $150, and to Tikal, $200, or $250 if you stay the night. You can cut the price to Guatemala by more than half if you take a Belizean taxi to the border and pick up a Guatemalan taxi in Melchor de Mencos. You just have to hope that a Guatemalan taxi is available when you show up. See the next chapter for more details.

Departing By Bus

Batty and Novelo buses for Benque Viejo pass through San Ignacio about every hour during the day, less frequently on Sunday. Batty departures from San Ignacio for Belize City are hourly from noon to 5 p.m. In the morning, catch a bus passing through from Benque Viejo. The first few stop at the town circle, near the police station and the bridge. Others pull into the parking area off Burns Avenue in the center of town. There are additional Shaw buses running between Belmopan and San Ignacio.

WHERE TO STAY

HOTEL SAN IGNACIO, *18 Buena Vista Road (P. O. Box 33), tel. 092-2034, fax 2134. 25 rooms. $25-$65 single/$30-$75 double, no service charge. Add $28 for three meals. Visa, Master Card, American Express.*

The best in-town hotel, located uphill about a half-mile from the Hawkesworth Bridge. On the outside, the hotel looks like a farm building, but inside it's rather pleasant, basically a concrete structure softened with extensive hardwood detailing, planters, a pool, deck with white-painted wrought-iron furniture, and lovely terraces overlooking the Macal River, the town of San Ignacio, the misty plain to the east, and the surrounding mountains.

All rooms have ceiling fans, balconies, and private bath; higher rates are with air conditioning and television. The dining room is breezy and pleasant, with a menu offering a range from rice and beans to kebabs and lobster, for $4 to $10 a la carte. The bar has Formica booths with Formica tables, vinyl seats, and tropical wood panelling and screens — a typically Belizean combination of the best native materials and imported accretions. Other facilities include a travel service, gift shop, laundry service, and meeting facilities.

Just up the road from the San Ignacio is the **HOTEL PIACHE** *(tel. 092-2109)*. The owners treat you as family, and the grounds are lovely and gardened, with many plant species labelled for your edification. The 17 rooms are basic concrete units, on the small side. With shared bath, the rate is $20 single/$27 double, an air-conditioned unit costs more. Rates may be lower out of season. Meals are provided on request at the adjacent thatched, sapling-sided bar, furnished with the oddest collection of castoff furniture.

Back down in the center of San Ignacio are three economy hotels on Burns Avenue, the main street: the **CENTRAL** *(No. 24)*, the **BUDGET** *(No. 22)*, and the **JAGUAR** *(No. 19)*. There are about 60 rooms between them, all quite simple. Rates are about $8 or less single, $12 double sharing bath. The Budget has some doubles with private bath at about $15 double. Rooms at the Central are light and airy and larger than those of its neighbors, and the place is generally more pleasant.

A step above these is the **VENUS HOTEL** *(tel. 092-2186)*, also on Burns Avenue, with 25 rooms on the second and third floors above the commercial level. Everything is brand-new and clean, and the rooms have fans and even wallpaper, though many are situated along inside corridors, with no outside windows. Take a look at your room first, especially in hot weather. The rate is about $20 single/$25 double with private bath, or $12 single/$15 double sharing bath.

The **NEW BELMORAL**, *17 Burns Avenue, tel. 92-2024*, has been totally renovated, and offers rooms with television, fan, private bath and other modern conveniences for $25 single/$30 double, which includes continental breakfast. Some of the rooms are quite large and pleasant. Master Card and Visa are accepted. The **PLAZA HOTEL**, *4A Burns Ave., tel. 092-3332*, has 12 new concrete rooms above a furniture store at $20 single/$30 double with ceiling fans, $10 more with air conditioning, Master Card accepted.

Bargain Lodgings

If these hotels are full, adequate accommodations are available at the **HI-ET**, *a block to the west, at West and Waight streets*. At $6 or so for a double, it's a Belizean budget bargain. The **HOTEL SAN JUAN** also has cheap rooms. And if absolutely everything in San Ignacio is full, cross the river to **MIKE'S GRAND HOTEL** *in Santa Elena*, where you can have a roof over your head for about $5 per person; or inquire at the Fruit-aplenty store for rooms.

Cottage Country

MAYA MOUNTAIN LODGE, *on the road south from Cayo toward the villages of Cristo Rey and San Antonio. Rates are $50 to $70 double, plus 15% service, and tax. There are also two shared-bath rooms at $40 double, making a total of 14 units. Children under 12 stay for free. Phone 092-2164 (fax 2029) in Belize, or 800-344-MAYA in the United States. The mailing address is Box 46, San Ignacio.*

This is a farm and mini-forest preserve, as well as a hotel.

Cottages are set on a breezy hillside among trees laden with orchids (including the black orchid, the national flower). Each has a private bath, and hammock outside the front door, and many have a bunk bed as well as queen-sized bed. Inside, under the high thatched roof, furnishings and finishings are: screening around the eaves, linoleum floor covering, pedestal fan, hardwood doors, and pebbly, rough stuccoed walls. Creature comforts here include full-time hot water and electricity. The view from most cottages is a slope of semi-cleared jungle. In the morning, there are bird and insect calls — but no mosquitoes.

The food at Maya Mountain Lodge is some of the best at any lodging place in Belize. Meals are served family-style on a covered patio, approached at night along a lantern-lit walkway. Help yourself to seconds — nobody's counting. It's not the usual Belizean fare — the bread and yogurt are homemade, and the vegetables are straight from the garden. I recently had a good lemon chicken. The menu is fixed, but changes daily, even the breakfast menu. Desserts are fruit cheese cake, pineapple upside down cake, and the like; juice is fresh-squeezed. Be sure to let them know if you'll be skipping any meal. Meals range from $7 for breakfast to $12 for dinner, and superb box lunches are available for day outings, including fruit beverages in a cooler. Mixers and ice are available if you bring your own liquor (none is served at the lodge).

Owners Bart and Suzi Mickler encourage visitors to get to know the country and countryside. A collection of books and monographs on archaeology, natural history, and things Belizean is available to guests, along with board and card games. A guide booklet helps you find your way along a network of forest trails to the lodge's very own Mayan ruin, advising due caution for black poisonwood and other uninviting species. Plants along the way are labeled. Talk to Suzi, and you can arrange a guided tour of the garden, with edible and decorative plants, from annato through cow's foot and croton to tamarind, with over 100 species in between. The style of service here includes a lot of personal attention, if this is suitable to your tastes.

The lodge also has its own canoes ($30 for a full day), horses for trail rides, mountain bikes, and vans for land tours, and a swimming spot along the river. Trips are operated to Mountain Pine Ridge, the Pantí Trail by boat, Xunantunich and Tikal (see below). Package tours using the lodge as a base are available in the summer. Example: $300 for a three-day, two-night package including a river trip, tours of Xunantunich and other western sights, meals, lodging, and airport pickup.

If you're traveling without reservations, and show this book, you'll get a discount on a space-available basis in shared-bath rooms. Call first from the telephone company office in town. To reach the lodge from San Ignacio, turn right just after crossing the Hawkesworth Bridge, then left and right again onto the Cristo Rey road. A taxi costs about $3. The lodge is less than a mile from the main road. Airport pickup is available for about $100 for up to four people.

I should disclose that I know Suzi from way back when, but I would recommend her place anyway.

About a mile and a half north of San Ignacio, at Branch Mouth, the confluence of the Mopan and Macal rivers, is **LAS CASITAS RESORT**. This is an idyllic spot, with three high-peaked cottages on a hilltop, and grounds nicely finished with lawns and bougainvillea and hedges and concrete steps. In fact, it's suited to a higher class of accommodation than what you get: bare cubicles with cement floors. The rate is about $25 double, and meals are available for about $5 each. For just a few dollars, you can arrange to sleep in the tri-level hammock tower, or to camp out.

To reach the hotel, take the local commuter canoe (fare 50¢ Belizean) from the end of the road, along with locals, who walk through the grounds at all hours to the adjacent village. *Telephone 092-2506, fax 2475 to leave a message.*

Out on the Bullet Tree Falls road, about three miles from San Ignacio and encircled by a loop of river, is **PARROT'S NEST**, which I endorse unreservedly because the proprietor is Fred Prost, creator of the Seaside Guest House for budget travelers in Belize City. Fred's new venture has four thatch-roofed units going for $20 double, and the name tells all: they're tree houses with some stilts for added support, and though they ain't for the birds, they get you right up there and into nature. Swim in the river, hire horses, hang out. *Call Fred at 092-3702, or write to him at General Delivery, San Ignacio, to hold your place.*

The **GROVE RESORT**, *in the flatter country off the Western Highway east of San Ignacio,* takes an estate-style approach to lodging, with extra creature comforts. There are six two-story pink concrete villas, with balconies, set among neat lawns dotted with plants on the edge of a citrus farm. The two suites in each villa are air-conditioned, and attractively furnished with imported wicker pieces, orthopedic beds, and small refrigerators.

A large second-floor bar-restaurant-clubhouse overlooks a good-sized pool (there is also creek swimming), and there is another pavilion bar at pool level. The kitchen equipment is *serious*, and even includes a pizza oven. Scuba lessons are available, and guests may use exercise equipment, rent mountain bikes, and ride horses.

The rate is $100 single/$125 double plus tax, and an additional $35 per person for three meals. More modest rooms at a lower price will eventually be added. To reserve, write to P. O. Box 1, San Ignacio, or call or fax 092-2421.

CHAA CREEK COTTAGES are 16 white units with Mayan-style roofs, furnished with Guatemalan blankets and weavings, but without electricity. Common facilities include a round dining pavilion with high ceiling, candlelit in the evening, and semicircular bar and lounge opening onto a deck with river view. The rate is under $200 double with meals. Located four kilometers along a rough road from a junction eight miles west of San Ignacio. *Book through travel agents, or call 2037 in San Ignacio.*

DuPLOOY'S, *Off a fork from the Chaa Creek road (currently being improved), and also four miles from the Western Highway. Afternoon tea and all meals are included in the lodge rate – $100 single, $145 double, plus 10% service, plus tax. Shared-bath units in an adjacent concrete house are $35 single, $45 double without meals. Credit cards accepted with surcharge. Telephone and fax 092-3301 or 2057 (U.S. representative tel. 800-359-0747, fax 212-749-6172). Guests can use the lodge's shuttle service (from San Ignacio at 9 a.m. and 4 p.m., $3 per ride, or free with three-night stay), or take a taxi from San Ignacio for $35; or, with advance notice, they can be fetched in a boat.*

Set in hills sloping down to the Macal River, accommodations in the stuccoed stone buildings of the main lodge are nine river-view rooms, two sharing bathroom facilities. All showers are tiled, and all guestrooms have hardwood vanities, good mattresses (not the case in every lodge in the area, sorry to say), and screened porch. There is also a separate, six-room house where the facilities are more modest, and bathrooms are shared.

Rock-paved walks lead to the common facilities. Meals (except for breakfast, served in a basket on your porch) are taken in a screened dining pavilion with a view to the limestone cliff tangled with vegetation on the opposite shore. For an afternoon and evening of relaxing with a drink in your hands, to the accompaniment of bird songs, continue to the **Hangover Bar**, cantilevered from the cliff edge and 30 feet above the river and anything solid.

Guests receive the attention of owners Ken and Judy duPlooy (from England and the United States, respectively). Ken takes people birding day and night — over 100 species have been sighted on the property. Other activities are hiking, and fishing for tarpon (occasionally) and tropical species that resemble snook and bass; swimming at a sandy bank (one of the few such spots in western Belize) and tubing and canoeing on the river; tours to Tikal, Mountain Pine Ridge and Xunantunich; horseback rides to Vaca Falls and to caves with Mayan pottery, with a return by canoe; and overnight jungle trips. A trip to Laguna Aguacate, near Spanish Lookout, for spotting keel-billed toucans, crocodiles and turtles, will cost $100 for up to four persons, a day trip to Tikal, about $90 per person in a group.

If you stay here, walk through the gardens to see the pineapple, limes, papaya, hot peppers, bananas, coconuts, tamarind, mangoes, oranges, watermelons, etc., before they are removed from their natural habitat and brought to the table. Beyond the gardens, the ground are mostly rolling and grassy. Or wander down to the tangled banks of the river, watch the leaves roll by, and listen to the music of the forest. Only the background hum of the generator, persisting until 10 p.m., reminds you that there are modern amenities here.

Also eight miles out of San Ignacio is the turnoff for **NABITUNICH** (Stone House) on San Lorenzo Farm, just a half mile to the north of the Western Highway over a good gravel road (Telephone 093-2309 to reach the farm). The eight simple cottages, each different, are on a slope below the farmhouse where an English-Belizean couple, Rudy and Margaret Juan, live with their seven children. Rooms are of varying sizes, some larger than others, not elegant, but neat, with basic furnishings, and naturally cool. The nicest is a sort of A-frame.

The view from the farm is commanding. Down through the meadow, across the river and up the hill are the Xunantunich ruins. You can walk to the site, fording a river on the way, or just gaze at the spectacular sunset behind them. Meals are copious, served in a lovely white dining room with great arched openings and a high thatched roof, and the menu changes every day.

There are no packaged tours, library or bar here, but you are not without diversions. Horseback rides can be arranged on trails that run through parts of the property that have been left otherwise untouched (cost is about $20 for the day), and there is a lovely swimming area down along the river. You can take off in a boat or canoe, or walk through the pasture and forest, pick allspice or a lime, go birding, or espy bromeliads and orchids overhead. Fishing for catfish can also be arranged without much ado.

The setting is genuinely homey, and the rates at Nabitunich are lower than at the other cottages: about $65 single/$75 double with three meals, $25/$35 for room only, tax and 10% service additional. Extra beds are available at $10. If you're not carrying too much luggage, you can take a Benque Viejo bus to the turnoff, and walk in.

If you *really* want to go back to nature, head for **RANCHO LOS AMIGOS**, *a bit over a mile out of San José Succotz, just east of Benque Viejo. The rate is about $15 per person per day, less for tent space, which includes breakfast and dinner. Dial 093-2483 to let them know that you're on your way.*

To get here, turn into town from the western highway, go past the soccer field, then left at the sign. As of recently, you can even make it in by car. Here you will find Ed and Virginia Jenkins and family, formerly of the States, who have selectively and respectfully carved a spread from 88 acres of jungle.

Guest units at Rancho Los Amigos are traditional Mayan cottages, built almost entirely from materials gathered on-site: lime plastered on a framework of sticks, with a thatched roof. But do not think for a minute that "traditional" means uncomfortable. The four rooms are cool and attractive, decorated with plants and floral curtains and brushy crafts from Punta Gorda. Much of the food is local produce as well, and water comes from springs. Meals may include fish or range beef, never pork or lard, or you can specify vegetarian. The kitchen is open-sided, and food is cooked both over an open fire and in a traditional oven. The sweetener is honey produced on-site. Trails run though the forest, where you can observe the birds and animals, and, with some advice, pick herbs. There are also some caves within hiking distance.

This is a *jungle* retreat. You use pit toilets (to keep the springs uncontaminated), and showers are outdoors. And yet, everything is so well thought out, and flows so naturally from the resources available, that there is little sense of roughing it.

Ed claims that Virginia is the best cook in Belize.

WHERE TO EAT

EVA'S BAR, *at street level below the Hotel Imperial on Burns Avenue*, serves breakfasts, and meals of steaks, and chicken and rice and beans, sometimes tamales and mole and chicken curry. A meal costs $4 or less, and is not at all bad.

But you don't come to Eva's just for the food and the Belikin. Eva's is the hub of the *Greater Cayo jungle telegraph*. This is where visitors get together to plan excursions to Mountain Pine Ridge and elsewhere, where the local taxi driver can tell you about growing up in the bush and treating illness with native plants, where the Mennonite whose faith is not firm slouches over a rum and Coke, where the fellow who's been here a few days longer than you will give you the total lowdown. The expatriate owner scurries among the tables and behind the bar, seeing to every need of his customers.

Scores of postcards from past patrons are tacked onto the walls. Hand-lettered posters announce new cottage colonies, tours, goods for sale. And there are NOTICES from the management. (NOTICE is a common Belizean word, you will find out.) Guatemalan handicrafts are on sale, to satisfy a market lacking in local production. I am sure Eva's will be immortalized in some novel of the Belizean jungle.

At 27 Burns Avenue, the **SERENDIB** is a pleasant restaurant and bar. Burgers and sandwiches are served, along with beef dishes and Sri Lankan curries and seafood. Your check comes on a little tray with two hard candies. "A" for effort. *Closed on Sundays, and between 3 p.m. and 6:30 p.m.*

The **RED ROOSTER BAR & GRILL**, *2 Far West St., tel. 92-3016, fax 2057*, hosted by folks from Colorado, has an open kitchen so you can see the cooking, and serves pizza, nachos, and liquid nourishment. They cater to rafters and canoers and bikers and everyone else.

For a change of scene, try dining at one of the lodges outside San

Ignacio. Most will accept outsiders for dinner, and the surroundings are certainly more refined than at any restaurant in-town. **MAYA MOUN-TAIN LODGE** has consistently good food, served on a sheltered terrace approached by a lantern-lit walkway, to the mysterious accompaniment of the calls of forest animals. *Call 2164* to see what's for dinner (about $15 with service charge), if they have room for you, and to reserve. Ask around among your fellow travelers as to the state of culinary affairs at the other lodges outside of San Ignacio.

MAXIM'S, a Chinese restaurant, *is on Far West Street*, which is a block over from West Street proper. There is no Farther West Street. The atmosphere is typically Chinese-Belizean — small, dark, plastic tablecloths — and so is the food — egg foo, mein, fried rice, and curries with chicken on the bone. So-so, at $4 to $7 for a meal.

For snacks, the **FARMER'S EMPORIUM**, a general store *below the Hotel Central*, sells fresh-baked bread, granola, yogurt, and cups of the most delicious chilled, fresh-squeezed orange juice. *Across the street*, the **JAGUAR INN** serves hamburgers, and sometimes has game such as deer or gibnut.

CAHAL PECH

Surprise! In a spot of dense jungle right above San Ignacio is **Cahal Pech** (Place of the Ticks), one of the most attractively and genuinely restored Mayan ceremonial center in Central America.

Unlike Mayan cities excavated years ago, Cahal Pech's center has not been denuded of shading trees, and the park-like archaeological site is alive with birds and forest mammals. Most of the structures were found standing and intact, so there has been little guesswork in the restoration. Laborers under the direction of Dr. Jennifer Taschek of the University of Oregon have simply taken structures apart, de-rooted the pieces, and put them back together, with a strong mortar topping to withstand modern foot traffic. For now, visitors have an unusual opportunity to look over the shoulders of working archaeologists.

Like most Mayan sites, Cahal Pech was occupied for centuries, during which its buildings were renewed, reconstructed, and covered over. It probably flourished in the Classic period, until about 900 A.D.; but some features, porticoes of corbeled arches, suggest a post-Classic occupation under the Toltec-influenced Maya of the Yucatan. And it could well have been an important center as early as 200 A.D. Dr. Taschek suggests that Cahal Pech functioned more as a noble family estate, or castle, than as a political capital, and was originally occupied by Maya-related peoples as early as 850 B.C. Cahal Pech is just one of the Mayan centers that occupy virtually every hilltop in the Cayo area.

ARRIVALS & DEPARTURES

To reach Cahal Pech, walk or drive past the Hotel San Ignacio, along the curve toward Benque Viejo. The ruins are on a rise off to the south.

TOURING THE RUINS

The main constructions of Cahal Pech are situated around two principal plazas. Most of the buildings, of the type generally called palaces, are long and low-lying. The eastern side of the main plaza is lined with noble tombs, long ago violated by looters, while "official"-type structures form the other sides. Some of the surfaces have been re-covered with lime plaster in the Mayan manner. Rooms are large by Mayan standards, and corbeled archways are wider than elsewhere, perhaps due to the strength of the mortar made from local limestone.

The building known as the **Audiencia**, on the west side of the main plaza, was probably used for public ceremonies, to judge by the rise in the middle of each wide tread of its stairway, a trick of perspective to center attention on any ceremonies performed there. The outer structure dates from the ninth century, but parts of the stairway and foundation platform, dating from a century earlier, are left exposed and unplastered to show of their earlier appearance.

Climb the steps of the Audiencia, and you will look down onto a smaller plaza that once served as some sort of official reception area. The large temple on the south side, the tallest structure here, can be ascended by a stairway and path for a general view of the site. About a third of the way up is an inset that archaeologists call a throne room and seat of power.

At the northwest corner, a narrow passageway leads through the complex. A dump found below its exit suggests that this was a service passage. To the southwest of the tallest structure is yet another courtyard, possibly a private reserve for the noble family. Excavations suggest that the residents lived in increasing privation, as Classic Mayan civilization declined after 800 A.D.

The ruins also offer spectacular views of San Ignacio (also available from the nearby disco known, as well, as Cahal Pech). Look for the red sheet-concrete roof of the new museum-visitors center, where artifacts from nearby sites are displayed. Exhibits are planned to illustrate the daily life of the Maya. The center is meant to educate Belizeans about their heritage, to encourage preservation, and to discourage looting. There is a small admission charge.

Tipu, another site in the Cayo area, is the locale of an old Spanish mission church, one of the few that were established in what is now Belize. **Pilar**, a few miles west of San Ignacio, is a Mayan ruin that has not been extensively investigated. Both sites are unrestored, with little to attract the casual visitor.

NIGHTLIFE

On any weekend night, and most nights during the week, drift along toward the sound of reggae music to find a place to unwind. The most distinguished name in dance in the Cayo area is currently the **Cahal Pech disco**. You cannot miss it, green and concrete and open-sided, with soaring thatched roof, on the hilltop south of town, next to the radio tower and microwave dish and Cahal Pech archaeological site. Cahal-Pech-the-disco is the dancing spot with the mightiest views in all Belize. It's almost within walking distance of the Hotel San Ignacio, though you should take a taxi to your dancing date after dark.

EXCURSIONS

Easy destinations during day trips from San Ignacio are Mountain Pine Ridge (described above), the Mayan ruins at Xunantunich, and the Pantí Medicinal Trail (see below). The Caracol site has just re-opened to visitors. San Ignacio is also a good base for longer runs to the Belize Zoo, to several caves, the Crooked Tree reserve, and even to Tikal in Guatemala.

Tour Services to Area Excursions

The cottages in the vicinity of San Ignacio offer tours to all possible attractions. Those run by the **Maya Mountain Tours** (*at Maya Mountain Lodge, tel. 092-2164*) provide the services of a naturalist. Maya Mountain Lodge will take a group of four into Mountain Pine Ridge for $165 for a full day; to Tikal for $300 for the day, or about $200 per person for an overnight trip; to Xunantunich for $70. A boat trip upriver from the lodge to the Pantí Trail costs $120 for two, $40 per additional person.

DuPlooys' runs a half-day excursion by car or horseback to Xunantunich for $50, a half-day boat trip on the Macal River for $60 per person, and a day trip to Tikal for $200.

A current provider of adventure excursions is Chris Heckert, who takes his clients out in a Unimog, which is a combination of Jeep and armored personnel carrier. Ask Herr Heckert to take you to Caracol. In a group, figure about $60 per person. He also takes groups on day trips to Mountain Pine Ridge ($18 per person), to Vaca Falls, and to a cave with Mayan inscriptions, using old logging roads impassable in conventional vehicles.

Mountain Pine Ridge

Mountain Pine Ridge is the most popular day trip from San Ignacio, and various operators put together groups, at about $18 per person. To get aboard, inquire at Eva's for Louis or for Chris Heckert.

Red Rooster Inn (see below) takes groups into the reserve for $30 and up per person, including lunch.

A full day tour of Mountain Pine Ridge by taxi will cost about $100, though some drivers will try to give you a shortened trip for the same price.

SPORTS & RECREATION

Canoes

Inquire at Eva's for Toni ("Bob's brother-in-law"), *or call 2267*, to arrange to rent a canoe for a float down the Macal River. An all-day trip, unaccompanied by guide, costs $30 and up, depending on where you arrange to be retrieved, and there are hourly and half-day rates. Canoes are also available from **Float Belize**, about a mile-and-a-half out of town on the road to Guatemala.

Rafting

You can also arrange canoe trips, and rafting, at the **Red Rooster Inn**, *2 Far West St., tel. 092-3016, fax 2057*. A full-day float trip on the Mopan River (Class I and II rapids) costs from $30 to $50 per person, depending on the number in the group. Included are lunch, snacks and equipment. Half-day biking/rafting tours cost the same or slightly more, again depending on numbers.

For more adventure, Red Rooster also has river trips extending over two, three and four days, at about $40 per day. Pickup at hotels in San Ignacio is included, and there are small additional charges to fetch passengers at country lodges.

Horseback Riding

Various of the lodges around San Ignacio will have horses brought in for guests. Or, if you wish, check in at Easy Rider stables, less than a mile up the road to Bullet Tree Falls, where you can have a full horse for half a day for $30. They can also set you up for river fishing.

The Pantí Trail

The unusual **Pantí Trail**, *a few miles west and south of San Ignacio*, is where visitors may learn about native medicinal plants. One plant is used to stop internal bleeding; another provides pure water; another cures dysentery; others are poisonous. These are more than curiosities: many modern medicines are derived from the plants of the tropical forest, and the race is on to discover the secrets of the jungles before they are destroyed by land-clearers, and before university-trained doctors totally displace traditional healers. The trail is named for Mayan healer Eligio Pantí.

Plants, which are all growing in their natural environment, are labelled in English, Spanish, Mayan, and Latin.

The Pantí Trail is located at **Ix Chel**, a farm named for a Mayan goddess and belonging to Rosita Arvigo, an American disciple of Pantí. *To arrange a visit, call the Environmental Information Center at 45545 in Belize City; or dial 2188 in Cayo*; or contact a travel agency. You can reach Ix Chel, which is adjacent to Chaa Creek Cottages, by taxi from San Ignacio, or by boat along the Macal River. A tour will cost about $15.

Dr Arvigo also gives five- and seven-day seminars in herbal healing, and even dispatches herbs by mail order (in case you're strictly an armchair traveller). *Write to Ix Chel Farm, San Ignacio, Cayo, for details.*

PRACTICAL INFORMATION
Banks
The Belize Bank and Atlantic Bank have branches in San Ignacio. There are no other banks on the way to the west, but there are money changers right at the border of Guatemala.

Telephone Office
The **telephone office** (B.T.L.) *is on Burns Avenue.*

Post Office
The **post office** *is above the police station, up near the Hawkesworth Bridge.*

General Information
For general information about the Cayo area, your best source is the bartender at Eva's.

BENQUE VIEJO

About 80 miles from Belize City, **Benque Viejo del Carmen** is the last settlement in Belize on the road to Guatemala. The name of the town is probably a Spanish-English corruption of *old bank*, bank being a riverside logging camp. The name bespeaks the time when the border between Belize and Guatemala existed more in theory than in fact, and English-speaking loggers and Spanish-speaking chicleros, or chicle gatherers, both exploited the forests. The town's population of about 3000 includes many Mopan Maya Indians.

Though Guatemala is just a short jog away, Benque is a typically Belizean-appearing village of two-story clapboard houses with tin roofs overhanging second-floor porches, set amid haze-shrouded hills. Benque sprawls, its houses set wide apart one from another. If you're coming in from Guatemala, you'll be impressed by the rather substantial services available in a little Belizean town — a large police barracks, clean running water, even a fire station. It's also Hispanic. You won't find a city hall in Benque, but rather, a *Palacio Municipal.*

ARRIVALS & DEPARTURES
Arriving By Bus
Batty Bus departures from Belize City (Mosul St. at Bagdad, a block from East Collet Canal, *tel. 72025*) are at 6, 7:30, and 9 a.m. Novelo's Bus Service (19 West Collet Canal, *tel. 77372*) buses depart every hour from 11 a.m. to 7 p.m., and at 9 p.m., from noon to 5 p.m. on Sundays. *For Belize City*, Novelo's departures from Benque are every hour from 4 a.m. to 11 a.m., from 5 a.m. on Sundays. Batty departures from the border for Belize City are at 7 a.m. and 2 and 3:30 p.m.

Departing: Crossing the Border
The Guatemalan border post is about a mile beyond Benque Viejo. The 6 a.m. Batty Bus from Belize City goes right to Melchor de Mencos on the Guatemalan side, connecting with a bus for Flores, the main city of the Guatemalan department of El Petén. With luck, you can connect at the El Cruce junction with a bus for Tikal. If you take a later bus for Benque, you'll have to walk or take a taxi to the border.

From Flores, you can travel onward into Guatemala by bus or plane, or to Palenque, in Mexico, by a combination of bus and riverboat. See the next chapter for details.

The Guatemalan Consulate is a few miles back from the border, along the Western Highway in Succotz, near the Xunantunich ferry.

SEEING THE SIGHTS
The major attraction of the area is the nearby **Xunantunich** archaeological site, described below. But, as elsewhere in Belize, the human landscape is also fascinating.

Just outside of Benque is the Mopan Maya village of **San José Succotz**. The inhabitants are descendants of migrants from San José village in the Petén department of Guatemala, and the ancient Mayan customs and folklore have been more faithfully maintained in isolated Succotz than in modern San José. Mopan is the first language, and the fiesta days of St. Joseph (March 19) and the Holy Cross (May 3) are celebrated every year.

WHERE TO STAY
Benque has some simple hotels, if you have to stay here. **OKI'S**, *on George St.* (the main drag), charges $6 per person. **THE MAYA HOTEL**, *on the same street*, charges $4 per person.

HOSPEDAJE ROXY, *at 70 St. Joseph St.*, on the way out of town toward Guatemala, is r-r-really basic. For better lodgings, if you're driving, look in at **NABITUNICH COTTAGES** (mentioned above) and the other lodges *on the way to San Ignacio.*

XUNANTUNICH

The site of **Xunantunich** (Maiden of the Rock) *is just northeast of Benque Viejo, near the confluence of the Mopan and Belize rivers.*

The ruins of Xunantunich comprise the largest archaeological site in the Belize River valley. Indications from pottery and from stelae inscribed with date glyphs are that Xunantunich was occupied until about 850 A.D., somewhat later than other sites of the Classic period. The eminently defensible situation of the ceremonial center, with its commanding view of the surrounding countryside, might have had something to do with this relative longevity.

Though known to archaeologists since the late nineteenth century, Xunantunich was not excavated until 1938. A Cambridge University team explored the site extensively in 1959 and 1960, and started the work of stabilizing the structures. More recent excavations took place after looting. Only limited restoration and reconstruction has been done.

Bring a snack and something to drink, as there are no facilities for visitors.

ARRIVALS & DEPARTURES

To reach the ruins, walk or drive from Benque Viejo toward San Ignacio, about two miles, to the village of Succotz, where a hand-operated cable ferry winches cars and people across the Mopan River. Service is from 8 a.m. to 4 p.m., and there is a small charge on weekends. Follow the dirt road from the ferry landing another mile uphill to the entrance, where an admission fee is collected.

TOURING THE RUINS

At the heart of Xunantunich are three adjacent plazas laid out roughly along a north-south line. Dominating all is **El Castillo** (structure **A-6**), the massive pyramid at the south end of the main complex. At 130 feet in height, it is the tallest building even in modern Belize, but for the recently measured Sky Palace at Caracol, to the south.

The outer shell of El Castillo is the last of a series of temples and pyramid bases superimposed one atop the last over a period of centuries. Its corbel-vaulted temples were decorated with stone and stuccoed friezes, though these have mostly been destroyed over the years by wind, rain, and penetrating jungle vegetation. One frieze on the east side, from an underlying earlier temple, shows through the damaged outer layer, and has been partially restored. Its carvings represent astronomical symbols. The temple complex was probably once covered by a roof comb, long collapsed. A wide terrace, about one-fourth of the way up, once supported lesser temples.

The main temple at the top of El Castillo is a typical Mayan structure. Interior rooms are capped with the corbelled, or false, arch, layers of stones protruding successively inward. This technology allowed only short spans, so Mayan interior rooms are narrow and cramped.

El Castillo can be climbed on a trail that winds back and forth across its face — certainly a less intimidating experience than going up the steep staircases of such extensively restored structures as those at Tikal. Near the top, a set of concrete steps winds diagonally up the western face, an accretion as un-genuine and atrocious as will be found in any reconstruction. On the opposite face, in a more protective approach, a wooden stairway rests above the temple and shields it from damaging foot traffic.

Whichever route you take, from the top you can see steaming, undulating rangeland and jungle, stretching away for miles to the east; the Maya Mountains to the south; and Benque Viejo, and the lowlands of the department of the Petén in Guatemala, to the west. It is one of the most impressive views in Belize.

Excavations at Xunantunich have yielded up objects of stone and obsidian, an abundance of seashell and jade items, a spindle whorl used to make thread, and what appears to have been a jeweler's workshop, complete with flint hammers and stone chisels. These, the variety of pyramids, palaces and ball courts, and the friezes and glyphs that decorate the buildings, are indications of a complex and well-ordered society. The Cambridge University team discovered substantial damage to the site from an earthquake, which might have been the immediate cause of the city's demise.

About a mile and a half north of Xunantunich are the **Actuncan** ruins. Pottery similar to that of Xunantunich was found there, indicating that Actuncan might have been a satellite of the larger center.

SOUTHERN BELIZE

The overland route to southern Belize is less than straightforward. Vehicles must follow the Western Highway from Belize City to Belmopan, then double back to the southeast along the Hummingbird Highway; or take a newer cutoff to the south at Democracia, 31 miles west of Belize City. The road distance to Dangriga, the biggest southern town, is 107 miles by the first route, 77 by the second, while the sea route is 36 miles long. The waterlogged terrain directly south of Belize City accounts for the switchback.

Public transportation in the south is poor. On most days, four buses run up from Dangriga to Belize City in the morning, and return in the afternoon. Two buses a day leave from Dangriga for Punta Gorda, and one for Mango Creek. Service to Placencia is less than daily. Confirm schedules before you head south, especially if coming from the west and changing buses in Belmopan.

From Belmopan, the Hummingbird Highway is paved for about twelve miles through flat country of low bush, much of it once forest that has been logged out, to Caves Branch. The road then rises and runs along the northeastern skirt of the Maya Mountains, through an area of eroded limestone hills. Here the earth is honeycombed with caves — many of which still contain ancient Mayan altars and offerings — and underground streams, and topped with misty tropical hardwood forest dense with orchids, bromeliads and ferns.

ST. HERMAN'S CAVE & BLUE HOLE

Off the road, *in the vicinity of mile 13*, is **St. Herman's Cave**. To reach it, take the unmarked road leading to the west, about a mile south of the roads department depot at mile 12. A thousand yards in, take the path up and then the steps down into the cave. It's an enchanting area, with mist and sunlight filtering through ferns and trees, and jungle vegetation tumbling down the limestone face.

You'll need a powerful flashlight and extra batteries to go any distance in. There are extensive passageways, and a small river. Knowledgeable speleologists downgrade this cave. But at least it's accessible, and for the less-than-knowledgeable, it's quite impressive. Mayan Pottery found here is kept in the vaults of the Archaeology Department in Belmopan.

About two miles farther south along the highway is the **Blue Hole**. You'll know you're at the right place when you see "Warning Thieves Here" painted onto the road surface. Comforting. Some chaps are known to hide in the bush and raid the unattended cars of visitors. Lock your vehicle, or leave somebody on guard.

From the roadside, take the steps down, to where water flows up from underground. The hole is, indeed, blue and deep and lovely, with vines and plants cascading down the enclosing little canyon. The waters flow off in a clear stream, then into a cave and back into the earth. Bye-bye. Dye tracings show that the waters that emerge at the Blue Hole come from St. Herman's Cave, and ends up in the Sibun River. Take a refreshing swim, if you're not too worried about your car.

A nature trail, about 1.5 miles long, connects the Blue Hole and the entry to St. Herman's cave, through the forest and away from the highway. *Do not walk it alone.*

Notable bird species at Blue Hole, according to the Belize Audubon Society, include the slaty-breasted tinamou, spotted wood quail, black hawk eagle, white hawk, keel-billed toucan and nightingale wren.

SPORTS & RECREATION
Spelunking

Adventurous Belize, operated by Ian Anderson, offers caving, among many available capers, on a 60,000-acre leased plot near Belmopan, perforated by hundreds of caves. Underground run the waters of the inland Blue Hole, which re-surface on the site, and disappear into yet another cavern.

Some caves are of the walk-in type, others require a rappel down ropes from surface openings. Some are considered archaeologically sensitive, with fossilized Mayan footprints, ancient sculptures, and crystallized skeletons in place. Some caves hold waterfalls.

Camping and day trips range from "soft" to "hard" in difficulty. An underground river tubing trip, suitable even for timid folk, runs from light shaft to light shaft, up to the surface and down under again, around pillars several feet thick carved with Mayan images, with breaks to walk through the jungle where logs have floated through and jammed the thoroughfare. Trips to remote sites last as long as a week.

Adventurous Belize has a few bedrooms available in a couple of farm houses off the Hummingbird Highway, south of Belmopan, a sort of hostel, with bed and meals for $60 per day, less if you stay in a tent, plus $25 to $30 for each day's outing (more if you're staying elsewhere). There is no electricity and no running water but for a basic cold shower.

There are also walking trails lined with identified native flora transplanted from the vicinity. Observation decks are being constructed at canopy level.

THE STANN CREEK VALLEY

At mile 24, the valley begins to widen. Plantations of little cacao trees, no bigger than a man, are sighted. Then come the vast citrus groves that dominate the **Stann Creek Valley**. Canned fruit juices and concentrates made from grapefruits and Valencia oranges of the valley are one of Belize's main exports.

DANGRIGA

Known until recently as Stann Creek, **Dangriga** is one of the principal settlements of the **Black Caribs** (*Garífunas*, or *Garinagu*), the people of mixed African and American Indian origin who live along much of the Caribbean coast of Central America. The Caribs trace their arrival in Dangriga to 1823, when their ancestors fled Honduras in the wake of a failed rebellion. The anniversary of their landing is celebrated on November 19 every year.

Although only 36 miles apart in a straight line, Dangriga and Belize City have little in common beside their seaside locations and a preponderance of wooden buildings. Belize City is in a swamp; but in southern Belize, the rivers rushing down from the Maya Mountains have, over the many centuries, deposited a wide and thick layer of soil, making the coastal belt agriculturally rich and eminently habitable. With a population of about 8,000, Dangriga is almost a metropolis in people-scarce Belize, clean, bustling with the commerce associated with the citrus industry.

Telephone dialing code for Dangriga is *05 from Belize, 011-501-5 from the U.S.A.*

ORIENTATION

The sea views from Dangriga are lovely. Two rivers that flow through, North Stann Creek and Havana Creek, are populated at most times of the day by fish, people, and boats of every size, in equal numbers. Dangriga is jolly, cheery, lively. The church is usually packed. But Dangriga is flat, and physically not too interesting or attractive.

The Garifuna culture, about which much has been said and written, is not easily penetrable unless you stay in town for a while, get to know a few people, and are yourself an open person. You might be offered coconut bread by a street vendor, but other traditional Garifuna food, such as *cassava*, is usually eaten at home. Garifuna dancers are most evident on Garifuna Settlement Day. But the celebrations continue off and on until the end of the year.

Masked John-Canoe (or *Yankunu*) dancers perform in the streets before Christmas for gifts of money, rum or candy. Conch shells are blown at midnight on Christmas Eve. Other ceremonies are rarely seen by outsiders. One is the *dugu*, a healing ritual in which a priestess communicates with the dead while in a trance. The dugu takes place over the course of a week, to the accompaniment of drumming and dancing, and sacrifices of chickens and pigs.

You'll see the studios of several Garifuna artists in the area below North Stann Creek. The most noted is Mr. Pen Cayetano. Hours are whimsical. Garifunas are also known for their home-made instruments, especially drums.

GETTING AROUND TOWN

Vans are available for rent, with driver, at the **Pelican Beach Hotel**, for about $150 per day. You can also try **Rosado's Tours**, *35 Lemon St., tel. 22119*, for inland and fishing tours, or **Lester Eiley**, *25 Oak St., tel.*

22113, for boats. All of the above will also arrange fishing trips and transport to the cayes.

ARRIVALS & DEPARTURES

Arriving By Bus From Belize City

Z-Line buses (Magazine Road, *tel. 73937, 22211 in Dangriga*) leave at 8 and 10 a.m. and 2, 3 and 4 p.m., Monday through Friday, with more limited service on weekends. Fare about $4. The James bus (Pound Yard Bridge on West Collet Canal, *tel. 07-2056*) leaves Monday, Wednesday, Friday and Saturday at 9 a.m.

These are the schedules via the Hummingbird Highway. Inquire for any routings via the newer Democracia-Manatee road.

Arriving By Air

Maya Airways flights leave Belize City for Dangriga daily at 6:30 a.m. (except Sunday), 9 a.m., noon (except Sunday) and 2 p.m., continuing to Big Creek and Punta Gorda. Northbound flights from Big Creek and Punta Gorda also touch down here. Fare is about $25 from Belize City to Dangriga. *Telephone 77215 in Belize City for the latest information.*

The airstrip in Dangriga is in the Pelican Beach Resort's back yard.

Departing By Bus

Buses park in Dangriga *Riverside*, the south end of the bridge over North Stann Creek. Z-Line departures for Belize City are at 5, 6, and 9 a.m., and 3 p.m.; James bus Tuesday and Friday at 1 p.m., Sunday and Thursday at 6 a.m. These are the schedules via the Hummingbird Highway. Inquire for any routings via the newer Democracia-Manatee road.

Every day but Sunday, buses leave Dangriga for Punta Gorda at 12:30 and 7:30 p.m., for Mango Creek at 3:30 p.m.

A bus leaves for Placencia on Monday, Wednesday, Friday and Saturday at 2:30 p.m. The James Bus from Belize City also continues to Punta Gorda on the four days when it's running.

And that's all the southbound bus transport there is.

Departing By Air

Maya Airways flights leave for Belize City at 8:40 a.m. (except Sunday), 11:05 a.m., 2:05 p.m. (except Sunday) and 4:05 p.m. Southbound flights continue to Big Creek and Punta Gorda. Buy tickets at the Pelican Beach Resort next to the airstrip, or at a shop on Dangriga's main street with a Maya Airways sign.

WHERE TO STAY

PELICAN BEACH RESORT, *P. O. Box 14, tel. 05-22044, fax 22570).
20 rooms. $57 to 70 single/$75 to 85 double, plus 10% service plus tax, slightly
lower March through October. Add $25 for three meals. Visa, Master Card,
American Express.*

Pelican Beach is located at Scotchman Town, a mile north of
Dangriga, next to the airstrip. Rooms are upstairs in the main lodge, and
in an annex. About half face the water. They're plywood-panelled with
hardwood floors, ceiling fan, vinyl easy chair, large night table — typical
of no-frills rooms in the cayes, but much larger, and with a real tub in the
bathroom. The dining room is pleasant, with sea views through louvers,
and the goofy combination of elements that you will have come to expect
in Belize: Star Trek table lamps, formica counters, bamboo accessories,
a stuffed sailfish, overhead fans, and sagging ceiling panel — altogether
perfect. A large common area has table tennis.

The best feature, though, is the lovely, wide, palm- and pine-shaded
beach, fringed with sea grapes, that extends to the veranda of the hotel.
There are plenty of chairs under the second-floor overhang, where you
can sit and watch the fleets of pelicans.

Boats, fishing excursions, cottages on South Water Caye ($115 for the
trip out, $100 for the cottage per day) and jaguar reserve tours ($150 for
five persons), windsurfers and snorkeling equipment are all available at
a price. As the only resort, there are some slight extra charges built in to
staying here — a less advantageous exchange rate than at the bank, and the
fact that taxis charge a relatively steep tab *per person* for the one-mile trip
from town.

JUNGLE HUTS MOTEL, *Ecumenical Dr., tel. 05-23166. 6 units. $30
single/$35 double, or $43/$50 with air conditioning.*

You will know them when you see them: four little square cottages by
the bridge that carries the highway into Dangriga. For those who prefer
not to be right in the center, these are a good choice.

Dangriga's in-town hotels are more modest and have fewer amenities.
The **HUB GUEST HOUSE** (*573A South Riverside, P. O. Box 56, tel. 05-
22397), just south of the bridge at North Stann Creek*, is a clean concrete
bungalow, with seven rooms going for $18 single, $25 double with private
toilet and shower. Ask here about boat rentals, and excursions. Credit
cards are accepted with a surcharge.

The **RIVERSIDE**, *in the center of Dangriga at 135 Commerce St.*, has
small rooms at $10 per person with shared bath. Homey atmosphere. The
owners also have a lodge on one of the cayes offshore, where the daily rate
is $125 per person with all meals. It's another $125 to get out there.

Rooms at the **CAMELEON CENTRAL**, *119 Commerce St., are barer
than at the Riverside*. The rate is about $8 per person. The **RÍO MAR INN**,

977 Waight Street (Southern Foreshore), tel. 22201, has just a few rooms at less than $10 per person.

The **BONEFISH HOTEL** *(15 Mahogany Rd., P. O. Box 21, tel. 05-22165, fax 22296, 10 rooms, $45 single/$60 double),* on the seafront, does, indeed, have the air conditioning and cable television that it advertises, but the rooms are concrete with musty carpeting and the barest of furnishings, though it's clean. An all-day fishing trip (for bonefish, naturally) can be arranged for $150. Located two blocks south of the bus park, then two blocks east to the sea. *In the U.S., call 800-798-1558 to reserve. (Ask for Byron.)*

WHERE TO EAT

Restaurants are generally open in Dangriga at meal times only, i.e., 7 to 10 a.m., noon to 3 p.m., and from 7 p.m. Two Chinese restaurants *on the main street*, the **SUNRISE** and the **STARLIGHT**, serve sandwiches, rice and beans, and assorted chow meins. **THE BURGER KING** (no relation to anything else by that name) serves rice and beans, fried chicken, conch soup, and burgers, too. The tab runs to $2 for a sandwich at any of these eateries, $5 to $6 for a main course.

COCKSCOMB BASIN WILDLIFE SANCTUARY

The world's first and only jaguar reserve, the **Cockscomb Basin Wildlife Sanctuary** *is located off the Southern Highway south of Dangriga.* Just a few years ago, jaguars were hunted as big game, and were in danger of disappearing from Belize, as they have from most other countries in the Americas. Now they're a protected species.

Largest of the hemisphere's cats, jaguars *(panthera onca)* grow up to six feet in length and weigh up to 350 pounds. Armadillos and gibnuts (pacas) are among their favorite foods, though they'll eat animals of all sizes, from deer and peccaries to rats and birds. Despite local tales, there's no evidence that they have a special taste for humans. Jaguars use old roads and trails to get around the reserve, which includes several abandoned logging camps.

The Cockscomb basin is an area of moist tropical forest bounded on three sides by ridges of the Maya Mountains, crossed by two large rivers and numerous creeks. The forest reserve was established in 1984; the wildlife sanctuary within it in 1986, with the support of public and private organizations, including the Jaguar car company.

The wildlife sanctuary takes in the habitats not only of the jaguar, but also of Belize's other cats: pumas, jaguarundi, margays and ocelots. Local wildlife also includes brocket deer, paca *(gibnut),* and peccary; Baird's tapir *(mountain cow),* and kinkajou *(nightwalker),* boas, iguanas, tree frogs, and much else. Common bird species are toucans (*billbirds*), king vultures (*King John Crow*), curassows, and scarlet macaws.

The 100,000-acre reserve also includes at least one Mayan site, Kuchil Balam, chanced upon only a few years ago by scientist Alan Rabinowitz.

ARRIVALS & DEPARTURES

To reach the sanctuary, take a bus or drive to Maya Center, at mile 14 on the Southern Highway. The reserve is seven miles westward.

WHERE TO STAY

Bunk beds are available in dormitories, at a fee of less than $10 per person, and camping is permitted, also at a charge. Bring your own food. There are also several nature trails, and exhibits illustrating local species.

TOURING THE RESERVE

Before going, inquire about facilities and seasonal conditions at the **Audubon Society**, *12 Cork St., Belize City, tel. 77369.* Or call at the Pelican Beach Resort in Dangriga, which is in radio contact with the reserve.

Have no fear if you plan to walk in — jaguars don't frequent the entry road. In fact, though you might sight jaguar tracks, your chances of seeing a live jaguar are better even at the Belize Zoo than here. What you'll espy is evidence of the jaguar's nocturnal presence: tracks and droppings. Expect mainly to enjoy the nature trails, in a rain forest that has been little altered even by loggers.

It takes about two hours to reach the camp on foot from the Southern Highway. Remember that the rainy season in this area runs from June through January, and that with from 100 to 180 inches of precipitation per year, it is *wet*.

PLACENCIA

About a hundred miles south of Belize City is the idyllic **Placencia Peninsula** (also spelled **Placentia**), a skinny, 16-mile long finger of beach and coconut palms that points southward from the mainland. Placencia village, at the southern tip, is home to just a few hundred Creole fishermen and their families. A generator at the fishing dock hums around the clock, providing electricity to make the ice that preserves the catch. Otherwise, Placencia could just as well exist in another age. The principal means of transport are the wheelbarrows that ply the village's mile-long sidewalk.

The center of Placencia is everybody's back yard. There's no hustle and bustle, in fact, there's no street, just open sand, wooden houses scattered under the coconut palms, and the concrete sidewalk. The point of arrival, and the point of departure for orientation, is the fishing co-op's dock at Placencia Point, the very bottom of the peninsula. Gasoline is available nearby (in case you're driving).

The center for all communications in Placencia is the combination post office/telephone office/gas station/charter fishing operation/air line ticket agency, at the end of the road on the west side of the village.

A Belize Defence Force detachment is present in Placencia, near the co-op: a few chaps lounging in t-shirts and shorts and listening to reggae at a pre-fab building. Without the sign, you'd take them for vacationers.

The advent of all-year road connections will no doubt change the sleepy character of Placencia. Already, chartered buses arrive on some weekends, filling most hotels with vacationers from Belize City. Plan to go in the middle of the week, but do go now, before the yacht harbor, air terminal, travel agency, "in" bars, and glass-bottomed-boat sightseeing tours are in place.

From the top of the peninsula, there's water to both sides: the reef-protected Caribbean to the east, and the mangrove-lined Placencia lagoon to the west, with the Maya Mountains towering in the distance. Being on the Placencia Peninsula is just like being on a tropic isle, and until the road was completed, that's just what Placencia, in effect, was.

Telephone dialing code for Placencia is *06 from Belize, 011-501-6 from the U.S.*

ARRIVALS & DEPARTURES

A recently constructed road provides all-year access to Placencia from a turnoff at mile 23 on the Southern Highway. From this point, it's seven miles to the sea and the beginning of the peninsula; 16 miles to **Maya Beach**; 19 miles to the Garifuna village of **Seine Bight**; and 22 miles to the end of the road at Placencia.

Arriving By Bus

One bus leaves Dangriga for Placencia on Monday, Wednesday, Friday and Saturday at 2:30 p.m. The ride takes about three hours. If coming from Belize City, confirm connections by calling the Z-Line bus company *(02-73937)*. A bus departs Dangriga at 3:30 p.m. daily for Mango Creek, where you can hire a boat to Placencia (see below).

Arriving By Air

Flights land at the Big Creek airstrip on the mainland opposite Placencia. **Maya Air** departures from Belize City are at 6:30 a.m. (except Sunday), 9 a.m., noon (except Sunday) and 2 p.m., via Dangriga, continuing to Punta Gorda. *Telephone 77215 in Belize City* for the latest information. One **Tropic Air** flight lands in the afternoon. Northbound flights from Punta Gorda also touch down at Big Creek.

If you have a reservation at one of the resorts north of Placencia village, you'll be picked up.

Arriving By Boat

Otherwise, you'll have to find a boat that's going over, either from Big Creek or nearby Mango Creek. A charter run costs about $20. Stop in at the Billbird Lodge to enjoy a drink while the staff phones and arranges for you to be fetched. *Or find a phone yourself and call the Placencia post office (06-22046) to have someone sent over.*

Departing By Bus

One bus leaves Placencia for Dangriga on Monday, Wednesday, Friday and Saturday at 3 a.m. Buses pass through Independence, adjacent to Mango Creek on the mainland, twice a day northbound and southbound. Inquire at hotels for exact schedules.

Otherwise, you'll have to cross to the mainland to catch a plane or bus. If you're looking to leave town, Mrs. Leslie at the post office will call around and find a boat to take you over. On Monday, Wednesday and Friday at about 2 p.m., you can ride over with the mail for $5 per person. The return trip is at 2:45 p.m. You can sometimes find boats leaving for the mainland between 8 and 9 a.m. from the co-op dock, which will take passengers for $5 or so through mangrove-lined channels to Mango Creek.

Departing By Air

Flights between Belize City and Punta Gorda touch down about five times daily at the Big Creek airstrip. Reserve through the Billbird Lodge in Big Creek *(tel. 06-22092)* or the post office in Placencia *(tel. 06-22046)*.

WHERE TO STAY

SINGING SANDS, *Maya Beach, tel. 06-22243. (P. O. Box 662, Belize City, tel. 02-30014, fax 02-32747). 6 rooms. $65 single/$75 double, plus $30 for three meals. Master Card, Visa, American Express.*

A "low-impact" beach cabana lodge, 16 miles from the junction on the Southern Highway. Individual thatched units have 12-volt fans and lighting. Copious fixed-menu meals, water sports equipment, extensive beach, long dock with thatched shelter, fishing and snorkeling arranged.

SERENITY RESORT, *tel. 06-23232, fax 23231. $75 single/$85 double. $25 per extra adult, $10 for children. Add $30 for three meals. U.S. reservations: tel. 800-331-3797. Off-season rates available.*

The most substantial resort in the Placencia area, the new Serenity consists of 12 rooms, most cottage-style and separate from each other, with large beds and sofas, ceiling fans, and private terrace. Some can be combined for families. The grounds are large, with 2000 feet of beach frontage. Guests bring their own alcohol. Fishing and inland trips arranged.

RUM POINT INN, *tel. 06-23239, fax 23240. 8 cabins. $170 single/$200 double plus 10% service and tax, with three meals, including transfer from Big Creek airstrip. Rates about 20% higher from Christmas to June. American Express, Visa, Master Card. Reservations: Toucan Travel, 32 Traminer Dr., Kenner, LA 70065, tel. 800-747-1381, fax 504-464-0325.*

A couple of miles up the coast from Placencia Point, Rum Point Inn lodges its guests in unique free-form concrete cabanas — they look something like mushrooms. The main house is a typically Belizean seafront structure, with the dining area and bar upstairs to catch the breeze. The food is quite good. In addition to the usual Belizean activities of fishing, diving, birding and tours to ruins and Indian villages, guests have the use of a book and video library.

KITTY'S PLACE, *tel. 06-22017. 3 units. A small apartment upstairs in a beach tower, with butane refrigerator, cooktop, two beds and full bath, goes for $70 per day; the two rooms downstairs, sharing bath, for $30 single/$40 double, plus 10% service plus tax.*

Another apartment with separate bedroom goes for $90 plus service charge, rooms with private both for $50 single/$60 double. The extensive grounds include coconut palms and cashew trees, and assorted chickens, ducks and rabbits, not to mention the ante-bellum sports bar.

TURTLE INN, *tel. 062-3244. 6 cottages. $45/$50, plus $30 for three meals, no service charge. Visa and Master Card. Rates are slightly lower June through September. U.S. reservations: 2190 Bluebell, Boulder, CO 80302, tel. 303-444-2555.*

Talk about low-key — there's not even a sign to identify the Inn. The guest units are thatch-roofed bamboo structures lined with reed mats, raised to catch the breeze. Each has an RV-type toilet. All electricity is from solar panels, so the background generator hum found at many Belizean resorts is missing. Meals are mainly seafood. A two-bedroom beach house is available by the week. The American owners specialize in inland, sea and river float trips, along with rain forest treks and overnight stays.

MOTHER OCEAN'S TROPICAL ENVIRONMENT AND RESEARCH STATION, *formerly The Cove, P. O. Box 007, tel. 06-22024, fax 22305. 6 rooms. $75 per person daily, plus 10% service plus tax, with three meals, or $65 per person from May through October. American Express, Visa, Master Card. U.S. reservations: 800-662-3091.*

These are clapboard cottages on stilts, all with private bath and ceiling fans, about a mile north of Placencia. Each has two queen-sized beds. The screened porches have hammocks, and there's a tennis court. Scuba,

snorkeling and fly fishing and trolling are available, along with hosting of
fishery and oceanic research.

SONNY'S RESORT, *12 units. Reservations: tel. 06-22103 (Placencia) or
13 and F streets, King's Park, Belize City, tel. 02-44975.*

Right in Placencia Village, and only in Belize: house trailers pulled up
onto the sand, with screened porches added on. More attractive are six
cabanas. Each is panelled inside, has a ceiling fan, tiled bathroom with tub,
mini-refrigerator and coffee pot. The rate is $50 for up to four people.
Trailer rooms are $30 single/$40 double.

RANGUANA LODGE, *tel. and manual fax 06-23112. Visa and Master
Card accepted.*

The fanciest cabana units in Placencia, each with one double and one
single bed, a bathroom with tub, refrigerator, coffee pot, porch, and
genuine wood panelling, though the beds could be better. The rate is $70
double with tax.

Budget Lodging

Several establishments in the center of Placencia Village charge $10
to $15 double — not a bad price, but don't expect luxury. **RAN'S** is a cool
house shaded by palms, back from the sea. The **HOTEL HELLO** has
simple rooms, some with private bath, right on the beach. Pleasant. Look
for the white house with blue trim. The **SEASPRAY**, *also on the seafront,*
is comparable. **MISS LYDIA'S**, *100 yards north of Jene's restaurant (tel. 06-
23117)*, has clean little rooms with fans, sharing toilet and shower
facilities. The proprietor will also make coco bread on order.

More substantial (though still unluxurious) are the rooms at the
PARADISE VACATION HOTEL (formerly Dalton's E-lee), *the clapboard
building 200 yards west of the co-op's pier at the southern tip of Placencia, next
to the Tentacles bar.* Airy rooms upstairs go for $10 per person with sea view,
balcony, and shared bath. Less breezy rooms downstairs, with private
baths, are $25 double.

WHERE TO EAT

JENE'S restaurant and bar, *opposite the Seaspray hotel*, is a comfortable,
dark-wood-panelled room that suits Placencia to a "t". Meals run from $4
for rice and beans to $10 for lobster, with chow mein, conch, shrimp and
steak in between. Also sandwiches and breakfasts. Try the turtle steak.
Good food, attractively served. They also have an assortment of wine, as
well as hard liquor and beer, and sea weed, a milk shake made with marine
flora, and liquor if you wish. A *notice* advises that British Forces are
excluded, due to consistently rowdy behavior.

Other, tourist-style bars have arrived, and more no doubt will come.
The **KINGFISHER** is a large thatched pavilion facing the sea, serving fish,

pork chops, t-bone steak, shrimp and lobster for from $6 to $15. **TENTACLES** is a bar and steak house that extends over the water, at the very south of the peninsula. You can get fish fried, poached, or broiled, or shrimp sauteed in butter — something more elegant than the usual back-country food.

The **GALLEY**, *along the sidewalk south of downtown Placencia*, serves burgers, fries, fish and juices at all hours during the day. (Most eateries are open from 7:30 or 8 a.m. to 2 p.m., and from 7 to 11 p.m.)

North of town by more than a mile, **KITTY'S PLACE** is the sportsman's bar and restaurant, in a balconied plantation-style house, a great second-story area open to the sea, with fans overhead, extensive nautical decoration, loads of books and tapes, and television usually showing the most important football, baseball or basketball game from somewhere in the world. The set meal for $12.50, served upon reservation, usually includes seafood; breakfast and sandwiches are available as well.

EXCURSIONS

The barrier reef offshore is still little visited, and, in some places, unexplored. Small cayes are protected by the reef. Diving and picnicking trips can be arranged at the **Placencia Dive Shop** at **Kitty's Place**, *north of the village near the airstrip, tel. 06-22027; and with Geno at the post office (tel. 06-22046)*. Any of the resort hotels to the north will make arrangements as well. At Kitty's place, the rate for a day's excursion with two dives is $70 to $80, depending on how far you go; certification courses run $350, day snorkeling trips with lunch $40 and up.

SPORTS & RECREATION

Shorter snorkeling trips cost less, as little as $10 with Geno at the post office/telephone office.

Kitty has several inland tours to the Jaguar reserve and Mayan ruins, and a boat trip available to Monkey River, a fishing village down the coast. She also rents a canoe, windsurfer, bicycles, and assorted gear for diving and snorkeling.

A small boat for fishing can be rented for $100 to $150 per day, depending on who you're dealing with and how far out you're going and the time of year (rates are lower in July and August, when things are slow).

Mike and Bonnie Cline arrange trimaran trips. Inquire at the yellow house up from Placencia Point, *or call 23154*. And you will find signs posted by Captain Joel, Conrad, at Miss Lydia's rooms *(tel. 06-23117)* and many others offering fishing and snorkeling.

NIM LI PUNIT

Located about a half mile off the west side of the Southern Highway, in the vicinity of mile 75, is the **Nim Li Punit** archaeological site. No restoration work has been done, and the site is only partially cleared; but it makes for a nice picnic spot if you're driving through.

Nim Li Punit (Big Hat, from the head gear shown on one of the stelae) was discovered in 1974 during exploration for oil, and, as often happens to Mayan ruins, was soon looted. A tomb of a noble, overlooked by the robbers, was uncovered by archaeologist Richard Leventhal in 1986.

Nim Li Punit includes several groups of buildings set on plazas, and a ball court. Only the southmost group can be visited. Twenty-five stelae have been found. One, 31 feet high, is the tallest carved stela in Belize. Or it would have been, had it ever been erected. It appears to have been unused because of an error in carving.

Stelae at Nim Li Punit bear dates, in the western equivalent, between 700 and 800 A.D. As many as 5000 people might have lived at the site in that period. Similarities in architecture, and proximity, suggest a connection with the larger site of Lubaantun, to the southwest.

Access to the site is by a trail from the Southern Highway. A sign points the way. If you're heading south and see the Whitney lumber mill on the east side of the road, you'll know you've gone too far.

Just to the south of Nim Li Punit is **Big Falls**, where the Southern Highway crosses the Rio Grande. Nearby are the only known warm springs in Belize, on the Peter Alaman farm. Mr. Alaman runs a general store, and can direct you to the springs. Ask for permission if you're interested in camping. Big Falls is a popular weekend bathing and picnicking spot.

PUNTA GORDA

Nearly two hundred miles by road from Belize City, or half that distance by sea or air, **Punta Gorda** (population 3000) is the last town of any size in southern Belize. Predominantly a **Carib** settlement, Punta Gorda also includes assorted Creoles, Mopan Maya, Kekchi, Chinese, Lebanese and East Indians in its ethnic quilt.

Once exclusively a fishing village, Punta Gorda has been converted into an agricultural market town by the construction of roads to the interior and to Belize City. Beans and rice, produced by Carib and Indian farmers, are the major food crops.

Telephone dialing code for Punta Gorda is *07 from Belize, 011-501-7 from the U.S.*

ARRIVALS & DEPARTURES
Arriving By Ferry

A ferry leaves from Puerto Barrios, Guatemala, on Tuesdays and Fridays at 7:30 a.m. for Punta Gorda. Fare is about $6.

Arriving By Bus

Z-Line buses leave Belize City (Magazine Rd. west of Collet Canal, *tel. 73937*) for Punta Gorda daily at 8 a.m. and 3 p.m., via Dangriga. Fare is about $8, and the trip can take up to eight hours, depending on road conditions.

Arriving By Air

Flights on **Maya Airways** *(tel. 02-77215)* operate from the Belize City airstrip for Punta Gorda at 6:30 a.m. (except Sunday), 9 a.m., noon (except Sunday) and 2 p.m., via Dangriga and Independence/Big Creek. One daily **Tropic Air** flight operates to Punta Gorda. Fare is about $50.

Departing By Ferry

A ferry leaves for Puerto Barrios, Guatemala, on Tuesdays and Fridays at 2 p.m. Fare is about $6. Get your ticket as early as possible in the two-story brick building on Middle St., next to the Maya Indita store. *Call 07-22065 to verify the current schedule.* Check out with immigration before boarding, with your Guatemalan visa or tourist card in hand.

If you miss the boat, a charter trip can be arranged in a skiff for something like $100.

Departing By Bus

Z-Line buses leave for Belize City at 5 a.m. and 11 a.m.

Departing By Air

Maya Airways flights operate northbound at 8:20 a.m. (except Sunday), 10:45 a.m., 1:45 p.m. (except Sunday) and 3:45 p.m. One daily **Tropic Air** flight operates northbound at 7 a.m., connecting with flights at the international airport.

Tickets on both airlines are sold at Bob Pennell's hardware store/insurance agency on Main Street in Punta Gorda. Reserve as far in advance as possible. Fare is about $50 to Belize City.

WHERE TO STAY

The clean and airy seafront **NATURE'S WAY GUEST HOUSE**, *at 65 Front St., at the south end of town (tel. 07-22119, P. O. Box 75)*, is an off-beat place, a wooden house with odd corners and nooks. There are only eight rooms, each with one large bed and a small upper bunk. Access to local ways is facilitated if you stay here, as the owners are an American-Belizean couple. They keep a collection of books and source material on the peoples and places of southern Belize. About $15 single/$20 double, no service charge, no credit cards. Most of the rooms are with shared bath.

The **MIRA MAR HOTEL**, *a concrete building near the center of town at*

95 Front Street (tel. 07-22033), has rooms in several tiers with private bath and fans, above the Chinese restaurant. Rates range from $19 to $55 single/$30 to $74 double, including tax. The surprising top rate gets you air conditioning, cable television, and mini-refrigerator.

Away from the water, the **SAINT CHARLES INN**, *23 King St. (tel. 07-22149, 15 rooms, $16 single/$25 double)*, is a substantial house with fair-sized rooms, all with fans, most with private bath with hot water, and cable television. If nobody is visible to serve you, inquire at the general store next door. **G & G's Inn**, *49 Main Middle St., tel. 22086*, has rooms in the same price range.

Your basic lodging houses, at $10 per person or less, include **PALLAVI'S HOTEL**, *19 Main St.*; the **ISABEL**, *on Front St. near the town center*; and **MAHUNG'S HOTEL**, *11 Main St. (tel. 22044)*. Mahung's is probably the best bet for cleanliness, though the late hours bar across the street might not be an asset. The **WAHIMA HOTEL**, also with cheap rooms, *is along the seafront just north of the Texaco gasoline station.*

Hotels North of Punta Gorda

SAFE HAVEN LODGE, *Office at 2 Prince St., Punta Gorda, tel. 07-22113. $100 single/$140 double with meals.*

A fishing and diving lodge, located on the Rio Grande, a few miles north of Punta Gorda, and just off the sea. Packages include meals, lodging, and transport from Punta Gorda. Fishing packages do not include tackle. Non-sportsmen ("eco-guests") are allowed use of a boat. Currently, there are five cabanas with two rooms each, and a few rooms in the fishing lodge, which is a large house with beamed ceiling and veranda. Food is mostly seafood, with some local and Chinese plates, and special requests honored.

ACCESS BELIZE, *adjacent to Safe Haven, is in development as a lodge free of barriers to the disabled and elderly. For information, contact Alda M. Lyons, 95 Washington St. no. 217, Weymouth, MA 02188, tel. 617-843-0404, fax 617-331-1785.*

Stay in a Mayan Village

There's an unusual program afoot in Punta Gorda to spread the benefits of tourism by arranging for visitors to stay with families in the interior.

This involves spending hundreds of dollars for your ticket, taking time off from work, and ending up somewhere in the bush to sleep on a hard bed or in a hammock in a thatch-roofed hut with a dirt floor, stumble in the dark through the scratching chickens to an outhouse, eat rice and beans, and wash with cold water, and if you see it strictly in these terms, skip to the next section, please.

So what's in it for you? Meeting local people as people, who go about their daily business to survive and enjoy life, not as servants to outsiders. Learning how corn is soaked in lime water and prepared for making tortillas; how wild herbs are used in cooking, and to cure illness; how local materials are harvested from the forest to build houses; how crops are grown with a minimum of chemicals. Tilling corn and beans, splitting firewood, beating clothes on rocks in a river. Hiking to caves and visiting ancient cities with native guides. Seeing how it's possible to live without cars and piped gas and electricity, and also how radios and satelliteTV have made their way to some of the more remote places on earth. And giving indigenous peoples the assurance that they have something to contribute to the west of the world, as well as some of the cash that normally flows to more go-getter types in the tourist trade.

If you're interested, contact the **Toledo Visitors Information Center** at the wharf. Most of the families speak English and Spanish, as well as their native tongue.

In strictly monetary terms, the price of lodging is under $15 per person per night, and meals are less than $5 each, and there is a registration fee of about $10 with the Toledo Visitors Information Center.

More formal guest houses are being organized in participating villages, with western-style toilets. And it's possible to stay as a paying house guest by making your own inquiries in villages in the bush. One reader has recommended the house of the José and Amillia Oh family, near San Pedro Columbia, as "the cleanest place I stayed in Belize." She had a room in the family sleeping house with a private entry, explored for medicinal herbs, and visited the ruins and caves of the area in the company of Mr. Oh. The Ohs can be reached through a neighbor's phone *at 07-22303* — call in the evening, and tell when you will call back.

WHERE TO EAT

This is not one of the high points of Punta Gorda, but things are gradually improving. **NATURE'S WAY GUEST HOUSE**, in continuing evolution, serves meals on an airy, garden-bordered porch. $3 gets you a breakfast of eggs and beans and huge slabs of home-baked bread. Lunch or dinner, with rice and beans, and chicken or beef or fish and salad, runs $4 to $5. Ask to sample Mayan and Carib dishes. For just sitting and watching the palms and the sea, this is the place.

The **MORNING GLORY CAFÉ**, *59 Front Street*, is clean, open for breakfast, reasonably priced, and affords a sea view.

The **KOWLOON**, *opposite the Maya Indita store on Middle St.*, has a real menu, with hamburgers and other sandwiches for $2 or less, and meals with fried fish, chow mein and assorted Chinese and non-Chinese main courses for $4 and up. They can modify something to order if it's not too much trouble. A plain and simple place, with video parlor in the front room, but clean.

SEEING THE SIGHTS

Punta Gorda is airy, breezy, open, hill-fringed, and quiet and affable. The center of town is more or less the area by the pier, where there is a lovely verandahed post office-governmental services building, and a pole on which a signal beacon is run up at night. The market is at Queen and Front streets, but there's generally not much activity.

The seafront in town is not for swimming — sewer pipes run into the water, for one — but the narrow, long beach to the north is attractive.

Then there are the Gurkha and British troops stationed nearby to make sure that the Guatemalans don't take their claims to Belize too seriously. Harrier jets from Belize City roar down along the coast and perform impossible turns in full view of the residents of Punta Gorda, and, more importantly, of the Guatemalans. Helicopters ferry soldiers to hilltop jungle observation posts, from which, unofficially, they saunter down to shops over the line to buy packs of cigs, watched, but not stopped, by their Guatemalan opposite numbers.

Nightlife consists of the **Dreamlight Disco**, *on Main St. opposite Mahung's Hotel*; and walking under the glow of stars, and of the lights atop the Voice of America radio towers.

If you are not continuing into Guatemala, the **Maya Indita** store *on Middle St.* has one of the best selections in Belize of Guatemalan weaving and other craft items.

To be taken as an old hand, always refer to Punta Gorda as "P.G."

Across the Bay of Honduras from Punta Gorda is **Livingston**, *in Guatemala*, also a mainly Carib settlement. A regular boat service is maintained between the two towns. Offshore, the southern end of the barrier reef, and the Sapodilla and Ranguana Cayes — little frequented picnicking and swimming spots — are accessible by boat. Punta Gorda itself is the most rain-soaked spot in Belize, and vegetation in the area is suitably exuberant.

Just north of Punta Gorda are the remains of their Toledo settlement, where sugar cane was planted. The settlement slowly disintegrated, as the descendants of the original refugees tried their luck in other parts of Belize, or returned to the United States.

Later years brought laborers deported from India, Creoles from up north, and Indians from Guatemala.

EXCURSIONS

The **Nature's Way Guesthouse**, *65 Front St.*, runs trips in a van to sites near Punta Gorda. For six persons, a trip to **Blue Creek** or **Lubaantun** costs $75; slightly more if you stop at both sites. They'll also arrange boat trips: $75 to **Moho Caye**, $150 to **Hunting Caye**, or $225 to the **Río Dulce in Guatemala** — and back. And they have camping equipment and a sleep-aboard trimaran available for rent, a sailboat, inflatables and windsurfers, and can help with arrangements for fishing.

Julio Requeña, *12 Front St., tel. 07-22070*, also offers boat charters and van trips.

The **Toledo Visitors Information Center** *(P. O. Box 73, Punta Gorda, tel. 07-22470)*, a private operation, located at the wharf, specializes in low-impact tourism, village stays with Kekchi and Mopan families (see below), and river, fishing and caye trips.

There are also a few taxis — the rate is about $120 for a day-long excursion — but otherwise, not much in the way of an organized tourism industry. A few roads poke back into the hinterland of Punta Gorda, over flat ranch and rice land, and into pocket canyons in the jungled foothills of the Maya Mountains.

LUBAANTUN

Located on the outskirts of San Pedro Columbia, **Lubaantun** (Fallen Stones) is the major Mayan archaeological site in southern Belize. The ruins were first reported to the outside world by refugee Southerners of the Toledo settlement, in 1875, and have been explored at various times by archaeologists and adventurers, among them Thomas Gann. Recent excavations were carried out by Norman Hammond.

The ceremonial center of Lubaantun, like that of Xunantunich, to the northwest, is atop a ridge that dominates the countryside. A series of plazas, each surrounded by stone temples and palaces, ascends from south to north, conforming with the rising ridge line. The structures are mostly terraced, and overlie earlier buildings. Around the ceremonial center are hillsides that show signs of also having been terraced, and faced with masonry, either as an esthetic continuation of the plaza architecture, or for agricultural purposes.

ARRIVALS & DEPARTURES
By Car

To reach Lubaantun from Punta Gorda, drive west to a mile and a half past the Shell gasoline station at the junction of the Southern Highway, then turn right — currently, there's no sign. Two miles ahead is San Pedro Columbia. Continue to the left around the church, then right and downhill, over a concrete bridge, for about a mile. To the left is the trail to the site, passable in vehicle in the dry season for part of the way. Park at the turnout before the rotted plank bridge.

SEEING THE SIGHTS

There are Mayan hilltop structures stretching all over the area beyond the excavated part of Lubaantun. About three miles to the northwest, along the Columbia Branch of the Rio Grande, is **Uxbentun** (Ancient Stones), also on a leveled hilltop, and largely unexcavated. The related site of Nim Li Punit is to the northeast, just off the Southern Highway.

The major structure at Lubaantun is 40 feet high and 100 feet in length, and the plazas are relatively long and wide. But the natural hills that Lubaantun's temples cap give the impression that structures are taller. On a clear day, an observer atop the temples can see to Punta Gorda.

Unusually, temples and palaces at Lubaantun were constructed of precision-cut stones, fitted together without mortar. The corners of some structures are rounded, a characteristic also of some sites along the Usumacinta River to the north. Sides of structures are formed of two-stone courses, with the upper stones protruding. Superstructures atop the temples were probably made of perishable materials, such as wood and thatch, for nothing remains. Some of the original lime-mortar facing and flooring can still be seen. A ball court indicates that some kind of game was played, either for recreation or as part of a religious or political ritual. Three ball-court markers, removed for safekeeping, are the only carved monuments discovered so far at the site.

Life in Lubaantun

Excavations at Lubaantun have yielded a wealth of materials that reflect the way of life of the ancient inhabitants. The most interesting discoveries are molded whistle figurines, an art form uncommon among the Classic Maya. Found in burials, the figurines, as well as bespeaking an interest in music, illustrate Mayan styles of dress, and show that weaving techniques included tapestry and tie-dying, still used by Maya-related peoples in Guatemala. Black and red and green powders might have been used as facial makeup and body paint, applied using iron pyrite mirrors.

Grinding stones indicate that corn was prepared for tortillas just as it is today. One grinding stone showed traces of flint, which was ground and added to clay to make pottery. Conch shells and fish bones might have come from **Wild Cane Caye**, a Mayan maritime outpost. Jade beads, obsidian knives and turquoise came from a considerable distance away. The inhabitants of Lubaantun probably traded with the highlands of present-day Guatemala, using cacao beans as their currency. The figure of a skull made from a transparent, glass-like quartz (the so-called "crystal skull") is of uncertain origin—it might have come from Brazil as late as the sixteenth century, though the daughter of Mitchell Hedges, the archaeologist who discovered it, claims an ancient Mayan origin for the piece.

The materials found at Lubaantun indicate that the city reached its peak toward the end of the eighth century A.D. All building of ceremonial structures came to an end soon after.

The little-visited Lubaantun site is open from 8 a.m. to 5 p.m. The temples are overgrown with trees, not prettified by modern reconstruction, but beautiful in their existing state. The caretaker will show you where various items — caches of mollusk shells, a human jawbone — were discovered, point out what might have been a prison for captives, and indicate where native religious rituals have been performed even in recent times. Bring your own refreshments.

4. HONDURAS
& THE BAY ISLANDS

HISTORY

Honduran history can read like the enumeration of generations in the Bible. From the time the Spanish left until the present, there have been more than 100 presidents, chiefs of state, military rulers, and similarly designated persons-in-charge. Buccaneers and English traders held sway for years in parts of the country, and the capital shifted back and forth, in colonial times and after independence, until a hundred years ago.

No ancient villages or monuments remain from the earliest inhabitants, but pottery fragments found near the Caribbean coast have been dated as far back as 2000 B.C.

More is known about the native inhabitants of central, western and southern Honduras of pre-Hispanic times, for many were living in settled communities when the Spanish arrived, and others, the ancestors of some of these peoples, erected monumental cities that can still be visited.

Of the early inhabitants, the **Maya** were the most powerful and advanced. The Maya dominated what is now western Honduras for at least a thousand years, made numerous significant discoveries and advances, and then faded mysteriously, though their descendants are still present in Honduras and neighboring countries.

People readily identifiable as Mayan, by their pottery and other artifacts that have been found by modern archeologists, began to appear as far back as 1000 B.C. in an area that today includes southern Mexico, Guatemala, and Honduras. Soon after the time of Christ, Mayan settlements began to contain not just houses, but ceremonial structures at their centers. Temples were erected on great platforms throughout the Early Classic period, from 300 to 600 A. D. Some were the tallest buildings in the hemisphere until this century.

Mayan cities, such as **Copán**, in Western Honduras, contained numerous plazas surrounded by temples, multi-roomed structures, ball courts, and what might have been specialized buildings such as sweat baths. The cities were built with the most simple, back-breaking techniques, of rubble carried to the construction site without the aid of wheels or machines, piled into platforms behind retaining walls faced with limestone blocks and plastered over with lime mortar. Limestone was easily worked, and occurs everywhere in Mayan territory. The landscape was also remade as necessary: hilltops were cut off, cisterns constructed, streams diverted, swamps cut by canals for transport and drainage, and built up to create raised gardens. Corn and cassava and yams were planted, and nuts were harvested from the forests.

In the city centers, *stelae*, or carved stones, were erected in the plazas to record important events, especially those in the lives of royalty. Those at Copán were the most beautiful works of art of any pre-Columbian people. Probably only the nobility and priests could be accommodated in the few, small rooms that could be created under the primitive Mayan arch, or corbel — a single capstone over two walls protruding inward toward each other. Nobility were buried in tombs under temples, which were decorated with painted friezes, and hieroglyphic writing.

In Honduras, the descendants of the Maya survived as separate, remnant nations, alongside groups that migrated from the lands to the north, and others that were either conquered by migrants from Mexico or largely succumbed to foreign influences and rule. Major Maya-related groups are the **Chortí** and **Lenca** peoples. The **Pipil**, of Nahuatl descent, lived along the southwestern mountain slopes, toward the Pacific.

By the time the Spanish arrived, the natives of western Honduras had declined from the levels of achievement of the Maya. There was no central authority ruling over a large area, and interregional trade was limited. Without knowledge of outsiders of other races, there was no solidarity, and warfare occasionally raged not only between nations, but sometimes among people speaking a common language. It was by subduing and subsequently allying themselves with different native groups that the Spanish were able to conquer.

The first encounters between natives and Spaniards in what is now Honduras were peaceful. **Christopher Columbus** himself sailed along the Caribbean coast in 1502, and in July of that year landed on the island of Guanaja, which he called **Isla de los Pinos** (Pine Island).

It was at the time of this first European visit that Honduras received its modern name, though there are several versions of just whence the name comes. Some say that *Honduras* — literally, "depths" — was applied to describe either the deep seas or low-lying lands of the adjacent coast. Others say that *hibueras*, the native word for floating gourds, was cor-

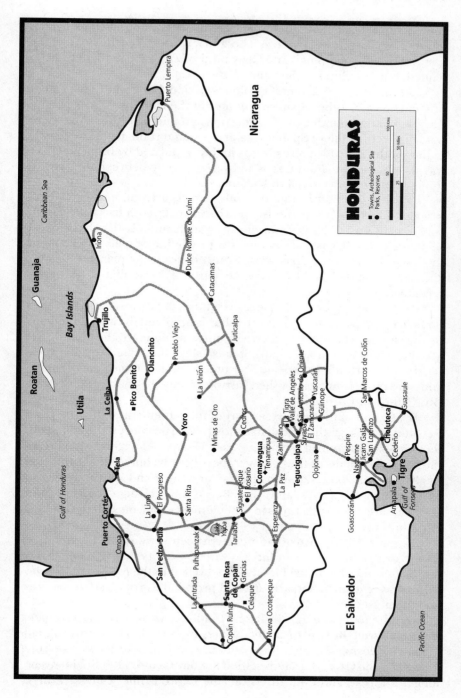

rupted into *higueras*, Spanish for fig tree, and later into *Honduras*; or that the aboriginal name was Ondure. The land was also called the Coast of the Ears, after native ear-plugs; and Guaymura, after a tribe thought to be so named; but Honduras is the name that stuck.

Honduras was settled in the colonial period, but never to the extent of Guatemala or other Spanish colonies in the isthmus. Discoveries of silver led to the founding of **Tegucigalpa** as a mining center. And there was some settlement of Spaniards along the land route from Guatemala in the southwest, which already was highly populated by Indians. There was also interest in Honduras as an overland route between the oceans, though that role was to fall to Panama.

Far from the mother country, with a small garrison, sparsely settled, vast Honduras was only tenuously held by Spain. Pirate attacks on Spanish convoys increased in the Caribbean. Dutch and British buccaneers sheltered in the Bay Islands, behind the protection of reefs that kept out the larger boats of the Spaniards. British buccaneers, planters, loggers and sailors landed in and occupied parts of Mosquitia in the early seventeenth century.

By the opening of the eighteenth century, the British had a firm grip on Belize, and protectorates over the Bay Islands and the Miskito Indians on the Honduran coast. Provided with guns and liquor by the English, the Miskito and Sumos attacked any Spanish ships that dared to enter their territory. British forces repeated occupied and lost Omoa and Trujillo, and were more firmly established eastward along the coast at Black River (Río Tinto) and Brus.

By the end of the century, as part of the settlement of the American Revolutionary War, the British had mostly been pushed off the mainland, though Spanish control remained weak. Hampered by Spanish mercantile policy, residents of the colony traded illegally, but willingly, through English intermediaries, moving lumber and sugar and gold and silver to and through the Bay Islands and Belize, in exchange for cloth and manufactured goods. At times in the colonial period, most of the trade of Honduras involved smuggling.

Honduras at the turn of the nineteenth century was a highly stratified society, with a broad base of Indians with few rights. Above them were a few blacks, and the mixed bloods who dwelled in the towns. Those who worked as craftsmen and artisans and provided European-style services had the most prestige.

Despite independence in 1821, Honduras' weakness and disorganization allowed Britain to maintain and expand its claim to disputed territories during the early independence period. British subjects from Belize and the Cayman Islands settled the **Bay Islands** after Spain was no longer a threat, and even threw out the Central American garrison in

1838. Since Britain dominated trade with Central America, taking strong action against the interlopers was a chancy matter.

The **Wyke-Cruz treaty** with Britain in 1859, during the presidency of José Santos Guardiola, provided for British withdrawal from the Bay Islands, with guarantees for the religious freedom of the islanders. British influence along the coast of Honduras gradually came to an end over succeeding decades.

While British influence was on the wane, that of the United States was increasing. A promoter named Ephriam George Squier, who had once served as U.S.consul, attempted to start up a railroad across Honduras in 1853. No track was constructed until 1871 — money intended for the railroad had a way of going to arms purchases instead — and the railroad never operated. In the process, though, various American business interests learned of and invested in Honduras. Mining was the key attraction at first, and later, banana plantations on the north coast.

Under President Luis Bográn, from 1883 to 1890, Honduras was once again influenced by Guatemala. The last of a string of three conservative presidents was deposed just three years later by Policarpo Bonilla, a liberal, with Nicaraguan aid. Bonilla oversaw the revision of many laws to streamline administration and encourage foreign investment, and signed Honduras to a union with El Salvador and Nicaragua that never came about. Bonilla was backed by a more formal political party structure than Honduras had previously known.

Succeeding presidents were generals Terencio Sierra and Manuel Bonilla, the latter using a show of force as well as votes to get into office in 1903. Guatemala invaded in 1906, and when Bonilla made peace, Nicaragua invaded the following year and kicked Bonilla out. Bonilla staged a revolt against his successor, Gen. Miguel Dávila, and the presidency was settled on yet another person, Francisco Bertrand, through U.S.-sponsored negotiations.

While an elite of politicians and generals from Honduras, Nicaragua, and Guatemala were playing out their power games in Tegucigalpa and regional capitals, it was in the north of the country that the real changes were unfolding, as Honduras was converted into a banana republic.

Around the turn of the century, banana traders in New Orleans began to look into Honduras as a reliable supplier of commercially grown bananas, which were being exported principally from Costa Rica. The predecessor of the Standard Fruit Company made the first shipments. In 1911, the Cuyamel Fruit Company, organized by Sam Zemurray, began operations, followed in 1913 by the United Fruit Company. Honduras soon became the leading exporter of bananas in the world, and bananas were to remain the mainstay of the modern sector of the economy for many years. The banana companies, through their assorted commercial ventures and worker welfare system, were to be, in effect, more important than the government for many Hondurans.

The elections of 1923 produced no majority for any candidate. With the country on the brink of a new civil war, and Augusto Sandino harassing the U.S. Marines in Nicaragua next door, the United States once again brokered a political solution. New elections were won by Miguel Paz Baraona of the National Party whose leader, Gen. Tiburcio Carías Andino, had gained the most votes in 1923, but, to everyone's surprise, had refused to take power by force.

Carías was a Renaissance man of the times, an intellectual who for a while held his party above his personal ambitions. Carías himself came to power in the 1932 elections. His party allegedly stood for good management, reconciliation, and free elections, but Carías managed to stay in office until 1948, through constitutional amendments. Revolts and opposition flourished at the beginning of his term, but the nation eventually became resigned to his authoritarian rule. Political exiles were encouraged to return home, but those who continued to speak out were subject to arrest.

Early in the Carías regime, Panama disease caused the banana industry to go into a tailspin, and world war cut off trade. During Carías' tenure, the economy diversified somewhat, into mining and ranching and timber exports, and coffee production. Carías selected his successor, Juan Manuel Gálvez, who took office in 1949, his Liberal opponent having conveniently withdrawn. Gálvez cooperated with the Central Intelligence Agency in promoting the overthrow of the populist Arbenz government in Guatemala and restoring the position of the United Fruit Company in that country. After another election which produced no majority, Vice President Lozano seized the government.

While Honduran leaders were helping to meddle in Guatemala, in their own country, banana workers became increasingly dissatisfied and went on strike, and unrest spread throughout the small sector of the economy where people labored for wages. The strike ended with significant increases in benefits for United Fruit and Standard Fruit workers, and recognition for the first time of their right to bargain.

Lozano exiled one of his political opponents, Ramón Villeda Morales, allegedly for helping to foment the "leftist" United Fruit Company strike — certainly not the last time the specter of labor unrest and communism would be used against an opponent. In the end, the army seized power and sent Lozano packing.

A constituent assembly brought in a new constitution in 1957, and selected Ramón Villeda Morales of the Liberal Party as president. During Villeda's term in office, the Central American Common Market took shape. Import restrictions were removed, and many products that formerly were imported into Central America began to be manufactured in the region. But most of the new factories went up in Guatemala, El Salvador and Costa Rica, where there were more roads, more shipping facilities, and more sophisticated investors, and Honduras was left behind, in many cases helping to finance the development of its neighbors.

Under Villeda, schools were built and labor rights were strengthened, though unrest continued in the realm of the United Fruit Company. As elsewhere in Central America, a social security system was installed to take care of the medical needs and pensions of a limited number of workers. The border with Nicaragua was finally determined through arbitration, after the neighboring country threatened to invade the newly delineated and sparsely populated Gracias a Dios department. Villeda was turned out of office in 1963 on the eve of new elections by Air Force Col. Osvaldo López Arellano, whose accession was handily "confirmed" by a constituent assembly.

Over the preceding decades, many Salvadorans, crowded by a coffee-plantation economy, had come to settle in Honduras, crossing an ill-defined border and squatting on uncultivated lands. As the numbers of Salvadorans grew, they faced increasing discrimination, and with no documentation, were subject to arbitrary actions by both government and ordinary Hondurans. In 1969, the situation came to a head with the expulsions of many Salvadorans, and exploded after a soccer match between the two countries. In five days of bitter fighting, El Salvador, then called "the Israel of Central America," drove into Honduras along the Pan American Highway and around Nueva Ocotepeque. The air force of Honduras managed to damage a refinery in El Salvador, but the country was rescued from disaster only by a cease-fire declared by the Organization of American States. A sullen Honduras refused to cooperate further with the Central American Common Market, and despite a peace treaty signed in 1980, hard feelings from the war continue.

López turned the government over to civilians in 1971, but took power again in 1972, this time spouting the reformist populism that was the rage among the military in parts of Latin America. In 1978, a new junta, lead by Policarpo Paz García, seized the government.

Military rule began to wind down once again in 1980, with the convening of a constituent assembly. Still another constitution was implemented in 1982, and Roberto Suazo Córdoba became president. Military buildups in Honduras were significant under Suazo, as the United States poured in weapons in response to the Sandinista victory in Nicaragua. "Contra" opponents of the Sandinistas found refuge and set up bases with American support and Honduran connivance, and American troops staged maneuvers on a near-permanent basis.

Following a traditionally inconclusive election in 1985, José Azcona Hoyo became president, after the various factions of his party, though not Azcona himself, together gained more votes than the leading Liberal, Rafael Leonardo Callejas Romero. Callejas ran again in 1989. This time he scored a clear victory, and was sworn into office in January 1990. The verdict is not yet in on how well the current president, Carlos Roberto Reina, is doing.

In recent years, there has not even been enough money available to buy fertilizer. The uneven balance of trade and waffling about paying a large foreign debt led to an overvalued currency, and, in turn, a decrease in foreign investment.

Other problems faced by the government were continuing ones: poor agricultural management and a lack of infrastructure; inadequate schools, poor technical education, and deficient health care; a population growing almost as fast as production; a lack of roads and railroads, except in the banana country of the north; limited port facilities. But Honduras has many material and human resources, it is near potential markets, and its weather and attractions make it a prime candidate for touristic development. With stability returning to the region, the prospects for the nation are promising.

LAND & PEOPLE

Honduras is a fertile country. It rains enough almost everywhere. There are many valleys, with expanses of flat land, there is plenty of sun and rich soil. Everything grows here, from apples and wheat and peaches at the higher altitudes to pineapples down in the wet, hot lowlands.

But Honduras does not have a simple landscape, anything but. It's a bit disordered, even messy. There are mountains here and there, spots of desert, jungle, with no continuation of anything. Nevertheless, it is possible to make something intelligible out of the ensemble.

Honduras covers 112,088 square kilometers (43,644 square miles), about the size of the state of Tennessee. By Central American standards, Honduras is big, second in size after Nicaragua. But this is a sparsely populated land, with just under 5 million inhabitants. El Salvador, next door, has about four times the population density of Honduras.

Honduras stretches between 13 and 16 degrees north latitude, and from 83°15' to 89°30' west latitude. Though its peaks do not reach dramatic heights, it is the most mountainous country in Central America, and most of the land is more than a thousand feet above sea level.

Along the north is the 800-kilometer (500-mile) Caribbean coastline. On the east, an 870-kilometer (545-mile) border with Nicaragua runs south and west from the Caribbean to the Pacific. The distance along the west side of the country is almost as long — 339 kilometers (211 miles) southwest with Guatemala, then 341 kilometers (212 miles) to the southeast with El Salvador, ending at the 145-kilometer (90-mile) Pacific coastline along the Gulf of Fonseca. Apart from this huge chunk of mainland, there are also the **Bay Islands** off the north coast, and farther out in Caribbean waters, the Swan Islands, or Islas del Cisne.

Mountains cover more than two-thirds of the land thus enclosed. Spread almost haphazardly, they create numerous valleys with small expanses of arable land, mostly isolated one from another. Some valleys, north and east of Tegucigalpa, are broader than the others, covered with savannas. Major ranges are the Merendón and Celaque, running roughly from southwest to northeast, with peaks as high as 2800 meters (over 9000 feet). The Nombre de Dios range, with peaks up to 8000 feet, lies just back from the Caribbean shore, forming the spectacular southern boundary of the department of Atlántida. The Entre Ríos range parallels the Nicaraguan border in the sparsely populated northeast region. The Bay Islands are just a short above-water expression of an undersea continuation of the Merendón mountains.

The economy is still dominated by just a few crops: bananas, and the African oil palm, cacao, pineapple, and other fruit products promoted and exported by American companies. Farther east, the landscape is a waterlogged terrain of mangrove and swamps and lazy rivers, of hardwood and rubber trees and palms and wide sandy bars near the sea, and stretches of scrub Caribbean pine on sandy soil inland, and a few settlements along the rivers. Honduras mahogany of renowned quality, growing sparsely, is cut and shipped out, but few other uses are made of the land.

Honduras is rich in minerals: gold and silver that first attracted avaricious Spanish adventurers; and lead, zinc, tin, iron, copper, coal and antimony. Some of these have been exploited for centuries. There are deposits of gypsum, strata of marble, and limestone, used since Mayan times to make a durable mortar.

Dozens of rivers drain the mountains of Honduras, combining and renaming with their flow as they near the oceans. Major waterways are the Goascorán, Nacaome and Choluteca in the south, and the Ulúa and Chamelecón in the north. Farther east along the Caribbean, the Coco and Patuca were once highways for pirates and English adventurers, and are still major routes in an area where few roads penetrate.

Flora

In your travels around Honduras, you'll mainly see the crops that Hondurans commonly farm for home use and for sale. These include corn, beans, and sorghum at the temperate altitudes toward the center of the country; coffee on mountains slopes; tobacco in warm valleys; and in the hot lowlands, sugar, coconut, manila hemp (*Abacá*), pineapple, cotton, African oil palm, and that signature crop, bananas. Garden crops and fruits include cassava, common vegetables such as tomato and cabbage, cacao, and tropical fruits such as mangoes, avocados, *zapote*, *anona*, tamarind, guava, papaya, *nance*, and *jocote*.

Outside cultivated areas, Honduras' forests are a treasure trove of tropical variety that has only recently been set aside, in part, as national parks and biological reserves. Atop mountain peaks and along the crests of ridges are cloud forests, the "weeping woods" where abundant moisture allows ferns and vines and orchids and broadleaf plants to thrive at every level, from the rich humus of decaying matter at ground level, up to the crooks of tree branches, where bromeliads take their nourishment from passing detritus blown on the wind, and capture the moisture in the air. Live oaks and wild avocados are common in most cloud forest areas; the exact plant variety varies according to particular moisture conditions.

Practically beside some of these wonderlands are patches of desert, starved of moisture by nearby peaks that catch the clouds on the prevailing winds. Pines and firs cover vast stretches of highland Honduras below the peaks, and toward the wetter lowlands, mahogany, *ceiba* (silk-cotton), Spanish cedar, and rosewood are typical, with palms along the beaches, and mangroves in the water-soaked coastal areas. Acacias and even cactus are typical of the savannas of the northeast.

Fauna

Assorted common forest animals typical of Honduras: anteater, armadillo, coyote, deer (white-tailed and brocket), raccoon, kinkajou, coati, turkey, cats (puma, ocelot, jaguarundi, margay, jaguar), opossum, white-lipped and collared peccary, monkeys (howler, spider, capuchin, marmoset), gray fox, gopher, porcupine, tapir, turtles, lizards (iguana, skinks, gecko, etc), snakes (boa, worm, coral, bushmaster, rattlesnake, fer de lance), sloths, cottontail rabbits, rodents (flying squirrel, mice, rats, porcupines, agoutis, paca [*tepezcuintle*]), skunk, river otter, bats).

Near and in the water are assorted crocodiles, caymans, turtles (leatherback, Ridley, loggerhead, hawksbill, green), manatees, salamanders, and frogs and toads.

Fish, aside from game species mentioned in connection with the Bay Islands, include catfish, minnow, cichlid, gar-pike, mud-eel, sea catfish, sharks, guapote (a bass-like river fish), mojarras (cichlids), top minnows (mollies), and black bass introduced in Lake Yojoa; and there are such mollusks as snails, lobster and fresh-water crabs.

For coral and fish watchers, a good reference is *Guide to Corals and Fishes of Florida, the Bahamas and the Caribbean*, by Idaz and Jerry Greenberg (Miami: Seahawk Press, 6840 S.W. 92 Street, Miami, FL 33156), available in a waterproof edition. Natalie's fish-sighting list includes: green moray, spotted moray, barracuda, sand diver, trumpet fish, squirrel fish, fairy basslet, tiger grouper, yellowtail snapper, French and Spanish grunt, porkfish, banded butterflyfish, reef butterflyfish, queen angelfish, rock beauty, French angelfish, yellowtail damselfish, blue and brown chromis, parrotfish, black durgon, blue tang, ocean surgeon, white spotted filefish, hawksbill turtle, coral crab, spiny lobster, spotfin butterflyfish, moon jellyfish, octopus and urchin.

Birdwatchers, take along your bird books. A comprehensive checklist of Honduran birds, mentioning over 700 species, is available for about $2 from Natural History Tours, P. O. Box 1089, Lake Helen, FL 32744. *Field Guide to Mexican Birds*, by Roger Tory Peterson and Edward L. Chalif (Boston: Houghton, Mifflin) includes about 93 percent of known Honduran species. The most notable locale for birding is the Lancetilla Botanical Garden near Tela. But there are many others, some of them mentioned in passing in this book.

Among typical or notable species (and these are mentioned just to indicate the range of species in Honduras):

The quetzal, an elusive cloud forest trogon in iridescent red and green, with an arc of tail feathers several feet long, which every Central American country claims as its own; nightingale thrush (*jilguero*), black robin (*sinzontle*), wood hewer, clorospinga, hummingbirds (more than twelve varieties), motmots, curassows (*pavones*), chachalacas (wild hen), tinamou, quail, parrots and macaws, toucans, partridge, wrens, grebes, cormorants, pelicans, hawks, falcons, ospreys, vultures, herons, ibises, ducks, swallows, flycatchers, warblers, dippers, orioles, jays, blackbirds, cuckoos, rails, plovers, gulls, terns, pigeons, owls, kingfishers, swifts, mockingbirds, jacana, storks, flamingos, guans, limpkins, sun bitterns, potoos, puff-birds, manakins, honey creepers, finches, sparrows, frigatebirds, boobies, anhingas, egrets, spoonbill, doves, roadrunners, woodpeckers, tanagers, cardinals, turkeys, chickadees.

People

What do you notice first about the people of Honduras? They are friendly and they are helpful. They are easy-going. They are approachable. They are not at all hard to get along with.

To me, this is slightly surprising. For Honduras is a poor country, indeed. Yet in this place, you do not feel the inequalities, the seething social tensions that form a backdrop to a visit to so many other places that are far better off. There are rich people, indeed, in Honduras, but the out-and-out exploitation of the masses that has characterized the history of neighboring countries has been in Honduras less pronounced, if not totally absent.

Hondurans comprise many of the races of the earth. Whites, blacks, Amerindians, Orientals, Lebanese, and every mixture thereof can be found, either as part of the national culture, or as a group maintaining its own separate ways. Spanish is the national language, but American Indian tongues and English dialects are also spoken. Hondurans, as are many of the peoples of poorer countries, are mostly young, mostly country people, and mostly farmers. But there are notable differences between the different groups.

Ladinos

Most of the five million Hondurans, those you typically think of as Hondurans, and who think of themselves as Hondurans, are Mestizos, or **Ladinos**, people who have both European and American Indian ancestors. About 88 percent of Hondurans fall into this category. Native Americans are the next largest group, as much as ten percent of the population. Blacks, whites, and assorted other groups and mixtures make up the rest.

Ladinos live everywhere in Honduras, but mostly in the more heavily populated west-central corridor of the country, running from San Pedro Sula to Comayagua to Tegucigalpa to the Gulf of Fonseca. Other groups reside in specific areas, mainly near the perimeter of Honduras. They are overwhelmngly Catholic.

PLANNING YOUR TRIP

Climate & Weather

• Temperatures are warm all year, and you can get good weather somewhere in Honduras in every season. But some months are better than others. Or, to put it another way, you can decide what weather you like, and go to the appropriate area of Honduras at the appropriate time.

• Tegucigalpa, along with most of Honduras, has moderate, spring-like temperatures throughout the year. In central Honduras, temperatures get cooler the higher you go. May is the warmest month, but it is rarely uncomfortably hot in the capital.

• It rains for six months of the year in Tegucigalpa and most of central Honduras, from May through October, for a few hours a day, and it is dry on most days during the rest of the year (*verano*, or "summer"). But even in the rainy season (*invierno*, or "winter"), precipitation isn't too high. You can visit Tegucigalpa at any time of year without concern for the weather.

• The south coast along the Pacific has a rainy season, just like Tegucigalpa, but the wet is wetter, and the temperatures are generally hotter. But half of the year is very dry.

- The Caribbean coast on the north, and the Bay Islands, get rain throughout the year. The trade winds that blow from the northeast bump up against the Nombre de Dios mountains that lie just inland from the shore, causing clouds to dump their moisture. Tela and La Ceiba get more than three meters (ten feet!) of rain in a year. Montreal, Houston, and New York get about one meter in an average year. While October through November is the rainiest time, you always have to expect some rain along the coast. But you can expect sunny periods on every day as well. There are occasional hurricanes during the rainiest times along the coast.

- Temperatures throughout the lowlands are hot all year. But right along the water, there is usually a breeze, especially from October through April. Along the Caribbean coast, it is always very humid, so you might need air conditioning for sleeping. Nothing dries, and everything is a little bit rotten.

- Out on the Bay Islands, away from the mountain ridge, rainfall is lower than right along the coast, and though the chart doesn't show it, humidity is lower. January through September are considered good months to visit the Bay Islands. But if you can stand some rain mixed with your sunshine, the rest of the year is okay as well.

HOLIDAYS IN HONDURAS

Here are the holidays, both familiar and unfamiliar, to watch out for in Honduras. Banks and businesses will be closed, and you won't be able to make a plane reservation or book a tour, on these days.

January 1	*New Year's Day*
Moveable	*Holy Thursday*
Moveable	*Good Friday*
	(Many businesses close all week)
April 14	*Day of Americas*
May 1	*Labor Day*
September 15	*Independence Day*
October 3	*Day of Francisco Morazán*
October 12	*Columbus Day (Día de la Raza)*
October 21	*Armed Forces Day*
December 24-25	*Christmas Eve and Christmas*
December 31	*New Year's Eve*

In addition to national holidays, every town has its own local celebration day.

Entrance & Exit Requirements

I have to tell you to re-check with your airline or a Honduran consulate before you leave on your trip. Entry requirements are subject to change, and vary by nationality.

U.S. and Canadian citizens currently require only a passport to enter Honduras. U.S. citizens may also enter with a tourist card.

As of recently, no visa is required of citizens of: Argentina, Australia, Belgium, Chile, Costa Rica, Denmark, Ecuador, El Salvador, Finland, Germany, Guatemala, Iceland, Italy, Japan, Netherlands, New Zealand, Nicaragua, Norway, Panama, Peru, Spain, Sweden, Switzerland, United Kingdom, and Uruguay.

Citizens of the above countries are initially granted permission to stay in Honduras *for 30 days*. After that period, they must request an extension to remain in the country, just as if they held an expired visa.

Visas

Visas are not required of transit passengers. When required, visas are issued by Honduran consulates. A visa will usually allow an initial stay of 30 days. To remain longer, you'll have to apply to the immigration department.

Tourist Cards, which can be used in place of a visa by nationals of certain countries, are sold for $2 at the check-in counter by airlines serving Honduras, and by some travel agencies. You can also buy a tourist card upon arrival at an airport in Honduras, but it's safer to have one beforehand. To get a tourist card, you need to show a passport, a birth certificate, or some other convincing evidence of your citizenship. A tourist card is initially valid for 30 days, and can be extended by the immigration department in Tegucigalpa, La Ceiba, or San Pedro Sula.

When you arrive in Honduras, whether by land or air, you *could* be required to show that you have either a return ticket, sufficient funds to cover your expenses, or both.

Entry points along the borders with neighboring countries are generally open "officially" from 8 a.m. to 5 p.m. weekdays, but you can cross outside these hours for an extra fee (see below).

Vaccinations

No vaccination is required unless you're arriving from an area where there is currently an outbreak of some dread disease, such as yellow fever.

Entry & Exit Fees

There's an arrival tax of about $2 per person to pay when you enter Honduras, and fees totalling about $10 to pay when you leave by air. Children are exempt. In addition, there are fees of several dollars to pay for cars, for crossing land borders outside regular business hours, and for assorted other reasons.

In addition, and aside from any official increase in charges, there are *unofficial welcome and goodbye fees* that can range up to $10 per person. Call them tips, bribes, or what you wish. You'll find that they can be negotiated downward if one person in your group is in charge of paying for everyone, and even eliminated entirely sometimes if you ask for a receipt, or to speak to a supervisor (who may acknowledge that a slight mistake was made by the man at the point of public contact).

You may be asked to identify yourself at any time, usually near borders. *Carry your passport* or tourist card with you at all times, and if lost, contact your embassy immediately to obtain new travel documents.

The *exit tax* when departing Honduras by air is a hefty 95 lempiras — almost $19 at the current exchange rate!

Staying On

Most visitors are granted an initial stay of 30 days, though this may be shorter, especially if you enter overland and are short of funds. Extensions of permission to stay are processed at immigration offices in major towns: Comayagua, San Pedro Sula, La Ceiba, Tela, Santa Rosa de Copán, and other departmental capitals. With more difficulty and delay, they may be processed in Tegucigalpa, at **Migración**, *6 Calle, 11/12 Avenidas.*

CUSTOMS - ENTERING HONDURAS

You're allowed to bring in anything reasonable for a vacation trip to Honduras, along with gifts and new personal items up to a value of U.S. $1000. For children, the limit is $500. You're limited to two liters of liquor, and 200 cigarettes or 100 cigars or about a pound of tobacco. Firearms require a permit, and fresh fruits and vegetables should not be carried.

For questions and clarifications about customs, contact the **Dirección General de Aduanas**, *Avenida Juan Lindo, Colonia Palmira, Tegucigalpa, tel. 382566 (tel. 331290 at the airport, 562154 at the San Pedro Sula airport, 420013 in La Ceiba).*

CUSTOMS - RETURNING HOME

If you're going back to the States, you have an exemption of $400 for goods purchased in Honduras, which can include up to a quart of alcoholic beverages and 200 cigarettes. Many handicraft products that you might buy in Honduras are totally exempt from U.S. customs duty.

Canadians can use their yearly $300 exemption, or $100 quarterly exemption, with a cap of 200 cigarettes and 1.1 liters (40 ounces) of liquor.

Whatever you take home, don't include pre-Columbian articles or yaba-ding-dings; coral; fish; or shells. These could be confiscated on your way out of Honduras or into your home country and/or land you in jail or delayed with a court case.

USING TRAVEL SPECIALISTS

I think that you're best off using the services of a travel agency near your home with which you've dealt before. However, it's perfectly possible that the folks near home won't have much to offer.

- **Roatan Charter**, *Box 877, San Antonio, FL 33576, tel. 800-282-8932, fax 904-588-4158.* Helpful people, with a line on everything new in the Bay Islands and the rest of Honduras.
- **Great Trips**, *P. O. Box 1320, Detroit Lakes, MN 56501, tel. 800-552-3419 or 218-847-4441, fax 218-847-4442.* The folks at Great Trips know a lot about both the mainland of Honduras and the Bay Islands, and make reliable arrangements.
- **Triton Tours**, *1111 Veterans Blvd., Kenner, LA 70062, tel. 800-426-0226 or 504-464-7964, fax 504-464-7965.* Triton is one of the original travel agencies serving the Bay Islands.
- **Bahia Tours**, *1385 Coral Way, Miami, FL 33145, tel. 800-443-0717 or 305-858-5129, fax 305-858-5020.* Represents Anthony's Key and other dive resorts and live-aboard boats.
- **Elegant Vacations**, *1760 The Exchange, Suite 150, Atlanta, GA 30339, tel. 800-451-4398, fax 404-859-0250.* Represents several hotels, and arranges inland tours.
- **Maya World Tours**, *9846 Highway 441, Leesburg, FL 34788-3918, tel. 800-392-6292 or 904-360-0200.*
- **Journeys**, *4011 Jackson Rd., Ann Arbor, MI 48103, tel. 313-665-4407, fax 313-665-2945.* Operates monthly tours that emphasize the marine life of the Bay Islands, and a family tour.
- **Laughing Bird Adventures**, *P. O. Box 131, Olga, WA 98279, tel. 800-238-4467.* A small adventure travel company, offering sea kayaking in the Bay Islands, mountain hikes at Pico Bonito, and river kayaking.
- **Landfall Productions**, *39189 Cedar Blvd., Newark, CA 94560, tel. 800-525-3833 or 510-794-1599.* Specialists in dive vacations, offering especially detailed information about the resorts they represent.
- **Americas Tours and Travel**, *1402 Third Avenue, Seattle, WA 98101, tel. 206-623-8850, 800-553-2513, fax 206-467-0454.* Founded by Mr. Javier Pinel, a Honduran who is now back home and looking after things at that end. Mr. Pinel runs a week-and running week-long package tours of Honduras throughout the year. These folks claim to be able to get lower rates than other agencies at certain resorts in the Bay Islands..
- **South American Fiesta**, *910 W. Mercury Blvd., Hampton, VA 23666, tel. 800-334-3782, fax 804-826-1747.*

Travel agencies *in* Honduras are mentioned in various parts of this book. But here are a few that you might want to consult from home, in case the above agencies are unable to give you the service you require.

- **Explore Honduras**, *P O Box 336, Med-Cast Bldg., Blvd. Morazán, tel. 311003, fax 329800 in Tegucigalpa; tel. 526242, fax 526239 in San Pedro Sula.* Explore Honduras has a superb reputation for reliability, and is the ground operator for many U.S. agencies offering Honduras travel.
- **Cambio C.A.**, *P. O. Box 2666, San Pedro Sula, tel. 527274, fax 520523.* Specializes in low-impact, sustainable, ecologically oriented excursions, including canoe trips in Mosquitia, quetzal and manatee watching, hiking in cloud forest, and rafting on the Chamelecón River near San Pedro Sula and the Cangrejal River near La Ceiba. One week-long adventure trip includes camping, trekking with pack mules, and floating down the Cuyamel and Patuca rivers through the remote northeast, with opportunity to observe endangered wildlife and visit remote Indian villages. Services in English, German and Spanish. Cambio C.A.'s services are available through most of the U.S. agencies that specialize in Honduras, or they can be contacted directly.
- **La Mosquitia Ecoaventuras**, a younger company than Cambio C.A., specializes in ten- to fourteen-day low-impact adventures in the vast forests of Mosquitia, including the Río Plátano Biosphere Reserve, with emphasis on birding, wildlife viewing, and non-intrusive contacts with native peoples. *Information is available from La Mosquitia Ecoaventuras, P. O. Box 3577, Tegucigalpa, tel. 370593, fax 379398.*

GETTING TO HONDURAS

Arriving By Air

For a country that almost nobody knows about, Honduras is amazingly easy to get to.

To start with, most little countries have only one point of entry by air. Honduras has three. You can land in Tegucigalpa, the capital. Or, if you're just visiting the Caribbean area, you can fly into San Pedro Sula or La Ceiba. A short connecting flight takes you from La Ceiba to Roatán in the Bay Islands.

AIRLINES WITH DIRECT SERVICE TO TEGUCIGALPA

American	*Miami*
800-433-7300	
Taca	*Belize, Guatemala, San Salvador*
800-535-8780	

AIRLINES WITH DIRECT SERVICE TO SAN PEDRO SULA

Continental	*Houston, Belize*
800-231-0856	
Lacsa Airlines	*New Orleans, New York, Cancun, Guatemala*
800-225-2272	*Los Angeles, Mexico City, San José*
American	*Miami, New York*
Taca	*Miami, Guatemala, San Salvador*
Iberia	*Miami*
Aero Costa Rica	*Orlando*
Copa	*Mexico City, San José, Panama*

Cancun Connections

If you can get to Cancun, Mexico, on an inexpensive charter, you can also get to Honduras cheaply. **Lacsa Airlines**, among others, flies daily between Cancun and San Pedro Sula, at a round-trip fare of only $200. Not only is this a low-cost way to get to Honduras, it also saves many of the landings, takeoffs and changes of plane often involved in taking scheduled carriers all the way.

Charters operate to Cancun mainly from major Canadian cities.

Always try to buy a round-trip ticket before you leave home. You'll usually get a better price, and there are significant taxes to pay if you buy your return ticket in Honduras.

Arriving By Car

Unleaded gasoline is not available in Honduras, so you'll have to disconnect your catalytic converter after crossing through Mexico. Gasoline prices are slightly higher than those in the United States, lower than in Canada. In general, it's wise to drive during daylight hours, and to look for a gasoline station when your tank is half full.

While labor for auto repairs is inexpensive in Honduras, parts always cost more — sometimes double the price in the country of manufacture — and sometimes they're not available for your make of car. Don't drive anything too exotic, or in bad condition. Volkswagens, Toyotas, Datsuns and U.S. pickup trucks are good choices.

Tourists may enter their vehicles for an initial period of 30 days. Renewals are available through customs offices to extend your stay for up to six months. I recommend that you enter Honduras through Guatemala, rather than via El Salvador.

Arriving By Bus

Here's another feat that's possible, though I wouldn't want to go non-stop by bus from North America to Honduras. As part of a measured overland journey, though, it can be fun, and the fare is about $100 from the U.S. border.

Basically, you have to take a first-class bus to Mexico City. This will take from ten hours to two days, depending on where you cross the Mexican border. In Mexico City, catch a Cristóbal Colón bus for the Guatemalan border. There are at least two each day, and the trip takes sixteen hours. Connecting buses take you to Guatemala City, where you catch the Rutas Orientales bus for Esquipulas, then a mini-bus to Agua Caliente on the Honduran border. From this point, it's easiest to travel to San Pedro Sula, or to the ruins of Copán. You can also travel from Guatemala via San Salvador and the Pan American Highway to Tegucigalpa, but you should verify current conditions in El Salvador before doing so.

GETTING AROUND HONDURAS

By Air

Honduras has a well-developed domestic air transport network. You can't go everywhere, but you can fly the long distances, and continue by bus, taxi, or boat.

Isleña and **Sosa** connect with the Bay Islands and operate along the north coast to Mosquitia.

Fares in all cases are reasonable. The top tariff is about $150 round trip from Tegucigalpa to the Bay Islands. A one-way hop from La Ceiba to Roatán costs from $25 to $40.

By Bus

They're not Greyhounds, but on major routes in Honduras, buses are comfortable enough. You'll get a padded seat on something that looks on the outside like a school bus. Standards for leg and hip room might be lower than what you would desire, but for a ride of a few hours from Tegucigalpa to San Pedro Sula, the bus will be tolerable.

As you venture off the main routes, the level of service becomes less desirable. Minibuses and microbuses — vans — serve the less-traveled, bumpier routes, for example, from San Pedro Sula to La Entrada and the ruins of Copán. Seats are small and stiff and crowded together to provide no knee room. Buses may be underpowered, and whine along in low gear at low speed, turning short trips into ordeals. Sometimes, out of greed, or sympathy for passengers who have no other way to travel, the passenger load is beyond reasonable safety limits.

To increase your comfort, wherever you're going by bus, try to start your trip at the terminal point. Line up early to get a reserved seat. Generally, you'll have more leg room, and less bouncing, at the front of the bus, near the driver. Buses usually leave the terminal fully loaded; if you flag one down along the road, you could be obliged to stand.

Bus stops along roads are never marked. Ask the driver to let you off where you want to get off, and flag down a bus when you want to get on.

In all cases, bus fares are low. For example, you'll pay about $3 to travel from Tegucigalpa to San Pedro Sula, a distance of 250 kilometers.

By Car

What's it like to drive in Honduras? Well, you have a good chance of getting lost if you're not careful, if you don't ask questions, and if you don't have a good sense of direction. Road signs hardly exist. You'll see some kilometer posts, stop signs, and arrows to indicate the flow of traffic and one-way streets. But directional signs that tell you where to turn to get to a village or town are practically unknown. Always follow your map carefully, and when you reach a junction, stop and ask for the way to your destination. It's the only way.

The major paved highways in Honduras are the **Pan American Highway** crossing from El Salvador to Nicaragua in the south; the highway through Tegucigalpa to the north coast; part of the route along the north coast; and the western highway that roughly parallels the border with Guatemala. There are some other paved stretches, but travel off these main routes will often involve unpaved roads either dusty or muddy, according to the season, over winding, unbanked routes that are the descendants of the mule trails that once snaked through the mountains of Honduras.

Repairs can be accomplished in Tegucigalpa and San Pedro Sula on most familiar passenger cars and pickup trucks. Outside of major centers, you'll probably have to send for parts. Sports cars, turbos, and similar unusual vehicles (for Honduras, anyway) should stay home, rather than face servicing by unfamiliar hands, or a lack of parts.

RENTING A CAR

Cars are available for rent in Tegucigalpa, San Pedro Sula, La Ceiba and Roatán. I think that taxis are a better way to go, especially in Tegucigalpa. In addition, you can obtain only limited insurance protection in Honduras.

By Taxi

Getting around by taxi is cheap — if there's two of you, it's cheaper than taking a bus in North America. For a five-kilometer ride, you might pay as little as $3. Or you can hire a taxi by the hour for $7 or so.

By all means, take a taxi! Just make sure that you agree on the fare with the driver before you start out. And on any out-of-town trip, give the vehicle a once-over to make sure that you'll make it to where you're going.

HOTEL RATES

In the United States, you often pay for a hotel according to season, with discounts sometimes available if you're an AAA member or have some other affiliation, or if your employer has negotiated a corporate.

In Honduras, *what you pay depends on who you are.*

The highest rate is the **rack rate**, which is generally what you'll be charged as a foreigner, whether you make your reservation through a travel agency, a toll-free telephone reservation service, or directly with the hotel from abroad. Usually, the rack rate is the rate I've quoted in this book. The 7 percent tax is included, unless otherwise mentioned.

At some resorts in the Bay Islands, you'll pay an additional 10 percent service charge, but this is not the practice throughout Honduras.

Since Honduras is a poor country, and many rooms are empty outside the high season, **resident rates** are often available to Hondurans, resident foreigners, military personnel, peace corps volunteers, and Central Americans. If you feel that you qualify for a discount under any category, by all means *ask for it.* Sometimes it takes a little forwardness, sometimes it takes a little fluency in Spanish, but you can often cut your hotel bill just by asking.

In addition, some travel agencies (very few, actually) claim that they can get the Honduran rate for foreigners. Do some price comparisons to check out any such claims.

Note that this double-rate structure applies only at the high-end hotels. You'll look pretty silly if you ask for a resident's discount at a budget hotel that has mostly Hondurans among its clientele.

BASIC INFORMATION

Here's some basic information matters, in alpabetical order:

BUSINESS HOURS

Hondurans are early risers. In a country where many do not have electricity, people get up at sunrise, and don't go out much after dark.

Businesses are generally open from 8 a.m. to 11:30 a.m. or noon, and from 1:30 or 2 p.m. to 5 or 6 p.m. Along the hot coast in the north, businesses may open even earlier. On Saturday, businesses keep morning hours only.

Exceptions: Banks are generally open from 9 a.m.–3 p.m. Monday–Friday. Government offices are open from 7:30 or 8 a.m. until 3:30 p.m.

ELECTRICITY

Most electricity is supplied at 110 volts, 60 cycles, just as in the U.S. However, some locales operate only on 220 volts, so inquire before you plug anything in.

Sockets take standard American-type plugs with parallel blades and no grounding prongs.

HEALTH CONCERNS
Before You Go

If you are taking any medications regularly, pack twice the quantity you think you'll need. Brand names in Honduras might be different from the ones you're familiar with. Also prepare a small emergency kit.

It's important to be current with your routine vaccinations, such as tetanus, diphtheria, and polio. Vaccination against typhoid, and gamma globulin as a precaution against hepatitis, are also recommended. There is some malaria in rural areas. Get some antimalarial pills from a doctor before you go, and take the pills as directed.

In Honduras

If you don't drink the water, and watch what you eat, you shouldn't have any health problems.

In general, you should stick to foods that have been well cooked, and are still hot when served. Fruits and vegetables are okay if they have a peel, or are cooked. But avoid salads, and sandwiches that are decorated with fresh vegetables. Don't hesitate to leave anything doubtful sitting on your plate. Water is not safe to drink from the tap in *any* city in Honduras. Stick to bottled beverages, or take along Halazone tablets or laundry bleach (two drops to a quart, allow to stand 30 minutes).

Your medical kit should include: a sunscreen containing PABA (sunburn can be a problem if you're not used to being outdoors); insect repellent (the best brands, such as Cutter's or Muskol, contain methyl toluamide); condoms (if there is any chance of a new sexual relationship); personal medications; anti-malarial tablets; Halazone or bleach for drinking water; sterile pads, bandages, antiseptic soap, and analgesic pills.

For longer stays, consult a public health or travelers' clinic. Useful publications include *Health Information for International Travel* (Department of Health and Human Services), available from the U.S. Government Printing Office, Washington, D.C. 20402; and *Health Guide for Travellers to Warm Climates*, available from the Canadian Public Health Association, 1335 Carling Avenue, Suite 210, Ottawa, Ontario, Canada K1Z 8N8. The International Association for Medical Assistance to Travellers may be able to provide a list of English-speaking doctors, in Honduras and other countries, for a small fee. Write to **IAMAT**, 736 Center St., Lewiston, NY 14092.

In Tegucigalpa and San Pedro Sula, and in any town of any size, there's *always* a pharmacy open at night. Look for a lighted *de turno* sign on the outside. "*De turno*" pharmacies are also listed in many newspapers.

LEARNING SPANISH

The **Escuela de Español Ixbalanque** ("Ish-ba-lan-keh" Spanish school) in Copán Ruinas (site of the greatest Mayan city in Honduras) offers one-on-one instruction in Spanish for four hours a day, five days a week. Students board with local Spanish-speaking families, or have the option of staying at a hotel.

Contact Darla Brown, Escuela Ixbalanque, Copán Ruinas, Honduras, tel. 983432, fax 576215.

MONEY & BANKING

The current exchange rate as of press time is about 9 **lempiras** to the dollar.

You pay for goods and services in Honduras in lempiras, the coin of the realm, named after the native chief who died fighting the Spanish invaders. The exception is the Bay Islands, where, in some resorts, everything is priced in dollars, and lempiras may not even be welcome.

Lempiras come in bills, and in coins of 1 lempira, 50 **centavos**, 20 centavos, 10 centavos, 5 centavos, 2 centavos, and 1 centavo. Once upon a time, U.S. coins were in circulation here, leaving *daime* ("dime") as the nickname for the 20-centavo coin of the same size, and *búfalo* as the name for the 10-centavo coin, after the buffalo on the American nickel. A 50-centavo piece is a *tostón*, and sometimes you'll hear of, but never see, a *real* (ray-AL), or "bit." Two *reales* are 25 centavos.

> *In this book, prices are expressed in U.S. dollars, based on the current exchange rate of about 6 lempiras to the U.S. dollar. In the case of hotels, especially in the Bay Islands, that quote prices only in U.S. dollars, I give the actual rate in dollars charged by the hotel.*

Black Market, Gray Market, Free Market

Honduras has a black market, but it's so open and tolerated, that you might as well call it the gray market, or, even better, the free market.

How do you change money on the free market? Generally, you don't have to look for it, it will find you. Taxi drivers, hotel clerks, owners of stores that sell imported goods will all offer their exchange services, or can direct you to somebody looking for dollars. Money changers speak enough English to consummate the deal—more than bank clerks. They'll take travelers checks without much ado, and their hours are certainly flexible. Street money changers generally don't hold more than the equivalent of $100 or $200 in local currency. To change more than that amount, try a store.

Of course, this information is subject to change. Verify the current official and free-market rates as soon as you arrive.

Exchanging Money

Then there are the *casas de cambio* (exchange houses), which, for the moment, are legal, and offer a quicker exchange service than that provided by banks, with more security than you'll get with street changers. Some are said to launder money for the drug trade, and some have minimums of $200. Their numbers are growing, and you should spot one near your hotel; if you don't see one, look for ads in *Honduras This Week*.

Exchange houses will handle the currencies of other Central American countries, which can be difficult otherwise to exchange.

Banks

Banks will give you a less advantageous exchange rate, generally about five percent less than what you'll get at an exchange house, and you'll often face discouraging lineups. And hotels and other services catering to tourists usually give you even less for your foreign money.

Wherever you end up changing money, at a bank or on the free market, you'll find that only U.S. dollars, in cash or travelers checks, have any value. Currencies of neighboring countries can be exchanged at the border, or sometimes at exchange houses, but Canadian dollars, sterling, German marks and other solid currencies might just as well be play money in Honduras.

Credit Cards

Visa, Master Card and American Express are widely accepted at middle- and upper-range hotels in Honduras. Your charge slip will be processed at the bank rate of exchange — certainly no advantage.

For **cash advances** on a Visa card, try any bank that displays the Honducard-Visa symbol. Bancahsa and Bancahorro can make cash advances throughout the country. Otherwise, for Visa or Master Card cash advances, contact **Credomatic**, *second floor, Interamericana de Seguros building, Tegucigalpa, tel. 326030; or Ficensa building, San Pedro Sula, tel. 532404*; or try any bank with a Credomatic, Ficensa or Futuro sign.

POST OFFICE & COURIER SERVICES

Post offices are generally open from 7 a.m. to 6 p.m. during the week, from 8 a.m. to noon on Saturday. There could be some variation in small towns. I should tell you that everything that I've ever mailed from Honduras has arrived safely in Canada.

Alternative Mail Services provide express air shipment of urgent letters out of Honduras, avoiding delays and other possible contretemps in the local mail system. One company offering quick delivery of letters and packages is **EMS**, *tel. 224971 in Tegucigalpa, 570707 in San Pedro Sula*.

From North America, you can find express service to Honduras from some cities with Hispanic communities. Check the yellow pages under Courier Service for a company with a Spanish-sounding name. Express letter services charge more than the post office, but a fraction of what large courier companies collect. If nothing else is available, DHL and some other courier companies will deliver letters and documents to Honduras at a minimum charge of about $40 from North America.

SHOPPING

Honduras isn't famous for its shopping, but there are some products that are rather typical of the country, and of special quality.

What you'll see everywhere in Honduras, in gift shops and hotels and markets, is hardwood, especially mahogany, made up into assorted useful and decorative items: bookends, sculptures, oversized salad servers, and lamps. Straw hats from Santa Bárbara are of especially good quality, come in many sizes and colors, and are useful during your travels, as well as making attractive souvenirs. Wicker work is intricate and of excellent quality, especially near and along the north coast, where, along the highways, you will find animals, suspended chairs, rockers, and all kinds of utilitarian and decorative items, many of them, unfortunately, too large to take home easily. Leatherwork, jewelry, baskets, t-shirts and beachwear and embroidery are also available, along with primitive paintings, which are a special favorite of mine, and of many other people as well.

Honduran crafts are supplemented by crafts from neighboring countries. You can buy fine weaving from Guatemala, and textiles from El Salvador. You should also keep an eye out for more mundane bargains that are offered in *pulperías* (corner stores) and larger outlets: ground coffee, tropical fruit jams, rum, and assorted sauces.

Bargaining is common in Honduras, but you won't get the big discounts you'll find in some other countries.

TAXES

A 7% tax is added to all room and meal bills. On beverages, the tax is 10%. Departure taxes at airports total about $19.

Indirectly, you'll be paying import duties on anything you buy. Much of government funding in Honduras comes from taxes on both imports and exports, rather than from income taxes. Innocent items like film and tape cassettes, as a result, sell for double what they would cost in the United States or Canada.

TELEPHONES

The national telephone system, operated by Hondutel, serves only a few of the major towns of Honduras.

Calls within Honduras can be made conveniently from hotel phones, or from pay phones where they are available.

You'll find coin telephones — they work with ten-centavo pieces — on the main streets of Tegucigalpa and San Pedro Sula, but nowhere else, for the moment, as most of the country lacks direct-dial service.

Calling Hone

Rates to the States and Canada are approximately $2.50 per minute during the day, less at night. Collect calls may be placed to the United States, Canada, Mexico, the Bahamas, and all Central American countries except El Salvador.

For international calls, try to use a private line if possible. Direct-dial service to foreign countries is *only* available from Tegucigalpa, San Pedro Sula (phones beginning with 53), La Ceiba, the Bay Islands, and a few other locales. Hotels can arrange foreign calls — it's not so expensive, and easy to get a line. Or you can go to an office of Hondutel, the telephone company, but you'll often face a long lineup and confusing procedures.

USA Direct is available from many public phones (coin deposit required) in Tegucigalpa, and from USA Direct phones at Toncontín airport and certain Hondutel offices. *From public phones, dial 123 to reach an English-speaking AT&T operator.*

TIME

Honduras is on Central Standard Time, equivalent to Greenwich Mean Time less six hours.

TIPPING

Generally, you can leave a ten-percent tip in any restaurant, and be considered generous. Many local people will leave less, or nothing at all, especially in small, informal eating places. You can give one lempira (about 25¢ U.S.) to anyone who carries your bag, more in fancier hotels. Taxi drivers don't get anything on top of the negotiated fare.

Some hotel restaurants add a ten-percent service charge to your bill, in which case there's no need to leave an additional tip, except for exceptional service.

WATER

In general, do not trust the tap water for drinking, anywhere in Honduras. There are exceptions to this rule of thumb. You may find clean spring water flowing from the tap in the Bay Islands. But unless you're assured that the tap water is safe, don't drink it. In most places on the mainland of Honduras, the water is hard — it has a high mineral content. It's not easy to take a shower, and you'll need plenty of shampoo.

WHERE TO FIND INFORMATION ABOUT HONDURAS
The Tourist Office
For a map of Honduras, and assorted pamphlets, try writing to the **Honduras Tourist Bureau** *(Instituto Hondureño de Turismo), P. O. Box 3261, Tegucigalpa, D.C., Honduras.* They take up to six months to respond — sometimes they don't respond at all — and don't answer specific questions, so try other sources of information as well.

All the News
Honduras This Week is a gold mine of information about Honduras, and the indispensable tool for keeping up with the latest developments. New hotels, restaurants and travel services are profiled, and at least one page is devoted to ads for diving services, hotels, restaurants, and other facilities of interest to visitors.

Honduras This Week is available in major towns in Honduras, mainly through hotels. You can often find a copy in a Honduran consulate. *To subscribe (for $40 annually in the United States), write to Apartado Postal 1312, Tegucigalpa, D.C., Honduras, or call 315821, fax 322300.*

Consulates & Embassies
Honduran consulates and embassies generally handle trade matters, but in some cases might be able to answer questions about the retirement law or travel in the country.

In New York, the consulate *is at 80 Wall St., New York, NY, 10005.*

In Washington, D.C., the embassy *is at 3007 Tilden St., NW, Washington, DC, 20008 (tel. 202/966-7702).*

SPORTS & RECREATION
Honduras offers more than phenomenal beaches for those of you looking for sports and recreation. The fun includes:

CRUISE THE ISLANDS & THE COAST
Sail Down in Your Own Boat
The definitive handbook for these waters is *Cruising Guide to the Honduras Bay Islands,* available from Wescott Cove Publishing Co., P O Box 130, Stamford CT 06904. This book includes numerous maps, charts, and customs information that will get you safely to, through, and out of the Caribbean waters of Honduras.

Charter a Sailboat
To have a sailboat waiting for you, contact a travel agency that specializes in Honduras, such as **Roatán Charter,** *Box 877, San Antonio, FL 33576, tel. 800-282-8932, fax 904-588-4158.*

Take a Cruise

The Ukrainian-registered *Gruziya* ("Georgia") sails regularly from St. Petersburg, Florida, to Cozumel, Belize, and onward to Puerto Cortés, Honduras. The five-deck vessel has two restaurants, a casino, pool, disco, and a crew offering an unusual Russian and Ukrainian experience in the Caribbean. Rates for a one-week cruise range from about $1000 to $2000 per person, with deep discounts for the third and fourth person sharing a cabin. Contact **Odessa America Cruise Company**, *170 Old Country Rd., Mineola, NY 11501, tel. 800-221-3254.*

To arrange diving in conjuction with the cruise, contact **Maya World Tours**, *9846 Highway 441, Leesburg, FL 34788-3918, tel. 800-392-6292 or 904-360-0200.* The folks at Maya World plan a cruise package that includes diving in Mexico, Belize and off Roatan for a package price of under $1000 per person.

Charter a Boat

Motor vessels without sails can also be secured through **Roatán Charter**, and through many of the hotels in the Bay Islands.

DIVING

Here's an activity that you will enjoy exclusively in the Bay Islands.

Skin Diver magazine regularly publishes articles covering diving and accommodations in the Bay Islands, and classified and display advertisements for hotels and diving packages. Available at newsstands, or by subscription from *Skin Diver, P. O. Box 3295, Los Angeles, CA 90078.*

FISHING

For the most part, sport fishing is something you'll participate in from resorts in the Bay Islands.

On the mainland of Honduras, the most famous fishing hole is **Lake Yojoa**, known for bass weighing in at about ten pounds on the average. The few hotels along the lake have limited equipment available for rent. If you own your own gear, it's advisable to bring it along.

A fishing license is required, and is usually obtained in advance through a travel agency.

HUNTING

Southern Honduras, around the city of Choluteca, is known as the dove-hunting capital of the world. The season is from November 1 to March 15, and a daily limit of 50 doves is imposed.

Hunting requires a license; details are best handled through a travel agency. One company familiar with procedures is **Dockside Tours**, *339 Hickory Ave., Harahan, LA 70123, tel. 800-235-3625, fax 504-737-2998.*

Within Honduras, contact the **Departamento de Caza y Pesca** (Department of Hunting and Fishing).

NATIONAL PARKS

Here's another of the surprises of Honduras. In just a few years, Honduras has moved into the forefront of Latin America in protecting and preserving its natural treasures. And treasures there are aplenty — over 700 species of birds, 500 piscine species, and flora that includes scores of species of orchids alone.

Paradoxically, the backwardness of Honduras has left this ecological bonus intact. Few roads — and poor ones at that— underpopulation, and limited industrial agriculture, except in bananas, have left nature alone in much of the country. The Mosquitia region along the border of Nicaragua is one of the last largely undisturbed lowland forests in Central America. And there are pockets of highland cloud forest that the magnificent resplendent quetzal, the holy grail of birders, still calls home.

But the remaining untouched forests of Honduras are now in danger. Multinational companies are turning envious eyes toward stands of pine and deposits of minerals. Farmers from the exhausted soil of the central part of the country are seeking new lands to clear and plant.

Over a dozen treasure troves of nature are now protected as national parks, reserves and refuges, and many more sites are under consideration for inclusion.

For now, things are in a rudimentary state. Most parks have no trails, camp grounds, guides or guards. But a start has been made, and the establishment of the parks and reserves is holding off loggers and farmers who might otherwise be cutting down the trees and chasing off the animals. And in the not-too-distant future, Honduras is sure to join Belize, Costa Rica and Guatemala as a destination for visitors interested in getting to know tropical life forms beyond the kinds that are attacked with insecticide.

Current information about conditions in National Parks may be available from the following sources:

- **Ministerio de Recursos Naturales** *(Department of Natural Resources), Blvd. Miraflores, Tegucigalpa, tel. 328723.*
- **Asociación Hondureña de Ecología** *(Honduran Ecology Association), Colonia La Reforma C-2423, tel. 383383.* The Ecology Association, in an unusual arrangement, manages La Tigra National Park for the government. It publishes guides to the mammals and ecosystems of the country.
- **COHDEFOR** *(Forestry Development Corporation), Carretera al Norte, tel. 228810.*

NATIONAL PARKS

Unless specific facilities are mentioned, parks are not yet ready for visits on your own.

- **Montecristo-Trifinio** – *near Ocotepeque. No trails, continues into Guatemala and El Salvador. 54 square kilometers.*
- **Cerro Azul** – *10 km northeast of Florida (Copán Department). Along Guatemalan border, includes caves, cloud forest and recovering forest. The lake atop Cerro Azul mountain, known as Laguna de los Pinares, is frequented by migrating birds. 150 square kilometers.*
- **Celaque** – *5 km west of Gracias. Includes Mount Celaque, highest peak and cloud forest in country, and colonial fort and hot springs. Campsites available. 270 square kilometers.*
- **Santa Bárbara** – *in Santa Bárbara. Includes caves, and Marancho, second highest mountain in Honduras. 130 square kilometers.*
- **Cusuco** – *20 km west of San Pedro Sula. Includes cloud forest with quetzal habitat, trails. 10 square kilometers.*
- **Cerro Azul Meambar** – *30 km northwest of Comayagua. Forest and watershed reserve above the eastern side of Lake Yojoa, with falls and rapids.*
- **Pico Pijol** – *east of El Progreso. Cloud forest. 114 square kilometers.*
- **Pico Bonito** – *south of La Ceiba. Includes high tropical forest on Bonito Peak. Trails. 68 square kilometers.*
- **Montaña de Yoro** – *south of Yoro. Adjacent to Torupane Indian reserve. 155 square kilometers.*
- **Capiro-Calentura** – *in Trujillo.*
- **Sierra de Agalta** – *Olancho. Includes dwarf forest. Trails and camping. 255 square kilometers.*
- **Montaña de Comayagua** – *13 km east of Comayagua. Includes archaeological site and regenerating forest. 62 square kilometers.*
- **La Tigra** – *11 km northeast of Tegucigalpa. First national park (established 1980), protecting Tegucigalpa's watershed. Trails, dormitories. 75 square kilometers.*
- **Punta Sal** – *6 km west of Tela. Includes beaches and reefs, trails. 419 square kilometers.*
- **El Armado** – *in Olancho. Includes Montaña del Armado. 1 square kilometer.*
- **La Muralla** – *8 km north of La Unión, Olancho. Cloud forest, trails. 16 square kilometers.*
- **Cuero y Salado** – *20 km west of La Ceiba. Coastal area with river estuaries and navigable canals, includes manatee habitat. Access by boat. 85 square kilometers*
- **Laguna Guaimoreto** – *East of Trujillo. Includes Lake Guaimoreto. 50 square kilometers.*

RAFT & KAYAK THE JUNGLE RIVERS

Honduras has white water! It's rapid, it's exhilarating, it's ecological, it's adventurous, it's off-beat, it's inexpensive, but best of all, it's warm.

There are major rivers throughout Honduras, but rafting operators mainly use those on the north coast, where water levels are most reliable during the rainy season from October to May.

The **Cangrejal River**, inland from La Ceiba, rated at Class II to Class III, has some significant rapids, as well as many sedate stretches, where you can take a break from paddling to view the banana fields, riverside forest trailing vines into the water, and colorful tropical birds fluttering into and out of the foliage.

The **Cuero River**, running through **Cuero y Salado National Park**, west of La Ceiba, is a stereotypical lazy jungle river, lined by dense forest and abandoned coconut plantations, perfect for visitors who want to enjoy birding and wildlife observation.

The **Chamelecón River**, running to the east of San Pedro Sula, is generally more sedate than the Cangrejal, with exciting stretches.

Rafting organizers provide all necessary equipment: raft (or kayak, where appropriate), helmet, life jacket, and paddles. Participants should wear bathing suit and t-shirt or lightweight jogging outfit as protection against the sun, and tennis shoes or surf shoes. Take along a change of clothing for when you're done!

Despite the excitement, there is little danger in rafting the rivers of Honduras. Passengers wear life jackets, and in the case of an occasional capsize, you're soon washed away from any rocks into deeper, safer water.

One-day trips out of La Ceiba or San Pedro Sula, generally costing about $75 per person, are offered by:

• **Caribbean Travel** (*Ríos Honduras*), *Hermanos Kawas building, Avenida San Isidro, La Ceiba, tel. 431361, manual fax 431360. Guides are from the Rocky Mountain Outdoor Center in Colorado.*

• **Cambio C.A.**, *P. O. Box 2666, San Pedro Sula, tel. 527274, fax 520523.*

ECOTOURISM

Talk of rain forests, talk of eco-tourism, talk of adventure travel. Whatever you call it, Honduras is the last frontier of travel in Central America, where an adventuring soul can still be one of the few outsiders to drift along a lazy river bordered by centenary trees, listen to the roar of howler monkeys trooping through the jungle canopy, spot a limpkin wading in the shallows, wonder at petroglyphs carved by mysterious ancient civilizations.

Though the pressures of logging companies and land-hungry peasants are inexorable, and more forest has been destroyed in the last few decades than in all the centuries since the Spaniards arrived in the New

World, there are more jungles left in Honduras than elsewhere in the region. The forests are protected, at least nominally, in such areas as the **Río Plátano Biosphere Reserve**.

Low-impact tourism by adventurous visitors represents one of the few viable ways to make those lands valuable in a capitalistic world, without destroying their ancient treasures of medicinal plants, animal life, water-storing lowlands, and mangroves where fish breed.

The pioneer travel operator in low-impact tourism in Honduras, and one worthy of your consideration (this is not a paid ad!) is **Cambio C.A.**, which limits the size and frequency of its trips in order not to destroy what you are going out to see.

Here's what they have to say:

"Our travelers journey in dugout canoes through unspoiled, little-travelled tropical rain forest. They see the Caribbean unmarred by high-rise hotels and souvenir touts. Our travelers eat, travel, and live much as the indigenous people of the region do, and our unhurried pace allows us to get to know the local inhabitants as fellow humans and not as carnival attractions or museum pieces. . .

Our programs are designed to inform the traveler about the environmental, cultural, social, and political settings of the land through which we journey. . . . Our leaders carry basic medical supplies, two-way radios, and the many small comforts that make the difference between an adventure and an ordeal."

Among offerings from Cambio are canoe trips in **Mosquitia**, quetzal and manatee watching, hiking in cloud forest, and rafting on the **Chamelecón River** near San Pedro Sula and the **Cangrejal River** near La Ceiba. One week-long adventure trip includes camping, trekking with pack mules, and floating down the **Cuyamel** and **Patuca** rivers through the remote northeast, with opportunity to observe endangered wildlife and visit remote Indian villages. Guides speak English, German and Spanish.

Cambio C.A.'s services are available through most of the U.S. agencies that specialize in Honduras, or they can be contacted directly: **Cambio C.A.**, *P. O. Box 2666, San Pedro Sula, tel. 527274, fax 520523.*

TEGUCIGALPA

Tegucigalpa as a settlement dates back to 1578, when silver was discovered, on September 29, St. Michael's Day. The town that grew up around the mine was called Real de Minas de San Miguel, in the saint's honor, with *de Tegucigalpa* — "of the Silver Hill" in the *Nahuatl* language — appended to distinguish this San Miguel from many others. In time, Tegucigalpa was the part of the name that stuck.

Throughout the colonial period, Comayagua was the capital, but Tegucigalpa continued to grow in importance, and, after independence, the seat of government alternated between the two major settlements. In 1880, the administration of the country was installed once and for all in Tegucigalpa. Officially, the capital bears the suffix "D.C." for *Distrito Central*, the central administrative district that also takes in adjacent Comayagüela. The city is known as *Teguz*, pronounced "Tegoose."

Tegucigalpa Today
With more than 800,000 people, metropolitan Tegucigalpa is the most populated city of the country, but it is lacking in some of the attributes of a capital. Tegucigalpa has no railroad. The Pan American Highway bypasses the city, and an all-weather road to the north coast was completed only in the middle of this century.

Tegucigalpa and adjacent Comayagüela are poor cities. But Honduras has had the dubious advantage of being relatively uniformly poor, and the seething social tensions of neighboring lands are less apparent here. You can stroll around Tegucigalpa during the day and feel safe and unbothered. Only occasionally does a beggar or street vendor dare to approach a stranger. Tourism is a fledgling industry, with all of the advantages and disadvantages this implies.

ARRIVALS & DEPARTURES
Arriving By Air
International airlines serving Tegucigalpa, or with sales offices, are:
- **Alitalia**, *tel. 3729322*; and **Lufthansa** *in the Midence Soto building downtown, tel. 376900.*
- **American Airlines**, *Palmira building, tel. 321347.* To Miami, New York.
- **Continental Airlines**, *Toncontín Airport, tel. 337676.* To Houston.
- **Iberia**, *Palmira building, tel. 315253.*
- **KLM**, *Ciicsa Bldg., Col. Palmira, tel. 326410.*
- **Lacsa**, *Los Jarros Bldg., Blvd. Morazán, tel. 311525.*
- **Taca International**, *La Interamericana building, Blvd. Morazán, tel. 312472. To Guatemala, San Salvador.*

Airport
Toncontín Airport *is just five kilometers south of downtown Tegucigalpa.* The runway is in good repair, and that's the good news. The other news is that it isn't much of an airport. When you arrive, there are no visible airline counters, and the information desks are likely to be unattended. If you need anything, go to the departure area (if it is open).

Entry formalities, like everything else at the airport, are minimal.

Airport hours are 6 a.m. to 8 p.m. Nothing lands at night. There's an **airport bank**, but you might as well change your money with the fellows out front. The **post office counter** is open from 8 a.m. to 3 p.m., and is one of the fastest ways to send anything home. **Hondutel**, the national telephone monopoly, has an airport outpost. There are also AT&T USA Direct phones, which you can pick up to reach an operator in the States.

Getting to Town from the Airport

Once you go outside the terminal, you'll find a hubbub of **taxi drivers** and money changers — disconcerting, perhaps, as your introduction to Honduras, but not dangerous in any way. There's a fixed tariff of about $5 to go from the airport by "yellow cab" to any location in the capital. Or, you can walk to the main road a couple of hundred meters from the terminal and pick up a regular city taxi for about half that price.

City buses to town also pass regularly. It's inexpensive enough to reach the airport from town by taxi, but the Loarque or Río Grande bus will also take you. One central stop is on 6 Calle (Av. Jérez) in front of Super Donuts.

Budget has a car-rental counter, and there are other companies not far away.

Departing By Air

Isleña Airlines, *tel. 331130 at the airport,* flies to the Bay Islands and to La Ceiba as well. One local air taxi service is **Aeroservicios**, *tel. 331287, fax 341633.*

Departing By Bus

There's no central bus terminal in Tegucigalpa, but many buses for suburban and distant destinations leave from private stations in Comayagüela.

Among the bus operators:

• **To Comayagua and San Pedro Sula:** Empresa El Rey, 6 Avenida, 9 Calle, Comayagüela, *tel. 333010.* This station looks like a bombed-out garage. Buses leave every 90 minutes from before dawn to 10:30 p.m. Fare is less than $4 to San Pedro, less than $2 to Comayagua. Buses are comfortable and uncrowded. Also Hedman-Alas (better than other companies), 11 Avenida, 13/14 Calles, Comayagüela, *tel. 377143,* and Transportes Sáenz, 12 Calle, 7/8 Avenidas, Comayagüela, *tel. 376521,* hourly departures from 8 a.m. to 6 p.m. The ride to San Pedro Sula takes about four hours.

• **To Juticalpa and Olancho department:** Empresa Aurora, 6 Calle, 6 Avenida, Comayagüela, every hour; and Rutas Olanchanas, 8 Calle, 6/7 Avenidas.

• **To Danlí:** Discua Litena, near Jacaleapa market, *(tel. 327939)* five kilometers from downtown in southeast Tegucigalpa. Danlí and Paraíso: Emtraoriente, 6 Calle, 6/7 Avenida, Comayagüela, *tel. 378965*, 6 departures daily from 6:30 a.m. to 4:30 p.m.

Other Honduran and Foreign Destinations By Bus

Bus service for other destinations is given with descriptions of various other towns. From downtown Tegucigalpa, the Villa Adela bus will pass near many of the Comayagüela bus stations.

To reach Guatemala by bus, you can to travel via San Pedro Sula and Santa Rosa de Copán. Otherwise, cross through El Salvador. For El Salvador, take a bus for El Amatillo from the Belén market. For Nicaragua, take a bus from the Mi Esperanza station, 6 Avenida, 24/25 Calles, Comayagüela *(tel. 382863)*, as far as Guasaule, on the border. Through bus service between Central American capitals is much more limited than it once was.

ORIENTATION

It is easy to get disoriented in Tegucigalpa. The city does not have straight streets like those of San Pedro Sula, except at the very center. It's more like the pattern of a souk in the Middle East. The topography of the valley is far from flat, and you have small hills everywhere. The city is divided into units called b*arrios* and *colonias* (neighborhoods and suburbs), each of which is more or less homogeneous in its social class.

Downtown is Tegucigalpa proper, or **Barrio El Centro**, and across the Choluteca River, connected by four bridges, Comayagüela, the poorer and flatter part of town, with few significant buildings or governmental operations. Everything of any importance occurs in Tegucigalpa, which runs northward up the slopes of Mount Picacho, and wraps around the eastern side of Comayagüela.

Streets wind this way and that through and between the different barrios and colonias, straightening out for a while, then snaking along and up a hill again. The same street will have different names, both traditional and numbered, and one or the other version will be posted.

The first step in finding any location, if you're not familiar with the city, is to ask for its *barrio* or *colonia* (neighborhood or district) and find that area on a map. Barrios are generally older or more centrally located than colonias. Once you're in the general area, ask for the street that you're seeking. Sometimes, an address will be given as a street name with a house number. Sometimes, you'll get the name of the street, and the nearby cross streets. For example, the Hotel Istmania is at 5 Avenida, 7/8 Calles (between 7 and 8 Calles, or streets). These are the lucky cases. As often as not, though, an address will be given simply as a location relative to a well-known landmark: *media cuadra del Hotel Honduras Maya* (half a block from the Hotel Honduras Maya). Ask for the hotel, and you're halfway there. Now, start looking!

GETTING AROUND TOWN

Auto Rental

If you are going to rent a car, think first about hiring a taxi. Not only is it cheaper, but roads are bad around Tegucigalpa, with many potholes, and traffic is crazy (though it doesn't move too fast, at least), and traffic signs are only an afterthought.

Generally, you will be substantially responsible for damage to a rented vehicle, even if you buy local insurance, which provides only limited coverage. Verify if your automobile insurance from home or your credit card will provide any additional coverage (such coverage is gradually being eliminated).

Among car-rental companies are:

• **Budget**, *at the Hotel Honduras Maya and at the airport, tel. 335171 and 335161, fax 335170.*
• **Avis**, *Hotel Honduras Maya, tel. 320088, and airport, tel. 339548.*
• **Hertz**, *Centro Comercial Villa Real, tel. 390772.*
• **National Car Rental**, *Hotel Honduras Maya and airport, tel. 332653, fax 339769.*

These companies have toll-free numbers in the United States and Canada, useful for making reservations and getting the latest rates. Sometimes, by reserving in advance, you can get a lower rate than you might obtain locally.

Some local car-rental companies are:

• **Amigo**, *Boulevard Morazán, tel. 315135, fax 374445.*
• **Maya Rent A Car**, *Blvd. Morazán at Av. República de Chile, tel. 326133.*
• **Molinari**, *Hotel Honduras Maya, tel. 328691; airport, tel. 331307.*
• **Toyota Rent A Car**, *Colonia El Prado, Comayagüela, tel. 334004.*

DRIVING IN TEGUCIGALPA

Driving can be a problem in Tegucigalpa, especially at rush hours – about 7 a.m. to 9 a.m. and 3 p.m. to 7 p.m. It's not that there are a lot of cars. There just aren't enough streets, and those that exist are narrow and potholed. There are only a few routes to and through downtown, and they are often gridlocked. This explains why bus terminals are on the periphery of Tegucigalpa or in Comayagüela.

Right turns are allowed on red lights, but proceed with caution. Road signs hardly exist, and if you have a choice of driving or not driving, I think you will have a better time not driving.

By Bus

Buses exist in Tegucigalpa, and it's even possible to get a sheet from the tourist office listing the number of each route, and the neighborhood where it starts and where it ends. This, however, will be useless for most visitors, as it gives no idea of the route the bus takes as it winds from one hillside neighborhood down and up to another through Tegucigalpa's tortured geography.

Local buses can be crowded, and the lineups stretch and curve like so many strands of spaghetti. Many of the points of any interest to visitors are in the small downtown area, and those that aren't can be reached inexpensively by taxi for under $3. If you're staying at a hotel away from the center, such as the Alameda, ask the staff for guidance as to which bus will take you into the city and back out, if you don't want to take a taxi.

Fares on buses are low, the equivalent of about 10¢ U.S. Bus drivers and fellow passengers are very helpful.

By Taxi

Taxis are everywhere in Tegucigalpa. They're inexpensive, at about a dollar per person for a run around downtown, $2 for a ride to any place on the outskirts of town, $5 to the airport in the Yellow Cab taxis or $3 in a regular taxis. I highly recommend taxis as an alternative to the crowded and confusing service provided by public buses. They're also easier on your nerves than renting a car for local excursions, and usually cheaper, at about $6 per hour for time actually used.

Since taxis are not metered, it is essential to agree on the fare with the driver before you get in.

Try to find a taxi that looks well maintained. Some are frighteningly dilapidated. The better-kept fleet of Yellow Cabs is based at the Honduras Maya Hotel, and charges about double the going rate for trips.

Don't be surprised if a taxi stops to pick up another passenger on the way to your destination. It's part of local practice.

Tourist Office

The tourist office is amusing. It is located in the **Europa building** *east of downtown in Colonia San Carlos (Calle República de México, Avenida Ramón E. Cruz)*. Look for the Lloyds Bank branch on the first floor — the tourist office is two floors up. They have no hotel information, other than a list, but they sell attractive posters as well as maps. As for buses, they will tell you where to catch them, but they have only a sketchy idea as to schedules. If you don't expect much, you won't be disappointed.

To reach the tourist office, take any eastbound Lomas bus from the main square, and get off at Hospital San Felipe. Walk one block west, then left one block on Av. Ramón E. Cruz.

WHERE TO STAY

Better Hotels

HOTEL HONDURAS MAYA, *Avenida República de Chile at 2 Calle, tel. 323191, fax 327629. 200 rooms. $107 to $120 single/$120 to $135 double, $200 to $350 in suites. $13 per extra adult, no charge for children, nominal charge for crib. Visa, Master Card, American Express. U.S. reservations, tel. 800-448-8355.*

Located just east of downtown Tegucigalpa, the Honduras Maya is one of the city's landmarks, a high-rise in local terms, at 12 stories, with a trademark sculptured vertical frieze on its main tower meant to reflect the Mayan tradition of Honduras. It's the top hotel in town (though not super-luxurious and getting somewhat worn at the edges), where diplomats stay on the first days of their assignments. Rooms have the expected air conditioning, and televisions offering U.S. programs via satellite. Beds are comfortable, though furnishings are on the bland side.

Service is more than adequate, the pool is huge and heated, and views are scenic. An on-site health spa includes a sauna and steam bath. There are several restaurants, including a 24-hour coffee shop, brand-new convention and meeting facilities, extensive protected parking, and plenty of shops and services (auto rental, barber shop, travel agencies, etc.) both on the extensive hotel grounds and in the surrounding neighborhood. There is no charge for local phone calls, a plus if you're in town on business. Also complimentary (at least recently) is the buffet breakfast. Uniquely among Tegucigalpa hotels, the Honduras Maya has a casino, where the gaming includes blackjack, roulette, and slot machines.

HOTEL PLAZA SAN MARTÍN, *Colonia Palmira on Plaza San Martín, P. O. Box 864, tel. 372928, fax 311366. 110 rooms. $90 single/$110 double/ $115 triple, $130 in suites. American Express, Diners Club, Visa, Master Card.*

Tegucigalpa's newest major hotel, just east of downtown, is a blocky Mayan fortress of a building, with bare, slightly sloping facades terraced to the roof comb (in this case, a machine enclosure). Rooms are plainly furnished but quite comfortable, each with a balcony, refrigerator, sitting area, television, phone, and central air conditioning. Facilities include coffee shop, restaurant, bar, exercise room and indoor parking, but no pool.

HOTEL ALAMEDA, *Blvd. Suyapa (P.O. Box 940), tel. 326920, 326902, fax 326932. 75 rooms. $75 single/$90 double/$105 triple plus tax. U.S. reservations: tel. 305-226-7500. American Express, Visa, Master Card.*

This is one of the few hotels on the outskirts of the capital. It's about three kilometers from the airport in the hilly Alameda district southeast of downtown, and though it's not near any attractions, I can recommend it if you're interested in a quiet location. The hotel is built in a colonial-influenced style, with a white exterior, balconies, and red-tile roof. All rooms are carpeted, with color television, and the enclosed grounds include two swimming pools, one for children, and one quite large. There are also a sauna and steam bath, travel agency, car rental, barber and beauty shops, and conference rooms.

HOTEL PLAZA, *4 Avenida at 4 Calle (P.O. Box 175), tel. 372111, fax 372119. 83 rooms. $60 single/$75 double/$85 triple. American Express, Visa, Master Card.*

Centrally located on the pedestrian mall of downtown Tegucigalpa, opposite the post office, the Plaza offers good-sized air-conditioned rooms, all with queen-sized beds, and televisions with U.S. programming. Some of the standard rooms have sofa beds as well. Possible negative points for some visitors will be the lack of a swimming pool, and of shops inside the hotel, though most required services are available nearby. There are two restaurants here, including an all-night coffee shop, the Papagallo. Protected parking.

HOTEL LA RONDA, *6 Calle (Avenida Jérez) at 11 Avenida, Barrio La Ronda (P.O. Box 849), tel. 378151, fax 371454. 46 rooms. $50 to $70 single/ $55 to 80 double. U.S. reservations: tel. 800-742-4276. American Express, Visa, Master Card.*

A nice hotel, though hardly luxurious, conveniently located downtown. Certain rooms have no view at all, but most are quite large and comfortable, with carpets, telephone, color television and air conditioning. Small apartments are available, with kitchenette and dinette. Adjacent parking, restaurant and bar.

SUITES LA AURORA, *Avenida Luis Bográn 1519, Colonia Tepeyac, tel. 329891, fax 320188. 46 units. $36 single/$42 double with fan, $60/$65 with air conditioning.*

These are furnished apartments in a relatively quiet neighborhood; the units are fully equipped with kitchen, air-conditioning and television. Also on site are a convenience store, pool, sauna, steam room, restaurant, bar and protected parking.

Moderate Hotels

HOTEL ISTMANIA, *5 Avenida, 7/8 Calles, No. 1438 (P.O. Box 1972), tel. 371914, 371638, 371639, fax 371446. 34 rooms. $30 single or double. Visa, Master Card.*

Centrally located near Dolores church, and a few blocks from the Cathedral and Central Park, the Istmania is a modest, clean, businessmen's hotel, housed in a narrow modern building.

HOTEL EL PRADO, *3 Avenida, 8 Calle, tel. 370121, fax 372221. 68 rooms. $75 single/$85 double/$100 triple plus tax. American Express, Visa, Master Card.*

A modern building located near the back of the Cathedral. Rooms are air conditioned and have televisions.

GRAN HOTEL KRYSTAL, *6 Avenida/6 Calle (P. O. Box 283), tel. 378804, fax 378976. 59 rooms. $19 single/$30 double. American Express, Visa, Master Card.*

A good-sized businessperson's hotel, located in the center of *everything* in Tegucigalpa, and a good value for the price.

Budget Hotels

HOTEL IBERIA, *Peatonal Dolores, tel. 229267. $7 single/$9 double shared bath, $10 single/$12 double private bath.*

On the pedestrian mall near the Dolores Church. Well maintained, clean, friendly, and safe. Rooms on the second floor are better. There's a pleasant living room. I don't think that you can do better for the price. The market across from the hotel is colorful.

HOTEL IMPERIAL, *5 Avenida 7/8 Calles No. 703, Callejón Los Dolores, tel. 221973. $4 single/$6 double.*

Budget lodging in a good location.

NUEVO HOTEL BOSTON, *6 Calle no. 321, Barrio Abajo, tel. 379411. $8 to $9 single/$10 to $11 double.*

Well-located near Dolores church, and very good for the price. Take a room that doesn't face the street (which costs less). Management is English-speaking and friendly.

HOTEL MARICHAL, *5 Calle at 5 Avenida, No. 1115, tel. 370069. $8 single/$14 double.*

A large hotel with many basic, clean rooms, varying in size and quality. Near the Plaza Dolores.

HOTEL GRANADA, *Avenida Gutemburg 1326, tel. 374004. 46 rooms. $9 single/$12 double.*

At the eastern end of downtown, also a good buy, with a relatively quiet location. Additional rooms are available in a newer annex, a couple of blocks away *(tel. 220597).*

HOTEL RITZ, *5 Avenida, 4 Calle (P.O. Box 743), Comayagüela, tel. 222769. 23 rooms. $10 to $12 double.*

This hotel is not luxurious, but a good value if you need to be near the bus stations in Comayagüela. Most rooms are modest, many with shared bath.

HOTEL COLONIAL, *6 Calle, 6/7 Avenidas, Comayagüela, tel. 375785. $8 singe/$10 doubles.*

Convenient to the bus stations, all rooms with private bath, clean, good for the price.

HOTELITO WEST, 10 Calle, 6/7 Avenidas, Comayagüela, tel. 379456. $12 double. A budget hotel recommended by some readers.

Pensiones

Many of the cheaper places to in which to stay are in the area of the **Dolores church**, *on Peatonal Dolores (a pedestrian street that starts in front of Dolores church and runs down to the main pedestrian street, 4 Calle)*. Right by the church is **HOSPEDAJE TRES DE MAYO.** Another one nearby is **HOSPEDAJE SUREÑO**, clean and basic, with airy rooms, and a rate of under $5 per night. Hospedaje Montoya, also in this area, is much less attractive. **HOTEL FORTUNA**, at the corner of Dolores and Paulino Valladares, at about $6 for a room sharing bathroom, is clean and calm, okay for the price.

WHERE TO EAT

I can't say that Tegucigalpa has all the gourmet delights of a major capital. There isn't enough of an audience for fine cuisine to be very common. But if you attune yourself to what's available, you won't be disappointed — not at all.

Downtown

LA TERRAZA DE DON PEPE, *5 Calle (Avenida Colón), downtown (opposite the "Pequeño Despacho")*. The specialty is charcoal-grilled meats — *"carnes a la parrilla"* — which are as tasty as you'll find in Tegucigalpa. But you'll also come here for the old-time ranch atmosphere. Large, friendly, and relaxed. About $5 for most main courses.

BURGER HUT, *next to the church of La Merced (2 Calle, 8 Avenida)* is one of many, many fast-food places. And you can also get the real thing. Burger King has an outlet on the Peatonal mall downtown, as well as a couple of outposts in outlying areas.

PIZZERIA TITO, *Callejón Los Dolores (the north-south pedestrian street, by Bancahasa)*, is one of many pizzerias, this one Italian-owned, with an unpretentious menu that includes pastas. All items attractively served. Don't be tempted by the wine. It is not good. They also have a branch on Boulevard Morazán.

RESTAURANTE Y PIZZERIA NINO, *on Callejón Dolores near 5 Calle*, is a small establishment owned by a Honduran-Italian family, with not only an assortment of pizzas, but hearty soups and pastas (the latter at up to $5) and saltimbocca, calamari and other specialties (up to $8).

AL NATURAL, *near Morazán Park, just behind the cathedral on a narrow street*. This is a restaurant that I recommend highly, set in an interior courtyard, quiet and peaceful despite the downtown location. The cuisine is vegetarian-style, though not strictly so, a good bet for travelers who are fearful of upsetting their tummies (or have done so already), attractively served.

PIZZA BOOM, *Avenida 6, Calles 6/5*. A step up from your usual pizzeria, with a fireplace and fountain. About $8 for a family-size pizza. They have a branch on Morazán Blvd. at the Guadalupe church.

MEDITERRÁNEO. *Adjacent to Pizza Boom near Plaza Dolores*. Inexpensive Honduran home cooking with a Greek touch.

Boulevard Morazán

For fast food, head to **Boulevard Morazán**, *the strip that runs east from downtown Tegucigalpa. Follow 3 Calle onto Avenida República de Chile, past the Hotel Honduras Maya, then turn left (east) onto Morazán*. There must be about 30 outlets on this street, modern and clean-looking, with names familiar and almost familiar.

SALSA, *on Blvd. Morazán*, serves light meals of Tex-Mex food: tacos, burritos and quesadillas, with soft drinks and pie for dessert . . . and rhythm. **TACO LOCO** has similar items.

For Chinese food, you can head to the same area for a choice of eateries. The **CHINA TOWN PALACE** has the usual extended Cantonese menu, with some Szechuan items, including shark-fin soup, shrimp with bamboo shoots, hot spicy chicken, and assorted combinations. About $7, more for shellfish or one of the house specialties. **ON LOK** is also pretty good.

KLOSTER, *on Blvd. Morazán, next to the On Lok Chinese restaurant (two blocks east of Av. República de Chile)*, is a popular spot for quaffing beer. But they also have genuine German food and, unusual for Tegucigalpa, take-out service. *Dial 327676 for delivery to your hotel or wherever you happen to be*. About $8 for a main course.

You'll find steak houses along Morazán as well. One with a Mexican flavor is **EL ASADOR**, *about three blocks up from the corner of República de Chile*. **JACK'S STEAK HOUSE**, *on Morazán at Las Lomas shopping center*, is a branch of the long-established restaurant of the same name in San Pedro Sula.

EL ARRIERO, *half a block south of the Hotel Honduras Maya on Av. República de Chile at no. 516*, specializes in steaks and seafood grilled in Uruguayan fashion, as does **EL NOVILLERO**, *on the same street*. **JIMMY WEST**, *Avenida República Argentina no. 322*, is a steak-and-barbecue-rib house. Main courses from $4 to $8.

A well-established seafood restaurant is **HUNGRY FISHERMAN**, *Av. República de Chile, also near the Honduras Maya*. Prices for lobster and shrimp are a bit high, but the fish, in garlic or assorted sauces, is reasonable, at under $10 for a main course.

Right in the Hotel Honduras Maya, you'll find the relatively formal **LA VERANDA** restaurant, where the cuisine is reliable, and, though high-priced for Honduras, not at all a bad value for what you get.

Higher on the price scale, **ALONDRA**, *on República de Chile, opposite the Honduras Maya*, serves a continental menu, and caters to groups. Expect a tab of $20 or more, with a drink.

EL BISTRO, *Sendero San Juan (off Av. República de Chile one block below the Hotel Honduras Maya)*, is a French-operated establishment with light European bistro fare. Also serving French food is **CA FÉ DU MONDE**, *near the Hotel Plaza San Martín and the Honduras Maya, on Avenida Juan Lindo*.

Avenida La Paz

Avenida La Paz, *the eastern continuation of 6 Calle, is, like Boulevard Morazán*, a thoroughfare through some of the better-off neighborhoods of the capital, and there are some attractive restaurants out this way.

GAUCHOS, *Av. La Paz No. 2410, by the Alpha y Omega cinemas*, specializes in Uruguayan-style steaks, roasted by an open fire. About $10 for main courses.

The **DON QUIJOTE** restaurant *on Av. La Paz* specializes in paella, codfish stew, and similar hearty traditional Spanish fare, along with more familiar steaks and chops. Meals are about $6 and up.

Panoramic Dining Views

For a meal with a panorama, ask for the road (or take a taxi) to **Hatillo**, *above the city to the north*, where **LA CUMBRE** serves German and Hondurans food and drinks. Also here, **THE TANNERY** has American and European meals, at $5 or so for a main course.

BARS

You're in the wrong town if you're looking for exciting nighttime entertainment, but there are several places where you can enjoy a quiet drink without hassle.

Within the **Hotel Honduras Maya**, the bars serve snacks with drinks, and if you go at around 5:30 in the evening, you'll find the offerings fairly substantial.

Nearby, the **Hungry Fisherman** and **Ca Fé Allegro**, mentioned above as eating places, will also serve you just a drink; or, continue to one of the snack-and-drink spots along Blvd. Morazán.

Downtown, the **O'Henry Bar** of the Hotel Plaza, 4 Avenida at 4 Calle, has a happy hour from 6 to 7 p.m. daily except Sunday. Music often plays, and snacks are served with the drinks.

To find a student crowd, head toward the university on Suyapa Blvd., either by bus from the San Isidro market in Comayagüela, or, preferably, by taxi. There are bars in the area, and sometimes informal sidewalk entertainment.

SEEING THE SIGHTS

Downtown

Central Tegucigalpa, still somewhat colonial-flavored, is small enough that you can get a sense of the city during a walk of just a few hours. There are some fine old examples of colonial and nineteenth century architecture, city squares in which to linger, and pedestrian streets for shopping and observing the flow of city life.

A good place to start your excursion is the main square, or **Parque Central**, also known, more formally, as **Plaza Morazán**. On the east side of the square is the twin-towered **Cathedral of Tegucigalpa** (or Cathedral of San Miguel), the construction of which was started in the middle of the eighteenth century. The facade of the cathedral is noted for its inset, or engaged, columns with horizontal grooves and pillars in the form of mermaids. While the Cathedral is similar in many respects to others of the period in Central America, the pleated columns are a peculiarly Honduran characteristic that occurs here, and on some of the churches in Comayagua. *Open weekday afternoons from 2:30 p.m. to 6 pm., and on Sundays from 10:30 a.m. to 12:30 p.m.*

South of the Cathedral, across 3 Calle, is the **Palacio del Distrito Central**, which houses the municipal government of Tegucigalpa and Comayagüela. On this site stood the old *cabildo*, or town hall, where the Declaration of Independence of Central America was ratified on September 28, 1821.

At 5 Avenida, another branch of the mall runs northward, to the twin-towered **Iglesia Los Dolores** (**Dolores Church**), containing, as does the Cathedral (which it predates by about twenty years, to 1732, though it wasn't completed until 1815), gold-plated altars. The pilasters on the facade are decorated with rosettes, and windows are finished with busts of angels on top and depictions of fruits underneath.

Farther west, across 3 Avenida and then south down a side street, is **Teatro Manuel Bonilla** (**Manuel Bonilla Theater**). Every Central American capital has one grand, significant performance area, and this is Tegucigalpa's, completed in 1912. The facade is neoclassical, while inside, there is an ornate double horseshoe tier of seating above the main floor, a copy of a contemporary theater in Paris.

Farther afield, *on the edge of downtown, four blocks north along 2 Avenida*, is **Parque La Concordia** (**Concordia Park**), a block-sized square that contains small-scale replicas of Altar Q and Stela C of Copán, as well as a model of a temple at Chichén Itzén in Mexico. This is meant to be a small botanical garden as well, with assorted non-Maya statuary, pools, and plantings. Couples frequent the Bridge of Sighs and hold hands alongside the Lake of Love.

Walking back to the Central Park, *then south along 7 Avenida (Calle Bolívar)*, you'll come to a small square called **Parque Merced**, after the

Iglesia La Merced (Merced Church) on its east side. This church dates from the seventeenth century, and includes some colonial paintings and an elaborate altar. Farther south is the **Palacio Legislativo**, or **Congreso Nacional (Legislative Palace**, or **National Congress)**, a campus sort of building that dates from 1955, and is quite peculiar among the older and more elaborate governmental edifices in the city.

Walking down toward the river, you'll see the **Puente Mallol (Mallol Bridge)**, the oldest bridge in the city. Construction was started in 1818.

Back up along 6 Avenida, you'll reach the well-guarded, fortress-like former **Casa Presidencial (Presidential Palace)**, *at the corner of 1 Calle*, completed in 1919. The massive, light-pink, wedding-cake Moorish-Italian architecture, with a dome at one end, ogive arches, and keyhole openings, overwhelmingly defensive, says much about the turnovers of government through the years.

Back at the Parque Central, *go east along 4 Calle to 10 Avenida* to reach the **Church of San Francisco.** This is the oldest of the churches that remain in Tegucigalpa, started in 1592 (by Franciscans, of course), and greatly altered starting in 1740, when Mudéjar elements characteristic of southern Spain were added to the original simple structure. Inside are gold-plated altarpieces and colonial paintings. Next door is the building that formerly housed the San Francisco monastery.

Comayagüela

In **Comayagüela**, *southwest of downtown Tegucigalpa*, you'll find no high-rise buildings, only numerous bus stations, a few cheap hotels, and assorted other nondescript concrete commercial and residential structures, along with several sights that are not as historically interesting as those in Tegucigalpa proper, but every bit as rewarding for visitors who are interested in the way the broad class of Hondurans lives.

The heart of commercial Comayagüela is the **Mercado San Isidro (San Isidro Market)**, the largest in the city. Here you can find everything, and you can bargain for anything. Yet it's not a frenzied place at all, in fact, it's very calm, and not dangerous (though, as in any market, you should keep valuables out of sight, and money in a hidden pocket).

If you don't find what you're looking for at the San Isidro Market, try the **Artesanías (Handicraft) Market**, held on weekends adjacent to **Parque El Soldado (Soldier Park)** *at 4 Avenida and 15 Calle, toward the south end of Comayagüela*. Aside from the goods, the park itself is pleasant, with caged birds, and luxuriant vegetation.

Southeast of Downtown

East of Comayagüela, and south of downtown Tegucigalpa, the hill called **Juana Laínez** juts up alongside the road from the airport. At the top is the

Monumento de la Paz (Peace Monument). A walk or taxi ride up to the top will give you a panorama of Tegucigalpa and the surrounding hills.

The monument itself is a double-vision image of a flying saucer and complementary rings, set on concrete pillars. I'm not sure of the imagery, but it certainly isn't warlike. At the foot of the hill is the **National Stadium.** A large fruit and flower market operates here on Friday and up to noon on Saturday.

North of Downtown

North of downtown is the peak called **El Picacho** (1310 meters), one of several mountains surrounding the city. Picacho is included in **Parque Naciones Unidas (United Nations Park).** First of all, before you go to Picacho, ask at your hotel about current conditions — a fire recently did severe damage to the vegetation on the hill, and regrowth is under way. Also, take a sweater.

There are several ways to get here. From downtown, you can walk due north, following 9 Avenida. Once you cross 6 Calle, the streets — many of them cobbled — become more winding and narrow. You pass through the neighborhood called La Leona, where some of the large, old houses have been restored to their past glory. The streets give way to paths, and with some help from passersby, and an eye toward the summit, you should be able to make it to the top. Or, you can go up in a taxi for about $5 round trip, including a wait of a half-hour.

The main reward of a visit to Picacho is the view to the whole valley spread out before you. You get a good orientation to the city. And by looking around, you'll understand why it was that your plane made a couple of sharp turns before touching down at Toncontín Airport, which is on a small plateau, one of the few flat pieces of land in this valley.

You'll also find a small zoo, in decrepit state with the animals badly cared for, and some reproductions of Mayan ruins, including pyramids. In the absence of regular maintenance, the park has become something of a ruin itself. There is long grass everywhere, and evident vandalism. There are also outdoor grills, in case you want to cook your lunch. The area is crowded on Sundays.

Also north of downtown, the **Instituto Hondureño de Antropología e Historia (Honduran Institute of Anthropology and History)** has a museum housed in a mansion. It's really all quite limited. Part of the building is conserved as a monument to itself, and to the ex-president and his first lady. Other exhibits illustrate the lives of the Jicaques, Lencas, Chortís, Miskitos and Sumos, native peoples whose ancestors occupied the land before the Spanish arrived. And there are exhibits of fossils and colonial life. In any case, it's a quiet place with nice gardens, and good views of the city. Closed Monday and Tuesday, open from 8 a.m. to 3:30

p.m. other days, small admission charge. Take a taxi, or ask for directions from your hotel if you're walking.

It's on Calle Morelo, off 3 Avenida, seven blocks north of the post office downtown. You can stop here on the way to United Nations Park.

SHOPPING

What you will find when shopping in Tegucigalpa, and in Honduras in general, is quite limited: leatherwork, wood carving (especially in mahogany, including boxes and statuettes), furniture, hammocks, leather bags, beadwork, silver and gold jewelry, baskets, pottery, and clothing items. And, oh yes, cigars.

The wood carvings are the most typical souvenirs of Honduras, and if you have some use for an oversized set of salad servers, well, this is the place to find them. But I have to tell you that you needn't spend a great effort looking for extraordinary crafts. With some exceptions, you won't find them.

For the most fun shopping, you should head to the markets. **The Artesanas (Handicraft) Market** *is held on weekends at Parque El Soldado in Comayagüela.* Also in Comayagüela, nearer to downtown, is the **San Isidro market**, where you'll find not only handicrafts, but hundreds of simple utilitarian items that seem to date from a past age.

Aside from the markets, almost every hotel has a souvenir shop, where, of course, you'll pay more for anything. And there are dozens of other stores, among them:

Tienda del Artesano, *facing the south side of Valle Park (No. 1001),* is operated by **ANAH** (*Asociación Nacional de Artesanos de Honduras*), a national guild of craftsmen, and has a selection of *everything* made by artisans in Honduras. *Hours are 9 a.m. to 6 p.m. during the week, to 4 p.m. on Saturdays.* Other shopping possibilities include:

Tikamaya, *on 3 Calle at 10 Avenida, by Valle Park.*

Candü, *opposite the Hotel Honduras Maya, on Avenida República de Chile* has some interesting paintings, and a stock of maps of Honduras and Tegucigalpa. There are other souvenir shops in the immediate area — this is where the money is in Tegucigalpa.

Exposición de Arte Celajes *(tel. 391971), 501 Plaza San Martín, by the Hotel Plaza San Martín,* has a fair selection of crafts, as well as paintings and other fine arts. The owners are English-speaking.

Mundo Maya, *in the Hotel Honduras Maya, and also in Colonia Palmira.*

El Mundo Maya, *Calle Adolfo Zuñiga 1114 (two blocks behind the cathedral),* stocks original paintings as well as more standard souvenirs, and also provides travel information.

Honduras Souvenirs, *in the Lomas del Boulevard shopping center on Blvd. Morazán,* also has an assortment of gift items.

Lesanddra Leather, *in the Los Castaños shopping center on Blvd. Morazán*, has more finely made leather items than you'll find in handicraft stores or markets.

PRACTICAL INFORMATION

Banks

Major banks downtown are:

- **Bancahsa**, *5 Avenida, 5 Calle, tel. 371171.*
- **Banco Atlántida**, *7 Avenida, 5 Calle, tel. 321742.*
- **Banco Sogerin**, *6 Calle, 6 Avenida, tel. 374551.*
- **Banco de Honduras** (*Citibank subsidiary*), *Midence Soto building, main square, tel. 371155, and Boulevard Suyapa, tel. 326122.*
- **Lloyds Bank**, *Europa building, Calle República de México, Avenida Ramón E. Cruz, Colonia San Carlos, tel. 321864.*

For **cash advances** on a Visa card, try any bank that displays the Honducard-Visa symbol. Bancahsa (see above) and Bancahorro are authorized to make advances, *or call 381111 for assistance.* Otherwise, for Visa or Master Card cash advances, contact **Credomatic**, *second floor, Interamericana de Seguros building, tel. 326030,* or try any bank with a Credomatic, Ficensa or Futuro sign.

Embassies & Consulates

Call first before visiting an embassy or consulate, in order to obtain office hours, and to get directions. Among the representatives of foreign nations are:

- **Belize**, *Colonia 15 de Septiembre No. 1703, Comayagüela, tel. 331423.*
- **Canada** (*consulate only*), *Los Castaños building, 6th floor, Boulevard Morazán, tel. 314545.*
- **Costa Rica**, *Colonia El Triángulo, tel. 321768.*
- **El Salvador**, *Colonia San Carlos, No. 205, tel. 321344.*
- **France**, *Avenida Juan Lindo, 3 Calle, Colonia Palmira, tel. 321800.*
- **El Salvador**, *Colonia San Carlos, tel. 321344.*
- **Germany**, *Paysen building, Blvd. Morazán, tel. 323161.*
- **Guatemala**, *Colonia Las Minitas, 4 Calle No. 2421, tel. 321580. (Consulate, Colonia Palmira, Avenida Juan Lindo, tel. 325018).*
- **Israel**, *Midence Soto Building, tel. 372529.*
- **Italy**, *Colonia Reforma, Avenida Principal No. 2602, tel. 383391.*
- **Japan**, *Colonia Reforma, 2 Avenida, tel. 326828.*
- **Mexico**, *Colonia Palmira, Calle del Brasil, tel. 326471.*
- **Netherlands** (*consulate*), *Colonia Lomas del Mayab, Calle Copán, tel. 315007*
- **Nicaragua**, *Colonia Tepeyac, tel. 324290.*

- **Panama**, *Palmira building, Colonia Palmira, tel. 315441.*
- **Sweden**, *Colonia Miraflores, Avenida Principal No. 2758, tel. 325935.*
- **Switzerland**, *Colonia Alameda, 4 Avenida, 7 Calle No. 1811, tel. 329692.*
- **U.S.**, *Avenida La Paz. Tel. 323121 to 9.*
- **United Kingdom**, *Palmira building (near Hotel Honduras Maya), tel. 325429.*

Laundry

There's exactly one coin-op (or more exactly token-operated) laundry near downtown. **Mi Lavandería** *(tel. 376573) is in Comayagüela on 2 Avenida (Calle Real) between 3 and 4 Calle, opposite the Repostería Calle Real (a sweet shop).* They're open every day, including Sundays, and they'll also do your laundry and dry cleaning on a drop-off basis. There are other establishments scattered through Tegucigalpa that will do your laundry at a piece rate if you want to save a few dollars over your hotel's charges.

Movies

Look for advertisements for movies in the daily papers, and in *Honduras This Week*, which lists the original English-language title. Most of the films are foreign, and are shown in the original language, with Spanish subtitles. Ads never give addresses, so ask at your hotel as to where any cinema is located. Admission costs about a dollar in most cases.

You'll find a *simpático* atmosphere in movie houses. People smoke, talk, laugh out loud, and cheerfully share the premises with some permanent residents: the bats in the rafters.

Post Office

The **central post office** *is on the pedestrian mall (Calle 4, Peatonal) at 4 Avenida, opposite the Hotel Plaza. Hours are from 8 a.m. to 8 p.m.* I have found the service reliable, at least for letters mailed from this location: my letters to Montreal took about six days to arrive.

Telephones

You can make international telephone calls, with persistence, from **Hondutel**, *5 Calle at 4 Avenida.* The lines are long, and once you get to the front and order your call, you have no idea if you'll get through. A far better way is to call from your hotel, if it offers long distance service, even at a surcharge; or from a private phone, if you can get your hands on one.

International direct dialing is available from Tegucigalpa, but not from most phones in the country. If you're calling the States, the easiest route is to dial 123 for AT&T's **USA Direct** service. From a pay phone, drop in a coin before dialing. There are dedicated USA Direct phones at the Hondutel office.

**EMERGENCY AND SERVICE NUMBERS
FROM TEGUCIGALPA**
- *191– Long distance in Honduras*
- *192– Telephone number information*
- *196 –Time of Day*
- *197– International long distance*
- *198– Fire*
- *199– Public security (police)*

Water

Officially, the U.S. embassy says the water is *not* safe to drink from the tap. Drink bottled beverages and soda water. In any case, water is a scarce commodity in Tegucigalpa, and if you're not staying in one of the better hotels (which have pumps and storage tanks), you could well find nothing more than a dribble when you turn on the tap.

Weather

In terms of temperature, Tegucigalpa, like much of Honduras, has just one season, a sort of moderately warm summer. Average daily high ranges from a maximum of 86 degrees Fahrenheit (30 degrees Centigrade) in April to 77 degrees F (25 degrees C) in December and January. Average low temperature runs from a maximum of 65 degrees F (18 degrees C) in June to a minimum of 57 degrees F (14 degrees C) in January and February.

Rainfall, however, can run to extremes. The dry season in Tegucigalpa lasts from November through April. Average rainfall in November is just an inch and a half (38 mm), and drops to a trace by March. On most days in the dry times, there's hardly a cloud in the sky. Rain picks up quickly in May — May and June have the heaviest annual rainfall, 7.1 and 7.0 inches (180 and 177 mm) respectively. July and August see a drop to 2.8 inches (70 mm), then rainfall increases somewhat in September and October before tapering off again.

Even in the rainy season, however, Tegucigalpa is not a hard place to take: usually, fewer than half the days in any given month have any noticeable rainfall.

During the months of low rainfall in Tegucigalpa, especially past February, everything is dry — the air, the yellowed grass, the dust that blows up constantly from unwatered and unpaved streets on the frequent gusts of wind. The breeze can make the temperature feel cooler than it really is. But a light sweater is as much as you'll need to keep warm. The higher elevations nearby will require a bit more covering.

Tours & Travel Agencies

• **Agencia de Viajes Marcris**, *5 Calle, 11/12 Avenidas (near Hotel La Ronda), tel. 222151.* This general travel agency can arrange local and regional tours.

• **Agencia de Viajes Brenda**, *Midence Soto arcade (P. O. Box 1349), tel. 375039.*

• **Agencia de Viajes Concorde**, *4 Calle, 9/10 Avenidas, No. 905, tel. 378207.*

• **Agencia de Viajes Jupiter**, *6 Avenida, 2/3 Calles (half block north of Presidential Palace), tel. 375644.*

• **Agencia de Viajes Intercontinental**, *5 Calle, Avenida Colón, no. 404, tel. 378370.*

• **Eco-Hiking Eco-Tourist Expeditions**, *P.O. Box 30037 Toncontín, Comayagüela, tel. 331208.* This new company offers expeditions in four-wheel-drive vehicles to remote Lenca communities, where bases are organized for treks into countryside rarely seen by outsiders.

• **La Mosquitia Ecoaventuras**, *P. O. Box 3577, Tegucigalpa, tel. 370593, fax 379398.* This company specializes in ten- to fourteen-day low-impact adventures in the vast forests of Mosquitia, including the Río Plátano Biosphere Reserve, with emphasis on birding, wildlife viewing, and non-intrusive contacts with native peoples. *Information is available from Geotours, Lomas del Boulevard shopping center, Blvd. Morazán, tel. 320466, fax 311058.*

• **Honduras Tours**, *J.S. Bldg., Blvd. Morazán, tel. 324415, fax 310178.*

• **Honduras Copán Tours**, *Edificio Comercial Palmira (opposite the Hotel Honduras Maya, P. O. Box 1373), tel. 326769, 329964, fax 326795.* One of the larger agencies in Tegucigalpa.

• **Explore Honduras**, *P O Box 336, Med-Cast Bldg., Blvd. Morazán, tel. 311003, fax 329800, operating through most hotels.* Excursions to Copán, San Pedro Sula, Lake Yojoa and Pulhapanzak falls. Explore Honduras has a superb reputation for reliability, and is the ground operator for many U.S. agencies offering Honduras travel.

• **Agencia de Viajes Cosmos**, *3 Calle, 6/7 Avenidas, tel. 370395.*

• **Jet Tours**, *1 Calle, 1 Avenida, Barrio San Rafael (next to Hotel Honduras Maya), tel. 325555.*

• **Maya Travel Service**, *Midence Soto Building, tel. 376979.*

• **Mundirama Travel Service** *(American Express representative), Fiallos Soto Bldg. 132, tel 376111, fax 228258;* branch at Ciicsa Building near Hotel Honduras Maya, tel. 323909, fax 320072.

• **Viajes Mundiales**, *2 Avenida No. 205, Comayagüela, tel. 371837.*

VISITING NEARBY TOWNS
SUYAPA

The religious capital of Honduras for the overwhelmingly Catholic majority, **Suyapa** is a suburb of Tegucigalpa, about eight kilometers east of downtown. The attraction for pilgrims is a six-inch statue of the Virgin, imbued with miraculous powers, which, according to tradition, was discovered in a corn field in 1743, and, no matter how many times it was moved, returned to its original place. The image was credited with the cure of a captain of the grenadiers, who organized the construction of a church in its honor.

The faithful arrive at all times of the year, but especially for the **Feast of the Virgin** on February 2, and during the following weeks.

Suyapa rates as an attraction for those with an interest in the religious ways of Honduras, or for those with some extra time. If you go, catch the number 31 bus from the San Isidro market in Comayagüela, or take a taxi for about $3.

SANTA LUCÍA & VALLE DE ANGELES

The trip to these two towns will take a half-day in a car, by taxi, or on a tour, or a full day by bus if you go to both places. The bus leaves from near San Felipe Hospital, about two kilometers east of downtown on Avenida La Paz, a continuation of 6 Calle, at 7 Avenida. (Take a Lomas bus from Plaza Morazán to Hospital San Felipe; walk one block east, one block south on Av. República Dominicana, then one block east on Calle Bustamente y Rivero, an unpaved street. Departures are about every hour.)

A tour costs about $10 per person, a taxi about $20. The road is paved all the way, and in excellent condition.

Santa Lucía

Santa Lucía is *17 kilometers from Tegucigalpa*, on a 2.5-kilometer spur from the main road, a small, picturesque village, its main street paved with cobblestones. Santa Lucía was once an important mining center, early in the colonial period, but as the mines were worked out, it became a backwater.

There's a colonial church, with old paintings and a statue of a black Christ that is said to have been a gift of King Philip II, sculptured in Spain more than 400 years ago. A shop sells handicrafts, and there are pleasing views of tile-roof houses and hills and patches of corn all around. There are no restaurants or hotels aimed at visitors.

Valle de Angeles & Vicinity

Eleven kilometers onward, **Valle de Angeles** is a larger colonial-style town of whitewashed, lime-plastered adobe houses with red tile roofs, massive wooden lintels, and porches with roofs supported by rough wooden posts. Valle de Angeles is cooler than Tegucigalpa (bring a sweater), quiet, clean and friendly, not too different from the hill villages above the Spanish coast that prosper from the visits of tourists.

There are restaurants on the main street and central plaza, and assorted boutiques selling the leather, wood and ceramic articles for which the town is known. You might be able to visit the school where some of these crafts are taught. **Lessandra Leather** is one of several shops with luggage and purses made for the tourist trade. **La Casa del Chocolate** is a tea room where you can buy home-made cookies for consumption with hot chocolate.

More formal is **POSADA DEL ANGEL**, a comfortable inn where you can take a break from walking around the village. Rooms are available for under $15 double. *Phone 362233 to reserve.*

The **RESTAURANTE TURÍSTICO VALLE DE ANGELES**, *tel. 762148,* set in the pines on a hill above town, serves Honduran home-style cooking — grilled meats, fried plantains, beans, enchiladas, mountains of tortillas — which is difficult to find outside of private homes, at a tab of up to $6. Open from 10 a.m. to 6 p.m., closed Monday.

And there are other establishments offering inexpensive country cooking, as well as a branch of the **DON QUIJOTE** Spanish restaurant.

LA TIGRA NATIONAL PARK

Above San Juancito, **La Tigra** is a cloud-forest peak where the wonderland of vegetation that once covered much of the high part of Honduras still survives in parts and is regenerating in others. Covering 238 square kilometers, La Tigra National Park protects a watershed that supplies almost half of Tegucigalpa's water. Seventy-five square kilometers are an absolute reserve, the remainder a buffer zone.

Elevations in the protected area are as high as 2290 meters. As many as half of the plant species present in La Tigra are considered rare in other parts of Honduras.

La Tigra's botanical bounty is due to its location near the continental divide, and the prevailing winds that bring rain through much of the year. Broad-leafed plants, vines, mosses, bromeliads and orchids and ferns live not just on the ground, but on the trunks and branches of trees, taking up water from the air and from the ground, sending out huge leaves to take advantage of what light filters through the canopy, and roots to absorb nutrients from decaying plant matter. In parts of the park below 1800 meters, there are also pines more typical of lowland Honduras.

Birds make their nests in the trees and are attracted to the flowers that are always in bloom; the quetzal, iridescent red-and-green with an arc of tail feathers several feet long, is regularly seen, along with the goldfinch and green toucan. Animals that inhabit the park include tapirs, jaguars, ocelots, monkeys and mountain lions, many of them only at the highest and least accessible elevations.

A bus to San Juancito and La Tigra leaves the San Pablo market in Tegucigalpa daily at 10 a.m. Take the Colonia 21 bus from the main square to reach the market. From San Juancito, it takes about an hour at a slow pace on an ascending trail to reach the administrative office of the park, in a former mining camp, where basic lodging is available. Without reservations (by telegram to Parque Nacional, Campamento Rosario, San Juancito), it's best to come during the week with a sleeping bag. Arrangements can also be made to sleep in private houses.

A second route to La Tigra is north from Tegucigalpa by the El Picacho road through El Hatillo to Jutiapa, where there is another visitors' center.

Bring along a sweater — it's windy and relatively cool at La Tigra. Hiking shoes are useful, though any comfortable old shoes will do. Make sure you stay on the trails. Not all are well-marked, so if you lose your way, re-trace your steps until you find trail markings again.

Management of the park has been in the hands of a private foundation, Amigos de La Tigra, since 1992.

OJOJONA

Ojojona is yet another picturesque hill town with cobbled streets, white houses with red-tiled roofs, and colonial churches — three of them, in fact, with paintings that date from before independence. Ojojona is also known for its pottery, especially water jugs made in the shape of roosters. Other local craft specialties are woodcrafting and leatherwork. A small museum contains the work of Pablo Zelaya Sierra, one of the most noted painters of Honduras.

Ojojona sits on a small plateau among mountains. The name of the town means "greenish water" in Nahuatl, the language of the Mexican Indians who accompanied the Spanish conquerors. The original town, now called **Pueblo Viejo**, stood three kilometers from the present site.

Ojojona is located 30 kilometers from Tegucigalpa, on a spur (at kilometer 24) from the main highway for the coast. Buses for Ojojona leave from 4 Calle, 8/9 Avenidas, Comayagüela, about every hour. There is an inexpensive pension in town.

Santa Ana, a nearby village, has a couple of colonial churches. **Lepaterique**, (**Tiger Mountain**) to the west, is also picturesque. The **Montaña Yerba Buena Biological Reserve**, just north of the town, has swimming pools.

TO THE NORTH

North from Tegucigalpa is the heartland of Honduras, the connecting rift valleys between the Caribbean and the Pacific that first attracted Spanish settlers, where Honduran culture was forged as invaders and natives met and contested and finally merged, where even today the population of Honduras is concentrated. But this was a well-developed area even before the Conquest. A culture known as the **Yarumela** flourished near Comayagua more than 1500 years before Christ. Marble pieces decorated with human faces have been found from a culture called the **Ulúa**, which existed after the fall of Mayan civilization.

For all its importance to the country, it is a measure of the underdevelopment of Honduras that even much of this route was, until relatively recently, off the beaten track. Only a dirt track, interrupted by a ferry over **Lake Yojoa**, connected the two major cities of Honduras for most of the last hundred years, and only in the last twenty years has it been possible to drive this route on a paved highway. Elsewhere in Central America, the lack of roads was compensated by railroads, but in Honduras, there was nothing.

For the visitor, there is much majestic countryside to be seen during a journey along the major highway, along with **Comayagua**, the old capital where colonial churches still stand; small and little-visited towns where old ways and a slow pace of life still hold sway; and Lake Yojoa, as pleasant a stopping point and vacation area as will be found on the mainland. At the end of the route is **San Pedro Sula**, the metropolis of the north, and of modern Honduras, and beyond are the coastal cities, beaches, and the special world of the **Bay Islands**.

COMAYAGUA

For more than 300 years, **Comayagua** was the capital of colonial and independent Honduras. But "capital" is a grand term for what was, in fact, just the major settlement and administrative center of a backwater colony of little importance in the imperial scheme, or in the world in general. Tthe colonial period was the heyday of Comayagua. After independence, congresses met alternately in Comayagua and Tegucigalpa. The city was burned by the invading army of Guatemala in 1827, and, as Honduras settled into an existence as a satellite of other Central American countries, Comayagua never re-assumed its preeminence.

In 1880, Comayagua received its final deflation. President Marco Aurelio Soto, whose Indian wife was snubbed by the Comayagua's high society, snubbed Comayagua in turn, and moved the government permanently to Tegucigalpa. People moved away too, and Comayagua became just a stopping point on the overland mule trail to the Caribbean coast.

And its churches and few governmental buildings, no longer much attended or used, remained fairly unaltered, so that today, parts of the town constitute a museum of nineteenth-century Honduras.

ARRIVALS & DEPARTURES

By Bus

Comayagua is about an hour's drive from Tegucigalpa, or 90 minutes by bus. All San Pedro Sula buses (from Tegucigalpa) stop along the highway, a kilometer from the town center. To catch a bus to Tegucigalpa or San Pedro Sula, walk or take a taxi to the Texaco station along the highway. One yellow bus shelter is located on each side.

As well, buses operate to Villa San Antonio hourly from 9 a.m. to 3 p.m.; to San Sebastián at noon and 1 p.m. from near the market. Buses to La Paz leave from the Texaco station about every fifteen minutes. There are slower buses to Tegucigalpa from the center of town.

From Tegucigalpa, catch buses for Comayagua and San Pedro Sula at Empresa El Rey, 6 Avenida and 9 Calle, Comayagüela (departures every hour or more frequently, from before dawn to 10:30 p.m.). Fare is less than $3. Buses are comfortable and uncrowded.

Hedman-Alas, 11 Avenida, 13/14 Calles, *tel. 377143*, and Transportes Sáenz, 12 Calle, 7/8 Avenidas, Comayagüela, *tel. 376521*, also offer hourly departures from 8 a.m. to 6 p.m.

ORIENTATION

Comayagua has a population of about 30,000. The altitude of about 300 meters makes it warmer than Tegucigalpa, but not a sweltering tropical town by any means.

To reach the market, follow the street that passes in front of the Cathedral, toward the south, past the colonial museum. Local fiesta days are February 2 through 11 in honor of the Virgin of Lourdes, December 8 (Immaculate Conception), and December 12 (Virgin of Guadalupe, especially celebrated by Indians of the surrounding area).

WHERE TO STAY

Be advised that given the proximity of the **Soto Cano air base**, some of these hotels do an hourly trade.

HOTEL IMPERIAL, *Barrio El Torondón, tel. 720215. 24 rooms. $8 single/$12 double.*

A two-story hotel with a few colonial details on the façade. Simple rooms. Well protected, though the street here is not well lit.

HOTEL EMPERADOR, *on El Boulevard, the access road to town from the main highway. Tel. 720332. 19 rooms. $12 per person.*

Simple, adequate rooms.

HOTEL NORYMAX, *tel. 721210. $18 double. On the same street as the Emperador.*

Clean and pleasant, charming balconies. Nice, modest rooms, and quiet. Small handicraft store. Washing machine available. Restaurant for breakfast. A good buy.

HOTEL LUXEMBURGO, *Boulevard Comayagua.*

Bare rooms, but the beds are clean. About $10 double.

HOTEL QUAN, *Barrio Abajo, tel. 720070, 720190. 20 rooms. $6 single/ $10 double with private bath and fan; $20 double with t.v. and air conditioning. Visa. U.S. contact: Avenues to the World, 1091 Industrial Blvd., San Carlos, CA 94070, tel. 415-592-2090, fax 415-591-8986.*

A more than adequate hotel for the price, especially in the air-conditioned rooms. From the end of the Boulevard, go half a block north.

Other small and inexpensive hotels are near the main square and around the market.

WHERE TO EAT

PÁJARO ROJO. *Located one block north of Hotel Emperador on the entry road.* The "Red Bird" is a more formal restaurant than others in Comayagua, with meals of paella, grilled steaks, seafood and chicken served on an attractive patio. Main courses range up to $6, sandwiches and snacks are lower-priced. There are dancing and live music on some evenings. The same owners operate the **PÁJARO AZUL** ("Blue Bird"), an eatery with breakfast and lighter fare *right along the highway.*

The **CHINA** restaurant *a couple of blocks west of the square* is what it sounds like; and there is another Chinese eatery on the square itself.

SEEING THE SIGHTS

What remains of colonial architecture in Comayagua dates mainly from the eighteenth century. The rustic churches and palaces of the early Spanish administrative center were repaired, expanded, rebuilt and relocated as the town and colony matured. A new flurry of building followed earthquake damage in the middle of the eighteenth century. But independence brought conflicts between government and church, and endemic civil turmoil. Construction fell off, and the architectural fashions of the late colonial period lived on.

The florid rococo style in Spain, known as *Churrigueresque*, had its own peculiar expression in the Americas in the eighteenth century, taking into account local conditions. Heavy, thick-walled, ground-hugging structures were built, on the theory that they would vibrate less and so suffer more limited damage in earthquakes. Decorative detail — flutings, plaster decorations of flowers, saints placed in niches, metal and wood grilles — relieved the heaviness of the buildings. Columns set into walls are especially characteristic of Comayagua and Honduran colonial architecture. Many of the buildings of Comayagua fell into disrepair, as the population declined following the definitive relocation of the capital. Some eventually were replaced by nondescript structures. But, with time, many of the principal buildings of the old capital have now been restored. These, and the cobbled streets and red tile roofs that predominate, lend to Comayagua the air of a city from the past.

Church of La Merced

The **Church of La Merced** was started in 1550 under Bishop Cristóbal de Pedraza. Tradition has it that the church was built on the site of the first mass in Comayagua. It was consecrated as the first Cathedral of Comayagua in 1561 and remained the principal church for fifty years. The square on which it stands was, at the time, the main plaza of the city, the location of the market and of all notable public events.

Originally a rudimentary structure of mud on a framework of sticks, with a thatched roof, La Merced was reconstructed around 1590, of stone and adobe. In 1644, it received an altarpiece as a gift from Philip IV of Spain. To judge by the building seen today, the present structure largely dates from the early 1700s. One of the two bell towers was demolished after it was damaged in earthquakes in 1774.

Cathedral of Comayagua

Three blocks north of the Merced Church, and one block west, is the **Cathedral of Comayagua**, or **Iglesia de la Inmaculada Concepción** (Church of the Immaculate Conception).

The multi-tiered façade of the Cathedral is especially rich in decoration and detail. Two niches to either side of the door contain figures of St. Augustine and St. Jerome. St. Gregory and St. Ambrose are placed in niches on the level above, while on the third level is the figure of the Immaculate Conception, flanked by St. Joseph and St. John the Baptist. Above them rises Christ, with His hands extended. Palms and grapes are depicted in low relief throughout, and characteristically Honduran engaged columns climb the entire height. Unfortunately, all of this is white on a white background, and stands out only when the sun strikes in such a way as to create an interplay of light and shadow.

Alongside the Cathedral is the bell tower, jutting forward and supported by buttresses, with arched openings in four tiers, and crowned with a cupola covered by two-toned ceramics. The smooth walls contrast the detail of the Cathedral fa_ade. The tower clock, crafted by Moors in Seville 800 years ago, reposed in the Alhambra of Granada, before it was donated to the original Cathedral of Comayagua by Philip II. It is quite possibly the oldest working clock anywhere.

Inside, pillars allow natural light to flood the main nave. Formal pews, numerous altarpieces, mosaic floor and paintings are a sharp contrast to the bare, country-church aspect of the other colonial monuments of Comayagua. The Cathedral holds some of the treasures of colonial art in Honduras. The pulpit and three retables are richly carved—one retable, in a side chapel, dedicated to the Holy Sacrament, has a wrought silver front. Solid silver accessories were gifts from Philip IV. The many paintings include the Martyrdom of St. Barth by Murillo, and there are notable statues of saints.

Other Cathedrals & Museums

The **Regional Museum of Archeology**, *located off the street that runs in front of the Cathedral, one block to the north. Hours are Wednesday to Friday 8 a.m. to noon and 1 to 4 p.m., weekends 9 a.m. to noon and 1 to 4 p.m; the museum may sometimes be visited on other days.* The museum is located in the building that was the house of government when Comayagua was capital of the republic. One-story, attractive, it reflects simpler times when the administration of an entire country, such as it was, could be carried out from what today would barely contain a municipal bureaucracy.

La Caxa Real (or *Caja* in modern Spanish), begun in 1739 and finished 1741, was the depository for royal taxes. The building suffered in earthquakes, and now only the front wall remains. If nothing else, its naked state, bare of the plaster and decoration of restored edifices, illustrates colonial construction techniques. Massive stone blocks, bricks, and rubble from older buildings were piled and mortared to form walls up to a meter in thickness.

The **Column of the Constitution** dates from 1820, the eve of Central American independence. The name of the monument refers to nothing local, but to the 1812 Spanish constitution, which was an inspiration for liberal thinkers in the Spanish colonies. Locally, it's called **La Picota** ("the gibbet"), since the gallows and stocks of the town were adjacent.

The **Church of San Francisco** was constructed starting in 1574. The Franciscans were the second religious order in Comayagua, after the Mercedarians, and erecting this church was their first task, and a continuing one. The building was renovated numerous times — in fact, this is the second site of the church. Damaged in a mid-eighteenth century earthquake, its roof crashed down in 1806. In another earthquake, in 1809, the bell tower collapsed.

In the northern part of Comayagua, the **Church of Caridad Illescas** is one of the lesser churches of the town, as it was meant to be. This was a neighborhood parish, serving Indians and mixed-bloods who were required to come here for indoctrination. Construction was started in the early nineteenth century, and not completed for another hundred years.

Basically in baroque style, the Church of Caridad Illescas has a pediment over its main door, and, characteristic of Comayagua churches, a round window toward the top of the façade. The decoration along the top is more flamboyant than that of the earlier Merced church, but the general aspect is simple.

SPORTS & RECREATION

Climbing and hiking have some enthusiasts in this area. If you're interested, *ask for the Alianza Francesa* (Alliance Française), which has a mountaineering club.

PRACTICAL INFORMATION

There are several banks in Comayagua, including Bancahsa, Calle del Comercio; Banco Atlántida, Calle del Comercio; and Banco de Occidente, Calle de Comercio.

Amigo Renta A Car has an agency in Comayagua, *tel. 720371*, and **Cramer Tours** has a branch in town.

North of Comayagua

The main highway continues through the warm, fertile **Comayagua Valley**. From kilometer 94, there is a steep climb, to a pass at kilometer 105, on the continental divide. On one side, waters flow toward the Caribbean; on the other, toward the Pacific. The descent is to the **Siguatepeque plateau**, which is forested with pines, the Honduran national emblem.

Siguatepeque, "Hill of Women," *is four kilometers off the highway, from a junction at kilometer 114*. There is a good American Adventist hospital here, and, at 1140 meters, the climate is relatively cool. From the highway junction, another road cuts to the southwest, to the towns of Intibucá and La Esperanza. Buses operate to Siguatepeque from 8 Avenida, 11/12 Calles, Comayagüela *(Transportes Maribel, tel. 373032)*.

Near kilometer 131, you can see from the road a large kiln, where people burn lime for use in mortar, an activity that has gone on since the time of the ancient Maya. Modern cement still has not replaced old methods. You also see small-scale sugarcane mills — *trapiches* — emitting great plumes of smoke. The view in this region is spectacular, out to multiple peaks, and pastured hills and mountains. Unexpectedly, in the midst of a tropical country, it looks as if you were in Switzerland.

At kilometer 137, a kilometer before **Taulabé**, after an abrupt descent, you can visit the caves called Tarule, or Taulabé. There are stalactites and stalagmites, and, if you look straight up, bats. A boy will guide you through at no charge, though you should leave a few lempiras as a tip. The cave is 400 meters long.

The road is very good this way, but watch out for unexpected potholes. There are many small shops and eateries, where you can stop for a drink, and a plain, home-cooked meal.

Northwest of Taulabé, via a branch road, is **Santa Barbara** (population about 16,000), a regional center that dates from the late colonial period. There are several inexpensive hotels. Palm hats woven here are sold all over Honduras and in neighboring countries.

LAKE YOJOA

At kilometer 149, you get your first spectacular view of **Lake Yojoa** (yo-HO-ah), surrounded by mountains. One of the beauty spots of mainland Honduras, Yojoa has clear waters, and, for a mountain lake of its size and depth (175 square kilometers, up to 40 meters deep), its waters are surprisingly warm. The altitude along the shore is about 600 meters.

Yojoa is best-known, perhaps, for its bass. These are not indigenous — they were stocked, years ago — but they have taken well, and the lake is now a sport fishing center. Anybody can swim, of course, and the few hotels usually have boats and water-skiing equipment available for rent.

ARRIVALS & DEPARTURES
By Bus

Buses on the Tegucigalpa-San Pedro Sula route will let you off at either the Motel Los Remos or at the turnoff for the Motel Agua Azul, near kilometer 164. From the latter point, buses run along the north shore of the lake about every half-hour.

ORIENTATION

Lake Yojoa lies beside the main north-south highway, which follows its eastern shore. From the road, you'll see marshes, and trees growing out of the water, draped in Spanish moss. It is a true paradise for birds. From kilometer 165 (about 80 kilometers from San Pedro Sula), a branch road traces the northern shore, and it is mainly along this route, and right at the junction with the main highway, that you will find the few lodging and eating places and boating facilities that serve visitors.

From the western shore of the lake, a secondary road reaches San Pedro Sula by way of the falls of Pulhapanzak. Hills and mountains overlook the lake, the highest being Mount Marancho, to the west.

Weather & Climate

The Lake Yojoa region gets copious amounts of rain, from clouds trapped by **Mount Marancho**, or Santa Bárbara (2744 meters). September, October and November are the rainiest months around Yojoa, though most of the rain falls at night. February through June are dryer.

During these months, farmers burn the land to ready it for the next crop season. Sometimes, you cannot see the mountains for all the smoke.

Around Lake Yojoa

The lake itself is largely fed by underground streams. It acts as a natural humidifier — everything around is green, and you can feel the moistness. If you spend any time in the area, inspect your camera lens for fungus. Two islands poke out of the lake. The larger is near the south end.

The flat lands around the lake, well-watered and well-drained, afforded good access by roads, are intensively farmed. Sugar cane, coffee and pineapple are the main crops. Coffee especially is grown — the abundant water means that the coffee bush and the trees that shade it can both prosper.

Shade allows for a slow ripening of the coffee bean, and a maximum development of flavor. Gradually, the fruit of the coffee (the *cereza*, or "cherry") turns from green to red, at which point it is ready for picking. The outer skin is removed by simple machines, then the coffee is dried in the sun, which causes the "parchment" layer to flake off. Further drying is accomplished with hot air blowers fueled by oil. The beans then are classified by size and quality. Different sizes and types go to different markets. Italians get small beans sorted by hand. Mechanically sorted coffee ends up in the States (though experts say that the shape has no effect on the taste).

You can visit the coffee dryer at **Peña Blanca** village (see "West of Lake Yojoa" section below), and the coffee plantation at the Adventist school on the road to El Mochito from Peña Blanca. Or ask any farmer in the area for permission to look around. People are very friendly.

The expansion of agriculture in the rich lands around Lake Yojoa has some notably unfriendly effects. The forests on the slopes of Mount Marancho and nearby are legendary for their wildlife. But as trees are cut, some of the jaguars, pumas, ocelots, deer and bears are, in fact, becoming nothing more than legends. There is also concern that agricultural runoff and mining are poisoning the lake's waters.

WHERE TO STAY

There isn't much in the way of accommodation around the lake, and the hotels are scattered.

HOTEL AGUA AZUL (*telephone 527125 in San Pedro Sula*) *is located along the north shore of Lake Yojoa, about 3.5 kilometers from the junction at kilometer 165. There are 21 units. You'll pay $16 double in regular rooms, and up to $25 for a "chalet" (cottage) with six beds.*

Rooms are simple, with old furnishings, but comfortable, and the water from the taps is hot. Maybe I should call this a well-kept fishing

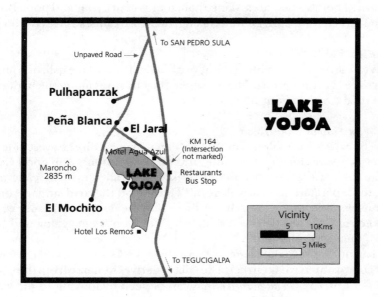

camp. The hotel makes arrangements for bass fishing and boating and water skiing. And the bird watching in the area is excellent. The gardens and landscaping are a fantasy world, and everything is quiet, but for the forest noises, and the nocturnal burps of giant frogs. And there's a pool, if you don't want to jump into the lake.

If you're just passing through for the day, the Agua Azul's shaded lake-view terrace is a good place to try black bass, available here as a filet (you can get it bones and all from any number of roadside stands). They also have a full menu of steaks, chicken and sandwiches, with nothing over $6.

LOS REMOS *(tel. 570955 in San Pedro Sula; there are 19 sleeping rooms in total; the rate is about $15 per person)*

A cluster of motel units and cottages at the south end of the lake, where the road from Tegucigalpa reaches the shore. It's not a luxury place by any means. But everything is clean, and the balcony of the restaurant offers good views. The owners will make arrangements for fishing and boating. There's a launching ramp, in case you're towing your boat.

The **BRISAS DEL LAGO**, *10 kilometers from the highway turnoff, has about 72 rooms going for $60 double, along with several suites at a higher rate. For reservations, call 527030 in San Pedro Sula, 222874 in Tegucigalpa, or fax 533341.*

Some rooms here are air-conditioned and have television and lakeview balcony. There's a play area, dance hall, tennis courts, bar and pool. Boats can be rented for fishing or for cruising; there are canoes and pedal boats.

WHERE TO EAT

You can eat reasonably at the above hotels. Try the lake fish, of course. There are also numerous eateries where the bus stops along the highway, but I'd be careful about them.

The West Side of Lake Yojoa

The road from kilometer 164 to Peña Blanca, on the west side of Yojoa, is one of the nicest in Honduras (in my opinion), with good views to the lake and the surrounding peaks. You will see sugar cane and pineapple plantations. The village of **El Jaral** is off the road, and was once of considerable importance. It was there that the ferry across Lake Yojoa docked, in the days before the highway between Tegucigalpa and San Pedro Sula was completed.

Farther on is **Peña Blanca**, where the paved road ends. The view is attractive from the main street. The village derives its name from the white peak, or outcrop (*Peña blanca*), that can be seen by looking to the west. Buses run between Peña Blanca and the main highway about every half-hour.The **HOTEL MARANTA** *in Peña Blanca* charges less than $10 double for clean, basic rooms. There's a snack bar at the store next to the hotel, charging less than $4 for a home-cooked meal.

El Mochito, to the southwest of the lake, is a mining center for lead, copper and silver, exploited in colonial times.

PULHAPANZAK

About 11 kilometers to the north of Peña Blanca, via a rough road, the **Pulhapanzak Falls** drop down to a natural pool, a great place for swimming. The site is a park, and there's a small admission charge. Groups from San Pedro Sula crowd the facilities on weekends.

To reach the falls by public transport, take the bus from Peña Blanca that runs to San Pedro Sula. One passes about every hour. Ask the driver to let you off at Pulhapanzak village. Or, if you're starting from San Pedro Sula, take the bus for El Mochito. It's a slow ride with many stops. The falls are a kilometer from the village.

There are some Mayan ruins, but to inexperienced eyes they look like hillocks covered with vegetation. Farmers around the lake have discovered numerous Mayan artifacts, though there has been little intensive exploration of the local ruins.

MOUNT MARANCHO
& SANTA BÁRBARA NATIONAL PARK

It is possible to hike to the top of **Marancho** (also known as **Santa Bárbara** mountain), but this is a task for expert adventurers. According to Michael Bell of the U.S. Peace Corps in Honduras, hikers should:
- be experienced;
- have a topographical map, obtainable from the Instituto Geográfico Nacional in Tegucigalpa, and a good compass;
- carry plenty of water;
- have overnight camping equipment; and • carry a machete to clear trails when necessary. The ascent, for people in good condition, takes 15 hours — that's a two-day excursion.

Rainfall is high at the top of the mountain, and vegetation is largely as it was created by nature, due to the difficulty of access. You will walk where no human has gone before, and see vegetation and animal life that looks as if it came from a prehistoric world: giant vines dangling from trees and twisting through vegetation, and huge transparent butterflies. At some places, the ground-level layer of living and rotting vegetation is a meter thick. This is all a very special experience.

Santa Bárbara National Park, covering 130 square kilometers, includes the Yojoa basin, as well as Mount Marancho with its cloud forest, and several caves. The core area covers 5500 hectares. A buffer zone comprises 7500 hectares in which agricultural activities and wood-cutting are controlled. Mount Marancho and its underground sink holes, caves and hollows feed Lake Yojoa and numerous streams, forming one of the major watersheds of Honduras.

SAN PEDRO SULA

One of the oldest cities in Honduras, **San Pedro Sula** is also the newest, the center of industry and trade in the fastest-growing part of the country, with a population of over 300,000. *San Pedro Sula is just 246 kilometers from Tegucigalpa*, and a continent away.

Tegucigalpa has venerable governmental buildings and institutions of learning. San Pedro Sula has factories. Tegucigalpa is where the Mestizo culture of Honduras was formed. San Pedro Sula, if not polyglot, is multicultural, with evident African and Levantine strains. Tegucigalpa, in the mountains, has hills and winding streets. San Pedro Sula, in the lowlands, is flat. Tegucigalpa has buses. San Pedro Sula has buses *and* a railroad. Tegucigalpa developed as the isolated capital of a backwater. San Pedro Sula knows no limits. In the Honduran context, it is Chicago.

Today, San Pedro Sula is a clean, modern, growing town. Yet it is still of a manageable, or human, aspect. Prosperity is obvious, and everything looks efficient. There are no beggars, or few of them. And strangely, there is no visible military presence, which can make you feel uncomfortable if you've become used to seeing soldiers around, as you will in some other parts of Honduras.

Downtown San Pedro Sula is small and mostly uncongested, reflecting the rapid growth of the city after the period of motorization. There are pockets of wealthy suburbs, and little evidence of grinding poverty. There is also very little in the way of points of interest or attractions, except for some annual feasts and celebrations. But San Pedro Sula is *the* starting point for excursions to many other places. You can fly right in from abroad, stay in good accommodations, and continue by road to the ruins of Copán and to points along the coast, on day or overnight trips.

ARRIVALS & DEPARTURES

By Air

• **Aero Costa Rica**, to Orlando, Florida.
• **Continental**, *Gran Hotel Sula, tel. 574141; 574740 at airport.*
• **Copa**, *10 Avenida, 1/2 Calles SW, tel. 520883 (562518 at airport).* To Mexico City, Panama, San José, Costa Rica.
• **Isleña Airlines**, *tel. 562218.* To La Ceiba (three flights daily).
• **Lacsa**, *8 Avenida, 1/2 Calles SW, tel. 526888,* to Costa Rica, Guatemala, Miami, New Orleans, Cancun, Mexico City, New York.
• **Taca**, *9/10 Avenidas, 1/2 Calles NW, tel. 532646.* To San Salvador, Guatemala, Miami.
• **Aero Servicios**, *Gran Hotel Sula, 10 Avenida, 9 Calle NW, No. 9, Los Andes, tel. 534401.*
• **American Airlines**, *Firenze Bldg., Barrio Los Andes, tel. 580518; 682356 at airport.* To Miami, New York
• **Aviateca**, *2 Calle, 1/2 Avenidas NW, tel. 532580.* To Guatemala

The Airport

Ramón Villeda Morales Airport *is located about 12 kilometers east of San Pedro Sula, off the road to La Lima.* A taxi will take you out for about $6. Buses for La Lima will leave you more than a kilometer from the terminal.

The airport has a large duty-free shop, well stocked with perfumes, cigarettes and liquors. Both lempiras and dollars are accepted, and you can buy goods *when you enter* Honduras at this airport, as well as when you're leaving, which saves possible breakage.

By Bus

At least three bus companies provide hourly or near-hourly service between Tegucigalpa and San Pedro Sula. The ride takes about four hours, and the fare is less than $3.

San Pedro Sula to Tegucigalpa: Empresa Hedman Alas 3 Calle, 7/8 Avenidas NW, *tel. 531361*, hourly, with newer buses than those of other companies; Transportes Sáenz, 9/10 Avenidas, 9/10 Calles SW, tel. 531829; and Empresa de Transportes El Rey, Avenida 7, Calles 5/6, tel. 534264, every 90 minutes.

Tegucigalpa to San Pedro Sula: Empresa El Rey, 6 Avenida, 9 Calle, Comayagüela, every hour or more frequently from before dawn to 10:30 p.m. Buses are comfortable and uncrowded. Also Hedman-Alas, 11 Avenida, 13/14 Calles, Comayagüela, and Transportes Sáenz, 12 Calle, 7/8 Avenidas, Comayagüela, hourly departures from 8 a.m. to 6 p.m.

To Puerto Cortés: Empresa Impala, 2 Avenida, 4/5 Calles NW; and Empresa Citul, 7 Calle, 5/6 Avenidas SW, *tel. 530070*. Buses operate about every 20 minutes until 6 p.m.

La Lima, Tela, and La Ceiba: From the Tupsa station, 2 Avenida, 5/6 Calles SW, every five minutes to La Lima (the banana capital) and Progreso. Change buses in Progreso for Tela; or take a La Ceiba bus to the Tela junction, and a taxi into town (less than a dollar for the taxi ride). Buses leave every hour for La Ceiba.

Copán Ruins: Empresa de Transportes Torito, 6 Calle, 6/7 Avenidas SW, *tel. 534930*, has buses going to Santa Rosa de Copán. To reach the ruins of Copán, take this bus as far as La Entrada (two hours), where you can pick up another bus for Copán Ruinas, 64 kilometers and almost two hours and a travel-sickness pill onward. A couple of direct buses are operated daily by Etumi, 6 Calle, 6/7 Avenidas SW, at 10 a.m. and 1 p.m.

Santa Rosa de Copán: Every hour or more frequently by Empresa Torito, 6 Calle, 6/7 Avenidas, SW and Transportes Copanecos, 6 Calle, 4/5 Avenidas SW.

To Guatemala: There are several choices. Continue by bus from Copán Ruinas; take a bus to Santa Rosa de Copán, then continue by bus to the border past Nueva Ocotepeque; or Transportes Impala, 2 Avenida, 4/5 Calles SW with several through buses a day to Nueva Ocotepeque and the border.

Departing By Train

A slow, cheap train leaves in the morning for Puerto Cortés and Tela (with a change of train en route) from the station near 1 Avenida and 1 Calle. *For information, call 531879 or 532997.* If you're a train buff, hurry up and climb aboard before the service is discontinued.

ORIENTATION/GETTING AROUND TOWN

The central area of San Pedro Sula is divided by 1 Calle (running east-west) and 1 Avenida (running north-south) into four quadrants, or zones: *Noreste* (*NE*, or Northeast), *Noroeste* (*NO*, or Northwest), *Sudoeste* (*SO*, or

Southwest) and *Sudeste* (*SE*, or Southeast). Streets are numbered, and addresses in the central area always give the quadrant, using the Spanish abbreviation. (For convenience, I will use the English NW and SW for Northwest and Southwest).

Calles run east-west, *avenidas* run north-south. 4 Avenida downtown is a pedestrian mall (*peatonal*). Avenida Circunvalación is the ring road around the central area. There are also various *colonias*, or suburbs.

Car Rental

Among car-rental companies in San Pedro Sula are:
- **Avis**, *1 Calle, 8/9 Avenidas NW, tel. 530955, fax 578877.*
- **Auto Usados**, *3 Avenida, 19 Calle NW, tel. 534038.*
- **Molinari**, *Gran Hotel Sula, tel. 532639, fax 522704.*
- **Budget**, *tel. 526749, 522295, fax 533411. At Gran Hotel Sula and airport.*
- **Maya Rent a Car**, *3 Avenida, 7/8 Calle NW, tel 522670, and at the Hotel Copantl and the airport.*
- **Blitz**, *1 Calle, 3/4 Avenidas NW, tel. 522405.*
- **Toyota Rent a Car**, *4 Avenida, 2/3 Calles NW, tel. 572644.*

Tourist Office

The local **tourist office** *is on the third floor of the building at 4 Calle, 3/4 Avenidas NW.* They're not very helpful, but if you're starting your Honduras trip here, you can pick up some free maps and accurate information on buses, and weed through the piles of fact sheets that are lying on various counters.

WHERE TO STAY

GRAN HOTEL SULA, *1 Calle, 3/4 Avenidas NW (P. O. Box 435), tel. 529999, fax 576215, 527000. 118 rooms. $85 single/$96 double/$107 triple, $128 in suites. U.S. reservations: tel. 800-223-6764. No charge for children under 12.*

This is a nine-story building right on the main square of San Pedro Sula. The staff is competent and friendly. The rooms (and the hotel in general) are very clean, the mattresses are excellent, and all are provided with coffee makers. All rooms in the main tower have balconies (I recommend those with a view to the pool, a courtyard work of tiled art, complete with cascades and tributaries), and suites have kitchenettes and sleep sofas. There are also some poolside units. Other amenities include a restaurant, 24-hour coffee shop, casino, and assorted boutiques, entry to health club, and twice-daily maid service (extraordinary!).

Discounts — significant ones — are available to Hondurans and resident foreigners.

HOTEL COPANTL SULA, *Colonia Las Mesetas (P. O. Box 1060), tel.*

530900 or 537656, fax 573890. 205 rooms. $90 to $95 single or double. U.S. reservations, tel. 800-328-8897, fax 512-341-7942.

This is the *other* large hotel in San Pedro, located on extensive grounds on the southern outskirts of the city, on the way in from Tegucigalpa, more a grand hotel than any other in town. It's nice, clean, quiet, and modern, with a soaring, dark, multi-story lobby, bar, disco, and country-club facilities that include an Olympic-size pool with diving blocks, pool snack bar, four tennis courts, handball courts, sauna and whirpool, exercise equipment, and massage service for a fraction of U.S. prices.

A free shuttle bus runs every half hour to downtown during daylight hours on weekdays and till noon on Saturday, otherwise you'll have to take taxis or have a rental car if you're going anywhere in town. When the hotel is not full, you might try asking for the corporate rate, the military rate, the resident's rate, or some other discount.

HOTEL BOLÍVAR, *2 Calle, 2 Avenida NW No. 8 (P.O. Box 956), tel. 533224, 531811, fax 534823. 70 rooms. $28-$30 single/$32-$38 double. American Express, Visa, Master Card.*

This is a good, middle-range hotel, a modern building with an excellent central location and attractive grounds, though it could be better maintained. There is air conditioning on the top (third) floor and in poolside rooms. Main courses in the restaurant run $6 or less, with an emphasis on seafood. Protected parking. The hotel is well publicized and often booked up, so reservations are advisable.

JAVIER'S HOUSE, *Calle 9, Avenida 23-24 SW (house 239D), tel. 576322. $45 double with breakfast. U.S. contact: tel. 1-800-553-2513.*

Something new, a bed-and-breakfast, operated by Javier Pinel, a Honduran travel agent who lived many years in the States.

HOTEL AMBASSADOR, *5 Avenida, 7 Calle SW, tel. 576824, fax 575860. 39 rooms. $27 single/$32 double.*

A low-rise, motel-style building in a shopping center the southwest part of San Pedro. Rooms are air-conditioned, some have balconies, there is a coffee shop, and protected parking is provided.

HOTEL PALMIRA. Two locations under one management: **Palmira 1**, *6 Calle, 6/7 Avenidas SW, tel. 576522, 26 rooms*; and **Palmira 2**, *7 Avenida, 4/5 Calles, SW, tel. 522363, 19 rooms. $19 single/$34 double with fan, slightly more with air conditioning.*

In either location, your money buys you a modern, plain room, short on decor and soothing surroundings, but clean and secure.

Businessman Hotels

Somewhat similar to the Palmiras in facilities and atmosphere, or lack of same — Central American businessmen's hotels — are:

HOTEL TERRAZA, *6 Avenida, 4/5 Calles SW, tel. 533108. 42 rooms. 10 and up single/$18 and up double.*

Restaurant, bar, air-conditioned rooms.

HOTEL COLOMBIA, *3 Calle, 5/6 Avenidas SW, tel. 533118 or 575345 . 25 rooms. $17 single/$35 double.*

HOTEL LA SIESTA, *7 Calle, 2 Ave SE, tel. 522650 or 529290. 44 rooms. $10 per person.*

A plain hotel with plain rooms. Some have balconies, facing a busy street.

WHERE TO EAT

There are few restaurants worthy of mention in San Pedro Sula. I have found good eating in some of the better hotels, especially the two noted below:

GRAN HOTEL SULA, *1 Calle, 3/4 Avenidas, NW.* On the first floor, you'll find the 24-hour Skandia diner, with good, simple meals for just a couple of dollars. On the second floor, the more formal Granada restaurant offers a buffet at noon for about $6, and full dinner at night, and, sometimes, entertainment. The cuisine is genuinely continental, and excellent, aside from which it is a very good value. Even Peace Corps volunteers, who stay in two- and three-dollar hotels, come out to dine at the Gran Hotel Sula.

Comparable food, with a higher tab, will be found at the **HOTEL COPANTL SULA**, *on the southern outskirts.*

Chinese

Chinese restaurants with standard Cantonese fare include the **COPA DE ORO**, *2 Avenida, 2/3 Calles SW No. 4*; **LUCKY**, *3 Calle, 3/4 Avenidas, just south of the main square*; the **CENTRAL PALACE**, *4 Calle, 6/7 Avenidas No. 43, SW*; **CHINA TOWN**, *5 Calle, 7 Avenida SW*; and **TAIWAN**, *5 Avenida, 2/3 Calles, NW.*

Other Fare

PAT'S STEAK HOUSE, *out of the way at 5 Calle, 17 Avenida SW (on the ring road, in the vicinity of the Hotel Copantl Sula)* is your best choice if you're looking for a thick cut of beef or a surf 'n turf combo. $10 and up for a meal. Owned by an American, it's often full. *Phone 530939 to reserve before going out.*

LAS TEJAS, *nearby along the curve in the ring road at 9 Calle, 16/17 Avenida*, also serves grilled meats, to a hacienda theme. **JOSÉ Y PEPE'S**, *on Circunvalación at 6 Calle SW*, has steaks, seafood, and Mexican specialties. *They have a more pleasant branch above town in Colonia Palmira, at Avenida República de Panamá 2027.*

CHARLIE'S CHICKEN is a huge roast chicken emporium *at 4 Avenida and 15 Calle NE, near the ring road*. The fare won't hurt your stomach, and it's a good place to take kids if you've had too many burgers with them.

SEEING THE SIGHTS

If I told you there were sights to see in San Pedro Sula, in the usual touristic sense, I would be pulling your leg. Despite San Pedro's long history, all of the city is modern, and there are no notable parks or museums or public institutions. Even the **Cathedral**, with its neo-colonial appearance, is a post-war structure.

You can, however, stroll the streets and get a sense of the commercial life of the town, or shop for handicrafts; though the city is hot for much of the year, especially from April to October, without the cooling sea breezes of the coast. If you're not here for business, you will use San Pedro as a base for visits to Copán, banana country, and the coast to the north.

For an in-town excursion, you can go up to the **Mirador Caprí** (viewpoint) *west of the city*. This is just a parking area and a Coke stand on a hill, about four kilometers from downtown. Take a taxi ($5 or less) or your own car. There are no buses. On a clear day you can see for miles, to the mountains that look over Lake Yojoa to the south.

SHOPPING

The **Mercado de Artesanías Populares**, *6 Calle, 8/9 Avenidas NW*, sponsored by the tourist office, has a variety of sculptures in wood, straw items, pottery, hammocks, silkscreen prints, and primitive paintings. Another large store is **Dicias Novedades**, *4 Avenida mall, 2/3 Calles SW, a half-block from city hall*.

The **Central Market** is *at 6 Calle and 2 Avenida SW, a few blocks south of the main square*. The wares are foods and spices, but if you go without great expectations, you might find straw hats or utilitarian items to your liking. The **Guamilito Market** *is at 6 Calle and 8 Avenida NW*, with more handicrafts than at the Central Market.

Look on the side streets around the Gran Hotel Sula for handicraft shops, and at the small booth in the Central Park. Items offered include wood carvings, paintings, and leather items. And don't pass up the pi_atas and many other items intended for local use that make for interesting knick-knacks once you get them home.

Alongside the highway to Puerto Cortés are stands with fabulous wicker creations: baskets in the form of animals, pendant chairs, benches, sofas, love seats, and much more. You'd need a shipping container to get the big stuff home, but don't let that keep you from stopping and shopping for the small items.

AIDS WARNING

San Pedro Sula is said to have an AIDS infection rate of as high as four percent – comparable to that in Haiti and Thailand. According to journalist Larry Luxner, the prevalence of prostitution, a high incidence of cervical cancer (which leaves women vulnerable to infection), and the proximity of Puerto Cortés with its transient population of sailors, are all factors in this alarming statistic.

Whatever the causes, San Pedro Sula is not the place in which to take risks.

PRACTICAL INFORMATION

Banks

Banco Atlántida, *1 Calle, 3 Avenida NW, tel. 531215*; Banco Central de Honduras, *5 Avenida, 3 Calle SW, tel. 533804*; Banco de Honduras (Citibank), *3 Avenida, 1 Calle NW, tel. 523151*; Banco Continental, *3 Avenida, 2/3 Calles SW, tel. 522744*; Banco Mercantil, *1 Calle, 2/3 Avenidas NW, tel. 534444*; Lloyds Bank, *4 Calle, 4 Avenida SW, tel. 531379.*

For cash advances on a Visa card, contact Bancahsa, *5 Avenida SW No. 46*, or any bank with a Honducard-Visa sign, *or call 580323*. For a cash advance on Visa or Master Card, contact Credomatic, *Ficensa building, tel. 532404*, or any bank with a Credomatic sign.

Consulates

- Belgium, *4 Calle, 4 Avenida No. 28, tel. 527989.*
- El Salvador, *Edificio Rivera y Cía, 5th floor, tel. 534604.*
- Germany, *Berkling Industrial, Puerto Cortés road, tel. 531244.*
- Guatemala, *8 Calle, 5/6 Avenidas No. 38, tel. 533560.*
- Italy, *5 Avenida, 1/2 Calles NW, Constancia building, tel. 523672.*
- United Kingdom, *Teminales Cortés, tel. 532600.*

Fiesta

The big local celebration is on **June 29**, in honor of Saints Peter and Paul. The festivities run for an entire week — at least.

Movies

What the heck, they're cheap. Newspapers don't give the addresses of the cinemas. **The Tropicana** *is at 7 Av, 2 Calle SW*; **The Aquarius** *at 11 Avenida, 2 Calle NW*; the **Presidente** *on 1 Calle west of the park; Los Andes on the ring road.*

Post Office
3 Avenida, 9 Calle SW, No. 75.

Telephones
Hondutel, for long-distance calls, *is at 4 Avenida, 4 Calle SW.* Emergency numbers in San Pedro Sula are the same as in Tegucigalpa:
- **191** – Long distance in Honduras
- **192** – Telephone number information
- **196** – Time of Day
- **197** – International long distance
- **198** – Fire
- **199** – Public security (police)

Tours & Travel Agencies
- **Maya Tropic** *in Gran Hotel and Copantl Sula, P.O. Box 480, tel. 522405, 525401.* Arranges bass-fishing trips to Lake Yojoa, tours to the Bay Islands, and day trips and longer excursions to the ruins of Copán, banana plantations, and along the coast. Maya Tropic is the company that arranges many of the side trips to the mainland offered in conjunction with Bay Islands dive trips.
- **Eco Tours**, *Calle 9, Avenida 23-24 SW (house 239D), tel. 576322. U.S. contact: tel. 1-800-553-2513.* Operated by Javier Pinel, recently of Americas Tours and Travel in Seattle. Mr. Pinel keeps a boat at Lake Yojoa, and arranges custom trips, as well as operating a week-long "Honduran Highlights" tour.
- **Cambio C.A.**, *P. O. Box 2, Trujillo, Colón, tel. 527335 in San Pedro Sula,* arranges rafting trips on the Chamelecón River and hikes in Cusuco National Park (see below), at $90 per person per outing and up.
- **Explore Honduras**, *Paseo del Sol Building, 2 Avenida, 1 Calle NW, tel. 526242, fax 526239.* Considered a reliable operator of trips in northern and western Honduras.
- **Transmundo Tours**, *6 Avenida 2/3 Calles SW No.15, tel. 534752.*
- **Cramer Tours**, *on the Peatonal (4 Avenida SW No. 2, near the Central Park, tel. 577082, fax 576867) and at the Hotel Copantl Sula.* Tours to banana plantation, Copán, the Lancetilla garden.
- **Alas tours**, *3 Calle, 4/5 Avenidas SW, tel. 530345.*
- **Brenda Tours**, *2 Calle SW No. 25-D, tel. 530360, 531770, fax 528129.* Mainly they offer excursions to the Bay Islands.
- **Mundirama Travel Service**, *Edificio Martínez Valenzuela (American Express representative), 2 Calle SW, 2/3 Avenidas, tel. 530490.*
- **Agencia de Viajes Mundiales**, *8 Avenida, 1/2 Calles SW, Roma Building, tel. 532309.*
- **Cosmos**, *10 Avenida, 3/4 Calles, NW, tel. 527270.*

LA LIMA

Two kilometers past the airport is the turn for **La Lima**, capital of bananas. You are surrounded by bananas for as far as you can see. In La Lima, turn right, and you will cross a bridge over the brown Chamelecón River. Alongside is another, pedestrian bridge. Above, **Chiquita** on the water tank watches over.

Past the bridge, on the left side, are the banana company operations, which you can visit if you arrive between 7 a.m. and 10 a.m., or from 12:30 p.m. to 2:30 p.m. It is all impressive. I have eaten bananas all my life, yet until I went to La Lima, I was in the dark about the basics of cultivating this fruit and transporting it to markets worldwide.

The guides will show you everything. Bunches of bananas are covered with plastic to protect the fruit from insects. Plants at different stages of maturity are color-coded. Branches laden with bananas are supported with a special tool while they are hacked off the plant with a couple of expert strokes of a machete. The whole mature plant is then cut down, but for a single shoot that will grow up to replace it. The stem of bananas, meanwhile, is transported to the processing plant, where fruits are washed, separated into bunches, sorted, and washed again. Chemical treatment retards ripening, then the fruit is packed and weighed. Blemished fruits go their separate way, to be processed into baby food. As industrial tours go, this one is off-beat, and well worth taking.

Beyond La Lima, just two kilometers before Progreso, there is a smaller banana processing plant on the left side of the road. With a small tip, you can arrange to visit it, and it takes less time than to see the one at La Lima.

Buses operating on the route to Tela will take you to La Lima for less than 50 cents. While you're out this way, you can also view the classic two-level arrangement of banana towns: standardized housing for the field laborers, which, though it is better than what most people would otherwise inhabit, is still visually dreary and sterile; and pools, golf courses and attractively designed and landscaped residential bungalows for the upper ranks of employees.

DEPARTMENT OF YORO

Most travelers will head north from El Progreso to Tela, La Ceiba (takeoff point for the Bay Islands) and, possibly, Trujillo. To the east, however, is an area little visited and lightly populated, the **department of Yoro**, covering the long valley sheltered from the coast by a ridge of mountains. Some of the residents are the remaining Jicaque Indians who were displaced from the coast by migrations of Black Caribs, and, under the influence of missionaries, adopted settled corn agriculture, much like the Indians of western Honduras.

The **town of Yoro**, capital of the area, dates from 1578. The name derives from the Nahuatl for "center." Many place names in Honduras are in the language of the Mexican Indians who accompanied the Spanish conquerors.

An odd phenomenon is said to re-occur every year between June 14 and 25 in **El Pantano**, just over a kilometer to the southeast of the center of Yoro, when a fierce combination of downpour, thunder, lightning and winds leaves in its wake a scattering of stranded fish. This **"rain of fish"** has given rise to many theories as to its causes. One is that fish from the Atlantic, at the end of their life span, sense and follow an extreme low-pressure system up the Aguán valley to Yoro, and jump ashore when the storm is at its worst.

Montaña de Yoro National Park, covering 155 square kilometers of rain forest south of Yoro, is adjacent to Torupane reserve of the Jicaque Indians. **Ayapa Volcano**, south of Yoro, holds caves with pools inhabited by blind fish.

Olanchito, 243 kilometers from San Pedro Sula, is the center of one of the fastest-growing agricultural areas of Honduras, along the Aguán River. The town was founded in 1530, moved to a new location, and never flourished until recent times. Accommodations for visitors are available at the **HOTEL VALLE AGUÁN**. There are frequent buses to La Ceiba.

Tocoa, to the east, is a bustling commercial center with good, plain accommodations at the **HOTEL SANABRIA**, *tel. 443400.*

THE NORTH COAST

The northwestern lowlands of Honduras — a strip about 50 kilometers wide, backed by mountain ridges for almost 200 kilometers — are the banana republic of Honduras. I don't mean this in any demeaning, stereotyping way. It's just that banana cultivation and commerce in bananas have made this area what it is today.

Farther east, toward the border of Nicaragua, where the land is poorly drained and considered mostly uncultivable, things are much as they were 100, 200, even 300 years ago. Hardly a road penetrates the marshes and forests, transport is mainly by boat, and Indian bands live in scattered groups. The **Garífunas**, or **Black Caribs**, near Trujillo and Tela, and the **Miskito**, **Sumo**, and **Paya Indians** along the eastern stretches of coast, are little known, and little understood, outside their territories.

The main attraction of the north coast, however, is beaches. There are miles and miles and miles of sandy strip, bordered by palms, as idyllic as any. The most accessible parts, near the ports, have some hotels, and even a few rather good resorts. And if it's isolation that you're after, you do not have to travel very far from any coastal town to find a stretch, away from major roads, where hardly anybody has gone before you.

PUERTO CORTÉS

Puerto Cortés is the major port of Honduras, and one of the largest in Central America, with modern container facilities, stretching for five kilometers along a bay near the mouth of the Chamelecón River. Located 57 kilometers from San Pedro Sula and 303 kilometers from Tegucigalpa, it's a hot and humid place, with more than 100 inches of rainfall every year, though some sea breezes relieve the heaviness of the climate.

The modern city of Puerto Cortés dates from 1869, when it was founded on swampland across the bay from the old Spanish port, as the terminus of a new interoceanic railway. The railway never got very far, but Puerto Cortés prospered anyway, as a banana port, and later as a center for oil refining. Oddly, it was also the base of the Louisiana lottery from 1893 to 1895, after a run-in with the U.S. Post Office.

ARRIVALS & DEPARTURES
By Bus

Lodging and eating places are limited; consider taking a local bus for the day to Puerto Cortés from San Pedro Sula. Departures are about every 20 minutes until 6 p.m., from 2 Avenida, 4/5 Calles NW (Empresa Impala) and 7 Calle 5/6 Avenidas SW (Empresa Citul). In Puerto Cortés, the Impala station is at 3 Avenida, 3 Calle, *tel. 550606*. Local buses will take you along the coast to Omoa and Pinalejo.

By Train

A narrow-gauge banana-era train leaves for San Pedro Sula in the morning, and there is daily service to Tela with a change of train. Hurry up and buy your ticket! The railroad has been in a decrepit state since the banana companies switched to trucks and shipping containers, and could disintegrate without prior notice.

By Sea

Puerto Cortés is a port, you are within your rights to insist that it is possible to continue to somewhere by sea. Indeed you can, but patience is required. Large canoes sometimes leave for the Carib towns of Lívingston in Guatemala and Punta Gorda in Belize. This can be a soaking voyage even in mild seas. If you find such a trip, make sure you get your passport stamped before you leave, at the Oficina Regional de Migración on the main square *(tel. 550582)*. The officials there might be aware of any pending departures.

If you're heading up the coast, you'll usually spend less time if you go the long way around, by Copán, to Esquipulas in Guatemala, and then to Puerto Barrios.

ORIENTATION/GETTING AROUND TOWN

For the visitor, Puerto Cortés is almost a dead end. Despite its proximity to Guatemala, there's no way out from here by scheduled transport. Of interest, though, are the old Spanish fort at Omoa, just up the coast, and the beaches nearby. Local buses will take you to the Garífuna villages of **Travesía** and **Baja Mar** just east of Puerto Cortés, or you can walk. There are few facilities.

For use of a beach with services (restaurant, boats, horseback riding), try the Hotel Playa or the Costa Azul.

Maya Rent A Car has an agency *at 3 Avenida, 2/3 Calles, tel. 550064, fax 550218.*

WHERE TO STAY

HOTEL MR. GGEER, *2 Avenida, 9 Calle, tel. 550444, fax 550750. 30 rooms. $25 single/$35 double.*

No, I didn't misspell the name, nor will I explain it. This is a modern hotel, the best in the port, with restaurant and bar, air conditioning, and carpeted rooms with television. A buffet lunch is available most days.

Around Puerto Cortés, you'll find pleasant beaches along the road to the west. And not far from downtown, in the opposite direction from the port, there's one acceptable hotel, the **COSTA AZUL**, *tel. 552260, fax 552262, at the El Faro beach area, $45 single/$50 double.*

HOTEL PLAYA, *Barrio Cienaguita, tel. 551105 or 550453, fax 552287. 25 rooms. $45 single/$50 double.*

This hotel is on the outskirts of Puerto Cortés, four kilometers toward Omoa, then half a kilometer down a side road. Rooms in motel-style low-lying wings, practically on the water, have hardwood panelling, t.v., air-conditioning, phone, and a double and single bed; and there are larger apartments. Landscaping and public areas are somewhat harsh in aspect.

WHERE TO EAT

Two restaurants in Puerto Cortés have no unexpected surprises for your tummy. **EL TORITO** ("The Little Bull") specializes in red meat, and **PLAYA AZUL** ("Blue Beach") serves sea creatures.

PRACTICAL INFORMATION

Banks include **Bancahsa**, **Banco Atlántida** *(2 Avenida, 3/4 Calles)*, **Banco de Occidente** *(4 Calle, 2/3 Avenidas)* and **Lloyds Bank** (2 Avenida, 3 Calle).

OMOA

Omoa dates from late in the colonial period, when the captain-general of Guatemala ordered the founding of a new port, in 1752. The purpose was not only to protect insecure Spanish sea lanes and control smuggling, but to halt the advance of the British, who already had outposts in Belize, the Bay Islands, and at Black River (Río Tinto) in Mosquitia.

Situated east of the mouth of the **Motagua River**, at a deep harbor, Omoa was well situated to serve not only the commerce of indigo from Guatemala, but of silver from Honduras as well, and it remained the major port on the coast for many years.

A major port required a major defense, and in 1759, work was started on the construction of the **Castillo de San Fernando (Castle of San Fernando)**, named for the saint of King Ferdinand VI of Spain, who ordered its construction. Despite its age, the fortress of San Fernando, solidly built, remains in excellent condition. Triangular in shape, it is roughly 200 feet on a side, with walls 12 feet thick and 18 feet high.

Offshore, ships are known to have foundered with Spanish treasure, and at least one wreck with a trove of gold coins was found, in 1972.

ARRIVALS & DEPARTURES
By Bus
Local bus service is available on **Transportes Omoa** from the center of Puerto Cortés to Omoa and the beaches nearby. There are other companies operating directly to the center of Omoa only.

VISITING THE FORT
The **Fortress of Omoa**, *70 kilometers from San Pedro Sula, is open to visitors weekdays from 8 a.m. to 4 p.m., Saturday and Sunday from 9 a.m. to 5 p.m.* A nominal admission charge is collected at the visitors center alongside, an old building with displays that include maps, illustrations regarding Honduran history, cannon, cannonballs, and an anchor. If you insist on taking a camera into the fortress, *they* will insist in turn on collecting a fee of about $5.

The fortress is *massive*, and yet, oddly, it has today the air of a blinded giant, surrounded as it is by pasture and banana fields. A utilitarian work, it is bare of decorative detail, topped by ramparts, with a lower outer wall with corner turrets.

Arched chambers line the interior courtyard, some of them replastered and restored. Certain of the chambers were used as lodgings by Spanish officials, others as kitchens, a chapel, a prison, a gunpowder store. One contains hundreds of cannonballs.

Visitors can walk on the ramparts, where rusting cannon lie, and look out over the fields toward the now-somewhat-distant sea.

Note: Be aware that most of the Fortress of Omoa is unrestored, and conditions are not up to those at tourist sites in countries that have more experience in handling visitors. Restrooms are filthy. Beggars and car-watchers grope tourists. There are no refreshment facilities. However, Omoa is a potential gem, and things can only get better.

Adjoining the fortress is **Centeno Lagoon**. Variations in water level, or perhaps seismic movements, cause its waters to turn sulfurous during the dry season, poisoning many fish.

WHERE TO STAY/WHERE TO EAT

HOTEL ACANTILADOS DE OMOA (*Caribbean Cliff Marine Club*), *P. O. Box 23, Chivana, Omoa, tel. 551461 (526182 in San Pedro Sula), fax 551403. 18 units. Visa, Master Card.*

New and attractive stone-and-stucco cabanas facing the sea on a grassy hillock dotted with pines and bushes. Each unit has a porch and hammocks. There is no pool, nor television, but this is the best hotel in the area, with air-conditioned rooms, private beach, bar, and restaurant. Rates range from about $40 for a unit with a queen and single bed, to $60 for a room with two double beds and refrigerator, to just over $100 for a cottage with two bedrooms and space to sleep eight or more persons. Discounts are available midweek.

The hotel, *about four kilometers east of Omoa*, is part of a recreational complex, and available on site are a convenience store, marina, disco, fishing and other rental boats, and a couple of watering holes and a second restaurant.

Right in Omoa are several inexpensive pensions, the **TULIA**, the **PUERTO GRANDE** and the **CENTRAL**, none of which can be considered "tourist-class," but they'll do if you're on a budget, at $10 or less for a single or double room.

Aside from Acantilados, mentioned above, the safest places to eat near Omoa are the stands on the beach, which offer fried fresh fish and Carib-style conch-and-coconut soup for a couple of dollars and up.

LANCETILLA EXPERIMENTAL STATION

Just south of Tela is the **Lancetilla Experimental Station**, a wonderland of tropical effusiveness and variety. United Fruit established this center in 1926, as part of a program to diversify its plantings in Central America.

The amphitheater of hills around the Lancetilla site protects it from the worst extremes of tropical weather, while the elevated situation provides natural drainage for the copious amounts of water that drop from the sky and flow from the surrounding mountains. By the time the property was turned over to the government of Honduras in 1974, following extensive hurricane damage and rising costs, over a thousand varieties of plants had been established. Some of them were notable success stories. The African oil palm has supplanted bananas on many

United Fruit plantations; and eucalyptus and teak have also shown themselves to be comfortable here.

But the longtime director of the gardens, famed botanist Wilson Popenoe, to whom they are dedicated, did not limit plantings to crops with commercial potential. Ornamental plants have also been an important feature from the beginning, and these, in turn, attract a great variety of birds.

ARRIVALS & DEPARTURES

To reach Lancetilla, take the road from Tela out to the San Pedro Sula highway. The Lancetilla turnoff is about a kilometer out of Tela. Follow the dirt road for three and a half kilometers to the entrance. It's also a rather pleasant walk from Tela of about an hour.

LANCETILLA'S TREES AND PLANTS

Among the many, many species of trees at Lancetilla:

Mahogany, which occurs naturally in the surrounding hills, is notably non-gregarious: one mahogany tree is isolated from the next in the forest or on a plantation. Mahogany wood is used for carving, and for furniture.

Teak, also used for furniture and dishes.

Bamboo plants, examples of different types gathered from all over the world. Some are more than 50 years old, and over 50 feet tall.

Nutmeg trees, which come as male-female pairs.

Cinnamon trees in several varieties.

Strychnine trees, which you cannot even touch without serious consequences, including, possibly, death. If you go out in the morning, you can see the bodies of birds that pecked at strychnine trees and dropped dead on the spot. Only certain ants can consume this tree.

A tree native to Africa produces a fruit that can be eaten only during four days a year, when cyanide compounds are absent. The rotting fruit is deadly. (Could this be the original forbidden fruit?)

Another tree produces a delicious fruit after 35 years of growth, under the best of conditions — obviously not a candidate for commercial plantations. I'm also told that there are coca plants in the park, which you might recognize by the parallel veins in their leaves.

The orchid collection can also be viewed, and plants are available for purchase. Check import regulations before leaving home, or else pass up this opportunity.

Everything at Lancetilla is labeled with color-coded tags: *yellow* for ornamental, *red* for fruit, *green* for timber, and *black for poisonous.*

HOURS

The garden is open from 7:30 a.m. to 3:30 p.m. weekdays, 8:30 a.m. to 4 p.m.

on Saturday and Sunday, closed on Monday except for the nursery. You should arrive an hour before closing at the latest in order to see anything.

I recommend that you go in the early morning, about 6 a.m., if you're on foot, in order to beat the heat, and to see all the birds that congregate in the trees along the way, toucans and many other parrots, motmots, oropendulas, and the Central American curassow, among others. There are more than 200 species, in fact, which can be seen in the area and in the park. A checklist is available at the visitors' center.

PRACTICAL INFORMATION

There is a restaurant at the entrance of the park, or you can picnic in designated areas. A map is given to visitors, but you should look into guide service when you arrive. There is no fee for a tour, but a tip is appropriate. Not all guides speak English.

SAN JUAN & TORNABÉ

Several small **Garífuna** villages lie along the coast not far from Tela. **San Juan** is four kilometers to the west, and **Tornabé** is another three kilometers beyond. Both are reached by local bus from Tela.

The Garífunas, or Black Caribs, speak a language all their own, which is said to be of Amerindian origin, though some of their vocabulary can be recognized as coming from Creole English. Their houses are of bamboo and thatch, and blasting out from them is reggae music. In fact, Garifunas walk as if they are dancing. They are interested in visitors, not least to be included in their photos.

If you're lucky, you can join the Garífuna in a meal of conch soup or some other stew-type dish based on seafood. Or, at the very least, buy coconut bread.

Buses for Tornabé leave from Tela as they fill up. The fare is minimal, or you can take a collective taxi from the main square for less than a dollar.

Punta Sal Marine National Park, *adjoining the Garífuna villages*, is a protected area of beach and sea that includes reefs, wrecks, beaches, swamp, wet savanna, coastal lagoons, and cliffs — a varied combination in a small area. Wildlife in the park includes ducks, manatees, caimans, and various species of monkey. The park stretches inland over more than 400 square kilometers.

Access is on foot or by boat from Tela. There are trails in the most easily accessible sections, and a couple of isolated fishing villages offer supplies in a pinch.

WHERE TO STAY IN TORNABÉ

THE LAST RESORT, *P. O. Box 145, Tela, tel. 482591.*
A new colony of eight bungalows on the edge of Tornabe, offering

one of the few comfortable beach accommodations outside a major town. Managed by a Swiss-and-Honduran couple, the complex has a bar, restaurant, palm-shaded deck, and individual units that sleep up to five persons, equipped with fans and private bathrooms. Water craft (including a catamaran) are available for exploration of the adjacent Micos and Diamond lagoons, and of nearby Punta Sal National Park, and diving and snorkeling can be arranged. The resort also has a van available for excursions to Lancetilla Gardens and other coastal attractions, and to pick up guests in Tela.

LA CEIBA

La Ceiba, *65 kilometers east of Tela*, is Standard Fruit's town, a banana port where ships move in, and sailors move about, with all their traditional carousing. Hondurans say that "Tegucigalpa is where we think, San Pedro is where we make money, and La Ceiba is where we have fun." This is the only city in Honduras where *Carnaval* is celebrated in the great fashion of the Caribbean islands. La Ceiba's *carnaval*, nominally in honor of San Isidro, takes place during the third week in May, with dances, parades, beauty queens, floats, and general fooling around.

In the annals of banana exploits, La Ceiba and Standard Fruit are known for developing the giant Cavendish variety of banana to substitute for the *gros Michel*, which is regularly laid low by Panama disease. Out in the market, Standard is better known by its brand name, Dole. Dole pineapples as well as bananas now keep the port busy. For visitors, La Ceiba is the main jumping-off place for the Bay Islands.

ARRIVALS & DEPARTURES
By Air
Service is provided from **Golosón Airport** west of town (about $2 by taxi) by:

Isleña Airlines, *Av. San Isidro at the main square, tel. 430179, fax 432632.* To San Pedro Sula (four flights daily), Tegucigalpa (two flights daily), Bay Islands, Puerto Lempira, Palacios.
- To Roatán *(Bay Islands)*: at least five times daily, currently at 6:30 a.m. (except Sunday), 8 a.m., 10 a.m., 2 p.m. and 4:30 p.m.; fare $20 one way.
- To Guanaja *(Bay Islands)*: daily except Sunday at 6 a.m., 12:30 p.m. and 4 p.m.
- To Utila *(Bay Islands)*: daily except Sunday at 6 a.m. and 4 p.m.; fare $15 one way.

Lansa Airlines, *Avenida San Isidro by Central Park, tel. 422354.* To Bay Islands.

Aerolíneas Sosa, *tel. 430884.* Flights in coastal region, to Tegucigalpa and Bay Islands in Twin Otters.

By Bus

The bus station is off Calle 11 at Blvd. 15 de Septiembre — go south, then west from the main square. Tupsa buses direct for San Pedro Sula depart every one to two hours from 5:30 a.m. to 5:30 p.m., stopping only at El Progreso. Fare is about $3.

Buses leave about every two hours for Trujillo, from 4 a.m. to 3:45 p.m. Service to Tela is almost continuous, and there are less frequent buses to other regional towns.

By Train

The morning train will take you from San Pedro Sula to Tela. An early afternoon train will take you back.

By Boat to the Bay Islands

If you want to go to Utila, Roatán or Guanaja by boat, head for the pier and ask around for the next boat out, or inquire at the San Carlos bar. Usually, boats leave two or three times a week, and charge $5 or less for the trip. Travel time is four to five hours, depending on the craft.

Boats leave when they are full — and you'll learn what "full" really means. As for the crew, you'll see characters with one tooth, and I'm told that a Captain Hook-type is sometimes espied. Some boats go to Roatán only, some stop at Utila or Guanaja. Just let me remind you here that the air fare is reasonable and the flight is short.

GETTING AROUND TOWN

La Ceiba, with a population of about 60,000, is low-lying and hot, but, despite its banana-port history, it's a surprisingly pleasant place. Streets are paved, and clean. Breezes blow through. Along the sea is a single great pier, culminating in a lighthouse, and, until repairs are made, severed neatly in two, a hurricane casualty. A canal with clean water cuts through, lined by the shady, broad-crowned *ceiba* trees (silk-cotton, or kapok) for which the city is named.

Car Rental
• **Molinari**, *Gran Hotel París, tel. 420055 or 432371.*
• **Maya Rent A Car**, *Hotel La Quinta, tel. 430224.*

Tourist Information

Visitors' information is available in the office *at 1 Avenida and Avenida San Isidro, near the sea.*

WHERE TO STAY

HOTEL COLONIAL, *Av. 14 de Julio, 6/7 calles, tel. 431953, fax 431955. 60 rooms. $22 single/$32 double.*

A newish hotel with conference facility, sauna and whirlpool (if no swimming pool), rooftop bar, restaurant, and souvenir shop. Rooms have air conditioning, telephone and color television. Safe-deposit boxes available, protected parking. And as the name suggests, decor is wrought iron and dark wood.

GRAN HOTEL PARÍS, *Parque Morazán (P. O. Box 18), tel. 432371, fax 432391. 89 rooms. $40 single/$45 double.*

The Gran is the oldest of the good hotels in La Ceiba, a secure, three-story office-type building overlooking Ceiba's main square. Rooms are clean and air conditioned, there is a nice, clean pool, and personnel are well trained and helpful; though this is hardly a luxury hotel, and maintenance could be better. Take a room on the pool side, which is quieter. If you miss your connecting flight to the Bay Islands, because of bad weather, delays into the night, or whatever, this is where you'll probably end up. Coffee shop, good restaurant, parking.

HOTEL PARTENON BEACH, *Barrio La Isla, Calle de la Barra 12 tel. 430404, fax 430434. 45 rooms. $22 single/$28 to $34 double/$57 in suite. Master Card, Visa.*

A modern, new beachfront hotel. Rooms are carpeted, with private bath, air conditioning, television. On-site are a pool, one of the better restaurants in Tela, and car-rental agency. A good value — and rooms without sea view are slightly lower priced. Reliably answers faxed reservations requests — unusual in Honduras!

HOTEL LA QUINTA, *tel. 430223, fax 430226. 113 rooms. $30 to $40 single/$36 to $40 double/$50 for four persons.*

Booming La Ceiba's most booming hotel is opposite the golf course, about ten minutes from the airport. Recently enlarged, La Quinta consists of motel-style rooms surrounding a pool, each air-conditioned, with carpeting, television, and phone. Some rooms have refrigerators. The beach is ten minutes away, with transportation available from the hotel.

GRAN HOTEL CEIBA, *Avenida San Isidro, 5 Calle, tel. 432737. 40 rooms. $25 double. Master Card, Visa.*

This is a plain, modern hotel with an eighth-floor view terrace, air-conditioned rooms, bar, and coffee shop. Only the name is grand. Second-best in town, centrally located. Rooms have private bath and phones.

WHERE TO EAT

RICARDO'S, *Avenida 14 de Julio at 10 Calle.* This could be where you'll have your best meal in Honduras. Owned by a Honduran-American couple, Ricardo's offers air-conditioned seating, or dining on a very nice terrace, decorated with plants and protected from the rain.

There is a variety of seafood, beef and pasta dishes, and a good selection of wines. Service is excellent. For what you get, it's not all that pricey, $10 per person or less.

PARTENÓN BEACH, *at 12 Calle on the way to the Tela highway*, offers Greek-style food. The seafood crepes are excellent.

The **GRAN HOTEL PARÍS** is also said to set a good table.

NIGHTLIFE

For many visitors, and for many Ceibeños as well, night and dancing and drinking are what Ceiba is about.

Among dance halls (locally called *discos*), popular spots include the **Coco View**, *in Barrio Potreritos*. Music is decidedly Caribbean, including reggae and the punta rock of the local Garifuna people. The dance area is air-conditioned, and patrons are required to leave their shooting irons at the door. (This is a fact, and it is not necessarily the case at other establishments.)

La Costa, *along the beach*, specializes in salsa and other popular Latin music, and serves light meals. The **Ocean Club**, *located where Avenida 14 de Julio meets the beach*, is owned by gringos, and as of recently, was not charging admission. Music is Latin and rock, and burgers and undergraduate-style filling foods (spaghetti and meatballs) are served. **El Cayuco** is a dancing shack *right at the water's edge*, active at almost every hour. Away from the beach, *in Barrio La Isla*, **Black and White** is popular for all-night dancing, and piñata-busting on Sunday afternoons.

Cover charges of a dollar or so, more on weekends, are collected at most dance halls.

The **San Carlos Bar** (with hotel rooms) *is near the Hotel Iberia*. Don't forget your cowboy hat and kicker boots. Park your horse in front and flop the saloon doors open.

SHOPPING

Various shops offer wood crafts and the like; one is **El Buen Amigo**. **Deco-Arte**, *near Ricardo's Restaurant*, has handicrafts and works of art selected with good taste, and of a quality much higher than you'll generally find in Honduras. Unusually, they have crafts from other Latin American countries as well. Other shops are **El Regalito**, *north of the Plaza*, and the large **El Buen Amigo** store, which sells maps.

PRACTICAL INFORMATION
Banks

Banco Central de Honduras, A⸱ ⸱ la República, tel. 420622;

Bancahsa, *9 Calle, Avenida 14 de Julio/San Isidro, tel. 430547*; **Banco Atlántida**, *Avenida San Isidro, tel. 431008*; all these in addition to street money changers on the main square (parque central) in front of the Gran Hotel París.

Insects

For visitors interested in insects, the high point of La Ceiba will be a visit to the **entomology museum (museo de entomología)** at the **Regional University Center of the Atlantic Coast (CURLA)**. More than a thousand specimens are on display, including many, many spectacular butterflies, and a rare homoptera known as the peanut head.

Hours are 8 a.m. to 5 p.m. during the week, and a free bus to the campus leaves every half hour from Manuel Bonilla Park, downtown.

Travel Agencies

For assistance in getting to the Bay Islands, or out of the country, try:
- **Lafitte Travel**, *Hotel Iberia, tel. 420115, fax 431391.*
- **Caribbean Travel**, *Hermanos Kawas building, Avenida San Isidro, tel. 431361, manual fax 431360.* Rents houses in Utila and arranges **rafting** trips on the Cuero and Cangrejal rivers. The cost is about $75 per person, including lunch and pickup at your hotel or at the airport. The season runs from October to May, and the guides are from the Rocky Mountain Outdoor Center in Colorado.
- **Transmundo**, *Hotel París, tel. 422820.*
- **Honduras Tours**, *Calle 12, Avenida 14 de Julio, tel 432828.*
- **Cambio C.A.**, *P. O. Box 2, Trujillo, Colón, tel. 431399 in La Ceiba*, specializes in low-impact nature-oriented trips (also known as ecotourism). They offer tours to Cuero y Salado National Park (see below), hikes through rain forest in Pico Bonito National Park to the south of La Ceiba, and arranges rafting on the Cangrejal river. Rates range upward from $60 per person per outing.

Near La Ceiba

As elsewhere along the coast, beautiful and near-deserted beaches lie to the east and west of town.

At **Perú**, a fishing village *about 10 kilometers east of La Ceiba*, there are roofed shelters with barbecues and picnic tables available for day use, for a nominal fee.

Corozal, a Garífuna beach village *about 15 kilometers east of La Ceiba*, can be reached by hourly bus. Along the way is **Piedra Pintada** ("Painted Rock"), a greenish-yellow outcrop in an otherwise flat landscape. And there are other fishing villages with attractive and little-visited beaches in both directions from La Ceiba.

Esparta and **El Porvenir**, *to the west,* aside from their sands, are known for the so-called "crab invasions." In July and August, the creatures race through town in the thousands toward inland destinations.

CUERO Y SALADO NATIONAL PARK

Cuero y Salado National Park, *roughly 20 kilometers west of La Ceiba,* takes in 85 square kilometers of coastline, river estuaries and navigable canals lined by lush vegetation, and includes the major protected manatee habitat on the Caribbean coast of Central America. Spider, white-faced and howler monkeys, crocodiles and caimans, jaguars and many kinds of small mammals also inhabit the area. Plant species include water lilies an royal palms.

Access to Cuero y Salado is by hand-operated coconut railway cars (*"burras"*) from the village of La Unión, just off the highway — the park includes old coconut plantations, canals dug by United Fruit, and villages. Dormitories, campsites and trails are being developed. Limited sleeping and eating facilities are available at the moment.

For details of current conditions, inquire at the **"Fucsa"** *(Cuero y Salado foundation) office in La Ceiba, on 1 Calle at Avenida Atlántida, near the sea,* or at **COHDEFOR**, *tel. 420800.* Fucsa can arrange overnight stays.

MOSQUITIA

Seeing Mosquitia with a Tour Group

Organized excursions to the forests and tribes of the interior are offered by **Cambio C.A.**, the low-impact travel service based in Trujillo. Among offerings are a visit to the Tawahka, a Sumo group three days' journey from the coast, who have maintained their traditions.

La Mosquitia Ecoaventuras, a younger company than Cambio C.A., also offers ten- to fourteen-day low-impact adventures in Mosquitia, with emphasis on birding, wildlife viewing, and non-intrusive contacts with native peoples. *Information is available from La Mosquitia Ecoaventuras, P. O. Box 3577, Tegucigalpa, tel. 370593, fax 379398.*

Seeing Mosquitia On Your Own

There are no guarantees about getting into, through, or out of Mosquitia. There are only a few dirt tracks into the region that radiate from Puerto Lempira. Most transport is by water (unscheduled, of course), and hotels and pensions are difficult to find, or non-existent in many localities.

Arriving By Air

Isleña Airlines, *in La Ceiba (Av. San Isidro at the main square, tel. 430179, fax 432632)* operates at least one flight daily to Puerto Lempira and Palacios along the coast of Mosquitia, fare $35 to $45. Air taxis can also take you to the landing strips in the interior (if you happen to have a contact with a missionary who will put you up).

ORIENTATION

If you arrive in Palacios or Puerto Lempira on your own, you certainly won't be the first gringo adventurer. You can find a room, and there are people who will hire out dories and dugouts for trips along the waterways. You can hike along the beaches from village to village, and rent sleeping space or pitch your tent (above high tide, please). Boats can be found to take you across estuaries, and at the village of Plátano, pilots will negotiate trips of up to several days into the Río Plátano Biosphere Reserve, though you can't expect any mercy when it comes to rates.

Stocks of food in the few stores are limited, so take your own reserve. Insect repellent, water purification equipment, jungle camping equipment, tropical boots, rain protection and plenty of time and tolerance and patience will also come in handy.

Río Plátano Biosphere Reserve covers a huge mass of land from the Caribbean inland to the fringe of Olancho department, where a rising population threatens the survival of primeval forest and the plant and animal species that inhabit the region. Agricultural and hunting activities by settlers are supposed to be controlled within the reserve, but in practice, land is cleared and animals are hunted with little restriction.

Río Plátano reserve includes **petroglyphs**, designs carved into rocks by ancient peoples. The banks of the River Plátano are especially rich in these prehistoric remnants. Other such designs are found in the caves of the Ayasta Canyon in south central Honduras, and cave paintings have been found in Nueva Armenia, south of Tegucigalpa. The Plátano petroglyphs, on riverside boulders, are generally serpentine in appearance, though at least one notable figure, at Walpunbantara, is recognizably an iguana.

A "lost" city called **Ciudad Blanca** is also said to lie within the confines of the reserve, the remains of a vast city built by a mysterious ancient culture. While no individual metropolis has been found, any of the petroglyph sites could well have been the origin of the legend of the lost city. Some consider that the archeological site known as Limonsito is, in fact, the lost White City.

Smaller reserves to the east include **Caratasca**, surrounding much of the Caratasca Lagoon, and the **Río Kruta** reserve, on the border with Nicaragua, where the rare harpy eagle is found.

THE BAY ISLANDS

More than a stretch of water separates mainland from islands. Mainlanders speak Spanish, while Bay Islanders speak English (sort of). Mainlanders are farmers. Islanders are fishermen and mariners and boatbuilders. Mainlanders are mostly *mestizos*, descended from Spaniards and native Americans. Bay Islanders are largely descended from Africans and Englishmen, from slaves and buccaneers and pirates.

And for the visitor, the Bay Islands are a world removed not only from the mainland, but from everywhere else in the universe, a paradise of beach and rain-forested peaks in the sea, with few telephones, clocks, or cares, and some of the best fishing and diving in the hemisphere.

Before the Spanish came to the Americas, the Bay Islands were most likely populated by Paya Indians. Many old dwelling sites have been identified, and pieces of pre-Columbian ceramic are still occasionally found.

Early English settlers came in peace. The Providence Company colonized Roatán in 1638 with Puritan farmers from Maryland. They called the place Rich Island, cut logwood trees for export, and grew tobacco and indigo, and cassava as a staple. Their colony, possibly located near today's Old Port Royal, lasted four years. In 1642, the Spanish threw out the Puritans, helpless and defenseless as civil war raged in England.

Spain followed a policy of keeping *everybody* out of the islands, so that no food could be grown, no shelter erected, that might be used by enemies. This policy turned many Indians into allies of the English pirates who continued to use the islands, despite the best efforts of the Spanish. A pirate camp at Port Royal was overrun by the Spanish in 1650, and all natives who could be found were exiled to the mainland. But pirates still returned to take on fresh water from island streams, hunt wild pigs, and dry turtle meat. Some say the loot from Morgan's 1671 raid on Panama is buried on Roatán.

In 1742, the British government moved to take the islands as part of a military campaign against Spain. New Port Royal on Roatán was fortified. Spanish attacks failed to dislodge the British, but diplomacy did the trick. The British evacuated in 1748.

When war between Britain and Spain broke out again in 1779, Roatán became a refuge for woodcutters displaced from the coast. Troops and refugees resisted bitterly at Fort George in 1782, but were obliged to surrender after two days. As many as 500 dwellings are said to have been burned. The fort was destroyed, and the black survivors sold into slavery.

The islands were nearly deserted once again, but not for long. In 1797, Britain marooned 5000 Black Caribs on the Bay Islands. The unfortunates, descendents of Carib Indians and shipwrecked African slaves, had rebelled against British rule on the island of Saint Vincent.

Spain, still maintaining a no-go policy, obliged the Caribs to move to the mainland near Trujillo, by that time virtually abandoned due to repeated British attacks; though some managed to stay on at Punta Gorda on Roatan's north shore.

The modern culture of the Bay Islands really dates to Central American independence. After 1821, Central America maintained a garrison in the islands, but the weak, decentralized country was no longer able to defend its territorial claims. White Cayman Islanders, fearful of black domination after the abolition of slavery, began to migrate to the Bay Islands, which some knew from fishing and turtling expeditions.

In 1849, the residents applied to be governed by the authorities in Belize. A local 12-man legislature was established, and in 1852, England formally annexed the Bay Islands. The new British expansion caused a fury, however, especially in the United States, despite the long tradition of British involvement in the islands and along the coast. In 1859, Britain gave in to U.S. pressure, and ceded the islands to Honduras.

For many years thereafter, despite the abolition of English-language schools under Honduran administration, and the settling of small numbers of mainlanders, the islanders were mostly ignored by the distant government in Tegucigalpa, and continued to live lives apart from the mainland mainstream. The Bay Islands developed an export agriculture of coconuts and plantains long before the mainland.

Today, many islanders are still merchant seamen and skilled boatbuilders. And fishing, for the dinner table or for the market, remains the most important occupation. Though tourism is fast becoming the mainstay of island life, and migrants from the mainland are becoming a more and more significant part of the population.

ARRIVALS & DEPARTURES
By Air

Guanaja and Utila have airstrips, while the runway on Roatán can handle jets. The new **Roatán International Airport Terminal** just opened as this book went to press.

Approximate schedules from La Ceiba, San Pedro Sula and Tegucigalpa to the islands are given elsewhere. From Tegucigalpa, the round-trip fare to the islands is about $130; from La Ceiba, about $40. Runways on the islands have no electric lighting.

If there is an evening delay in your connection, you could be "forced" to overnight on the mainland at San Pedro Sula or La Ceiba before continuing to the islands the next morning. If you have a confirmed connection, the airline picks up the tab, and you get to see more of Honduras than you might have otherwise.

Private planes must land and clear customs first on the mainland, most conveniently at La Ceiba.

By Boat

Yachties and others of that ilk can consult the *Cruising Guide to the Honduras Bay Islands*, available from Wescott Cove Publishing Co., P O Box 130, Stamford CT 06904. Fuel is available at the larger towns. Seas are generally choppy, with steady south-southeast winds of about 15 knots.

If you don't sail down, you can find a sailing vessel for hire in the Bay Islands. Start your search by contacting **Roatán Charter**, *Box 877, San Antonio, FL 33576, tel. 800-282-8932, fax 904-588-4158.* One of the vessels they represent is the 46-foot sloop *Honky Tonk*, currently for hire at $900 per person and up on a weekly basis, including beach barbecues and nights spent in ports and coves throughout the Bay Islands.

Passenger boats operate to the Bay Islands several times a week from La Ceiba, though it's generally more convenient to fly.

Bay Islanders are famed boat builders. Many craft are *dories*, elongated and similar to sailboats, and now often fitted with rudders, though traditionally they have had none; and dugout *cayucas*, canoe-like vessels made from hollowed logs.

ORIENTATION

Located about 60 kilometers offshore, the islands, running in a 125-kilometer arc, are the tips of undersea mountains that extend out from the mainland's Omoa ridge. Their peaks, rising as high as 400 meters (1300 feet), are covered with oak and pine and cedar and dense, broad-leafed undergrowth, and studded with caves and cliffs. Coral reefs, often within swimming distance of shore, virtually surround most of the islands, forming natural breakwaters, and creating ideal, calm pools for diving, fishing, swimming and sailing.

Roatán is the largest of the Bay Islands, with the major towns, though there are also settlements on **Utila** and **Guanaja**. The smaller islands are **Morat, Helene** (Santa Elena) and **Barbaret** (or Barbareta). With more than 60 smaller cays offshore, the Bay Islands cover about 92 square miles.

Population

About 22,000 persons inhabit the Bay Islands altogether, about 15,000 on the main island of Roatán, about 5500 on Guanaja, and 1500 on Utila. In addition to fishing and boatbuilding, some make a living harvesting and drying coconut meat, or copra, and many keep gardens of root vegetables, especially cassava. Local cuisine is heavy on fish, of course, but also on coconut, as in coco bread.

SPORTS & RECREATION
DIVING

What can you say about the diving? First, diving is what the Bay Islands are most known for. Second, the water is warm. Temperatures range between 79 and 84 degrees Fahrenheit (26 degrees to 29 degrees C). Third, underwater visibility is good. The water is not as clear as in Bonaire, but it is crystalline nevertheless. Visibility can vary with the weather. The sea is calm within the fringing reefs, and there are practically no drift currents along the south side of the islands.

And if you like **coral reefs**, you'll find the corals around the Bay Islands spectacular, intact, and very much alive (coral can get silted up and damaged by hurricanes, among other things).

The islands are each surrounded by coral reefs, from 20 to 40 feet down. Almost all of the coral types specific to the Caribbean can be found in the reefs off the Bay Islands. One of the most unusual and characteristic types is pillar coral, which reaches several feet in length. Others are elkhorn, star, lettuce and brain coral. And there are multi-hued rope, vase, finger and barrel sponges, flittering sea fans, and schools of rainbow colored fish, indigo hamlets, parrot fish, rock hinds, chromis and others that favor the reefs, seahorses, sea urchins, anemones, polyps, and more ordinary snappers and jacks and groupers and sea turtles. In deeper waters are manta rays.

The underwater landscape features wandering clefts and caverns, sheer walls, cracks, tunnels, caves and ledges, reverse ledges, and dropoffs of 100 to 200 feet. Walls start as little as twenty feet under the surface, which affords more natural light than is usually available in wall diving.

Famous sites include **Mary's Place**, off Brick Bay, a huge crack in the ocean floor (called the Grand Canyon of wall diving, and currently off limits because of over-visitation); **Bear's Den**, a formation that in earlier times was a waterfall, until the shifting of continental plates submerged it; the **Enchanted Forest**, planted with black coral and sea fans; **West End Wall** and **CoCo View Wall** off Roatán, and **Captain's Crack**, off Guanaja.

Wrecks include the *Prince Albert*, off CoCo View Resort on Roatán, and the *Jado Trader*, off southern Guanaja, and there are proprietary wrecks near some of the resorts. Others, reputed to be from colonial times, are only discussed in whispers.

I'm told there are few sharks, and, for what it's worth, I haven't seen any.

Most of the resorts that offer diving make life easy. The diving equipment and compressors are on the dock, right at the diving boat. There is nothing to lug, and no loss of time. Diving sites are usually no more than 20 minutes away. Many hotels have interesting coral formations and submarine landscapes within easy range of shore dives.

DIVING HIGH POINTS

Major points to consider about diving in the Bay Islands:
- *Decompression chamber available (at Anthony's Key Resort)*
- *Wall diving a major feature*
- *Several wrecks to dive*
- *Easy diving from shore – unlimited at a number of resorts*
- *Excellent variety of coral and fish*
- *Lowest package diving prices in the Caribbean*
- *Diving available on opposite shores of Roatan – sheltered diving off the south when winds are up on the north side.*
- *Live-aboards available*
- *Minimal travel time to dive sites–minutes in many cases.*
- *Many small resorts and representative agencies willing to answer visitors' questions before money is put down*

DIVING LOW POINTS

- *Sand flies are a nuisance on shore*
- *Limited entertainment and other non-diving resort amenities*
- *Limited dive shops outside of resorts*
- *Diving is built into most rates. Non-diving companions get little or no discount*

Waters are generally clearest for diving during the periods when there is the least rain: mid-February to mid-September. The onset of hurricane season and winds can churn up the waters during the late months of the year. But the same conditions help to distribute the nutrients in the water, and encourage growth of undersea life.

You *must* be certified to dive at Bay Islands resorts. If you're not, you can arrange to take courses for PADI or SSI certification.

Airlines have the usual baggage limits of about 45 pounds or two pieces.

Diving Live-Aboards

Terrific diving is within easy reach of almost any hotel on the Bay Islands, even if you just wade out from shore. Absolutely superb diving, at sites where the sea creatures are not yet accustomed to seeing masked humans, is a little farther out. To reach a number of such sites requires dragging your gear to the dock every morning, setting out for a long ride, returning for lunch, setting out again, and returning to your hotel, followed by repeated packing up and unpacking as you move on to your next diving base.

Or, you can live aboard your dive boat, and roll off the dive platform shortly after you roll out of bed.

Live-aboards come at a price. A week-long trip, with six days of diving, runs from $1000 to $1500, based on double occupancy. And the diving can be tougher. You'll spend more time in the water, probably at greater depths than if you dive from a shore base, sometimes in uncharted seas. Medical help in an emergency is *not* at hand.

But live-aboards also come with amenities: sundecks, video libraries for evening entertainment, good-sized rooms, and often photo-processing facilities. And since the diving is usually limited only by decompression tables and safety considerations, the cost *per dive* can turn out to be even more reasonable than from a land base. As many as five daily dives are scheduled.

Here are some of the live-aboards currently operating in the Bay Islands:

The *Bay Islands Aggressor*, 110 feet, carries 18 passengers in air-conditioned cabins (two to four persons each). Showers and toilets are shared. Features include sun-and-shade deck, video entertainment, bar, equipment and underwater cameras for rent, and on-board slide processing. Certification and specialty courses are available. The rate is about $1400 per person for a weekly trip with five-and-a-half days of diving throughout the islands and the Hog Cays, *with discounts available from September to February*. Resort and certification courses are available on board. *Contact Aggressor Fleet, P O Drawer K, Morgan City, LA 70381, tel. 800-348-2628 or 504-385-2416, fax 504-384-0817. For information within Honduras, contact Romeo's Resort, tel. 451127, where the boat docks.*

The *Isla Mia*, 75 feet, takes 14 divers in seven air-conditioned cabins, each with private bathroom, to sites around Roatan, Morat and Barbareta. Also on board are sundecks, slide-viewing tables, video player, two compressors, and a small library. The ship avoids using anchors on reefs, and offers naturalist seminars during selected weeks. The cost of an eight-day, seven-night package with unlimited diving is $1000 at any time of year, slightly more during seminar weeks. Guests are expected to be certified, in order to avoid excessive guiding. *For information, contact Isla Mia, 1315 Post Office St., Galveston, TX 77550, tel. 800-874-7636 or 409-765-1776, fax 409-765-1775. In Roatan, contact the French Harbour Yacht Club, tel. 451478, fax 451459.*

The *Maid'en Desert* is a 60-foot air-conditioned sailing ketch with just three double rooms and compressor, available at a weekly rate of $900 to $1250 per person. *For bookings, contact Roatán Charter, Box 877, San Antonio, FL 33576, tel. 800-282-8932, fax 904-588-4158.*

Costs

Diving in the Bay Islands is almost always part of a package included with your hotel booking, and if you compare prices, you'll find that a week of diving will cost several hundred dollars less than in Belize. Partly, this is because Honduras is a real country, that grows its own food and provides many of the services that must be imported for visitors elsewhere in the Caribbean.

If you're not in the Bay Islands on a dedicated dive vacation, here's an a la carte price list for services and rentals at Reef House Resort, which are representative of the *high end* of what you'll pay throughout the area: $25 per single tank dive, $35 per two-tank dive, $30 per night dive, $75 for a resort scuba course, $350 for full certification. Daily tank rental $7; regulator $10; buoyancy compensator, $8; masks, fins and snorkel, $7; dive light, $5.

What to Bring

When resorts talk about inclusive dive packages, they generally mean that air tanks, weights, guides and boat transport to dive sites are provided. You should bring your own regulator with tank pressure gauge, buoyancy compensator, and depth gauge, along with fins, masks, and, optionally, booties, gloves (to protect against abrasions), underwater light and dive watch. Anything you don't bring can be rented.

And don't forget your certification card.

FISHING

This is the how most resident islanders make their livings, either directly or indirectly. Traditionally, fish have been caught and kept fresh in pens made of closely placed stakes driven into the shallow seabed offshore, then transported to markets in La Ceiba and elsewhere on the mainland. But commercial catches of lobster and shrimp for export are becoming increasingly important.

Sport fishing isn't quite as developed as in some other Caribbean locales, though not for the lack of resources. Among the species found in the shallows near shore are bonefish and permit, which are caught all year, and grouper, snook, and all sorts of snapper, including yellowtail and red. Tarpon has a more limited season, generally from February through June.

Deeper waters have mackerel (king and Spanish), bonito, blackfin tuna, and wahoo, kingfish, and, seasonally, marlin, while jewfish are caught around the Hog Cays. Commercially fished are shrimp and lobster, red snapper, and conch ("conk," or sea snail), a somewhat tough species that is consumed locally but not much exported.

Tournaments

An annual **billfishing tournament** operates out of the Fantasy Island Resort and Marina on Roatán, usually at the end of September or beginning of October. The fee for participation has recently been just $50 per angler, and the winning fish in 1992 was a 400-pound marlin. Boat rentals can be arranged with registration. *For information, contact Fantasy Island at tel. 800-676-2826 in the U.S., or 451222 on Roatan.*

Fishing Gear

Choice of equipment can be limited, however. For bonefishing in shallow waters, a light spinning rod is suitable, with 200 yards of four- to six- pound test line (or eight-pound line, according to some anglers), and light lures. Heavier line and tackle are suitable for casting from shore, or for trolling. Take an assortment of lures to suit different conditions, jigs (hair, nylon, white, yellow, pink), hook sizes 1-0, and tipped leader 20- to 30-pound test, 18 to 20 inches long.

PRACTICAL INFORMATION

Beasts, Bugs, Bites, & Bonks

There are no poisonous snakes or dangerous wild animals in the islands, though sandflies ("no-see-ums") are placed by some in the latter category. I should say that this is without justification. There are some sandflies, but if there is even the slightest wind, they will not be a problem. On a still day, it would be hard to stay for very long on the beach unless you have insect repellent, so come prepared with your favorite brand. Residents place their houses on stilts above the level of molestation.

Hikers and treasure hunters venturing into the hills need have no concerns about wildlife, such as deer, lizards, rabbits, and parrots.

Don't nap under coconut palms on the beach. Plummeting coconuts can cause serious injury or death. In a storm, do not shelter under a coconut palm. Ample fallen palms are evidence that they don't have much of a supporting root structure.

Costs

Things cost more in the Bay Islands than elsewhere in Honduras, but it's still possible to live cheaply in the towns. Everything depends on where you stay. At Anthony's Key, the price of a beer is triple the price at the best hotel in La Ceiba. But this is not how things are everywhere.

Island Talk

Open belly? It's just how you say diarrhea in the local language, which is English, sort of, with many, many modifications. Bay Islands sayings have been collected in a fascinating illustrated booklet entitled *Wee Speak*, by American resident Candace Wells Hammond, which you'll find on sale here and there. Black Caribs, or Garifunas, speak their own language, and a perfectly intelligible version of English.

Standard English is also understood and tolerated. And since the Bay Islands have been part of Honduras for the last hundred years, you'll find that some people speak Spanish as well, though residents of Hispanic origin usually have to learn some English in order to get along.

Land

Oddly, the entire area of the Bay Islands is classified as urban, which, among other things, allows foreigners to own land along the water (prohibited in rural areas). Real estate operators have moved in, in a small way, and you can buy a piece of the islands from one of them. Can time-sharing be far away?

Phones & Fax

Now that phones have reached the islands, the easiest way to reach any hotel is to dial direct. Mail is slow, telegrams are fast and expensive. Many hotels have fax machines.

Souvenirs

Avoid picking, carrying, harvesting, buying, or otherwise acquiring to take home the following: coral (black or otherwise), fish, shells, and pre-Columbian artifacts (in plentiful supply, and commonly known as *yaba-ding-dings*). It's either illegal to take these out of Honduras without a license, or illegal to bring them back to your own country, or both, and it doesn't help to conserve what you came to see and do. This leaves t-shirts and hardwood carvings.

Weather

If you like rain, come in October or November or, with less certainty, in December — 50% of the yearly total falls just in these three months. If you have just a week of vacation, and don't want it spoiled by rough seas or airplane delays, come from January to September. The best months are March to August.

Expect to see some rainfall at any time of year, as storms blow through the Caribbean. Average rainfall in October and November is about 450 mm (almost 18 inches). The lightest months are March, April and May, with under 75 mm (less than three inches) of rain. January and February — when the islands are heavily visited — see moderate rainfall of about 200 and 125 mm (8 and 5 inches) respectively.

Temperatures are generally perfect in the Bay Islands. The yearly average is about 27.5 degrees C (81 degrees F). The coolest month is

January (25.8 degrees C, 78 degrees F), the warmest month is August (28.8 degrees C, 84 degrees F). With a sea breeze usually blowing, it's not hard to take.

On the average, a serious hurricane strikes every ten years.

UTILA

Utila is the nearest of the Bay Islands to the mainland, *just 35 kilometers from La Ceiba*. Measuring about 14 kilometers east to west, and almost five kilometers across, it is the island that sees the fewest visitors. Mostly this has to do with the island's geography. It is low-lying, something like an atoll, and the central portion, taking up a good two-thirds of the surface, is mangrove. A fringe of dry land surrounds this near-lake. Most of the high ground is at the east end — the absolute high spot is 200-foot Pumpkin Hill in the northeast, a walk of less than an hour from town. A canal through the mangrove bisects east-central Utila.

Utila is where most of the white Cayman Islanders settled after 1830, and to this day, most of the inhabitants are fair-skinned.

You don't find any big resorts on Utila, though you can see the foundations of a resort that was planned for a hilltop. Utila is difficult to reach, and has a small population. There are no beaches.

But these "disadvantages" for big-time tourism make Utila a great place to go and rest and hang out, away from the crowds, and from touristy expectations. People are friendly, and there are small stores, bars and restaurants where you can get to know them. Prices are lower than elsewhere.

There is one road, running a few hundred yards from the airport to East Harbour (identified on maps as the town of Utila), and two to three cars have been occasionally reported on it. Other settlements are on Pigeon Cay and Suc-Suc Cay, offshore to the southwest, connected to each other by an over-water walkway; and at West End. Most of the patch coral reef near the island is between these two places — the small offshore cays are surrounded by coral, making for good diving. There are some good walls and slanting reefs, though most dive sites are farther from shore than those off Roatan.

ARRIVALS & DEPARTURES

Arriving by Boat

Boats run irregularly from La Ceiba on the mainland to Utila and to the other islands, and you can inquire for captains at the San Carlos bar in La Ceiba or at the tourist information office.

But as I have said elsewhere, it is more certain to take the plane.

Arriving by Air

Isleña *(tel. 430179)* schedules flights to Utila daily except Sunday at 6 a.m. and 4 p.m. from La Ceiba, in Canadian-built Twin Otter short takeoff craft, or in DC3s, for a fare of $15 each way. Return flights are at 6:30 a.m. and 4:30 p.m. When demand warrants, Isleña operates an air bridge, ferrying passengers to Utila as the plane fills up.

Passengers on diving packages will be met at the airport. A truck meets incoming planes and will take you into town for $2 or so, or you can walk in — it's under a mile.

Departing by Boat

Boats can be hired to continue to Roatán; there is no current scheduled service. Otherwise, fly back to La Ceiba.

WHERE TO STAY

TRUDY'S, *East Harbour, tel. 453195. 20 rooms, $30 double.*

Owned and operated by Miss Trudy herself. Don't expect luxury, but this is a clean, pleasant, homey place, within walking distance of the airport, with views of the water. You can eat here, too, and make arrangements for diving and snorkeling.

SONNY'S VILLA, *6 rooms. $10 per person.*

A little place right by the water. Meals are served, and you can also arrange fishing and diving here.

CAPTAIN SPENCER'S HOTEL, *tel. 453161. 8 rooms, $8 per room.*

Clean rooms, but no special features, and no views.

UTILA LODGE. *8 rooms. U.S. reservations: 800-282-8932. Week-long dive package $650 per person including airport pickup, three daily boat dives and two night dives per week, tanks, weights, belts; non-diving $600. Single supplement $300. Week-long fishing package with five days of fishing from $995 in the flats to $1195 offshore. Heavy tackle included for offshore fishing; bring your own light tackle.*

A new lodge in the village, built right over the water on two levels. Each air-conditioned room has a ceiling fan, front and rear porch entry, a single and double bed, and equipment closet. The bar has inexpensive local drinks. Personal gear is *not* available for rent — bring your own, or make arrangements beforehand for rental through a local dive shop.

Utila Lodge is one of the few hotels in the Bay Islands ready, willing and able to receive sport fishermen. There are two fully equipped diesel-powered boats, and the specialties are marlin in the deeps, tarpon and permit and snook closer in, and bonefish in the flats.

For an occasional fishing day, the rate is $118.50 for a single fisherman on a skiff, about $150 per fisherman offshore. Marina facilities are available, with 14 slips on a 130-foot dock.

Other Lodging

You can also ask around for rooms in private homes.

Rooms and houses can also be found on Pigeon Cay and the Cayes nearby; camping is permitted on Water Cay, reached by boat from Pigeon Caye. There is an inexpensive lodging place at Blue Lagoon, at the end of the peninsula to the southwest of East Harbour; boat operators can tell you if it's currently open.

WHERE TO EAT & DRINK

Food is served in any number of small eateries *in East Harbour*. Fish, of course, is your best , fresh but always either fried or in a soup. And you'll find Caribbean-style pastries and spice cakes and coconut bread. Call the fare wholesome at best.

Of numerous bars, the **Bucket of Blood** is one popular gathering spot. The **Bahía del Mar** has a dock.

PRACTICAL INFORMATION

Services in East Harbour include a couple of banks; several Protestant churches; and shops with items fashioned from coral. You should not purchase the latter under any circumstances. Coral jewelry could be confiscated when you return to the United States.

THINGS TO DO

There are now a few dive shops on Utila. Try **Utila Dive Centre** or **Cross Creek Divers** *(tel. 453134)*. Prices at Cross Creek are somewhat lower than if you book through a dive resort: about $35 for two one-tank dives, and beginners are welcome. They have an introductory course over four days for about $200, including basic lodging.

Or ask around for other dive operators. But check the condition of the equipment before going out. Diving is an unregulated business in Honduras, and unless you go through a hotel that offers dive packages, you can't be sure of what you're getting.

You can also visit a cay. At Miss Trudy's, for example, you can arrange to be dropped off for a day for snorkeling, and picked up, box lunch included, for $10 per person or less. It's like having your own private island for the day. Make arrangements a day in advance.

Water Cay, *off the southwest of the main island*, is said to have good snorkeling off the south shore. Or, from town, walk out and snorkel off the airstrip.

Also found, without too much difficulty, are caves both over water (especially on **Pumpkin Hill**) and under water, **Blue Lagoon** along the south side of the island, waterways through the mangroves to explore by canoe, and trails across the island's interior.

ROATÁN

Roatán is the largest of the Bay Islands, roughly Cuba-shaped, stretching about 40 kilometers, and usually no more than three kilometers wide. Separated by a passage almost narrow enough to step across, at the eastern end, is the island of **Helene** (or Santa Elena), and slightly beyond are **Morat** and **Barbaret** (Barbareta).

If you like sun, beaches, swimming, a nice island away from it all, genial people, you'll find all that on Roatán. It is everything that you might hope for from a perfect Caribbean island, and it is not yet too commercial.

If you like diving, you might as well call it paradise.

And that's not the end of it. If you're a birder, you can see a wealth of tropical birds. And to round things out, there is even a lot of barely touched forest, for seafaring, rather than agriculture, has been the heritage of the islanders.

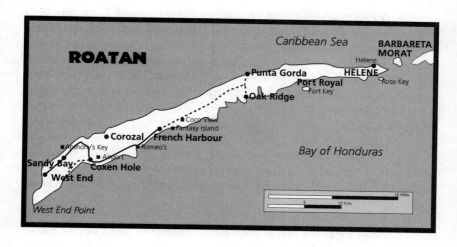

Landscape & Seascape

There is a long, irregular mountain ridge inland on Roatán, with hilltops reaching up to 235 meters, but these are just the peaks of the mountains that lie below the waters. Beaches and cliffs punctuate the north shore. It was the inlets and bays on the south, some with deep water, all protected by reefs, that attracted the first European pirates and loggers, and, in modern times, divers.

Reefs line the north coast, a few hundred meters from shore; along the south, coral formations are, in many places, within just steps of the beach. With easy diving, hotels, frequent air service, towns, and even a small road network, Roatán is what most people think of when they think of a vacation in the Bay Islands.

With the exception of a couple of "Spanish" settlements inland at **Corozal** and **Juticalpa**, the people of Roatán live right along the coast — many in white clapboard tin-roofed stilt houses set right above the water that is their highway and disposal system. Most are English-speaking blacks, though Black Caribs inhabit the village of Punta Gorda on the north side of the island. Inland, much of the hardwood forest in the hills has been virtually untouched since English woodcutters and their slaves took timber more than 150 years ago. Hikers occasionally find pieces of pottery made by the Paya Indians who lived here in pre-Columbian times.

Versions differ, but the name of the island might be a corruption of "rattan," from the vines of the island's forests, or a derivative of the Nahuatl expression for "place of women."

ARRIVALS & DEPARTURES

By Air

Isleña Airlines *(tel. 451088 in Coxen's Hole)* operates Canadian-built Twin-Otter short takeoff craft, as well as DC3s. Five flights are scheduled most days from La Ceiba, (currently at 6:30 a.m. (except Sunday), 8 a.m., 10 a.m., 2 p.m. and 4:30 p.m.) but if there's a demand beyond the schedule, they'll simply fly back and forth until everyone has been accommodated. The flight takes about 20 minutes, the fare is about $20.

Aerolíneas Sosa, *tel. 451154 in Coxen's Hole*, has operated flights from La Ceiba.

From October through December, expect some delays from bad weather and darkness. Airports are sometimes closed because of strong winds, as well as rain. But everything passes. Don't expect a delay of more than one day.

If you are connecting to the Bay Islands from an international flight, there's always a chance that you'll have to spend the night in La Ceiba if the international leg of your flight is delayed. They won't hold the domestic flight for too long.

The airport (or airstrip) is located two kilometers from Coxen's Hole. Facilities include a snack bar, gift shop, and a tourist office, the latter forever closed. If you have reservations, you'll be picked up and carted off to your lodgings. Taxis at the airport are plentiful, and high-priced. Bargain hard. If you walk, it's just ten minutes to Coxen's Hole.

By Boat

Boats also operate from the single pier in La Ceiba to the islands, and irregularly between the islands. To return to La Ceiba by boat, ask around in Coxen's Hole. There's usually a boat in the afternoon.

GETTING AROUND

Unlike the other islands, Roatán has some significant roads, generally in excellent condition. A single paved road runs northward across the island from Coxen's Hole to West End; and eastward from Coxen's Hole to French Harbour.

An unpaved road runs from Coxen's Hole west to Flowers Bay. From French Harbour, a dirt road continues inland through the hills, with branches to Oak Ridge and Punta Gorda.

If you absolutely *must* drive, **Roatán Rent a Car**, *tel. 451097*, rents vans, cars, pickup trucks and motorcycles. **Amigo Renta A Car** has a desk at the airport, and at Fantasy Island. *Call 451128.* **Toyota Rent A Car** *has a desk at the airport, tel. 451166.*

By Bus or Boat

Buses operating on the island are small, with 15 to 30 seats. All start from Coxen's Hole and go in either direction, departing about every 30 minutes, or more frequently between 7 and 9 a.m. and 3 and 6 p.m. The friendly driver knows everybody along the way.

To get around, you flag down a bus (or other passing vehicle if no bus arrives) and pay the driver's helper for the ride — about a dollar on most routes during the day, more at night. On Sundays, you have to take taxi.

Or else you're fetched to wherever you're going by boat.

DIVING & FISHING BOATS

Most of the resorts mentioned below have diving boats, and some have fishing boats. In addition, the *Bay Island Aggressor*, a cruising boat designed to accommodate 20 divers, is based at Roatán, as are the *Isla Mia* and the *Maid'en Desert*. You arrive by plane, and off you go from one dive spot to another, sleeping on board. Another live-aboard that regularly operates in the Bay Islands is the Isla Mia.

TOWNS & ACCOMMODATIONS ON ROATÁN

As I mentioned earlier in the book, there are hotels on Roatán that price everything in U.S. dollars, though Lempiras will be accepted if you insist. Generally, these are the resorts outside of towns, though there are exceptions, which are noted.

COXEN'S HOLE

From La Ceiba or anywhere on the mainland, you buy a ticket for Roatán, but once you arrive at the town's airstrip and are talking to locals, you better ask for **Coxen's Hole**, the local name, which recalls Captain John Coxen, a pirate of past days.

Coxen's Hole has an attractive, small central plaza, and clapboard houses and small general stores and lumber depots and outboard motor repair shops, and one or two larger general stores that style themselves "supermarkets." The wharf can be lively, with the landing of the catch, and processing and re-loading for export to the United States. If you like fish, it's enough to whet your appetite. Coxen's Hole is the capital of the islands, but, with just a few thousand inhabitants, effectively conceals any self-importance.

WHERE TO STAY

HOTEL CAY VIEW RESORT, *tel. 451202, fax 451179. 15 rooms. $30 single/$40 double.*

This is the best hotel in Coxen's Hole, good and clean, and the location is advantageous. Yes, they have a terrace with a view of a cay, as well as a bar and restaurant, and they'll make arrangements for diving and fishing. They sell nice black coral figurines, but then, if you have any conservation conscientiousness, you shouldn't be buying black coral. The Cay View is where groups from cruise ships land about once a week, for a half-day stay in the Bay Islands.

HOTEL EL PASO, *Coxen's Hole, tel. 451059. $10 single or double.* On Coxen's Hole's main street, with restaurant.

ALLAN'S, *tel. 451243*, is clean and simple. $5 single/$10 double. Under the bridge.

HOTEL BRISAS DEL MAR is a small hotel *just beside the Cay View*, with eatery. About $6 per person. Similarly inexpensive is the **HOTEL CORAL**, *tel. 451080*. The basic but clean **HOTEL SHILA**, *tel. 451015*, has rooms for about $10 single/$15 double, serves meals, and arranges diving, fishing and horseback riding.

WHERE TO EAT

There's a **BURGER HUT**, with imitation American hamburgers. The **RESTAURANT BRISAS DEL MAR** serves more local cuisine, *just opposite the Hotel Cay View*. Most of the hotels have eating rooms where you can consume fried fish, coconut bread, boiled bananas, and lots of Port Royal beer.

PRACTICAL INFORMATION

Banks

Banks include **Bancahsa, Banco Atlántida, Banffaa, Banco Sogerin** *in the Cay View Hotel.*

Dive Shops

Various dive shops rent equipment (which you should look over carefully) and offer diving trips, though the offerings may be better at West End (see below).

Gift and Book Shops

Being the island metropolis, Coxen's Hole has more amenities, shops, and services than are found elsewhere in the islands, including several souvenir shops. One, the **Traveller's Rest Gift Shop**, in the Bay Islands Company building (across from the airline offices) sells maps and books, and has a Xerox machine.

Other Services

There is a post office, and a **Hondutel** office for international phone calls.

Near Sandy Bay

This area is known for good scuba diving and snorkeling, and several dive resorts are located nearby:

ROATAN BEACH RESORT, *tel. and fax 451425. 10 rooms. $125 per person with daily diving, $90 non-diving. U.S. reservations tel. 800-395-5688 or 708-537-2381, fax 708-520-3908. Week-long diving package: $695, including three daily boat dives, meals, transfers, and one night dive. Non-diving package, $595.*

A new, intimate resort, said to offer excellent diving at north shore sites. Rooms are either individual or two to a cottage, fairly soundproof, air-conditioned, with sea views. Good for getting away from the crowd.

ANTHONY'S KEY RESORT, *Sandy Bay, tel. 451003, fax 451329. 50 units. U.S. office: 1385 Coral Way, Suite 401, Miami, FL 33145, tel. 800-227-3483 or 305-858-3483, fax 305-858-5020.*

Weekly dive packages from $775 to $975 per person, including three one-tank boat dives daily and two night dives per week, dolphin encounter and dolphin dive, and all activities. Additional nights $132 to $139 single/$220 to $234 double with meals and diving. Non-diving rate, $140 single/$240 double. Children 3 to 11, $45. About 15% lower in summer.

Everything about Anthony's Key can be described in superlatives. The landscaping alone makes it a paradise. The resort flows down a slope, and across to a small cay. There are units in the lodge on a hill, bungalows set into the foliage on the slope, and slat houses along the edge of the cay, on stilts in the water, reached by a 60-second boat ride. Macaws and hummingbirds flap and gyre about. Rooms are clean and somewhat sparse, but easy on the senses. Meals are simply prepared, and hearty. The bar is quite expensive.

The emphasis is on diving, as elsewhere on the island, with many boats and good instructors and equipment. Numerous groups come here.

The location near the west end of the island allows easy access to diving spots on both shores. Rates are higher than elsewhere, but Anthony's Key has a lot more: horseback riding, weekly beach picnic, swimming with dolphins, a dinner party on the key, island-style entertainment, crab races, tennis, and use of canoes, kayaks, pedal boats and small sailboats are included in the daily rate (non-guests can use the sailboats for a fee).

There are also a wildlife sanctuary with trails on nearby **Bailey's Key**, the **Museum of Roatán**, a decompression chamber, a doctor on-site, and secluded beaches. Fishing can be arranged, and snorkeling equipment is available for rent. Also available: resort diving courses, PADI instruction, underwater photo courses, and videos in which you can star. The souvenir shop has a good assortment of trinkets, and a photography shop offers processing, and rentals of cameras and underwater equipment. There's even the Casino Royal, if you're interested in gambling between dives.

Anthony's Key is one of the best resorts on the island, and highly recommended.

OCEANSIDE INN, *Sandy Bay, tel. 451552, fax 451532. 8 rooms. $25 single/$40 double. U.S. reservations, tel. 800-241-5271.*

Package price from $331 per person for seven days, including airport pickup, meals, picnic, and night out in French Harbour. Dives cost an additional $20 each, $22 with equipment, even less (!) for a package of ten dives.

Located alongside Anthony's Key (and right next to their dolphin pen), Oceanside Inn has good-sized hardwood-panelled rooms, all upstairs with sea view, steady breeze, and ceiling fans. The louver style of building is quite similar to that used in the cottages at Anthony's Key, though the facility is brand-new, and more modest and homey. Food is said to be quite good, emphasizing seafood prepared American-style— lobster, shrimp, pan-fried grouper, etc., served in a breezy dining room. The hotel also has two sun decks, a patio bar, and gift shop. A dolphin show can be included, optionally, with a package stay, for $75. Other excursions and options are dive certification ($260), horseback riding ($12) and rafting on the mainland ($89, including air transport and lunch). The owners of Oceanside are Hondurans who have returned after successful business careers in the States, so they know the worlds of both the islands and their guests.

There are assorted other small places that rent rooms in the area. **THE BAMBOO INN**, with seven rooms, charges about $18 per person for the night, and you become part of Dora and J.J.'s family.

Gardens, Institutes, & Museums

Carambola Botanical Garden, *across the road from Anthony's Key Resort*, has plantings of native and exotic species, including spices, elephant ear, hibiscus, bird of paradise, and many, many others. The locale is excellent for birding. The hilltop, reached via a 20-minute hike, offers good sea view.

The **Institute for Marine Sciences** (IMS) at Sandy Bay uses the facilities of Anthony's Key to care for, train and investigate a dozen or so bottle-nosed dolphins. Visitors are invited to swim with the dolphins in limited numbers. IMS is also a sanctuary and rehabilitation center for ailing marine mammals, sea turtles and birds.

IMS offers classes on marine mammals and coral reef biology, and, of course, the reef surrounding Roatan makes for a superb field laboratory. Students, according to their resources, stay at Anthony's Key Resort or at the Institute's dormitory. Degree credits may be available in cooperation with various universities. For information, contact the Anthony's Key office in the States, or Anthony's Key directly (see above).

The **Roatán Museum**, *in the same building as the Institute for Marine Sciences*, houses exhibits on the ethnology of the Bay Islands. Displays include Paya and Mayan artifacts, and a video presentation on the islands' past and prospects.

WEST END

West End is a quiet town *on the north coast of Roatán, opposite and west of Coxen's Hole, about ten kilometers away.* There are beaches and palm trees, and for the visitor, things are cheap. Rooms may be rented by asking around of locals. The going rate is $10 per person per night, or less. You can always find a place, except at Easter week.

Restaurants are really simple. Many are tiny affairs run by housewives. Chino's has Chinese food, and also rooms to rent. Vivian and Foster's Restaurant is located on pillars in the water, not far from the Lost Paradise, serving an honest and unpretentious soda-shop menu of hamburgers and sandwiches. Mr. Foster really exists. He has a lot of muscles, but he is a friendly giant. They also have rooms at West End Point for about $25 double, including the boat ride out.

The reef off West End is protected as part of the **West End Marine Sanctuary**.

Access to West End is by island bus from Coxen's Hole. A taxi from the airport should cost under $10.

WHERE TO STAY

(Aside from generic rooms in town)
ROBERTS HILL HOTEL, *tel 451176. 8 rooms. $20 double.*
These are individual units opposite the beach.
LOST PARADISE INN, *tel. 451306, fax 451388. 34 rooms, $40 per person, including three meals and airport transfer.*
This is a simple motel, at the end of the road . . . you'll feel that you've

finally found the Lost Paradise. Simply furnished rooms have showers, but nothing extra and nothing fancy. You pay an honest price and get honest accommodations, with helpful owner and employees. There are no diving facilities on site, but there are several dive shops in West End Town, five minutes away on foot. Free boat rides are given to nearby beaches. The motel is near the beach on a bay, but not all rooms have sea views.

SUEÑO DEL MAR, *tel. 451498. 8 rooms. $75 single/$110 double/$145 triple with meals ($50/$60/$70 without meals), plus 10 percent service and tax. Children 2 to 12 half price. U.S. reservations, P. O. Box 5240, Sierra Vista, AZ 85636, tel. 800-377-9525 or 602-378-6055, fax 602-378-6155.*

Dive packages from approximately $90 per person per day, including three boat dives, unlimited beach diving, meals, and one night dive per week.

The newest accommodation at West End, right on the beach at the end of the road, near the Lost Paradise Inn. The lodge is built in sedate plantation style, two-storied, L-shaped and hugging the beach, of varnished wood, with generous porches. Rooms are large, with walk-in closets, private bath, and two queen-sized beds. Guests on a diving package can take their meals at any time in the restaurant, which is open to the public.

Sueño del Mar, like a couple of other resorts in the vicinity, is *small*. There could be some drawbacks, but on the plus side, everyone is on a first-name basis, one of the owners is always on site, and diving is scheduled and locations are selected according to the wishes of guests. There are three dive boats. Call the toll-free number, and chances are you can talk with one of the owners in Arizona and get detailed answers to your questions.

FOSTER'S COVE are two-bedroom palm-shaded beach houses, built of pine and raised well above sandfly level on high stilts, owned by Mr. Foster and his American partner, Robert Beels. Each has an ample deck, wicker furniture, and one king and two twin beds, solar electricity, and a gas stove. The rate is about $500 per week for a unit that sleeps four persons. Maid service is extra, and a cook can be hired. Children and pets are welcome. Access is by boat from West End village.

Packages with diving and meals can also be arranged from about $800 per person. For information in the U.S. or Canada, call Maya World Travel, tel. 800-392-6292.

SEAGRAPE PLANTATION, *tel. 451428. 16 rooms. U.S. reservations, 9846 Highway 441, Leesburg, FL 34788, tel. 800-392-6292.*

Weekly package with meals, two boat dives daily, one night dive and unlimited shore dives, from $500.

These are rooms with private bath, two each in eight individual bungalows built over coral on an expansive 11-acre site about a half mile from West End village. Though it's set well back from the sea, they have a good dive shop.

GETTING AROUND

The beach at West End Town is okay, but the best beaches are three kilometers away, at West End Point, the very tip of the island. Just ask for a boat near Foster's Restaurant. You can also walk along the beach. Or take a glass-bottom boat trip over the reefs — inquire at Foster's.

Bargain Diving

At last count, there were four or five dive shops at West End, either independent or attached to lodging places, such as Seagrape Plantation, with compressors, well-maintained equipment, knowledgeable divemasters — and a willingness to strike a deal, especially during slow periods. I've heard of five- or six-dive packages for something like $100. You can't expect to walk into a steal like this on just any day, and diving is reasonable enough in any case on a package basis in the Bay Islands. But if you find yourself with extra time but no extra funds, and an unrequited passion for diving, check out West End.

You'll also find wind surfing gear available, and, most likely, sea kayaks.

WEST END POINT

Some of the best beaches on the island are here. White sand, palm trees, crystal clear waters — a tropical fantasy come true. But be on guard for sunburn! The snorkeling is excellent 100 meters from the beach, where the water is only five feet deep. There are coral and fish in all sorts and varieties, and when the weather is good, there are no currents at all.

East of Coxen's Hole

ROMEO'S RESORT, *Brick Bay, tel. 451127, fax 451594. 30 rooms. About $96 per person daily with meals and diving, $88 non-diving. U.S. reservations: tel. 800-535-DIVE or 305-633-1221, fax 305-633-1102.*

Weekly dive package from $670 to $840 per person, lower in summer, including three daily boat dives and two night dives per week.

This is a quiet place off the road between French Harbour and Coxen's Hole, in a sheltered cove, run by the same Romeo who managed Romeo's Restaurant in French Harbour. Most rooms are in a long concrete building, the central section of which (with terrace restaurant, front desk and gathering areas) has a soaring roof that suggests the South Seas. The whole place is pleasant enough, with luxuriant vegetation all around and views everywhere to the mangrove-lined waters. And Brick

Bay (English Harbour) is a good place to anchor: Romeo's is the closest hotel to Mary's Place, one of the most famed dive spots in the islands.

Standard rooms have two double beds, ceiling fans, balconies, and lagoon views. Deluxe rooms on the lower level are air conditioned. A hillside house, Casa Pepe, can be reserved for groups. Facilities include a pool with wooden deck, pavilion dining area, bar, sea kayaks, dockside gear storage, slide film processing, and several dive boats. Onshore amusements include volleyball, Ping Pong, and island trips. The current management, the Silvestri family, has worked hard to develop this hotel (which formerly was a yacht club) as a complete dive and vacation center, and they personally look after the needs of guests in the best innkeepers' tradition.

FRENCH HARBOUR YACHT CLUB, *16 rooms, tel. 451478, fax 451459. $35 single/$45 double.*

Whence the hotel's name derives, I know not. It's near the harbor, but not on the water, though the hotel has docks and motor boats and dinghies, and a bar, a short walk away. Maybe it's for yachties who want to sleep ashore. You have good views in any case, in a hilltop, remodelled, traditional, tin-roofed island house, with verandas, and a six-acre buffer zone. And it's clean. Rooms come with hot showers and fans, each with one double and two twin beds, air conditioning, and a television. The location is on the main road, eight kilometers from the airport, a half-kilometer from town.

FRENCH HARBOUR

French Harbour *is about ten kilometers up the south coast to the east of Coxen's Hole.* Nobody here speaks French (I was disappointed to learn my first time out). The bay is quite big, and you will find a large processing and packing operation for shrimp and lobster traveling on to the States. The town itself is a small concentration of houses built on pillars over the water, which serves as transport route and disposal system. I wouldn't go out of my way to visit the place, but you'll pass through getting to some of the resorts nearby. Bus service is frequent from Coxen's Hole.

WHERE TO STAY

HOTEL DIXON'S PLAZA, *French Harbour, tel. 451317. $25 double. Air-conditioned rooms, t.v. room, even parking, if you've brought your car.*

BUCCANEER HOTEL, *tel. 451032, fax 451036. 30 rooms. $100 single/ $160 double with meals and airport transfer. Weekly diving rate approximately $550.*

In French Harbor along the sea. This is an attractive, modern hotel built of wood, with soaring ceilings and screened and glassed walls that let in plenty of light. Guest rooms, facing the water, extend along an elevated deck.

The beach is not as attractive as at some other resorts, but rooms are comfortable, wood-panelled and carpeted, and the place is easy-going and cozy, without any pretense. Diving and boat tours for swimming are available — you can't swim in the shallows right in front. Amenities include a restaurant, cable t.v., and hot water in some of the rooms. A gazebo set out in the water is fitted with lights to allow night views of tropical fish. The value here is quite good.

In French Harbour, if you don't have the money to stay at the Buccaneer Inn, the **CORAL REEF INN** *next door* will give you shelter from predators at $15 per person, and there are smaller places where you can find a room for $10.

WHERE TO EAT & DRINK

ROMEO'S RESTAURANT, the predecessor of Romeo's Resort, is one of the top eating places on Roatán, specializing in crab. Or, you can stop just for drinks, over piers lapped by Caribbean waters.

NIGHTLIFE

Celebrity, *in French Harbour*, is currently the disco of note on the island of Roatan, and if you stay anywhere for a few days, you're likely to spend at least a few hours here one night for reggae and salsa.

PRACTICAL INFORMATION
Banks

Bank agencies include **Banco Atlántida**, **Banco Sogerín**, and **Banffaa**.

Tour Information
Bay Islands Tour and Travel Center, *tel. 451184.*

Near French Harbour
FANTASY ISLAND, *tel. 451222, fax 451268. 75 rooms. $100 single/ $130 double/$150 triple; $40 per child. Daily diving (3 dives), $50. Visa, Master Card, American Express. Package rates with three meals per day, $150 to $170 single/$228 to $250 double/$414 triple. Week-long dive packages $1300 single/$2100 double/$2900 triple, including three boat dives daily and one night dive per week.*

U.S. reservations: 304 Plant Avenue, Tampa, FL 33606, tel. 800-676-2826, fax 813-251-0301.

This is a one of the newer resorts in the Bay Islands, opened in 1989, a marina-diving-beach complex with some of the most comprehensive facilities. From a distance, it looks like condominiums in ski country, two stories of attached clapboard units with peaked roofs. Up close, you'll espy the palm-shaded verandas, and a dining area with soaring roof and cupola. Rooms come with ceiling fans, air conditioning, carpeting, refrigerator, shower and tub, artificial plants, satellite t.v., and private balconies. There are three bars, and plenty of loud music to accompany your time at the crushed-shell beach (if that's what you're looking for).

The resort is located two kilometers east of French Harbour on a small (15-acre) cay, about 500 feet offshore. The last stretch of road is unpaved.

As at some of the other Bay Islands resorts, they try hard at Fantasy island, though in a country without a strong resort tradition, some things still don't come together perfectly at meal time, or in room furnishings.

For diving, Fantasy Island offers the most modern facilities on the island, with a dive gazebo, camera rentals, film processing, a fleet of custom dive boats, and easy access to both sides of the island.There is good snorkeling, and canoes and windsurfers are provided. And Fantasy Island also has tennis courts and a marina.

Less expensive packages are available during the slow season, from September 15 to December 15.

COCO VIEW RESORT, *French Cay, tel. 451013, fax 451011. 25 rooms (9 beach rooms, 4 luxury bungalows, 12 over-water cabanas). About $130 per person daily with diving and meals, $110 for non-divers ($110 diver, $90 non-diver after one week). U.S. address: Box 877, San Antonio, FL 33576, tel. 800-282-8932, fax 904-588-4158.*

Weekly dive packages from $725 per person with all meals, transfer from airport, two daily boat dives and unlimited beach and night diving; non-diver packages from $625.

This is considered by some knowledgeable folks to be *the* place for divers. Located on a peninsula on the south shore, it was a wild, remote place, when you could only reach it by boat from French Harbour. Now, it's just beside Fantasy Island, more accessible, but still quite nice. You don't sleep in an aquarium, but aside from that, everything is diving.

Units, all with overhead fans (no air conditioning) and hot showers, are in two guest houses, and in individual roundhouse bungalows (extra charge $50 per person on a weekly package) and cabanas built on stilts over the water. It's not luxurious, and the price is appropriate, a good balance between budget and comfort. The resort is ten minutes by boat from Old French Harbour (just east of French Harbour), and transportation from the airport is included in the rate.

There is spectacular wall diving 100 yards out, and there are reefs and channels nearby, accessible on two dive boats. The wreck of the *Prince Albert*, a 140-foot freighter, deliberately sunk in 1985, is directly in front of the resort, in 65 feet of water. Tanks, backpacks and weights are provided and stored at dockside, and other equipment can be rented. Processing for E-6 slide film is available.

Instruction capabilities include resort, certification and specialty courses.

Landside diversions include kayaks, board games, Ping Pong and picnics on a private islet. Sailing and fishing can be arranged.

Also available are rental houses at **PLAYA MIGUEL**, *the development adjacent to the hotel*, at about $800 per week. These have two or three bedrooms, full kitchen and sundecks. For four persons, the rate is $2700 to $2800 with diving and meals, or $1785 to $2000 for non-divers; and live-aboard boats with air-conditioned quarters, at about $650 per person per week. Children are not encouraged to come except during a specific family week in July.

OLD PORT ROYAL

Old Port Royal is not a town at all in modern times, but it was the site of pirate encampments in the seventeenth century, and English fortifications in the eighteenth century. The last great battle here was fought offshore at Fort George in 1782. The English were ousted after a two-day battle, though not for the last time.

The remains of four different forts still exist, two on Roatán, and two on Fort Cay offshore, and there are some vacation houses in the area, which is otherwise uninhabited. Wood from wrecks found offshore has been dated to before the arrival of Columbus, suggesting that Europeans visited this area earlier than is generally acknowledged.

Boats on diving and fishing excursions will sometimes stop to let visitors walk around the old fortifications; or you can hire a boat for a trip out from Oak Ridge. A trail reaches Port Royal from the end of the island road east of Punta Gorda — it's a hike through the hills to reach the site.

Port Royal Park and Wildlife Reserve protects Roatán's water supply, and not incidentally, is a haven for birds and small mammals, such as the opossum and agouti.

BARBARETA

Barbareta, *three kilometers from Helene* (the island that adjoins Roatán), is a five- by two-kilometer island covered with forests and fringed with coconut palms. Spring water is abundant, and a hotel has sometimes operated here.

Barbareta Marine National Park, covering Barbareta, Morat, and the eastern part of Roatán, protects Diamond Rock forest, the last remnant of tropical rain forest on the island, as well as coral reef and the largest mangrove area.

GUANAJA

Columbus called **Guanaja** the Island of Pines (he landed at El Soldado beach on the north shore), and there are still some pine and oak trees left, though logging and fires have considerably changed the landscape over the years. The island measures about 18 by 6 kilometers, and most of it is green and hilly — the highest point on the Bay Islands, 1400 feet, is here. There are more Spanish-speaking people on Guanaja than elsewhere in the Bay Islands.

If you like Roatán, you'll love Guanaja. It's like an earlier version of Roatán — no real roads, only a few resorts, but of the best type. And the people are genuinely friendly and glad to have you around.

The dive spots are excellent, with clear water and spectacular formations — walls, caves, channels, ridges, tunnels — certainly as good as Roatán's, or, according to local enthusiasts, better. The main diving is off the reef and cays that border the southern shore, and the walls that drop in the depths of the Bartlett Trough.

ARRIVALS & DEPARTURES

By Air

Isleña Airlines (*tel. 454208 in Guanaja, 430179 in La Ceiba*).

The airstrip is right next to the canal that cuts across Guanaja about a third of the way across the island, from its southwest tip. If you have a reservation, you'll be fetched and taken to your hotel. Otherwise, you can take a boat to Bonacca town for about a dollar, along with the locals.

BONACCA

Officially, this is the town of Guanaja, though locals call it **Bonacca**, or El Cayo. Bonacca is also known as the *Venice of Honduras*, and the similarity is genuine not only in the presence of canals, but also in their aroma. The architecture of Bonacca is not quite as grand as that of its Italian cousin.

Bonacca sits on Hog Cay and Sheen Cay, half a kilometer offshore, where Cayman Islanders settled and constructed stilt houses over the water. With time, new houses were added in outlying sections, and connected by walkways on stilts. Eventually, fill was dumped around the houses, dry land was built up, trees were planted, and some of the canals were closed off. Today, Bonacca is a labyrinth of zigzagging pathways and walkways, its houses built close one upon another.

SEEING THE SIGHTS

Guanaja Marine National Park covers 90 percent of the island and surrounding reefs. Sea Cave, along the south of the island, is a rock that rises 80 feet from the Caribbean, and is said to have been a headquarters for William Walker when that American adventurer was trying to take over Honduras more than a hundred years ago.

The *Jado Trader* is a wreck deliberately sunk off southern Guanaja in 1987, to form an artificial reef. The 260-foot ship remains intact in 90 feet of water, making for the premier wreck dive in the Bay Islands.

WHERE TO STAY

The **HOTEL ALEXANDER** on *Hog Cay (tel. 454326, fax 454179)* has 12 seafront rooms with private baths, and, unexpectedly, 24-hour satellite television. At about $30 double facing the sea, less inside, it's probably the closest to a vacation hotel that you'll find right in Bonacca. There's a slightly higher charge for air conditioning.

The **HOTEL MILLER**, *with 20 rooms (tel. 454327 or 454240)* charges about $30 per person. The **CARTER** charges about $10 a person. The **HOTEL ROSARIO** has rooms at about $15 double, more if you require a television and air conditioning. None of these, given the congested surroundings, can really be called a resort destination.

Around the Island

BAYMAN BAY CLUB, *tel. 454191, 454179 (430457 in La Ceiba). 16 cottages, $125 per day including diving and meals, $115 non-diving. U.S. address: 10097 Cleary Blvd., Suite 287, Plantation, FL 33324, tel. 800-524-1823, 305-370-2120, fax 305-370-2276. American Express.*

Week-long dive package, from $675 per person, including meals, two daily boat dives, and shore dives; non-diver, from $625, including meals.

This is one of the best resorts in the islands, located on the northwest side of Guanaja, an elegant club in the jungle. Individual varnished hardwood cottages are sited in the dense foliage of the hillside; all have balconies and ceiling fans and views down to the beach and out to sea. The location is isolated, and the atmosphere is quiet. The reef comes almost to shore, with a 300-foot-long dock.

The rate includes two daily boat dives, unlimited shore dives, one night dive, and a round of activities including buffet meals (good food here), picnics, cruises, excursions to Bonacca Town, and hikes. There is a three-level clubhouse, the center of all action, including a bar, game area with billiards, a collection of books, and observation deck. Dockside facilities include a dive shop and compressors. Uniquely, Bayman Bay Club has dive kayaks to take guests to diving and snorkeling sites.

POSADA DEL SOL *(Inn of the Sun). 23 rooms, tel. 454311. $134 to $145 daily per person for divers, $112 to 129 for non-divers (based on double occupancy), children under 12 half diver rate. U.S. Reservations address: 1201 U.S. Highway 1, Suite 220, North Palm Beach, FL 33408, tel. 800-642-DIVE, 407-642-3483, fax 407-627-0225. American Express, Master Card, Visa.*

Weekly dive package, $910 to $1150 per person, including three daily boat dives, unlimited shore diving, and two night dives per week; non-diver, $700-$750. Off-season specials from $1400, including air fare(!).

Posada del Sol is a classy, tan-colored, palm-shaded villa on a good-sized estate at the base of the hills on Guanaja's south side. Rooms have beamed ceilings, sea views, and tiled floors — in solid Spanish genre, rather than the usual island stilt style. There are also four detached hillside units, each with two rooms. The owners are former commercial divers.

The site is very nice and relaxing. There are lots of good diving places in the area and on the eastern side of the island, and the resort owns its own beach on the north side where picnics are staged. Aside from the usual compressors and the three diving boats with water-level platforms and instruction facilities, Posada del Sol has a hillside pool with hardwood deck and adjacent bar, tennis court, gift shop, exercise equipment, processing for E-6 film, underwater video camera rental, water skiing, Hobie Cat, and windsurfing. Deep sea fishing can be arranged (bonefish, permit and snook can be caught in the flats right in front of the hotel) and guest boats can be accommodated.

Posada del Sol is in a class with Anthony's Key and Fantasy Island as one of the Bay Islands' top resorts — well designed, attentively staffed, with very good food, and recommended.

CLUB GUANAJA ESTE, *14 rooms. About $120 double with meals. U.S. address: P.O. Box 40541, Cincinnati, Ohio 45240, tel. 513-825-0878.*

More modest than the other resorts on the island, the Club Guanaja accommodates guests in seven cottages built on stilts, on grassy plots just a few feet from the coconut-palm-shaded beach. All face the water, and have private bath and porch. Amusements are limited to a bar, taped music and radio, and a VCR. Diving is right from the dock, sailing and fishing are arranged, and fishing guides are available. Near the northeastern tip of Guanaja, twenty minutes by boat from the airport.

CASA SOBRE EL MAR, *tel. 454269. U.S. tel. 800-869-7295 or 615-443-1254.*

On Pond Key, off the main island, a private house with three guest rooms, built on concrete piles directly over the water and the coral reef (ideal for snorkeling right from the door). Each room has private bath. Spring water is piped from the mainland. Casa Sobre el Mar has its own compressor, and supplies tanks, boat, and guide for diving. There's a wreck right off the dock, 80-feet down, which is recommended for night diving. The package rate, with meals and dives, is $600 per person per week. A small extra charge is made for fishing, to cover fuel.

NAUTILUS RESORT, *tel. 454135. 6 rooms. U.S. reservations: P. O. Box 1472, Marble Falls, TX 78654, tel. 800-535-7063 or 512-863-9079. Tel. 370397 in Tegucigalpa. $80 single/$130 double with meals, $105 single/$180* *double/$240 triple with diving. One-week diving package with two daily boat dives, one night dive, unlimited shore dives, meals and airport transfers from $600 per person; non diving from $450.*

On Guanaja's south shore, within view of Bonacca Town, Nautilus resort is a former private retreat totally renovated in 1992. The concrete guest house, with generous balconies and overhangs, is set well back from the beach, with just three guest rooms on each level, furnished and decorated with Mexican and Central American crafts. Two rooms are air conditioned. Extras include a television and video, and the balcony has commanding sea views.

Set on 60 hillside acres and reached by boat, the hotel has a thousand feet of beachfront, and a fast dive boat to reach the best spots quickly, along with a compressor, ample tanks, and rental equipment. Courses from certification to rescue diving are available. There are also trails through the forest nearby, and horseback riding, fishing and sailing can be arranged. The wind is steady, and is said to help control the sand flies on the beach.

WHERE TO EAT

Bonacca has various eating places where locals gather for drinks and snacks, the **Ca Fé Coral** and **Glenda's** among them.

SPORTS AND RECREATION

Snorkeling trips to offshore cays and points around the island are organized on an ad-hoc basis from most of the hotels, usually at $10 per person or so. For diving, if you're not staying at one of the hotels that offer packages, inquire at Dive Inn at the Ca Fé Coral eatery (but look over the equipment). Fishing can be arranged with various skippers in Bonacca Town, if your hotel doesn't have the capability.

NIGHTLIFE

There's a disco, or juke joint, called **Mountain View**, which, while a basic sort of place with a large dance hall, such as you will find in any Central American village, affords unusual views of water and boats on three sides, and mountains on the other.

PRACTICAL INFORMATION

Bonacca has a bank branch (**Banco Atlántida**), several general stores, pharmacy, and a cable television system!

CAYOS COCHINOS (HOG CAYS)

The **Hog Cays** are off the coast of Honduras, *20 kilometers to the northeast of La Ceiba, and 30 kilometers south of Roatán*. Consisting of two main islands and thirteen smaller cays, they have coral reefs, coconut palms, small mountains, and hardly any inhabitants but for a few Garífuna (Black Carib) fishermen. The entire mini-archipelago is a marine reserve, **Santuario Marino Cayos Cochinos**.

Big Hog (Cayo Grande) and **Little Hog** (Cayo Pequeño) are the two major islands, the former U-shaped, providing a sheltered anchorage, and covered with hardwoods, palm, and cactus.

ARRIVALS AND DEPARTURES
By Air
Transport to the island is by air taxi from La Ceiba or San Pedro Sula to a landing strip on Cochino Pequeño Cay just across the water from the hotel, at $100 to $150 per person (sometimes included with off-season packages).

By Boat
There is also informal and irregular boat service to some of the Hog Cays from the Garífuna fishing villages east of La Ceiba. Ask in Nueva Armenia. If you go on your own, take a hammock and all your food and plenty of time; but what you will have to pay for camping and how you will return are unpredictable.

Moorings off the reef are available at Plantation Beach (see below) for visiting yachts.

WHERE TO STAY
PLANTATION BEACH RESORT. *10 rooms. U.S. address: 8582 Katy Freeway, Suite 118, Houston, TX 77024, tel. 800-628-3723, fax 713-973-8585. In Honduras, call or fax 420974. Weekly dive package $750 to $900 per person, including three daily boat dives and night dives; non-diver $700.*

To *really* get away from it all, you'll book a week at Plantation Beach on privately owned Cayo Grande, the largest island in the group — all of a mile across, and once a pineapple plantation. Guests stay in mahogany-and-stone cottages, with hammocks and decks, four rooms with sleeping lofts to each. There are also two small separate houses.

In addition to diving at some of the less-visited (and even unexplored) sites in the islands, there are hiking trails, a beach, snorkeling, windsurfing, and sailboats available for charter.

WESTERN HONDURAS

Western Honduras is mountainous, curving along the borders of Guatemala and El Salvador. It is fairly densely populated for Honduras (though it doesn't seem so), with the highest concentration of Indian inhabitants, some living in villages virtually isolated from modern life. There are few roads, most of them are unpaved, rutted, and little traveled.

The Road to Copán

Copán, site of the most important pre-Columbian ruins in Honduras, is just 225 kilometers by air from Tegucigalpa. But there are no scheduled flights, and the roads that meander out this way in a roughly direct route from Tegucigalpa are so poor, that most travelers go all the way to San Pedro Sula from the capital, then cut back to the south — a trip of close to 500 kilometers — or else charter a small plane.

COPÁN RUINAS

This town, also known at times in its history as San José de Copán, is quaint and small, with a population of under 5000. It's in a lovely valley surrounded by gentle mountains, not too cold, and not too warm, at an altitude of about 600 meters. The streets are cobblestoned, many buildings have tile roofs, and the plaza has a colonial air — all in all, a pleasant place just for resting and walking around. The ruins that give the town its name are a kilometer away.

ARRIVALS & DEPARTURES

By Bus

From San Pedro Sula, the Etumi bus company has at least two direct buses daily to Copán Ruinas, recently at 10 a.m. and 1 p.m., from 6 Calle, 6/7 Avenidas SW.

Empresa de Transportes Torito, 5 Avenida SW No. 34, *tel. 534930*, has buses departing hourly (or more frequently) to Santa Rosa de Copán. To reach the ruins of Copán, take this bus as far as La Entrada (two hours), then catch the bus for Copán Ruinas at the Texaco station, departing about every 40 minutes until 4:30 p.m. It's still a ride of another two hours or so from this point. The road is tortuous in both the back-and-forth and up-and-down senses, but not in bad enough shape to slow vehicles to a crawl, a combination that can lead to unpleasant consequences for passengers. Take a travel sickness pill if you're subject to that malady. Copán Ruinas is 64 kilometers onward.

To Guatemala

Guatemala is just 11 kilometers away from Copán, but anyplace interesting in Guatemala is farther removed, and transport from the border area is poor.

Vans leave Copán Ruinas for the border at El Florido every hour, starting at 7 a.m. Leave town by noon to make onward connections. Buses leave from the border at 8 a.m., 10 a.m. and 12:30 p.m. for Chiquimula, the first major town in Guatemala. Intermittent transport in pickup trucks is sometimes available at other hours. For more details, see *Guatemala Guide*, by Paul Glassman (Open Road Publishing).

THINGS TO DO

The Regional Museum, *on the town square*, is well done, and gives a good presentation of the Maya. Not only jade and shell and bone jewelry are housed here, but also some of the more valuable altars and monuments from both the main ceremonial center and outlying areas. You can see the reconstruction of a tomb, the jewels of a governor, the dried blood of an ancient sacrifice, a skull with jade filling in a tooth, a very male bat from Temple 22, an expressive sculpture called "the melancholy woman," and clay figurines.

The museum is well worth a visit. Hours are 8 a.m. to noon and 1 to 4 p.m., and there is a small charge.

Panoramic Views

For a panorama of the town of Copán Ruinas and the valley stretching beyond, walk up to the **Cuartel**, also known as **Fuerte José Trinidad Cabañas**, the remains of an old army outpost, on the hill four blocks directly north of the square — follow the road that passes the museum. Though of centenary appearance, with massive walls and corner towers, and empty inside but for a grassy expanse, it only dates from 1946.

WHERE TO STAY

Comfortable rooms are rather limited in number in Copán Ruinas, and if there's a tour group in town, facilities will be quickly overwhelmed. It's best to arrive with reservations, or in a rented vehicle so that you can backtrack to San Pedro Sula or continue to Guatemala if everything desirable is full.

Phone service to Copán Ruinas is limited. If you can't call a hotel directly, *dial 983010* and ask for the hotel you want. If this doesn't work, send a telegram (which is inexpensive within Honduras).

These hotels are all on the main square, or just a few blocks away:

HOTEL MARINA, *tel. 983070, 983071, fax 983072 (tel. 390956, fax 390957 in Tegucigalpa). 40 rooms. $64 single/ $75 double/$90 in suite, $11 per extra person, less in older rooms. Visa, Master Card, American Express. Add $25 for three meals.*

This gracious establishment, located on one side of the main square, is the best place to stay, a complex that has grown from a traditional town home to a resort complex, the only one in this part of Honduras with pool, air-conditioned rooms, sauna, tennis courts, and meeting facilities. The wings of the new section, built in traditional ranch style with covered outdoor passageways, barrel-tile roofs and red-tile floors, surround quiet interior gardens. Rooms have televisions and modern bathrooms.

Since the Marina is the only resort-class hotel in Copán Ruinas, it's often filled with visitors on package trips from San Pedro Sula or the Bay Islands; and a tour could well be your only option for getting a comfortable room in Copán Ruinas during the dry season. An overnight trip from San Pedro Sula generally costs $130 or more per person, including bus, meals, and guide service at the ruins.

The **HOTEL MAYA COPAN**, *near the museum*, with a courtyard covered with flowers and tropical plants, is attractive on the surface, though rooms are bare and rustic and just adequate, with little light. The rate is about $10 per person. Horseback rides and fishing can be arranged.

Inexpensive hotels are clustered along the road from the square out toward the ruins. The **BRISAS DE COPÁN** has simple, clean rooms — some have private baths. The **MINI-HOTEL PATY** has a few rooms behind the restaurant, sharing bath.

In the same area are **LOS GEMELOS** and the **HOTEL HERNÁNDEZ**. None of these are as atmospheric as the hotels on the square, where most rooms open onto a patio, but they'll do, especially with prices of $5 or so per person, or $10 with private bath. Take a look at what's available before you settle in.

WHERE TO EAT

Generally, you'll eat at the hotels. The **GLIFOS** ("glyphs") restaurant *of the Hotel Marina* offers the most extensive menu in the village, with everything from a club sandwich to Mexican-style chilaquiles (chicken, peppers and fixings served with sauce on tortillas) to steaks to chicken cordon bleu. Breakfast at the Marina costs about $4, lunch or dinner $10 or so for a complete meal.

LA LLAMA DEL BOSQUE ("flame of the forest"), a block and a half from the museum, also has good food.

The **TUNKUL**, a block south of the museum, is the local book exchange, gossip center, and not coincidentally, most popular spot for eating and imbibing. Bar food is served: sandwiches, salads, chicken, spaghetti and *baleadas* (Honduran burritos), all at $5 or less. Unusual for town eating places, pleasant North American music usually plays.

The **MINI-HOTEL PATY** serves a set meal for $2, including a tiny main course but extensive garnishings of plantains, beans, and rice. And there are cheap eating stands in the market.

LEARN SPANISH

The **Escuela de Español Ixbalanque** ("Ish-ba-lan-keh" Spanish school) offers one-on-one instruction in Spanish for four hours a day, five days a week. Students board with local Spanish-speaking families, or have the option of staying at a hotel. The directors of the school are a Texan and a Honduran, and all teachers are government-certified.

Since Copán Ruinas is pretty much a backwater town without the hordes of resident foreigners present in other Spanish-language study centers (Antigua, Guatemala, or San José, Costa Rica), students have ample opportunity to experience the language in an extemporaneous' manner. Which is to say, you can talk a lot in Spanish with real people in real-life situations.

Rates at Ixbalanque are modest, indeed — $125 a week, including room and board, if a room is taken with a local family. They'll even arrange pickup in San Pedro Sula for an additional charge.

To reserve class time and accommodations, contact Darla Brown, Escuela Ixbalanque, Copán Ruinas, Honduras, tel. 983432, fax 576215.

EXCURSIONS FROM COPÁN RUINAS

M.C. Tours, *working out of the Hotel Marina, tel. 983453 and 983454,* arranges package stays in Copán and excursions in the area. Offerings are a horseback tour of the coffee farm of the Welchez family, which owns the Hotel Marina; a visit to hot springs; a cloud forest hike; and a horseback visit to outlying ruins are available. Prices range from $25 to $30 per person. And, now that the phones are in, they can arrange package tours throughout the country.

Go Native Adventure Tours, *working out of Ixbalanque Spanish School (tel. 983432, fax 576215),* offers excursions to students and non-students alike. Destinations include Pico Bonito cloud forest, Cuero y Salado wildlife refuge, the forests, rivers and lagoons of Mosquitia, and a beach walk from Puerto Cortés to Tela. Rates vary accoridng to number of participants and the trip — about $150 to visit two reserves, including an overnight stay, $450 for a five-day trip through Mosquitia.

PRACTICAL INFORMATION
Exchanging Money

The free market for currency exchange is on the square. You can usually get rid of Guatemalan money here, or right at the border, if you're coming from that direction, but it will be hard to exchange Guatemalan currency anywhere else in Honduras. There's also a bank at one corner of the square.

Phone & Post

The Hondutel (telephone) office and post office are near the museum.

Laundry Service

Copán Ruinas is also the cleanup center for traveling grungy gringos. **Justo a Tiempo** ("Just in Time") laundry, *just off the square alongside the church*, offers same-day wash and dry. Arrive in the morning, drop off your clothes, see the ruins, and change for dinner. *Open 7:30 a.m. to 5:30 p.m., Monday through Friday.*

THE COPÁN RUINS

Copán was the Athens of the Mayan world, where art and astronomy flourished. There were larger Mayan cities to the north, in present-day Mexico and Guatemala, and the structures at Copán are relatively modest compared to those at Tikal and Palenque and Chichén-Itzá. But there are more carved monuments at Copán then elsewhere, and the intricate, swirling, decorative art surpasses not only that of other Mayan cities, but of any other civilization in the Western Hemisphere before the arrival of Europeans.

Copán might have been settled as early as 2000 B.C. The valley was fertile and well watered. Over time, harvests became more and more abundant, with the perfection of corn agriculture and of a calendar to guide planting. Gradually, more organized societies grew up in Copán and the neighboring areas, among the people that are today called the Maya.

Copán developed in much the same way as other Mayan cities. Simple thatched houses on foundations evolved into temples on substantial masonry platforms. Ironwood, or *chicozapote*, substituted for less sturdy materials in lintels. Relatively soft volcanic rock was dressed using harder rock, and later incised with obsidian tools. Household implements were made of wood and clay; as techniques improved, pottery became more complex, and beautiful, and was used for ceremonial purposes. Newer, more complicated, more beautiful buildings were erected right on top of older ones.

The custom developed of memorializing rulers and royal families and recording history on buildings and monuments and in tombs. Great stones were rolled down from nearby mountains, carved with glyph figures representing names and numbers and events, and erected in the plazas as stelae.

The Rise ...

None of this happened in isolation. The **Copán River**, which flows into the Motagua, in present-day Guatemala, probably served as a link to other Mayan centers, and as a route for trade in cacao and obsidian, and there were probably roads as well. There are some artistic similarities between Copán and Quiriguá in Guatemala, which could have been reached by water, and the same language was used for writing throughout the Mayan area.

The Classic Era at Copán spanned just a few hundred years, from 465 A.D., the first date inscribed on a monument, to 800 A.D. During this period of recorded history, construction and reconstruction and astronomical discoveries and artistic expression were most intense. Despite the general air of mystery that surrounds Copán, the names of some of its rulers are known, and some of its cultural history has even been uncovered: *Smoke Jaguar* lived to the ripe age of 82, and was succeeded by *18 Rabbit*, who broke the tradition of destroying monuments with each change in rulers and using the rubble as fill in new structures. 18 Rabbit's successor, *Squirrel*, commemorated rulers of old whose monuments had been destroyed, and rebuilt the ball court. Other rulers have been identified as *Leaf Jaguar*, *Smoke Monkey*, and *Dawn*.

... and Fall

But the creative impulse and energy of Copán were not to last forever. The city and its suburbs grew, perhaps to more than 15,000 inhabitants. Copán became no longer self-sufficient, and thus vulnerable. For some reason — perhaps war, disease, drought, famine, overuse of resources — building suddenly stopped, no more dates were inscribed, and maintenance came to a halt. Rain forest grew into the plazas and onto the temples, earthquakes tumbled temples, and the city was obscured. People still lived at and near Copán, but not as part of a great civilization.

Interest in Copán was lost, if not the city itself, for a thousand years. Then newly independent and newly opened Central America began to draw interest from potential trading partners. American diplomat John Lloyd Stephens visited Copán in 1839, and later published a description, accompanied by illustrations, in *Incidents of Travel in Central America, Chiapas and Yucatan*. He was so impressed that he bought the site — for fifty dollars.

Reviving Interest in Copán

Alfred P. Maudslay, arriving from England in 1881, was the first of a stream of archeologists to study Copán. For a time, the Carnegie Institution of Washington took charge of the ruins. The **Instituto Nacional de Antropología e Historia** assumed control in 1952. New excavations have been carried out in recent years. With ongoing work, interpretations of life at Copán, and of the Maya in general, are constantly being revised.

The main ceremonial center of Copán covers about 30 hectares, or 75 acres, but this is only a small part of the residential and administrative and ceremonial area that was built up by the Maya. Other areas which can be visited are called El Bosque ("the forest"), to the southwest, and Las

Sepulturas ("the burials"), to the east. While the main temples and stelae are in the ceremonial center, important monuments, some with detailed chronologies, were placed up and down the slopes of the valley.

ORIENTATION

The ruins are a ten-minute walk from town, about a kilometer away. You can follow the road, or, more pleasantly, take the trail that runs just to the side of the road, right alongside some mounds and carved monuments, or stelae. *The usual visiting hours at the site are from 8 a.m. to 4 p.m. An entry fee of several dollars is collected.*

The **visitors' center** is well organized and well maintained. There are some exhibits, and a model of the site, photos, pottery (including pieces of Olmec and Teotihuacan origin), sculptured pieces of bone, and jade pendants. Time-line charts show the rise of the Maya relative to contemporary civilizations. Take a good look before you go out among the ruins. Several guide booklets are available for sale, including one in English published by the Instituto Hondureño de Antropología e Historia.

There are two **restaurants**, the official one in the visitor's center, with limited offerings; and one across the road, which is owned by one of the guides, is inexpensive, and serves decent, simple food. Both restaurants have gift shops attached. There are also picnic tables in a citrus grove toward the ruins.

Hiring a Guide

Guides can be hired on-site. They have a lot more information, especially in the way of local lore, than is provided in this book or in the booklets you can buy at the site; and though some of what they tell you may be strictly anecdotal, and may conflict with published descriptions and analyses, I strongly recommend that you hire one in order not to miss anything. Expect to pay a guide $10 or more for a two-hour walkaround.

Walking Around the Ceremonial Center

From the reception center, walk across the airstrip. You approach the ruins via a wide trail lined with towering tropical trees.

• **Caution 1**: You can be heavily fined if you destroy or damage anything at the site — stone, plant or animal — or if you try to take home any souvenirs. Or you can go to prison for several years. Or both.

• **Caution 2**: There are irritating plants, sometimes ten feet high, which can cause a severe reaction. They have pale-green leaves and small spines.

The **Ceremonial Court**, or **Great Plaza**, is the long, open area that you reach first, at the northern extreme of the ruins. There are stairways on three sides, and stelae, or large stones, reaching as high as four meters, carved with some of the most beautiful art created by the Maya. All of the exposed facing stones were once covered with stucco, and painted.

In most cases, the stelae were erected to celebrate an important event, such as the coronation or accession of a ruler. The noble figure is depicted figuratively, with animals and fruits and trees as symbols of power and lineage and ruling forces. Elaborate glyphs depict dates and detail history. Everything is exaggerated, and interlaces in an Oriental manner, and indeed, some modern adventure-scholars have found notable similarities between Copán sculpture and art in Asia.

Most of the stelae show a noble, probably a king or other official of Copán, standing straight up with feet together, short arms crossed in front, holding a scepter, a flamboyant accoutrement upon his head. Additional figures and ornaments fill the front of the block, while glyphs on the sides and back relate the story of the ruler and his dynasty.

Stela A, dating from 731 A.D., at the south of the Ceremonial Court, includes the glyph symbols for Tikal and Palenque, indicating knowledge of and contact with those other Mayan cities. The chamber underneath this and other stelae held offerings of jewelry, ceramics, and sometimes animals. Stela 4, just north of Stela A, comes from late in the recorded history of Copán, and shows that art evolved toward more natural representation. A great round stone in front of Stela 4, looking like a four-foot-high Big Mac, was used to sacrifice captives and human offerings. The head of the victim was placed on a depression in the surface, and channels carried off the blood, making for a neat job.

Stela B, to the north of Stela 4, commemorates the accession of a ruler named 18 Rabbit. Symbols of power include the macaws' beaks at the top, miniature heads of previous rulers, and the detailed headdress. The beaks were once thought to be the trunks of elephants, imputing a direct knowledge by the Maya of things Asian. **Stela C**, unusually, has a figure carved on the back instead of glyphs, and shows traces of red paint, which might once have covered other monuments as well. Both an old and young figure are shown. A turtle-shaped stone lies alongside.

Stela D, next to the steps at the north end of the plaza, dating from 736 A.D., shows a double column of glyphs on the rear side. The short beard of the figure is an indication of youth. Sea shells and figures of gods appear on top. The figures on the altar before it are of Chac, the god of rain.

Along the east side of the plaza, **Stela F**, to the north, also with the remains of paint, shows a figure whose robes extend from the front around the sides to form a frame for the glyphs on the back. A representation of the sun is similar to those on stelae C and 4, and the same artist might well have carved all three. Next comes Altar G, a double-headed serpent with a glyph equivalent to 800 A.D., one of the latest dates written at Copán. **Stela H** shows an unusual figure in a skirt, who may be a representation of 18 Rabbit. A statue found underneath was made of gold that probably came from Colombia or Panama.

Stela I, inset in a stairway on the east side of the court, shows a masked figure, who may be Smoke Jaguar, who ruled from 628 to 695 A.D., and was the father of 18 Rabbit.

The **Central Court** is the area adjoining the ceremonial plaza, on the south. All the way at the eastern extreme is Stela J, covered completely by glyphs. The only similar Mayan stela known is at Quiriguá.

The **Ball Court** is just south of the Ceremonial Court, characteristically a narrow paved area with three sloped sides. Some glyphs along the platforms bear the Mayan equivalent of 775 A.D., and others represent royal macaws. The macaw was a sacred and symbolic bird for the Maya, and you'll see plenty of macaws around Copán today, especially on the fence at the entrance to the site. This court sits atop two earlier structures, the first built in the fifth century. The players probably had to hit markers along the side with a rubber ball. In ball games played elsewhere when the Spaniards arrived, the losers lost their heads.

The Ball Court is closed to foot traffic, and more and more areas of the site are being closed to casual visitors, as it becomes painfully clear that removing earth and debris, and exposing Mayan structures to the elements and to the footsteps of visitors, only hastens their deterioration.

To the south of the Ball Court is the most spectacular of Copán's treasures: the **Hieroglyphic Stairway**. More than a thousand glyphs set in the 63 steps — together constituting the longest known Mayan inscription — relate the history of Copán's rulers, up to 755 A.D., when the structure was dedicated under ruler *Smoke Shell*. Unfortunately, the glyphs can barely be read, since the stairway was rebuilt and the stones reset in random sequence.

Along the center of the stairway are four male sculptures that remain of the original five. An altar before the steps shows a head inside the jaws of a monster.

In 1989, archeologists excavating behind the hieroglyphic stairway stumbled upon a noble tomb, considered to be that of *Yax Cuc Mol*, King Quetzal-Macaw.

Along the south of the stairway plaza, **Stela N** is an especially beautiful work of art, dated at 761 A.D. The human faces on each side extend to the edges, almost as a precursor to a statue. Serpents and indications of the cardinal points can be seen on top. One glyph on the back represents Mars; the Maya also had symbols for Jupiter and Venus.

Altar O, opposite the Hieroglyphic Stairway, is a stone block with a depression that might have served as a seat. **Altar 41**, nearby, has a jaguar face and a snake at the north and south ends, respectively, of its front face, possibly representing a mythical struggle. "Altar" is a generic term, used in the absence of any real knowledge of what purposes these blocks served.

The group of structures to the south of the Hieroglyphic Stairway is called the **Acropolis**. Overlooking the Western Court of the Acropolis is **Temple 11**, with its staircase called the Reviewing Stand. Huge snails and grotesque gods, one of them *Ik*, the rain god, adorn the way up the steps to the Temple of the Inscriptions, with its glyph panels. "El Viejo" (The Old Man), the gap-toothed sculpture at the southwest corner of the superstructure, stares right at a stela on a distant mountainside. Temple 11 was built during the reign of *Yax Pac* ("King Dawn," also known as "rising sun"), who ruled from 763 A.D. until his death in 820, and oversaw the last major construction at Copán.

In 1993, a tomb was discovered under Acropolis, apparently that of *Yax Kuk Mo*, the fifth-century ruler who founded Copán's royal dynasty.

Along the eastern edge of the Western Court, **Altar Q** depicts the royal lineage of Yax Pac. Four royal figures are shown on each side of the rectangular block; together, they are Yax Pac, and his 15 ancestors.

The last major area of central Copán is the **Eastern Court** of the Acropolis. Like other open areas, this plaza was slightly sloped, and a Mayan drain still carries off rain water. **Temple 22**, on the north side, built under the reign of *18 Rabbit*, who ruled from 695 to 738 A.D., is another spectacular example of Mayan architecture as spectacle. The doorway to the structure at the top is flanked by sculpture that turns it into monstrous serpents' jaws. At the corners are figures of *Chac*, the long-nosed god of rain. These motifs are indications of influence from Mayan areas farther to the north. The inner doorway shows themes from Mayan cosmology, including death's heads at the base. Along the sides, figures called *Bacabs*, looking like caricatures of modern-day Maya, hold up heaven, with a two-headed serpent above.

A model of Temple 22 may be seen in the visitors' center.

On the west side of the Eastern Court is the **Jaguar Stairway**. Stone jaguars flank the steps. Their eye sockets, now empty, were once filled with polished obsidian.

Temple 20, largely sliced away by the shifting Copán River below, is on the eastern side of the court. The river was re-routed in 1935 to forestall further damage. Some protective work is still going on. The layers visible on the damaged side of the temple neatly illustrate how new buildings were erected directly atop older ones.

Nature Trail

Adjacent to the ceremonial center is a trail through a section of tropical forest that has been protected from agricultural development. A

Spanish-language guide booklet is available on site. The trail runs for about a kilometer, ending at **Ball Court B**.

Copán's protected forest is a sample of leafy mid-level rain forest, with its vegetation determined by elevation, rainfall and temperature. It's considered a seasonally dry forest, since rain falls mostly from May to November, and the trees shed their leaves during dry periods to conserve energy.

5. GUATEMALA

HISTORY

All over Guatemala are the vestiges of cultures that flourished before the arrival of the Spanish. In the Pacific lowlands are great sculptures of animals, and massive stone heads. In the highlands stand the ruins of ceremonial and defensive cities. Spread across the jungles of the Petén are Mayan centers so numerous that they are still being rediscovered.

The older the remains, the more mysterious they are. The highland cities are the least unknown, for in some cases they were still occupied when the Spanish began their conquest. The Maya had a system of hieroglyphic writing, which, along with intensive excavations of Mayan ruins, gives some idea of their history and way of life. **Kaminaljuyú**, near Guatemala City, is a puzzle because of the many similarities in its architectural and ceramic styles with those of Teotihuacán, an important center far to the north in central Mexico. Strangest of all are the sculptures around **Santa Lucía Cotzumalguapa** in the Pacific lowlands, found apart from anything that would give clues as to where the people who made them came from, or what became of them.

By the early part of the Christian era, many of the Mayan settlements were growing into ceremonial centers. The **Early Classic** period of Mayan civilization, extending from about 300 to 600 A.D., saw the development of **Tikal** as one of the major cities in the Americas. The temple pyramids of Tikal, which reached their greatest heights in the eighth century, were the tallest structures in the hemisphere until the development of office buildings in the nineteenth century.

After hundreds of years of development, the great Mayan cities of the Petén suddenly went through a period of sharp decline, starting in the ninth century A.D. Nobody knows why, but speculation brings up invasion, revolt, drought, epidemic and exhaustion of the land as possible causes.

But Mayan building and cultural development continued elsewhere until the arrival of the Spanish, and even afterward in the areas outside Spanish control. By the year 1000, the center of Mayan civilization was the Yucatán. There, the Maya came under the influence of the **Toltecs** of central Mexico, and many of the Toltec gods and culture heroes came into the Mayan pantheon. Toltec motifs found their way into the ceremonial centers, and the greater use of columns and wooden beams gave a new grace and spaciousness to buildings. More is known about the Yucatán Maya than about the Classic Maya of the Petén, for a few Spaniards took note of their customs, and some of their oral history was dictated after they were conquered.

Civil war eventually broke out in the Yucatán, and by the time the Spanish arrived, the ceremonial cities had been abandoned. It took the Spanish twenty years to assert control of the region, after suffering an initial series of disastrous defeats. And it wasn't until 1697 that the last outpost of the Maya, the city of **Tayasal** on **Lake Petén Itzá** in northern Guatemala, fell to the Spanish.

After the Maya migrated northward, other Indian nations flourished in the highlands. The languages they spoke were in most cases related to Mayan, and it's common to refer to them and their present-day descendants as Maya, though in fact they were a blend of the races and cultural currents that preceded them in the region.

The highland nations of Guatemala were almost continuously at war with one another. Unlike the Maya and the people who had inhabited Kaminaljuyú, they built their cities in inaccessible locations surrounded by ravines. From these fortified capitals, they ruled over their own territories and those of subject nations. In their art and architecture, they copied many of the stylistic elements of the Indian nations of Mexico, but their cities were relatively small, and bare of decoration.

The principal nation of pre-Conquest Guatemala was the **Quiché**, sometimes called the **Maya-Quiché**. The name of this people means *many trees*, taken perhaps from the forested highlands which they inhabited. They occupied the area running from the present town of Chichicastenango westward past Quezaltenango. Their capital was **Cumarcaj**, which the Spanish and their Mexican Indian allies called **Utatlán**.

The Quichés have left one of the few documents to describe Indian history before the Conquest. The *Popol Vuh*, their sacred book, was set down in the Quiché language using the Latin alphabet a few years after the Conquest. In a form and tone that bring to mind the Christian Bible, it tells of the creation of the world, and of the wanderings of the ancestors of the Quichés from a place called **Tulán**. There is good evidence that this Tulán was the **Toltec Tula**, which was shaken by internal struggles just a few years before the Quichés appeared in highland Guatemala around

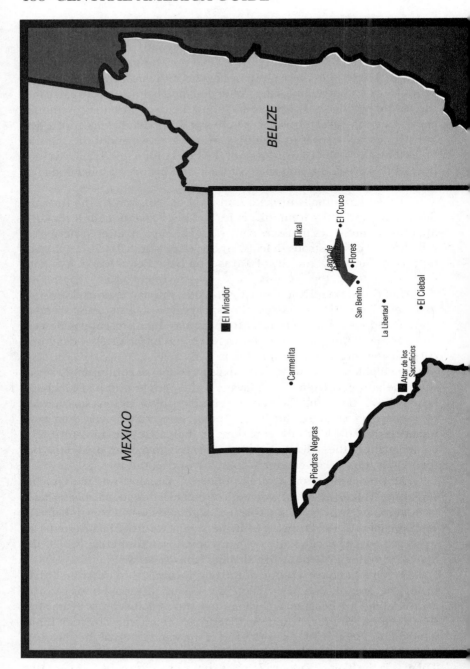

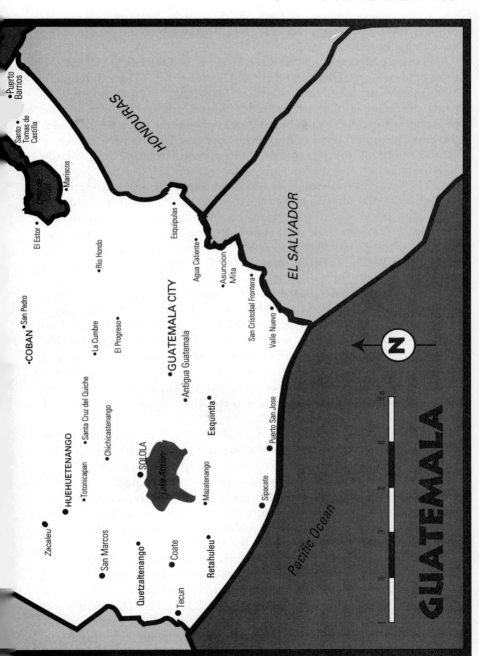

the year 1000. The migrants might have integrated with the natives of the area and adopted their language.

Pedro de Alvarado arrived in the lands of the **Quichés** in 1523, at the head of an army of Spanish soldiers and horsemen and **Tlaxcalan** Indian allies numbering less than a thousand men. Alvarado was supposed to bring the peoples of the area under the rule of the Spanish throne peacefully, if that were possible. But of course it was not, and Alvarado, 34 years old and a veteran of the bloody battles at Tenochtitlán, the Aztec capital, was hardly the man to show diplomacy and tact in dealing with the Indian nations.

The invasion route of Alvarado led through the jungle lowlands of southern Mexico, up the mountain pass in the shadow of the volcano Santa María, and toward the Quiché realm. After routing opposition in skirmishes along the way, the Spanish met the main Quiché army near where the city of Quezaltenango now stands, and thoroughly defeated it. During the battle, **Tecún Umán**, king of the Quichés, was killed by Alvarado himself.

The **Kingdom of Guatemala** of colonial times, ruled over by a captain-general, stretched from Chiapas to the border of Panama. In it, the Spaniards sought to erect a miniature Spain. The Spaniards who came to the New World did not see themselves as frontier dwellers doing without the comforts and familiar things of life at home. Towns were laid out according to the traditional Spanish pattern, with public buildings, a church and residential quarters set around a plaza and market. Governors, priests, judges, artists and craftsmen were imported to build and administer the Spanish order.

The capital of the kingdom was the third city of **Santiago de los Caballeros de Guatemala**, today's **Antigua**. It ranked with Mexico City and Lima as one of the great metropolises of the hemisphere.

The capital lived an uneasy existence from its founding in 1541. Floods, volcanic eruptions, famine, epidemic and earthquakes ravished Santiago from time to time. But the dead were buried, the rubble cleared, and buildings built and rebuilt as what wealth there was to be had in Guatemala became concentrated in the city.

In 1773, a series of earthquakes destroyed Santiago. In the wreckage of the capital, the conflict between church and civil authority came to a head. The captain-general favored relocation of the capital to a site that would, it was hoped, be less vulnerable to earthquakes. The archbishop insisted that the capital be rebuilt on its old site. The captain-general removed the civil government to the valley of La Ermita, but the church nobles and religious orders remained in Santiago and started reconstruction, staying even after the king ordered the transfer of the capital.

New Guatemala of the Assumption — Guatemala City — was officially founded in 1776, but it wasn't until 1780 that the archbishop gave up his struggle, under direct orders from the Pope. The Church was weakened in the conflict, but it remained a major force well into the period after independence.

Independence came, after a fashion, on September 15, 1821, when twelve prominent men of Guatemala City signed an **Act of Independence of Central America**. Soon afterward, **Emperor Iturbide** sent troops to force Guatemala to join his newly independent Mexican Empire.

Despite independe, Guatemala remained a backward country. Transportation was primitive, where it existed at all, and except for the other nations of Central America, which had to take it into account as the most populous and powerful state of the area, nobody outside its borders had much interest in Guatemala. What little trade there was, mainly the export of cochineal and indigo, declined after 1857, when synthetic dyes were developed.

Things changed drastically starting in 1871, when **Miguel García Granados** led his Liberal forces to victory over the government of Cerna. García Granados held the presidency for only a few months. His successor, **Justo Rufino Barrios**, began the systematic modernization of Guatemala. Under Barrios, a national bank was established, roads were built, church property was confiscated, and freedom of worship was declared. A national system of schools was set up, and the beginnings were made on a railway system.

Barrios was succeeded by a number of presidents who followed Liberal development policies. A concession was granted to the **International Railways of Central America** for the completion of the railroad system that Barrios had started. And large tracts of land in the nearly unpopulated Caribbean lowlands were turned over to an American firm, the **United Fruit Company**, for the planting of bananas.

After World War II, **Jacobo Arbenz Guzmán** started a program aimed at putting unused land into production, which provoked opposition from the United Fruit Company. Arbenz was overthrown in 1954 by **Col. Carlos Castillo Armas**, who was actively supported by the United States. After several coups and assassinations of military strongmen, a civilian, **Julio César Méndez Montenegro**, was elected president in 1966, though the military continued to influence government actions.

In the 1960s, Guatemala went through a period of industrial expansion, following the creation of the **Central American Common Market**. Companies geared up production on a larger scale for markets throughout the region. The processed-food, beverage, shoe, clothing and textile industries grew. Tires, cosmetics, paints, building materials, chemicals, drugs, and many other items that had formerly been imported, began to be produced in Guatemala. Foreign aid helped in the construction of health centers, schools, water-supply systems, market buildings, and new roads.

But with expansion and industrialization came increased social and political tensions. Paternalistic attitudes, developed over centuries of domination of Indian masses by Spanish and then Ladino elites, resisted adaptation to changed circumstances. Independent labor unions, land reform and welfare programs were seen by some powerful factions — and to a large extent still are seen — as threats to the social fabric.

During the term of Méndez Montenegro, the army conducted a campaign against insurgents in the northeast of the country. One of the leaders of that campaign, **Carlos Manuel Arana Osorio**, became president in 1970. He was succeeded by **Gen. Kjell Eugenio Laugerud García** in 1974. **Gen. Romeo Lucas García** took office as president in 1978. Charges of fraud accompanied every election.

Under Lucas, all protest was ruthlessly suppressed. Moderate politicians were regularly assassinated, and their murderers never pursued. Insurrection raged once again, this time mostly in the west of the country. Guerrilla bands attacked army outposts and patrols, the army rounded up suspected rebels and their supporters, and civilians were gunned down, or fled across the border to Mexico and Belize. The chosen successor to Lucas handily came out on top in the 1982 election, but before he could be sworn in, junior officers staged a coup and called on **Gen. Efraín Ríos Montt** to take over the government.

Under Ríos Montt, the anti-guerrilla campaign intensified. In an effort to strangle guerrilla support, Indians were conscripted into civilian defense patrols, and in some cases were concentrated into new settlements under military control. Somewhat of an odd man out among his fellow officers, as a preaching Protestant with social concerns, Ríos was replaced in 1983 by **Gen. Humberto Mejía Víctores** .

In the wake of turmoil in Guatemala and elsewhere in Central America, the economy went into a tailspin. Many of the mechanisms of the Central American Common Market ceased to function, export prices for sugar and coffee stagnated, tourists traveled elsewhere, unemployment soared, and the quetzal, long one of the strongest currencies in Latin America, lost more than half its value. Bad luck plagued the most promising development projects. A large nickel-mining project near Lake Izabal was mothballed as the world price of nickel declined, plunging prices took the gleam off newly developed petroleum reserves in Alta Verapaz, and even the intake tunnels of the huge Chixoy hydroelectric project were found to be leaky.

As the level of violence declined, the military moved toward washing its hands of responsibility for administering the country. Elections for a constituent assembly were held in 1984, and in 1985, power was turned over to the elected civilian government of Christian Democrat **Marco Vinicio Cerezo Arévalo**, after the army first declared a self-amnesty and assured itself continuing rural control.

World attention, when it was turned toward Guatemala, continued to focus on the government's ruthless repression of any dissent among the Indian majority. This was especially true when the 1992 Nobel Peace Prize was awarded to **Rigoberta Menchú**, a Quiché Indian activist most of whose family was murdered in military sweeps or after participating in peaceful demonstrations.

Jorge Serrano was elected to the presidency in 1991, despite well-publicized charges of shady business dealings. Whether the charges were true or not, once in power, his actions hardly calmed those who had misgivings. He dissolved congress and seized total power in mid-1993, after a military coup he allegedly had staged himself as a pretext for a power grab.

But Serrano soon was pressured to resign, and fled the country. His administration saw continued turmoil in the economy, with widespread electrical shortages. His administration recognized the independence of neighboring Belize, despite local opposition.

Following Serrano's departure, Guatemala experienced the most stunning peaceful turnabout in its history: Congress elected the former human rights ombudsman, **Ramiro de León Carpio**, to the presidency.

In early 1994, in a first-ever electoral ratification, an overwhelming majority of those voting (but still a considerable minority of the population) approved constitutional changes aimed at instituting effective separation of powers.

There have been some signs of a calming of the long-simmering war between the classes of Guatemala, and occasional efforts to punish those responsible for continuing abuses. The killer of **Myrna Mack**, a Guatemalan who was researching the treatment of Indians by the army in conflict areas, was sentenced to 30 years in prison in 1993, an action unthinkable not long before.

But despite occasional meetings between the government and the main guerrilla umbrella group, the **UNRG** (**Unidad Revolucionaria Nacional Guatemalteca**), and the return of some refugees from Mexico, armed opposition and mining of bridges, oil facilities, telephone towers, and other strategic targets continued into 1994.

LAND & PEOPLE

Guatemala, situated at the northern end of the Central American isthmus, borders on Mexico, the Pacific Ocean, the Caribbean Sea, El Salvador, Honduras, and Belize. It covers 132,000 square kilometers (42,000 square miles), an area just larger than that of the state of Ohio.

Packed into the country's relatively small area are towering mountains, tropical plains, near-desert river valleys, temperate plateaus, and lowland jungles and swamps.

The backbone of Guatemala is a branch of the **Sierra Madre** that enters from Mexico and breaks up into a series of smaller ranges spread through the southern half of the country. A chain of volcanoes runs parallel to the Pacific and on into El Salvador, forming the southern rim of the highlands, where most of the population lives. Guatemala means *the land of many trees*, and the name of the country was first applied to this area of pine and oak and fir. Over the years, much of the forest cover has been cleared off and the land planted in corn.

Between the mountains and the Pacific Ocean lies a wide plain broken by rivers rushing down from the highlands. The climate is hot and humid, but the gently rolling land, the ease of transportation, and especially the fertile soil make the Pacific lowlands the richest agricultural area of Guatemala, where most of the sugar cane, cotton and cattle are raised. Bordering this plain on the north is the narrow Pacific slope, where coffee is the chief crop.

To the north and northeast of the highlands, the land drops off more gradually than in the south. In **Alta Verapaz**, a coffee-growing area to the northeast of Guatemala City, the population density is lower than in the western highlands, and some of the native flora and fauna remain relatively undisturbed. Orchids flourish in the forests, and the *quetzal*, the rare bird that is the national symbol of Guatemala, can be seen occasionally.

Between Guatemala City and the Caribbean is the upper valley of the **Motagua River**, one of the few arid regions of the country, shielded from rainfall by the **Sierra de las Minas**. The relatively small Caribbean lowland region is, like the Pacific plain, a hot area with fertile soil. It rains all year along the Caribbean, while most of the country receives rainfall only from May to October.

The **Petén**, covering the northern third of Guatemala, is a vast, sparsely settled region of swamps, hardwood forest, grassy plains, and jungle. Wild boars, jaguars, and monkeys roam this remote area where the Maya once erected great cities. Today, roads are being pushed through the Petén, and new land is being opened for farming.

Because of the many climates of the country, almost anything will grow in Guatemala. Plants and trees are nearly endless in their variety. More than a hundred species of orchids are found in the forests. All the tropical fruits — mangoes, papayas, pineapples, and many others — grow in the warm areas, and apples and peaches appear at the higher altitudes. Flowers that are rare in other countries grow wild along the roadsides.

But mostly, what is grown in Guatemala is corn — on mountain slopes, in plots hacked out of the jungle, and in the hot coastal lowlands. Corn is seen everywhere, often with vines of black beans climbing the stalks. In terms of its monetary value, the returns on a corn harvest are low. But corn is what most Guatemalans eat — mainly in the form of tortillas — and what their ancestors ate centuries ago.

In the highlands, wheat is raised, though not enough to meet local needs. It's at the lower altitudes that crops for export are grown on a large scale. On the slopes between the highlands and the coastal plains, coffee and citronella are planted. And farther down are the great plantations of sugar, cotton, bananas and rice, and the large cattle ranches. To the north, in the Petén, some of the hardwoods are exploited.

Small deposits of lead, silver, gold, and jadeite in Guatemala's mountains have been worked since colonial times, but until recently, minerals have been relatively unimportant. Now, vast reserves of nickel-bearing ore have been found around **Lake Izabal**, near the Caribbean. Guatemala is capable of becoming a major exporter of this mineral. And enough petroleum has been discovered to assure self-sufficiency in oil.

GUATEMALA'S TALLEST VOLCANOES

Volcanoes with altitudes of more than 2000 meters, and the towns near which they're located:

Volcano	Altitude	Location
Tajumulco	4220m	Tajumulco, San Marcos
Tacaná	4093	Sibinal, San Marcos
Acatenango	3975	Alotenango, Sacatepéquez
Santa María	3772	Zunil, Quezaltenango
Agua	3766	Santa María de Jesús, Sac.
Fuego	3763	Alotenango, Sacatepéquez
Atitlán	3537	San Lucas Tolimán, Sololá
Siete Orejas	3370	San Martín Sacatepéquez, Quez.
Tolimán	3158	San Lucas Tolimán, Sololá
Cerro Quemado	3027	Quezaltenango, Quezaltenango
San Pedro	3020	San Pedro La Laguna, Sololá
Chicabal	2900	San Martín Sacatepéquez, Quez.
San Antonio	2750	San Antonio Sac., San Marcos
Lacandón	2747	Ostuncalco, Quezaltenango
Cuxliquel	2610	Totonicapán, Totonicapán
Pacaya	2552	San Vicente Pacaya, Escuintla
Jumay	2176	Jalapa, Jalapa
Alzatate	2045	San Carlos Alzatate, Jalapa
Suchitán	2042	Santa Catarina Mita, Jutiapa

Flora & Fauna

The northern jungles of the Petén are quite another story. There, on a visit to Tikal, one has a good chance of running across **spider monkeys** and **howler monkeys**, **armadillos**, **deer**, and **tepezcuintles** (spotted cavies). Off the beaten track are **jaguars**, **pumas**, and **wild boars**. The rush to settle the Petén has seen little provision for protection of jungle animals, and some could become extinct in the not-too-distant future.

Birds are too vast a subject for more than passing mention here. Guatemala's symbol of national liberty is the *quetzal*, a rare species of trogon reputedly unable to live in captivity. The quetzal has red, green, and white coloring, and a spectacular tail feather several feet long. In the few highland areas of Guatemala that are not densely populated, the quetzal can still be seen during its nesting season, generally in April and May. The upper slopes of volcanoes, the Zunil ridge east of Quezaltenango, the Chamá mountains in Alta Verapaz and the ridge of the Santa Cruz mountains north of Senahú, also in Alta Verapaz, are some of the areas where quetzals have been reported recently. A less lucky spot for sightings is the Biotopo del Quetzal (Mario Dary Reserve) in Baja Verapaz. If you won't be hiking, you can see stuffed quetzals at the National Palace, the Banco Agrícola Mercantil, and the Hotel Ritz Continental in Guatemala City.

Flora constitute a subject even more overwhelming and intimidating than birds, given the variety of climates in Guatemala. Most notable are the orchids that flourish in highland forests — hundreds of species, from those invisible at a casual glance, to brazen showoffs, including the national flower, the **monja blanca** (white nun). The national tree is the **ceiba** (kapok, or silk cotton), which shades the main square of many a lowland town with its long-reaching, leafy branches.

People

Most of the ten million Guatemalans are either **Indians** or **Ladinos**. After 300 years under Spanish rule, and another 150 years as an independent nation, Guatemala has not blended these two groups into a single culture.

The terms Ladino and Indian as used in Guatemala have as much to do with the way people live as with their racial heritage. The Indians of Guatemala — *naturales* or *indígenas*, as they prefer to be called — are the descendants of the peoples who lived in the country at the time of the Spanish conquest. Over the centuries, they have altered their clothing styles, their languages, their patterns of settlement and their religious practices.

But while changing their ways, they have maintained distinct regional cultures apart from the national life. Most of Guatemala's Indians live in the western highlands, and in Alta Verapaz and Baja Verapaz north of Guatemala City.

Ladinos are Guatemalans who are not Indian — there's no more exact way to define them. Racially, most Ladinos are **mestizos**, mixtures of Spanish and Indian blood lines. But a Ladino may also be of pure Spanish blood, or part black or oriental. Some Ladinos are pure-blooded descendants of Indians who have given up the Indian way of life.

Separate from all the other groups in Guatemala are the **Lacandón** people of the Petén and neighboring parts of Mexico. Never conquered by the Spanish, they speak a dialect that is thought to be closer to Classic Mayan than any of the other Indian languages of Central America. The Lancandones live in scattered encampments, and hunt and fish and cultivate corn. Their matted hair and rough cotton clothing give them a fierce appearance. Only a few Lacandones remain in Guatemala.

PLANNING YOUR TRIP
Climate & Weather

Despite the "eternal spring" label often applied to Guatemala, weather conditions vary considerably from region to region and season to season.

The difference between rainy season and dry season is most clearly defined in the highlands and along the Pacific coast. The dry season lasts from late October or early November through late April or early May. It's called *verano*, or summer, even though Guatemala is in the northern hemisphere. In the highlands, days are warm and sunny, except for a very rare rainstorm.

Nights are clear, ideal for stargazing when the moon's not out. With the absence of clouds, the day's heat dissipates quickly. Nights can be positively chilling at the higher altitudes, and winds add to the effect. A heavy sweater is a necessity if you're out late or getting up early. Temperatures sometimes drop below freezing above 2150 meters (7000 feet).

April is the warmest month in the highlands. Days are longer, and there are few breezes. Temperatures rise to about 85° Fahrenheit (30° Centigrade) for a few hours in the afternoon. During the rest of the year, the high will be from 75° to 80°F (25° to 27°C), with much variation according to altitude.

The rainy season (*invierno*, or winter) starts at the end of April or sometimes as late as the middle of May. Mornings are clear, but the sky is usually overcast for at least a few hours in the afternoon. Nights are warmer in the highlands during the rainy season, as the clouds hold in the heat of the day.

It's a rare day in the rainy season when there isn't at least some sun. The general pattern is for clear skies in the morning to be followed by the approach of dark clouds and then a downpour. The dark clouds usually give you enough warning to head for shelter. The rains may last for an hour or continue into the night. Usually, the skies clear up for a while in the afternoon. Rainfall is much heavier along the coast than in the highlands. June and September are the months when it rains most.

For rainy season travel, take along a raincoat or umbrella. There are enough sunny hours for swimming, walking and sightseeing.

To the north and northeast of Guatemala City, the rainy season isn't as well defined as in the southern part of the country. The Petén receives some rainfall throughout the year, though it's generally light from February to April. In Alta Verapaz and along the Caribbean, rainfall is lightest in December and from February to April, when there are only a few days of precipitation. As in the south, temperature ranges depend on altitude, though Alta Verapaz lacks the cold extremes of some of the higher elevations to the west of Guatemala City.

Near the Caribbean, the high temperature may approach 100°F (37°C) in May and June, while in January it's usually about 86°F (30°C). It's always cooler along the beaches.

NATIONAL HOLIDAYS

Businesses are closed on the days indicated below, as well as on local fiesta days. Holidays falling on weekends are celebrated on either Friday or Monday.

January 1	*New Year's Day*
	Holy Thursday
	Good Friday
May 1	*Labor Day*
June 30	*Army Day, and Anniversary of 1871 Revolution*
August 15	*Guatemala City fiesta. Businesses closed in Guatemala City only.*
August 29	*Postal Workers Day. Post offices sometimes closed.*
September 15	*Independence Day*
October 20	*Anniversary of 1944 revolution*
November 1	*All Saints' Day*
December 24	*Christmas Eve (afternoon only)*
December 25	*Christmas*
December 31	*New Year's Eve (afternoon only)*

Traveling with Children

In general, take the same precautions for children as for adults. Speak to your pediatrician or consult your community health department before you travel. If you're going to spend time in the sun — and it's practically unavoidable, even if you don't go to a beach — make sure that your child gets plenty to drink, and stays covered up at first. And of course, watch what your child puts in his mouth, and what other people give him.

Pack clothing items similar to those for adults. As well, take a few books and toys (the latter are expensive locally), including a pail and shovel for the beach. Take baby wipes for quick clean-ups. Children need their own identification for immigration purposes, even if they're included on your tourist card.

For babies, take changing supplies and bottle-feeding equipment, if needed. Disposable diapers are available in many towns, but not always in all sizes. The price is almost double that in the States, so you might want to take some along.

Gerber baby foods (instant cereals and strained vegetables and meats) are available in supermarkets in large towns, and sometimes in pharmacies in rural areas. Other readily available food items for babies include canned condensed milk, refrigerated pasteurized milk in some areas, canned fruit juice, cheeses, fruits, and powdered formulas.

With kids in tow, you'll spend considerable time in your hotel room. Be more selective than you might otherwise be. A television in the room and a swimming pool are attractive amenities for the kids, even if you don't need them for yourself.

Hotels in Guatemala rarely charge for children up to three years old. Older children will pay a small extra-bed charge.

If you decide to rent a house or stay in a hotel for an extended length of time, you'll find that you can hire a mother's helper for very little money. Or you can engage a short-term baby sitter through many hotels. A laundress can usually be found to wash and boil cloth diapers.

Private nursery schools and elementary schools in large towns will generally accept visitors' children for short-term enrollment. There are bilingual schools in Guatemala City and Antigua. Most schools are closed in December and part of January for summer vacation.

HOTEL RATES

These are set by a government agency, and in some cases make little sense. For example, you can stay in a lovely old inn in one provincial capital, with landscaped courtyards, great beamed passageways, spotless rooms with private baths and gracious service, and pay $12 for two persons. Or you can go up the street to a plain but newer hotel with no additional amenities and pay twice as much.

The rates I give include taxes totalling 17 percent, and are subject to change, of course. In the case of some newer and larger hotels, the official rates are largely fictitious. For these hotels, you will pay the approved rate only if you book through a travel agency or hotel chain, or travel at Christmas or Easter. You can sometimes get a lower rate — as much as 40 percent off the official rate — when you reserve directly with the hotel, either before you travel or from within Guatemala. In such cases, I give a lower "usual" rate. At the moderate and lower end of the scale, official prices are more realistic, and you can expect increases in some cases. Officially sanctioned rates are generally posted at the reception desk.

Though I haven't listed every hotel in every town, I've tried to give a range, from pensiones with no more than a bed and table in the room, to first-class establishments. In general, I'd plan to spend the night in towns for which accommodations are listed. When traveling to towns with limited accommodations, it is advisable to phone ahead to reserve, when telephone service is available.

You can find accommodations in many of the smaller towns, but they'll usually be far from luxurious. In any small town, the place to go for information about lodging or anything else is the town hall (municipalidad). Don't be afraid to ask questions. Officials will usually go out of their way to be of assistance.

HOTEL RATINGS

In addition to my own description and recommendations, I am including **star** ratings provided by the **Guatemala Tourist Commission**. These have nothing to do with quality of service, but reflect, rather, the physical plant and services available at the hotel.

- A **five-star hotel** (*****) in this parlance has air-conditioned rooms, shops, pool, meeting rooms, and everything else needed to host royalty and and foreign business executives, and more than you need as a tourist. There is less than a handful of such hotels in the country, — the superb Camino Real, the lesser Hotel El Dorado, and the Ramada in Antigua.
- A **four-star hotel** (****) may have no more than motel-class rooms, and might not even have a pool, though it usually does. It is usually a large hotel, in Guatemalan terms, with 30 or more rooms, shops, and tour services.
- A **three-star hotel** (***) is generally smaller than a four-star establishment, without shops or travel agency, but it may well provide better services and charge more for its rooms than a four-star joint.
- A **two-star hotel** (**) is generally a budget- to moderately priced establishment, with private baths. It might or might not have on-site eating facilities.
- A **one-star hotel** (*) is a budget establishment, often with shared baths.

Unrated hotels are either low-budget inns, or have not been officially classified for one reason or another. In outlying areas, some hotels may prefer to operate in semi-legal fashion rather than pay tribute to the tourist board (tourism taxes do not go into the general government fund.)

Use star ratings for a rough comparison of the availability of services in hotels.

PRICES

These are given in **US dollars**, based on recent exchange rates, and should be taken as approximate. While many prices have risen significantly in the last two years, Guatemala has always been an inexpensive country for the traveler, and costs remain relatively reasonable. A 7 percent sales tax (I.V.A.) applies to meals and most other purchases.

THE RUTA MAYA

What is it?

Ruta Maya is a concept first proposed by William Garrett in National Geographic magazine. Ruta Maya envisioned cooperation among authorities and travel organizations in the area once dominated by the Maya and still largely populated by their descendants: Guatemala, Belize, El Salvador, Honduras, and Yucatan and other southern Mexican states.

The aim was — and is — to make the archaeological sites, the rain forests, the caves, the lakes and the peoples of remote areas more easily visitable. Tourism would be used as an engine to protect the natural treasures of jungle, forest, wildlife and a treasure trove of flora threatened by logging, colonization, and refugee resettlement. Low-impact tourism could provide employment in areas where standing forest might otherwise be destroyed in order to devote the land to pasture or possibly unsustainable agriculture. Local people would serve as guides to birders, rafters, and those who simply want to wake up in misty, unspoiled forest to the roar of howler monkeys.

Several Central American government agencies and tour organizations have established **Mundo Maya (Mayan World)** as a central clearinghouse to mull over cooperation in tourist travel and promotion to the region.

The Ruta Maya has caught on, at least as a concept. Travel agencies and publishers use the tag of Ruta Maya (or Mayan Route, or Mayan Road, or Mayan World) to promote anything and everything touching on southern Mexico, Guatemala, Honduras, Belize, or El Salvador.

Ruta Maya Dreams

One day, there could well be seamless travel through the regions where the Maya once ruled. A single visa would allow tourists into the entire area. Highways and tramways envisioned by Mr. Garrett could be built through, and in harmony with, standing rain forest. Border procedures could be eased.

Ruta Maya Realities

Overland routes between the countries in the Mayan area are few. There is only one crossing point between Mexico and Belize, and there are only two highway crossings between Mexico and Guatemala. The road from Guatemala to Belize is sometimes barely passable.

Air travel is difficult in the Mayan area, except for flights between capital cities. In some cases, the availability of flights has been decreasing, as local airlines have gone under.

Many Mayan sites remain inaccessible for all practical purposes, except on adventurous river expeditions, or as single destinations from a capital city. It is difficult to visit several sites without backtracking.

Construction of new roads has led, without exception, to the degradation and destruction of tropical forest in Mexico and all Central American countries.

Rain forest continues to be destroyed in Guatemala, even in the Maya biosphere and other "protected" areas with little or no effective policing.

Easing tourism could well lead to more destruction. Promotion of so-called "ecotourism" generally brings hordes who stomp on delicate systems.

A legacy of distrust survives from almost 200 years of territorial claims and Central American wars. Every Ruta Maya country wants to be the hub for visits to the others.

TRAVEL AGENCIES

- **Far Horizons**, *P. O. Box 1529, San Anselmo, CA 94960, tel. 415-457-4575.* Archaeological tours.
- **Mountain Travel**, *1398 Solano Ave., Albany, CA 94706, tel. 800-227-2384*
- **Solar Tours**, *1629 K St. NW, Washington, D.C. 20006*
- **AIB Tours**, *2830 W. Flagler St., Coral Gables, FL 33134, tel. 800-AIB-TOUR*
- **American Express**, *1110 Brickell Ave. #302, Miami, FL 33131,tel. 800-327-7737*
- **Maya World Tours**, *9846 Highway 441, Leesburg, FL 34788, tel. 800-392-6292, fax 904-360-1077*
- **International Journeys, Inc.**, *17849 San Carlos Blvd., Fort Myers, FL 33931, tel. 800-622-6525.* Archaeological tours only.
- **Ladatco Tours**, *2220 Coral Way, Miami, FL., tel. 800-327-6162*
- **PCI**, *8405 N.W. 53 St., Miami, FL 33166, tel. 594-5684*
- **ABA Tours**, *1440 Canal St., New Orleans, LA 70112, tel. 800-654-7631*
- **Fantasia Travel**, *737 State St., New Orleans, LA 70118, tel. 800-348-9101*

- **Ocean Connection**, *16730 El Camino Real, Houston, TX 77062, tel. 800-331-2458*
- **South American Fiesta**, *10 W.Mercury Blvd., Hampton, VA 23666, tel. 800-334-3782, fax 804-826-1747*

GETTING TO GUATEMALA

By Air

From the United States, **Guatemala City** is served directly by:

- **Taca**, the Salvadoran airline, with non-stop service from New York, Houston, and Los Angeles, continuing to El Salvador. This flight can also be booked through Aviateca.
- **Lacsa**, from New York via Cancún or Honduras.
- **Aviateca**, the Guatemalan airline, from Miami, New Orleans, Chicago, Houston and Los Angeles.
- **Continental Airlines**, from Houston.
- **Mexicana**, from Los Angeles.
- **American Airlines**, from Dallas and Miami.
- **United Air Lines** from Miami
- **Iberia** from Miami.

Most of these flights operate daily.

By Private Plane

Private planes may enter Guatemala if the pilot and passengers obtain visas or tourist cards in advance. Pilots must call Guatemala radio (126.9) before entering the country. Radio frequency and navigation information for Guatemala City (TGE) can be obtained from aviation maps.

The standard visual navigation system for the approach from the Mexican border is to count seven volcanoes and then turn left to Aurora Airport. Pilots who have tried this system in cloudy weather have been known to end up in El Salvador, or even worse.

By Private Boat

Send a notice of arrival by wire to the captain of the port where you plan to enter Guatemala. All passengers should obtain tourist cards or visas in advance. The captain should present a list of passengers in triplicate, preferably notarized by a Guatemalan consul, as well as ownership documents, and sailing permit from the port of departure.

Boat permits are generally valid for 90 days. Boat owners who stay on for a while (this will generally be at the marinas on the Río Dulce) can renew their papers for another nine months. Apply in person at customs in Guatemala City, or through Mañana Marina on the Río Dulce. You can also arrange to leave your boat behind temporarily in Guatemala.

By Bus

The disadvantages of bus travel all the way to Guatemala are obvious — long hours in a sitting position, inconvenient connections, border delays, and much else. It's not even as cheap anymore: The border-to-border fare can be as much as $150, which, with meals, gets uncomfortably close to the price of a bargain air excursion. You can, however, see the sights along the way.

First-class buses, similar to Greyhound units, operate from all US border points to Mexico City, a trip of from 10 hours to two days, depending on where you cross the border. Buses of the Cristóbal Colón line, connecting with Guatemalan buses, depart Mexico City at least twice daily for the border points of Talismán and Ciudad Cuauhtémoc, each about sixteen hours away. From eastern Texas, the trip can be shortened by taking buses along the Gulf coast to Veracruz, avoiding Mexico City.

Mexican officials may require you to show a Guatemalan visa and buy a transit visa if you mention that your final destination is Guatemala. Keep your mouth closed. A tourist card or visa for Guatemala can be picked up at the Guatemalan consulate in Mexico City, Comitán, or Ciudad Hidalgo.

First-class buses operate through Central America to Panama. Fares from Guatemala City to the Canal should run about $50, and costs can be reduced by using less comfortable, slower, second-class local buses.

By Car

If your time is limited, don't even think about driving to Guatemala, with the possibility of breakdowns, difficult mountain roads, and unfamiliar conditions. But if you're going south for the winter, or are planning extensive travel in Mexico or elsewhere in Central America, if you're camping, or if your vehicle is simply indispensable, driving may be indicated. Rest assured that getting to Guatemala is eminently possible.

The shortest highway distance from Brownsville, Texas, to the Guatemalan border at Talismán is less than 2000 kilometers (1250 miles), following the Gulf coast to Acayucan, cutting south across the isthmus of Tehuantepec, then following the Pacific coast to Guatemala. On the last leg, you can also drive into the mountains by way of Comitán, in order to enter Guatemala in the highlands, at La Mesilla. Even from California, the going is easier and not much longer by following this route and avoiding mountain driving in central Mexico.

Mexican officials may — quite legitimately — demand transit fees of more than $100 if your final destination is Guatemala. When you enter Mexico, mention any town in Mexico as your final destination. Pay the appropriate deposit on your vehicle, and take at least five days for a leisurely drive down. Otherwise, you could be assumed to have lied about the purpose of your travel, and fined.

Your major requirement is a vehicle in good shape. Have it checked out, tuned up and greased before you leave home. Replace cracked or withering belts and hoses, bald tires, and rusting brake lines. If you're planning extensive travel off the main roads, consider taking a couple of spare tires, a gasoline can, water for you and the radiator, points, plugs, electrical tape, belts, wire, and basic tools. Otherwise, there's no reason to prepare for a safari, and the family sedan will serve you well. Consult your auto club for advice about dealing with the lack of unleaded gasoline.

If you stick to the main roads, driving should be only a bit more strenuous than at home. Most Mexican highways are two lanes wide, and gasoline stations are located only in major towns. Fill up when you can, with the highest grade of gasoline, and watch out for potholes, animals, people, and vehicles parked in the road.

ENTERING GUATEMALA

Regulations concerning visas and tourist cards change periodically, without any publicity to airlines and travel agencies. Verify the latest regulations with a Guatemalan consulate shortly before you leave home. Otherwise, you could be stranded en route when you try to change planes for the final leg of your trip, or deported as soon as you arrive.

Here are current regulations, subject to change and local interpretation by consulates and immigration officials:

Tourists entering Guatemala must have visas or tourist cards, with a few exceptions. Visitors entering by land may be asked to show sufficient money to cover their expenses. No vaccination certificate is required for travelers from most countries.

Tourist Cards

Tourist Cards, valid for up to six months, are available to citizens of the United States, and usually to citizens of Mexico, Britain, Canada and some other countries (the list changes regularly). They cost $5, and must be used within 90 days of issue. Tourist cards can be obtained from Guatemalan consulates, upon presentation of a passport, birth certificate, or other proof of citizenship.

Currently (subject to change — don't count on it!), tourist cards are issued at Aurora airport and at land entry points as well. Children under 12 may be included on the cards of their parents. Tourist cards must be renewed by the immigration department (address below) after the 30 to 90 days initially allowed upon entry. A tourist card can be used for multiple entries if it retains 30 days of validity. Holders of tourist cards should also carry a passport, which is the preferred identification for cashing travelers checks.

Passports & Visas

Citizens of most countries require a **visa** before visiting Guatemala as tourists. Visas are issued by Guatemalan consulates. The cost depends on your nationality and where the visa is issued. Citizens of the United States, Canada, the UK or Mexico may obtain a visa instead of a tourist card. Tourists may apply for a visa by mail. Businessmen generally must appear in person. Citizens of some countries, especially in Eastern Europe and Africa, must have their visit approved in Guatemala before a visa is issued.

Currently, visas are not required of citizens of: Argentina, Austria, Belize and other Central American nations, Belgium, Denmark, Finland, France, Germany, Holland, Israel, Italy, Japan, Luxembourg, Liechtenstein, Norway, Spain, Sweden, and Switzerland.

If you travel on a **passport** (whether or not you need a visa), and plan to stay more than 30 days, have your passport stamped by the immigration department (Migración), 8 Avenida at 12 Calle, Zone 1, Guatemala City. You'll have to apply again for permission to stay longer than 90 days. Ask at the information window for the form for a *prórroga* (extension), which may take a few days to process. You'll need an exit visa, unless you're a US citizen, if you stay in Guatemala for more than 90 days.

Minors traveling alone should have a letter of permission from both parents, notarized by a Guatemalan consul.

CUSTOMS

Tourists are allowed an exemption of $100 in customs duty. No more than three liters of liquor, two cartons of cigarettes, a still and a movie camera, and six rolls of film may be included in the goods on which duty is waived. Customs officers generally won't bother you if you bring some extra film or cigarettes. The exemption is in addition to clothing and personal items that a visitor would normally need. Firearms are permitted into Guatemala only with a permit issued by the Ministry of Defense.

BORDER HOURS & FEES

Air passengers pay no **entry fee**, and a **departure tax** of about $10.

Land borders are "officially" open from 8 am to noon and 2 pm to 6 pm, Monday through Friday; and from 8 am to noon on Saturdays. During these periods, you should pay a minor fee of under a dollar to enter, though hungry border officials often rake in a few dollars per person.

Pedestrians, bus, and car passengers may enter outside these hours, at an extra charge of about a dollar per person, again subject to minor graft.

A fee of a couple of dollars is charged all cars entering Guatemala. Vehicles entering or leaving outside regular hours pay an extra $5. A small toll is imposed at bridges on the Mexican border, on both persons and vehicles.

The **exit tax** is about a dollar for all persons leaving Guatemala by land or sea.

Penalty fees of about $2 per extra day are imposed if you've stayed beyond the validity of your tourist card, visa, or the entry permit that was stamped in your passport (if you didn't need a visa).

GUATEMALAN CONSULATES

US

- *2220 R Street NW, Washington, DC 20008, tel. 202-745-4952, fax 745-1908* (embassy)
- *2500 Wilshire Blvd., Los Angeles, CA 90057, tel. 213-365-9251, fax 365-9245*
- *870 Market Street, San Francisco, CA 94102, tel. 415-788-5651, fax 7885653*
- *300 Sevilla Ave., Suite 210, Coral Gables, FL 33134, tel. 305-443-4828, fax 443-4830*
- *180 N. Michigan Ave., Suite 1035, Chicago, IL 60601, tel. 312-332-1587, fax 332-4256*
- *World Trade Center 1645, 2 Canal St., New Orleans, LA 70130, tel. 504-525-0013, fax 568-0553*
- *57 Park Avenue, New York, NY 10016, tel. 212-686-3837, fax 447-6947*
- *508 Elizabeth St., Brownsville, TX 78520, tel. 512-541-3131* (honorary)
- *10200 Richmond Avenue, Suite 270, Houston, TX 77042, tel. 713-953-9531, fax 953-9383*

Canada

- *294 Albert St., Ottawa, Ontario K1P 6E6, tel. 613-224-4322, fax 2370492* (embassy)
- *736 Granville St., Vancouver, B.C., tel. 604-682-4831*

Belize

- *Mile 5, Northern Highway, and Benque Viejo*

Mexico

- *2 Avenida Poniente Norte No. 28, Comitán, Chiapas, tel. 963-22669*
- *Av. Central Norte No. 12, Ciudad Hidalgo, Chiapas, tel. 80193*
- *Obregón 342, Chetumal, Q.Roo, tel. 21631, fax 28585*
- *Av. Explanada 1025, Lomas de Chapultepec 11000, México 4, D.F., tel. 5407520, fax 2021142*
- *2 Calle Oriente 33, Tapachula, Chiapas, tel. 61252*

Costa Rica

- *Av. 1, Calles 24/28 (no. 2493), San José, tel. 314074*

El Salvador
- *15 Avenida Norte 135, San Salvador, tel. 712225, fax 713019*

Honduras
- *4a Calle 2421 (betw. Av. Juan Lindo and 1 Avenida), Col. Las Minitas, Tegucigalpa, tel. 325028, fax 321580* (embassy)
- *8 Calle B 14-15 NO, 148B, Barrio Los Andes, tel. 325018, fax 557748*
- *1 Av. Sur-Este, Ocotepeque*

Austria
- *Kantgasse 3, A-1010 Vienna, tel. 7152970, fax 7132421*

Belgium
- *Blvd. General Wahis 53, B1030 Brussels, tel. 7360340, fax 7361889*

France
- *73, rue de Courcelles, 75008 Paris, tel. 2277863, fax 47540206*
- *66, rue Grignan, F-13001 Marseille, tel. 542646*

Germany
- *Zeitenstrasse 16, D-5300 Bonn 2, tel. 358609, fax 354940*
- *Wagnerstrasse 31, D-4000 Düsseldorf 1, tel. 359124*
- *Wandsbeker Chaussee 1, D-2000 Hamburg 76, tel. 2503644, fax 2164426*

Israel
- *2 Rehov Ben-Eliezer, 46667 Hertzlia-Pituach, tel. 574594, fax 5467317*

Italy
- *Via dei Colli della Farnesina 128, I-00194 Roma, tel. 3272632, fax 291639*
- *Via Giotto, Lago 422, 20080 Bassiglio, Milano, tel. 4032478, fax 5358255*
- *Via Maragliano 1, I-16122 Genoa, tel. 562936*
- Also Como and Messina

Netherlands
- *2e. Beukelaan 3, 7313AN Apeldoorn, tel. 557421, fax 211768*

Spain
- *Calle Rafael Salgado 3, Madrid 16, tel. 4577827, fax 4587894*

South Africa
- *Greenmarket Square 54, Shortmarket St., Cape Town 8001, tel. 225787*

Sweden
- *Wittstocksgatan 30, S–115 27 Stockholm, tel. 6605229, fax 6604229*
- *Hogasplatsen 3, S-400-22 Göteborg, tel. 813010*
- *Carlsgatan 4 (Nordisk Trans. Sped.), S-201-24 Malmö, tel. 72230*

Switzerland
- *10 b, rue du Vieux Collège, CH-1204 Genève, tel. 289944, fax 49171*
- *14, rue du Midi, CH-1003, Lausanne, tel. 234223, fax 110639*

United Kingdom
- *13 Fawcett St., London SW10, tel. 3513042, fax 3765708*

GETTING AROUND GUATEMALA

By Air

Domestic service is limited to flights from Guatemala City to Flores, which serves as a gateway to Tikal and the Petén. There are numerous airstrips around the country, and direct flights in small planes and helicopters to towns and archaeological sites can be arranged through companies at the airport in Guatemala City, or through travel agents.

By Boat

There is scheduled boat service across Lake Atitlán from Panajachel, from Mariscos to El Estor on Lake Izabal, and from Puerto Barrios to Lívingston. Small boats can be hired for cruising on Lake Atitlán, Lake Izabal, and the Río Dulce.

By Bus

First-class buses comparable to those operated in North America run between Guatemala City and all major cities and border points. Fares are reasonable. It costs $10 or less to go from the capital to the Mexican border, San Salvador, or Puerto Barrios. Many first-class lines will reserve seats.

Ordinary **second-class buses** (*camionetas*) operating to all points in the country are another story. These are similar to American school buses (some of them actually are used American school buses), with stiff seats and up to seven passengers crowded into each row. Stops are frequent at small towns and junctions, where peasants will climb aboard, place their machetes next to the driver, argue about the fare (usually unsuccessfully), and get off a few kilometers down the road. Women may clutch a recently acquired chicken or nurse their children, and somehow, a lot of people manage to doze off despite the bumping and shaking and cramped quarters. Except for small parcels, all baggage rides atop the bus. Fares on second-class buses are very cheap, less than two cents (US)per kilometer.

By Car

Driving in your own or a rented car is one of the best ways to see Guatemala. Distances between most places of interest to visitors are short, so you can take it easy and enjoy the breathtaking scenery.

Entry permits for visitors' cars (and motorcycles and bicycles and boats) are initially granted for from 30 to 90 days upon presentation of registration and license at point of entry. Extensions may be requested at the customs office (Aduana), 10 Calle between 14 and 13 avenidas, Zone 1, Guatemala City. For a small fee, one of the customs men will write out your request for an extension on legal paper.

Insurance is not required, but it will save you possible detention if you're involved in an accident. Inexpensive short-term liability policies are available at the Granai y Townson agencies in Huehuetenango and Quezaltenango, and at many agencies in Guatemala City. Coverage for damage to your own vehicle is not available, so talk to your insurance agent before you leave home.

Road Signs

Warning signs using easily understood symbols are posted along the Pan American Highway and most major roads. On secondary roads, signs may be hand painted. Unless you know Spanish, you may think they're signs for somebody's store. The most frequent warnings and instructions are: *viraje obligado* (required turn in the direction of the arrow); *pendiente peligrosa* (dangerous grade); *frene con motor* (brake with motor); *derrumbes* (landslide zone); *túmulos* (bumps in the road surface — slow down!).

Many side roads are not posted with hazard warnings. Take it easy if you're driving a road for the first time.

LOCAL HAZARDS & PRACTICES

• *A tree branch on the road indicates a disabled vehicle ahead. Exercise caution. There's often no shoulder on which a vehicle in difficulty can pull off. If you break down, follow local practice and place a branch on the road to warn approaching traffic.*

• *Beep your horn when approaching a curve. Others might not do so, so be prepared to veer suddenly.*

• *The biggest hazard, aside from drunken drivers, is drunken pedestrians, especially on weekends and at fiesta times.*

• *The driver going up a hill has the right of way.*

• *Always carry your automobile documents with you. They may be checked at police posts.*

• *Unattended automobiles should be locked and, if possible, parked in a protected area. Remove all valuables. Never leave a broken-down vehicle unattended.*

Car Rental

Automobiles can be rented in Guatemala City at prices higher than those in most US and Canadian cities. You will be substantially liable for any damage to a rented vehicle, (locally purchased insurance will cover only part of the $2000 deductible) so confirm before leaving home that your own policy or one that comes with your credit card will protect you.

For a rental arranged in Guatemala, expect to pay about $50 per day, including tax, for the smallest car, with mileage included. Add gasoline and insurance, and you'll be out of pocket for up to $70 a day. You can sometimes get a better rate if you book ahead through the toll-free reservations numbers of the major car-rental companies. But if you make any changes in your pickup date or requested model of car, you'll be charged the higher local rate.

Exception: I've recently found Avis to be much more flexible than other companies about honoring discount rates when you make changes in your plans. Avis is also the only company that will not force you to purchase incomplete insurance coverage that you might not need.

By Taxi

If you're with a few other people, it's economical and convenient to go by first-class bus to a large town, and then hire a taxi for excursions to nearby small towns, to which bus service may be inconvenient or uncomfortable. Even intercity taxi runs are a practical alternative to cramped buses or tours. From Guatemala City to Panajachel on Lake Atitlán, a trip of 145 kilometers (90 miles), you might expect to pay about $75. Always get guidance about fares from the local tourist office before you engage a taxi.

By Tour

Tour buses operate from Guatemala City to all major areas of interest, except Tikal, which you can reach by a combination of plane and tour bus. Most excursions are for one day and take you back to the capital, although staying in the countryside is much to be preferred. Some of the available tours are mentioned in the Guatemala City chapter. From time to time, tours are available from Antigua, Panajachel and Quezaltenango as well.

Packages of hotel, meal and tour arrangements that you book with your airplane ticket vary from a few nights in a hotel in the capital to complete arrangements for a week of travel around the country. Low-price packages allow you to take advantage of cheaper air fares. The more complete packages, of course, spare you much planning and attention to details.

By Train

Service from Guatemala City to the Pacific lowlands and to Puerto Barrios is provided by Guatemala's rickety, low-priced trains

FOR MORE INFORMATION

For a list of hotels in Guatemala (without prices) and color brochures, call the **Guatemala Tourist Commission** at *800-742-4259 (or 305-442-0651, fax 442-1013)*; or write to:

Guatemala Tourist Commission, *299 Alhambra Circle, Suite 510 Coral Gables, FL 33134.*

From outside the United States or Canada, write to: **Instituto Guatemalteco de Turismo**, *7 Avenida 1-17, Zona 4 Ciudad de Guatemala Guatemala, Central America. Fax 502-2-314416.*

Other tourist offices have been established abroad, sometimes quite coincidentally where well-connected persons happen to be residing at the moment. Recently these have included the following addresses:

- *Bienenstrasse 63 CH4104 Oberwil/Basel Switzerland Tel. 61-4015032, fax 4015157*
- *11, Rue de Cronstadt 75015 Paris France Tel. 33-1-45301866, fax 42501878*
- *Via Arno g/4 00198 Rome Italy Tel. 39-6-8549431, fax 9123704*
- *Explanada 1025 1025 Lomas de Chapultepec 11000 México, D.F. Mexico Tel. 52-5-5407520, fax 2021142*
- *Pedro Henbríquez Ureño 136-A Santo Domingo Dominican Republic Tel. and fax 809-567-0115.*

Use the toll-free numbers given in this book to get as much information as you can on current hotel rates, automobile rentals, etc., and write to the addresses I've mentioned for language schools, bird lists and the like.

This Week in Central America, a respected newsletter that covers events in all the Central American countries, is published in Guatemala City and is available by subscription. Write to Apartado 1156, Guatemala City, or inquire at 12 Calle 4-53, Zone 1.

FUNDESA, a Guatemalan businessmen's organization, publishes *Guatemala Watch*, a monthly newsletter, and *Viva Guatemala*, a semiannual magazine. The first covers events in Guatemala, the second includes feature stories of interest to prospective visitors and to businessmen. For sample copies, write to FUNDESA, Apartado 865-A, Guatemala City.

Guatemala News Watch, a four-page monthly summary of events in Guatemala, with an emphasis on business, is available for $12 annually from **Guatemala Business Center**, *299 Alhambra, Suite 510, Coral Gables, FL 33134, tel. 800-741-6133* or *305-444-0600, fax 448-4237,* for information relative to doing business in Guatemala.

The weekly *Guatemala News*, with *New York Times* wire service stories as well as roundups of Guatemalan and Central American news and ads for travel services, is distributed free through hotels and restaurants where visitors have been known to turn up. If you don't find a copy, call 313664 in Guatemala City to inquire.

For a yearly subscription, send US$35 to **Guatemala News**, *F-23, Box 591999, Miami, FL 33159. In Guatemala, send Q100 to Apartado 1015, Ciudad de Guatemala.*

BASIC INFORMATION

Here's some basic information matters, in alpabetical order:

BUSINESS HOURS

Hours mentioned in the Guatemala City section apply generally throughout the country. Note that the midday break is rarely referred to as the *siesta*. It doesn't take long to get used to doing your shopping before noon or after 2 pm.

EARTHQUAKES

Earthquakes are frequent in Guatemala. Most are minor tremors, and if you're not used to them, you may mistake the rumblings of the earth for the vibrations caused by a passing truck. Major earthquakes, such as that of February 4, 1976, have occurred about every 50 years or so.

In the unlikely event that you're caught in a major quake, in Guatemala or elsewhere, stand in a doorway, or get outside if possible. The greatest danger is in collapsing roofs. The pretty tile roofs of houses in the highlands did much damage in the 1976 quake. In many cases they were supported by nothing more than rotting wooden beams.

ELECTRICITY

Electricity in Guatemala City and in most of the country is supplied at 110 volts alternating current. In a few smaller towns, service is at 220 volts. When you're outside of any large city, check the local voltage before you plug anything in. Sockets take standard American plugs without grounding prongs. Some isolated towns have their own generators, which may be turned on only at night.

HEALTH CONCERNS

A trip to Central America doesn't necessarily mean stomach cramps, mad dashes to find a toilet, and general malaise as unknown microbes attack your insides. With caution and some changes in your eating habits, you should be as healthy in Guatemala as you are at home.

Some pointers:

Keep up on your tetanus, polio and other general vaccinations. If you're planning to be in Guatemala for more than a few weeks and to go to out-of-the-way places, you should get a typhoid booster and a gamma globulin shot. For travel in the hot lowlands, take a malaria-preventive pill, such as Aralen, which is available locally without prescription. The usual dosage is two tablets per week starting two weeks before travel to a malarious area. Insect repellent will also come in handy.

Water in Guatemala City is chemically treated. In many towns the water is untreated. Stick to coffee or bottled drinks. If you must drink tap water, make sure that it's been boiled or filtered, or else treat it with laundry bleach (two drops per liter, let stand a half-hour) or a tablet such as Halazone.

All fresh meat should be cooked thoroughly. If your hamburger is pink in the middle, send it back to the kitchen. Fruits that grow on trees are generally safe to eat. Strawberries, lettuce, cabbage and other fruits and vegetables that might have been irrigated with contaminated water should be cooked or treated in a bath of a few drops of iodine in a gallon of water. If you have any doubts about whether such items have been treated, as you might in some of the more rustic eateries, leave them on your plate.

Generally, it's not in the cities that you have to worry about food preparation, or in the really remote villages where few visitors go, but in between. Be especially cautious of eateries frequented by travelers in small towns. Local sanitation methods may not be up to handling the constant influx of new germs. When you're ill, try not to eat out and spread your germs.

If you pick up dysentery (characterized by intermittent cramps and diarrhea) or some other intestinal ailment, you'll find many medicines available without prescription. Avoid overkill and try a mild preparation, such as Kaopectate or Pepto Bismol, along with fruit juice with honey and a pinch of salt, to replace lost body fluid. Carbon tablets, such as *Ultracarbón*, are helpful in some cases. Some readily available medicines for diarrhea, such as Entero-sediv and Enterovioform, contain ingredients that some doctors consider dangerous. If you've picked up worms from partially cooked fresh meat (symptoms are loss of energy and abdominal pain), try one of the milder preparations, such as Bryrel, first.

Take it easy on liquor until you are used to the altitude, and lay off it if you're sick. Liquor destroys the effectiveness of some medicines.

Stay away from fleabag hotels. Fleas are not only bothersome in themselves, but can carry disease. If you discover these or other crawlies, try Dermax, a locally available treatment for skin parasites.

None of the above should be taken as professional medical advice. If you become more than mildly ill, consult a doctor. Doctors' fees in Guatemala are usually quite reasonable. Relying on the advice of pharmacists, who may be poorly trained, is chancy.

On a somewhat different health tangent: keep your hands off the electric gizmos that heat the water (somewhat) in many hotel showers. Turn the water on to get them operating, and call the hotel staff to make any adjustments.

For late info: call the Central and South America travelers hotline at the Centers for Disease Control in Atlanta: 404-332-4559 in English; 404-330-3132 in Spanish.

LEARNING SPANISH

A number of Spanish-language study programs are offered in Guatemala. A typical four-week course includes classroom sessions, and several hours of individual instruction daily. The emphasis is on conversation. At $450 and up per month, including room and board with a Guatemalan family (or sometimes less!), these programs are a bargain. Some schools are flexible in the duration and intensity of their programs, and offer even lower rates.

Among the schools offering language instruction and recommended strongly by readers are:

- **Escuela de Español Casa Xelaju**, *Apartado 302 9 Calle 11-26, Zona 1, Quezaltenango Tel. 612628. US contact: 10221 St. Paul Ave., St. Paul, MN 55116, tel. 612-690-9471.* Casa Xelajú offers not only hot springs and volcano-climbing excursions with its instruction, but also cooking demonstrations and outings to a jail, a squatter settlement, cooperatives, the Guatemala City dump, and to join in road repairs. Talk about an introduction to a culture!

- **Kie-Balam Language School**, *12 Avenida 0-43, Zone 1 Quezaltenango. Tel. 612639 or 612610. US contact: Daniel and Martha Weese, 1816 North Wells, Chicago, IL 60614, tel. 312-642-8019 or 708-888-2514.* One-on-one instruction with university-trained students for five hours daily. The program includes contact with local community groups, some of which are directly aided by the school with both money and manpower for programs in health care, recycling and water systems. Trips to scenic and cultural areas can be arranged. Income is shared with community programs.

- **Juan Sisay Spanish School**, *15 Avenida 8-38, Zone 1 Quezaltenango. Tel. and fax 630327. US contact: 3465 Cedar Valley Court, Smyrna, GA 30080, tel. 404-432-2396.* Associated with social programs and reforestation.

- **I. C. A. (Instituto Central America)**, *1a Calle 16-93, Zona 1, 09001 Quezaltenango. Tel. and fax 09-631871. US contact: RR2, Box 101, Stanton, NE 68779, tel. 402-439-2943.* I.C.A.'s slogan is: *el monolinguismo* *es curable* (unilingualism can be cured). Tuition ranges from $100 to $120 per week, depending on the time of year, and includes five hours per day of private instruction, room and board with a local family, and contact activities that include visits to villages, hospitals and markets. Part of the modest tuition fees goes to support such projects as indigenous language instruction, scholarships, and reforestation.

- **Proyecto Lingüístico de Español**, *5 Calle 2-40, Zone 1 Apartado 114 Quezaltenango. US contact: tel. 718-965-8522.*
- **ProPetén Eco-Escuela Casa Ing.**, *Asturias Flores, Petén Fax 502-9-501370 US contact, Conservation International Eco-Escuela, 1015 18th St. NW, Washington, DC 20036, tel. 202-429-5660, fax 202-887-5188.* In San Andrés, on the northwest shore of Lake Petén-Itzá, the Eco-Escuela de Español is pioneering a combination of language study with immersion in the effort to save the rain forest. Beyond one-on-one Spanish instruction, lectures and field trips emphasize forest ecology. Students go off the usual tourist track, network with local residents instead of with tour guides, and stay with villagers.
- **Centro del Lenguaje América Latina**, *Apartado Postal 233 19 Avenida 3-63, Zone 3 Quezaltenango Tel. 616416. US contact: 635 Skyview Pl, Apt. 9, Madison WI 53713, tel. 608-255-0734.*
- **Escuela de Español Casa Xelaju**, *9 Calle 11-26, Zona 1, Quezaltenango. Tel. 612628. US contact: 10221 St. Paul Ave., St. Paul, MN 55116, tel. 612-690-9471.*
- **Sevilla Academia de Español**, *Apartado Postal 380 6 Calle Oriente No. 3 Antigua Guatemala, Sacatepéquez. Tel. and fax 323609.* Sevilla Academia offers many community-contact activities. Students pay their host families directly for room and board at a fixed low rate (a school's commission on this can sometimes be a sore point).
- **Instituto El Portal**, *1 Calle 1-64, Zone 3, Huehuetenango Tel. 641987.*
- **Centro de Estudios de Español Pop Wuj**, *1 Calle 17-72, Zona 1 Quezaltenango Tel. 618286. US contact, P. O. Box 43685-9685, Washington, DC 20010-9685.* References to former students will be sent on request. Enrollment is limited.
- **International Language School**, *15 Avenida 1-23, Zone 1 Quezaltenango Tel. 614451.* Classes are offered in the Mam and Quiché Maya languages, as well as in Spanish.

Write to the schools for information. Because there are so many language schools, especially in Antigua, there's no need to send a deposit or reserve a place unless your schedule is tight, or you have an especially strong recommendation to one of them.

Good advice from one student: try to change teachers every week in order to listen to different accents.

In general, because there are so many foreign students in Antigua, it's easy to succumb to the temptation to lapse into your own language. **Quezaltenango** is more of a "real" town, with a genuine workaday environment for practicing Spanish, though the surroundings may seem to some to be less romantic. By all means, try a couple of weeks in each place!

FIESTAS

Fiestas are the times of year when a whole town celebrates, usually in honor of its patron saint. In Indian towns, the *cofradías* carry their statues of saints in noisy processions, accompanied by the melody of the *chirimía* — a flute with the sweet sound of the oboe — and the beat of the *tun* — a drum made from a hollowed-out log, cut so as to sound two notes. Every few yards, the procession comes to a halt, and rocket bombs are fired as a symbolic form of communication with the gods.

Enormous sums of money — by local standards — are spent for the liquor, fireworks, food and costumes that are all part of the *cofradía* ritual. Traditional fiesta dances are performed, though they often deteriorate into drunken endurance contests. Itinerant photographers and food vendors may set up shop on the square, and along with the mechanical soccer games and games of chance, they give a town a carnival atmosphere for up to a couple of weeks before the main fiesta day.

In the less traditional Indian towns, and in Ladino towns, fiestas may include beauty contests, sporting events and social dances. The common denominator everywhere is liquor, plenty of liquor. Fiestas are times to let loose and forget about the everyday worries of work and survival.

Not everything about a fiesta is a delight. The fun of clumsy Indian ritual dancing and mass drunkenness is sometimes lost on outsiders. Fireworks are often set off with no safety precautions, and accidents can and do result. The amplified blaring of marimba orchestras for hours or even days on end may send you screaming and fleeing from town in search of peace and quiet. Buses going to a place where a fiesta is being celebrated are likely to be jam-packed, and hotel space may be unavailable. Guatemalans are used to such goings-on and inconveniences, but the foreign visitor, with different sensibilities, may react negatively. If you do plan to visit a town at fiesta time, make sure that you have hotel reservations, especially if you're traveling by bus.

MONEY & BANKING

Guatemala's currency is the **quetzal**, named after the national bird. The quetzal is divided into 100 **centavos**.

Guatemalan paper currency comes in 50-centavo, one-quetzal, and larger-denomination notes. All banknotes bear an illustration of the quetzal, as well as both Arabic and Mayan numerals. The 25-centavo coin has a portrait of a woman of Santiago Atitlán; the ten-centavo coin a stela from Quiriguá; the five-centavo coin the ceiba, the national tree; and the one-centavo coin a portrait of Friar Bartolomé de las Casas, protector of Indians in colonial times.

For decades the quetzal was worth exactly one US dollar. But foreign debt, low prices for Guatemala's principal exports, and loss of confidence in the economy and government led to a collapse in the value of the quetzal in the mid-1980s. At this time, it is worth approximately 17 US cents.

Currently, banks pay a "market" rate for US dollars slightly above the official exchange rate, and street money changers — who cluster around the main post office in Guatemala City — pay slightly more. There is some danger, of course, in changing your money with street characters who could abscond with your travelers checks. Try one of the stores near the post office, or ask a resident foreigner to steer you to an honest black marketer. If such dealings make you nervous, then by all means change your money at a bank, where the rate is only slightly lower and still gives you a lot of buying power.

Exchanging Money

Banks will accept US-dollar **travelers checks** for exchange into quetzales, but some will not take US cash. Canadian cash and other currencies are generally useless in Guatemala.

Spend or exchange your quetzales before leaving Guatemala. Exchange offices abroad pay unfavorable rates. Under recent regulations, you may repurchase up to 100 US dollars at the airport branch of the Banco de Guatemala just before you leave the country.

Travelers Checks can be cashed at most commercial banks in Guatemala City, when you present your passport. Outside the capital, cash travelers checks at branches of the **Banco de Guatemala** located in the major town of each department. *Hours are 8:30 am to 2 pm on Mondays through Thursdays, to 2:30 pm on Fridays.* In villages where there are no banks, and on weekends, travelers checks may be useless. Make sure you have local cash for the weekend and before setting off to small towns.

Money from Home

If you run short of money, the quickest way to get funds is to use your credit card to obtain a cash advance (see below).

Otherwise, have a bank at home order a telegraphic or telex transfer through one of the large banks in Guatemala City. Banks at home often send the money to a different bank from the one you specify, so if your money doesn't turn up, verify exactly where the money was sent.

Western Union transfers are not reliable outside of Guatemala City. A reliable but slow alternative is to have an international money order sent to you by registered mail. Regular money orders and personal checks are difficult to cash.

Credit Cards

American Express, **Diners Club**, **Master Card**, and **Visa** are accepted by airlines, by most hotels that charge $10 or more for a single room, and by many restaurants and stores in Guatemala City. **Master Card cash advances** can be obtained from some banks, and from **Credomatic de Guatemala**, *7 Avenida 6-26, Zone 9, Guatemala City*, with a five percent kickback subtracted from the proceeds. *Call (or have somebody call) 317436 for information.*

Banking machines should accept Master Card and Visa for cash advances in the near future. Your rate of exchange when using a credit card may be less favorable than what you get for exchanging cash or travelers checks — the situation varies from time to time.

POST OFFICE

The main post office in Guatemala City *is open weekdays from 8 am until 6 pm, until noon on Saturdays.* Elsewhere, weekday hours are 8 am to 4:30 pm, though there may be some local variation.

If you have any doubt about the proper postage, weigh your letter at the post office, and tell your friends at home to do the same. And never, never, ever send anything of the slightest value except by registered mail, and never send cash. Even registered mail provides only limited security.

Postal rates are quite cheap by world standards. It costs less than the equivalent of 10 cents US to send a five-gram letter (one sheet of air mail paper in an air envelope) to North America, for example; about 15 cents to Canada, and 25 cents to Europe.

Parcels should be wrapped securely in cardboard boxes (which are sold in most small stores), covered with brown paper, and tied with cord. The clerk may want to inspect the contents, so be prepared to unwrap. Insurance on new items is available to most countries for a small fee. Payment of postage is by the even kilo. The rate for air parcels to the US is about $3 for the first kilogram, and $2 for each additional kilogram; to Canada, $4 for the first kilogram and $2 per additional kilogram; to Europe, $5 for the first kilogram, $3 per additional kilogram. Air parcels take about two weeks to reach the US. Surface parcels have not been accepted recently.

Postal regulations are subject to local whim. In small towns, clerks may accept parcels only early in the morning, or may impose lower weight limits than the official ones (ten kilos to most countries). You could face a wait of hours when several tourists with parcels descend on a lone postal clerk in some un-metropolitan locale. Avoid hassles by mailing your parcels in Guatemala City, when possible. There are also agencies, such as **Get Guated Out** in **Panajachel**, which will take care of mailing.

RECEIVING MAIL

To receive general delivery mail, have it addressed to your name at **Lista de Correos** *in the town and department where you'll pick it up. For example:*

Harry Matamibas
Lista de Correos
Antigua Guatemala, Sacatepéquez
Guatemala, Central America

A small fee is charged for each general delivery letter picked up. Mail is held for a month, sometimes longer. Avoid having items sent to you in Guatemala. Though books, newspapers, magazines, and tape recordings will get through without any problem, almost all other merchandise must be picked up in Guatemala City after payment of a heavy customs duty. Tell the folks at home to send a money order instead (by registered mail).

Postal Alternatives

Courier services such as **DHL** provide a quick if pricey alternative to Guatemala's insecure postal system for documents.

For letters, many towns have **courier shops**, where letters will be accepted to be taken by air to Miami, where they enter the US Postal Service. The charge is generally a dollar or so per letter. Look in the phone book under *mensajería* if you don't spot a courier sign.

Comparable services by small Latin companies are available to Guatemala City but not to the interior of the country from many large US and Canadian cities. Check the phone book under "couriers" for such companies as **King Express** and **Cuzcatlán Express**. Or contact **King Express**, *P. O. Box 876180, Los Angeles, CA 90099-4411, tel. 213-483-8545.*

SAFETY

You will not fail to note evidence of civil unrest during any visit to Guatemala. Armed soldiers patrol the capital and all villages. You may be stopped at military checkpoints.

Despite this background, the precautions that you would take in any unfamiliar place should serve you well. I travel regularly to Guatemala, sometimes with my small children. However, I wish to caution all travelers to stay on the beaten track. Some visitors who have wandered away from towns and villages, even accompanied by local guides, have become targets of criminals. At this time, you should not hike or climb in the countryside, alone or in small groups, unless you have been assured by a reliable conservative source, such as your embassy, that the area you are visiting is safe.

Anybody who has traveled in countries poorer than his or her own, and anybody who lives in Guatemala, knows that you should take certain basic precautions.

The **Guatemala Tourist Commission** itself issues a pamphlet to visitors with these warnings:

- Only use authorized taxis.
- Leave valuables in the safe at your hotel (if there is one), and carry as little money as possible. Use a money belt.
- Lock your doors when driving in a city.
- Do not travel after dark.

Let me add:

- Leave the jewelry at home, including wedding rings.
- Never walk at night in unfamiliar areas.
- Never venture alone on hiking trips, and take a guide if headed for a little-frequented place near an urban center.

SHOPPING & BARGAINING

More than in most countries, one of the main activities of visitors in Guatemala is shopping. Hand-woven clothing and Indian textiles, heavy woolen blankets, jewelry, antiques, and such utilitarian items as hammocks, kitchen utensils and pottery, are all available at reasonable and sometimes ridiculously low prices.

One of the biggest choices is whether to buy in a store or in markets. Stores usually offer fixed prices, though in some cases you can get the price down. The larger handicraft stores in Guatemala City and in a few other towns frequented by visitors, such as Antigua and Panajachel, often have a more varied selection of higher quality items than you'll find in a market. The prices are usually higher than those you'll be able to obtain by going directly to Indian artisans. But unless you're planning to buy large quantities of one item or will be going to many of the smaller towns, you can do fairly well by shopping in stores.

Key Phrases

In markets, you'll be doing a lot of bargaining. Some of the key phrases in striking a deal are: *¿Cuánto vale?* (How much is it?); *¿Cuánto menos?* (For how much less will you sell it?); *¿Cuánto lo menos?* (What's your lowest price?) The vendor will say to you at various times in the bargaining process: *Hay trato, puede ofrecer* (You can bargain, you can make an offer); *¿Cuánto mas?* (How much more will you pay?).

What's A Fair Price?

Most likely, you'll have no idea of what is a fair price for any piece of merchandise. Test out the prices by negotiating with a few sellers. But remember that once you settle on a price, you have to buy. In any case, if an item is unique and you really want it, you're at the seller's mercy.

Don't hesitate to walk away when the seller reaches his "lowest" price. Prices drop when you start to leave. Prices will often come down to half the first figure. But there are many variations from item to item and market to market.

Hard bargaining is the mark of the intelligent buyer, but it can be at times a tedious and nerve-wracking process. Take plenty of breaks.

KNOW YOUR WEAVES!

One of the problems in looking at textiles is to distinguish cloth woven by hand on a backstrap loom from cloth made on a foot loom. Take a close look at the material. In cloth woven on a backstrap loom, the warp strands are much more visible than the cross-woven woof strands; the woof strands form "ridges;" a number of imperfections may be detected; and the ends need not be sewn across to prevent unravelling. Garments made from cloth woven on a backstrap loom consist of small sections sewn together, since the small loom limits the dimensions of the cloth produced. Foot-loomed cloth is more uniform, is used in larger pieces, and is often sewn across the ends to prevent unraveling. Both horizontal and vertical threads are easily visible.

Always look closely at what you're buying. With blankets, examine the ends to see if cotton warping is used or if the item is pure wool. Prices will vary according to the size of the blanket, quality of wool, thickness, and how much the blanket has been combed.

Some blouses and shirts are sold used, or are sewn partly from sections of used material. Examine such garments carefully for holes. If a section of used material is suspiciously bright, it has probably been run over with dye, and will run in the first wash.

Fabrics are woven in threads of varying qualities. The finest thread is *lustrina*, which defines the pattern much more sharply than the thread in lower-quality material. If the sewing and loose fit of some items of native clothing don't particularly suit you, you can have them altered by a local tailor, usually at a reasonable price, before you take them home.

To preserve the colors of most native fabrics, it's best to wash them in cold water with some salt and vinegar added. Be warned, however, that even with the best care, only the heaviest fabrics hold their shape and still look good after several washings.

STAYING OUT OF TROUBLE

Laws and customs, and the way they're enforced, may differ in Guatemala from what you are used to. In order to avoid problems, you should be aware of local practices. Some pointers:

Possession of any illegal drug, including marijuana, can lead to a prison sentence of from three to five years, as well as heavy fines and civil penalties. Be discreet. Even if you eventually beat a drug rap, you could languish in jail for months while a judge intermittently investigates the case. Your embassy will probably be of little use.

All travelers and vehicles are subject to search at any time, on the street, and at police and military checkpoints and roadblocks. Carry your passport or tourist card at all times, and vehicle papers if driving. Treat the authorities with deference..

Guns, of course, should not be carried, but pocket and hunting knives can also be considered illegal weapons. And, at times, customs, military and police officials have been known to regard fancy radios, electronics equipment and other unfamiliar items as suspicious. Avoid trouble by leaving the gizmos at home.

Though its tempting to try to extend your stay by working in Guatemala, even at low wages, without a work permit you'll have no protection against employer abuses.

Women should not go around unaccompanied at night, especially on weekends and at fiesta times, when liquor flows. According to veteran female travelers, if you're not interested in attention from local males, don't do anything that local women wouldn't do. Or at least do it discreetly. In any case, unwanted attention is just as likely to come from fellow travelers as from natives.

Be no less cautious about thieves than you would be anywhere else. Leave non-essentials at home. Store any valuables that you take along in a hotel safe, if there is one. Carry money and passport in inside or hidden pockets — several kinds are available at travel stores. In a pinch, use safety pins to close your pockets. A dangling passport case around your neck is an invitation to robbery. Pickpockets and thieves lurk at fiestas, in crowded markets, and wherever tourists go. One hotel owner advises guests to lock their doors even when going down the hall to the bathroom.

If you have a problem with the police, be polite and try to understand what the difficulty is. For minor offenses, such as drunkenness or creating a disturbance, it's probably best to submit to a small fine. For major offenses, you have the right to get in touch with your embassy.

TAXES

Most goods and services in Guatemala are subject to a 7 percent **value-added tax (I.V.A.)**. Goods bought in markets are exempt. Hotel rates are subject to an additional tax of 10 percent, bringing the total to 17 percent. At the airport, the exit tax is about $10. There are small taxes and fees when you cross into Guatemala at land borders.

TELEGRAMS

International telegrams are handled by **Guatel**, the telephone and communications company. Telegrams to the United States cost 45 cents per word or more, depending on the destination city, with a seven-word minimum. Rates are higher to most other countries. Address and signature are included in the word count. Where there is no Guatel office, the post office or the adjacent *Telégrafos* office will accept international telegrams, at higher rates.

Telegrams within Guatemala are handled by the post office or the adjacent *Telégrafos* office. The rate is just a few centavos per word, double for foreign-language messages and on Sundays and holidays. Use telegrams to reserve hotel rooms and otherwise communicate when your spoken Spanish may not be understood on the phone.

Telegrams from abroad to destinations outside of Guatemala City may be held for pickup rather than delivered, especially if the addressee has a non-Hispanic name. In such a case, you're generally wasting your money if you send a telegram.

TELEPHONES

The capacity of Guatemala's telephone system is limited. You could spend hours trying to place an international call through an operator, either at a Guatel (telephone company) office or from your hotel. If at all possible, try to dial direct from a private phone, without operator assistance. From Guatemala City, it's also fairly easy to reach an AT&T operator in the States from a USA Direct phone at the airport or at one of the major hotels.

Guatel office hours are generally from 7 am to 10 pm, with some local variation. A three-minute call to the United States costs $7 to $10 during the day, depending on the region called, slightly less at night and on weekends. To Canada, the daytime rate is $7 to $12. Calls to outside the hemisphere cost $20 or more for three minutes. Collect calls can be placed to the United States, Canada, Spain, Italy, Japan, Sweden, Mexico, and Central America.

Personnel rely on wristwatches to time calls, not always accurately, and incorrect rates are routinely charged. Keep track of the time on your own watch, and ask to see the rate schedule for wherever you are calling before you pay.

In some small towns, long-distance calls are handled by the telegraph office.

To reach a telephone outside the capital, dial 0 plus the six digits of the local number (061 plus four digits for Quezaltenango). To reach Guatemala City from elsewhere in the country, dial 02 plus the number. It's generally easier to place a long-distance call within Guatemala from a pay phone than through a hotel or Guatel operator. Just place a couple of 25-centavo coins on the rack before you dial. It's quite inexpensive to phone ahead — the equivalent of no more than 10 cents US a minute — so take advantage of the phones to make your hotel reservations.

CALLING GUATEMALA

Direct Connect Services:

190 *AT&T USADirect*
195 *US Sprint*
198 *Canada Direct provincial phone company consortium (English/Français)*

These numbers can be dialed direct from home phones. From public phones, you'll first have to drop in a coin — currently the ten-centavo minimum. Hotels may impose a hefty surcharge for direct-connect services — ask before you dial!

Almost any telephone company credit card can be used with direct-connect services. Or call collect.

CALLING GUATEMALA CITY

The dialing prefix for the capital is 02 from elsewhere in Guatemala. From the US or Canada, dial 011 (international direct dial) 502 (country code for Guatemala) 2 (city code) plus the number in Guatemala City. As an example, to reach the Hotel Camino Real:
- *__From the US__, dial 011-502-2-334633*
- *__From Panajachel, Guatemala__, dial 02-334633*
- *__From within Guatemala City__, dial 334633*

Messenger Calls

It's not unusual to call someone in Guatemala without knowing at which number to reach them, or if they have a phone at all (generally the case in Guatemala). Or, say, you know that your son or daughter is in Panajachel, but you have no telephone number.

The solution is to request a **messenger call** (*citación* in Spanish) through your long-distance operator. Give the name of the party you seek, the town, and indicate when you will be in to receive a return call. A runner will be sent to find the fetch your party to the local phone office. You'll pay at person-to-person rates, and a charge of 25 cents or so will apply at the other end. Quaint, homey, and usually effective.

To reach a number in Guatemala from abroad, follow directions in your phone book, or see dialing instructions given in this book with hotel listings for major towns.

Coin Telephones

Coin telephones are available, to a greater or lesser extent, in Guatemala City and some large towns. You'll generally find them outside the Guatel office, next to the town hall (municipalidad), on the main square, and, sometimes, in hotel lobbies.

TIME

Guatemala is on **Central Standard Time**, equivalent to Greenwich Mean Time less six hours.

TIPPING

In restaurants, a ten-percent tip is appropriate. Tipping is optional in small, family-run restaurants. In hotels, give the porter a quetzal if you need his help to carry your bags. If you stay a few days, you may want to leave a couple of quetzales for the maid or some other member of the staff. Guides extract generous commissions from stores and even from market vendors, so there's no need to tip them except for special favors. Don't tip a taxi driver once you have negotiated a fare. When in doubt about whether or how much to tip, remember that a tip is a reward for good service. Poor service means no tip.

WEIGHTS & MEASURES

Weights and measures in Guatemala are a hodgepodge of the metric system, the English system, and old Spanish measures.

Highway distances are measured in kilometers. Eight kilometers are equivalent to five miles. To convert kilometers to miles, multiply by 5/8, or .62. Distances along the railroad are measured in miles. And Indians will often speak of a certain town as being so-and-so many leguas distant. A legua is about four miles, or 6.7 kilometers, and informally refers to the distance a person will walk in an hour.

Meters and yards are both in use for measuring shorter distances, though yards, feet and inches are more common. A meter is equivalent to 39.37 inches, or a yard plus another ten percent. Native fabrics are often sold by the *vara*, a Spanish measure equal to .836 meters or about 33 inches. A standard *corte*, or length of skirt material, which you'll often find in the market, is usually six varas long.

Land measurement follows Spanish usage. The smallest unit is the square vara, or *vara cuadrada*. A *cuerda* is usually a square of land 32 *varas* on a side (equivalent to 716 square meters or 7701 square feet), though it may also be 40 *varas* on a side. A *manzana* is equivalent to about seven-tenths of a hectare, or 1.727 acres, and a *caballería* is equivalent to about 45 hectares, or 111.5 acres.

Weight is usually measured in pounds and ounces. 25 pounds make an arroba and 100 pounds a *quintal* (abbreviated qq.). At the post office, however, grams and kilograms are used. It takes about 29 grams to make an ounce and 454 grams to make a pound. A kilo is 2.2 pounds.

Gasoline is sold by the US gallon, equivalent to 3.8 liters. For other liquid measures, liters are usually used. Many products, including liquor, are sold by the botella, equivalent to three-quarters of a liter, or 25.4 ounces.

Is all this clear?

NATIONAL PARKS

On paper, at least, Guatemala has laws in place to protect sensitive areas. The **Protected Areas Law** declares wildlife to be part of national heritage, and authorizes the protection of sensitive areas with historic, scenic, genetic and/or archaeological value. In many cases, however, lands remain in private hands, and management rules are established for the owners.

Protected areas under control of the national government are a hodge-podge that range from urban parks to a vast jungle tract in the north.

MAYA BIOSPHERE RESERVE

The **Maya Biosphere Reserve**, formed in 1990, is one of 273 such conservation areas around the world, intended as a storehouse of natural wealth for all mankind.

Covering about 1.5 million hectares, it includes:
- **Tikal National Park**, **Río Azul National Park**, **Laguna National Park** in the northwestern corner of Petén, **Sierra del Lacandón National Park** along the Usumacinta River, and **El Mirador National Park**.
- The protected areas, or *biotopos* of the Petén: **Laguna del Tigre**, **Dos Lagunas**, and **El Zotz**.
- A multiple-use area of sparsely settled lands. Sustainable use of the land is encouraged. Examples: gathering of nuts, spices, and ferns.
- A buffer zone fifteen kilometers wide on the edge of the biosphere.
- Habitats that range from virtually untouched jungle to traditional *chicle* harvesting areas to wetlands to a part of the Maya Mountains.

Adjacent reserves in neighboring countries include **Calakmul Biosphere Reserve** in Mexico, and the **Orange Jungle** in Belize — making up a total protected area of four to five million acres (official measurements are inconsistent).

Cutting of forest and settlement in parks and biotopes is prohibited or limited, at least in law and theory. In practice, logging and farming continue out of view or beyond the control of responsible authorities.

PARQUE NACIONAL LACHUA

Parque Nacional Lachua (Lachua National Park) lies ten kilometers east of Playa Grande in the northern part of the department of Alta Verapaz, near the state of Chiapas in Mexico, 418 kilometers by road from Guatemala City. Covering 100 square kilometers, it is an example of subtropical rain forest, much of which has been destroyed in the neighboring area in the course of resettlement and land-clearing. At the center of the park is Laguna Lachua.

Typical trees here include mahogany, breadnut, ceiba and San Juan. Wildlife species that may be sighted include raccoons and coatis, peccary, and tapirs. Frequently sighted birds include parrots, toucans and macaws.

Access to Lachua is by cargo and pickup trucks from Cobán, the nearest large town, or by small plane from Cobán to the military airstrip at Playa Grande. The access road to the park branches from the main east-west road (*transversal del norte*) about seven kilometers east of Playa Grande.

PARQUE NACIONAL RÍO DULCE

Parque Nacional Río Dulce (Río Dulce National Park) covers a kilometer-wide strip on each side of the Río Dulce, the river that flows from Lake Izabal to the Caribbean, a total of 80 square kilometers of land, as well as the waterway itself, from Castillo de San Felipe to the river's mouth at Lívingston.

Typical wildlife in the area includes mollusks, sea birds, and such endangered species as tapirs, alligators, manatees, spider monkeys and turtles. There are also at least a dozen minor archaeological sites.

PARQUE NACIONAL EL ROSARIO

Parque Nacional El Rosario (El Rosario National Park) is a 1031-hectare tract of standing subtropical rain forest along the Río de la Pasión, three kilometers from Sayaxché in the department of the Petén. Typical trees include the ceiba (kapok, or silk cotton, the sacred tree of the Maya), mahogany, tamarind, and ironwood. Common animals include the coati, deer, tepezcuintle, and agouti.

PARQUE NACIONAL LAS VICTORIAS

Parque Nacional Las Victorias (Las Victorias National Park) is an urban reserve and recreation area covering 82 hectares in the city of Cobán, Alta Verapaz, along the river Cahabón and adjacent to the Calvary church and the soccer field. The park includes three small ponds and a nature trail.

PARQUE NACIONAL LAGUNA EL PINO

Parque Nacional Laguna El Pino (El Pino Lake National Park) is a 73-hectare plot near Barbarena in the department of Santa Rosa, about 45 kilometers southeast of Guatemala City.

SOME WAYS TO HELP

Avoid buying hardwood products unless you're sure the species is not threatened.

Do not buy tropical birds to take home, smuggled or otherwise.

Do not buy orchids or other plants of endangered species.

How do you know what's threatened? You probably don't. So stay out of the market for natural products, unless you first consult the list of the Defensores de la Naturaleza.

PRIVATE EFFORTS - AND YOU

Guatemala is a country where official efforts for the public good and the defense of natural treasures are always open to skepticism, dismay, opposition, and, too often, failure. Officially sanctioned parks and reserves are often nothing more than lines on a map, their boundaries violated by colonels who just happen to own nearby cattle ranches, or campesinos desperate for land to till or game for the table. Naturalist Mario Dary, who established the quetzal reserve in Baja Verapaz, ended up in a pool of blood (though not necessarily because of his conservation efforts). "Defense" against perceived domestic enemies, the luring of foreign investment, and other items are higher on the government's priorities list than conservation.

So it is that private efforts are essential, not only as a practical way of protecting and enhancing the natural environment where the government usually steps aside; but also as a way of involving ordinary Guatemalans, and implanting a conservation ethic as part of basic values.

Among the bright elements is the **Funcación Defensores de la Naturaleza (Defenders of Nature Foundation)**, *7 Avenida at 13 Calle (Cúpula building, second floor), Zone 9, Guatemala City, tel. 325064,* a mainline foundation whose aim is to protect biological diversity in Guatemala.

The foundation owns and protects the **Reserva de la Biósfera de Sierra de las Minas** (the **Sierra de las Minas Biosphere Reserve**), a 600-square-kilometer stretch of cloud forest in an area that has been repeated ravaged by fires. Included are five ecosystems, 70 percent of the mammalian, bird, and reptile species in Guatemala, and the country's most important watershed. The core area is owned by the foundation, which also manages a larger buffer zone, where land use is starting to be regulated.

Among their fund-raisers are coloring books of endangered species. And while they've picked up corporate sponsorship, you can stop by and see what you can do. Or become a supporter, for about $25.

SPORTS & RECREATION

Here is some of what Guatemala has to offer in this department:

BUNGEE JUMPING

Available off Río Dulce bridge at Fronteras. Contact **Maya Expeditions, Maya Expeditions/Expediciones Maya**, *15 Calle 1-91, Zona 10, first floor, tel. and fax 374666. (US address: Club 747-66, P. O. Box 527270, Miami, FL 33152.)* No further comment.

DIVING

Guatemala is not one of the great dive centers of the world, but some of the greatest diving is not far away, along the reefs of Belize. And for experienced or novice divers, deep plunges into Lake Atitlán and Pacific excursions are a novelty.

Several dive shops and schools are at your service for internationally recognized certification, tank fill-ups, and equipment rental and repair:
• **Colegio del Mar**, *5 Avenida A 6-59, Zone 2, Guatemala City, tel. 518833.*
   Internationally recognized certification is available.
• **Pana Divers**, *16 Calle 7-15, Zone 9, tel. 343870.*
• **Pro-Diver**, *6 Avenida 9-85, Zone 9 (Tivoli shopping center), tel. 312738, fax 782286 (with friends and associates at tel. 621433 in Panajachel, and 612707 in Quezaltenango).*

FISHING

Guatemala's lakes aren't especially known for their **sport fishing**. Mountain lakes such as **Atitlán** and **Amatitlán** are rich in mojarras, pepescas, pupos and butes, which will be familiar to some visitors as the cichlids, banded tetras, mollies and toothcarps that they keep in their aquaria at home. Such tropical fish are sometimes caught and eaten by locals, but they're not much sport.

Lake Atitlán also has eels, black bass (*lobina*) and crappies, though few hotels provide fishing equipment. Natives use spears to get the black bass. In **Lake Petexbatún**, in the Petén, snook and peacock bass are found, as well as tarpon at the height of the rainy season, in July and August.

In the lowlands, **Lake Izabal** offers snook (*róbalo*), tarpon (*sábalo*), and mullet (*lisa*) for sport fishing and eating, as well as sawfish. Out in

Caribbean waters are snook, snappers (*pargo*), tarpon, barracuda, tuna, mullet, amberjack, and crevalle jacks. There are also oysters, crabs and shrimp, and, along the reefs, turtles and mussels. Tarpon in large numbers enter the rivers, especially the **Río Dulce**, from March to June. In the flats near the Belizean border bonefish and permit are plentiful. Fishing boats and equipment are available at hotels along the Río Dulce.

On the **Pacific** side, there are yellow and black tuna, wahoo, snappers, bonito, crevalle jacks, roosterfish, and plentiful dorado (dolphinfish, or mahi-mahi) from about three miles out. Sailfish, also quite large, are farther out, and in deep waters, twenty miles offshore, are marlin. Except for some shrimping, not much fishing is done from Guatemala's Pacific ports, though the sports potential is great.

Serious sport fishermen should bring their own equipment insofar as is practical.

Fishing Excursions

Small-time fishing excursions for big-time spenders haven't yet arrived in Guatemala, though not for lack of raw material. At least one agency, however, will take care of your requirements:

• **Guatemala Offshore Fishing**, *5 Avenida 11-63, Zone 9, tel. 317222, fax 317225.* A one-day excursion from Likin, on the Pacific coast, runs about $200 on a 24- or 28-foot boat that holds up to four sport fishermen. The wahoo, dorado, sailfish, and sawfish are about 12 to 14 miles out.

RAFTING & RIVER TRIPS

Rafting and river trips are still relatively new to Guatemala. If you're interested in exploring in this way, you can have the satisfaction of being one of the first.

The raw material is impressive.

The **Usumacinta**, rising in the highlands of Guatemala and flowing toward the Gulf of Mexico, is the longest tropical river north of Venezuela. There is spectacular jungle scenery — towering centenary trees tangled with vines and alive with spider monkeys and darting macaws — but it passes by the ancient Mayan metropolises of Yaxchilán, Piedras Negras, and Altar de los Sacrificios. Other ruins lie along tributaries. The river is rated class II — unchallenging — with some class III stretches.

The **Cahabón River**, rising in Alta Verapaz and descending toward the lowlands and Lake Izabal, is a more difficult run — class III and class IV — with numerous rapids, some of them portaged because of their difficulty. A run down the Cahabón offers stops at hot springs, and the sight of birds from bluejays to macaws, and even quetzals. It may end with a switch to a motorized boat for a cruise down the Río Dulce.

The **Chiquibul**, recently opened to rafting by Maya Expeditions, runs through virtually untouched jungles, past 50-foot waterfalls and cascades of vines thick with bird life. Rated Class II-III, it can be traveled in combination with a visit to such ancient sites as Tikal and Lake Yaxjá.

The **Naranjo River**, near Quezaltenango, can be rafted in combination with a trip to the volcano Siete Orejas, and lowland archaeological sites.

The **River Motagua**, running from the central highlands of Guatemala toward the Caribbean, offers the only one-day river excursions of the type that have become popular in Costa Rica. A trip of six hours or so generally starts near Mixco Viejo, with a visit to the archaeological site there.

The major operator of rafting trips is Tammy Ridenour's **Maya Expeditions** (**Expediciones Maya**), *15 Calle 1-91, Zona 10, first floor, Guatemala City, tel. and fax 374666. (US address: Club 747-66, P. O. Box 527270, Miami, FL 33152).* Ridenour's brochure rings with remoteness and adventure:

> *Swim in the pristine travertine pools of Semuc Champey . . . native carriers help portage rafts and equipment around the unrunnable and deadly Chulac Falls . . . experience beautiful cliff walls, colonial Spanish bridges . . . the Usumacinta's shoreline is home to giant iguanas, turtles, the rare caiman, howler and spider monkeys, and the elusive jaguar. . . Ride underground on the Candelaria, through caves used by the ancient Maya.*

Not to mention that the water is warm, and you can still be among the first rafters on any number of rivers.

SAILING TRIPS

A catamaran trip operates every Friday down the **Río Dulce** in the lowlands of Guatemala. Twice a month, Captain John Clark sails from Hacienda Tijax, just downriver from the Río Dulce bridge, for a cruise across **Lake Izabal** under the stars, then downriver to visit to hot springs, falls, steam-filled caves, and the old Spanish fortress of San Felipe. The rate of about $70 per person includes two nights on board.

On alternate weeks, the catamaran cruises to the **Sapodilla Cays** of Belize, with stops at the manatee reserve, Lívingston, and Punta Manabique, for about $250 per person for six days. For information, contact **Aventuras Vacacionales**, *11 Avenida 32-64, Zone 5, Guatemala City, tel. and fax 310204 (or tel. 322613 in Antigua, 621252 in Panajachel).*

VOLCANO CLIMBING

For the Guatemalan who lives nearby, a volcano is a useful bit of real estate for growing corn or some other crop, and something to watch out for in case an eruption should spew ashes onto his crop or send a boulder flying through the roof of his house. Over the longer term, eruptions have their benefits. Weathered volcanic soil is rich in organic matter, phosphates and nitrates, and retains water. Volcanic products useful to the ancient Maya included **obsidian** (volcanic glass), out of which tools were made, **clay** (weathered ash), and **hematite**, or iron-oxide pigment.

For the visitor who doesn't see a volcano every day, and who perhaps has read a novel by Malcolm Lowry, a volcano is of great psychic and magical value, signifying the life-forces of the universe grumbling just under the surface of the earth. When one is this close, it's tempting to hasten up to the crater of a handy volcano, as evidenced by the people who climb Agua and Atitlán, sometimes by the dozen, and camp out at the top on the night of a full moon. The magnificent views are more than sufficient reward for most who make it all the way up and back.

There are, however, some possible drawbacks. For the visitor who is not in excellent physical shape, a successful ascent and descent will be followed by days of soreness, which could make the remainder of a vacation miserable. And an attempt to go up alone, or in the rainy season, or without camping equipment or food or warm clothing, or in ignorance of where the trails are supposed to go, could be fatal.

Then there's the crime problem. The most accessible of Guatemala's volcanoes are ascended regularly by tourists either alone or in small groups — perfect marks for muggers and rapists from nearby towns. **Pacaya**, south of Guatemala City, has become notorious as the locale of assaults on visitors.

The ascent of most of the volcanoes in Guatemala is an arduous task, not an easy daytime outing. And, in times in which mass communications have made the humble covetous of what you have, it is a task that should be tackled with qualified assistance, and not a sense of macho adventurism.

One travel agency in Guatemala City with expertise in organizing trips to numerous volcanoes is **Maya Expeditions/Expediciones Maya**, *15 Calle 1-91, Zona 10, first floor, tel. and fax 374666. US address: Club 747-66, P. O. Box 527270, Miami, FL 33152.*

GUATEMALA CITY

Guatemala City was founded early in 1776 after war and earthquakes had forced the abandonment, in succession, of the three colonial capitals known today as **Tecpán Guatemala**, **Ciudad Vieja**, and **Antigua Guatemala**. Colonial administrators laid out the city of New Guatemala of the Assumption in the fertile Ermita Valley. According to some sources, they thought that the ravines surrounding the site would absorb the shocks of earthquakes, and thus protect the city from the destruction that had befallen their previous capitals.

If that was their belief, they were dead wrong. An earthquake damaged the city in 1830, and a new pair of tremors on Christmas Day 1917 and January 24, 1918, destroyed the city almost completely. Because of the devastation early in this century, no colonial buildings remain, except for a few sturdy churches. The earthquake of February 4, 1976, wrought heavy damage and caused loss of life in a few of the outlying areas. But by and large, the newer buildings of the central city survived unscathed, or with only minor damage.

ARRIVALS & DEPARTURES
Airlines Operating to Guatemala City From Abroad
The main airlines are:
- **Aviateca**, *10 Calle 6-41, Zone 1, tel. 364181, 320302*
- **American Airlines**, *Reforma 15-54, Zone 9, office 4401, tel. 347415, 346933*
- **Continental Airlines**, *12 Calle 1-25, Zone 10, north tower, 12th floor, tel. 312051*
- **COPA**, *7 Avenida 6-53, Zone 4, tel. 316813, 318443*
- **Iberia**, *Reforma 8-60, Zone 9, tel. 320911*
- **KLM**, *6 Avenida 20-25, Zone 10, tel. 370222*
- **LACSA**, *7 Avenida 14-44, Zone 9*
- **Mexicana**, *13 Calle 8-44, Zone 1, tel. 336011*
- **TACA**, 7 Avenida 14-35, Zone 9, tel. 322360
- **United Airlines**, Reforma 1-50, Zone 9, tel. 322995

Service to Flores (for onward travel to Tikal) is provided daily (usually) by Aviateca and:
- **Aerovías**, *gate 9, Aurora Airport international terminal, tel. 345386 to 90*
- **Aeroquetzal**, *gate 9, Aurora Airport international terminal, tel. 311173 and 364482 to 5*
- **Tapsa**, *Avenida Hincapié, 18 Calle, tel. 314860*
- **Línea Aérea Maya**, *international airport, tel. 347682*
- **Aviones Comerciales**, *Avenida Hincapié, Calle 18 (hangar 21), tel. 67946*
Aeroquetzal also flies intermittently to Cancún.

ARRIVING & DEPARTING BY AIR
Aurora International Airport, serving international flights and some flights to Flores, is located on the south side of Guatemala City in Zone 13. Though modern in style, it has deteriorated into a third-world kind of facility. Packs of porters contest the custody of your bags, whether you need assistance or not. The metal detector at the terminal entrance has absconded with Pan Am, and of course the bathrooms are filthy. In other words, the airport is no showplace or haven from the realities of the world outside.

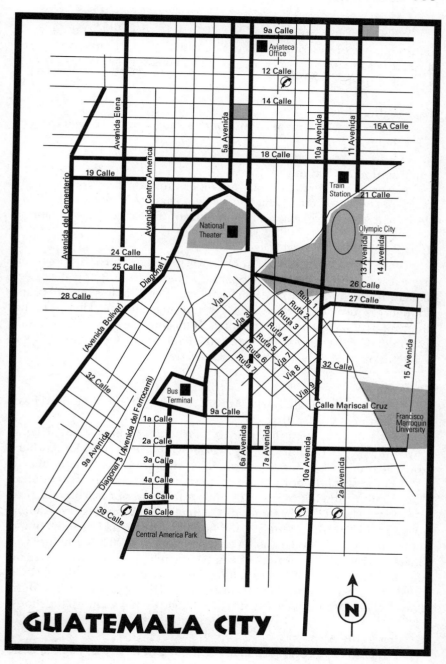

GUATEMALA CITY

When arriving on a flight, you'll first pass a desk staffed by a representative of the tourist office. You can pick up a tourist card here, if you don't already have one (subject to changing regulations), and book a room in town.

Exchanging Money

A **Banco de Guatemala** booth, for changing money, is open to meet most flights.

Immigration & Customs

Next come the immigration formalities, after which you pick up your baggage and go through what is usually a cursory customs inspection. Outside the door are taxis and the booths of the car rental companies.

Getting to Town

A taxi from the airport to any hotel will generally cost $10, even if you are exceptionally capable at bargaining. Bus 2, 82, or 83 on the street outside the terminal, will take you to zones 9, 4, or 1 for less than 10 cents, though it's usually a squeeze to get any luggage on. There are no limousines or collective buses to hotels. If the lower-level exchange booth is closed, take the outside stairway to the bank on the second level (open till 8 pm on weekdays, to 6 pm on Saturdays).

Departing

When taking a flight out of Aurora Airport, enter on the third level of the terminal via the driveway.

Check in with your airline, and if you're taking an international flight, pay your exit tax (about $10), then go down to the second level, where you'll go through immigration formalities when your flight is announced.

On the second floor are the cafeteria, duty-free shopping counters (low cigarette and liquor prices), handicraft shops, slot machines, a post office, and a branch of the **Banco de Guatemala** (hours: weekdays 7:30 am to 4:30 pm; Saturdays, Sundays and holidays 8 am to 11 am and 3 pm to 6 pm). Repurchase dollars here (currently up to a $100 limit) before you board your flight. The offices of **Guatel**, the telephone company, are on the second level, but if you're calling the States collect or with a Calling Card, you'll have better luck from the USA Direct phone on the third floor. When the bank is closed, try to exchange money at one of the shops.

Getting to the Airport

To get to the airport terminal, catch bus 2 or bus 82 or 83 on 9 Calle between 6 and 7 Avenidas, along 8 or 10 avenida in Zone 1, or along 6 Avenida in zones 4 and 9. Ask the driver if the bus is not clearly marked:

Aeropuerto? (Bus routes are frequently re-shuffled.) Taxis to the airport cost about $10 from Zone 1, slightly less from Zone 4 or Zone 9.

Service to Flores on some local airlines is provided from hangars on the east side of the airport, along Avenida Hincapié, as well as from the international terminal. Bus 203 from downtown passes nearby, but since flights depart early, a taxi is a better bet.

DEPARTING BY BUS TO MEXICO AND CENTRAL AMERICA

Obtain your visa or tourist card at the consulate of Honduras, El Salvador or Mexico before leaving Guatemala City.

Bus companies operating to Talismán El Carmen, on the Pacific coast route, will sell through tickets to Mexico City for $30 or so. The trip takes about 24 hours. See page 314.

To go to Mexico via the mountain route (Comitán, San Cristóbal de Las Casas, etc.), see listings for La Mesilla, pages 309-310.

To reach Honduras, take a bus to Esquipulas. There's frequent service from 19 Calle 8-18, Zone 1. Local buses provide service onward from Esquipulas to the borders of Honduras and El Salvador nearby.

Direct service from Guatemala City to San Salvador is available from:
• **Galgos**, *7 Avenida 19-44, Zone 1, tel. 23661, 536467.* Three daily departures.
• **Transportes Melva** and **Transportes Pezzarossi**, *3 Avenida 1-38, Zone 9, near the bus terminal, tel. 310874,* about every hour from 6 am to 2 pm.
• **Transportes Centro América**, *7 Avenida 15-59, Zone 1, tel. 84985,* one early departure, with pickup at your hotel.

DEPARTING BY TRAIN

Passenger service is provided from the station at *18 Calle and 9 Avenida, Zone 1 (tel. 83030),* to Puerto Barrios on the Caribbean and Tecún Umán on the border with Mexico. Service is slow — both trips take all day — with many stops at intermediate stations.

Service is steadily shrinking, and these trains may not operate for much longer. So if you're a train freak, you'll want to buy your ticket, pack a hamper of food, and enjoy the ride.

Trains for Tecún Umán, operating by way of Escuintla, Mazatenango and Coatepeque, operate on Saturday only, at about 7 am. A train for Puerto Barrios, operating by way of El Progreso, Zacapa and Quiriguá, leaves three times weekly (recently Tuesday, Thursday and Saturday) at 7:15 am. In both cases the fare is less than $3. Return trains operate the following days.

Verify all schedules at the station a few days before you intend travel.

ORIENTATION

Guatemala City is large, but quite manageable. The streets are logically numbered, and the places to which a visitor might go are concentrated in a few zones.

The commercial sections of the city are zones 1, 4, and 9, along the north-south axis of 6 and 7 avenidas. Office buildings and hotels line these streets, forming the backbone of the city. To the north and northwest, steep canyons bring the city to a dead end. The industrial areas and residential sections spread out to the east, south and southwest.

When locating an address in Guatemala City, always check the zone number first on a map (sold at most hotel newsstands). The same street numbers are repeated in different zones. Once you have the zone, finding the building is easy. The address of the Hotel Pan American, for example, is *9a Calle 5-63, Zone 1*, indicating that it's on 9a Calle (*Novena Calle*, or Ninth Street) between 5a Avenida and 6a Avenida (*Sexta Avenida*, or Sixth Avenue).

Numbers of streets from 1 to 10 bear the suffix "a" after the number (1a, 2a, etc.), indicating the equivalent of "first," "second," etc. To simplify matters, I've dropped the suffixes in all addresses that follow. To confuse things slightly, there are also capital-letter suffixes. 6 Avenida "A", for example, is a short street parallel to 6 Avenida, between 6 Avenida and 7 Avenida.

Only a few streets bear names instead of numbers.

GETTING AROUND TOWN

By Bus

Ordinary city buses run from about 6 am to 10:30 pm, depending on the route. The fare is currently 65 *centavos* (about 10 cents US) during the day, more on weekends and at night and on holidays. Low city bus fares are a sacred cow, and attempts to raise them have periodically provoked mass protests. Most buses are clunkers, and service is insufficient. At rush hours, passengers hang precariously from the front and rear doors.

Bus stops are generally poorly marked, but one telltale sign is a newspaper-and-candy stand accompanied by a lineup of people.

If you choose to ride the buses, you'll probably shuttle between zones 1, 4, and 9 on these lines:

Bus 203: Along 10 Avenida in Zone 1, Civic Center, along 6 Avenida and Ruta 6 in Zone 4, along Reforma in Zone 9 to the Obelisk. Also along 10 Avenida in Zone 1 to Reforma.

Bus 2, 63, 82, 83, 85: Along 10 Avenida or 4 Avenida in Zone 1, Civic Center, 6 Avenida in zones 4 and 9, 12 Calle in Zone 9 to Aurora Park. Bus 101 follows part of the above route.

Buses 2, 82, and **83** terminate at the international air terminal.

Buses 63 and **85** terminate in Aurora Park, near the zoo.

Other buses for the major attractions are listed in the zone-by-zone guide.

Metrobuses are newer buses that run on select routes in Guatemala City. They charge more than ordinary city buses, which keeps them less crowded. Most run southward from city hall in the Civic Center (the cluster of government buildings on the border of Zone 4 and Zone 1.

Metrobus 205 runs from the Civic Center along Avenida La Reforma, and past the obelisk to Avenida Las Américas.

Metrobus 201 runs to the Kaminaljuyú ruins and suburb.

Don't blame me if your bus doesn't appear where it's supposed to in Zone 1. The municipal government periodically orders route changes in an effort to decongest the city. Ask a cop or hotel clerk for directions. If you have trouble finding a bus to take you out of Zone 1, walk up 6 Avenida to 21 Calle, alongside the Fortress of San José, where most buses stop.

When confused by bus route numbers (which change periodically), pay attention to destinations posted on the buses. Any bus with a sign reading "Terminal" will pass the inter-city bus terminal in Zone 4. **Terminal Aérea** buses go to the international airport, and **Parque** buses (when northbound!) head for the main square in zone 1.

At night, after the buses have stopped running, you can get around by *ruleteros*, taxis and microbuses running along fixed routes until about 2 am You're mainly interested in the ones following the same route as bus 2. Fare is just slightly more than on buses, and varies with the distance traveled. To catch a *ruletero*, stand on a street corner and wait for a microbus, or for a taxi with its inside lights on. The driver or his helper will shout *Parque* or *Villa* or whatever the final destination is. If the driver shouts taxi, he's not running on a regular route, and you'll have to negotiate your fare.

By Car

If you're driving your own car, make sure it's parked in a garage or a protected lot overnight, and, preferably, in the daytime as well.

Traffic lights are turned off at night at many intersections. When they're off, and during the day at intersections that don't have signals, traffic on avenidas has preference over traffic on calles. Be ready to brake for drivers ignoring the rules.

Renting a Car

Most notably, all companies charge a deductible of about $2000, only part of which can be covered by locally purchased insurance. Rates vary, but are generally 25 to 50% higher than those in the US and Canada.

Among the companies are:

- **Tabarini**, *2 Calle A 7-30, Zone 10, tel. 316108*
- **Avis**, *12 Calle 2-73, Zone 9, tel. 316990, fax 321263*
- **Budget**, *Av. Reforma 15-00, Zone 9, tel. 316546, fax 312807*
- **Dollar**, *Reforma 6-14, Zone 9, tel. 348285, fax 326745*
- **Hertz**, *7 Avenida 14-76, Zone 9, tel. 322242, fax 317924*
- **National**, *14 Calle 1-42, Zone 10, tel. 680175, fax 370221*
- **Tally**, *7 Avenida 14-60, Zone 1, tel. 514113, fax 345925*

Some of these have agencies in the larger hotels and at the airport.

In the United States or Canada, call the toll-free numbers for Budget, Hertz, or National/Tilden to reserve a car and confirm the latest rates. From a consumer's point of view, it's desirable as a rule to rent from a franchise with a familiar name, in case you have any complaints to take to the head office. You can also sometimes get a better rate if you book in advance through a toll-free number. But several Guatemalan marques have good reputations, especially Tabarini.

By Taxi

Cabs have no meters, so many drivers will try to charge you more than the going rates. Even if you're not cheated, you'll find that fares are extortionate for this part of the world. There's little competition from the overworked public transit system, and no effective regulation.

Always agree on the fare before you get in a taxi. A trip of a few blocks will cost t least three dollars, and if you travel between zones, $5 will usually be the minimum fare. Figure about two to three dollars per kilometer for longer runs, and ten dollars or so from Zone 1 to the airport. From the airport, things are even worse. Expect to pay at least $10 to any hotel, even those only a kilometer or two away. If you bargain hard, you may ride for less.

Ask for advice about fares at your hotel, or from residents. If you are going from place to place during the day, the only way to go is to hire a taxi by the hour, at about $7 per hour for a minimum of three hours.

Taxis are hard to spot. They look like other cars, except that their license plates begin with "A." Best place to pick one up is in front of the major hotels, or at the taxi stands located at the Central Park or Concordia Park (15 Calle and 6 Avenida) in Zone 1. Some of the numbers are: *534124, 23226, 29290* (Central Park, Zone 1); *362882* (Conquistador Sheraton Hotel); *367951* (Bus Terminal); *374019* (Hotel Camino Real); *341686, 341975* (Airport).

Ruleteros—jitney taxis running along fixed routes—are mentioned in this section under Buses.

WHERE TO STAY

Better Hotels – Zone 4

HOTEL CONQUISTADOR RAMADA****, *Vía 5 4-68, tel. 312222, 341212 (reservations), fax 347245. US/Canada Reservations 800-228-9898. 170 rooms. $100 to $123 single/$128 to $146 double. Off-season rates may be available through the toll-free number.*

Recently renovated and redecorated, the Ramada (formerly the Sheraton) has a dramatic, multi-level atrium entry, decked with planters full of huge-leafed tropical plants and orchids. All rooms in the two towers have individual air conditioning, balcony, and cable television with US programs. Some suites have kitchens. Facilities include restaurants and night club, travel agency, bookshop, garage, and small pool. The location is in the banking and financial area of the city, not near most attractions for visitors.

Better Hotels – Zones 9 & 10

HOTEL CAMINO REAL*****, *Avenida Reforma 14-01, Zone 10, tel. 334633, fax 374313. US/Canada reservations 800-228-3000. 386 rooms. $164 and up single/$187 and up double, up to $1000 in certain suites.*

This is the hotel in Guatemala that gets it right. The Camino Real is a superb hotel, by far the best in the country, and near the top of the rankings in Latin America in terms of quality of rooms, services and facilities, all of which are constantly being upgraded.

Rooms: accommodations vary, but rooms are typically carpeted, with an easy-on-the-eyes pastel decor, television, phone, excellent beds, quiet air conditioning, textured wallpaper, art prints of the Guatemalan countryside, desk and dresser, table, and hardwood doors — in other words, comfortable and complete, down to the loofah and razor provided in the bathroom. Premier floors have their own concierge, extra amenities such as an honor bar and bathrobes, and breakfast buffet included in the higher rate ($234 single/$269 double).

Sports facilities: Two pools (including the more sheltered pool by the Biltmore tower), tennis courts, and health club.

HOTEL RADISSON VILLA MAGNA*****, *1 Avenida 12-46, Zone 10, tel. 329797, fax 329772. 98 units. US reservations, tel. 800-333-3333. $110 junior suite, $122 one-room suite, $146 two-room suite. Promotional rates often available through US reservation number.*

Suite units in an office-tower kind of building, a good value if you want to cook or settle in while doing business. Units are large, and include eat-in kitchenette complete with refrigerator, microwave and coffee maker. Rates include a breakfast buffet and welcome drink. Facilities: Restaurants in shopping plaza, room-service meals, whirlpool, exercise room with limited hours, indoor low-ceiling parking, conference room.

HOTEL EL DORADO*****, *7 Avenida 15-45, Zone 9, tel. 317777, 310817 (reservations), fax 321877. 250 rooms. $164 single/$187 double.*

The El Dorado is also a well-run hotel, and most of its rooms have been renovated over the last few years. All have balconies, and the decor is low-key pastel, with custom-woven fabrics — look for the quetzal motif. Bathrooms are on the small side, but furnishings are more than adequate — chairs, table, but no minibar. There are several good restaurants, but the outstanding feature here is the best sports facilities: two tennis courts, squash and racquetball, two pools, men's and women's gymnasiums, steam baths. Also: meeting facilities, shops and travel agency. Five-star rated, like the Camino Real.

HOTEL GUATEMALA FIESTA****, *1 Avenida 13-22, Zone 10, tel. 322555, 322572 (reservations), fax 682366. 205 rooms. $165 single/$190 double.*

Modern, but, thank goodness, the garish orange and lime-green decor prevailing in the guest rooms of yesteryear is being toned down to pleasant pastels in the course of renovations. Rooms are centrally air-conditioned, and the corner units, with balconies, are preferable. Facilities include exercise room and sauna, a small pool, bar, shops and travel agency, as well as underground parking. Guests report noisy discos in the area make sleep difficult.

HOTEL PRINCESS REFORMA, *13 Calle 7-65, Zone 9, tel. 344545. 90 rooms $105 to $140 single/$129 to $150 double. US reservations, tel. 800-327-3573.*

Brand new, in the most elegant part of the city. All rooms with cable t.v., and facilities include a gym, bar and restaurant, whirlpool and pool.

Better Hotels – Zones 13

HOTEL LAS AMÉRICAS, *Avenida Las Américas 9-08, Zone 13, tel. 316066. 100 rooms. $140 single/$152 double.*

A brand-new, sleek, arte moderne hotel in the Camino Real chain, a notch down from the parent hotel in terms of available services, but still quite good as a hotel. As for the location . . . it's in an upper-class shopping and residential area, but remote from any points of interest; and near the airport, but on the far side from the international terminal, and a fair-sized cab ride distant.

Moderate Hotels – Zone 1

HOTEL PAN AMERICAN***, *9 Calle 5-63, tel. 26807, 25587 (reservations), fax 26402. 60 rooms. $65 single/$70 double.*

Located a block from the main square, the Pan American is a long-standing favorite of the foreign community in Guatemala. The atmosphere is one of elegance well retained from the past, especially in the high-ceilinged lobby, and the service and food are excellent. Rooms are old-fashioned and comfortable, not elegant, with t.v. Noise is a problem on the 6 Avenida side.

HOTEL RITZ CONTINENTAL****, *6 Avenida A 10-13, tel. 81671, 80889 (reservations), fax 24659. 202 rooms. $119 single/$138 double. Much lower rates usually available.*

Large and centrally located, the Ritz and its tired fifties decor are getting a much-needed facelift. Some of the rooms are quite luxurious, with hardwood floors, large private sun terraces with spectacular views, marble vanities and tubs faced with Spanish tiles. Others are being upgraded. All have color televisions with satellite programming. Facilities include a pool, garage, and bar and restaurant.

Nobody should pay the official rate here. You should get a substantial discount on request — tell them I said so.

HOTEL DEL CENTRO****, *13 Calle 4-55, tel. 300208, 80639, fax 22705. 60 rooms. Up to $90 single/$110 double.*

Similar to modern Spanish hotels in decor — lots of dark wood and lamp fixtures. Recently refurbished, with comfortable rooms, though not deserving its four-star rating. Restaurant, garage, pleasant rooftop terrace, and cable t.v. in the rooms. Overpriced at the official rate, but negotiable.

HOTEL FORTUNA ROYAL, 12 Calle 8-42, Zone 1, tel. 500171, 517887, fax 512215. $50 single/$58 double.

Modest, new, with carpeted rooms, each with phone, t.v. and private bath. Bar and cafeteria. Not a wonderful area, but the rooms have everything except a decorator's touch.

CHALET SUIZO, *14 Calle 6-82, tel. 513786. 44 rooms. $28 single/$33 double.*

An old favorite among young travelers, but no longer the budget establishment of yesteryear, at least in Guatemalan terms. Some of the rooms are new and airy, a few are stifling, so make sure you look before you pay. Nice atmosphere, with a number of foreign guests usually sharing experiences in the courtyard.

The Chalet Suizo is enjoying a revival, expanding its stock of rooms, and its services. The Café Suizo serves breakfast; and light fare, including salads, soups and coffee, is available throughout the day.

POSADA BELÉN, *13 Calle A 10-30, tel. 513478, 29226. 9 rooms. $35 single/$42 double.*

One of the better of the smaller hotels and guest houses in Zone 1, a tranquil home decorated with colonial-style wrought iron, plants, and handicrafts from around the country. The friendly management is helpful in planning trips (they'll even arrange a full-week tour if you write in advance, or visits to a private reserve in the Petén), and keeps a library for guests. Breakfast is served (about $3), and other meals may be arranged with advance notice. Good beds, and a very quiet location.

HOTEL CENTENARIO***, *6 Calle 5-33, tel. 80381. 43 rooms. $26 single/$31 double.*

The rooms are cramped and the atmosphere is sterile, but the place is clean, the sauna is a nice feature, and you're right on the main square, if that's what you want.

Moderate Hotels – Zones 4

HOTEL PLAZA***, *Vía 7 6-16, tel. 362338, 363173. 57 rooms. $51 single/$58 double.*

This is a good buy for its facilities (American motel-style rooms, a very nice pool, squash court, reasonably priced restaurant); but street noise and fumes can be a problem, and though it's centrally located near some of the larger shopping complexes, it can no longer be considered a tourist accommodation.

Moderate Hotels – Zones 9 & 10

HOTEL VILLA ESPAÑOLA***, *2 Calle 7-51, Zone 9, tel. 323362, 323381, fax 365515. 67 rooms. $79 single/$88 double.*

Tiers of rooms in a three-story Mediterranean-style building above a courtyard. Protected parking. All rooms have color t.v.'s and fans. Not bad for the price, though the carpet burns in some rooms are getting historic. Restaurant, bar.

RESIDENCIAL REFORMA (LA CASA GRANDE)***, *Avenida Reforma 7-67, Zone 10, tel. and fax 310907. 28 rooms. $57 single/$70 double.*

A guest house in a Moorish-style mansion, a block from the US embassy. Rooms are individually decorated, and generally in good taste, though much plainer than the elegant public areas. Meals and cocktail service are available. Frequented by businessmen looking for a quiet ambience, among others, but readers complain that reservations may not be held.

APARTOTEL ALAMO***, *10 Calle 5-60, Zone 9, tel. 319817. 33 units. $58 single/$70 double, lower by the month. Visa, Master Card.*

Small, modern units, all with refrigerator and some with large sink (but no cooking facilities), but no restaurant or similar facilities found in hotels in this price range.

Moderate Hotels – Near the Airport

HOSPEDAJE EL AEROPUERTO (AIRPORT GUEST HOUSE), *15 Calle A 7-32, Zona 13, tel. 323086. 6 rooms. $25 single/$33 double.*

This modest middle-class home performs a real service for travelers. They'll save you a trip into town to find a bed for the night, so that you can get a fresh start on your travels in the morning; and they'll even give you ride with your luggage for the two blocks to the air terminal. Strictly no frills, bathrooms in most cases are shared, the beds are basic, the decoration isn't there, but the place is clean and airy, breakfast is included in the rate, and there's a t.v. room where guests actually talk to each other.

Despite the runways nearby, the neighborhood is quieter at night than almost any other in the city. A phone call is essential to make sure that there's room at the inn.

Budget Hotels – Zone 1

You generally won't have a private bathroom at a budget hotel, unless a range of prices is indicated. In that case, the higher price gets you a private toilet and shower.

HOTEL COLONIAL**, *7 Avenida 14-19, tel. 22955, 81208. 42 rooms. $19 single/$26 double.*

Comfortable, old-fashioned ambience, spotless rooms with comfortable beds. Most rooms with private bath. A good value. Breakfast is available.

HOTEL LESSING HOUSE, *12 Calle 4-35, tel. 513891. 7 rooms. $10 single/$15.*

A good, small hotel, usually booked up by a regular clientele from the provinces. Breakfast is available.

MANSÍON SAN FRANCISCO, *6 Avenida 12-62, tel. 25125. 40 rooms. $20 to $25 single or double.*

Clean and recently refurbished. Furnished apartments are available. Rooms at the higher rate are carpeted and have cable t.v.

HOTEL SPRING (PRIMAVERA), *8 Avenida 12-65, tel. 514207. 27 rooms. $21 single/$27 double, less with shared bath.*

Rooms are large in this big old hotel, though some have unvented showers that send out floods of steam. Another favorite of young and young-at-heart visitors. Convivial, but don't trust them to hold your reservation.

HOGAR DEL TURISTA, *11 Calle 10-43, tel. 25522. 11 rooms. $20/$25*

A plain, German-managed pension. Good value. Guests are expected to take their meals in the dining room.

HOTEL EL VIRREY, *7 Avenida 15-46, tel. 28513. 60 rooms. $10 single or double.* Central, only the rooms in the top tier are pleasant.

One of the many clusters of inexpensive hotels, in the vicinity of 15 Calle and 7 and 8 avenidas, includes these, among others:

HOTEL AJAU, *8 Avenida 15-62. tel. 20488. 28 rooms. $11 single/$13 double, more with private bath.* Clean, old, well-kept building, better than most in this range

Budget Hotels on Along 9 Avenida

HOTEL CENTRO AMÉRICA, *9 Avenida 16-38, tel. 83941, 83821. 52 rooms. $7 per person with private bath.*

HOTEL BELMONT, *9 Avenida 15-30, tel. 534662. 62 rooms. $7 single/ $9 double with shared bath, or $13 double with private bath.* In two buildings on opposite sides of the street.

HOTEL EXCEL, *9 Avenida 15-12, tel. 532709. 20 rooms. $19 single/ $$23 double.* New, and better than others on the block, with parking area.

HOTEL CAPRI, *9 Avenida 15-63, tel. 513737, 28191. 15 rooms. $12 single/$16 double, less with shared bath.*

HOTEL EL ALBERGUE, *9 Avenida 16-20. $5 per person.* Clean, rooms off a courtyard in an older building, not bad for the price.

WHERE TO EAT

Most of the inexpensive eateries are in Zone 1, while the more formal restaurants are clustered in zones 4, 9 and 10; but you'll find a range in prices, and good value for your money, in all areas.

Zone 1 – Downtown

My long-time favorite eating place in the capital is the dining room of the **HOTEL PAN AMERICAN**, *9 Calle 5-63.* There are many native-style touches, such as fiesta masks, waiters dressed in the men's outfit of Chichicastenango, and a brick hearth where a lady pat-pats tortillas into shape and cooks them over charcoal. Live piano music accompanies lunch. A buffet of native-style food is offered at luncheon Thursday, Friday, and Sunday. Even if you're not looking for a full meal, you might stop in for a pastry and a cup of coffee. Open at 6 am for breakfast (they have waffles). Prices are reasonable: lunch or dinner $5 to $10, breakfast or sandwich plates $4 and up.

Also a haven from the noise and bustle of downtown is the main restaurant of the **HOTEL RITZ-CONTINENTAL**, *10 Calle at 6 Avenida A,* which is being renovated into a large, open area with interior gardens. The food, usually served to organ music, can be excellent — the bread and even the potato chips are made fresh daily. And the luncheon special is one of the city's bargains. You can also get a variety of breakfast combinations starting at 6 am, long before most restaurants are open.

Prices are slightly higher in the **CANDILEJAS** restaurant of the *Hotel del Centro, 13 Calle at 5 Avenida,* where there are several lunch and dinner menus in rotation, featuring such items as Swedish meatballs and chicken breast in caper sauce. $7 or more for a complete meal, sandwich platters or breakfast for $3 and up.

Italian Food

The small **BOLOGNA**, *10 Calle 6-20*, serves pasta, pizza and meat dishes, usually to a full house. Arrive early for lunch or dinner. From $4. They have another, more attractive outlet in Zone 10. For cheap Italian food, there is no end of pasta and pizza palaces. At **AL MACARONE**, *6 Avenida 9-27*, the decor is garish lavender, the service is slow, but the food isn't bad. Pizza and burger combinations for $1 and up, portions of pasta and lasagne from under $3. They have branches around town. A similar chain is **A GUY FROM ITALY**, *with one branch at 12 Calle 6-23.*

Chinese Food

Many of the Chinese restaurants in Zone 1 are near Concordia Park, at 14 Calle and 6 Avenida. One of the better ones is **CANTON**, *6 Avenida 14-20*. Another fairly good Chinese restaurant is **FU LU SHO**, *on 6 Avenida at the corner of 12 Calle*. This is a hangout, with the dining area open to the street and food served until midnight. **RUBY**, *11 Calle 6-56*, serves the usual Chinese dishes as well as a filling non-Chinese lunch for less than $2.

Seafood & Spanish Food

ALTUNA, *5 Avenida 12-31*, is a thoroughly enjoyable place for a long lunch. You can eat in the pleasant bar in the center of the restaurant (the converted patio of a large old home), or in one of the small dining rooms that surround it. Closed Sunday.

EL MESÓN DE DON QUIJOTE, *11 Calle 5-27*, is one of those eccentric exile gathering spots that is more genuine than many a bar and restaurant back in the old country. Bullfight posters and celebrity photos decorate the stuccoed walls, bright red tablecloths are protected with plastic burned through by cigarettes, plants and lamps in baskets hang from the ceiling, ferns erupt from floors covered with pine needles. Rooms off the main hall have tables fashioned from barrels. **POSADA DEL TOBOSO**, *6 Avenida A at 11 Calle*, is an ever-lively great old multi-roomed house and bar, serving paella, Spanish omelettes, and seafood combinations. $5 and up.

German Food

A favorite of the German community is the **BAVIERA** , *on the second floor of the Maya Excelsior Hotel, at 7 Avenida 12-46*. There are daily specials served until closing.

For less gemülichkeit, try **DELICADEZAS HAMBURGO**, *at 15 Calle 5-34*, on Concordia Park. The set lunch is filling, and there are sausages, cakes, and fresh fruit drinks. $3 and up. **RANCHO MÜLLER**, *6 Avenida A 10-31*, next to the Hotel Ritz Continental, offers an odd combination of native-style barbecue and German deli. $2 to $5. There's a take-out counter for your picnics.

Mexican Food

EL GRAN PAVO, *13 Calle 4-41*, is genuinely Mexican, which means that the food is longer on sauces and shorter on cheese and other garnishes than the Mexican-American cookery you might know. Plates of tacos and enchiladas for under $2, mole, grilled meats and combinations for $4 to $7. **LOS CEBOLLINES**, *6 Avenida 9-75*, serves fajitas, tacos, tortas, small combination plates of Mexican standbys and daily specials for $3 and under, more substantial meat courses for $5 to $6.

Fast Food

Fast food has come to dominate the eating scene in Zone 1 in the last few years, and in some ways, it's not such a bad thing. The food is sanitary and reasonably priced, and it you're hungry, relief is at hand. Service in many a more traditional eatery is exasperating.

Here's a selection from the many establishments:

LAS SALSAS, *6 Avenida and 10 Calle* on the lower level of the Plaza Vivar building, is the most interesting fast-food outlet. Tacos, enchiladas, assorted combinations, and spoon on the sauces — from mild to roaring. $2 and up. Adjacent are **JIMMY'S HAMBURGER EMPORIUM** (see below), **PIZZA GRIZZLY**, and a quick Chinese eatery with a $2 lunch.

POLLO CAMPERO, specializing in fried chicken, has branches throughout the city. In Zone 1, you'll find one at the corner of *9 Calle and 5 Avenida*; and another at *6 Avenida and 15 Calle*. Both have parking lots. The chicken is spicier than the American fast-food variety. A complete lunch, with fries and Coke, goes for about $3.

CAFETERÍA LOS POLLOS, a chicken outlet on *6 Avenida between 14 and 15 calles*, is worthy of mention mainly because it stays open 24 hours. There's another branch at *7 Avenida 12-46*, on the ground floor of the Maya Excelsior Hotel. Unique among fast-food chains, **Los Pollos** has branches outside of Guatemala City, and they all have late hours.

Native Food

For Guatemalan cooking, try **LOS TECOMATES**, *6 Avenida 15-69*. The restaurant is cramped and unpretentious, but authentic. Also slightly larger than a hole in the wall is **RANCHÓN ANTIGÜEÑO**, *13 Calle 3-50*, and **LOS ANTOJITOS**, *15 Calle 6-28*.

Vegetarian

SOYA NUTRIAL, *16 Calle 3-64*. A complete lunch with soup, main course and fruit drink goes for just over $1. They also have bee pollen, turtle soap, and other health products. Off the beaten track, past the Central Market and near La Merced church, Señor Sol ("Mr. Sun") serves a set vegetarian lunch or dinner also for just over $1. Next door is **Soyavid**, where natural products and all kinds of herbs are sold.

Bars with Food

The **EL ZÓCALO** bar, at *18 Calle 4-39*, is a cavernous, busy and noisy place, heavy on local color. Order a beer, and you'll be served a mountain of *bocas* (snacks) that will include a bowl xof soup, a pile of tortillas, and assorted bits of meat.

Nearer the Central Park, in the arcade running off *6 Avenida between 8 and 9 calles*, is **EL PORTAL**, an old and woody drinking place, with mementos hung on the walls. Glasses of beer or shots of rum served with bocas for less than $1, light meals for $2 and up. At **EL MESÓN DE DON QUIJOTE**, *11 Calle 5-22* (mentioned above under Spanish food), the synthesizer is turned on after 11 pm, a performer steps onto the small stage, the electric guitar is plugged in, and music continues into the wee hours.

Inexpensive Food

The best cheap food is in the **central market**. *Enter along 8 Calle near 8 Avenida*, and follow the aroma of charcoal down to the eateries on the lower level. Squeeze in with the locals on a bench at a rough-hewn table, and fill up with stuffed peppers, grilled meat, omelettes, pacaya, plantains stuffed with beans, stew or *chuchitos*, all cooked before your eyes and served on enameled plates.

Zone 4
French Food

ESTRO ARMÓNICO, *at Vía 4 4-36*, is an international award-winning restaurant, and with good reason. Unpretentious on the outside, the locale is cozy on the inside, with arches, small dining areas, and an open fire. Try a tomato stuffed with shrimp as an appetizer, or leek, turtle or mushroom soup, then choose from daily specials that might include steak in bearnaise sauce, Tahitian shrimp, duck, or fish in a choice of preparations. I know of no other place where you will find *tepezcuintle* (paca), a Central American game animal, served in gourmet fashion. I take issue only with the herbed margarine. The entrance is opposite the rear of the Hotel Ramada. $15 and up for a full meal with a glass of wine.

Hotel Fare

There are also several restaurants in the **Conquistador Ramada Hotel**, if you're in the area. The attractive **PÉRGOLA** coffee shop has an assortment of continental fare, including fish almondine, pepper steak, and beef in native-style sauce for $7 and up, sandwiches for $4. Children's-size portions are available.

Spanish Food

One of the best bargains in town, and perhaps in all of Central America, is the **ALICANTE**, a simple, open-to-the-street restaurant *at 7 Avenida 7-46*. The atmosphere is more pleasant at the wooden tables on the balcony.

Seafood

AUTO MARISCOS, *at Vía 9, 5-04 (a couple of blocks from the Triángulo office building on 7 Avenida)*, is a big, US-style drive-up seafood house, brightly lit and short on atmosphere, but with very good food, including shellfish soup, paella, shrimp and lobster in various guises, and a salad bar. Choose beer rather than the house wine. $6 and up for fish, $10 for shrimp or lobster, less for the kids' menu. Sometimes there's a light lunch of fish, fries, and something fizzy for just a few dollars. Similar seafood is available in a more elegant atmosphere at **DELICIAS DEL MAR**, *Vía 5 3-65*, near the Sheraton. $7 and up for fish, $10 for shrimp.

Zones 9 & 10 – Zona Viva & Nearby

The **Zona Viva**, or *Lively Zone*, centered on the **Hotel Camino Real**, is where Guatemala's upper crust shops, dines, and otherwise entertains itself. The prices are sometimes un-Guatemalan, but they generally fall as you move toward the edges of the area.

French Food

At **LE RENDEZ-VOUS**, *13 Calle 2-75, Zone 10*, the dining is bistro-style on the patio and inside, past the parking up front. Popular and pricey. $7 and up for a light lunch of an attractive salad or a croque monsieur and a drink, $12 or more for steak-frites or anything substantial. **SIRIACO'S**, *1 Avenida 12-16, Zone 10*, more French-influenced than French, serves quiche, small steaks and salads in a pleasant art-gallery atmosphere drooping with plants.

Best of all is **ESTRO ARMÓNICO**, *15 Calle 1-11, Zone 10*, just around the block from the Camino Real's main entrance, a branch of the haute cuisine restaurant of the same name in Zone 4.

Mexican

EL PEDREGAL is as haute as you'll find in classic Mexican food between here and Oaxaca. What I mean is red snapper with fresh coriander, tequila shrimp, classic mole and crepes with cuitlacoche flowers, courtesy chilled coffee to top off your meal, and a classy environment that includes statuary on sheltered terraces, wicker chairs with leather cushions, and strolling Mariachi musicians. And you can appreciate it all at $10 and up per person.

Steaks

Don't hesitate to order steak in Guatemala City. When it's aged and cooked right, Guatemalan beef is marvelous, and at these steak houses, it comes in large portions. Figure $6 or more for a steak and a beverage.

PEÑA DE LOS CHARANGOS, *6 Avenida 13-60, Zone 9*. Gaucho ambience, with music, off the usual walking tracks.

HACIENDA DE LOS SÁNCHEZ, *12 Calle 2-10, Zone 10*. Pleasant, open-air pavilion.

EL RODEO, *at 7 Avenida 14-84, Zone 9*. Rustic and woody. Seafood, too.

GAUCHOS, *at the corner of 1 Avenida and 13 Calle, Zone 10*, is an Argentine-style steak house, in large rooms separated by arches. In addition to locally raised red meat, you can slide through imported Angus for $10 and up in this perhaps most pleasant of the carnivore corners.

Native Food

EL PARADOR, *Reforma 6-70*, serves tacos, country sausage, enchiladas, and marinated meats cooked on an open grill. A marimba band usually plays. $3 for a small combination plate, up to $7 for sirloin. Similar in price and food selection is **NIM-GUAA**, at *Reforma and 8 Calle*; and **LOS ANTOJITOS**, *Reforma 15-02*, where you can eat on an outdoor patio. If you hesitate to eat native-style snacks in the markets or on a bus, try **EL TAMAL**, *6 Avenida 14-49, Zone 9*. Tamales, tacos, chuchos and similar items cost 40 cents and up, to eat in or take out.

Mexican Food

EL GRAN PAVO, *12 Calle and 6 Avenida, Zone 9*, is a branch of the restaurant with the same name in Zone 1, though less atmospheric. **LOS CEBOLLINES** has a branch at *7 Avenida and 12 Calle, Zone 9*, larger and more pleasant than its Zone 1 outlet, another one downstairs in the Geminis shopping complex, *12 Calle and 1 Avenida, Zone 10*.

Seafood

PUERTO BARRIOS, *11 Calle and 7 Avenida, Zone 9*, is an attractive seafood house done up to look like a Spanish galleon. Ten dollars and up for shrimp or lobster, less for stuffed fish, chicken or steak. You won't find a place like this in the real Puerto Barrios. In the same compound is **TEPPANYAKI**, where Japanese-style steaks are cooked at your table. If you're not sure where to eat, consider that you'd pay a lot more than $10 for this kind of food almost anywhere else.

Asian Food

PALACIO ROYAL, at the corner of *7 Avenida and 11 Calle, Zone 9*, is the best Chinese restaurant in Guatemala City. The decor is genuinely oriental, and the menu is in Chinese as well as Spanish and English, a good sign. $7 and up.

Also good is **CELESTE IMPERIO**, *7 Avenida 9-99, Zone 4*. $6 and up, $10 for shrimp. More moderately priced, despite its location in the heart of the Zona Viva, is **EXCELLENT**, *13 Calle at 2 Avenida*. Many, many Chinese plates to choose from. $6 and up.

Tea and More

LA TERTULIA, *Reforma at 10 Calle, Zone 10*, is an old favorite of ol' timers and young timers, with assorted $2 breakfasts and $4 complete lunches, that latter including the likes of turkey, steak or shish kebab; and the $2 tea specials are light meals in themselves. Choose booths or tables under fans in a large room.

Family-Style

NAIS, *7 Avenida 6-26 and 5 Avenida 12-31, Zone 9, and 1 Avenida 12-47, Zone 10*, is similar to Lum's and other non-ethnic family restaurants that you'll find on suburban strips in the States. The specialties are tenderloin strip steaks, chicken, fondues and burgers. Fairly good, and reasonable at $5 and up for a meal, less for hamburgers.

Hotel Fare

The **Camino Real**, *14 Calle and Reforma*, has several restaurants. In **LA RONDA**, the cuisine is French and excellent. $15 and up. The **CAFETAL** coffee shop is good for elegant sandwiches with trimmings, salads, and native-style dishes. $6 for a deli sandwich or native-style combination plate, $12 and up for a complete meal. Also check their current schedule of theme buffets: Guatemalan, Salvadoran, breakfast, seafood, and others.

The restaurants in the **El Dorado** are also first-rate. The **GALEÓN** coffee shop has a garden-like atmosphere, with wicker furniture, and main courses for $6 or so; and the **CAFÉ-BAR** will do for informal, but not inexpensive eats (like lobster thermidor).In the **PARLAMENTO** restaurant, a daily buffet lunch is served for about $7. Lighter fare and hefty sandwiches are served in the Italian-style **CAFÉ-BAR**, adjacent to the main entrance. A full meal will cost $10 or more at either restaurant.

Kosher Style

LA MIGA DE YAACOV, *7 Avenida 14-46, Zone 9*, is a take-out deli. So where else will you find pastrami, salami and bagels? Daily specials, Closed from noon to 2 pm

Fast Food

The **POLLO CAMPERO** chicken restaurant at *7 Avenida and 10 Calle, Zone 9*, has a kids' play area. A **McDONALD'S** is at *14 Calle and 7 Avenida, Zone 9*. **BURGER KING** is on *Boulevard Liberación at 6 Avenida*. **LAS SALSAS** (for native food) and **JIMMY'S**, for hamburgers, have large outlets at *Reforma 13-59*, near the Camino Real, and nearby is **PIZZA HUT**, *Reforma 15-54*.

Lite

GITANO, *1 Avenida 13-31, Zone 10*, serves chicken on pita bread, deli sandwiches and fondues for around $4.

Inexpensive Food

Though it's nothing special as hotel restaurants go, the **COMPARSA RESTAURANT** in the **Hotel Fiesta**, *1 Avenida 13-22, Zone 10*, offers a fixed-price lunch (*almuerzo ejecutivo*) at about $2 ($4 by the time you add a beverage, tax and tip). Check out some of the other hotels in the area for similar if higher-priced deals.

You'll also find some bargains at noon in the office-shopping buildings of this so-called "lively zone." **A GUY FROM ITALY** has a 24-hour pasta outlet at *13 Calle 0-40, Zone 10*, just off Reforma.

BARS & NIGHTLIFE

Bars, discotheques, cozy clubs, restaurants and sleazy strip joints stay open into the early hours in Guatemala City. The nighttime scene is lively, and whatever it is you're looking for can be found. Here's a selection of places in addition to the bars and restaurants with entertainment mentioned above:

Some of the hotels are good bets for lively but hassle-free drinking, entertainment and dancing. Downtown, the **Ritz Continental** bar has a daily special mixed drink for $1. At the **Taberna** night club, adjacent to the main entrance of the Ritz, and downstairs, there's a happy hour from 6 to 8 pm, and evening entertainment.

In Zone 10, the **Lobby Bar** of the **Camino Real** sometimes has a piano player, a jazz singer, or some other pleasant surprise. In the *Zona Viva*, **Dash Disco** is downstairs in the shopping complex at *12 Calle and 1 Avenida, Zone 10*. **Le Pont Disco**, *13 Calle 0-48, Zone 10*, is attached to the Fiesta Hotel.

Many a bar in Guatemala City is a low-down place in which to get smashed. More yuppie-style places in which to get smashed include **El Establo**, *Avenida La Reforma 14-34*, pleasantly decorated with beamed ceiling, dim light, gardens and Spanish-style furniture, open from 5 pm; and **El Mostachón**, in the Plaza Montúfar shopping center on *12 Calle near 6 Avenida, Zone 9*. **Kloster**, downstairs in the commercial building at *6 Calle and 6 Avenida, Zone 9*, is the last thing you'd expect in Guatemala, a wood-panelled, dark Swiss den, where you can enjoy draft beer by the yard, a fair selection of wines, and fondues.

Mariachis

At night, stop by the **Trébol**, the cloverleaf intersection of *Avenida Bolívar and Carretera Roosevelt*, and you'll see mariachi bands in full Mexican outfits. The music is loud and brassy. Listen to a few tunes, and watch as locals drive up and haggle over the price of a song with one of the bands. The neighborhood around the Trébol is somewhat on the rough side, so go in your car or a taxi, or don't go.

CONCERT & EVENT INFORMATION

Concerts and sporting events are advertised in the Prensa Libre newspaper. The city has two especially interesting performance areas, the **National Theater** *in the San José Fortress, and the recently restored* **Teatro Abril**, *at 9 Avenida and 14 Calle.*

SEEING THE SIGHTS

Guatemala City is divided into 20 zones, but only those that contain museums, government offices, parks, monuments, hotels and restaurants that might interest most visitors are included here. The most important are within a few blocks of the National Palace in Zone 1. These can be seen in a day before you make forays into the countryside. Later on you can pick and choose among the sights that especially interest you.

Zone 1

Zone 1 is the old downtown area of Guatemala City, with its center at the **Central Park (Parque Central)**. (In any Guatemalan town, the main square is called the *parque*). The executive branch of the national government, the congress, and many hotels and businesses are located in this area.

The Central Park

The **Central Park**, *between 6 and 8 calles*, is technically two parks. To the west of 6 Avenida is **Parque del Centenario**; to the east, the **Plaza de Armas**, or **Plaza Mayor**. In the early days of Guatemala City, the park was a market, surrounded by the **Palace of the Captains-General** (where independence was declared in 1821), the mint, and lesser government buildings. All fell in the 1917 earthquake. The central square has had a facelift of sorts recently, and an official garage now underlies the Plaza de Armas, its barren surface dotted with several fountains.

Parque del Centenario, with its huge bandshell, is the more pleasant side. Even today, in the crowded, fumey, central-city environment, it manages to convey the air of a small-town square, where citizens of the capital read newspapers, chat, have their shoes shined, and observe the passing of the day from benches set among its flower beds, and humble visitors from the provinces rest between errands.

The National Palace

Now standing on the north side of the park is the **National Palace**, the center of the government of Guatemala. Built from 1939 to 1943, it was the last great public project of the dictator Jorge Ubico, who was overthrown not long after its completion.

Inside, the palace is far more pleasant and attractive than on the outside. The interior gardens and beams carved with coats of arms bring to mind the Moorish palaces of southern Spain. Around the two main interior stairways are a number of murals by Alfredo Gálvez Suárez depicting the history of Guatemala, from the semi-mythical times of the *Popol Vuh* to the wars between the Spanish invaders and the native kingdoms to the formation of a new society during the colonial period. Thrown in with these subjects is the unlikely theme of Don Quixote.

On the second floor is the **Reception Hall** (**Sala de Recepción**), a magnificent wood-panelled room with great chandeliers, used for state occasions. Stained glass windows depict the history of Indian and colonial Guatemala. But the most unusual feature is the stuffed quetzal — the bird that is Guatemala's symbol of national independence — which forms part of the coat of arms behind the rows of flags. If the Reception Hall is closed, ask one of the guards to let you in and to turn on the lights.

The Cathedral

The **Cathedral** (**Catedral Metropolitana**), *on the east side of the Central Park*, was begun in 1782 and finished in 1815. Bell towers and domes were added later. Built in the massive baroque style meant to resist earth tremors, the Cathedral has a bare white interior of little interest but for a number of altars covered with gold leaf.

Central Market Area

On the block behind the Cathedral is the modern **Central Market** (**Mercado Central**), which replaced the old market that was destroyed in the 1976 earthquake. A modern, low-slung concrete structure, the market starts with a pleasant plaza at street level, and continues for several stories below ground.

Visitors will be most interested in the scores upon scores of stalls on the upper levels where Guatemala's fine textiles, baskets, pottery, and other handicrafts are sold. But don't stop there. Onward and downward, vendors of pots and pans, meat, fruits, furniture and spices attract local customers, and some of their wares are worthy of your attention as well. On the first level are the eateries. And the commerce of the Central Market overflows to the shops and sidewalk stalls of all the nearby streets.

Almost all of the merchants at the Central Market are permanent vendors, who buy their wares from country people and middlemen. There are several other large markets around the city, including the sprawling terminal market in Zone 4.

On the opposite side of the square from the Cathedral is the **National Library** (**Biblioteca Nacional**). A massive, rectangular, and not especially attractive building, it features an intricate modernistic relief sculpture by Efraín Recinos on its main entrance stairway. *Around the block, with an entrance on 4 Avenida*, is the **Archivo General de Centro America** (**General Archives of Central America**), which stores documents of historical significance, including a manuscript by colonial chronicler Bernal Díaz del Castillo.

The Commercial Center

The stretch of 6 Avenida south of the square is the commercial heart of the city, lined with shops, slot machine parlors, movie houses and offices, and with restaurants and hotels located along the cross streets. 6 Avenida still retains a bustling, prosperous air, but on nearby streets you'll note the ills that afflict many an aging urban core. Bus after bus roars down an avenue, belching diesel exhaust from a poorly tuned engine, leaving hacking pedestrians and blackening buildings in its wake. Horns blare, trash is dropped in the streets, contaminants burn the eyes. The streets are cracked, and dusty and dirty with condensates of fumes. Pharmacies here (and in other parts of the city) dispense medicines from behind protective steel bars, and stores have armed guards.

Many a business and government agency has moved out of the central city, and many a street peddler has moved in to set up a stand and squeeze still more space from the congested sidewalks. Zone 1 is far from abandoned. A number of hotels and restaurants and shops maintain high standards. Still, in some establishments, floors crack, paint peels, nothing is repaired or replaced, and the clients have gone elsewhere.

At 7 Avenida above 21 Calle is the **Civic Center** (**Centro Cívico**), a complex of modern buildings housing offices of the city and national governments. The **City Hall (Municipalidad)** features a highly geometric interior mural by Carlos Mérida called *The Mestizo Race of Guatemala*. Mérida, Guatemala's leading modern artist, lived and worked for many years in Mexico. The outside relief sculpture on the east end of the building is by Dagoberto Vásquez. The combination of murals and sculpture with architecture in this and the other buildings of the Civic Center is a conscious attempt to revive the ancient Mayan tradition of integrating art with construction.

The other buildings in the Civic Center are those of the **Social Security Institute (IGSS)**, with a relief sculpture by Roberto González Goyri depicting the Conquest and the bloody clash of European and indigenous cultures; the **Bank of Guatemala**, also with relief sculptures by González; and the towers of the **Supreme Court**, the **National Mortgage Bank** and the **Ministry of Public Finances**.

Overlooking the Civic Center is the **San José Fortress**, a massive old defensive work. It's also a nice park, with carefully manicured lawns and flower beds, and cannon placed here and there along the ramparts. At the top stands the indoor-outdoor **National Theater** complex, which is skillfully integrated into the old structures.

On the east side of Zone 1 is the **Teatro Abril (Abril Theater)** *at 9 Avenida and 14 Calle*, recently reopened after extensive and painstaking restoration. The theater is an oddity in an otherwise run-down area, an artifact of an earlier age, when the separation of the cultured elite from the servile masses was even more of an accepted fact than it is today. Constructed in 1915 by cinema entrepreneur Julio Abril Valdez, the theater provided a European-style venue for legitimate Guatemalan theater and international touring companies.

The style is a secular adaptation of the ecclesiastical architecture of the period, with Corinthian columns, triangular and semi-circular pediments over windows and doors, vines in stucco, masks of comedy and tragedy on the balconies, and winged lions on the portico — all the correct symbolism, but otherwise with little decoration and quite bare and cold.

The **National Museum of Popular Arts and Crafts (Museo Nacional de Artes e Industrias Populares)**, *at 10 Avenida 10-72*, has on display a number of *huipiles*, or women's blouses, silverwork, pottery, paintings by Indian artists, fiesta masks, and ceramic and other objects used in native religious ceremonies. The collection is relatively slim, considering the artistic wealth of Guatemala; you can get a better sampling of native arts by visiting the handicraft stalls of the central market. A few of the *huipiles* are in styles that are rarely seen today. *Hours are from 9 am to 4 pm. Closed Monday and noon to 2 pm weekends. Small admission charge.*

The **National History Museum (Museo Nacional de Historia)**, which houses a limited collection of paintings and artifacts of Guatemalan history, is located *at 9 Calle 9-70*. If you drop in, take a look at Edward Muybridge's 1875 photos of Totonicapán. Many a highland town has a similar appearance even today. *Hours are 9 am to 4 pm, with a break from noon to 2 pm on weekends. Closed Monday.*

The **Church of Santo Domingo**, *12 Avenida and 10 Calle*, is one of the finer ecclesiastical structures in the city, finished in white and pastel cream stucco. It has two attached squat bell towers, one of which held the first public clock of Guatemala City. Inside is a large niched retable.

Farther north, *at 11 Avenida and 5 Calle*, is the **Church of La Merced**, dating from 1813, its gold-and-brown mosaic dome visible for many blocks around. The rather plain white exterior, typical of the period, with massive blank walls on three sides, has been undergoing extensive repairs of damage from the 1976 earthquake. Neoclassical columns and a sculpture of St. John the Baptist adorn the main entrance. The baroque interior is richly decorated with noted paintings and statuary, much of it brought from Santiago de los Caballeros (today's Antigua) after the 1773 earthquake. One painting in the sacristy, measuring over 65 square feet and representing the apotheosis of the Mercedarian order, was the largest executed during the colonial period in Guatemala.

Zone 2

Zone 2 is a pleasant old residential area just north of the city center that has changed little over the years.

The **Relief Map of Guatemala** in **Minerva Park** is the main attraction in this part of town. Measuring about 2500 square meters, it has a vertical scale several times that of the horizontal scale, so that the mountainous terrain of the country is shown quite clearly, though with a distortion that gives the volcanoes a strange, skinny appearance. Climb up to the viewing platforms, and you'll be able to trace the places you've been to and will be going to. The map was finished in 1905, and includes running water in all the rivers.

To get to Minerva Park and the relief map, take bus 1 north along 5 Avenida in Zone 1 to the end of the line.

Zone 4

Zone 4, together with the adjacent **Civic Center** of Zone 1, is Guatemala City's midtown commercial area, less congested than the old downtown. A railroad line divides the two zones. Most of the streets, except for through arteries, are called *vías* and *rutas*.

Just past the railroad line from the Civic Center on 6 Avenida is the **Centro Comercial de la Zona 4**, a shopping center and office complex. Most people wouldn't consider this a tourist attraction, but I find it interesting to wander the corridors, peer into shop windows, and probe the aisles of the supermarkets to see what people are buying and how much they're paying.

A block to the east, *on 7 Avenida*, on the ground floor of the **Inguat** building, is a **Visitors' Information** desk. Nearby is the sports complex known as **Olympic City (Ciudad Olímpica)**, consisting of a stadium, gymnasium, swimming pool, tennis courts, and an indoor arena. Guatemalans are more obsessed than most peoples with sports, and what seems to be an inordinate amount of space in the newspapers is devoted to the reporting of athletic events, especially the outcomes of soccer matches.

The **Yurrita Church**, also called **Nuestra Señora de las Angustias**, is located *on Ruta 6 a block east of the Triángulo*. Architecturally, it's one of the more interesting (or strange) of the city's churches, with twisting columns and concrete grillework that give it an appearance much like that of a medieval European fortress. It was built as a private chapel by a rich philanthropist before being opened for public worship. Inside is a fine carved altar.

Up Ruta 6 from the Yurrita Church, across Avenida La Reforma at the corner of 1 Calle, in Zone 10, is the **Botanical Garden (Jardín Botánico)**, my favorite oasis in the capital. The garden features a selection from Guatemala's incredible variety of trees and plants. If you're interested in flora, this is the place for an overview before going out to the countryside to identify plants. *Open Monday through Friday 8 am to 4 pm, closed December 1 to January 15. Enter through the building on Avenida Reforma.*

Bus Terminal & Terminal Market

West from the Triángulo, at 4 Avenida and 9 Calle, are the **Bus Terminal** and **Terminal Market**. The Terminal is a large lot covering several city blocks, jammed with buses that run to all parts of the country. Wedged between the buses, and scurrying for safety when the buses start moving, are hundreds of sellers of vegetables and fruits, dressed in the outfits of their towns. Here you'll see men of Sololá with great bundles of onions and garlic, women from San Pedro Sacatepéquez with baskets of cherries, and men of Nahualá in long woolen skirts, delivering metates, grinding stones.

Catching a bus at the terminal is vastly confusing. Some buses park in the main lot, others on the streets in the wholesale area to the south. But if you stand in one place, somebody will eventually come up to you, ask where you're going, and point the way. Fortunately, most buses to points of interest for visitors leave from elsewhere in the city.

Despite the madness and rush of the outside vendors, things are more organized on the two levels inside the market building, and in the temporary stalls that have sheltered vendors during continuing renovations. Here you'll find vegetables and herbs, flowers, handicrafts, cheap luggage, saddles and other leather products, hammocks and rope, baskets, piñatas, tropical birds, utensils made from scrap metal, and a thousand other items which you may or may not recognize. Butchers and grocers, merchants of beans, rice and wheat, sellers of every product that a working resident of Guatemala City might need for his daily life, offer their wares.

Any city bus marked "Terminal" will take you there. Buses back to Zone 1 pass outside the market along 4 Avenida.

Zones 9 & 10

Zones 9 and 10, Guatemala City's uptown, include the major luxury hotels, several museums, and the more tony restaurants and shops.

At the northern end of Zone 9, the main landmark is the **Tower of the Reformer (Torre del Reformador)**, Guatemala's answer to the Eiffel Tower, *at 7 Avenida and 2 Calle.* Dedicated to President Justo Rufino Barrios, it can be seen from almost any point in the city. The bell on top is rung only on June 30, the anniversary of the Liberal triumph in the 1871 revolution.

Avenida La Reforma, a wide, tree-lined thoroughfare *a block east of 7 Avenida*, forms the boundary between zones 9 and 10. Along it are embassies, residences of the wealthy, and apartment and office buildings.

On the top floor of the office building at Reforma 8-60 is the **Museo Popol-Vuh**, a museum associated with **Francisco Marroquín University**. Pre-Columbian sculpture and pottery from all parts of Guatemala are on display. There are also colonial ceramics, religious sculpture and paintings; and traditional native outfits. *Hours are Monday through Saturday 9 am to 5 pm, and there is an admission charge. A museum guide, in Spanish, is available at an additional charge.*

As a part of a university, the museum offers a comprehensive program that includes concerts, lectures, courses on such topics as Mesoamerican iconography and epigraphy, and, from time to time, tours to areas of cultural richness that are more highbrow than the condescending palaver on offer on many standard tours. Space is limited, and you should be fluent in Spanish to participate. *Stop by the museum or call 347121 for information.*

Just east of Reforma, *from 12 to 14 calles in the vicinity of the Hotel Camino Real*, is the area called the **Zona Viva**, or **Lively Zone**, where the city's most fashionable boutiques, trendiest discos and most expensive restaurants are clustered. Upscale Guatemala City is tree-lined, clean, and more low-key than lively.

A few blocks east of Reforma, *at 4 Avenida 16-27, Zone 10*, is the **Museo Ixchel**, which houses an outstanding display of Indian textiles. Included are many old-style town outfits and exquisite ceremonial costumes, which the visitor would not usually have the chance to see on excursions to Indian villages. Techniques of weaving and the evolution of native styles of dress are explained. Also on display are paintings by Carmen Pettersen of Indians in their traditional outfits. A stop here is highly recommended for anyone interested in Guatemala's native peoples and crafts. *Hours are 8 am to 5 pm daily, Saturday 9 am to 1 pm There is an admission charge of about $1.*

The main street of the district, after Reforma, is **12 Calle**, also known as **Calle Montúfar**. *At its junction with 7 Avenida* is the **Plazuela España**, a busy traffic circle. The fountain in the center of the plaza was originally the base for an equestrian statue of King Charles III of Spain. The statue was destroyed by a mob when Guatemala declared its independence, and President José María Reyna Barrios later had the fountain hidden. It was rediscovered in 1935 and placed in its present location. Farther east on 12 Calle are a number of shopping centers, stores and restaurants.

At the southern end of Zone 9 is the **Obelisk (Obelisco)**, a monument to Guatemala's independence, at the intersection of Boulevard Independencia and Avenida Reforma.

Bus 2 from along 10 Avenida in Zone 1 runs out along Reforma. Buses 82 and 83, which run along 6 Avenida in Zone 9 to 12 Calle, also stops within a couple of blocks of most of the above-mentioned places.

Zone 13

Out in Zone 13 in the southern part of the city are the airport and the attractions of **Aurora Park**. The airport is mentioned in the city directory, below.

Aurora Park on **Boulevard Liberación** is a pleasant place to spend an afternoon. Along the northern rim of the park are the remains of a colonial aqueduct. The park entrance is marked by a huge statue of **Tecún Umán**, the national hero of Guatemala who was slain in single combat with the Spanish conqueror Pedro de Alvarado. Just inside the entrance and to the left is the **Zoo**, which features lions, leopards, crocodiles, monkeys, peccaries, jaguars, panthers, snakes, alligators, iguanas, elephants, and roving photographers. Out in back are rides for the kids. One section, to the left of the main entrance, features wildlife of the Petén, including raccoons, coatis, agoutis, pheasants, jaguarundis and tepezcuintles (pacas, or gibnuts).

If you're not getting around by bus or taxi, you can easily stroll to the zoo from the Camino Real and other hotels in Zone 9 and Zone 10. Walk to the handicraft market, along the main airport boulevard, and turn west to the rear entrance of the zoo.

The **Museum of Natural History (Museo de Historia Natural)** has an excellent collection of stuffed birds, including macaws, owls, and, of course, the rare *quetzal*, Guatemala's national symbol. The museum is a good place for bird watchers to familiarize themselves with the local species. There are also jaguars and reptiles (also stuffed), some of them in displays featuring mockups of the animals' natural environments. Many of the birds are identified in English — a real plus for visitors. There are also numerous small stuffed mammals and fish, and mineral samples.

The **National Museum of Archaeology and Ethnology** houses an extensive collection, only part of which is on display at any one time. There are plaster models of archaeological sites, a carved wooden lintel from **Temple IV** of **Tikal** on which the glyphs standing out more clearly than in most stone sculpture, stone "masks" (facial sculptures), stelae, and pottery and many other artifacts. Many of the native outfits on exhibit were gathered thirty years ago, and are no longer in everyday use in Indian towns.

Next door is the **Museum of Modern Art (Museo de Arte Moderno)**, which houses a large mural by Carlos Mérida, one of the few modern Guatemalan artists to achieve an international reputation. There are also attempts by other artists at impressionism and cubism, but the visitor will probably appreciate more the representative works showing Guatemala's natural beauty and Indian life.

Hours at all the museums in Aurora Park are 9 am to 4:30 pm every day except Monday. On weekends there's a break from noon to 2 pm. There is a nominal admission charge to the archaeology museum. To reach the park, take bus 82, 83, or 6 from along 10 Avenida in Zone 1, or bus 82 or 83 on 6 Avenida in Zone 4 or Zone 9.

Zone 7
The Hill of the Dead

One of the major ancient cities of Mesoamerica, **Kaminaljuyú**, flourished within the limits of what is now Guatemala City. In the past few decades, most of the hundreds of mounds that once made up the great ceremonial center have been destroyed to make way for housing and commercial development. Some of the treasures of pottery and jewelry have been recovered and placed in the custody of the **National Museum of Archaeology and Ethnology**. But an untold amount was carted off by private collectors, or else now lies buried beneath the houses of Guatemala's middle class.

Kaminaljuyú — *Hill of the Dead* — predated the great Mayan centers of the Petén. Through studies of the structures and artifacts unearthed here, archaeologists have concluded that Kaminaljuyú was inhabited about 2000 years ago by a people skilled at sculpture and pottery, who used glyph writing. The styles of certain artifacts — tripod cylindrical vases and pieces with images of a god very similar to the Mexican Tlaloc — indicate a close relationship with Teotihuacán in central Mexico. It's possible that Kaminaljuyú became a southern outpost of Teotihuacán, or of a related center.

What today seem to be small hills scattered over the landscape are the remains of temple platforms, covered over with dirt and vegetation. The temples were set about patios and plazas, and each was built over a burial or a row of burials.

Among the items taken from the graves, in addition to pottery, are obsidian knives; mirrors consisting of iron pyrite pieces attached to slate; jade earrings, beads and amulets; incense burners in the shape of seated deities (formed so that smoke would escape through the eyes, ears and nostrils); and stone figures of fat men sitting on their haunches, similar in style to some found in the Pacific coastal region.

The temple bases of Kaminaljuyú are not impressively large when compared to those of later, Mayan centers. They consist of as many as eight superimposed structures. Most are made of adobe, with sloping outside walls that were covered over with a black, varnish-like finish to shed rain. Some of the earliest substructures consist of simple rectangular platforms with vertical walls, made out of either adobe or rubble and mortar.

Later temple bases were faced with pumice rock set in mud mortar, and covered with lime plaster. The structures consisted of up to three sections, each set back on the previous one, with narrow, heavy, un-adorned stairways ascending to the temple. Nothing has been found of the temples, so they probably consisted of wood and thatch, or of some similar perishable materials.

Situated on a broad plain, Kaminaljuyú differs from the archaeological sites of a much later period in that it was not a defensible place. Utatlán, Mixco Viejo, and Iximché were all built after the period of migrations from Mexico (about 1000 A.D.), when the highland nations were engaged in continuous warfare. These later cities were located on hilltops or on narrow tongues of land surrounded by canyons. But it would seem that the era when Kaminaljuyú thrived was a time of peace.

Visitors to Kaminaljuyú are sometimes disappointed at first by the appearance of what seem to be simple unexcavated earthen mounds. With a little looking, you'll find one of the excavation-restoration sites, roofed over to shelter the delicate adobe structures from the elements. The guard will let you in to wander down into a burial chamber set under five superimposed temple platforms. By the light of a candle or flashlight, you can see the remains of the skeletons of an adult and a child, along with ceramic vessels entombed with the body. It's an eerie trip into the past through a dark and damp tunnel. The second of the superimposed structures is being restored, not without some difficulty and conjecture on the part of those in charge of the project, since the building materials are so fragile.

Before you leave the excavation, you might want to take a look at a pile of pottery shards, lumps of obsidian, grinding stones and fragments of stone figures found here. The good stuff has been removed.

Elsewhere on the site is a second excavation, but the work has progressed far less than in the first area. Across the street is a shed containing some of the pieces of sculpture removed from the excavation.

Getting to Kaminaljuyú

By public transportation, the easiest way to get to Kaminaljuyú is to take a bus marked Kaminaljuyú from along 4 Avenida at the corner of 16 Calle in Zone 1. The bus also runs along 6 Avenida in Zone 4. Less frequently, Metrobus 201 runs to Kaminaljuyú from the civic center on the border of Zone 1 and Zone 4. The last stop is at the entrance to the site. If you're driving, follow Calzada Roosevelt west to 23 Avenida (at the Pollo Campero restaurant), then take a right turn to the site.

The excavations at Kaminaljuyú have been closed recently; don'tvisit the site unless you first verify that restoration work has been completed. *Call 516224 for more information. Hours are from 9 am to 4 pm.*

Zone 15

For a glimpse of some of the best and worst areas of Guatemala City, board bus 1 at the corner of 14 Calle and 10 Avenida, on the east side of Zone 1. The buses on this line are rarely crowded, despite the general disrepair and inadequacy of public transport in Guatemala City. You'll follow 12 Avenida southward. As you cross a bridge, look to your left, to a vast canyon where almost every inch of space is taken up by shacks of tin and scrap wood precariously clinging to the mud of the slopes. There are other such miserable squatter settlements in some of the canyons that ring the city.

The bus continues past a large military base (**Campo de Marte**), then down through another, unpopulated canyon, and up into a city of Frank Lloyd Wright-ish houses protected by barbed wire and shards of glass embedded in high walls. Despite appearances, most of the residents are not wealthy by the standards of the developed world, but in a country where many are poor, self-protection is inevitable. And in Latin America, in any case, family life typically unfolds out of public view.

You'll pass the **American Club** with its vast green spaces and tennis courts, the estates of private schools, and finally proceed down wide, tree-lined Boulevard Vista Hermosa. Ahead, on the hillside, are some of the better residential areas. Get off the bus at the **Super Centro Vista Hermosa**, a shopping mall, and take a look at the stores, among them a gardening center, a cosmetics boutique, and others more run-of-the-mill. Occasionally you'll hear English and other non-local languages, but this is no foreign colony.

Continue your tour with a stroll outside. There are more stores, some typical of Guatemalan neighborhoods and others catering to the special interests of the bourgeois. Residential streets are uncongested, atypically quiet. When you've satisfied your curiosity about the other half, catch bus 1 heading the other way.

MOVIES

Admission charges range upward from about $1, depending on the movie house and the feature. Current attractions are listed in the daily newspapers. Addresses of cinemas are rarely given, so ask at your hotel. Many movie houses are located along 6 Avenida in Zone 1. Sound tracks are usually in the original language, with subtitles in Spanish.

SHOPPING

The main center for native articles is the **Central Market**, where a visitor can spend many an hour gazing at and bargaining over the wares. If you're handicraft shopping, don't limit yourself to the inside vendors. On the streets all around are the emporia of many a specialized seller of textiles, toys, tinware and other specialties. Where else could a shop exist just by selling piñatas for a dollar and up?

Also interesting, if you can put up with the smells and confusion of the neighborhood, is the **Terminal Market** *in Zone 4*, where merchandise is more utilitarian. The **National Handicraft Market**, off the beaten track *in Aurora Park near the airport, in Zone 13*, is targeted specifically at tourists.

Much of what you'll see in the markets is also available in handicraft stores (*tiendas típicas*, or typical shops), where you can sometimes bargain. Some stores specialize in better-quality weaving, which the owners must search out or contract for, and the prices are fixed and higher. Among stores with a good selection of textiles are **Lin Canola**, *5 Calle 9-60*, Zone 1, near the Central Market; and **Sombol**, a*t Avenida La Reforma and 13 Calle*, Zone 9. And there are many, many others.

In some stores you'll find fine native textiles made up into stylish garments that can be worn at home and work in North America and Europe, which is often not the case with garments bought in the markets. You pay for the styling, of course, but usually not excessively. Among such shops are **Dzunún**, *1 Avenida 13-51, Zone 10*, in the *Zona Viva* (also an art gallery and somewhat avant-garde), and **Brigi**, *in the Triángulo building in Zone 4*.

Antiques — coins, ironwork, furniture and statues of saints — can also be found at some of the shops in Zone 1, especially **4 Ahau**, *11 Calle 4-*

53, a shop that also has especially fine antique weaving, masks, and carved saints; and in shops on 12 Calle between 3 and 4 avenidas. Nice to look at, even if you decide you can't lug the items home. Another locale for old items is along 5 Avenida between 8 and 10 calles. Beware of items of recent manufacture, and of pre-Columbian artifacts, which could be confiscated at US customs.

Don't overlook non-handicraft items. Cotton towels and bathrobes from El Salvador in attractive patterns are available at a fraction of what you would pay at home. Visit a supermarket if you have the time and stock up on coffee. **Café León**, **Café Mocca**, and **BBB** are good brands of ground coffee. A few stores have whole beans, which are less subject to losing their flavor (coffee is packed in cellophane). Also pick up peppers, hot sauces and exotic canned items, such as hearts of palm. Save your liquor purchases for the duty-free shop at the airport, where good local rum goes for about three dollars per bottle.

PRACTICAL INFORMATION
Air Quality
During the dry season, and during the rainy season whenever there is no current downpour, dust and dirt seem to be the major component of the atmosphere. Yes, Guatemala has more pressing problems than those bequeathed by industrialization. Just remember that, as you try to breathe.

Banks
Banking hours in Guatemala City are generally from 8:30 or 9 am to 2:30 or 3 pm, Monday through Friday. Some banks have after-hours windows open to 4:30 pm. Most, but not all, commercial banks will cash a travelers check for you. If you can't find a place to cash a travelers check on a weekend, try the airport branch of Banquetzal, open weekdays from 7 am to 8 pm, Saturdays from 8 am to 6 pm.

Among the major banks are:
- **Banco de Guatemala,** the national bank, *Civic Center, Zone 1*
- **Banco de Occidente**, *7 Avenida 11-15, Zone 1, tel. 531333, fax 514348*
- **Lloyds Bank**, *8 Avenida 10-67, Zone 1, and 6 Avenida 9-51, Zone 9, tel. 327580, fax 327641*
- **Banco Agrícola Mercantil**, *7 Avenida 9-11, Zone 1, tel. 511166, fax 510780* (*overseas department*)
- **Banco Industrial**, *7 Avenida 5-10, Zone 4, tel. 345111, fax 319437*
- **Banco Internacional**, *7 Avenida 11-20, Zone 1, tel. 512021, fax 27390* (*overseas department*)
- **Citibank**, *Reforma 15-45, Zone 10, tel. 336564, fax 336860*

Doctors

If you need to see a doctor, call your embassy and get a list of approved doctors who speak your language. In an emergency, try the **Centro Médico**, a private hospital with an excellent reputation, *located at 6 Avenida 3-47, Zone 10 (tel. 323555 to 323559, fax 326151)*. The Centro Médico has a 24-hour emergency service, and a staff of specialists in a number of fields.

Pharmacies

Note also that several pharmacies are open 24 hours on a rotating basis (*de turno*). Check the list posted at the nearest pharmacy.

Embassies & Consulates

Most of the addresses given below are for consulates. For countries not listed, see the blue pages of the telephone directory under *Cuerpo Diplomático* and *Cuerpo Consular*. Best time to visit any consulate is on a weekday morning. Many are closed afternoons and weekends.

- **Belgium**, *Reforma 13-70, Zone 9, tel. 316597*
- **Canada**, *13 Calle 8-44, Zone 10, sixth floor (P. O. Box 400), tel. 336102, fax 336153*. (Handles most matters concerning Canada for all Central America)
- **Costa Rica**, *Reforma 8-60, Zone 9, tel. 320531*
- **El Salvador**, *12 Calle 5-43, Zone 9, tel. 325848*
- **France**, *16 Calle 4-53, Zone 10, tel. 373639*
- **Germany**, *20 Calle 6-20, Zona 10, tel. 370028*
- **Holland**, *12 Calle 7-56, Zone 9, tel. 313505*
- **Honduras**, *16 Calle 8-27, Zone 10, tel. 373921*
- **Israel**, *13 Avenida 14-07, Zone 10, tel. 371334*
- **Italy**, *5 Avenida 8-59, Zone 14, tel. 374557*
- **Japan**, *Ruta 6 8-19, Zone 4, tel. 319666*
- **Mexico**, *13 Calle 7-30, Zone 9, tel. 318165*. Open weekdays 8:15 am to 2:30 pm
- **Nicaragua**, *10 Avenida 14-72, Zone 10, tel. 680785*
- **Panama**, *5 Avenida 15-45, Zona 10, Tower II, No. 708, tel. 320763*
- **Spain**, *6 Calle 6-48, Zone 9, tel. 343757*
- **Sweden**, *8 Avenida 15-07, Zone 10, tel. 336536*
- **Switzerland**, *4 Calle 7-73, Zone 9, tel. 313725*
- **Taiwan**, *7 Avenida 1-20, Zone 4, tel. 324888*
- **United Kingdom**, *7 Avenida 5-10, Zone 4, tel. 321602*
- **USA**, *Reforma 7-01, Zone 10, tel. 311541*
- **Venezuela**, *8 Calle 0-56, Zone 9, tel. 316505*

Laundries

Your hotel can arrange to do your laundry, but prices are often outrageous, so check first. There are plenty of commercial laundries and dry cleaners around town, many with rapid service. If you prefer to put your stuff in the machines yourself, try the laundries at *4 Avenida 13-89, Zone 1; and Ruta 6 7-53, Zone 4, opposite the Triángulo building.*

Post Office

The **main post office** is located *at the corner of 7 Avenida and 12 Calle, Zone 1.* To mail a letter, go to one of the counters on either side of the stairway that faces the entrance. Have your letters weighed and buy the proper postage. Deposit letters along the wall to the left. To mail a package, go to the rear, where you'll see a Parcel Post sign in English.

To pick up General Delivery mail, look for the *Lista de Correos* sign along the rear corridor. To send telegrams within Guatemala, turn right just inside the entrance. *Hours are 8 am to 7 pm weekdays, 8 am to 3 pm Saturday (other post offices have more limited hours).*

Telegrams

Telegrams within the country should be sent from the **main post office**, *7 Avenida and 12 Calle.* The cost is quite low, about 3 cents US per word. Telegrams for foreign countries are handled by **Guatel**, *8 Avenida and 12 Calle.*

Telephones

Coin telephones are in short supply. Good places to find them are pharmacies, the lobbies of some hotels, and outside the **Guatel** building, *7 Avenida between 12 and 13 calles, Zone 1.* Place coins of 5, 10 and 25 centavos on the rack to be swallowed as required. Long-distance calls within Guatemala can be dialed direct from coin telephones, and this is often easier than going through a hotel operator. Use 25-centavo coins in this case. Dial 0 plus a six-digit number.

Many small stores will rent their telephones to you at charges higher than those at coin phones.

Long-distance calls to foreign countries can also be dialed direct (have a pocketful of coins!), or placed from your hotel or from the offices of Guatel: *8 Avenida and 12 Calle, Zone 1; Avenida La Castellana and 39 Calle, Zone 8 (near the bus terminal); and at the airport.* It can take hours to reach a number abroad through an operator.

Faster telephone service to the States is available through USA Direct telephones at the airport and some hotels.

You may see a listing such as this for a telephone number: 456722 a 8, or 456722 to 8. This means that all the six-digit numbers from 456722 to 456728 will connect you with the place indicated. You'll have to dial them individually if one of the numbers is busy.

SOME EMERGENCY & SERVICE NUMBERS

120	*Police*
121	*Long distance within Guatemala*
122	*Volunteer Fire Department (Bomberos Voluntarios)*
123	*Municipal Fire Department (Bomberos Municipales)*
124	*Telephone number information*
125	*Red Cross (Cruz Roja)*
126	*Time of day*
127	*International Telegrams*
171	*International long distance*
174	*Information for international long distance*

Tourist Information

There are two information desks for visitors, one at the airport (just before the immigration counter, where you can make hotel reservations), and another on the ground floor of the **Inguat** building, *7 Avenida 1-17, Zone 4, near the Civic Center.* Some of the personnel speak English, French or German. Hours at the Zone 4 location are 8 am to 4:30 pm on weekdays, to 1 pm weekends. *For information by phone, dial 311333 (to 47).*

Water

The tap water in Guatemala City is chemically treated and safe to drink. If you don't like the taste, stick to bottled mineral water or beer. Some parts of the city suffer from periodic water shortages, but the better hotels have their own water-storage and purification systems.

Weather

Average daily high temperature during the year in Guatemala City is 25° Centigrade (77° Fahrenheit). Average low is 13°C (55°F). Warmest time of the year is April, when the average high is 27°C (80°F) and the average low 15°C (59°F). The coldest time is December, with an average range from 23°C (73°F) down to 12° C (54°F).

Occasional cold and windy spells occur in November and December. Rainfall is another matter. From November through April, there's hardly any rainfall at all. June and September are the wettest months of the rainy season in the capital, with about 260 mm (10 inches) of rain.

Even in these wet months, it only rains two out of three days, and then for only a few hours.

570 CENTRAL AMERICA GUIDE

EXCURSIONS FROM GUATEMALA CITY

Tours & Travel Agencies

Whether you take a tour depends on how much time you have, the money you have to spend, and whether you're up to traveling around the country on ordinary buses. The latter can be uncomfortable and disconcerting if you're alone and find it difficult to be continuously among people who don't speak your language.

It also depends on where you're going. For travel to the scenic western highlands, it's more enjoyable, and usually cheaper, if two or more persons share a rented car and make overnight stops in Antigua, Panajachel, and Chichicastenango. On the other hand, tours are a good bet for long one-day trips from the capital to the Pacific Coast, Copán and Tikal.

Tour prices don't vary too much from one company to another. Some samples of approximate prices for tours lasting a day or less: Guatemala City, $20 to $25; Antigua, $25 to $30; Mixco Viejo, $35 to $50; Chichicastenango and Lake Atitlán, $40 to $55; Quiriguá and Río Dulce, or Copán, up to $100; Tikal, $160 to $200.

When a tour covers a few towns or archaeological sites and includes overnight accommodations, the price rises considerably. Examples: Chichicastenango-Lake Atitlán-Antigua (two days), $150 to $200; Tikal (overnight), $250 and up; Copán and Quirigua (overnight), $125 to $150.

You'll probably book a tour with a travel agency in or near your hotel. If you don't like the service you get at the nearest travel agency (common abuses: credit-card surcharges, abysmal exchange rates, not placing hotel reservations as promised), I think you're best off using the services of a long-established agency, such as **Clark Tours**, *7 Avenida 6-53, Zone 4, second floor, Triángulo building, tel. 310213, fax 315919.*

Among other companies offering tours and travel services are:

- **Hayter Travel**, *9 Calle 4-69, Zone 1, tel. 519673*
- **ECA Tours**, *5 Avenida 13-21, Zone 9, tel. 314265, fax 321056*
- **Izabal Adventure Tours**, *7 Avenida 14-44, Zona 9, office 35*, works with museum groups in the United States, and can arrange stays at lodges in the Petén jungle that are difficult to reach on your own.
- **Maya Expeditions/Expediciones Maya**, *15 Calle 1-91, Zona 10, first floor, tel. and fax 374666. US address: Club 747-66, P. O. Box 527270, Miami, FL 33152.* Rafting and archaeological trips.
- **Museo Popol Vuh**, *Avenida Reforma 8-60, Zone 9, tel. 347121*, is a museum, not a travel agency, but they give tours to areas of cultural richness from time to time that are more highbrow than the condescending palaver on offer on many standard tours. Space is limited, and you should be fluent in Spanish to participate.

- **Expedición Panamundo**, *6 Avenida 14-75, Zona 9, tel. 317508, fax 317565*. Adventure excursions as well as standard tours.
- **Expedición Panamundo**, *6 Avenida 14-75, Zone 9, Guatemala City, tel. 502-2-317588*. A nine-day overland and river expedition to ruins in both the Petén and adjacent Mexico, including nights of camping along the Usumacinta River, costs about $1200; a three-day trip to Tikal and Lake Petexbatún comes in at about $300 — not bad for an introduction to the jungle.
- **Ney's Tours**, *13 Calle 0-56, Zone 10, tel. 370884, fax 335441*
- **Maya Tours**, *6 Calle 1-36, Zone 10, tel. 353575*
- **Agencia de Viajes Tivoli**, *6 Avenida 8-41, Zone 9, tel. 310067, fax 343297*
- **Tropical Tours**, *4 Calle 2-51, Zone 10, tel. and fax 323748*
- **Turismo Kim' Arrim**, *Vía 5 4-20, Zone 4, tel. 324931, fax 322791*

For others, check the telephone directory under *Agencias de Viajes*.

American Express has a representative at *Reforma 9-00, Zone 9, tel. 311311*; **Wagons-Lits** at *Reforma 12-81, Zone 10, tel. 313268, fax 346143*.

NEARBY TOWNS

The department of Guatemala includes sixteen *municipios*, or townships, besides Guatemala City. A few towns and one major archaeological site in adjacent departments are also readily accessible from the capital.

MIXCO

Mixco was founded in 1525 after the Spanish conqueror Pedro de Alvarado laid siege to and captured the Pokomam capital now known as **Mixco Viejo**. The Indian survivors of the battle were forced to migrate to a site where the Spanish would better be able to control them. For centuries, Mixco was a majority Indian town, but it is now part of the metropolitan area of the capital, populated mostly by working-class Ladinos.

Corn and beans are raised in the few parts of the township that remain rural, and in the urban areas there's some light industry. The land here is craggy and broken. The most outstanding feature of Mixco is the large domed church, which travelers can readily see as they pass through on the way from Guatemala City to the western highlands. Mixco was the scene of bloody battles during the civil war of 1829, and suffered severely during the 1976 earthquake.

SAN PEDRO SACATEPÉQUEZ

San Pedro Sacatepéquez is an agricultural center whose farmers sell their produce in the markets of Guatemala City. The textiles woven here are particularly beautiful, especially the women's *huipiles*, which from a distance consist of hundreds of bright watercolor splotches painted on cloth. The region was occupied by the Sacatepéquez nation at the time of the Spanish conquest, hence the name Sacatepéquez became attached to many towns in the area. The market is worth a visit.

Buses run frequently to San Pedro from the terminal in Zone 4.

SAN JUAN SACATEPEQUEZ

Largest Indian township in the department of Guatemala, **San Juan**, like San Pedro, supplies produce to the capital. Terraced slopes planted to a variety of flowers, for sale in the markets of Guatemala City and for shipment abroad by air, make the area around San Juan particularly colorful. Women's huipiles are woven in purple and yellow, and many bear the figures of two-headed eagles and horses. Women will often wear a second huipil to ward off the morning and evening chill.

Buses run frequently to San Juan from the terminal in Zone 4.

The hills along the road from Guatemala through San Pedro and San Juan are thickly forested, and many residents of the capital drive out this way to spend weekends at their country homes, or to enjoy the scenery and a meal at one of the roadside restaurants. A few kilometers after San Juan, where the dirt road leads off toward Mixco Viejo, the landscape starts to change. Vegetation is less abundant, except in river valleys, and the terrain is more broken. The high ridge of the **Sierra de Chuacús** is visible to the north. There are only scattered small settlements along the winding road.

MIXCO VIEJO RUINS

Mixco Viejo was the capital of the Pokomam nation, one of the warring peoples of pre-Conquest Guatemala. Dramatically set on a hilltop at kilometer 60 that commands the surrounding valleys, the city was a ceremonial center and also a bastion of defense.

Spanish forces laid siege to Mixco in 1525. For three months they tried to starve the warriors in the fortress, but the Indians held out, receiving supplies, according to legend, through a secret tunnel. Finally, the allies of the Pokomams abandoned the fight and revealed to the Spaniards the entrance of the tunnel. Alvarado blocked the supply route, and managed to storm the fortress by way of the only other access, a narrow and treacherous trail. The inhabitants were evacuated to the present-day Mixco near Guatemala City, and the fortress destroyed.

The site consists of pyramids, observation and defense platforms, ball courts, altars and walls. The buildings date from the fourteenth and fifteenth centuries, but older walls have been found under the platforms in the area called **Group A**. Many pyramids show Mexican stylistic elements that were typical of the period just before the conquest, such as double stairways and twin, flat-roofed temples. been found at the site, and archaeologists suggest that bodies might have been cremated, which would have been an unusual practice in the highlands. One of the more interesting details is a ballcourt marker in **Group C**, a copy of the original, which is in the shape of a snake with a human head in its mouth.

Despite the damage wrought by the 1976 earthquake, there's much to see at Mixco Viejo, and the setting is spectacular. If you're driving, it's an easy trip via San Juan Sacatepéquez, though the last part of the route is unpaved and winding. Turn left at the junction just after kilometer 59.

ARRIVALS & DEPARTURES

Buses for Mixco Viejo leave from the corner of 2 Calle and 1 Avenida, Zone 9, near the Guatemala City bus terminal. Verify departure times in both directions the day before you go (recently 10 am and 12:30 pm from Guatemala City). The bus drops you at the junction near kilometer 59. Walk uphill another kilometer to the ruins.

To return, walk back and wait for the bus at kilometer 58. You might not have much time at the ruins before the bus leaves, or a one-day round trip might not be possible.

CAMPING OUT AT THE RUINS

If you've got the equipment, the ruins are an ideal place to camp out. Nobody minds if you unroll your sleeping bag under one of the thatched shelters, as long as you leave the site clean. It's a lovely place for watching the sunset and sunrise, and for thinking yourself back into the times when religious rituals were performed at the temples here. Water and soft drinks are available at the site, but bring your own food.

SOUTH OF GUATEMALA CITY
AMATITLAN

Located along the shore of the lake of the same name, **Amatitlán** is a favorite weekend resort for residents of Guatemala City. The lake — 11 kilometers long, 3.5 kilometers wide, with a maximum depth of 40 meters — is a beautiful sight, with hills on the north and the volcano **Pacaya** towering over to the south. Hot springs bubble up from the earth all over the area, and at many points along the highway to Escuintla, you'll see steam coming out of the ground. But the lake has not been dealt with kindly by recent generations. A railroad crosses it at the center, its narrowest part, and a power plant belches smoke along its shore. Its waters are polluted.

Most of the area along the shore is privately owned and occupied by houses of the wealthy. One of the few places where visitors may approach the waterside is near the town of Amatitlán, at a small rocky beach lined with cheap eateries, and where boats offer rides on the lake. Bathhouses nearby offer one-hour sessions in hot tubs for a dollar or so. A highway circles the lake, and makes for a pleasant drive.

The area around Amatitlán was occupied before the Conquest. There are ruins about one kilometer east of the town center, consisting of mounds and the remains of ball courts, which appear to have been occupied from 500 to 800 A.D. The town is now a processing center for coffee, sugar, and dairy products.

From the shores of the lake, you can take an aerial tramway to **United Nations Park** (**Parque Naciones Unidas**), or you can drive up. The main asset of the park is the panoramic view of the lake. It's also somewhat of a lovers lane. For more serious visitors, there are a reconstruction of the temples of Tikal and archaeological artifacts on display; and the undisturbed plant life of the area is a bonus for naturalists. Pleasant for a picnic and for hiking, though, on a weekend, you'll have to search around for the parts that are uncrowded and unlittered. Small admission fee.

ARRIVALS & DEPARTURES

Buses for Amatitlán leave frequently from the corner of 20 Calle and 3 Avenida, Zone 1, Guatemala City. Trains for Tecún Umán also stop here.

WHERE TO STAY - TRAILER PARKS

The nearest trailer parks to Guatemala City are along the highway outside Amatitlán. Thermal swimming pools are located near or on the sites of all three. Rates run from 50 cents for backpackers to several dollars for motor homes.

- **La Red Trailer Park**, *kilometer 33*. If you're not staying at the park, you can use the pools for a small fee.
- **Las Hamacas**, *kilometer 32*. Pools are also available here for day use.
- **Auto Mariscos**, *kilometer 33*. Several hookups behind the seafood restaurant.

SAN VICENTE PACAYA

A small town in a coffee-growing area, **San Vicente Pacaya** is located on the slopes of the **Pacaya** volcano, which is the main attraction. The volcano is active, and from time to time spews lava from its cone. A trail starting near the school leads up the volcano's slopes, and on a clear day, when the volcano is belching, you can see some pretty nifty fireworks. It's a nice climb even when the peak is shrouded in clouds. The newer cone of the volcano can be viewed from the old cone above it. Try to find out before you come out whether the volcano has been acting up.

ARRIVALS & DEPARTURES

Buses for San Vicente Pacaya usually leave from the terminal in Zone 4 in the late morning and return the next day. Inquire about current schedules the day before you go. For climbing, it's more convenient to go in the early morning, either by driving or by taking an Escuintla bus to the junction for San Vicente and walking up to town.

CLIMBING PACAYA

It is absolutely essential to visit Pacaya in a group. Like an urban park at night in the United States, the slopes of Pacaya are near-deserted, but for tourists who are sure to turn up now and then, and criminals from the city who are just as sure to lie in wait. Visitors have, more than occasionally, been assaulted, robbed, beaten, and raped.

From Guatemala City, group visits with accomplished guides are offered by **Maya Expeditions**, *15 Calle 1-91, Zona 10, first floor, tel. 374666.* Inquire in Antigua for van tours to the volcano, currently operated by several travel shops.

THE WESTERN HIGHLANDS

The western highlands are the most densely inhabited part of Guatemala, and the home of most of the Indian population. Stretching from Guatemala City to the border of Mexico, the area includes the great mountain peaks of the **Sierra Madre** and the **Cuchumatanes** range, and temperate and near-tropical valleys. Guatemala's chain of volcanoes runs parallel to the Pacific, forming the southern rim of the region.

In the western highlands is the most dramatic scenery of Guatemala, including **Lake Atitlán**, surrounded by volcanoes and precipitous mountains, one of the most beautiful lakes anywhere. Roads climb to frosty heights, drop down in a few kilometers to plateaus planted with corn and wheat, and plunge into narrow valleys, their sides carpeted with trees, streams rushing through at the bottom. Spotted here and there through the landscape are clusters of whitewashed adobe houses with red tiled roofs, little hamlets of people dressed all alike in traditional clothing.

ANTIGUA GUATEMALA

In a valley surrounded by mountains, and by the towering volcanoes **Agua**, **Fuego**, and **Acatenango**, lies **Antigua Guatemala**. Today it is a pleasant city of cobblestone streets, houses and businesses with colonial-style facades and tile roofs, and of restored and vegetation-covered ruins of churches, palaces, convents and mansions. Just over 200 years ago, it was **Santiago de los Caballeros de Guatemala**, along with Lima and Mexico City one of the major centers of Spanish power in the Americas.

ARRIVALS & DEPARTURES

By Bus, Shuttle, or Van

Buses leave from the terminal and market three blocks west of the central park. For service to villages near Antigua, see "Excursions from Antiqua" later in this chapter.

The most convenient buses for Antigua leave from 15 Calle 3-65, Zone 1, Guatemala City, about every hour, from 7 am to 7:45 pm. On weekends, the service is every half hour. There are additional buses from 20 Calle and 3 Avenida. The main bus stop has moved around several times in the last few years, so if possible, re-check the departure point at your hotel desk.

Buses leave Antigua for Guatemala City from 6 am to about 7 pm.

Daily van service (*el shuttle*) is currently available from Antigua to the international airport and major hotels in Guatemala City. Fare is about $12. Phone 320011 in Antigua, 953374 in Guatemala City, or ask at the Ramada, the Hotel Antigua or Doña Luisa's restaurant for information. The same van operates three days a week to Panajachel on Lake Atitlán.

Another van service operates to the airport for only $5 from 1 Calle Poniente No. 12, tel. 322295; and yet another one can be reserved for about $7 by calling 323434. The competition is fierce.

To connect with buses heading for the western part of Guatemala (Lake Atitlán, Chichicastenango, Quezaltenango and Huehuetenango), take a bus to Chimaltenango. Departures are from the bus terminal about every 45 minutes, from 6:30 am to 5:30 pm.

ORIENTATION

Streets in the central part of Antigua are for the most part numbered. East-west streets are called *calles*. They bear the suffix *poniente* or *oriente* depending on whether they're west or east of the Cathedral. North-south streets are avenidas and carry a suffix of *norte* or *sur* (north or south). As a point of reference, the Cathedral is on the east side of the central park, or main square. Some streets are also marked with old colonial names.

FOR A NICE VIEW...

For a panorama of Antigua, walk or drive up to Cerro de la Candelaria, the hill north of town. Follow 1 Avenida Norte as it winds upward. The trip takes about 10 minutes by car from the central park, and a new set of steps makes the walk an easy outing. Best time is around noon, when there are no shadows to obscure details. A nighttime walk is out of the question.

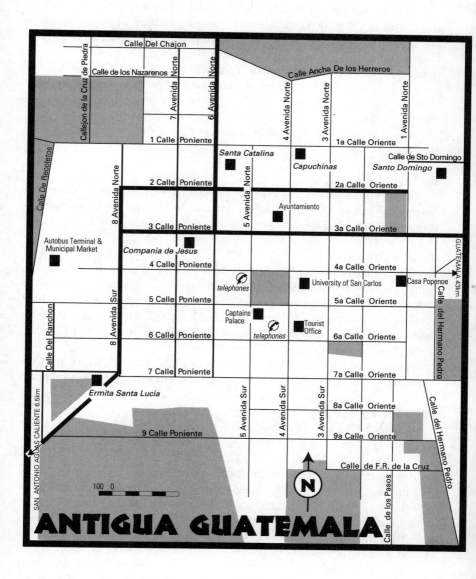

ANTIGUA GUATEMALA

GETTING AROUND TOWN

By Bicycle & Motorcycle

Bicycles are rented at 6 Avenida Sur No. 6 (go inside the auto repair shop) and at 6 Avenida Norte No. 11, among other places. Motorbikes are also available at some locations from time to time — recently at **Comercial Maravilla**, *6 Avenida Norte No. 6*, but they're hardly cheaper than cars. **Montaña Maya Bicycle Tours**, *6 Avenida Sur No. 12B, tel. and fax 323316*, arranges local rides, or multi-day trips to Lake Atitlán.

Renting a Car

Avis has an agency *on 5 Avenida Norte, opposite the Posada de Don Rodrigo*.

By Taxi

Taxis are abundant around the central park. The tourist office (see below) will advise you on what is a fair rate to Guatemala City or any of the neighboring villages.

Tourist Office

The tourist office in Antigua should be one of your first stops. Mr. Benjamín García López, who's often at the desk, will give you a map of the city and orient you to the major colonial monuments, tell you ghost stories, mention any new restaurants and hotels that have opened, try to find you a room in a private home when the hotels are filled up, and in general will make you feel at home.

The tourist office is on the ground floor of the **Palace of the Captains-General**, not far from the Cathedral on the south side of the central park.

WHERE TO STAY

CASA SANTO DOMINGO, *3 Calle Oriente No. 26, tel. 320079, fax 320102. US reservations tel. 800-223-9832 or 212-599-8280, fax 212-599-1755. 24 rooms. $158 single/$175 double/$199 triple, $210 to $350 in one-bedroom suites. Visa, Master Card, American Express.*

Prepare to lose your breath and your heart to the most romantic, most transporting, most unexpected, most Antiguan of the larger hotels in the old capital. The hotel Casa Santo Domingo is a colonial monument intact, the fifteenth-century monastery of Santo Domingo, re-invigorated as Antigua's premier luxury hotel.

All the facilities of a modern resort wind through the stabilized massive walls and sedate wings and halls and cells of the ecclesiastical structure, fusing the modern with a sedate and haunting ecclesiastical aura. Massive carved wooden chests and statues, antiques all, line the stone-flagged passageways, the waters of ancient fountains sway to music, volcanoes and neighboring monun⸻ and bougainvilleas in the gardens are framed through archways ⸻ Casa Santo Domingo is not a conventional building in any sense ⸻ 's almost a personality. The swimming area is a venerable pool, ⸻ ncient fountain at its center. Concerts are sometimes given on the s⸻us grounds. Candles illuminate the passageways at dusk, the numbe⸻ hidden nooks and remote corners are beyond counting.

The guest rooms are all in a modern wing designed to fit unobtrusively amid the ruins. Some have private terraces and whirlpools, all are carpeted, and have fireplaces, television, air conditioning, safe, heavy colonial-style furnishings, and old-fashioned board-and-batten ceiling.

RAMADA ANTIGUA***, *9 Calle and Carretera Ciudad Vieja, tel. 323002, fax 320237 (US/Canada tel. 800-228-9898). 155 rooms. $140 single/ $154 double. Lower rates available off-season through toll-free number – keep asking.*

Located on the road to Ciudad Vieja, in a modernesque-colonial complex. Farther from the center of town than other hotels (a walk of ten minutes or so), but the facilities are the best in Antigua: extensive gardens, three pools, tennis courts, a children's play area, sauna, numerous shops, and a large restaurant and bar. Every room has a fireplace, cable television, and enchanting views to the surrounding misted volcanoes. Recommendable as a base for travel around Guatemala, or simply as a winter vacation resort.

The Ramada has a desk in the arrival area of the international airport in Guatemala City and a courtesy van to transport arriving passengers from the capital.

HOTEL ANTIGUA***, *8 Calle Oriente and 4 Avenida Sur, tel. 320288, fax 320807 (tel. 532490, fax 535482 in Guatemala City). 60 rooms. $150 single/$164 double.*

Distinguished, colonial-style, with extensive gardens, fireplaces in all rooms. Lovely atmosphere. The hotel comes alive on Sunday, when a luncheon buffet of native and American food is accompanied by marimba music. Pool, restaurant, bar, shops, parking.

THE CLOISTER, *5 Avenida Norte No. 23, tel. and fax 320712. 7 rooms. $60 double, including breakfast.*

This is the most *Antigüeño* of the intimate lodging places in town, a sixteenth-century convent brought up to the most exacting modern standards, while retaining the elegance of bygone times. Individual suites of various sizes have been created, each with its own fireplace, library, and collectibles including antique oak furniture.

POSADA DE DON RODRIGO***, *5 Avenida Norte No. 17, tel. 320291 (318017 in Guatemala City). 33 rooms. $91 single/$104 double.*

This comfortable in⸻ear the center of town, is a restored and historic colonial house, the Casa de Los Leones, named originally for the lions sculptured in stone by the doorway. The furnishings and decorative details around the several cobbled and gardened patios are worth a look even if you're not staying here. Rooms are individually decorated. Try to get one with a volcano view. Restaurant, bar. Good value.

EL ROSARIO LODGE, *5 Avenida Sur and 9 Calle Poniente, tel. 320336. 36 rooms. $19 single/$23 double.*

Tranquil location on the edge of a coffee and orange farm. Plain, comfortable rooms, some with fireplaces. A few efficiency apartments are available by the month. Restaurant, parking. Reservations reported not held, theft from locked rooms has been a problem here.

MESÓN PANZA VERDE***, *5 Avenida Sur No. 19, tel. and fax 322925. 6 rooms. $37 double, $58 in suites.*

As lovely as the restaurant of the same name, a new, authentically re-created colonial atmosphere, from the cupola to the archways to the sedate courtyard. Rooms are huge, with high ceiling, wicker chairs, and French doors that open to the garden; and suites are even more ample, with fireplace, a dressing area bigger than most hotel rooms, and a tiled tub on a platform base.

HOTEL AURORA***, *4 Calle Oriente No. 16, tel. 320217. 36 rooms, $35 single/$40 double.*

A well-kept, family-run establishment in a large old home with courtyard. Colonial atmosphere, good value. Breakfast served.

HOTEL EL CARMEN, *3 avenida Norte No. 9, tel. 323850, fax 323847. 17 rooms. $34 to $44 single/$46 to $50 double/$46 to $58 triple with breakfast.*

A new, plain, modern concrete building with colonial references in the decoration, plain, functional rooms, and modern comforts that include television and carpeting — sort of the local idea of what visitors want. Sun terrace upstairs.

POSADA SAN SEBASTIÁN, *3 Avenida Norte No. 4, tel. and fax 322621. 8 rooms. $26 single/$30 double.*

Pleasant smaller hotel, rooms around grassy courtyard with hanging pots of plants and decorations of antiques. Some upstairs rooms have tiny balconies.

CONVENTO SANTA CATALINA, *5 Avenida Norte No. 28, tel. 320080. 11 rooms. $35 single/$40 double/$54 triple.*

As the name suggests, rooms in a restored convent, next to the Santa Catalina arch, all situated around a courtyard. The large rooms can be chilly, but the two blankets on the queen-sized bed are helpful, and furnishings, including armoire and desk, are more than adequate. The restaurant serves Italian food.

HOTEL SANTA CLARA, *2 Avenida Sur No. 20, tel. 320342. 14 rooms. $20 single/$25 double/$35 triple.*

Large rooms off the courtyard of an old home, most with high ceilings and hardwood bedstead, and massive armoire, some with skylight. A few of the rooms are in a newer section, less attractive, but farther from the street, and quieter.

POSADA LANDÍVAR, *5 Calle Poniente No. 23, tel. 322962. 11 rooms, $8 single/$10 double, $12 with private bath.*

Rooms crowded around a courtyard, clean and convivial, always with hot water.

POSADA SAN FRANCISCO, *3 Calle Oriente No. 19, tel. 320266. 14 rooms, $8 per person.*

A renovated budget sleeping place, still economical, now with hot water, closets and new furniture.

HOTEL DE LA PLAZA REAL, *5 Avenida Sur No. 8, tel. 320581. 34 rooms. $9 single/$14 double.*

Located above a large restaurant and movie house, noisy at times, but good for the price.

Budget Hotels

It's hard to go wrong at any of the hostelries offering budget rooms in Antigua. A sampling:

EL DESCANSO, *5 Avenida Norte No. 9, tel. 320142. 14 rooms. $14 single/$16 double.*

Relatively new, rooms are small but quite clean.

CASA DE SANTA LUCÍA, *Alameda Santa Lucía Sur No. 7. 12 rooms. $8 single/$10 double.*

Small, comfortable rooms with private baths. On the edge of town near the bus terminal and market. Quiet, and one of the best values in town.

HOTEL PLÁCIDO, *Avenida del Desengaño No. 25. 15 rooms. $6 per person, $7 with private bath.*

Out on the Chimaltenango road, and somewhat off the beaten track. But rooms face a courtyard garden, and a laundry area and the kitchen are available to guests. Good value.

PENSIÓN EL ARCO, *5 Avenida Norte No. 32. About $3 per person with shared bath.*

Simple, clean lodging, pleasant atmosphere.

ALBERGUE ANDINISTA, *6 Avenida Norte No. 34, tel. 323343*, has low-prices rooms, offers volcano trips, and will store your extra luggage at no charge while you travel around Guatemala.

Trailers

Inquire at the tourist office for parking spots. Currently, the Texaco station near the Hotel Ramada can accept a few campers.

Houses for Rent

You can sometimes pick up leads from the tourist office or resident foreigners. Comfortable houses with complete kitchens, closets and furnishings could rent for well over $1000 per month.

WHERE TO EAT

You can eat and drink to your heart's content in Antigua, usually at insignificant expense. A selection from the bounty of restaurants:

DOÑA LUISA'S (PASTELERÍA Y PANADERÍA DE DOÑA LUISA XICOTENCATL), *4 Calle Oriente No. 12.* Reuben and roast beef sandwiches, chili con carne, baked stuffed potatoes, excellent bread and pastries, granola, and assorted other down-home specialties. $4 and up. Also baked goods to take out. They pack 'em in, and sometimes as a result, service is I-don't-care.

EL SERENO, *6 Calle Poniente No. 30.* Perhaps the classiest restaurant in Guatemala. Exquisite atmosphere in a meticulously restored colonial mansion: beamed ceilings, decorative plantings, flowing fountain, roaring fire, subdued lighting, glowing candles, classical music, the works. The food is not quite up to the environment, but still well prepared. $20, or less if you have just a main course. *Telephone 320073 to reserve.*

WELTEN, *4 Calle Oriente 21A, tel. 320630.* A courtyard restaurant with adaptations of classic Italian and continental cuisine. $10 to $15 for a full meal, or $5 for a light lunch.

LA PANZA VERDE, *on 5 Avenida Sur opposite the Rosario Lodge,* is an elegant restaurant housed in a faithful reproduction of a colonial house, with cactus and Norfolk pines in the garden, hanging baskets of plants, brick arches against white walls, and balconies and dark beams and red tiles overhead. $10 and up, about $5 for the stir-fry vegetarian plates. *Open at meal times (noon to 3 and 6:30 to 10 pm), Sundays for lunch, closed Monday.*

Hotel Fare

Also good bets for atmospheric dining are some of the hotels. At **POSADA DE DON RODRIGO**, *5 Avenida Norte No. 9*, you have a choice of American-style steak, and native dishes. $8 and up. A marimba band often plays in the courtyard. In the **HOTEL ANTIGUA**, *4 Avenida Sur and 8 Calle Oriente*, service is excellent and the surroundings are elegant. There's a buffet on Sundays, but the $6 weekday lunch is the best buy.

The Hotel Ramada Antigua's **ALOM** feature's a changing continental menu with food cooked to order, and several readers have registered their raves. About $10 and up.

Vegetarian

The **RAINBOW READING ROOM**, *7 Avenida Sur No. 8, at 6 Calle*

Poniente, is currently the premier gathering center for visitors, a shop with used books, and patio reading room-cafe, where tofu, hummous, bagels, gazpacho, sandwiches and other vegetarian fare is served, with nothing priced over $2. During the day, everything is low-key and quiet, at seats at plain wooden tables in the courtyard. At night, videos are shown, and they light a campfire as a backdrop to impromptu singing, playing, and poetry recitals. Controlled kids and pets are welcome, too.

SUEÑOS DEL QUETZAL, *5 Avenida Norte No. 3*, serves hummous, tabouli, vegetable paté, moussaka and other yummies without meat, for $3 to $4.

Other Recommended Restaurants

RESTAURANT KATOK, *4 Avenida Norte No. 7*, is a modest and pleasant patio steak house, serving charcoal-broiled sirloin, chicken and sausages. $5 and up for main courses or breakfast, $3 for sandwiches.

PEREGRINOS, *4 Avenida Norte No. 1*, is the current outlet for Mexican *antojitos* (which are repeatedly reincarnated here and there in Angigua). Burritos, flautas, enchiladas and the like for $4 and up.

At **CASA DE CAFÉ ANA**, *in the Rosario Lodge, 5 Avenida Sur at 9 Calle Poniente*, the food is good and the portions are large. Complete breakfasts and lunches are prepared at meal times (starting at 7:30 am, 12:30 pm and 6:30 pm), a la carte Guatemalan specialties and meats at other hours. Pleasant, quiet. About $4 to $5 for the set meal, sandwiches available.

CAFÉ CAFÉ, *in the patio at 5 Avenida Norte No. 14*. Native specialties such as stuffed peppers and pepián, and sandwiches. $2 to $4. Pleasant.

LA CENICIENTA, *5 Avenida Norte No. 9*. Strictly desserts, and good ones: apple pie, carrot cake, brownies. $1.50 and up with coffee.

EL CAPUCHINO, *6 Av. Norte No. 10*. Italian-style. Pizza and pasta, as well as steak, shrimp and sandwiches. $4 for the set lunch, up to $8.

QUESOS Y VINO (*Cheeses and Wine*), *5 Avenida Norte No. 32*, just past the arch, has a limited menu of pizzas, calzone, and pastas made on site, all of it good. Closed Tuesday.

Budget Fare

For inexpensive meals, try the **SAN CARLOS** restaurant, your basic Guatemalan eatery, *on the north side of the central park, next to the corner pharmacy*. The restaurant in the **HOTEL DE LA PLAZA REAL**, *5 Avenida Sur No. 8*, is a local late-hours hangout, and inexpensive.

BARS

Bars in Antigua come and go, as in any touristy town. For a civilized drink, consider the **Posada de Don Rodrigo**, the **Hotel Antigua**, or the **Ramada** (where the peanuts at the bar are unusually excellent). The

Mistral bar and bistro, *4 Calle Oriente No. 11*, under Québecois management, has banquettes covered with blankets, a pleasant interior courtyard (okay, what doesn't have a courtyard in Antigua?), a limited menu of sandwiches, and tall lemonade as well as stronger stuff.

SEEING THE SIGHTS

Antigua is a city of monuments of the colonial past, both restored and in decaying ruins. The harshness of the 1773 disaster has been softened by time and creeping vegetation, creating the tranquil anachronism of Antigua today, set almost in a pocket of time in a green valley watched over by volcanoes and mountains.

Antigua is an eighteenth-century city. Though it lived as **Santiago de los Caballeros** for more than 200 years, much of the early architecture was lost to intermittent earthquakes, or modified over the years. Buildings partially destroyed by tremors were rebuilt in then-current styles. Most of what is left today was built after the 1717 earthquake, in the colonial-late baroque style.

The rebuilders of the city in the eighteenth century thought they had learned their lessons from the early disasters. Structures went up with massive walls of brick and rubble to resist the vibrations of earth tremors. Buildings were kept low to prevent walls from toppling. Short bell towers were set firmly into churches, or separated from them entirely. The squat, heavy aspect of the city was relieved by the flamboyant decorations of the Churrigueresque style that were worked into the plaster and stucco that covered walls. Delicate flowers in relief, flutings on columns, plaster statues of saints in niches in the façades of churches all hid the underlying massiveness of the buildings in an interplay of light and shadow, as did the wooden grilles and carved stone portals of private homes. Fountains, spacious plazas and an orderly plan of wide streets added to the sense of openness.

MUSEUM & RUINS HOURS

Museums and restored buildings are generally open daily, except Monday from 9 am to 4 pm (with a break on weekends from noon to 2 pm). There are nominal admission charges to some museums. The grounds of unrestored ruins are open from 8 am to 5 pm, closed on Mondays.

Start at the **central park**, with a look at the restored fountain in its center. In colonial times, the plaza was a place for assembly and public functions, for bullfights, tournaments, whippings and hangings, and for the daily market. This was a bare, open stretch of land, without the shade trees and benches that now make the plaza a pleasant place in which to sit and watch the passing scene. On three sides of the square, the facing sidewalks are sheltered by restored colonial archways.

The **Ayuntamiento** (**City Hall**), *on the north side of the square*, was the headquarters of the city government of Santiago de los Caballeros, and now houses the government of the present-day city. On the façade is the coat of arms of Santiago, showing St. James on horseback riding above three volcanoes, the central one in full eruption.

Part of the Ayuntamiento now houses the **Museum of Santiago**, a collection of artifacts depicting aspects of daily life in the colony. On exhibit are colonial ceramics and modern copies, ironwork, tools, uniforms, silver articles, paintings, musical compositions on parchment, and a sword that was used by Pedro de Alvarado. The great siege cannon on display was taken from Fort San Felipe on the Río Dulce. In the rear is a two-story prison that functioned until 1955.

Next door is the **Museo del Libro Antiguo** (**Old Book Museum**), in the part of the Ayuntamiento that housed the first printing press of the Kingdom of Guatemala. On display are assorted imprints, and illustrations of the progress of printing.

The **Palace of the Captains-General**, *on the south side of the central park*, was the headquarters of the government of the colony. Its façade is a two-story archway, now restored. The upper level was used by the nobility to watch spectacles in the plaza. Inside were the residence of the captain-general, courts of law, and the royal treasury.

The original building was damaged during the intermittent earthquakes that preceded the destruction of Santiago, and a new building was completed in 1764. It crumbled in the 1773 earthquake.

The front of the palace is now occupied by the local police detachment, the tourist office, and offices of the government of the department of Sacatepéquez, of which Antigua is the capital. Few signs remain in the ruined interior of the grand salons from which a kingdom was ruled. Visitors may enter the courtyard, and climb to the second floor of the restored part of the palace.

What now remains on the east side of the central park is the shell of the second Cathedral of Santiago. The original building, financed partly by Bishop Marroquín's sale of what remained of the cathedral in the former capital, was started in 1543, and rebuilt late in the seventeenth century, after earthquakes had caused much of it to fall. The second building was a maze of naves, chapels, domes, arches and belfries, lit by dozens of windows, its altars inlaid with precious metals, its columns sheathed in tortoise shell. The walls and niches were decorated with numerous paintings and statues of saints.

Beneath the floor of the first Cathedral were buried the remains of Pedro de Alvarado, his wife Beatriz de la Cueva, Bishop Francisco

Marroquín, Bernal Díaz del Castillo, and other dignitaries and dastardlies of the early years of the colony. The exact location of the tombs was lost after the partial collapse of the building.

The Cathedral's present façade is a composite of elements taken from the wreckage of the colonial building. Behind the façade, one of the chapels has been reconstructed as the **Church of San José**. Inside is a statue of Christ by Quirio Cataño, who also sculptured the Black Christ of Esquipulas. The remainder of the Cathedral is a vast jungle of ruined arches, rubble, broken columns, and crumbling walls.

The **University of San Carlos de Borromeo**, *on 5 Calle Oriente facing the Cathedral,* is a beautiful building in the Moorish style. The rooms are set off an arched passageway around the patio and central fountain. The arches are ornamented with curves and points and flutes, and the walls facing the courtyard are covered with geometrical decorations.

Today the university houses the **Colonial Museum**, an exhibition of art from the colonial period, and depictions of life in old Guatemala. A good part of the collection consists of paintings of religious personalities and saints, as well as wooden statues of saints, which are still a form of popular art in rural Guatemala. In Room 4 is an interesting diorama of a university classroom in colonial times, in which two students present a thesis and refutation, while the professor supervises the action from a pulpit. Room 5 features a large mural of a university graduation, as well as some recreations of colonial activities: blacksmithing, sculpture, pottery-making and evangelizing among the Indians.

Turning right on 1 Avenida and continuing two blocks, you come to the **Church and Monastery of San Francisco**. The partly restored church was as large as the Cathedral, its columns and arches towering in a combination of massiveness and grace. Next to the church, the monastery was the headquarters of the Franciscan order, which patronized the arts and science.

One of the Franciscan friars, Pedro de Bethancourt, is buried in a chapel adjoining the church. He is revered today as a healer of the sick. Brother Pedro founded a hospital, and is credited with having turned many a sinner from evil ways.

Down 7 Calle to 2 Avenida, then one block north to 6 Calle, are the **Church and Convent of Santa Clara**. The convent was founded by nuns who came from Puebla, Mexico, in 1699. It fell in the 1717 earthquake, and the second convent was completed in 1734. The church and the cloisters in two arched rows face inward to a large patio with a fountain at the center, forming an enclosed space that afforded the sisters plenty of privacy.

Four blocks north on 2 Avenida, at the corner of 2 Calle, are the ruins of the **Church and Convent of Las Capuchinas**, completed in 1736. This was another place where the sisters lived in splendor. The cells are built around a unique circular patio. Each had its own toilet, an incredible luxury for the time. The daily chores of the sisters are said to have included tending their gardens and doing the laundry of the priests of Santiago.

The **Church of La Merced**, *at 1 Calle Poniente and 6 Avenida Norte*, now largely restored, is a massive structure with a Churrigueresque façade of arches, winding stems of stuccoed flowers and vines, and lace-like patterns. The designs cover almost every square inch of the central section, and of the niches where figures of saints are placed. The church and monastery, home of the Mercedarian friars in Guatemala, were completed a few years before the 1773 earthquake, and suffered little damage while the rest of the city fell around them. The plaza out front is more peaceful than Antigua's central park, with taller trees, and at its center, a nice fountain with medallions.

The **Church of San Jerónimo**, *at the corner of 1 Calle Poniente and the Alameda de Santa Lucía, near the bus terminal*, is a small building in ruins, set next to a monastery whose thick walls surround a central fountain. The church was built in 1757 and closed a few years later, when it was discovered that the Mercedarians had never obtained a building permit. It was later used as the royal customhouse.

The ruins of **La Recolección** are *down the dirt street next to San Jerónimo*. With the exposed brick work of great columns and arches, one might think oneself in the ruins of ancient Rome. But a glance upward to the coffee and shade trees all around, and the volcanoes towering overhead, reminds the visitor that this is the New World. The setting of the church and monastery is probably the most magnificent in Antigua.

The church was founded early in the eighteenth century on the outskirts of town, since Santiago was already quite closely built. There was some opposition to the establishment of yet another ecclesiastical structure in the city. The two-story monastery included a large library, medical facilities and study areas. The church, of which not much remains, was a treasure house of works by European and Guatemalan artists.

NIGHTLIFE & ENTERTAINMENT

Nights are quiet during the week in Antigua, which is very conscious of its role as a cultural center. There's not much to do except sit and converse over coffee or a drink, or go to a movie. Weekends are livelier, however, with many visitors driving into town from Guatemala City.

The **Colonial cinema** is on *5 Avenida Sur*, which runs along the west side of the central park. Admission to most movies is a dollar or more. Check the posters in the lobby to see what's playing, and to get starting times.

Videos to the taste of gringos are shown at several locations around town, among them (at least as of today): **Cine Café Oscar**, *3 Avenida Norte No. 2*; **Frisco Video Bar**, *1 Avenida Sur No. 15*; **Géminis**, *5 Calle Oriente 11A*; **Cinemala**, *3 Avenida Norte No. 9*, **Café Flor**, *4 Avenida Sur No. 1*; and **Rainbow Reading Room**, *7 Avenida Sur No. 8*. If you don't find what you want, you can always set up shop for yourself.

Chamber music and classical marimba concerts are held intermittently throughout the year. Check with the tourist office to see if any are on tap, as well as for any other special events. There are also open-air concerts on Sunday mornings and some evenings on the central park.

Marimba concerts are usually given on weekend afternoons at the Hotel Antigua.

A disco operates in the **Hotel Ramada**.

REST & RELAXATION

Antigua Spa Resort is a self-pampering center a few block past the Hotel Ramada Antigua – ask there for directions. They have a heated swimming pool, whirlpool, beauty treatments, gym and restaurant, in case your hotel doesn't offer any of these services. Some services are available by membership only, and the gender divide is currently as follows: male, Monday to Saturday 5 to 8 am and 6 to 9 pm, female, 8 am to 6 pm on the same days, Sunday for ambos sexos (both kinds), as they say locally.

And if you're in the mood to swim, the **Hotel Antigua** *and the* **Ramada Antigua** *will let you use their pools for a fee if you're not a guest. For a hot-springs swimming pool, see* **San Lorenzo El Tejar***, listed below under "Excursions from Antigua."*

SHOPPING

The specialties of Antigua are textiles from nearby towns, available at the market, at handicraft shops around town, in the central square of Antigua on weekends, and in the village of **San Antonio Aguas Calientes**; ceramics, at the market, handicraft shops, and at the workshops mentioned above; antiques, at some of the handicraft stores; carved jade; and silver jewelry, at the factory in **San Felipe de Jesús**.

Most shops that cater to visitors are located on *5 Avenida Norte* and *4 Calle Oriente*. Some, such as **Colibrí**, *4 Calle Oriente No. 3B*, benefit development or aid projects. Jade is sold at several factory showrooms along *4 Calle Oriente*, one near the park, another *above 1 Avenida*. **Un Poco de Todo**, *on the square*, sells rubbings of Mayan and colonial monuments.

Several interesting shops are away from the town center, among them **Concha's Foot Loom**, *7 Calle Oriente No. 14*; **Casa de Los Gigantes**, *7 Calle Oriente No. 18*; and **Casa de Artes**, *4 Avenida Sur No. 11, tel. 320792, near* *the Hotel Antigua*, which has some of the highest quality artisanry, paintings and antiques.

The Market

The **Market** is located *at the bus terminal, three blocks west of the central park*. Every day is market day, but business is busiest on Mondays, Thursdays and Saturdays. Before the 1976 earthquake, the market was held in and around the old Jesuit monastery. The new location is considerably more ample, if less central, with large sections set aside for handicrafts of various sorts, as well as groceries, fruits and vegetables. Enter and wander about at your leisure. This market is less ordered than most, having taken root on a "temporary" site.

Pottery Factory

The **Montiel factory** uses traditional techniques to produce glazed white pottery in Antigua's distinctive *mayólica* style. Clay is ground by large stone wheels turned by hand, and pottery wheels are operated by foot power. The factory once had many employees, but as cheaper pottery and plastic vessels came into use, business declined. It's now operated as a small family enterprise.

To reach the factory, go north on 6 Avenida Norte to the diagonal street on the edge of town, about six blocks from the central park. Go left one block on the diagonal street, then turn right, and walk up to number 20. If you get lost, ask for the *fábrica de loza Montiel*. You're welcome to examine the techniques, and to buy if you wish.

Ceramic birds are a specialty of the Ródenas family. One workshop can be visited *at 1 Calle del Chajón no. 21* (a couple of blocks north of the market, near La Recolección), and other family members work elsewhere in the neighborhood.

PRACTICAL INFORMATION

Banks

- **Lloyds Bank**, *at the northeast corner of the central park, tel. 320444, open 9 am to 3 pm*
- **Banco de Guatemala**, *on the west side of the central park, open 8:30 am to 2 pm, to 2:30 pm on Fridays*
- **Banco del Agro**, *also on the park, tel. 320793*
- **Banco G&T**, *5 Avenida Norte No. 2, tel. 320639*

Coffee

The Antigua area produces some of Guatemala's finest coffee. Coffee trees are small and delicate, and are shaded by taller trees. They're planted on almost all available flat land around Antigua and in many places within the town. The small white flowers bloom at the beginning of the rainy season, after which the green berry (called the *cereza*, or cherry, in Spanish) develops and ripens to a deep red. The bean is inside, under the skin of the berry and an inner skin. The harvest takes place at the close of the rainy season.

Cultural Resources

Assorted places not mentioned elsewhere include **CIRMA**, a resource center and library specializing in Middle America, *at 5 Calle Oriente No. 2E*; **Casa de la Cultura**, *next to the Cathedral*, which sponsors art exhibitions, talks, and musical performances; **Alliance Française**, *3 Calle Oriente No. 19A*; and **Instituto Italiano**, *4 Calle Oriente No. 21*. The **El Sereno** restaurant often has exhibitions of art, antiques, and prints.

Doctors

Dr. Aceituno, a general practitioner, has his office at *2 Calle Poniente No. 7, tel. 320512*. He speaks English.

Fiestas

The traditional fiesta of Antigua on July 25 honors St. James the Apostle, the patron saint of the city. The biggest religious celebrations, however, take place between Ash Wednesday and Easter Sunday.

On Sundays during Lent, processions from the churches of Antigua and from nearby villages wind their way through the streets of the city. On Fridays, vigils are kept at special altars.

The celebration of **Holy Week** (*Semana Santa*) starts with processions and vigils on Palm Sunday. On the night of Holy Thursday, elaborate carpets of flowers and colored sawdust are laid out in the streets. On Good Friday, a solemn procession reenacts the progress of Christ to his crucifixion. Penitents carry on their shoulders the heavy platform bearing the image of Jesus and the cross. During the morning, the members of the procession dress in purple, but after 3 pm, the hour of the crucifixion, they change into black. Funereal music accompanies the ceremonies, which are attended by the devout from all over Central America.

The major Good Friday procession leaves the **church of La Merced** at 8 am. A few blocks from the church, it passes through the Calle Ancha over some of the most beautiful sawdust carpets.

Colorful processions also take place in Antigua at Corpus Christi and during the days preceding Christmas.

Groceries

One store particularly well-stocked with cheeses, meats, liquors and the usual staple items is *located at 6 Avenida Norte No. 1*. There are similar but smaller stores in the area, and in the market as well. The **Troccoli** hardware store, *at 5 Avenida Norte and 6 Calle Poniente*, has a good selection of liquor.

Guides

Guides are ubiquitous in Antigua. Ask for credentials, or hire one at official rates through the tourist office. If you go shopping with a guide, he'll get a cut from the merchant, and the price to you will be higher.

Horses

Several persons have provided guided horseback trips in recent times, among them Hanna *at 2a Avenida del Chajón No. 3*. Günter Wamser, *Alameda Santa Lucía No. 7*, has organized two-to-four hour scenic rides, and can arrange more adventurous treks lasting from two to twelve days. **Adventure Travel Center**, *4 Calle Oriente No. 7, tel. and fax 323228*, offers rides to San Antonio Aguas Calientes for $30. Or inquire at **Viajes Tivoli**, *above Un Poco de Todo*, the bookstore under the colonnade on the west side of the main square.

Indigenous Music

At **Casa K'ojom**, *Calle Recoletos No. 55 (near Alameda de Santa Lucía)*, there is an outstanding exhibition of native musical instruments. A daily tour at 10:30 am affords explanations of the origin of each instrument, and when it is played, followed by an audio-visual presentation. Sometimes there are live performances as well. Open daily except Sunday from 9:30 am to 12:30 pm and 2:30 pm to 6 pm.

Language Schools

These are Antigua's growth industry. More than a dozen schools offer instruction in the Spanish language. Through them, you can arrange to board with a Guatemalan family. As one student put it: "The whole town is geared to helping you learn Spanish. They'll listen to you and speak slowly. Go to the park and the shoeshine boys will give you a free lesson." Even street sharpies hustle schools, along with lodging places and tours.
Among the established schools are:

· **Sevilla Academia de Español** , *Apartado Postal 380, 6 Calle Oriente No. 3, tel. and fax 323609*. Sevilla Academia offers many community-contact activities. Students pay their host families directly for room and board at a fixed low rate (a school's commission on this can sometimes be a sore point).

· **Professional Spanish Language School** , *7 Avenida Norte No. 82, tel. 320161* (associated with a private aid program)

· **Proyecto Lingüístico Francisco Marroquín** , *7 Calle Poniente No. 31*

• **Tecún Umán Linguistic School** , *6 Calle Poniente No. 34*

And there are dozens of others. Fees range upward from about $450 per month for half-time instruction.

Laundry
Washers and dryers are available at **Lavarrápido**, *5 Calle Poniente No. 7A*. There's a quick wash center at *1 Avenida Norte No. 21, tel. 320691*.

Post and Telegraph
The **Post and Telegraph Office** is located *on the Alameda de Santa Lucía at 4 Calle Poniente, opposite the market.*

Telephones
The office of **Guatel**, the telephone company, is *at the corner of 5 Avenida Sur and 5 Calle Poniente, on the central park.* Pay phones are located *next to the San Carlos restaurant and along the arcade on the central park.*

Public Toilets
Public toilets are located *across from Lloyds Bank, at the northeast corner of the central park.*

Warnings
I've received assorted complaints about foreigners who have set up services as tour guides, handicraft shop owners (especially for "charitable" ends), auto renters . . . I'll just remind you not to trust anyone solely because he or she speaks with a familiar accent.

The ill-lit outskirts of Antigua are not for nighttime strolls, especially Candelaria Hill.

Ask for references when you engage a guide, or hire one through the tourist office.

I could go on and on . . . it's just that Antigua is an extraordinarily pleasant place, and it's easy to let down your guard in the presence of the inevitable bad eggs.

EXCURSIONS FROM ANTIGUA
Travel Agencies
Tivoli Travel, *tel. 323041, fax 320892, is one flight up from Un Poco de Todo, on the west side of the park.* **Turansa** has an office *on the Ciudad Vieja road, tel. 320011,* and they'll also help you out at the **Mistral** bar, *4 Calle Oriente.*

VOLCANOES

Agua, *south of Antigua, measures 3766 meters (12,356 feet) above sea level. An earthquake in 1541 caused water dammed in its crater to wash away the second capital of Guatemala, now known as Ciudad Vieja. The peak can be reached from the village of Santa María de Jesús. There's a basic pension in town where you can stay in order to get an early start. Agua is the easiest to climb of the three volcanoes near Antigua. From its summit, the Pacific Ocean can be seen clearly to the south across the coastal plain, as can the peaks of the chain of volcanoes stretching from Mexico to El Salvador.*

*Fuego and **Acatenango** lie southwest of Antigua. Acatenango is the one to the north. Fire-scarred Fuego, measuring 3763 meters (12,346 feet), was in eruption at the time of the arrival of the Spanish, and still belches fire, lava and ash intermittently. Its continuing activity has caused its profile to change over the years. Acatenango measures 3975 meters (13,042 feet). Fuego and Acatenango are reached from La Soledad farm (finca), past Ciudad Vieja. The ascent is arduous, and should be attempted only by those in excellent physical condition.*

For more details about climbing these volcanoes, see Benjamín García at the Antigua tourist office, consult the Antigua guide by Mike Shawcross, or inquire at the Asociación de Andinismo, 6 Avenida Norte No. 34.

Volcano expeditions have been offered recently by several operators. Daniel Ramírez Ríos, at 6 Avenida Norte No. 34, is fluent in English, and also operates a guest house. And the folks at his house are a treasure chest of all sorts of information about Guatemala. They'll also answer written inquiries.

Gran Jaguar, *at 4 Calle Poniente No. 30, tel. 322712, also operates trips, offering a ride part way up Pacaya in a van, followed by a 90-minute hike. At about $10 per person, they're a bargain. And considering the multiple risks of going on your own (losing your way, assault by criminals), a guided trip is the only safe way. Ask for references to recent participants, or ask around among your fellow travelers as to whether they've been satisfied with the services of this or another operator.*

SANTA MARÍA DE JESÚS

Santa María de Jesús, on the slopes of the **Agua** volcano, was founded shortly after the Conquest, and populated with Indians of the Quiché nation brought from the area of Quezaltenango. It was moved up to its present site early in the eighteenth century, after a flood destroyed the original village.

A picturesque town with many thatched houses, Santa María is one of the few places in the region where some of the men as well as the women wear the traditional town outfit. Men's shirts are red, with woven figures of flowers and animals.

Santa María is the usual starting point for climbing the Agua volcano, and a guide can sometimes be secured by inquiring at the city hall. A small Pensión provides basic overnight accommodation.

ARRIVALS & DEPARTURES

Buses for Santa María leave from the Antigua terminal about every hour from 10 am to 5 pm. The last bus returns from Santa María at 6 pm It's also a pleasant walk downhill for about 10 kilometers along the dirt road back to Antigua, through forests, meadows, and, finally, coffee plantations in the area of San Juan del Obispo, with many impressive views along the way. The road beyond Santa María continues to Palín on the highway to the Pacific. It's best driven in a jeep. A branch road climbs part way up the volcano Agua.

SAN ANTONIO AGUAS CALIENTES

San Antonio Aguas Calientes, like the surrounding small towns, is a center for the cultivation of corn, beans and coffee, as well as citrus and vegetables. But the attraction here is the weaving, some of the best in Guatemala in terms of tightness of the weave, designs and color combinations. Characteristic designs include flowers and geometric shapes, usually done on an orange background. Local huipiles, napkins and wall hangings are displayed for sale all over town, along with pieces from other parts of the country.

The main activity for visitors to San Antonio is to admire and buy textiles at the open stands on the plaza. If you're going to be around for a while, you can contract with one of the women for weaving lessons.

ARRIVALS & DEPARTURES

Buses operate from Antigua to San Antonio Aguas Calientes by way of Ciudad Vieja about every hour, starting at 7 am. The last return bus leaves San Antonio at 5 pm. The walk from Ciudad Vieja (dusty in the dry season) takes about 45 minutes.

SAN LUCAS SACATEPEQUEZ

San Lucas Sacatepéquez existed at the time the Spanish arrived, but was moved to its present location a couple of decades after the Conquest, with its population augmented by Indians brought from Rabinal. In 1871, it was the site of a great battle in which Liberal revolutionaries defeated government forces.

San Lucas is important nowadays as a junction for Antigua on the Pan American (Inter-American) Highway. On weekends, residents of the capital on excursion crowd the numerous restaurants and the roadside market.

You'll notice a few motels in the area. In Guatemala, as elsewhere in Latin America, many motels are locales for romantic trysts, and don't cater to the family trade. Which is why they're usually not mentioned in travel literature.

ARRIVALS & DEPARTURES

Buses operate about every hour to Santiago Sacatepéquez from 2 Avenida and 2 Calle, Zone 9, near the terminal in Guatemala City.

BETWEEN ANTIGUA & CHIMALTENANGO
JOCOTENANGO

Adjoining Antigua, **Jocotenango** is a center for processing coffee beans grown in the area. There's an Adventist herbalist institute at Calle Real No. 30, if you're interested in natural cures, massages and steam baths. Closed Saturdays.

San Lorenzo El Tejar, part of the township of **Pastores**, is the site of a small and pleasant hot-springs swimming pool. To get there, take any Chimaltenango bus from Antigua, and ask to be let off at San Luis Las Carretas. From there, it's a walk of about two kilometers to the pool. Ask for the balneario. If you're driving, take the right-hand fork at San Luis Las Carretas. Admission is less than a dollar, hours are 9 am to 5 pm.

CHIMALTENANGO

Situated on the continental divide, **Chimaltenango** was an important town of the Cakchiquel kingdom before the Conquest. The present city was founded by Pedro de Portocarrero in 1526. In 1527 and 1541, Chimaltenango was considered as a possible site for the capital of Guatemala.

Today, it is a busy trading center, home to some light industry (sawmills, a thread factory), and capital of the department of Chimaltenango. It's also headquarters for a number of foreign evangelical missions, which run schools and churches, and are active, with some success, in converting the inhabitants from their traditional religion.

The department of Chimaltenango was one of the worst-hit sections of Guatemala in the 1976 earthquake. The rubble is long gone, but the area has been permanently altered. Traditional and attractive — but structurally dangerous — homes of adobe with heavy tiled roofs have been replaced by safer houses of wood and concrete blocks, with tin overhead.

ARRIVALS & DEPARTURES

Buses leave frequently from the corner of 20 Calle and Avenida Bolívar, Zone 1, Guatemala City. Last bus about 4 pm. Buses run from Chimaltenango to Antigua about every 45 minutes, the last at 5 pm.

TECPÁN GUATEMALA

First Spanish capital of the Kingdom of Guatemala, **Tecpán** is one of the more important market centers of the highlands. The surrounding plain is a major wheat-growing area, and in the town are flour mills, as well as sawmills for processing lumber from nearby forests.

IXIMCHÉ RUINS

Located about three kilometers from Tecpán, at Pueblo Viejo, **Iximché** *was* the capital of the **Cakchiquel nation** when the Spanish arrived in Guatemala. Of the archaeological sites in the highlands, it is the one that suffered the least destruction during the Spanish conquest and in succeeding centuries.

Iximché was founded around 1470, when the Cakchiquels began a period of conflict with the Quichés. A fortified capital (like others of the same period in the highlands), it was surrounded by deep ravines and a man-made ditch which isolated the ceremonial centers and dwelling places of the nobility from the plebeians who lived outside. Although the Cakchiquels were almost always at war, construction and expansion of the capital continued until the arrival of the Spanish, through the levying of labor and material contributions on subject tribes.

The Cakchiquels received the Spanish peacefully in 1524, and Pedro de Alvarado established Tecpán Guatemala nearby as his headquarters for governing the colonial Kingdom of Guatemala. The Cakchiquels had been allies of the Spanish against the Tzutuhils and the Quichés, but in the face of demands for treasure by Jorge de Alvarado, they rose in revolt, and waged a guerrilla war against the Spaniards until 1530.

ORIENTATION

The site of Iximché consists of four large ceremonial plazas and two smaller plazas, each with one or two temples, house platforms, smaller ceremonial structures, and, in two cases, ball courts. The plazas were built with slight inclines to allow for drainage. The substructures of stone and mortar have survived the highland climate over four centuries, and are now partially restored. But the adobe superstructures, which were probably roofed with straw or some other perishable material, have largely melted away.

Visitors to Iximché can see the remains of murals painted on the stucco that covered the buildings. Archaeologists attribute the three layers of mortar and paving to the practice of renewing streets and structures whenever a king died.

The largest complex at Iximché is the **Palace**, consisting of altars and a nucleus of houses around a patio. Knives, grinding stones, comales for cooking tortillas, and other implements of domestic life have been found here, but all have been removed. Nearby is a pyramidal base with a stone block, used for sacrifices. Like the Aztecs and many other tribes of Mesoamerica, the Cakchiquels tore out the hearts of their victims.

Among the artifacts excavated at Iximché are large cylindrical incense burners, ceramic objects of various types, obsidian knives, skulls of beheaded humans, and a flute made from the femur of a child. These are illustrated in a guide book in Spanish by Jorge Guillemín, available at the site.

Visiting hours at Iximché are 9 am to 4 pm.

FACILITIES

No food is available at the ruins. Stock up on snacks before you set out. You can stop at one of the roadside restaurants near Tecpán, kilometer 87. If you're continuing westward, try **CAFETERÍA CHICHOY**, *at kilometer 102 on the south side of the highway,* for inexpensive Guatemalan home cooking, and a look at the handicrafts of a widows' cooperative.

ARRIVALS & DEPARTURES

Buses directly to or passing Tecpán operate frequently from the corner of 20 Calle and Avenida Bolívar, Zone 1, Guatemala City, from 6 am to 4 pm Travel time is about two hours. For first-class service, take a Quezaltenango bus (see Quezaltenango listings).

From Tecpán, you'll have to walk (or drive) to the ruins. Ask for Iximché or Pueblo Viejo. It's a pleasant hike along a winding dirt road through corn fields and forests.

After your visit, flag down a bus for Guatemala City on the Pan American Highway. If traveling westward, make sure you get back to the highway by 3 pm.

HIGHWAY NOTES

West of Tecpán, the **Pan American Highway** climbs through forested countryside. There are only scattered small settlements along the road at these altitudes, up to 3000 meters above sea level. Along the way are junctions for roads to **Godínez** and the coast (kilometer 117), **Chichicastenango** (kilometer 127), and **Panajachel** and **Lake Atitlán** (kilometer 130).

Back at kilometer 69, another road cuts south from the Pan American Highway toward Lake Atitlán, passing through **Patzicía** and **Patzún**. This route, with many hairpin turns, steep grades and unpaved stretches, is not considered safe for travel beyond Patzún.

LAKE ATITLÁN

The late British author Aldous Huxley once called **Atitlán** the most beautiful lake in the world, and only a few hard souls have been known to disagree with that judgment. Located about 65 kilometers west of Guatemala City in a straight line, or more than double that distance via the winding mountain roads, the lake is a gem in its natural beauty, in the flora and fauna of its waters and the surrounding area, and in the rich traditional Indian life of the villagers who live along its shores. Three volcanoes — **San Pedro, Tolimán**, and **Atitlán** — tower over the southern shore, while mountains rise to a thousand meters above the northern rim.

Thousands of years ago, the eruptions that formed the volcanoes closed off several river valleys, and in the process created Lake Atitlán. New eruptions sealed the lake's river outlet about 500 years ago, and today, its waters drain through underground seepage into rivers leading to the Pacific.

ORIENTATION

The lake's surface is 1562 meters (5125 feet) above sea level, though the figure varies somewhat from year to year, as the waters rise and fall. The maximum recorded depth is 324 meters (1063 feet), but the waters are probably deeper in parts. The length is 18.5 kilometers, the width varies from 7 to 12 kilometers, and the total surface area is 130 square kilometers (50 square miles). Eighteen small islands dot the surface, but some disappear during years of high water.

The area around Lake Atitlán is a region of brilliant natural color. The shades of the sky vary from sunrise to sunset. The lake is a light blue when the **Xocomil** (Sho-ko-mil) wind blows up from the coast in the late morning, a deep blue when the sky is cloudless, and a gray sea when the evening fog rolls in. Everywhere are the colors of wildflowers along the roadsides, white coffee flowers or red coffee berries, and the hibiscus and bougainvillea and countless other plants cultivated in gardens.

SURROUNDING VILLAGES & VILLAGERS

Twelve villages (or more, if some of the smaller hamlets are counted) line the shores of Atitlán. Their inhabitants are for the most part descendants of the Cakchiquel and Tzutuhil nations that inhabited the area at the time of the arrival of the Spaniards. Some of the villages are modern in the manner of other highland settlements, with many of the inhabitants speaking Spanish, traditional native dress going out of

fashion, and orthodox Catholicism and Protestantism replacing the old religious organization.

But in a few of the villages, a visit by an outsider is still a rare event. Life goes on much as it has for centuries. Men till fields of corn and patches of vegetables, and raise coffee, avocados, anise, onions and strawberries as cash crops. Women weave and tend to household chores in tile-roofed, whitewashed adobe homes. In many ways, the lake villages represent the great spectrum of life styles seen in the Indian towns of all of western Guatemala today.

While some natives use *cayucos*, dugout canoes with sides built up of rough planks, the lake figures little in the daily life of the people who live along its shores. Most will trudge along a lakeside trail with their cargo on their backs, in the manner of the people of other highland towns, rather than use a canoe. Few natives ever learn to swim, and there are hardly any legends about the lake. Fish has never been an important part of the Indian diet, and the stocking of the lake with black bass some years back nearly wiped out the native fish population.

Hotels and restaurants are concentrated in Panajachel, on the northern shore. Good roads allow day excursions from Panajachel to Chichicastenango, Quezaltenango, smaller highland towns, and the Pacific lowlands.

As for the name, Atitlán signifies *place of much water*, or simply *lake* in Nahuatl, the language of the Mexican Indian allies of Pedro de Alvarado.

ARRIVALS & DEPARTURES

From Guatemala City, the easiest route to Lake Atitlán is via the Pan American Highway. A road winds southward from the junction at kilometer 130 to Sololá, and then down a steep grade to Panajachel. Total distance is about 147 kilometers.

Along the way, at kilometer 120 on the Pan American Highway, a roadside rest area affords breathtaking views to the lake far below and the volcanoes beyond. At kilometer 117 on the Pan American Highway, **Las Trampas**, is the junction for a scenic, winding road to Panajachel via **Godínez**, above the eastern end of the lake. Total distance via this route is about 160 kilometers. The narrow old road via Patzicía and Patzún, through several canyons, is in a near-abandoned state, is considered dangerous, and should be avoided. From the coast highway, an excellent paved road starts at kilometer 113, and continues to **San Lucas Tolimán** on the southern shore of the lake, and Godínez on the north side.

LAKESIDE TOWNS
PANAJACHEL

Located in a broad river delta, **Panajachel** is the main center from which to see the lake area. It has a number of hotels and restaurants covering a wide range of prices and service.

Along a few side streets near its center, Panajachel is still a typical highland town, where shops, pool hall and eateries huddle one against another in similar thick-walled adobe buildings. Toward the lake are substantial vacation homes behind stone walls, each with a family of caretakers who cut the grass with machetes and keep the bougainvillea trimmed for when the owner shows up. A couple of small inns recall the days when this was a sleepy village known to a limited number of outsiders.

But Panajachel has turned the corner from tradition to trade. Advertising signs, concrete-block hotels, and mini-shopping centers have sprouted, along with street stalls, and rickety plank buildings that see alternating service as handicraft shops, eateries, and lodging places. Older buildings are being renovated into bars, pizza joints, and video parlors. Land that has been family-held for generations and generations comes onto the market. Idiosyncratic new houses perch precariously on hillsides. On one street is an informal bazaar where native peddlers and visitors on indefinite stays offer textiles and trinkets, among dust and paper kicked up by the late-morning wind. Some gringos say that other gringos have spoiled Panajachel, but Guatemalans flock to town on weekends to take it all in.

Still, along the back paths, where the native inhabitants live in small adobe houses and cultivate irrigated plots of vegetables, Panajachel is timeless. Many women wear the traditional red *huipil* and blue skirt.

Despite the evident influence of tourism, agriculture is, for now, the main occupation of the townspeople, and when seen from the approach roads winding down the mountainsides, the coffee plantings and vegetable patches give Panajachel the appearance of a great garden.

ORIENTATION

Though not very large in population, Panajachel is quite spread out, in contrast to other highland towns, and you're bound to do a bit of walking to get from place to place. The streets have various formal and informal names, but none are posted.

The road from Sololá, which is the main street, enters Panajachel near the lake, then angles away from the water toward the town center. The major reference point for getting your bearings is the **Mayan Palace Hotel**, at the intersection of the main street and the street leading to the beach (**Avenida Santander**).

Across the river from the center of Panajachel is the neighborhood called **Jucanyá** (*across the river* in Cakchiquel), a quieter and mostly Indian area. The road that fords the river (starting at the bakery on the main street) continues to the lakeside villages of **Santa Catarina Palopó** and **San Antonio Palopó**. In addition to the streets in Panajachel, a network of narrow trails makes it possible to get from one place to another without seeing anything more than Indian houses and coffee trees along the way.

Officially, Panajachel has recently been divided into zones and numbered streets, in the Guatemalan fashion. The unofficial Avenida Rancho Grande, for example, is now 2 Avenida, Zone 2. The numbers haven't yet caught on, except, perhaps, on tax bills, so you'll still find your way around by asking for streets by their traditional names.

Planning-wise, Panajachel is a nightmare. Noisy restaurants, noisier bars, and, noisiest of all, evangelical churches, go up wherever there is space, and often where there isn't, without regard to existing uses, need for services, availability of water, and, uh, drainage, etc.

ARRIVALS & DEPARTURES

Buses will stop for you anywhere on the main street, but the main unofficial bus stop is in front of the Mayan Palace Hotel.

Guatemala City to Panajachel: Transportes Rebuli from 21 Calle 1-34, Zone 1 (tel. 513521), approximately every hour from 6 am to 4 pm Fare on either line under $2. There is no first-class bus service. To travel part of the way in more comfort, take a Quezaltenango bus from Guatemala City and change at Los Encuentros, or take a van (see below). Travel time from Guatemala City by bus is about four hours.

Panajachel to Guatemala City: Rebuli has twelve departures between 5 am and 3 pm Inquire as to the latest schedule at the Rebuli office on Panajachel's main street, near the town hall. For Antigua, take a Guatemala City bus and connect at Chimaltenango.

Bus Alternatives

Van service (*El Shuttle*) is available daily at 6 am to Guatemala City (via Antigua on Wednesday, Friday and Sunday), returning to Panajachel in the afternoon. Fare is a hefty $20 each way. *Phone 621555 or or 621474* or stop in next to the Al Chisme restaurant to arrange pickup at your hotel.

Or, perhaps better, have one of the Panajachel taxis fetch you from Guatemala City or somewhere else. Try Luis Maca, *at 621571.*

To Chichicastenango, Quezaltenango, Huehuetenango and Mexico: Take any Guatemala City bus and connect at Los Encuentros. There are also several direct buses for Quezaltenango from 5:30 to 7:45 am, and at 11:30 am and 2:30 pm. Direct buses for Chichicastenango also pass several times during the morning. Recent schedule: 7, 7:45, 8:45 and 10:30 am. The last direct return bus from Chichicastenango is at 2 pm; later buses provide connections at Los Encuentros junction on the Interamerican Highway. A slow bus for the Mexican border at La Mesilla has operated on most mornings recently at 6:15 am.

The people who operate the van shuttle to the capital also run a tour to Chichicastenango, starting at 8 am on Thursday and Sunday, for $35. Inquire at Panajachel Tourist Services, next to the Al Chisme restaurant on Avenida Los Arboles.

To Sololá: Take a Guatemala City bus, or, if you fear not for your life or the grief of your loved ones, one of the rickety vans or station wagons that operate every hour or so.

To the Coast: Direct buses to San Lucas Tolimán and the coast highway at Cocales pass through about every hour, more frequently before 8 am The last bus passes at about 3:30 pm. Connect at Cocales for lowland destinations and the Mexican border. The 7 am bus connects at San Lucas with a bus for Santiago Atitlán.

GETTING AROUND TOWN

Taxis park near the post office. *Dial 621571 to call one to your hotel.*

WHERE TO STAY

HOTEL DEL LAGO**, *Tel. 621555, fax 621562 (tel. 316941, fax 348016 in Guatemala City, US reservations tel. 800-327-3573). 100 rooms. $93 single/$111 double.*

A multi-story resort hotel on the public beach, without question the best-run of the larger hotels along the lake, with the most comprehensive facilities. Rooms are light, bright and cheery, with colorful bedspreads and the obligatory weavings on the walls, and terraces with a view to the lake and its bordering volcanoes. The huge large dining room looks out to the water and the food isn't bad; the pool is large, with ample deck, and there are shops and small health club.

HOTEL ATITLÁN**, *Tel. 621429 (tel. and fax 340640 in Guatemala City). 60 rooms. $140 single/$158 double, less during non-holiday periods.*

Amid coffee lands on the shore of the lake two kilometers from town (toward Sololá), a colonial-plantation-style building, with a most attractive atmosphere of away-from-it-all elegance. The bar is especially pleasant, and volcano views are excellent, the public areas with brick-tile floors and soaring ceilings and whitewashed walls suggest another era. Beach and tennis courts, and pool. Getting to town is an up-and-down hike, or a drive. Two important considerations: hot water supply is intermittent, and you'll probably want to eat elsewhere.

CACIQUE INN*, *Tel. 621205. 33 rooms. $50 single/$60 double.*

At the entrance to town on the Sololá side. Pool, fireplace in each of the large, attractive rooms. A good value, the food here is consistently better than at any other hotel, and the owner-manager speaks English.

HOTEL TZANJUYÚ*, *Tel. 621317 (310764 in Guatemala City). 32 rooms. $56 single/$64 double.*

An older hotel, not without faded elegance, but also with faded service, at the entrance to town from Sololá. Swimming pool, bar and extensive bare grounds. The large corner rooms have the best views, but you should take at look at where you'll sleep before you put down money — some of the rooms have at times been invaded by creatures. Food not great.

HOTEL PLAYA LINDA*, *Tel. 621159. 18 rooms. Up to $41 single/ $53 double.*

On the rocky public beach, off-beat, with nice gardens and a flock of caged fowl, common and otherwise, out front. All rooms have lake-view terraces.

PARADISE INN**, *Tel. 621021. 12 rooms. $25 single/$30 double. Visa, Master Card.*

Nice compound near the lake — follow the river up from the public beach. Rooms are plain, but all have fireplaces, and there is protected parking.

HOTEL VISIÓN AZUL*, *Tel. 621426. 25 rooms. $$51 single/$58 double.*

Off the Sololá road. Attractive rooms, all with lakeview terraces facing an expanse of pasture between the hotel and lake. Beach (the nicest at any hotel, available to non-guests for a fee of a couple of dollars), pool, horses for rent, and coffee shop. Coffee plantation next door. Get written confirmation of the rate when you check in.

MAYAN PALACE, *Tel. 621028. 24 rooms. $10 single/$15 double.*

Nice rooms for the price, but the hotel is on the main street at the noisiest intersection in town.

RANCHO GRANDE INN*, *Tel. 621554 (764768 in Guatemala City). 11 rooms. 16 rooms. Up to $60 double.*

Comfortable rooms with fireplaces, and homey, inn-style furnishings in cottages on well-tended grounds edged with bougainvilleas — you get considerably more privacy here than in other Panajachel lodgings. The price includes an enormous breakfast. Good value. At the midpoint of Avenida Rancho Grande. (This is a classy neighborhood, by the way. The author lived next door for a number of years.)

MÜLLER'S GUEST HOUSE, *Av. Rancho Grande (2 Avenida 1-81, Zone 2), tel. 760409, fax 344294 in Guatemala City. 4 rooms. $40 double, $50 triple with breakfast.*

A ranch-style country house (guest rooms all open to a sheltered passageway), on extensive grounds, with polished wood floors (unusual in this region, and quite welcome), and attractive weaving decorations. In good taste, and occupying the middle range, where accommodations are increasingly hard to find. Protected parking.

HOTEL REGIS, *Tel. 621149. 20 rooms. $43 single/$49 double.*

On Avenida Santander, always one of the better values in town, the staid old Regis has been spruced up and given a hefty dose of speed and liveliness under its new Swiss management. The fence along the street constitutes one of the main hangouts (literally) of Panajachel's battalions of street vendors (the wall of my own house is still another), but the spacious grounds with children's play area are a haven amid the bustle. Well-maintained rooms with television and phone, restaurant with standard food.

HOTEL GALINDO, *10 rooms. $15/$20.*

On the main street. The flowered courtyard is the nice feature here. The hotel also has cottages near the lake.

MINI MOTEL RIVA BELLA*, *Tel. 621353. 7 rooms. $15 single/$20 double.*

Modern, clean, cottage-style units in a compound off the main street, near the Texaco station. Very comfortable, and a good value if you don't need to be near the lake.

FONDA DEL SOL, *Tel. 621162. 20 rooms. $10 per person with private bath, less with shared bath.*

Pleasant woody rooms above the restaurant of the same name. On the main street.

HOTEL MAYA KANEK, *Tel. 621104. 30 rooms. $8 per person, or less with shared bath.*

On the main street in the center of town, venerable (I happily stayed here for a month twenty years ago) but recently renovated. Hot water and protected parking — good features for a budget hotel. Give my regards to Arturo.

Bungalows

There are several compounds of bungalows where you can settle in for days and weeks, do your own cooking, and generally feel more at home than in a hotel. **BUNGALOWS GUAYACÁN** are set in a coffee plantation in the Jucanyá neighborhood, across the Panajachel river. The daily rate is $25, with discounts by the month, and includes weekly maid service. A deposit may be required. *For information, inquire at the Las Vegas store or the Mini Motel Riva Bella on Panajachel's main street, or call 621479.*

Less attractive pre-fab cement cottages, but nearer to the lake, are **BUNGALOWS EL AGUACATAL**, *by the Hotel del Lago. Telephone 621482 to reserve.* The rate is about $49 daily. Others are **BUNGALOWS EL ROSARIO**, *near the public beach, nine units, tel. 621491 (761582 in Guatemala City)*, $47 single/$64 double/$105 for four.

Budget Hotels

It's easy to find lodging for $4 per person or less — sometimes much less — at any of the places that advertise their "rooms." Best of these budget pensions is **ROOMS SANTANDER**, *on Avenida Santander*, not far from the main street. Most popular — I don't know why — is **MARIO'S ROOMS**, *farther down the same street.* **ROOMS MI CHOSITA** is on the same street as the Last Resort bar, *off Santander*, and there are others on Avenida Rancho Grande, the next street over.

On a budget at the beach, **HOSPEDAJE RAMOS** has ten concrete rooms and protected parking, at $7 single/$12 double. Nearby, the **HOSPEDAJE CONTEMPORÁNEO** is a slight cut above, with ten rooms at $9 single/ $14 double.

Houses for Rent

Rents range from $30 to several hundred dollars per month, according to amenities and what the traffic will bear. Most quarters are secured simply by asking around. Try any of the compounds of bungalows, including those rented on a daily basis (see above).

WHERE TO EAT

Health Alert!: Before you eat anywhere in Panajachel, consider the sanitary conditions that prevail. Toilets flush into irrigation ditches, which overflow onto the streets. The most basic sanitary measures are unknown, or blithely ignored. At the very least, you can pick up hepatitis, colds, or whatever else your fellow travelers and long-term residents have on their hands and tongues. I believe that the places mentioned below are safe, but don't fail to reel back at anything you may see.

There is a sewage drainage system in Panajachel, constructed with European Community funds. But the projected treatment plant, to have been built with local money, is another story.

FLYIN' MAYAN YACHT CLUB, *at the center of town by the Mayan Palace.* Best pizza in the country, dripping with cheese, in assorted decorations and sizes, from $3.50. Clean, centrally located, inside-outside seating, including a street-watching terrace, and a reedy, trellised room where the exiles gather.

AMIGOS, *on Av. Santander just off the main street,* looks like a mysterious Mexican lair, with low ceilings, worn tile floors, and white-washed walls. Crowd in, and you'll find that in addition to burritos and enchiladas (garnished with guacamole and all the trimmings, for about $4), there are daily gourmet offerings. The toilets are clean. (It matters!)

EL PATIO. Popular and informal, inside-outside, *in the Patio shopping area on Avenida Santander.* Char-broiled steaks, cassoulet, Szechuan chicken (not the real thing), pepián (chicken in dark sauce) and other interesting plates for $4 and up, served with real butter, also sandwiches, and wine by the glass.

At **AL CHISME**, *on Av. Arboles,* the surroundings are new and clean and shopping-center plain. As of a recent date, this was the most popular eating and gathering spot in Panajachel, and with good reason. The chicken roulade, with ham filling and vegetables in a cream sauce, is just excellent. $5 for and up for lunch or dinner, $3 and up for breakfast or a sandwich and beverage. Surcharge on credit cards.

HOTEL DOS MUNDOS, *Av. Santander near lake,* has Italian fare prepared by a real Italian: lasagna, scallopini, whole fish, brochette, at $6 to $12 for a meal, served under a thatched enclosure with large windows. Visa, Master Card.

LA UNICA, a.k.a. the **Deli-Restaurante**. *In a courtyard off the main street, opposite the Centro de Salud (health center).* You can't tell what surprise will turn up next on the menu, but right now you'll find pastrami and

Virginia Ham sandwiches, sausage and sauerkraut, bagels, falafel, tofu, stuffed potatoes, herbal drinks, waffles, and all kinds of eggs. $2 to $4 for a light meal, $3 for a complete pancake breakfast. And so popular that there's a Deli 2 at the end of Avenida Santander, by the lake.

EL CISNE, *on Av, Rancho Grando*, about halfway to the lake. A most pleasant and unpretentious place, with perhaps the best blue-plate lunch in town, for under $3, and complete dinners for $3 to $5, with tortillas in a cloth napkins, Andean music, and tables both inside and on the porch. Worth the walk over.

LA LAGUNA. Dining on the porch or inside a large house set back from the main street. Steak in various forms, chicken and shrimp, paella by appointment. $5 and up, sandwiches $2.

COMEDOR HSIEH, *down the street from the Blue Bird*. Vegetarian. Daily specials, for about $2, include lasagna, curried vegetables, pizza and stuffed peppers. Also breakfast combinations, yogurt, granola, tempura, salads, and sandwiches.

EL BISTRO, *at the end of Avenida Santander*, is a delightful eating place. Sit in one of the inside rooms, or, preferably, at a table in the garden, among herbs planted by the owner-chef. The menu varies. $10 or more for meat or fish. Annoyances include a hefty obligatory service charge, and bread fees. No kids allowed at dinner (from 7:30 pm).

At the beach, **LOS PUMPOS** and **BRISAS DEL LAGO** offer sandwiches and light dinners. Pleasant to sit outside at these two places and watch the volcanoes, the lake and sunset, which is what you're paying for. $5 and up, $2 for sandwiches at Las Brisas, slightly more at Los Pumpos (they have tablecloths). **EL TOCOYAL**, *opposite the Hotel del Lago*, is glassed-in, more formal, offering views even in the rainy season, and pasta and steaks for $6 to $10.

BARS

The **Flyin' Mayan**, mentioned above for its pizza, also has the least expensive drinks among places where a visitor might imbibe. The **Last Resort**, *off Avenida Santander near the elementary school*, is Panajachel's most venerable non-traditional watering hole. Drinks for about a dollar, and generous meals of lake fish, chicken and ribs for $4, as well as sandwiches and pizza.

I don't vouch for the service, and drinks are more expensive than elsewhere; but one of the pleasures of Panajachel is to walk out to the **Hotel Atitlán** at sunset, and sip your drink in the bar or on the terrace as you look over gardens to the lake, the mist, and the clouds folding over the ridge between volcanoes in the distance. Surely one of the better views from any bar, anywhere.

SEEING THE SIGHTS

Aside from people-watching and shopping, appreciation of beauty is the main activity for visitors to Panajachel. One can easily spend a number of days observing the nuances of color in the sunset or the waters of the lake, or staring at the clouds rolling overhead and creeping around the peaks of the volcanoes.

If you don't feel like leaving, but don't know what else to do, here are some suggestions: Wander along the back paths of Panajachel. Visit one of the nearby towns by car, by bus, or on foot. Take a walk on the trails along the lake, or into the mountains. Take a bus ride to Cocales, down through a landscape that changes from cool highland to coffee slopes to sugar and citronella fields to steaming cattle pastures, the coastal flats and sea often visible in the distance.

Continue onward, perhaps, to the archaeological sites around Santa Lucía Cotzumalguapa. Climb a volcano; swim; rent a boat; or take a ride on one of the scheduled boats.

NIGHTLIFE & ENTERTAINMENT

The best entertainment after a day's swimming or marketing is to watch the sunset, or the coastal lightning reflected against distant clouds during the rainy season (a show!). **Movies** are shown occasionally at the auditorium next to city hall, with Mexican thrillers (e.g., *Saint Against the Mummies of Guanajuato*) predominating. More reliable are the **videos** shown at the bar next to the El Patio restaurant, at **Grapevine Video**, and several other locales up and down Av. Santander. The stock is recycled every week or so.

SHOPPING

Native textiles are the local specialty, in the market of Panajachel, in the many handicraft stores in town and the stalls that line the main streets, and in the markets of Sololá and Santiago Atitlán. Non-traditional arts and crafts include imaginative hand-painted and printed t-shirts; oil paintings of village scenes and of the lake, some quite good, some not so good; and assorted bead necklaces, silver jewelry, and sketches by itinerant artists.

The **market** is on the main street at the eastern end of town, just past the town hall. Market day in Panajachel is Sunday, but things are also fairly busy on Saturdays. On these days, stalls are rented by vendors of textiles from all the major highland towns, as well as spice and kitchen-utensil merchants, itinerant shoemakers, and sellers of fish and pineapples and assorted other exotic produce from all corners of the republic. On non-market days, there's always a good selection of local produce in the morning.

Market days at towns readily accessible from Panajachel are: Sunday, Chichicastenango, Nahualá; Tuesday, Sololá, San Lucas Tolimán; Thursday, Chichicastenango; Friday, Sololá, Santiago Atitlán, San Lucas Tolimán; Saturday, San Lucas Tolimán.

PRACTICAL INFORMATION FOR THE PANAJACHEL-LAKE ATITLÁN AREA

Banks

Banco Agrícola Mercantil, *in the same building as the Mayan Palace Hotel. Open 9 am to 3 pm weekdays.* As the senior bank, this one has long lineups. You might find quicker service for cashing travelers checks at **Banco Industrial**, *on Avenida Santander near the telephone office*; or at **Banco Inmobilario**, *on Avenida de los Arboles, near the center of town.* There's also a branch of **Banco Granai** *in Sololá*, but there are no other banks in the lake region. Make sure you have sufficient cash before setting out for nearby towns.

Beaches

The **public beach**, which is the edge of the wide delta of the Panajachel River, has in recent years become less and less savory for swimming. Prosperity has brought many a flush toilet to Panajachel, and in some cases the untreated outflow travels via irrigation ditches right to the lake. For swimming, stick to the hotel pools, or take a walk well away from town. Best time to swim in the lake is in the morning, before the Xocomil wind comes up and turns the water choppy. The water's cold (this is a high mountain lake), but it becomes quite tolerable, even refreshing, once you go under.

Limit your activity at the public beach to sunning and volcano watching and people watching and taking a meal in any of the two dozen eateries housed in blue sheet-cement cottages. The beach is where locals wash themselves and park their *cayucos* (canoes) for the night, where drivers bathe their buses, where the ladies from Santa Catarina press their woven wares upon you, and where late-night drunks pitch bottles to watch them crash and smash on the recently built, currently collapsing rock terraces (your hotel taxes at work). The beach is never dull, but nor is it an idyllic, sun-drenched, endless stretch of white sand. Pebbles, rocks, and plain old dirt are ample, and driving rains rut the surface.

Parking is permitted at the beach, with a small fee imposed when there are enough visitors to make it worth sending somebody to collect (usually on weekends). Camping is sometimes permitted, sometimes discouraged. And changing rooms are available for a fee.

A private and cleaner beach, at the **Hotel Visión Azul**, is open to visitors for a fee. Campers can also rent space there. Or arrange to use the meandering pool at the Hotel del Lago, for a fee of about $2 for the day.

Bicycles

Bicycles are rented just off the main street, *opposite the Mini Motel*; and at a location *down the street from the Last Resort bar, off Avenida Santander*. Motorcycles are rented near the Catholic church, at about $5 per hour.

Boats

Current schedules are clearly posted at the tourist office on the main street. Recent scheduled services, all daily, are:

- **Panajachel-Santiago Atitlán** : 8:35, 9, 9:30, 10:30 am, 3 and 4 pm from the public beach. Return departures from Santiago Atitlán at 6, 7 and 11:45 am, 12:30, 1, 2, and 5 pm.
- **Panajachel-San Pedro La Laguna** : 9:30, 11:30 am, 2:45 and 5 pm from the Hotel Tzanjuyú, some runs with stops in Santa Cruz; 8, 9, and 11 am, noon, 1:15, 2, 4, 5:30 and 7:30 pm from the public beach. Return departures from San Pedro at 4, 5, 6, 8, 10, 11 am, noon, 2, 3, 5 pm, among others.
- **Panajachel-San Antonio Palopó-San Lucas Tolimán** : 9:30 am from public beach. Return departure at 1 pm.
- **Panajachel-San Pedro-Santiago Atitlán-San Antonio Palopó-Panajachel**: Daily 9 am boat tour, with a stop of about an hour in each village, from public beach. Fare about $7, minimum four passengers, can be booked at tourist office in Panajachel. Return to Panajachel at 3 pm.
- **Santiago Atitlán-San Pedro La Laguna** : about every hour from 7 am to 5 pm.

Except as noted, fare is just $1 to $2.50 on any of these runs.

By combining runs, you can make any number of circle trips starting from Panajachel, or, for convenience, take the daily boat tour. Additional boats operate on fiesta days.

Rowboats can be rented *at the boatyard at the foot of Avenida Santander*. Go out in the morning, when the waters are calm. **Motorboat tours** to lake villages, and water skiing, can be arranged at the same place. Group trips are also available at the Hotel Atitlán, the Hotel Tzanjuyú, and the Hotel del Lago (more expensive), and from the boatyard of Mr. Rosales across the river, near the cemetery (cheaper). And you can sometimes barter with the owners of canoes and motorboats at the public beach to take you to Santa Catarina Palopó and San Antonio Palopó.

Diversions Balam, *at the beach, tel. 622242*, offers kayaks, canoes and water skis for rent.

Doctors

For emergencies, try the **health center** (**Centro de Salud**) or the

national hospital in Solalá. Dr. Hernández has his clinic near the Texaco station, there's a doctor near the pharmacy in the shopping center on Av. Santander, and there are usually some interns in the Solalá hospital resident in town.

Fishing

It's a big lake, but except for some large-mouth and small-mouth bass (lobina), the fish are small. Hooks and line can be purchased at any general store. You might catch some crappies or tilapia if you drop your line near shore; the black bass are farther out, and are usually speared by natives.

Goods & Services

Anthropologist Sol Tax wrote extensively, forty years ago, about the "penny capitalism" of Panajachel, a flourishing of small-scale entrepreneurs of fruit and vegetables and tinware and transport in a village that, unlike most in Guatemala, has no great hinterland for the cultivation of the staple crops of corn and beans.

Today, in an otherwise bleak national economic environment, the tradition of trade represents hope and profit not only for native Panajachelenses, but for indigenous traders displaced from their home villages by civil conflict, Ladino promoters, and foreign entrepreneurs of every stripe from drifter to yuppie to big-time talker in versions of several languages. You can study Spanish here (**Centro Internacional de Español of Antigua** has a branch *near the town center, tel. 621378*); fax your business documents around the globe; drop off your purchases for one-stop export labelling, packing and shipping at **Get Guated Out**, *on Avenida de los Arboles, upstairs tel. and fax 622015.*

There are also: **ChoCopán**, Dina's chocolate store *on the main street* (also with books — why not?); an herbal cure emporium; self-service laundries; a travel agency (intermittently); several dozen cottage clothing factories; subdivisions with building lots for sale (but no streets); and dentists who will fix up your teeth and gums at a fair price, if you're going to be in town for a while — one is Dr. Lavarreda at the Hotel Maya Kanek.

Laundry

If your hotel doesn't do laundry, or if you don't like the price, you'll find several places with self-service machines. Or, you can employ any of several ladies who will pound your linens into cleanliness at a set price per dozen (a dozen anything, handkerchiefs to jeans), though modern, high-tech fabrics don't stand up well to this treatment. Look for the laundry sign on Avenida Santander, or ask somebody who's been around town a while.

Massage

Try the health club at the **Hotel del Lago**, where a one-hour massage goes for under $10 — a real bargain, if you've ever had a massage in North America. And there are resident foreign practitioners elsewhere in Panajachel. Ask at any herbal store, such as the one on Avenida Los Arboles.

Post Office-Telegraph-Telephones

The post office is located along the side street by the Catholic church, near the town hall. Try to mail packages early in the morning. Domestic telegrams are handled next door. For telephone calls and international telegrams, go to the **Guatel** office, *in the red-brick building on Avenida Santander*. Look for the microwave tower. Coin phones are located outside **Guatel**, and next to the town hall.

School Days

The **Robert Müller International School** operates on the American school calendar with a global curriculum and a United Nations of kids, in English and Spanish, with one teacher to six kids. *Call 622142 to sign up.*

Spanish School

Yes, you can study Spanish in Panajachel as well as Antigua and Guatemala City and Quezaltenango and Huehuetenango. **Centro Internacional de Español** has operated recently *along Callejón Londres, an alley off Av. Santander*, with two students per teacher (most schools elsewhere offer one-on-one instruction).

Weather

During the **rainy season**, from May to October, temperatures will reach about 81° Fahrenheit (27°C) during the day. At night, there are usually enough clouds lingering to hold in the warmth of the day, but the temperature may drop to as low as 54 ° F (12°C). A sweater will come in handy.

During the **dry season**, daily highs range from 73° to 84° F (23° to 29°C), but at night, the mercury can fall to the high thirties and low forties F (3° to 5°C). Frigid winds are common at night during the dry season, so a couple of sweaters or a coat are necessary. Above the lake, around Sololá and at the higher altitudes, frost is common early in the morning in the dry season. I have even seen snow flurries along the Pan American Highway late at night in February.

Winds

Of the many currents that blow across the lake from the surrounding valleys, the most constant is the **Xocomil**, *the wind that carries away sin* (in Cakchiquel). The Xocomil rushes up late every morning from the coast, and suddenly turns the waters of the lake from calm to choppy. Afternoon winds usually blow in from the north, bringing rain from May to October. Winds on the lake are ever-shifting, which makes sailboating difficult.

EXCURSIONS FROM PANAJACHEL
Tourist Office

On the main street near Avenida Santander, closed noon to 2 pm, Monday afternoon, and all day Tuesday. The man in charge, Víctor Manuel Salguero, can help out with air reservations and confirmations. When the office is closed, boat schedules are posted on the door. Unofficially, information and useful services are available at **El Toro Pinto**, opposite the Texaco station.

Volcanoes

Three volcanoes tower over the south shore of Lake Atitlán. Look at them, and you can read the history of the lake, which was formed by their eruptions. **San Pedro**, to the southwest of Panajachel, rises to 3020 meters (9909 feet) and can be climbed in a day, starting from the town of San Pedro La Laguna. To the southeast is **Tolimán** with its twin craters, one at 3134 meters (10,283 feet), the other at 3158 meters (10,361 feet). Behind Tolimán, to the south, is **Atitlán**, the highest of the lake volcanoes, at 3535 meters (11,598 feet). Atitlán last erupted in 1853. Steam still seeps from the craters of both Atitlán and Tolimán. The climb to the top of either, starting at the town of San Lucas Tolimán, usually requires an overnight stay at the crater or in the saddle between the volcanoes.

Between Tolimán and the lake is **Cerro de Oro**, a volcanic mound. Its crater once held a Tzutuhil fortress, but is now given over to corn and bean cultivation. Cerro de Oro can be climbed in less than an hour.

Other Lakeside Villages

The villages around Lake Atitlán can be reached from Panajachel by water, of course, and, with three exceptions, by existing roads that descend from the surrounding highlands or run back from the shore. A new and ill-conceived waterside road is currently being blasted by the US Army Corps of Engineers, the main effect of which will be to displace natives from their lands and disrupt traditional life.

CHICHICASTENANGO

Santo Tomás Chichicastenango has long been one of the magical destinations of the Americas. A great market center for the Indians of the western highlands, it is inundated on Thursdays and Sundays with traders who bring their produce, textiles and handiwork from all the towns of the region. It is also a place where the traditional, mystical ways of Guatemala's indigenous peoples still visibly hold sway.

In former times, traders would carry their wares for hours along dirt roads or back paths to reach Chichicastenango, often setting out the day before the market and sleeping out on the plaza. Visitors from the outside had to face grueling hours on dusty roads from the capital to get to see the great market, the mix of pagan and Catholic ritual amid clouds of incense at the Santo Tomás church, the rolling hills and steep canyons of the forested and farmed countryside often shrouded in mist.

Chichicastenango still maintains a separate government for its Indians. A first and second mayor and councilmen, as well as an Indian court, take care of matters that concern the Indian community exclusively. Operating parallel to the Indian government is the religious organization based on *cofradías*, groups of men devoted to a particular saint. Duties in the cofradías are alternated with service in the government, as a man slowly but steadily rises in position in each.

The *cofradías* and *chuchkajaues* — native prayer men — have always been more important than the institutional church in the religious life of Chichicastenango. While baptisms take place in church, and are all-important in setting a person on the proper course in life, marriages and funerals are under the charge of chuchkajaues.

The *cofradías* number fourteen. The most important is the *cofradía* of St. Thomas, the patron saint of Chichicastenango. On the day of the saint of each *cofradía*, the saint's image is carried in procession, and installed in its place of honor in the house of the new cofradía chief, or alcalde.

All the *cofradías* participate in the feasts of the more important saints. Images of the major saints bring up the rear of the processions. The *cofradía* officers wear ceremonial jackets over their regular outfits, and carry varas, staffs of office capped with silver suns and wrapped in ritual cloths. The beat of the *tun* (a drum) and the melody of the *chirimía* (a flute) provide musical accompaniment. Every few steps, the procession comes to a halt and a rocket bomb is fired from a launching pipe. Candles, incense burners, feathers, and fruit decorate the thrones of the saints.

The processions are only the visible part of the activities of the *cofradías*. All during the year, the head of a cofradía hosts meals for his members. At fiesta times, the *cofradía* dresses up its saint and members drink heavily. The expenses born by a *cofradía* leader are heavy, sometimes running into more than what he earns in a year, and so he often must go into debt to finance his position of honor.

The *chuchkajaues*, or prayer men, act as mediators between individuals and the saints and idols. In the folk Catholicism of the highlands, the saints and idols are seen very much as active powers who can intervene in the world to set things right or punish wrongdoers. A prayer man, phrasing things in the proper way, can appeal to an idol for help, ask for forgiveness, seek a cure for illness, or give thanks for a bit of fortune. By using a kit of seeds, a chuchkajau can tell the future. The ceremonies of *chuchkajaues* take place at the church, at household shrines, and at stone idols set up in the hills outside town. When the ceremony is held at an idol, a sacrificial chicken may be thrown in with offerings of candles, flowers and liquor.

ARRIVALS & DEPARTURES

To drive to Chichicastenango, follow the Pan American Highway (CA1) to **Los Encuentros** junction at kilometer 127. Turn right for the road to Chichicastenango. Near kilometer 135, there's a small turnout on the left where you can stop to look down on Chichicastenango. In the distance is the city of Santa Cruz del Quiché, on its own hilltop. Beyond this point, the road descends into a canyon on switchbacks, and climbs back up to the plateau on which Chichicastenango sits. A small parking fee is collected on market days at the town entrance.

Galgos, 7 Avenida 19-44, Zone 1, Guatemala City, tel. 23661, 536467, has been running a bus to Chichicastenango at 6:30 am on Thursdays and Sundays, with an afternoon return.

Ordinary, crowded buses of the Masheña and Reina de Utatlán lines leave from the terminal in Zone 4, Guatemala City, about every hour on market days, about every two hours on other days. Take any bus marked Quiché or Chichicastenango. Most stop at 20 Calle and Avenida Bolívar, Zone 1, on the way out of the capital.

Otherwise, for a comfortable ride part of the way, take a bus from Guatemala City toward Quezaltenango (Rutas Lima, 8 am from 8 Calle 3-63, Zone 1, or Galgos, as above, 8:30 am) and connect with another bus at Los Encuentros.

Many local buses also operate from Chichicastenango to Los Encuentros, where connections can be made for Guatemala City, Panajachel, and Quezaltenango. Don't start out too late in the day. Los Encuentros is a lousy place in which to get stuck. It's 2600 meters high, and cold and windy in the early morning and from the late afternoon on. The temperature drops below freezing at night in the dry season. There's a small restaurant at the gas station.

WHERE TO STAY

MAYAN INN***, *tel. 561176 (60213 in Guatemala City). 30 rooms. Usual rate: $65 single/$75 double. Authorized rate: $75 single/$85 double/ $105 triple.*

One of the best hotels in the country, in two traditional tile-roofed buildings west of the square, furnished with antiques and antiquities gathered from all over the country. Pleasant gardens, and views to the surrounding valleys from the terraces. Altogether a superb hotel, except, perhaps, for some aspects of the food service. Horseback trips and car tours arranged. Also a good place to hear the marimba, Guatemala's best-known native instrument, usually played on market days in the courtyard of the bar. Add about $30 per person for three meals.

HOTEL SANTO TOMÁS**, *tel. 561061, fax 561306. 43 rooms. $90 and $114 single/$99 and $114 double/$114 triple.*

On the entrance street, next to the Chevron station. A pleasant, relatively new hotel in tasteful colonial style, with a number of modern amenities, including heated pool, whirlpool, sauna and exercise facilities. All rooms have fireplaces. Marimba music is almost always playing in the courtyard, the gardens and colonnaded passages are lovely, and in a crowd on market day, you could easily feel that you had wandered into a medieval fair. Add $8 for lunch or dinner.

HOTEL VILLA GRANDE CHICHI, *(tel. 348136, fax 348134 in Guatemala City). 66 rooms. $57 single/$65 double, $90 to $108 in suites.*

For many years a concrete shell of a time-share that stood incomplete due to war and a real estate scandal, the Villa Grande, on a hillside grandly overlooking Chichicastenango, has finally come into service. Suites have fireplaces, an alcove, a second bed on a stuccoed base, a large bathroom with tub. About three-quarters of a kilometer from the square in Chichi.

PENSIÓN CHUGÜILÁ**, *tel. 561134. 27 rooms. $28 single/$33 double.*

North of the square on the street leading through the arch. A pleasant, traditional place built around a courtyard. Many rooms have fireplaces. Lower prices are with shared baths. Good value. Add about $4 each for a large lunch or dinner, $2 for breakfast.

MAYA LODGE**, *tel. 561177 (29367 in Guatemala City). 10 rooms. $25 single/$31 double.*

On the square in the middle of the action, rooms in a meandering and charming old house, simple and clean. Meals available for about $5 each.

Budget Hotels

HOTEL GIRÓN, *tel. and fax 561156,* is on the street one block north of the square, behind an arcade of stores. Recently upgraded, it has 17 rooms with a few extra comforts and frills (wooden headboard, night table) for $10 single/$15 double with private bath and hot water. Meals are served for $3 to $5.

POSADA BELÉN, *12 Calle 5-55, Zone 1, tel. 561244. 14 rooms. $7; single/$11 double ($10 single/$14 double with private bath).*

A three-story, slim concrete structure, this is perhaps the only budget hotel in Guatemala with a New York contact *(tel. 212-349-7020* — the owner lived in my home town for a number of years, and speaks the language, along with some Greek and Chinese). And, if nothing else, they have a view to Pascual Abaj and a lovely valley from the rooms. Rooms are bare, with no tables or closet, but one has a fireplace. Eggs and sandwiches are available for a couple of dollars. Take the first side street to the left past the gas station after entering Chichi.

HOSPEDAJE SALVADOR, *near the Belén*, has 42 rooms on three levels around and above a courtyard in a family-style compound decorated with potted plants. It's pleasant to look at, but, once again, bare once you're installed. *$6 single/$8 double ($11/$14 with private bath, more with fireplace).*

HOTEL PASCUAL ABAJ, *tel. 561055*, is a couple of blocks from anywhere else, through the arch and then another block downhill. Seven rooms have private bath and go for $8 single/$11 double. Good for getting away from the noise.

WHERE TO EAT

The **HOTEL SANTO TOMÁS** serves a set lunch for about $11, and it is a bargain as much for the atmosphere as the fixings.

The **EL TORITO** restaurant, *upstairs in the Girón commercial center, a block toward the arch from the square*, offers kebabs, something *they* call a *filet miñon*, and a steak-and-bean *(típico* plate) for $5 to $6, served in a dark and dusty salon with views through lace curtains to the street below. A marimba plays in the courtyard.

Restaurant row in **Chichi** is a half-block back from El Torito. The **TZIGUÁN TINAMIT**, *on a corner a block from the square toward the arch*, offers fare similar to that at El Torito, but the place looks cleaner. *Next door*, **KATOKOK** is cheerier, with whitewashed walls, canned marimba music, waiters in uniform, and lower prices than any of the above.

Budget & Moderate Fare

For cheap food, go to the booths in the market, or the small eateries on the entrance street east of the plaza.

Inexpensive and moderately priced meals are available at the **MAYA LODGE**, *on the square*, and at the **PENSIÓN CHUGÜILÁ**.

SEEING THE SIGHTS

The **Church of Santo Tomás** *on the east side of the plaza* is a whitewashed colonial structure, built around 1540. On the steps, prayer men burn *copal* resin on a stone platform, and *estoraque*, another resinous incense, in hand-held burners. The altarpieces inside are of wood and silver, decorated with faded paintings and statues of saints.

The impressive part of the church is not its physical structure, but the ceremony that takes place amid clouds of incense on the front steps and around low wooden platforms placed along the aisles. After burning incense on the front steps, a *chuchkajau* enters with his client, and stops at the door to explain the purpose of the ceremony to the guardian spirits of the church. Prayers are said at the altar railing, and then at the platforms, each of which is associated with a specific group of ancestors. Candles, flowers and liquor are offered to the souls residing in each area. The *chuchkajau*, using the exact combination of words appropriate for the act, calls on the saints, the souls of the departed and the lords of all the natural forces of the Indian universe to hear his plea.

To the side of the church is a former monastery, now used for church offices. Laid out in its garden is a model in concrete of the ceremonial staff of the St. Thomas *cofradía*.

In the parish archives, the Spanish priest **Francisco Ximénez** discovered the manuscript of the **Popol Vuh**, the sacred book of the Quichés, early in the eighteenth century. Regarded as a masterpiece of American indigenous literature, the *Popol Vuh* consists of two parts. The first reads somewhat like the Christian Bible, and tells through allegory, poetry and symbolism the early history of mankind. Man was created from a paste of corn, according to the *Popol Vuh*, after initial attempts using wood and clay produced excessively rigid and fragile human beings. The second part is an account of the wanderings of the forebears of the Quiché nation, from their ancestral home in the Toltec lands of Mexico to the highlands of what is now Guatemala, and the establishment of a powerful kingdom. This part seems to have a strong factual basis, at least to the extent that historians and ethnologists can compare it with archaeological evidence and the few other written accounts available to them.

Visitors to the church should enter by the side door through the monastery, and stay off the front steps so as not to interrupt the ritual. Sunday mass starts at about 8 am, and is attended by the members of the cofradías, who arrive early and sit near the altar.

El Calvario is the chapel *on the west side of the plaza*. Inside is a figure of Christ in a glass case. Incense is burned on a stone platform at the top of the steps, and rituals similar to those of the Santo Tomás church take place inside.

The **Museum** is located *on the south side of the plaza* and contains the jade collection of Ildefonso Rossbach. Rossbach came to Guatemala as an accountant, studied for the priesthood in the United States, and returned to Guatemala to serve in Chichicastenango until his death in 1944 at the age of 74.

The museum is open every day except Monday, from 8 am to 2 pm on market days, from 8 am to noon and 2 to 4 pm on other days.

Pascual Abaj, or **Turkaj**, is a stone idol located *on a hilltop about a kilometer from town*. In local religious practice, idols complement the saints as representations of the natural forces that govern the world. Unless a ceremony is in progress, with candles and incense burning and perhaps a chicken being sacrificed, the shrine itself, a stone figure surrounded by stones, with an incense-burning platform nearby, won't seem particularly impressive. Views of Chichicastenango and the surrounding valleys from the hilltop, however, are excellent.

To reach the idol, take the street that leads south from the plaza between the church and the museum, turn right at the first corner (9 Avenida, or Chi Turkaj), and follow the road down the hill and out of town, past the *morerías*, the shops where masks and costumes are prepared for fiestas. Feel free to stop and look in. Where the road bears right, continue straight (you can drive as far as this point) on the trail to Turkaj.

SHOPPING

The **Market** on Thursdays and Sundays is the principal attraction for most visitors. The specialties are Chichicastenango *huipiles* (women's blouses), sashes, carved and painted boxes, and masks. But handicrafts from all over the highlands are brought to town for the benefit of tourists. The selection is better than in other markets, but asking prices are higher, so be prepared to bargain hard.

The jostling and the frank commerce can be unsettling at times, and it takes patience and detachment to wade through all that is available, decide what you really want, and try to strike a deal. By late afternoon, most of the vendors are packing up, and peace returns to the plaza, amid the litter and discards of the day's commerce.

With all the noise and madness of market day, and all the merchants from outside who come to town, it's often difficult to see through the activity and focus on the town itself. Visitors might want to arrive a day early or stay for a day after the market to get a picture of Chichicastenango at peace.

FIESTAS

Fiestas are the times of year when the *cofradías* honor their saints and install new officers. Most of the ritual takes place in the house of the outgoing head of the *cofradía*, amid food and drink. The saint is brought to the church the night before the day dedicated to him, and the next morning is carried in procession after mass, and later placed in the house of the new cofradía head.

The fireworks specialists, responsible for all the noise of the celebration, have their own guardian figure called **Tzijolaj**, a small horse and rider carried by one of the members of the fraternity as he dances about.

Tzijolaj, who may represent St. James, is a messenger who communicates between man and the governing forces of the universe. Tzijolaj is thought to have originated at the time of the Conquest, when men on horses were taken by the natives to be gods.

The **Feast of St. Thomas**, starting on December 14 and culminating on December 21, is the main Chichicastenango fiesta. Processions and liquor and dances also appear during Holy Week (Easter), at Christmas, on All Saints' and All Souls' days (November 1 and 2), at the October harvest festival, on Corpus Christi, and on the feast days of the saints of each of the cofradías, most notably January 20, March 19 and June 24.

PRACTICAL INFORMATION

Travelers checks can be changed at the **Banco del Ejército** *on 6 Calle, the main street, about a block from the square.* **Telephone calls** can be made at the **Guatel** office *on the entrance street, next to the pig market.* The **post office** is nearby.

QUEZALTENANGO

Quezaltenango is on the surface a provincial sort of place, with narrow streets winding up and down hills, a scarcity of traffic in the center, and a peaceful and dignified air. Yet the city is the second largest in Guatemala, the hub of the highlands, the center for trade between the coast and the highlands, and for the movement of the produce of the area to the capital.

The vicinity of Quezaltenango was inhabited by the **Mam** nation until two centuries before the Spanish conquest, when the **Quichés** took over the region. The Quichés called their walled city **Xelajuj**, *under the ten hills,* and today most Guatemalans refer to the town as **Xela** ("SHAY-la").

It was near Xelajuj that the Spanish under Pedro de Alvarado defeated the forces of Tecún Umán. In what was to become a pattern, the old Indian city was abandoned, and the new city of Quezaltenango was founded nearby as a center of Spanish power.

Quezaltenango was to become a rival of Guatemala City. In the years after Central American independence, when travel was difficult and regionalism was stronger than it is today, Quezaltenango first declared its allegiance to Mexico, then finally joined the Central American Federation as capital of the state of Los Altos. Los Altos was incorporated into Guatemala in 1840, but in 1848, another attempt at secession was put down by armed force.

Late in the nineteenth century, much of the Pacific slope of Guatemala was planted in coffee, and Quezaltenango grew as a commercial center from which the beans were shipped to Pacific ports. Foreign traders moved in to take charge of the commerce of the town, and many of Guatemala's richest families trace their wealth to the trade boom of those days. The city's expansion was halted suddenly by the earthquake of 1902, which destroyed Quezaltenango and brought ruin to its merchant class.

The city was rebuilt, and a railroad was constructed to facilitate commerce between highland and coast. The railway was washed out in the thirties and never reconstructed, but a road eventually took its place. Quezaltenango recovered from the disasters, but was never again to rival Guatemala City.

Today, Quezaltenango is a city proud of its cultural heritage. Many of Guatemala's best writers, musicians, and scholars have lived there, and are honored with statues in front of the municipal theater. The neoclassical architecture preserved from the beginning of the century gives the town a dignity that contrasts sharply with the helter-skelter construction of Guatemala City and coastal towns. Quezaltenango's setting is one of grandeur, under cultivated hills and the perfect cone of the Santa María volcano.

Quezaltenango is one place where many an Indian has prospered in commerce. In other highland towns, business is often the exclusive realm of Ladino merchants. But many of the stores in Quezaltenango are tended by women in huipiles and pleated skirts of foot-loomed material, working not as hired hands, but as owners.

The Weather

If there is an eternal springtime in Quezaltenango, it's felt for only a few hours a day. Nights are cold, and during the dry season, the temperature sometimes drops below freezing. Throughout the year, people arise late in order to avoid facing the morning chill, and only by midmorning has the sun warmed the air sufficiently for the inhabitants to go about without wraps. In the evening, a crispness returns to the air, and the Quezaltecos don sweaters and shawls again.

Farming & Weaving

The department of Quezaltenango has been one of the more densely populated areas of Guatemala since colonial times. The highland parts are given over to the cultivation of corn and wheat, and to sheep grazing. Textiles are woven in great quantities, using techniques ranging from the backstrap looms of small towns to the foot looms of Salcajá to the modern machine looms of the town of Cantel. The Pacific slope is largely planted in coffee, while the lowland parts of the department, around Coatepeque, are areas of large-scale sugar and cotton farming. All around the city of Quezaltenango, the earth's depths open to the surface through hot springs and active volcanoes.

HIGHWAY NOTES

Beyond **Nahualá** (kilometer 155), the **Pan American Highway** twists and climbs to frosty altitudes of over 3000 meters, through bare, sheep-grazing country. This area is often shrouded in fog at night. The road is in excellent condition, but poorly tuned cars will huff and puff on the way up. The road winds down from the summit to the **Cuatro Caminos** junction (kilometer 185), from which the white church of **San Francisco El Alto** is usually visible, far above. Roads from the junction lead to **Totonicapán** and **Quezaltenango**. The junction for **San Francisco El Alto** and **Momostenango** is a few kilometers farther along. If you're going to either of the latter two towns, take the second turn for an easier climb from the highway. The main highway continues over another mountain pass to Huehuetenango.

The branch road to Quezaltenango passes through Salcajá. A few kilometers before Quezaltenango is the junction called **Las Rosas**. A sharp turn at the police post takes you around the prison farm (*granja penal*) and onto the paved highway to **Cantel**, **Zunil**, and onward down to the coast. At **El Zarco** junction, this road joins the **Pacific Highway**.

ARRIVALS & DEPARTURES

Most buses leave, rather inconveniently, from the terminal out in Zone 3. Few buses leave after 4 pm. To reach the bus terminal, take bus 2 or 6 from the central park. First-class buses to Guatemala City and buses for towns nearby leave from locations nearer the central park.

Guatemala City to Quezaltenango: First-class service on Rutas Lima (8 Calle 3-63, Zone 1) 7:45 am, 2:30, 4, 8 pm; Galgos (7 Avenida 19-44, Zone 1): 5:30, 8:30, 11 am, 2:30, 5, 7, 9 pm; América, 2 Avenida 18-47, Zone 1, at 5 am, 9 am, 3 pm, 4:45 pm and 7:30 pm Second-class service on Tacaná (2 Avenida 20-49, Zone 1).

Quezaltenango to Guatemala City: Rutas Lima (2 Calle 6-32, Zone 2, a few blocks east of the square, just off the road to Guatemala City), 5:30, 8 am, 2:30, 7:30 pm Galgos (Calle Rodolfo Robles [Calle 0] and 18 Avenida, Zone 3, near the La Democracia shopping area), 5, 8:30 and 10:30 am, 12:30, 3, 5 and 6:30 pm; and América (7 Avenida 3-33, Zone 2), at 5 and 9:45 am and 1, 3:45 and 8 pm Also Tacaná, four daily second-class buses from the Zone 3 terminal.

Panajachel (Lake Atitlán): From the terminal at noon and 1:30; Higueros (12 Avenida and 7 Calle off the central park): 4 am and 3:30 pm Chichicastenango: direct buses from the terminal at 1:30 and 2 pm At other times, take a Guatemala City bus and transfer at Los Encuentros for Panajachel or Chichicastenango.

San Marcos: Rutas Lima: 11:45 am, 8:30 pm (both first class); various companies from the bus terminal about every two hours.

Huehuetenango: Rutas Lima: 5 am (continuing to La Mesilla and Mexican border), and from the terminal about every hour. Or take a bus from behind the Centro Comercial near the Central Park to Cuatro Caminos, and flag down a bus on the Pan American Highway.

Tecún Umán/Talismán/Mexican Border: two daily buses from the terminal; or change buses at Coatepeque on the Pacific highway. Rutas Lima has a direct early-morning bus to Talismán.

GETTING AROUND TOWN
By Taxi

For $2 or less, you can reach any destination in town. The tourist office will advise you about fares if you want to hire a taxi to one of the nearby towns. *To call a taxi to your hotel, dial 8121.*

WHERE TO STAY

PENSIÓN BONIFAZ, *4 Calle 10-50, Zone 1, tel. 614241, fax 612850. 53 rooms. $52 single/$60 double. In Guatemala City, tel. 80887.*

Quezaltenango's dowager hotel, colonial-style and elegant, with impeccable service, pleasant public rooms, and roof terrace for views of the city. Excellent restaurant, bar, protected parking, and, as far as I'm concerned, the only place to stay in Quezaltenango if budget is not a limitation. The portable room heaters are welcome on cold highland nights. Highly recommended.

CENTROAMERICANA INN, *Blvd. Minerva 14-09, Zone 3, tel. 630261. 12 rooms. $14 per person.*

Near the Democracia commercial area, with neatly furnished rooms in a rambling compound of spruced-up wooden and stuccoed buildings—an odd collection, but really quite pleasant.

HOTEL DEL CAMPO*, *Las Rosas junction, tel. 618082, fax 630074. 100 rooms. $28-35 single/$35-$48 double.*

A modern roadside motel, at the junction for the highway to the coast. Warm pool. Rooms are clean and plain, and apartments are available for larger groups. Suitable if you have a car (as is the hotel at Las Georginas hot springs, mentioned a few pages ahead).

CASA KAEHLER, *13 Avenida 3-33, Zone 1, tel. 612091. 6 rooms. $8 single/$10 double ($10/$15 with private bath).*

Small and cozy.

CASA SUIZA, *14 Avenida A 2-36, Zone 1, tel. 630242. 19 rooms. $10 single/$12 double, or slightly less sharing bathroom.*

A small, older place, with rooms around a courtyard. Good value.

HOTEL KIKTEM JA, *13 Avenida 7-18, Zone 1, tel. 614304, 20 rooms. $11 single/$14 double.*

Colonial-style, thick-walled, musty, with a few ghosts. Good value.

HOTEL RADAR 99, *13 Avenida 3-27, Zone 1. 15 rooms. $4 per person, less with shared bathroom.*

Only the two top rooms, with a terrace and views to the city and hills, have any compensations. I don't know where the hotel's name comes from.

WHERE TO EAT

PENSIÓN BONIFA, *just off the square*, offers the most elegant dining in town. The cream of Quezaltenango society gathers at the Bonifaz; often a few older German-Guatemalan ladies are here at midday, remnants of the old foreign commercial elite of coffee country.

Breakfast & Light Fare

Early risers heading to nearby markets might have trouble finding breakfast. Most restaurants in Quezaltenango take their time in opening. However, the dining room of the **HOTEL MODELO** starts serving at 7:15 am, and offers eggs, pancakes, and juices at reasonable prices — $2 and up — in a pleasant atmosphere. Also open early is the **CAPRI**, *at 11 Avenida and 8 Calle, just down from the central park*. The cooking is native style: eggs served with tortillas, meat garnished with a topping of tomatoes and onions. Smoky atmosphere, brick walls, big wooden chairs, and locally woven tablecloths. $2 for breakfast, lunch or dinner.

Another choice is **LA POLONESA**, *14 Avenida A 4-71, near the post office*. They serve basic breakfasts for just over $1, as well as hamburgers and sausages. **BAVIERA**, *5 Calle 12-50*, has light fare of sandwiches, pies, and soups, and you're welcome to come in just for a cup of coffee. **PIZZA RICCA**, *14 Avenida 2-42*, serves an acceptable pie, if you want to be sure of what you're getting.

Country-style Dining

Try the **RESTAURANT PANCHOY**, *on the outskirts of Xela, on the road to San Marcos*. The food is fairly good — mostly steaks and chicken cooked over coals. $8 and up. Take bus 6 from the central park to just past kilometer 205. If you're driving, follow 4 Calle in Zone 3 past Minerva Park and out of town.

Chinese Food

For fair Chinese food, try **SHANGHAI**, *4 Calle 12-22*. $3 and up, less for non-Chinese items. For fast chicken, there's a 24-hour **LOS POLLOS** outlet *at 13 Avenida and 6 Calle*.

BARS

Tecún, *in the passageway off the central park, at 12 Avenida 4-32*, is a cavernous, down-at-the-heels bar with decaying wooden tables and two juke boxes (called by their trademark, rockola, in Guatemala). Beer, rum, and little plates of stuffed peppers, spaghetti and eggs are served. Drinks are less than $1. Definitely a place in which to get smashed.

At 1 Calle and 14 Avenida, opposite the municipal theater, **Taberna Don Rodrigo** serves up burgers, coffee, and draft beer.

SEEING THE SIGHTS
Around the Central Park

Quezaltenango possesses one of the most attractive main squares in Guatemala, lined with buildings from early in the century. Officially called **Parque Centro América**, the square is a rectangle a few blocks long, sloping uphill to the north. In it are stone benches and fountains and statues, and all around are stone-faced buildings in the neoclassical style, with triangular pediments, fluted columns, and a Moorish octagonal window thrown in here and there.

Standing along with these dignified buildings housing government offices, banks and the cultural center, are the **Cathedral** with its colonial baroque facade, the old market with its massive, fortress-like walls, a couple of tall (three stories, which is tall for these parts) old brick commercial buildings, and some newer nondescript store structures. There are always people sitting out on the stone benches of the park watching the passing scene, and traffic is usually light. The air often has a bite to it, which seems to slow things down.

The Cathedral, *on the east side of the park,* presents an old and florid façade with a squat bell tower alongside. This front wall is all that remains of the original building, which fell down some time ago. In back is a newer building, bubbling with domes.

The **City Hall (Palacio Municipal)**, *on the next block up from the Cathedral,* is one of the main neoclassical buildings on the square. If the gray stone on the outside looks somewhat forbidding, take a look at the beautiful gardens in the courtyard.

The **Natural History Museum** is located *on the south side of the park* in another neoclassical building called the **Casa de Cultura del Occidente (House of Culture of the West)**. There are small exhibits here, some of them rather trivial, such as a mirror shattered by lightning. But most of the displays are interesting, and include pottery from the Pacific lowland area, pre-Columbian ceramics and jade, native costumes, stuffed animals and birds, herbs and mushrooms, a pickled human brain, and blurbs for local industries. This mishmash of subjects is not all natural history, but it's a fun collection of manageable size, in a dusty, small-city museum.

Downstairs, the musical collection includes numerous native-style instruments, among them tzijolaj flutes made from cane, drums fashioned from logs and animal skins, and old-style gourd marimbas. There are also a number of fiesta masks. If you haven't come across a real fiesta in your travels, stop in to see a part of what you've missed.

Exhibitions of paintings are often held in the salon next to the museum entrance. *The museum is open Monday through Friday, 8 am to noon and 2 to 6 pm.*

Also in the Casa de Cultura is the **Tourist Office**. The local delegate of the tourist commission keeps extensive files on bus schedules, local cultural events, and new restaurants. A city map is available. *Hours are 8 am to noon and 2 to 6 pm, Mon.-Fri.*

Behind the museum is the **Mercadito**, the old little market which nowadays is mainly a place where women peddle cheap meals. *The main market is in Zone 3.* Across from the Mercadito is the **Centro Comercial Municipal**, a modern three-story shopping center, and in between is a public amphitheater built into the slope.

Elsewhere in Quezaltenango

The **Municipal Theater (Teatro Municipal)** is a few blocks up from the square, *at 1 Calle between 14 Avenida and 14 Avenida A.* It's another of the neoclassical buildings, with Doric capitals on its columns. The plaza in front is decorated with busts of local artists and scholars.

Farther on, the great old **La Democracia market** in Zone 3 is no more. A modern "**Centro Comercial**" is under construction to take its place. But this area, seven blocks north and three blocks west of the central park, remains a thriving area of small stores and tradesmen. *At 4 Calle and 15 Avenida in Zone 3* is the **Church of San Nicolás**, a gray Gothic structure with flying buttresses of reinforced concrete, looking somewhat like an illegitimate offspring of the cathedrals of northern Europe.

Just over a kilometer to the west, *along 4 Calle*, is **Minerva Park**, a large, green, tree-shaded area, pleasant for spending a free afternoon. *Right in the middle of 4 Calle, at the entrance to the park*, is the **Templo de Minerva**. A glut of such temples was erected throughout Guatemala during the reign of Estrada Cabrera, who figured himself a promoter of education, and dedicated monuments to the appropriate Roman goddess. The one in Quezaltenango stood incomplete for decades, but the finishing touches were put on a few years ago.

To reach Minerva Park, take bus 6 from the central park.

Nearby, *off 4 Calle*, are the **main market** of Quezaltenango, and the **terminal** from which buses leave for the small towns of the department, the coast, and other parts of the highlands. If the main square of the city is deceptively quiet, the frenzy of activity at the bus terminal and market gives some idea of the commercial importance of Quezaltenango.

MOVIES & ENTERTAINMENT

Movies are shown at the **Cadore**, *13 Avenida at 7 Calle, a block from the central park*. Mexican flicks predominate.

On Sunday mornings, the **Trencito Estrella**, a train of cars pulled by a tractor, takes kids and grownups on rides around town, starting at the Municipalidad on the park. Nominal fare.

AREA VOLCANOES

The major volcano in the area is perfectly formed **Santa María**, *3772 meters (12,376 feet) high, which peeks out over the ridge to the south of Quezaltenango. A crater on its slope,* **Santiaguito**, *was formed in 1902, and is in constant eruption.*

For a view of the fireworks, take a bus from the Zone 3 terminal to Llanos del Pinal, or else drive there by following 8 Calle and Diagonal 11 west from the central park, or take a taxi. From **Llanos del Pinal**, *take the trail near the military reserve (polígono de la brigada militar). You can climb a ridge and look down into the crater. Best time for viewing is just before dawn. It's a strenuous climb, but the sightings of bromeliads and the birding are worth the effort. And as visitors become more frequent, it will probably be a good idea to take a guide to show you the way, and for safety. Inquire at the tourist office in Quezaltenango, or in the village of Llanos del Pinal.*

A couple of other high peaks south of Santa María are **Zunil** *and* **Santo Tomás**. *A few years ago, the National Geographic Institute stripped these mountains of their status as volcanoes. The institute decided that what appear to be craters are in fact eroded peaks.*

SHOPPING

There are many handicraft stores in the **Centro Comercial** (shopping center) just down from the central park. Most feature merchandise from the Quezaltenango region. A large **Artexco** (handicraft cooperative) outlet is located *at 7 Avenida and 16 Calle on the road out of town toward the Pan American Highway*. Take a Las Rosas city bus from the square.

A **handicraft market** operates the first Sunday of every month on the square, and there is a handicraft exhibition, locally touted but similar to other shops, *at 14 Avenida 3-36*. You can also look at the market in Zone 3. And, of course, the nearby towns are full of handicraft specialties.

PRACTICAL INFORMATION

Banks

Several banks are located *around the Central Park*, including **Banco de Guatemala** and **Banco de Occidente**.

Doctors

Dr. Isaac Cohen, *17 Avenida 1-56, Zone 3, tel. 614658*, speaks some English. Or try the **Policlínica** *on 14 Avenida near Calle 1, Zone 1.*

Groceries

In addition to many small shops around the city, the best-stocked place is **Minimercado La Democracia**, *on 15 Avenida near 1 Calle in Zone 3*. Near the central park, try the **La Selecta** and **Metro Centro** supermarkets, *both at the corner of 4 Calle and 13 Avenida*. A large, modern shopping center is located *at 4 Calle and 24 Avenida in Zone 3, on the way to Minerva Park.*

Hospital

The best is the **Hospital Privado**, *Calle Rodolfo Robles 23-51, Zone 1, tel. 614381.*

Insurance

If you've just driven from Mexico, buy liability coverage at **Granai y Townson**, *14 Avenida 3-31, Zone 1, upstairs*, or **Seguros de Occidente**, *13 Avenida 5-38, Zone 1.*

Language Study

Quezaltenango, like Antigua, is becoming a center for learning Spanish, and numbers of readers have sent me encomiums full of praise for the local language schools. While "Xela" doesn't have the colonial charm of Antigua, and the air has a definite bite on a February morning, the living experience here, and the use of language, are more workaday and realistic. Quezaltenango is also somewhat of a university town, with branches of Guatemala City institutions

Among the language schools of Quezaltenango are:

• **Kie-Balam Language School**, *12 Avenida 0-43, Zone 1 Quezaltenango, tel. 612639. US contact: Daniel and Martha Weese, 1816 North Wells, Chicago, IL 60614, tel. 312-642-8019.* The school helps support community health and environmental services, and the program includes visits to markets, craft centers and villages.

• **I. C. A. (Instituto Central America)**, *1a Calle 16-93, Zona 1, 09001 Quezaltenango, tel. and fax 09-63187. US contact: RR2, Box 101, Stanton, NE 68779, tel. 402-439-2943.* I.C.A.'s slogan is *el monolinguismo es curable* (unilingualism can be cured.) Tuition ranges from $100 to $120 per week, depending on the time of year, and includes five hours per day of private instruction, room and board with a local family, and contact activities that include visits to villages, hospitals and markets.

Part of the modest tuition fees goes to support such projects as indigenous language instruction, scholarships, and reforestation.

- **S.A.B.E.**, *1 Calle 12-35, Zone 1, tel. 612042, fax 8878,* has been in operation for many years, in association with a travel agency;
- **Escuela de Español Casa Xelaju**, *Apartado 302, 9 Calle 11-26, Zona 1, Quezaltenango, tel. 612628. US contact: 10221 St. Paul Ave., St. Paul, MN 55116, tel. 612-690-9471.* Casa Xelajú, offers not only hot springs and volcano-climbing excursions with its instruction, but also cooking demonstrations and outings to a jail, a squatter settlement, cooperatives, the Guatemala City dump, and to join in road repairs. Talk about an introduction to a culture!
- **Juan Sisay Spanish School**, *15 Avenida 8-38, Zone 1, tel. and fax 630327. US contact: 3465 Cedar Valley Court, Smyrna, GA 30080, tel. 404-432-2396.* Associated with social programs and reforestation.
- **Centro del Lenguaje América Latina**, *Apartado Postal 233, 19 Avenida 3-63, Zone 3, Quezaltenango, tel. 616416. US contact: 635 Skyview Pl, Apt. 9, Madison WI 53713, tel. 608-255-0734*
- **Centro de Estudios de Español Pop Wuj**, *1 Calle 17-72, Zona 1, tel. 618286. US contact, P. O. Box 43685-9685, Washington, DC 20010-9685.*
- **Proyecto Lingüístico de Español**, *5 Calle 2-40, Zone 1, Apartado 114, Quezaltenango, tel. 612620. US contact: tel. 718-965-8522.*
- **Proyecto Lingüístico Santa María**, *Apartado 230, 14 Avenida A 1-26, Zone 1, Quezaltenango, tel. 612570, fax 618281. US contact, j287 Harvard St., No. 61, Cambridge, MA 02139, tel. 617-547-7806.* Involved with community development projects, tuition is higher than at other schools.
- **International Language School**, *15 Avenida 1-23, Zone 1, tel. 614451,* with classes in Quiché and Mam, as well as Spanish.
- **International School of Spanish**, *8 Avenida 6-33, Zone 1.*

Laundry

For coin-operated machines, try **Minimax** *at the corner of 1 Calle and 14 Avenida.*

Mexican Consulate

In the **Pensión Bonifaz**, *just up from the central park.* Inquire at the front desk if you need a Mexican tourist card.

Post Office-Telegrams

The post office is *at the corner of 15 Avenida and 4 Calle, Zone 1.* Local telegrams are sent from here, international ones from the telephone office.

Telephones

For long-distance calls, the **Guatel** office is *at the corner of 15 Avenida A and 4 Calle, Zone 1.*

HUEHUETENANGO

The **department of Huehuetenango** is one of the richest in Guatemala in tradition and color. The vast majority of the people are indigenous, most speaking some dialect of the Mam language. The Mam kingdom covered the greater part of the western highlands centuries before the Conquest, until Quiché warriors pushed the Mam back to the present-day departments of Huehuetenango and San Marcos.

Now, living in the towns where the Spanish overlords concentrated their ancestors, many still follow their mixed pagan and Catholic traditions.

ARRIVALS & DEPARTURES

Most buses leave from near the market, though there is the possibility that some services will relocate to a new market-terminal off the road to Guatemala City. For destinations not mentioned here, see individual town listings, or inquire at bus company offices along 1 Avenida between 4 and 1 calles, preferably the day before you travel.

Guatemala City to Huehuetenango: El Cóndor (19 Calle 2-01, Zone 1), at 4, 8 and 10 am and 1 and 5 pm; Los Halcones (7 Avenida 15-27, Zone 1): 7 am, 2 pm, large buses; Los Flamingos (6 Avenida A 18-70, Zone 1): 12:15 and 5:30 pm; Rápidos Zaculeu (9 Calle 11-42, Zone 1): 6 am, 3 pm.

Huehuetenango to Guatemala City: El Cóndor (5 Avenida 1-15), at 4, 7:45, 9:45 and 10:45 am and 12:45 pm; Los Halcones (7 Avenida 3-62), 7 am, 2 pm; Los Flamingos (4 Calle 1-51): 5 am, 12:30 pm; Rápidos Zaculeu (3 Avenida 5-25): 6 am, 3 pm.

Quezaltenango: Rutas Lima (4 Calle 3-30), 3:30 pm (first class). Other departures about every hour from market area.

La Mesilla/Mexican Border: Pick up your Mexican tourist card at the consulate in Huehuetenango. El Cóndor, 6 and 10 am, 12:30 and 3:30 pm Rutas Lima: 8 am (first class). Other departures approximately every hour from along 4 Calle and 1 Avenida, until 2 pm.

Sacapulas: 4:30 am and 11:30 am from 1 Avenida 2-46. Other buses operate to Santa Cruz del Quiché and Nebaj via Sacapulas.

ORIENTATION

In the department of Huehuetenango are frosty mountain peaks and dry plains and dense jungle, ravines and valleys, lakes, and vast forests. To the north of the city of Huehuetenango rise the Cuchumatanes mountains, highest in Guatemala, with frosty peaks over 3000 meters. It's too cold at the heights to plant many crops, and the inhabitants depend on sheep-raising.

Many of the towns of the department were reached by roads only in the last twenty years. Much traditional trade still takes place on market days, when men carry heavy loads for many kilometers over narrow, steep and winding trails in order to earn a bit of cash. Sometimes exchanges take place over the border with Indian towns in the Mexican state of Chiapas, whose peoples are closely related to those of Huehuetenango in language and heritage.

The city of Huehuetenango is a quiet and provincial sort of place, populated mostly by Ladinos. The area around the **market** is crowded with Indian traders from all parts of the department, often dressed in the colorful outfits of their home villages. Trucks filled with Indian workers on their way to plantations on the coast pass through at all hours. There's some light industry — flour mills, shoemaking and the like — but mostly, Huehuetenango is a trading center for handicrafts and agricultural products moving out of the towns of the department, and cloth and thread and manufactured goods coming in.

The **square** is a quiet center of town life that has remained unchanged for many years. Archways shelter the sidewalks, a band shell looks out over the park from the second floor of the city hall, and a wedding-cake tower sprouts from the departmental government building to a height that must have seemed awesome many years ago. Laid out in one corner of the tree-shaded park is a relief map of the department, interesting for tracing the ups and downs of the winding roads going to the more isolated towns. The colonial church is off to one side, and on some central streets are schools and other buildings in the neoclassical style that was popular in the nineteenth century, after the Liberal revolution.

GETTING AROUND TOWN

Taxis park near the central park. I can't imagine any need for a taxi to get around town, but you might want to hire one to go out to the Zaculeu ruins or to a nearby town. Always bargain on fares.

WHERE TO STAY

HOTEL ZACULEU, *5 Avenida 1-14, tel. 641086. 38 rooms. $30 single/ $36 double.*

An old-time hotel with rooms opening off a flowered courtyard, and public areas decorated with regional handicrafts. Some rooms are relatively bare, others are little suites, with separate sitting areas and dark wood cupboards and tables.

HOTEL PINO MONTANO, *tel. 641637 (531394 in Guatemala City. 18 rooms. $12 per person.*

On the Pan American Highway at kilometer 259 (two kilometers past the junction for Huehuetenango). Accommodations are in semi-detached units on pleasantly landscaped grounds. Restaurant, pool. This is your best bet if you have a car.

HOTEL MARY*, *2 Calle 3-52, tel. 641-618. 25 rooms. $8 single/$11 double.*

New, clean brick building. Some rooms with private bath. Good buy.

HOTEL CENTRAL, *5 Avenida 1-33. $3 per person.*

Nice old place with large rooms. All rooms are bathless, but the common sinks have hot water, which is often absent in cheap hotels. You don't have to stay here to eat in the dining room, which offers the best food bargains in town. Tasty, filling meals go for $1.50. Breakfast is served at 7 am, lunch at 12:30, dinner at 6:30 pm

HOTEL MAYA, *3 Avenida 3-55. $4 per person ($2 sharing bathroom).*

A cement-block hotel, with small but well-lit rooms. Good value.

AUTO HOTEL VÁSQUEZ, *2 Calle 6-67, tel. 641338. 20 rooms. $4 per person.*

Concrete block rooms, characterless. The name means it has parking.

WHERE TO EAT

If you find a really good restaurant in Huehuetenango, let me know. Meanwhile . . .

In the $5 range: The **REGIS RESTAURANT** *in the Hotel Mary, 2 Calle 3-52*, is clean-looking and serves meals with beef or chicken as the main course, and sandwiches. **LAS BRASAS,** *4 Avenida 1-53*, has a few Chinese items on the menu, and meat cooked over coals.

In the $3-to-$4 range: **MAXI PIZZA,** *2 Calle 5-35*, serves spaghetti and lasagne for $2, hamburgers, and pizzas in assorted sizes for $3 and up. Cleaner than most. For a couple of pieces of fried chicken, try **RICO MAC POLLO,** *on 3 Avenida* next to the Hotel Maya. **LOS POLLOS,** *at 3 Calle 5-38*, the fast chicken chain, has a fluorescent-lit 24-hour branch a half block from the square. The **RESTAURANT MAGNOLIA,** *at 4 Calle and 6 Avenida*, is a big hangout where locals sit over beers late into the night. Open at about noon.

NIGHTLIFE & ENTERTAINMENT

Not much happens at night in Huehuetenango. Try a movie at the **Cine Lili,** *3 Calle 5-35*. Films in English are often shown. If you're lucky, you might catch an evening band concert in the central park.

SHOPPING

Specialties in Huehuetenango are hand-woven *huipiles*, shirts, bags, sashes and other items of Indian clothing from all over the department.

Look in the market, in the **Artexco cooperative** *(look for the double pine tree sign on 4 Calle opposite the market)*, and in stores near the central park.

PRACTICAL INFORMATION

Banks

Change your travelers checks at **Banco de Guatemala**, *5 Avenida and 2 Calle*. Open 8:30 am to 2 pm (Fridays to 2:30 pm) If you're heading to Mexico, unload your extra quetzales here for dollars, if any are available. Rates over the border are less favorable.

Groceries

For pasteurized milk, cheeses and cold cuts, try any of several small stores located on *3 Calle between 2 and 3 avenidas*, or the **Sáenz** supermarket at *3 Calle and 5 Avenida* on the central park, or the **Comisariato** *in back of the pharmacy at 3 Avenida and 3 Calle.*

Insurance

Automobile liability insurance is available at **Granai y Townson**, *5 Avenida 4-23.*

Language Study

A language school that has functioned recently is **Fundación 23**, *at the corner of 7 Calle and 6 Avenida*. Another, recommended by readers, is **Instituto El Portal**, *1 Calle 1-64, Zone 3, tel. 641987.*

Mexican Consulate

In the **Farmacia del Cid**, *4 Calle and 5 Avenida*. They charge a dollar or so for a tourist card. No telling what you'll be charged if you show up at the border without one.

Post Office-Telephones-Telegraph

2 Calle 3-54. Go in back to mail a letter.

LA MESILLA/MEXICAN BORDER

Located at kilometer 341, **La Mesilla** is the hamlet on the Guatemalan side of the border; a few kilometers down the road on the other side is Ciudad Cuauhtémoc, in the Mexican state of Chiapas.

If entering Guatemala at La Mesilla, you'll first go through immigration procedures at the station on the border. Tourist cards are sometimes available, but it's best to pick one up in advance at the Guatemalan consulate in Comitán. The customs post for baggage inspection is a couple of hundred meters up the road from the border.

ARRIVALS & DEPARTURES

To Huehuetenango: Various bus companies about every 90 minutes from 5:30 am to 4 pm Travel time to Huehuetenango is two to three hours. To Guatemala City and intermediate points: El Cóndor buses at 6, 7, and 10 am, and 2 pm At other times, connect at Huehuetenango. Leave San Cristóbal de las Casas on the first bus of the day to meet the 10 am bus.

Guatemala City to La Mesilla: El Cóndor (19 Calle 2-01, Zone 1) at 4, 8 and 10 am The 4 am bus offers the best onward connections, or start later in the day from Quezaltenango or Huehuetenango. There is also a bus to this border point from Panajachel.

On to Mexico

Buses for San Cristóbal and points beyond leave from the Mexican side at about noon. Others depart from the Mexican customs post about three kilometers up the road, and you'll have to walk or take a taxi to catch them. It's best to have a Mexican tourist card in hand. If you get stuck, a couple of rooms are available at one of the cafés opposite the main Mexican customs post.

TO THE CARIBBEAN

Northeast of Guatemala City is the long valley of the **Motagua River**, a near-desert region for almost 200 kilometers from the capital, then a lush, green, lowland area, where the river winds through cattle and banana country, to empty finally into the Caribbean at the border of Honduras.

The lowlands along the Caribbean are small compared to the Pacific lowlands, and though the temperature is often in the nineties (Fahrenheit), distances to be covered are relatively short, so I wouldn't worry too much about the discomforts of bus travel. Rain is another matter. The wet season isn't as well defined to the north and northeast of Guatemala City as in the western highlands or on the Pacific coast. Storms can blow in from the Caribbean at any time of day on any day of the year, bringing short and heavy downpours.

Take along a raincoat or umbrella. Anyone spending a lot of time in the area, or staying in cheaper accommodations that might not be adequately screened, should take a malaria preventive.

THE QUETZAL RESERVE

At kilometer 161, the **Biotopo del Quetzal**, or **Quetzal Reserve**, was set aside to protect the flora and fauna of the rain forest in the **Chuacús** mountain range. A rich variety of plant life flourishes in the high humidity blown in by prevailing winds throughout the year and trapped by mountain ridges. In an enchanted, fairy-tale environment, orchids, bromeliads, mosses and ferns mask the branches of trees, and vines and plants with gigantic leaves penetrate into all levels. Roots of trees and plants as well as lowly worms mine and recycle decaying material, whether it lies on the ground or in the crook of a tree.

ARRIVALS & DEPARTURES

With an early start, a visit to the reserve can be a day trip from Guatemala City, though you'll probably continue to Cobán or stay overnight nearby. To reach the reserve, drive or take a Cobán bus to kilometer 161.

WHERE TO STAY

There are two choices for overnight stays. At kilometer 156.5 is **POSADA MONTAÑA DEL QUETZAL***, an attractive lodging compound with 18 motel rooms and cabins, and two pools, one for kids. The hillside cabins, all with fireplaces, are faced with stone and stucco, and the atmosphere, with clouds folding over the forested ridge, fern-lined walkways, and cool and misty air, is perfect. *The rate is about $40 single/$50 double. Phone 314181 in Guatemala City to reserve.* This is also a good place to stop for lunch — $4 for the daily special, and an a la carte menu with some native-style dishes and sandwiches. If you don't have a car, flag down a bus along the highway to take you from the reserve to the Posada. Tradesmen who stop at the posada are usually good about giving rides back to the reserve.

Adjacent to the reserve, *about 300 meters toward Cobán*, is the hillside **HOTEL RANCHO EL QUETZAL**. Rooms are in the most basic cane huts, but they're there, at least, in case you can't find onward transport. *The charge is about $4 a person.* This is the nearest place to the reserve to get a drink.

Visiting the Reserve

The Biotopo covers 2849 acres, but only a small portion, 62 acres near the highway, is open to visitors. This is as things should be at a reserve, but even this limited area will allow you to see a good cross-section of cloud forest. Comfortable walking shoes are helpful, but heavy boots are not a necessity. Well-made steps, rock-paved causeways, and paths of loose stone banked by logs and rough-cut lumber invite you to penetrate the forest without making an ordeal of it. Off the trails, the ground is more squishy than muddy.

Since this is a cloud forest, you'll often be walking through penetrating mist, and rain protection won't keep you dry.

Camping and cooking in the reserve are prohibited.

At the information center just above the road is an odd assortment of exhibits — ocelot feces, nuts and fruits, and illustrations of mammals and birds that frequent the reserve and surrounding area. These include margays, spider monkeys, green toucans, and hawks, among others. The most noted species, though, is the *quetzal*, the bird with iridescent red and bluish-green plumage, and an arc of tail feather several feet long, that is the national emblem of Guatemala.

The quetzal nests in the trunks of dead wild avocado trees at altitudes of from 900 to 3200 meters, and feeds on fruits and nuts. Courting takes place in February and March, and incubation of eggs in April and May — as good a time as there is to see the quetzal (though other lightly inhabited, less accessible ridges, such as that to the north of the Polochic Valley, are better for spotting the bird than this reserve). *Quetzal* habitat, once estimated to cover 30,000 square kilometers in Guatemala, is now at about a thousand square kilometers, and still falling as forests are cleared for corn plots.

Take a look at the map of the reserve, and pick up a guide folder (currently only in Spanish), before you set out on your walk. *Musgos* ("mosses") trail leads from the reception center up and along the mountain face, then back down to the highway. *Helechos* ("ferns") trail, branching from the main route, is a shortcut back to the starting point.

LANQUÍN

In the hot country of Alta Verapaz, near the Cahabón River, is **Lanquín**, a small and picturesque town of wooden and adobe houses and a colonial church, surrounded by mountains. Nearby are some of the natural wonders of Alta Verapaz.

ARRIVALS & DEPARTURES

A narrow, unpaved, rutted road descends through beautiful rainforest country to Lanquín, 63 kilometers from Cobán. Attempt to drive the route only in a vehicle with high clearance, and watch out for the surprisingly heavy traffic of trucks, which service the oil fields at Rubelsanto.

A bus leaves Cobán at about 6 am and gets to Lanquín at 1 pm. There is an early afternoon bus as well — check the day before you go at the station in Cobán. Two rather basic pensions provide rooms and meals for a couple of dollars each. A bus back to Cobán passes through town at about 8 am, or you can go on to Cahabón, from where buses operate to El Estor when the road is dry.

SEEING THE SIGHTS

The **Lanquín Caves** (**Grutas de Lanquín**), *within walking distance of town*, stretch for a couple of kilometers underground. Though not extensive by the standards of speleologists, the caves are fabled in Guatemala. Electric lights near the entrance will be turned on for a fee. (Inquire first at the municipalidad [town hall — they might have to rouse the attendant.) To go in beyond the lights, you'll need your own flashlight and spare batteries. The blue **Lanquín River** resurges from the caves, and provides some good swimming. You can camp at the cave entrance.

About nine kilometers from Lanquín, is **Semuc Champey**, a natural limestone bridge in the gorge of the **Cahabón River**, here the river plunges underground, to reappear several hundred meters downstream. Above the hidden river is a series of natural pools in every shade of blue, separated by rocks and hillocks carpeted in grass and bromeliads, linked by streams and falls rushing over rocks.

Semuc Champey is a natural water park, with clean water and currents for do-it-yourself water slides. But there are no lifeguards or safety measures. The rims are sharp, and a carless slide over boulders can result in injury. Watch out! Get an early start if you venture out this way, or take camping equipment.

To reach Semuc, take the road from Lanquín, and cross the bridge on the Cahabón River, then follow a trail off to the right for about 1500 meters. There's a shorter but more difficult up-and-down trail from another point on the road. Inquire locally.

WHERE TO STAY

HOTEL EL RECREO LANQUÍN CHAMPEY, *tel. 512160, has 25 rooms at $18 single/$24 double.*

PARQUE NACIONAL LACHÚA

Parque Nacional Lachúa (**Lachúa National Park**) lies ten kilometers east of Playa Grande in the northern part of the department of Alta Verapaz, near the state of Chiapas in Mexico, 418 kilometers by road from Guatemala City. Covering 100 square kilometers, it is an example of subtropical rain forest, much of which has been desroyed in the neighboring area in the course of resettlement and land-clearing. At the center of the park is Laguna Lachua.

Typical trees of the park include mahogany, breadnut, ceiba and San Juan. Wildlife species that may be sighted include raccoons and coatis, peccary, and tapirs. Frequently sighted birds include parrots, toucans and macaws.

Access to Lachúa is by cargo and pickup trucks from Cobán, or, more easily, by the road from Sayaxché, to the north, which is kept in better shape by petroleum companies. There's also a regular service by small plane from Cobán to the military airstrip at Playa Grande for under $20. The access road to the park branches from the main east-west road (transversal del norte) about seven kilometers east of Playa Grande. Rowboats and a basic **campsite** are available, and there is a trail running about four kilometers through the protected area.

DOWN THE POLOCHIC

The **Polochic River** valley was for many years Cobán's opening to the outside world. Until better roads were built in the last few decades, goods and people would move by road to **Papaljá**, board the trains of the **Verapaz Railroad** for **Panzós**, and continue by boat across **Lake Izabal** and down the **Río Dulce** to **Lívingston** and **Puerto Barrios**. The journey took a couple of days, and required an overnight stay in malaria-infested Panzós.

A road now leads all the way to Lake Izabal, ending at **El Estor**, which is no paradise, but which is where you'll have to spend the night before catching the ferry to **Mariscos** on the south shore. If you're driving, you will probably have to retrace your route, since the ferry doesn't carry cars, and the branch road to **Cahabón** isn't always passable. You might want to go only as far as the lowlands around **La Tinta** in order to appreciate the changing scenery as the road descends to near sea level, and then turn around.

The valley of the Polochic, except for El Estor, where a nickel mine opened and closed in the seventies, is pretty much a backwater area, passed by as transportation routes changed. Hardly an outsider comes through these days to take a look at what's going on. But the valley is an area of great natural beauty, from the narrow highland canyon, where the steep slopes that hem in the rushing river are covered with coffee plantations, to the great lowland plain, where the full river lazes through rice paddies and steaming pastures dotted with corozo palms.

ARRIVALS & DEPARTURES

Getting to El Estor from Cobán by bus is a seven-hour trip. All along the way, Indians going to market or work in valley towns get on and off. It's a measure of the isolation of this area that the driver speaks to them in their own languages, since few can speak more than a few words of Spanish.

Buses leave from the terminal lot in Cobán twice a day for El Estor (recently at 8 am and noon). If the trip seems long, you can take a bus to Tamahú or Tucurú (preferably on a market day) and wander around for a while until the bus for El Estor comes along, or else wait for a return bus to Cobán or Tactic.

If you're up to hiking, the highland part of the valley is a beautiful area for walking and bird watching. Follow the road from Tamahú or Tucurú for a while, or the river, then flag down a bus. Buses usually stop in La Tinta or Telemán long enough for passengers to catch a meal (the Indian passengers usually remain on board and wait patiently while the driver eats), but the food isn't very good in any of the small diners. You'd do better to pack some snacks.

THE PETÉN

Guatemala's last frontier was the **Petén**, the vast and sparsely settled department covering the northern third of the country. Thousands of years ago, the Maya settled the area. They burned away jungle to plant patches of corn, traded by way of rivers and laboriously constructed roads, and built great ceremonial cities that endured for centuries. They abandoned the Petén for unknown reasons, though a later group of Toltec-Maya immigrants from the Yucatán settled near Lake Petén Itzá and remained unconquered by the Spanish until 1697. After the Petén was nominally brought under Spanish control, only a few scattered settlements were established in the wilderness.

The Petén is an area of dense hardwood forests and dry jungle, of grassy savannas and small hills and valleys, dotted with lakes and seasonal swamps, cut here and there by rivers draining into the Gulf of Mexico and the Caribbean. In the southeast part of the department, the **Maya Mountains** rise to 500 meters, but most of the land is much lower. Thick layers of underlying sedimentary rock give evidence that much of the Petén was covered by the sea 200 million years ago, then slowly emerged and eroded into its present form.

Until relatively recently, about the only product that came out of the Petén was chicle, the raw material for chewing gum, bled from chicozapote trees in the forests of the north by a rough-and-tumble breed of workers, and shipped out by plane. There were no roads running into the area from the rest of Guatemala, and so the forests remained unspoiled refuges for birds, wild boars and dogs, jaguars, and other animals that had disappeared long ago from the settled parts of the country.

Today, the face of the Petén has changed. Thousands of people from the crowded and overworked lands of the south have moved to the virgin lands of the north. Forests are cut and burned off to create new farmland, simple pole-and-thatch houses are quickly erected, and whole communities spring up where maps still show empty land. In the last twenty years, population has soared from 65,000 to 300,000.

Buses from Guatemala City to Flores can take forever, and sometimes longer. The run is scheduled for 12 hours, but muddy roads, breakdowns and rest stops often extend the trip into an ordeal of up to 20 hours. The buses are usually crowded, and the trip in most parts isn't as visually interesting as one might expect, since there's little unspoiled forest along the road, and slash-and-burn agriculture soon becomes boring.

FLORES, SANTA ELENA, & SAN BENITO

The island city of **Flores**, founded in 1700, is the successor to the last stronghold of the Maya. Centuries after Tikal and other cities of the Petén had been abandoned, some of the inhabitants of Chichén-Itza in the Yucatán migrated southward and founded **Tayasal** on an island in Lake Petén Itzá .

By the time the Spaniards moved into the area, the old Mayan causeways had long been covered with jungle growth. Though the building of a road through the Petén to Belize remained a dream for many years, nothing was done about it, and Flores — known in colonial times as Remedios—and the towns of the area remained isolated outposts, subsisting on corn-and-bean agriculture, cattle grazing, and sugarcane farms. By the end of the last century, virtually the only important economic activity was the bleeding of chicle from trees in the jungle.

With the opening of the Petén, first by airplane and later by highway, the area around Flores has boomed. Most of the growth has been in Santa Elena and San Benito, opposite Flores on the mainland. Flores itself sits on a small island, with no room for expansion. It remains a charming and quiet old place, with only a bit of dust kicked up now and then by vehicles traveling the road around its rim.

ARRIVALS & DEPARTURES
By Air

All scheduled service to Flores is somewhat theoretical, subject to delay and cancellation. Plan accordingly — visit Tikal and the Petén early in your trip, rather than at the very end, when a delay might cause you to miss your flight home.

Round-trip fare between Guatemala City and Flores ranges between $100 and $125. But the competition is fierce, and discounts are often offered outside of peak periods. Rainy-season fares can be as low as $50 round-trip. And if you're a resident of Guatemala, or can convince the ticket sellers that you're a resident, you'll get a discount in any season.

Aviateca flies larger planes to Flores than those of other companies, usually Boeing 737s, at 7 am and 3 pm. Return flight to Guatemala City is at about 4 pm. The Aviateca schedule can be confirmed in the United States or Canada by phoning 800-327-9832. Or reserve at the Aviateca office in Guatemala City on 10 Calle at 6 Avenida A, Zone 1, tel. 38222, or 501337 in Flores). Note that though this flight is shorter than those of other companies, buses don't leave for Tikal until the other flights are in.

Other airlines, with similar fares and virtually identical departure times from Guatemala City are:

- **Aerovías**, *at the international terminal of the airport (tel. 345386 in Guatemala City, 500513 in Flores)*, with flights to Flores in 50-passenger propeller craft.
- **Línea Aérea Maya**, *international airport, tel. 347682*
- **Tapsa** *(tel. 314860, 500596 in Flores)*
- **Aviones Comerciales**, *Avenida Hincapié and Calle 18, Zone 13 (hangar 21, tel. 67946).*

Bus 20 from downtown Guatemala City serves the Aviones Comerciales hangar, Buses 2, 82 and 83 (or any bus marked terminal Aérea) go to the international terminal; but you'll probably take a taxi to make your early flight.

The airport for the Flores area is located about two kilometers east of the center of Santa Elena. Taxis run to town, or you can walk to one of the nearby hotels, or continue directly to Tikal (see below).

Belize & Mexico Connections

Island Air and **Tropic Air** have flying tours to Tikal from San Pedro (Ambergris Caye) and Belize City, when demand warrants. A tour bus meets the plane in Flores for the 40-mile ride to the Tikal archaeological site. Morning and afternoon visits to the ruins are included, along with lunch. Return to Belize City and San Pedro is by late afternoon. These trips operate daily with a minimum of four passengers.

Reserve at any travel agency, or call Island Air in Belize at 02-31140 or 026-2484 Tropic Air at 02-45671 or 026-2012. The price is about $200, or more if you book through certain travel agencies.

On several days of the week (currently Tuesday, Saturday and Sunday), the Aerovías flight from Guatemala City continues to Belize City, and returns in the afternoon. On Wednesday and Friday, continuing service is provided to Chetumal, in southern Mexico.

By Bus

For recent schedules and information about new routes, inquire at the Hotel San Juan on the main street in Santa Elena. The terminal for the Flores area is in Santa Elena, a couple of blocks south and east of the causeway.

Guatemala City to Flores: Fuente del Norte, 17 Calle 8-46, Zone 1, tel. 83894, has *servicio especial* buses (supposedly making fewer stops than others) departing for Flores 13 times a day, hourly from 1 am to 9 am, then every two hours until 11 pm. Travel time can be up to 13 hours, depending on weather, road conditions, road repair work, how much cargo has to be crammed on at villages along the way, military inspections, police inspections, traffic, etc. Book your seat the day before you travel.

Flores to Guatemala City: Buses depart the terminal in Santa Elena about every two hours from 1 am to 11 pm.

Buses to Poptún leave Santa Elena at 6 and 10 am, and 1 and 4 pm. Buses for Guatemala City also pass through Poptún.

For buses to Tikal, and remote border areas, see pages 412-413. Service is also available to other Petén towns (see town listings later in this chapter).

ORIENTATION

Even if there were no spectacular ruins accessible from the town, Flores would be a pleasant place in which to spend a vacation. The *cayucos* (dugouts with sides built up of planks) plying the surface of Lake Petén Itzá, the thickly forested surrounding hills, the tropical bird life, and a sense of remoteness all give the place a unique atmosphere.

Flores is located at a bend in the southwest corner of **Lake Petén-Itzá**, which covers 99 square kilometers (38 square miles) and is dotted with a number of smaller islands. The lake is a large depression filled with ground water, fed by a few small streams and emptied by underground seepage. The name Petén was applied by the Itzá Maya to the island where Tayasal was located. It was later used as a name for the lake and finally for the whole region.

For **swimming**, you can jump in the lake anywhere, though the water around Flores is encrusted with vegetation and is not too appetizing. Head for a spot away from the settled area, either on foot or in a canoe.

For the **best views** from Flores, walk up to the town square (in this case a circle) at the crest of the island. You'll be able to look down on the western end of the lake, and over to the low surrounding hills.

Until the causeway connecting Flores with Santa Elena was built, the only way to get to the island was in small *cayucos*. A commuter service of motorized cayucos still operates between Flores and San Benito. The fare is a few cents.

GETTING AROUND TOWN

Jeeps are rented by Koka Rentauto, Calzada Rodríguez Macal *at 1 Avenida B (tel. 501233)*, and at the **airport** *(tel. 500526)*; by Enrique Garrido, at the airport, and at the Hotel San Juan in Santa Elena. Rates are about $50 daily for a Jeep, subject to bargaining when things are slow. It's often a better bet to hire a taxi for the day. $35 to $40 will get a group of four a round trip to Tikal.

Travel Agencies

Travel agencies include **Tivoli Travel**, *4 Calle 0-43, Santa Elena, tel. and fax 500575*; and **Tropical Tours**, *2 Calle 6-80, Zone 1, Santa Elena*, around the corner from the Hotel del Patio, *tel. 500535, fax 500033.*

WHERE TO STAY

In Santa Elena

HOTEL TZIQUINAHA***, *tel. 501359 (20258 in Guatemala City). 36 rooms. $55 single/$65 double.*

Within walking distance of the airport (if you don't have much luggage), and a couple of kilometers from the center of Flores. There's no noise problem, since only a few planes land during the day. Air conditioning, pool, cable t.v., restaurant. Food not great.

JAGUAR INN, *Calzada Rodríguez Macal 879, tel. 500002. 18 rooms. $18 single/$25 double.*

A haven for travelers, new, cheery, built around a gardened courtyard. Comfortable rooms have ceiling fans and attractive woodwork, and are decorated with locally woven crafts. One of the owners speaks English, the other is English. Restaurant. Turn left just before the Texaco station as you approach from the airport. This street is less trafficked (and less dusty) than others in Santa Elena. Under the same management as the Jaguar Inn at Tikal.

HOTEL MAYA INTERNACIONAL**, *tel. 501276. In Guatemala City: 8 Calle 1-75, Zone 10, tel. 348136, fax 348134. 22 thatched cottages. $59 single/$66 double.*

Near the causeway to Flores — look for the large thatched dining pavilion. The units are currently reached by rickety walkways over the watery grounds. Well maintained. Jeep tours arranged.

HOTEL EL PATIO***, *tel. 501229, fax 501104 (tel. 371963, fax 374391 in Guatemala City, 800-327-3573 in the US). 22 rooms. $75 single/$82 double.*

Located back from the lake, near the Maya Internacional, on the road in from the airport. A substantial two-story colonial-style structure with archways around a relatively cool central courtyard. The neat, modern rooms have overhead fans and cable television.

HOTEL COSTA DEL SOL**, *Calzada Rodríguez Macal, tel. 500336 (530361 in Guatemala City). 29 rooms. $28 single/$35 double.*

A motel built around a large swimming pool along one of the main streets in Santa Elena — lots of dust can blow in, but the rooms are airconditioned and have cable television, the management is friendly, and the restaurant isn't bad. A good buy.

HOTEL SAN JUAN, *tel. 500041. $10 single/$12 double. On the main street of Santa Elena.*

Bare rooms with shared bath. So-so, but a good travel base, as buses for Tikal leave from the hotel.

In Flores

Hotels on the west side of the island, with a view to San Benito and some open water, are preferable to those on the south side, where you'll only see the causeway, and traffic kicking up dust in Santa Elena.

HOTEL PETÉN**, *tel. 501392. 21 rooms. $23 single/$28 double, less with shared bath.*

West side, in two buildings. The main building of this hotel is more pleasant than it appears from the street. Rooms are in tiers, some with good lake views.

HOTEL LA JUNGLA, *11 rooms. $12 single/$15 double.*

LA MESA DE LOS MAYAS (*tel. 501240, $23 single/$29 double*), one of Flores' old-line restaurants, has recently made several guest rooms available.

HOTEL CASONA DE LA ISLA, *north side, tel. 500692. 27 rooms. $24 single/$36 double.*

The newest hotel in Flores, with air-conditioned rooms, restaurant, parking. A good buy.

THE HOTEL ITZÁ, on the south side, is a dive: no soap, no towel, no customers, unless everything else is full.

In San Benito

San Benito, the red-light district of metropolitan Flores, is a hodge-podge of buildings strewn around a market. It's not the most pleasant place in which to stay, but there are a couple of dreary hotels with rooms for about $3 per person.

Outside Flores

HOTEL VILLA MAYA****, *tel. 500086. 28 rooms. In Guatemala City: 8 Calle 1-75, Zone 10, tel. 348136, fax 348134. $90 single/$98 double.*

Located beside little **Lake Petenchel**, surrounded by jungle and palms and forest and swamp eight kilometers east of Santa Elena on the way to Tikal, then another four kilometers north on a rough road. Villa Maya is currently in only partial operation. Rooms, in hillside jungle houses, have red-tiled floor, hardwood bed and built-in furniture, prints of toucans, and a small terrace facing the lake, as well as odd and interesting shapes. There are fans only to cool you off. The restaurant serves a basic menu of fish and beef dishes, and usually has tepezcuintle, and sometimes other game.

Monkeys, pheasants and assorted other wildlife are on the grounds, both caged and roaming free, or, in the case of multiple macaws, sitting on perches and watching you; and everything is as well manicured as it can be in a land of exuberance. All structures are roughly Mayan in design, but unmistakably modern — a metal palapa (pavilion), stone terraces, and a pool on several levels.

In El Remate

HOTEL CAMINO REAL-TIKAL*****, *tel. 500204, fax 500222 (800-327-3573 in the US, 334633 in Guatemala City). 72 rooms. $164 single/$175 double.*

On a hillside at the northeast corner of Lake Peten-Itzá, about three miles from El Remate and 31 kilometers from Flores, the Camino Real is the Petén's premier resort. There are no pretensions to roughing it — the rooms, in proto-Mayan buildings capped with thatched roofs have cable t.v., balcony and lake view. Windsurfers, mountain bikes, kayaks, canoes and sailboats are all available to guests, scuba diving can be arranged, the hotel has its own boat for lake trips, and there are a pool and meeting rooms. And then there's easy fishing for a species known locally as white snapper.

Despite the frills, the emphasis is on fitting in with the environment. A treatment plant keeps the lake water clean, and kitchen waste is recycled into an experimental farm and greenhouse where some of the hotel's produce is grown.

WHERE TO EAT

Elegant cooking is nearly unknown in the Petén, which is still largely a frontier area. Chicken is invariably rubbery, and your filet mignon will be something tough and unrecognizable. Don't let yourself in for disappointment by ordering something that local hands aren't up to preparing.

On the other hand, the Petén is now settled enough to have its own moyenne cuisine, based largely on such native game as *tepezcuintle* (paca, or gibnut in Belize), wild boar and turkey, and deer. I wouldn't pass up the chance to try these. At the **MESA DE LOS MAYAS** in Flores, you can enjoy a meal with local game that is not elegant, but wholesome, well-cooked, and reasonably priced at about $5. You're also safe with fish, beef on skewers, and Guatemalan-style steak in onions and tomatoes. This is an unpretentious place, with reed mats decorating the walls. There are simpler menus, without game, at the less attractive **RESTAURANT GRAN JAGUAR** and **LA JUNGLA**, both nearby in the center of Flores.

Otherwise, for predictable fare, you're probably better off to stick with the dining facilities of hotels, which better understand the requirements of visitors. The **JAGUAR INN** serves comprehensive dinners for about $5 to $7, including soup and dessert. The cafeteria at the **HOTEL SAN JUAN**, the base for buses to Tikal, is open at 6 am.

PRACTICAL INFORMATION

A post office and a branch of the **Banco de Guatemala** are located in the center of Flores. **Guatel**, the telephone company, is on the mainland in Santa Elena, about three blocks west of the causeway. Look for the microwave tower.

Travel Information

The **tourist office** is at the airport in Santa Elena.

The **Hotel San Juan** in Santa Elena is a good place to get recent travel information. Several bus lines are headquartered there, and air tickets are sold.

TIKAL

Tikal, greatest of all Classic Mayan cities, is northeast of Flores, towering above a dense jungle. In this remote area, one of the greatest civilizations of its time established a city that endured for centuries.

Tikal is a place for wondering, not only at the engineering accomplishments of the Maya, but at the jungle splendors of the Petén. The site of Tikal is a national park, one of the few accessible areas of the Petén that has not been taken over by agriculture, and where the native flora and fauna still flourish relatively undisturbed.

The park is dense with mahogany, chicozapote, cedar, ceiba and palm trees, and intertwining vines. Howler and spider monkeys swing in the treetops, snakes prowl, and foxes, coatimundis, pumas and wild turkeys roam the ground. The hundreds of bird species include toucans and macaws, easily visible for their size and bright colors, the harpy eagle, curassows, egrets, vultures, road runners, motmots, Montezuma's oropendolas, tinamous, and the oscillated turkey.

ARRIVALS & DEPARTURES

By Air

Tikal has an airstrip, but there is no direct service unless you charter a small plane in Guatemala City. Scheduled flights operate to Flores, 60 kilometers away by road. A bus from the Jungle Lodge meets all planes and charges about $5 per person for the trip to Tikal, or more if there are few passengers. Return buses leave Tikal in time to meet flights departing for the capital. You can also take a taxi for about $25, rent a car at the airport, or take local buses from Flores.

By Bus

There are daily buses and express microbuses from Flores to Tikal. Buses leave Tikal for Flores promptly at 6 am and 1 pm. The microbus leaves at about 3 pm, and you're assured of a seat only if you've booked from Flores. To travel to Belize, take the Flores bus from Tikal as far as El Cruce, and wait there for a bus to Melchor de Mencos on the Belize boundary.

By Car

From Flores, follow the road east to El Cruce (kilometer 29), then turn north for Tikal. Most rental-car companies do not let you take their vehicles overland from Guatemala City to Tikal. Jeeps can be rented in Flores.

PLANNING YOUR VISIT TO TIKAL

The ruins of Tikal are extensive, and you should allow two days to see them, if you have the time. You can fly to Flores one morning, take the bus up, and fly back to Guatemala City the next afternoon; or you can go back to Flores for the night, since overnight facilities at Tikal are limited.

An admission fee of about $6 is collected when you arrive at the park entrance, about 17 kilometers (10 miles) from the visitors' center of Tikal — and it might be higher by the time you reach the gate.

THE DEVELOPMENT OF TIKAL

As is the case with all Mayan sites, the origins of Tikal are only barely discernible. Findings of pottery dating from a few hundred years before Christ give evidence that the Tikal was inhabited at that time, perhaps by people who were attracted by the height of the site above surrounding swamps, and by deposits of flint, useful for making tools. No intact buildings have been found from the earliest periods of Tikal settlement, since the Maya were in the habit of destroying old structures in order to use the materials for new buildings.

By the time of Christ, the **Great Plaza** had already taken its basic form, with platforms and stairways constructed on the north side. Over the next few hundred years, the city grew in extent and height, as old buildings were razed or covered over with new ones, and tombs set into the plaza floor. The corbeled arch came into use, as did new-style pottery vessels painted in three or more colors. Similarities in artistic styles, tools and materials suggest that the pre-Classic Maya of Tikal were in contact with other peoples of Mesoamerica.

Tikal's Golden Age

The Classic era of the flourishing of Tikal lasted from about 300 to 900 A.D., more or less the time when Copán and Palenque were also at their heights. In addition to raising their temples to ever greater heights, the Maya of Tikal worked changes on the landscape. Ravines were dammed to form reservoirs for seasonal rains. Causeways were built to connect different parts of the city, and to provide trade routes to other Mayan centers. Trade developed with far-away peoples who could provide jadeite, obsidian and other useful raw materials.

Some sort of residential city grew around Tikal, though its nature is a matter of debate. The great buildings in the center are assumed to have been temples and palaces for religious purposes, though they might also have been residences for the noble classes. Scattered for more than four kilometers in every direction from the center of Tikal are thousands of platforms that might have been the foundations of houses of stone and wood.

As many as 50,000 people lived in Tikal and its hinterland, perhaps many, many more. Estimates of the population depend on interpretations of how many people would have lived in one house, whether all houses were occupied at one time, and, perhaps most importantly, on how much food could have been produced in the surrounding area.

The most visible evidence of a large population, a bountiful agriculture, and a highly developed social organization, is, of course, the very magnitude of Tikal. Many laborers had to work over long years to carry the rock and rubble needed to fill the bases of temples. While the fill was being set in place, masons had to build retaining walls, and later to face structures with carefully cut blocks. Meanwhile, lime mortar had to be made by burning limestone, a process that required the cutting of immense quantities of wood. All this had to be done with brute human labor, for the Maya did not know the use of the wheel, nor of iron, nor did they have beasts of burden.

While all this hard labor was going on, artisans were at work scraping away at limestone to form the low-relief sculptures of stelae, and incising designs into beams of *chicozapote*. This wood, carved when fresh and soft, takes on an iron hardness when exposed to air. The original temple lintels of Tikal, the finest examples of Mayan wood carving, have endured the jungle climate for centuries.

Additional workers had to patch up fallen bits of plaster, replace missing blocks of limestone, keep the temples painted, plaster over plaza floors worn with use, and maintain the reservoirs. Artisans created jewelry and beautiful pottery vessels with painted scenes of daily life, and jadeite jewelry and mosaics of shells and stones for personal decoration and as funerary offerings. Priests had to preside over human sacrifices, the victims of which might have been secured in raids on neighboring peoples (if one is to believe recent interpretations of scenes depicted on some Classic Mayan pottery vessels). Other priests and officials had to supervise matters ranging from ball games to the administration of justice to the calculation of the calendar.

All the people who were tending to the organized activities of civilization in Tikal could hardly have devoted much time to growing food. So in addition to the workers and nobility of the town, there must have existed a large class of farmers. Mayan agronomy was in many respects more advanced than that of modern tropical farmers. The Maya of Tikal took seemingly dreadful jungle swamps, with their store of water, and reworked them into resources that supported large population centers. Drainage canals were dug, and dirt piled up to create raised planting beds. Cassava, yams, corn and ramon nuts could have provided a complete and varied diet, along with wild game.

Today, one can sit atop a pyramid, gaze at the Great Plaza and roof combs rising up from the sea of jungle, and imagine the times more than a thousand years ago when the plaza was alive with activity and the city was surrounded by cultivated fields dotted with houses. But one can do little more than imagine. There is no coherent history of Tikal and there may never be one. Bits and pieces of information are picked up from drawings on pottery and bone, finds of tools, similarities in artistic styles between Tikal and other Mayan and non-Mayan centers, and the few glyphs that have been deciphered up to now. Written dates on stelae at Tikal range from the fourth century A.D. to 869 A.D., which is thought to have been the period during which civilization in the city reached its greatest development.

Tikal's Decline

Some short time after the last stela was erected, Tikal entered a period of rapid decline. Buildings were left unfinished, and population decreased dramatically. A number of possible explanations have been proposed: exhaustion of the land, drought, disease, revolution, invasion, perhaps the coming of a prophet who led his people back into the jungle. It's all a matter of speculation. Whatever happened at Tikal might have occurred at Copán and Palenque as well, for those cities began to decline at the same time.

After the fall of civilization at Tikal, the city was inhabited intermittently, but there was never the kind of highly organized social system that characterized Tikal at its height. Tombs were occasionally looted, monuments were moved, and buildings were left to decay. Trees took root among the temples, their roots holding the stone and plaster together, and the stelae were covered over with moss.

Archaeological Excavations

The first systematic exploration of Tikal was carried out by Modesto Méndez and Ambrosio Tut, officials of the government of the Petén, in 1848. The report of Méndez awakened European interest in Tikal. A Swiss scientist showed up and carried off some of the temple lintels, and Alfred Maudslay arrived from England in 1881 to start clearing and photographing the ruins. Over the next fifty years, exploration was carried out by archaeologists sponsored by the Peabody Museum of Harvard University and the Carnegie Institution of Washington. From 1956 to 1969, the University Museum of the University of Pennsylvania undertook a massive excavation and reconstruction project in cooperation with the government of Guatemala. Work at the site is now supervised by the Institute of Anthropology and History of Guatemala.

Tikal consists of thousands of constructions ranging from temples on pyramid bases to palaces to ball courts to tombs and burial chambers to stelae. Many of the structures remain in the form of mounds into which they collapsed during centuries of abandonment of the site, and many others lie buried under later buildings. Most of the restored and partially restored structures date from the Late Classic Period, which lasted from about 550 A.D. to 900 A.D. The major monuments are in clusters, some in the vicinity of the Great Plaza, others in outlying areas reached by following causeways built by the Maya.

WHERE TO STAY

JUNGLE LODGE**, *32 rooms, tel. 501519 in Flores. $70 single/$82 double, less with shared bath. In Guatemala City: 29 Calle 18-01, Zona 12, tel. 768775, fax 760294.*

Modern cottage rooms, airy and light, whitewashed inside, each with two double beds, tiled shower, marble vanities, closet, pastel bedspreads, ceiling fan, porch . . . all in all, quite unexpected. The large lobby-dining room, screened and open to jungle sounds, is a pleasant gathering area, though food offerings are quite limited. Electricity is available only a few hours a day. And the rate, considering the lack of amenities, can be a sore point.

THE TIKAL INN**, *$100 double with dinner and breakfast, or $75 for two without meals in bungalows, less in hotel rooms.* Also much improved. The hotel is concrete and airy, and a thatched roof and wicker furnishings provide a pleasant environment. The best feature is the swimming pool.

THE JAGUAR INN has just two room*s, which go for about $35 double with meals, and two safari-style tents with night tables, mattresses, and electric lights, available at about $15 double. Call 500002 in Santa Elena (Flores) to reserve space.* Transport can be arranged from Santa Elena/Flores, where the owners operate a larger lodging place under the same name.

Camping

There's an ample grassy campsite right at the entrance to the visitors' reception area, with running water, shower and toilets, open thatched shelters, and plenty of room for vehicle parking. The charge is about $6 per night (an unofficial and variable arrangement). The diners nearby rent hammocks and mosquito nets for a couple of dollars a night, with a deposit required. A blanket will be useful in the dry season (December through May) since it can get surprisingly cold at night. Mosquito repellent will come in handy in the rainy season. There are fireplaces for cooking, and plenty of firewood is available for gathering. Campers should note that dogs are not allowed into the national park.

Try to choose your spot as soon as you arrive. Conditions at the campsite are a great improvement over those just a few years ago, when you had to fetch water from a crocodile-infested pond. The crocodiles are gone now, but so, unfortunately, are a couple of workers.

WHERE TO EAT

At the **JAGUAR INN**, on the north side of the airstrip, meals are served in a pleasant and cool thatch-roofed pavilion. The food is as good as you'll find in Tikal. Breakfast costs about $3, lunch or dinner $5, and there are sandwiches, vegetarian dishes, and an a la carte menu more varied than you'd expect way out here. They'll also pack a picnic. The Jungle Lodge serves meals, at slightly higher prices in its cool and pleasant dining area, but offerings are limited.

The restaurant at the visitors' center, has an ambitious menu, with a few non-jungle main courses, such as pepper steak and fettucine, at $6 and up, though you should not expect the food to live up to its description.

South of the airstrip are a couple of inexpensive diners.

PRACTICAL INFORMATION

Facilities at the Tikal reception area include a temple-style **visitors' center**, holding a mock-up of the ruins, an exhibit of some stelae, and a restaurant (see above). There's also a **post office**, the **museum**, and a jungle **nature trail**. And if you spend any time around the visitors' area, ask for directions to the treehouse. That's all.

THE MUSEUM

The **Tikal Museum**, located just north of the airstrip, contains a collection of some of the artifacts discovered during excavations at the ruins. Most interesting is a reconstructed tomb complete with skeleton and offerings of jadeite jewelry and pottery. A number of rubbings on rice paper show the designs of stelae more clearly than does a direct glance at the sculpture in daylight.

The museum is open from 9 am to 5 pm, weekends to 4 pm. Other stelae are housed in the visitors' center. An additional entrance fee is collected, higher for foreigners than for Guatemalans, but nominal nevertheless.

NATURE TRAIL

The **Camino Interpretativo El Caoba** (*Mahogany Interpretive Trail*), which starts by the Jaguar Inn, is still being developed. It passes through a chicle-gatherers' camp. This is a chapter of the Petén's history that has just recently closed, with the substitution of ingredients in the manufacture of chewing gum. Take a walk of an hour or two, depending on your interest and condition.

TOURING THE RUINS

Before You Start Out

Wear light cotton clothing and a hat when you go out to the ruins. The sun is usually strong, though you can escape it for a while by ducking under a tree or into a temple. Carry some fruit or a canteen of water, or both. Bottled sodas are sold at various sites in the ruins, but no food. The Jaguar Inn will pack a box lunch if you've come without a hamper. Wear shoes with non-slip soles for climbing temples. Getting up the long flights of steps is no problem, but if you've got a fear of heights, getting down can be hairy. A flashlight will be useful for looking into temples and underground chambers.

Hours

The site is open from 6 am to 6 pm, though the guards start to clear visitors out at 5 pm. You can get into the ruins during the full moon if you request permission at the *inspectoría*, a little building beside the trail from the airstrip.

THE ANCIENT CITY OF TIKAL

The **Great Plaza**, dominated by **Temples I and II**, sits on an artificially leveled tongue of land between two ravines, at the center of Tikal. The grassy plaza was originally covered over with lime mortar, which was renewed every few centuries.

Temple I

Temple I, also called the **Temple of the Giant Jaguar**, rises 44.2 meters (145 feet) over the east side of the plaza. The base is formed of nine terraces with sloping sides, supporting a platform on which sits a three-room temple building. (Note that the standard descriptive terms are somewhat confusing. The word "temple" refers both to the entire construction, including the great rubble-filled base, and to the relatively small superstructure.)

The crowning roof comb appears to have been mainly decorative. Roof combs were hollowed out to lighten their weight, and faced with carved limestone blocks. The eroded figure of a seated person can barely

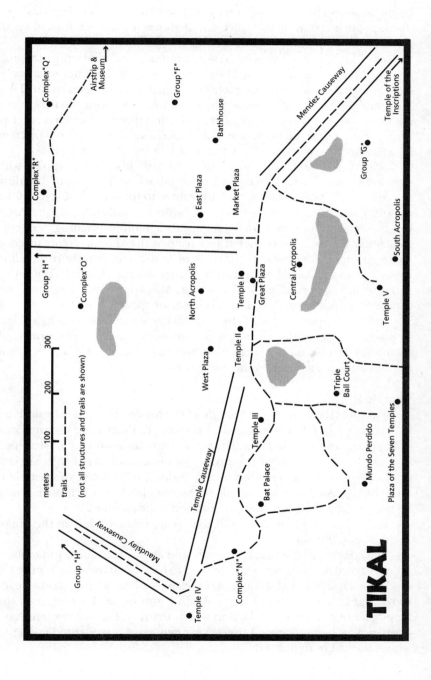

TIKAL

meters

100 200 300

trails

(not all structures and trails are shown)

be made out on the comb of Temple I. The stairway now visible was used during construction. It was once covered over by a more formal set of steps.

The Maya built temples by creating mountains and placing molehills on top. At the base of Temple I (and under most of the other temples) is a great burial vault, a reconstruction of which may be seen in the Tikal Museum. The body of a noble was placed on a masonry bench in the chamber, along with offerings of ceramics and pieces of jewelry. Inscriptions indicate that the noble was called *Ah Cacau* (Lord Cacao), and that he ascended to power in 682 A.D. and ruled for almost fifty years.

A corbeled arch was built above his chamber and capped with wooden beams, after which began the laborious process of building retaining walls, filling the spaces with rubble to form the first layer of the pyramid base, then building successive layers to the desired height. After the artificial mountain had been raised, a temple building was constructed at the top. The corbeled arch used by the Maya to create interior space in temples consisted of layers of stone successively protruding inward, until they could be capped by a single block. This arch could span only a narrow width, so massive Mayan structures contain claustrophobically small amounts of interior space.

Inside Temple I, some of the original carved wooden beams are still in place. Lintels at the entrances to temples were left undecorated. A secondary burial, dating from after the completion of Temple I, was found beneath the floor of the rear room.

Temple II

Temple II, known as the **Temple of the Masks** for the decorations on its stairway, reaches a height of 38.1 meters (125 feet) over the west side of the plaza. With its roof comb intact, it might have stood almost as high as Temple I. The walls of the inside rooms are scribbled with ancient graffiti. No tomb has yet been found under the base, but the temple is thought by some to honor the wife of the ruler buried in Temple I. It may be her portrait that decorates an interior wooden lintel.

Both Temple I and Temple II date from relatively late in the life of Tikal, about 700 A.D.

Placed around the plaza are stelae and associated altars, some plain, others carved in low relief. Many appear to have been moved after the fall of Classic civilization at Tikal. Later stelae (the date glyphs can be read) were larger and sculptured more skillfully out of harder rock than the limestone of the earlier stelae, on which many of the inscriptions have worn away. The portraits on the stelae might have represented nobles to whom they were dedicated.

The North Acropolis

The North Acropolis, fronting on the north side of the Great Plaza, is one of the most heavily constructed areas of Tikal. Hidden under the visible structures are many superimposed earlier buildings.

Excavations in **Structure 5D-34** revealed a tomb cut into the bedrock deep below, containing the skeletons of a noble and his retainers, along with turtles, a crocodile, and pottery. In **Structure 5D-33**, facing the plaza, a number of layers of construction are visible. Here, the outer layer has been removed on the left side, revealing a great "mask" (large facial medallion) decorating one of the earlier buildings. On the right side, a matching mask may be seen by entering an excavation in the intact outer structure. Still another temple base covered the outer structure seen today, but was so badly eroded that most of it was stripped away during the reconstruction of the North Acropolis.

Stela 31, now in the Tikal museum, was found buried in the second-layer building. One of the most beautiful of the early stelae at Tikal, it was defaced prior to the building of the now-destroyed outermost temple. Paradoxically, burial in rubble preserved it from further damage. Pictured on it is a ruling noble whose name glyph has been read as Stormy Sky. This may be the person whose mutilated skeleton was found in a tomb under the structure.

Some archaeologists now believe that the Sky family were hereditary rulers of Tikal. Glyphs on another tomb in the North Acropolis identify an earlier ruler of Tikal called *Curl Nose*, who might have come from Kaminaljuyú.

South of Tempe I is a small ball court. Scenes painted on pottery suggest that players hit the ball with padded knees and hips. South of Temple II, another pyramid contains no ruins on top, suggesting that it might have been capped with a perishable thatched structure. Excavations in the plaza floor southeast of the stairway of Temple II have revealed *chultuns*, chambers carved in bedrock and filled with what appears to be trash. Many of these chambers have been found, though their original use remains unknown.

The Central Acropolis

Adjoining the south side of the Great Plaza is the complex of buildings known as the **Central Acropolis**. The buildings here are called palaces, not because they were royal residences — nobody knows what they were used for — but to distinguish them from the temples and pyramids elsewhere around the Great Plaza. The palaces are relatively long, low buildings surrounding small plazas, or courts, on different levels. Many are unrestored.

The palaces were constructed at different times, sometimes on top of older buildings. Alterations went on after construction was completed, with the addition of doorways, second stories, and outside stairways. The interior rooms have benches, which might have been used for seating or as sleeping platforms. The palaces are multi-story structures only in a primitive sense, since the upper floors are set back and supported mainly by a layer of rubble fill behind the rooms of the lower floors. Only one of the palaces, fronting on Court 6, has an interior staircase. Many of the palace facades were decorated with low-relief friezes, only a few of which survive intact.

The Palace Reservoir

The Palace Reservoir, just south of the Central Acropolis, was created by damming a ravine and sealing the porous limestone with clay. Nearby terraces were sloped so that water would drain into the reservoir.

Along the eastern end of the northern base of the Central Acropolis is the Late Classic **Structure 5D-43**, a platform supporting a two-room building. The rectangular molding on the base, and the sections jutting out above and below the molding, are similar to architectural features at Teotihuacán in Central Mexico, indicating a possible flow of architectural influence from that site, or from Kaminaljuyú, a Teotihuacán outpost in present-day Guatemala City.

North of Structure 5D-43 is the open area known as the East Plaza. On its east side is a ball court, beside which is a quadrangle of buildings called the Market Place. Farther to the east is a large, rubble-filled platform which might be the foundation of a temple left uncompleted. On the east rim of the platform is a building believed to have been a steam bath, with a low doorway and an inside firepit. Temple 4D-38, to the southeast of the plaza at the entrance to the Méndez Causeway, is notable for the cache of human skulls discovered under the base of a stairway, which suggests that human sacrifice was practiced at Tikal.

West Plaza & Tozzer Causeway

The **West Plaza**, to the northwest of Temple II, includes a large palace on the north side, an unfinished temple covering a tomb on the west side, and a number of stelae, which might have been moved from their original positions after the fall of Classic civilization at Tikal.

Leading west from the West Plaza is the **Tozzer Causeway**. The causeways at Tikal were wide, raised roads paved with mortar. Most are now named for archaeologists. A foot trail winds among the buildings to the south of the Tozzer Causeway.

Temple III & Complex N

Temple III, 54.9 meters (180 feet) high, is also known as the **Temple**

of the Jaguar Priest, after the figure on an interior lintel of a fat man in a jaguar skin. A stela at the base of the stairway contains a date glyph equivalent to 810 A.D., indicating that Temple III was probably built in Late Classic times. Near Temple III is the **Bat Palace**, or **Window Palace** (so called for the unusual window openings on one side), another Late Classic structure, the second story of which fell down long ago.

Beyond Temple III is **Twin-Pyramid Complex N**, a set of structures of a kind peculiar to Tikal and Yaxjá. Two identical flat-topped pyramids with stairways on each side face each other across a plaza. A row of uncarved stelae and altars stands in front of the east pyramid. Off to the side is an enclosure containing a stela and altar. In the case of Complex N, these are among the finest examples of stone sculpture at Tikal. Complex N is dated 711 A.D. Dates on stelae in similar complexes elsewhere in Tikal indicate that such complexes were erected every twenty years.

Temple IV

Temple IV, at the end of the Tozzer Causeway, is the tallest known structure in the Mayan world, with a height of 64.6 meters (212 feet). It might also have been the tallest structure in pre-Columbian America, depending on whether one takes into account the base platform. The top is reached by a difficult trail (the stairway is gone), and affords spectacular views of the other temples. The three-room temple at the top contained two exquisite lintels, which were carried off to Switzerland. Impressions of the carvings on the top sides of the beams may be seen in the interior doorways. Glyphs on the lintels date Temple IV at 741 A.D.

Other Sites Near Temple IV

From Temple IV, a trail follows the **Maudslay Causeway** through the jungle to the northeast, ending at **Group H**, which includes two twin-pyramid complexes. The first, **Complex M**, was partially destroyed, possibly when the causeway was built. Complex P includes some relatively large rooms, the walls of which are covered with ancient Mayan graffiti.

The **Maler Causeway**, with a footpath down its center, runs from Group H back to the East Plaza. Midway is a set of twin-pyramid complexes. **Complex Q**, the easternmost of the group, is the only twin-pyramid complex to have been partially restored.

Back to the center of Tikal. From the East Plaza, the **Méndez Causeway** runs to the southeast, passing **Group G**, a complex of palace-type buildings, the walls of which are scribbled with graffiti. At the end of the causeway, about a twenty-minute walk from the East Plaza, is the **Temple of the Inscriptions**, named for the many glyphs on the roof comb and on the temple trim.

South of the Central Acropolis lies the **Plaza of the Seven Temples**, reached most easily by a trail running south from Temple III. This group is named for a series of temples in a north-south row. The central one features decorations of crossed bones and a skull. On the north side of the plaza is the **Triple Ball Court**, an unusual series of parallel playing areas.

To the west of the Plaza of the Seven Temples is the area recently re-christened **Mundo Perdido** (*Lost World*), which is only now being explored intensively by archaeologists. The **Great Pyramid (Structure 5C-54)** rises 32 meters (105 feet) above the Lower Plaza. It consists of five superimposed pyramids constructed between 700 B.C. and 250 A.D., the last at the end of the pre-Classic period. Stairways ascend on each side of the outermost, visible layer. Two mascarones (masks, or facial sculptures), of the original 16, survive on the western side of the pyramid, and are sheltered by thatched roofs.

Temple V

Beyond the Plaza of the Seven Temples to the east is **Temple V**, last of the great pyramid temples of Tikal, 57.9 meters (190 feet) high. Unusual features include a stairway finished with moldings along the edges, rounded corners on the base and superstructure, and an interior room small even for a Mayan structure.

After a look at Temple V, you can continue with explorations of the outskirts of Tikal, if you wish. From the southwest corner of the Mundo Perdido complex, follow a trail down steps and over a stick bridge, and 300 meters onward to a recent excavation site. You can enter a thatch-covered trench to inspect several large stone sculptures of faces. The trail continues back to Group G. If you search around, you may find other such little-visited areas on the periphery of Tikal where you can see restoration work in progress.

LAKE YAXJÁ

At kilometer 61 on the road from Flores toward Belize, a branch road leads north for eight kilometers to the twin lakes called **Yaxjá** and **Sacnab**. On the north shore of Lake Yaxjá are the **Yaxjá ruins**, unusual among Mayan sites in that small sections appear to have a grid street pattern. Other ruins, on Topoxte Island near the south shore of the lake, show elements of the Yucatán Maya style, indicating that a migration from the north to this area might have taken place after Classic civilization in the Petén had come to an end.

A jeep trail, passable in the dry season, leads from the end of the branch road to the Yaxjá ruins. Or try to hire a boat at the village at the end of the branch road in order to reach Yaxjá and Topoxte Island. The lake is a pleasant place to stop if you're traveling in a camper.

WHERE TO STAY

CAMPAMENTO EL SOMBRERO, alongside Lake Yaxjá, offers campsites and cottage rooms as part of a package that includes pickup at the airport in Flores, and visits to Nakum and one or two other ancient sites rarely seen by outsiders. Stay longer, and you can arrange to ride horseback to Tikal, along trails once used by rough-and-ready chicle gatherers, and now reverting to jungle.

For information, call 505553, or 314051 in Guatemala City.

THE MAYA BIOSPHERE RESERVE

Formed in 1990, the Maya Biosphere Reserve is one of 273 such conservation areas around the world, intended as a storehouse of natural wealth for all mankind. Covering about 1.5 million hectares, the Maya Biosphere includes:

• Tikal National Park, Río Azul National Park, Laguna National Park in the northwestern corner of Petén, Sierra del Lacandón National Park along the Usumacinta River, and El Mirador National Park.

• The protected areas, or "biotopos" of the Petén: Laguna del Tigre, Dos Lagunas, and El Zotz.

• A multiple-use area of sparsely settled lands. Sustainable use of the land is encouraged. Examples: gathering of nuts, spices and ferns.

• A buffer zone fifteen kilometers wide on the edge of the biosphere.

• Habitats that range from virtually untouched jungle to traditional chicle harvesting areas to wetlands to a part of the Maya Mountains.

Adjacent reserves in neighboring countries include Calakmul Bioshpere Reserve in Mexico, and the Orange Jungle in Belize – making up a total protected area of four to five million acres (official measurements are inconsistent).

Cutting of forest and settlement in parks and biotopes is prohibited or limited, at least in law and theory. In practice, logging, farming, chicle gathering, and the hunting and capture for export of endangered species continue out of view or beyond the control of responsible authorities.

6. PANAMA

HISTORY

The Post-Columbian era began with the arrival of **Rodriguo de Bastidas**, who discovered the Isthmus of Panama in 1501. The region was occupied by various Indian tribes at the time: the Cuna, Chocó, Guaymí, and many others. As with other Indian tribes who encountered foreigners, many succumbed to Spanish cruelty as well as the diseases they brought with them. The first Spanish settlement, Nombre de Dios, was founded at the mouth of the Río Chages by another explorer, Diego de Nicuesa.

Farther down the coast another settlement, Santa María la Antigua del Darién, was founded in 1510. It was shortly after this, in 1513, that **Vasco Nunez de Balboa**, searching for gold, 'discovered' the Pacific Ocean and claimed it for the King of Spain. In 1519, about 5 miles east of where it stands today, Balboa moved the city of Santa Maria across the isthmus to the Pacific side, renaming it **Panama** (abundance of fish). Because of its strategic position, Panama City became a crossroads of Spanish exploration and expansion into Central and South America. The ruins of the old settlement are still there, in **Panamá Viejo** (Old Panama).

Panama and Nombre de Dios became the two main ports on the Pacific and Caribbean coasts, connected by the Las Cruces Trail, until Nombre de Dios was destroyed by the English pirate **Francis Drake**. As a result, Portobelo and Fort San Lorenzo at the mouth of the Rio Chagres became the priority ports to the Caribbean. Gold from Peru and other colonial treasures were brought there along El Real Camino (the King's Highway). To protect their treasures from pirates, the Spanish built fortresses to ward off attack, which are still intact today.

In the end, even with the new fortresses, the Spanish were no match for the strength of the British ships. The English pirate **Henry Morgan** managed to penetrate the Spanish barrier and overpower Fort San Lorenzo. After which Morgan sailed up the Río de Chagres, then

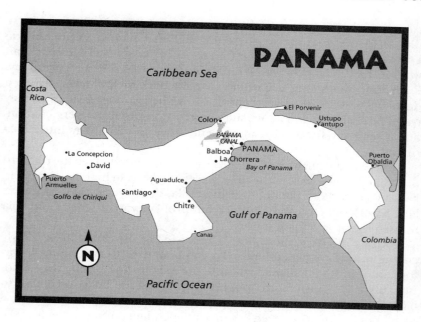

conquered and destroyed Panama. Not long after this attack, the city of Panama was rebuilt west of the original site on the land where it stands today. Soon after the attack on Panama, the Spanish were dealt another blow when Portobelo fell to the British Admiral Edward Vernon.

Accepting defeat, the Spanish began sailing around Cape Horn to transport their plunder and supplies. As Spain began to lose more and more vessels to piracy, they started to lose interest in Panama. As a result, Panama declined in importance and was absorbed into Nueva Granada, which later became Colombia.

In 1819, Venezuela and Colombia gained independence from Spain and joined Gran Colombia, which included Columbia, Venezuela, Ecuador, Peru and Bolivia. This confederation dissolved in 1830, but Panama still remained a part of Colombia.

About this time the major powers of the world once again became interested in Panama. They realized that Panama had the narrowest distance between the Atlantic and Pacific Oceans. Seizing the economic oppurtunity, the United States signed a treaty with Colombia in 1846 to build a railway across Panama, which included a provision allowing the US free transit and the right to protect the railway with military forces. During the five years it took to build the railroad, France and other nations began the planning stages for an inter-oceanic canal.

Building a canal was not a new idea, since in 1524 King Charles V of Spain ordered the first survey to be made. But it wasn't until 1878 that a contract to build such a canal was awarded to Lucien N. B. Wyse. Wyse then sold the contract to a French diplomat named **Ferdinand de Lesseps**. De Lesseps' *Compagnie Universelle du Canal Interocéanique* began work in 1880. The plan was to build the canal alongside the US railway. Everyhting was going according to plan until yellow fever struck a devasting blow to the project. The diseases killed workers faster than they could be replaced, and as a result construction problems were continuous. Eventually fiscal mismanagement drove the company into bankruptcy.

The French, unable to complete the canal, wanted to sell the rights to the United States who, at the time, were interested in building a canal in Nicaragua. In 1903 Phillipe Bunau-Varilla, de Lesseps' chief engineer, began work on a transfer contract, but problems arose when Colombia refused to enforce the transfer.

During this time, the political climate in Panama was shifting, slowly edging towards independence. To compound matters, Colombia was forcefully drafting Panamanians into the military and seizing their land. Bunau-Varilla, grasping the opportunity, asked the US government to back Panama if it claimed independence. With America's support, a revolutionary junta declared Panama independent on November 3, 1903. The US recognized the new government immediately. On November 18, 1903, a canal treaty was signed by Bunau-Varilla and US Secretary of State John Hay. The treaty gave the United States much more control than the original draft treaty rejected by the Colombians. Unfortunately, Bunau-Varilla did not consult with the newly independent government he represented when formulating the treaty.

Despite the problems with the treaty, the construction of the canal continued in 1904. Construction took ten years during which the project battled disease and frequent engineering difficulties. Today the project still remains as one of the greatest engineering feats of the 20th century.

Colombia finally recognized Panama in 1921, after the United States paid the Colombian government a small gratuity of 25 million dollars as compensation for its loss of land.

In 1936, the original treaty was replaced by the **Hull-Alfaro Treaty**. In this later treaty's stipulations, the US had no rights to intervene outside the Canal zone (8 miles on either side), no right to seize land on behalf of the Canal, and would increase its annual sum for canal use. Prior to this treaty the United States was able to intervene in Panamanian politics at will. As result of these new restrictions on the United States, the Panamanian military's power grew, and in 1968 the **Guardia Nacional** took control of the government, placing **General Omar Torrijos Herrera** as the new Panamanian leader.

General Torrijos plunged Panama into massive debt as a result of his public works programs and his modernization programs for Panama. But in 1977 he also negotiated a new **Canal Treaty** gradually phasing out US control over the Panama Canal, culminating in the eventual ownership transferance on December 31, 1999. At the same time another treaty was established ensuring that the canal shall remain open and neutral to all nations in times of peace and war. A year later the US Senate attached conditions to the Treaty allowing the United States limited intervention rights and the right to defend the canal beyond the 1999 deadline.

In 1981, Torrijos was killed in a plane crash and was succeeded first by Colonel Paredes and then by the now-infamous **Colonel Manuel Antonio Noriega Moreno Noriega**, former head of the Panamanian secret police and CIA operative, consolidated his leadership, enlarged the Guardia Nacional, censored the press, and created paramilitary squads who informed on those not completely loyal to the Noriega regime. In 1987 he was accused by the US Government of drug trafficking with the Colombian drug cartels, murdering opponents, and rigging elections.

In 1988, the US imposed economic sanctions on Panama, resulting in a popular revolt against Noriega. This was easily and violently suppressed. In 1989 free democratic elections were held in Panama, but Noriega declared them null and void when his candidate failed to win. Noriega's forces proceeded to physically beat the legitimate winner and his vice-presidential candidates on live televison – never a good idea – which resulted in another popular coup attempt which was again supressed by violence.

On December 15, 1989, the legislature that Noriega put in place declared him president and announced that Panama was at war with the United States. The next day an unarmed US Marine in civilian clothes was killed by Panamanian soldiers.

The United States reacted quickly by launching an attack on Panama City in **Operation Just Cause**. The mission was ordered by President George Bush to protect American lives, maintain the security of the Panama Canal, restore democracy to Panama, and to capture Noriega. On the fifth day of the invasion Noriega was found seeking asylum in the Vatican's Embassy. Pressure on the Vatican was great, and their ambassador convinced Noriega to give up by threatening to cancel his asylum. On January 3, 1990, he was flown to Miami and charged with multiple criminal charges. He remains in a US federal prison today.

Eventually, **Guillermo Endera**, the legitmate winner of the 1989 elections was sworn in as president, but still problems remain. The invasion had severely damaged parts of the city, leaving areas without water or electricity. Opinion is split in Panama City over the invasion; many are glad that Noriega is gone, but others question whether deomocracy is really taking root.

LAND & PEOPLE

Land

The Republic of Panama occupies the isthmus connecting the North and South American continents. The country is approximately the size of South Carolina. On the north it is bounded by the Caribbean Sea; on the south by the Pacific Ocean. To the east lies Colombia, and on the west Costa Rica.

Panama has two well defined regions: the **Atlantic Watershed** covered by tropical rain forest, and the **Pacific Watershed**, whose narrow valleys and coastal plains receive less rainfall. Mountain ranges form the backbone of the isthmus. Although there are some portions of this mountainous range with peaks of over 11,000 feet, the *cordillera* descends in the canal area to a height of only 290 feet.

Overall, Panama has a tropical climate. Rain falls sporadically throughout the dry season, which is January through April. The rainy season extends from May through December, with the heaviest rainfall between September and November. Temperatures vary only slightly during these seasons and throughout the country. During the rainy season the humidity is an average of 80%; in the dry season approximately 60%. The average temperature in Panama City is 80° F, with a maximum of 87° F and a minimum of 73° F. At night, you can look forward to constant breezes that give some relief from the heat.

Tropical rain forest is the dominant vegetation in the canal area, along the Caribbean coast, and in most of the eastern half of the country. Panama's position as a 'bridge' between the two continents has given it a variety of plant and animal life. The **Parque Nacional del Darien** protects one large tropical rain forest.

The **Panama Canal Commission**, in conjunction with a binational board of directors, operates the 43-mile canal that passes through the isthmus between the Atlantic (Caribbean) and Pacific Oceans. Under the Panama Canal Treaty of 1977, the Commission will remain a US Government Agency until December 31, 1999. At that point, the canal will be under the control of the Panamanian government but the "canal will remain neutral in times of peace and war for all nations." Spanish is the official language of Panama, but English is widely spoken.

People

The population of Panama is a little over 2 million. Most of these people live in three of Panama's nine provinces: **Panama**, **Colon**, and **Chiriqui**.

At the time of Columbus, more than 60 Indian tribes were living on the isthmus. Today Indians make up only 6% of the population. While the majority of these are **Cuna**, located on the northeastern Caribbean coast and the San Blas Islands, other groups include the **Guaymi** in western Panama and a small group of **Chocoe** Indians in the southeastern part of Darien Province.

Direct descendants of the Spaniards who colonized the country remain influential, but no longer dominate Panama's social, economic, and political life. Mixed-blooded Panamanians share prominent political and professional status with the Spanish-descendent group. Much of the population in Panama is a mix of Spanish-Indian and black-Hispanic ancestry. Immigrants from China, India, Europe, the Middle East and South and Central America can be found in the growing middle class of the country. Blacks of West Indian descent, whose ancestors provided much of the labor during the construction of the canal, tend to be concentrated in provinces of Panama and Colon. North American influence on Panama's Hispanic culture is also evident in Panama City and Colon. Combining the history and heritage of these distinct ethnic groups has formed the modern Panamanian way of life.

The interior provinces of Panama are ethnically more homogeneous. The Spanish-Indian mix is dominant and North American influence here is relatively minor.

PLANNING YOUR TRIP
GETTING TO PANAMA

Many call Panama *the* crossroads of the world: sea vessels from all over travel through the canal, travelers often pass through on their way to South or Central America, and Panama is also a major hub for air travel. When leaving Panama, if you are headed for Costa Rica, Colombia, or Venezuela, you'll need an onward or return ticket before you board a plane or cross the border.

By Air

The international airport **Omar Torrijos** is at **Tocumen**, northeast of the city center. **Copa** is Panama's national carrier. The major American cities that have connection flights to Panama are Miami, New York, Washington DC, Houston, Dallas and Los Angeles. A number of airlines connect Panama with all other Central American countries, South America, North America and the Caribbean.

Usually a ticket can be arranged with a free stopover in a variety of places; check with the airline you're flying. For example, Taca, the El Salvadoran airline, offers a free stopover in San Salvador.

Service from North America is provided by:
• **American**, *US 1-800-832-8383; Panama City (69-6022)*
• **Continental**, *US 1-800-231-0856; Panama City (63-9177)*

Service from Europe is provided by:
- **Iberia**, *US 1-800-772-4642; Panama City (27-3671)*
- **Aeroflot**, *US 1-800-429-4922; Panama City (25-0497)*

Service for Central and South America is provided by:
- **Copa**, *US 1-800-359-2672; Panama City (27-5000)*
- **Lacsa**, *US 1-800-225-2272; Panama City (25-0193)*
- **Taca**, *US 1-800-535-8780; Panama City (69-6066)*

By Boat

You would think that getting to and from Panama would be a snap by boat, but this is not the case. Most of the ships passing through are freight ships and do not take passengers.

By Bus

Most buses will take you to the Panamanian border at either Guabito or Paso Canoas. From there you can continue on to Coasta Rica by switching buses. There are also daily bus runs offered by **Tica-Bus** *(tel 62-6275)* between San Jose and Panama City and between San Jose and David. You must have an onward or return bus ticket if you are entering Panama or Costa Rica.

By Car

There are three border crossings between Panama and Costa Rica. Paso Canoas, on the Inter-American Highway (heading toward Panama City); Rio Sereno, which is usually not as busy; and the northernmost crossing at Guatibo. *The border crossing at Paso Canoas is open from 7 am to 10 pm (with a few hours off for lunch and dinner). The one at Guabito is open from 7 am to 5 pm (it also closes for a few hours at lunch time).*

The Panamanian government does not like foreigners selling cars in Panama, and the assumption is that you might want to do so, which means a hassle for you. There is a great deal of paperwork involved. I you want to take a vehicle between Central and South America, you will have to ship it around the **Darien Gap** (the highway reaches a dead-end at the Darien Gap). This can be very expensive, but the price of shipping on cargo boats is sometimes negotiable. Flights will ship cars as well. If you cannot stay with your vehicle at all times, don't be surprised if something is stolen from it. Detach all removables (hubcaps, windshield wipers, etc.), double lock everything, and keep everything out of sight. Campers are a special target, so lock up tight.

In addition, if you are planning on taking your car to South America you need a carnet de passage along with customs, shipping, and other paperwork. The carnet is a bond guaranteeing that you will not sell your vehicle in South America. This bond is partially refunded when you leave the continent and prove that you still have the vehicle. You can arrange a carnet with the **South American Explorers Club** *in Denver, Colorado 80218 (303) 320-0388).*

THE DARIEN GAP

There are two ways through the Darien Gap: travelers can take the northern coast via the San Blas archipelago and Puerto Obaldía, using boat services and involving minimum walking; or yoou can go through the jungle from Yaviza (Panama) to the Río Atrato in Colombia's Los Katios national park. You'll need to walk most of the way (a guide is suggested when taking this route, because drug traffickers use this route often and gringos are then suspected of running drugs or being DEA agents). Either of these routes should take you no longer than a week, but count on more, especially for the jungle route.

Remember, both Panama and Columbia require onward tickets (also check consulates for exit and entry stamps at the border towns: Sapzurro, Panama; Boca de Cupe, Panama). Save yourself some time and purchase these before your adventure across the border. Take dried food with you and plenty of water; this is a hot region making water a precious commodity. Be equipped to purify water if you need to.

ENTERING PANAMA

Most people who travel to Panama will need a visa or a tourist card, depending on your nationality: British, Spanish, Swiss and Germans do not need a visa or tourist card to stay up to 3 months and a return travel ticket. US and Canadian citizens need only a tourist card and a return ticket, but it is wise to check with the embassy to determine whether you need the visa or tourist card. If a visa is required a Panamanian embassy or consulate can issue one within 24 hours for approximately $15. In addition, upon entering the country travelers may be asked to show 'sustainability' at the point of entry (about $300).

To extend your stay in Panama, travelers need to go to the **Migracíon y Naturalizacíon** office in Panama City, David, Santiago, or Chitré. You will need two passport size photos, a letter stating your reasons for staying in the country, a return or onward plane ticket, and $11. You may be asked to present proof of solvency (bank book from home or bank statement).

If you do extend your trip in Panama, you must obtain a permit to leave (a *permiso de salida*). For this permit you need your passport and a *Paz y Salvo* form that you can get at the **Ministerio de Hacienda y Teroro**. It's a bit of a hassle but worth the trouble.

The United States has Panamanian consulates in Atlanta, Houston, Los Angeles, Miami, New Orleans, New York and San Fransico, along with the embassy in Washington DC. Panamanian missions in other countries include:

- **Australia**, *PO Box 276, Kenmore, Queensland 4069*
- **Belize**, *PO Box 7, Belmopan (tel 8-2504)*
- **Colombia**, *Calle 87, No 11A- 64, Bogota (257-5068)*
- **Costa Rica**, *del Higuerón de la Granja de San Pedro, 600 meters south & 25 meters east, Casa Esquinera, San José 1000 (tel 25-3401)*
- **El Salvador**, *21 Avenida Las Bugambilias, Colonia San Francisco, San Salvador (tel 98-0773)*
- **Guatemala**, *Vía 5, No 4-50, Zona 4, Edificio Maya, Guatemala City (tel 32-5001)*
- **Honduras**, *Colonia Palmira, 2nd Floor, opposite Hotel Honduras Maya, Tegucigalpa (tel 31-5441)*
- **Mexico**, *Campos Elyseos, No 111, Dept 1, Colonia Polcano, Mexico 5 DF (tel 250-4245)*
- **Nicaragua**, *Pancasán; from Hotel Colón, 1 block east, 4 blocks south & 1 1/ 2 blocks north, No 61, Managua (tel 72-202)*
- **UK**, *24 Tudor Court, London EC4Y (tel 071-3533 4792)*
- **US**, *2862 McGill Terrace NW, Washington DC 20008 (202) 483-1407)*

GETTING AROUND PANAMA

Getting around Panama is much easier than other Central American countries. The US presence has created a modern and well-structured transportation facility.

By Air

Panama has several domestic airlines leaving from La Paitilla airport:

- **Areoperlas** serving Panama City, Colon, David, Changuinola, Bocas del Toro, Isla Contadora and San Migual, *tel 69-4555*
- **Alas Chiricanes** serving Panama City, David, Changuinola and Bocas del Toro, *tel 64-6448*
- **Ansa** serving Panama City, David, Archipiélago de San Blas and Puerto Obaldiá, *tel 26-6881*
- **Chitréana de Aviación** serving Panama City and Chitré, *tel 26-4116*
- **Parsa** serving Panama City, and the Darien province (La Palma, Sambú, Garachine, El Real, Yaviza, Jaqué), *tel 26-3422*
- **Transpasa** serving Panama City and Archipiélago de San Blas: this airline also charters flights anywhere in the country, *tel 26-0932*

By Boat

Traveling in-country is fairly easy by boat, especially if you are traveling to the islands of San Blas and the Bocas del Toro island archipelagos. Boats leave from Panama City.

By Bus

The bus system serves all accessible areas in the country. Buses arrive and depart from the Interior bus station on Avenida Balboa. Buses servicing David, Chitré, and Los Santos depart hourly; buses to Las Tablas depart every two hours; and, buses to Darien once in the morning depending on the season.

By Car

There are many competitive car rental agencies in Panama City and in David. The average price is $30 per day, but this varies.
- **Avis Rent-a-Car**, *tel 64-0111*
- **Budget**, *tel 63-8474; (airport) tel 38-4069*
- **Discount**, *tel 23-6111*
- **National**, *tel 64-8277; (airport) tel 38-4144*
- **Hertz**, *tel 64-1729; (airport) tel 38-4081*

By Train

During the invasion of 1989 the train was destroyed.

Tourist Information

The **Instituto Panameño de Tourismo, IPAT**, has an information counter *at the Atlapa convenmtion center (tel 26-7000) and is open Monday through Friday, 8:30 am to 4:30 pm.* There is also an IPAT counter *at the international airport (tel 38-4322, ext. 311, open everyday, 8 am to 11 pm.* The offices give out free city and country maps and a tourist book on things to do. They also keep current listings on hotels and their prices, tours and boat schedules. There are IPAT offices also in Colón, Portobelo, David, Santiago and Chitré.

For more information on national parks and flora and fauna, contact Intrenare, the Instituto de Recuros Naturales Renovables, tel 32-4325, located outside of Panama City and/or Ancon, the **Asociación Nacional para la Conservación de la Naturaleza**, *tel 64-8343, located in Panama City.*

SPORTS & RECREATION

The best place for **scuba diving** and **snorkeling** in Panama is the **Bastimentos National Park**, near **Bocas del Toro**. This is the only park in the country that protects marine life. You can dive and snorkel off most islands, but the **Archipelago de San Blas** and **Isla Grande**, both on the Caribbean coast, are especially good areas. Check with the IPAT office for more snorkeling information.

Fishing is also popular in Panama (remember that Panama means *abundance of fish*). There are plenty of rivers, coastline, and islands that are good fishing grounds. Deep sea fishing is also possible in **Lago Gatún** on the Panama Canal and trout fishing running down the **Volcán Barú**, near the towns of Boquete, Volcán, Bambito and Cerro Punta.

Surfing beaches along the Pacific coast are pretty good. The two most popular are **Playa El Palmar**, near San Carlos (west of Panama City and easily accessible); and **Playa Venado**, on the south end of the Penísula de Azuero.

If you like to hike there are plenty of places to do so. From Boquete, you can hike to the top of **Volcán Barú**, Panama's highest peak. Near Panama City, on the shores of the canal, **Soberanía National Park** has a section of the old **Las Cruces trail** used by the Spanish to cross the isthmus – a great way to spend an afternoon.

The most famous walk of all is the hike through the **Darien Gap**. It's just you and the rainforest! You can only do this in the dry season.

The islands are plentiful here, more than 1600. Among the more interesting is the **Archipelago de San Blas**, with its traditional Cuna culture, the **Archipelago Bocas del Toro**, protected by the Bastimentos National Park, and the tiny **Isla Grande**, just off the coast the Caribbean near Portobelo. On the Pacific side there is the **Archipelago de Perlas** and the **Isla Taboga**. And don't overlook **Isla Barro Colorado**, in the Canal, which is a tropical rainforest research station run by the Smithsonian Institution.

BASIC INFORMATION

Here is some basic information about Panama:

BUSINESS HOURS

Business hours are normally Monday through Friday, 8 am to noon and 1:30 pm to 5 pm, and Saturday 8 am to noon. Government offices are open Monday through Friday from 8 am to 3–4 pm, without closing for lunch. Banks are open Monday through Friday, 8 am to 1 pm.

ELECTRICITY

Be wary of the electrical currents coming out of sockets. They may be either 110 or 220 volts, so doublecheck before plugging in.

HEALTH

Tap water is safe in almost every part of Panama, so eat what you want and load up on the ice cubes if you're so inclined.

Malaria is not a problem in Panama City, but travelers should check with their doctors about malaria medication. Anti-malaria medication is recommended if venturing outside the city. If traveling to the Darien region and the area of the San Blas islands, you should take extra precautions because there have been cases of Chloroquine-resistent malaria strains.

Panama is hot and tropical. Take care of your skin by wearing a wide-brimmed hat and slap on some extra sunblock! Don't forget to drink plenty of liquids; you can dehydrate quickly in the heat.

MONEY

Panama uses the US dollar as its currency. The official name for it is the Balboa, but it is exactly the same bill and in practice people use the term *dólar* and *Balboa* interchangeably.

Coins are made of the same value, size, and metal as US coins. Coins include 1, 5, 10, 25, and 50 *centavos*; there are 100 *centavos* to a Balboa.

NATIONAL HOLIDAYS

January 1	*New Year's Day*
January 9	*Martyrs' Day*
March-April	*Good Friday, Easter Sunday*
May 1	*Labor Day*
August 15	*Founding of Old Panama (Panama City only)*
October 12	*Hispanic Day*
November 1	*National Anthem Day*
November 2	*All Souls' Day*
November 3	*Independence Day*
November 10	*First Call for Independence*
November 28	*Independence from Spain*
December 8	*Mother's Day*
December 25	*Christmas Day*

In addition to the holidays listed above, there are a number of different celebrations and cultural events throughout the year, depending on the city or town. But by far the best celebration is **Carnaval**, the Panamanian version of Mardi Gras, held on the four days before Ash Wednesday. It is a major holiday in Panama and is celebrated with costumes, music, parades, dancing and general festivities. The final day, Shrove Tuesday, features a huge parade. The celebrations in Panama City and Las Tablas are by far the best and worth the extra effort to attend.

SAFETY

As with any city, there is crime in **Panama City**. Be smart and stay out of crummy areas, be alert in the cheaper parts of town, and don't flash anything unnecessary (jewels, fancy watches, and the like). **Colón** by far is the most dangerous city in the country. The poverty and general state of disrepair breeds thieves – even in the middle of the day.

SHOPPING

For many people, Panama provides the finest shopping south of Miami. The international atmosphere brings the selection and prices of everything from bond issues to boa constrictors, many at duty-free prices.

Panama's ethnic diversity also allows for a variety of traditional products including woodcravings, weaving and textiles, ceramics, masks, straw goods and many other handcrafts. Some of the more famous Panamanian goods are the colorful hand-stitched appliqué textiles made by the Cuna Indians called molas, and the pollera, the intricately stitched, lacy dress of the Península de Azuera.

TELEPHONE & MAIL

Intel is the national telephone service with offices throughout the country. The offices offer international telephone connections, telex, telegraph, fax, and sometimes modem services. In-country telephone calls can be made anywhere at phone boxes, which cost about 5 cents for 3 minutes.

The mail service in Panama is pretty reliable. Letters from Panama to the United States take about 5 to 6 days. If you want to receive mail address it to :

Name
Entrega General
Town & Province
República de Panamá

TIME

Panama is in the same time zone as New York and Miami. It is five hours behind Greenwich Mean Time and one hour behind the rest of Central America. If you're coming from Costa Rica, be sure to set your clock ahead an hour.

WEIGHTS & MEASURES

The official measure in Panama is the metric system, but the American system of pounds, gallons, miles is also used.

PANAMA CITY

Panama City is a thriving modern city with international banking, business, trade and transport. The city was originally founded in 1519 by **Pedro Arias Dávila**, not long after Balboa claimed the Pacific for the Spanish throne. The city soon became a crucial post for the Spanish empire, as the Pacific center for goods transported along **El Camino Real** (the royal highway) to the Caribbean. It also was the country's center for the government and church.

Panama's importance as a trading center made it a target for many British, Dutch, and French pirates that roamed the seas during this time. In 1671, the city was attacked and destroyed by English pirate Henry Morgan, leaving only the ruins of **Panama Viejo** that still stand today. The city was reestablished west of the original site (about 8 miles) on a small peninsula. This location made the city easier to defend and was never successfully attacked again (until 1989). In 1767, when the Spanish stopped using El Camino Real, Panama city lost its luster and declined in importance until the 1850's, when the Panama Railroad was completed. Gold rush prospects traveled through the country (and continued all the way up to California), revitalizing the city.

Panama was declared independent of Colombia on November 3, 1903, and Panama City became the capital of the new nation. Since the completion of the canal, Panama City has become an international hub of sorts.

ARRIVALS & DEPARTURES

See pages 665-667 for arrival and departure information.

ORIENTATION

Panama City runs about 10 km along the coast, from the Panama Canal at the western end to the ruins of Panama Veijo to the east. Near the Canal are the US Air Force Base, Fort Amador, and some wealthier suburbs occupied by US personnel and canal workers. The colonial part of the city, called **San Felipe** or **Casco Viejo**, is on the western side of town jutting out into the sea.

From Casco Viejo two major roads run east, **Avenida Central**, running past the Cathedral in San Felipe to Plaza 5 de Mayo, and **Via Espana** which branches off Avenida Central bringing you into the buisness and finance district. Avenida Central turns into Avenida 1 Norte, Avenida Simon Bolivar, and finally Via Transistmica heading out of town towards Colón. Avenida 6 Sur branches off Avenida Central shortly after San Felipe, running past the Paitilla airport towards Panama Viejo.

The city of Panama is not set up in grid formation, so it is difficult to explain the layout of the city. When you arrive, head for the closest IPAT office and obtain a free map of the city. The city has a well-established bus system that can take you almost anywhere.

GETTING AROUND TOWN
By Bus

The bus system is well organized in Panama City. Buses run throughout the city everyday from 5 am to 11 pm.

By Car

If you plan on renting a car you may want to wait until you venture outside the city. The intercity bus system is very efficient.

By Taxi

Taxi's are plentiful. Fares are zone-based, so try and look at a zone map before getting in the cab. Most fares in the city will cost you a couple of dollars. If you need to call a cab try **Ama** *(tel 21-1865)*, **America** *(tel 23-1928)*, or **El Parador** *(tel 66-3111)*.

By Bike

To rent a bike call **Alquiler de Bicicletas Moses** *(tel 28-0116)*.

WHERE TO STAY

Casco Viejo

Casco Viejo is the least expensive area in the city – but it is also not the safest at night, so be careful if you're staying in this area.

HOTEL VASQUEZ, *Avenida A and Calle 3, across from Arco Chato, tel 28-8453. Inexpensive.*

The nice owner here keeps the place clean but the rooms get warm at night. All rooms share a common bath.

HOTEL COLONIAL, *Calle 4 at Plaza Bolivar, tel 62-3858. Inexpensive.*

This hotel faces Plaza Bolivar and gets a little noisy. Some rooms offer a view of the ocean, and some double rooms come with a private bath . There is a small restaurant.

HOTEL FOYO, *Calle 6 and Avenida A, tel 62-8023. Inexpensive.*

A pleasant place with rooms surrounding an atrium. Doubles are available with or without a private bath.

Calidona/Bella Vista

PENSIÓN LAS PALMERAS, *Avenida Cuba at Calle 42, tel 55-1195. Inexpensive.*

A clean place to hang your hat for cheap. Singles and doubles cost about the same. All rooms have private bath.

RESIDENTIAL EL DORADO, *Calle 37 between. Avenidas Peru and Cuba, tel 27-5767. Moderate to Expensive.*

A wonderful spot offering a visitor's choice of rooms with fans or air-conditioning, or rooms with air-conditioning, TV, and hot water. All rooms come with private bath.

HOTEL CALIFORNIA, *Via Espana at Calle 43, tel 63-7844. Moderate to Expensive.*

The rooms here offer air-conditioning, TV, and hot water. All rooms come with a private bath. The hotel has security personnel and its own restaurant and bar.

RESIDENCIAL JAMAICA, *Avenida Cuba at Calle 38, tel 25-9870. Moderate to Expensive.*

A nice, clean hotel with private bath, hot water, air-conditioning and TV.

HOTEL EL PANAMA, *Panama 1, tel (507)69-5000. Expensive.*

One of Panama's finer hotels with 3 resturants, indoor tennis courts, a modern casino, discoteque, and pool. All rooms have a private bath and air-conditioning.

MARRIOT CESAR PARK HOTEL, *Panama 6a, tel (507)26-4077. Expensive.*

A five-star hotel offering beautiful rooms, 3 resturants, nighttime entertainment, casino gambling, tennis courts, a pool and a number of shops.

WHERE TO EAT

LA CASCADA, *Avenida Balboa at Calle 25, tel 62-1297. Take bus 2 from Plaza 5 de Mayo, open Monday through Saturday, 3 pm to 11 pm.*

If you are really hungry, try this place. The servings are enormous and the menu is quite extensive. It is set in an open air patio with a view of the bay.

EL TRAPICHE, *Via Argentina, 2 blocks off Via Espana, tel 69-2063, open daily 7 am to 11 pm.*

Reasonably priced Panamanian food. There is indoor and patio seating.

LAS BOVEDAS, *Plaza Francia, Casco Viejo, tel 28-8058, 28-8068. Open daily.*

Dungeons under the defensive sea wall of the Casco Viejo (Old Town) converted into a French resturant. Lots of atmosphere here and a mouth watering menu. Live jazz on Thursday, Friday, and Saturday evenings.

PAPARUCCHI'S, *Via Argentia No 59, tel 23-2870.*

Operated by Italians who have a reputation for great pizza. Patrons are served either inside or on a sidewalk terrace.

BAR RESTURANT LESSUPS, *Via Espana CL 46, La Cresta, tel 23-0749.*

Named after the Frenchman who built the canal, this mansion boasts 19th century elegance with a beautiful art nouvaeu decor. The cuisine is classic French with specialties of escargot, tenderloin steak with bearnaise sauce, lobster, seafood, and more.

EL TRAPICHE, *Via Argentina, El Cangrejo, tel 69-4353.*

This restaurant specializes in great Panamanian cooking.

MEDITERRANEA, *Calle 50 and Uruguay, tel 69-8211.*

For something a little different and unexpected try this Middle Eastern restaurant, complete with belly dancer for your nightly entertainment.

TINA JAS, *Calle 51 No 22, Belle Vista, tel 63-7890.*

This restaurant offers a pleasant atmosphere with traditional folklore shows Tuesday, Thursday, Friday, and Saturday. Authentic Panamanian food is served.

SEEING THE SIGHTS

Panama City has plenty of tourist attractions. Some sites are outside the city, so plan for a few day trips in your schedule.

A good place to start is the **Casco Viejo** neighborhood. The cobblestone streets bring you back to a time long ago. **Plaza de la Independencia** (Plaza Central) is at the middle of Casco Viejo and one of the major hubs of the city..

The **Iglesia de San Jose** is a must-see *(Avenida A at Calle 8)* housing the legendary altar of gold. Close-by is the **Arco Chato** (Flat Arch), which has stood unsupported for more than three centuries. The missing keystone reassured canal builders that Panama was not prone to earthquakes. *The arch is located at Avenida A at Calle 3.*

At the **Paseo de las Bovedas** (Promenade of the Dungeons), *at the end of Avenida Central (the southern tip of the penisula)*, visitors can walk along the top of the sea wall built by the Spanish to protect the city. From here people can see the ships lining up to enter the canal and the **Bridge of the Americas** arching over the canal. Below the wall is the **Plaza de Francia**, where large stone tablets tell the story of the canal's construction. The plaza is dedicated to those who lost their lives from yellow fever and maleria. This is where you'll find **Las Bovedas**, restored dungeons that are now a restaurant and gallery.

At the **Mercado Publico**, vendors will sell you anything from pencils to a whole side of beef. For those of you who have trouble with the smell of food after its been hanging around in the tropical climate, you may not want to venture here, but it is a wonderful glimpse into Panamanian life. *Avenida E. Alfaro between Calle 11 and 13. Open daily, 5 am to 6 pm.*

The **Museum of Colonial and Religious Art** has some interesting pieces, *located in Casco Viejo in an 18th century chapel next to the Flat Arch.* Another interesting museum is the **History Museum**, *also located in Casco Viejo*, offers a complete history of Panama. The three periods include colonial, union with Colombia, and Republicanism. *Cathedral Plaza, tel 28-6231. Open Monday through Friday, 8:30 am to 3:30 pm.*

A third museum well worth the visit is **Reina Torres de Arauz Anthropology Museum**, a wonderful museum displaying artifacts dating back thousands of tears. The many cultural influences shown here give visitors a true perspective of this international country. Highly recommended. *Plaza 5 de Mayo, tel 28-7687. Admission is 50 cents, open weekdays 9 am- noon and 1 pm to 4 pm.*

Teatro Nacional, *Avenida B at the waterfront. Donations requested, open daily 8:30am to 4:30pm*, and the **Palacio Nacional** next door was designed by Ruggieri, who also designed La Scala in Milan. The European influences are obvious and beautiful, with the painted ceilings, gold balconies, and chandeliers. The national symphony orchestra usually plays here and is worth checking out.

Panama Viejo is about four miles east of the city. These ruins comprise the original Panama City. After Henry Morgan destroyed the city in 1671, he took the wealth of the city but overlooked the golden altar now housed in Iglesia de San Jose. Apparently some nuns covered the altar in mud so Morgan would not think to take it. *The ruins are easy to get to; just take any Panama Viejo bus from Plaza 5 de Mayo.*

Just north of the city sits **Parque Natural Metropolitano**, a tropical nature preserve filled with flora and fauna. The trails in the park will lead you to a lookout point with a spectacular view of Panama City and the canal. *From Plaza 5 de Mayo, take SACA bus toward Fort Clayton and ask the driver for the park's visitor center. If driving, take Calle Curundi at Avenida Juan Pablo, tel 32-5552. Admission is free, open Tuesday through Sunday, 9 am to 3 pm.*

Atop a hill north of the city sits the **Baha'i House of Worship**. The Baha'is have constructed a beautiful temple. Visitors who just want to check it out or spend an afternoon in meditation are welcome. Men should wear long pants and women long skirts. *Located at Transistmica Mile 8; take Transistmica bus, but first ask the driver if he goes all the way. The driveway to the temple runs between the Banco Nacional and a Ron Bacardi Building. It takes about 15 minutes, walking, to get to the top.*

SPORTS & RECREATION

If you're into hiking, call or visit **Eco-Tours of Panama**. This group has excellent day hikes into the rain forest and treks across the Darién. The guides are very knowledgeable and well worth the money. *Calle Ricardo Alfaro (Tumba Muerto), on the upper level of the Centro Commercial La Alhambra, tel 36-3076, open Monday through Saturday, 8 am to 5 pm.*

If you want to discover Panama's underwater wonderland, check out **Scuba Panama**; they'll rent you full scuba gear if you are a certified diver for around $30 a day. If you want to get certified there is a one-week course, including equipment and a trip to Isla Mamey on the Caribbean Coast. This will cost you approximately $130; student rates are available with a ISIC card. *Urbanization Herbruger El Carmen, across from the Teatro* *en Circulo, tel 61-3841, open weekdays 8 am to 6 pm, Saturday 8 am to 1 pm.*

PRACTICAL INFORMATION
Money
Since the US dollar is the official currency it is easy to cash travelers checks, although   almost any currency can be exchanged here. The business and trading district is located on Via Espana. You shouldn't have any trouble exchanging cash.

The **American Express Office** *is on the 12th floor of the Union Bank Building, 5 Avenida Samuel Lewis, a block from Via Espana (tel 63-5858).* **Banco del Istmo** and **Chase Manhattan Bank** sell and cash Visa travelers checks and will give cash advances on Visa and Mastercard.

Post
The main post office is on the **Parque Catedral** *in the San Felipe district, in the building that was once the French headquarters for building the canal. It is open Monday through Friday, 7 am to 5:45 pm, Saturday, 7 am to 4:45 pm.*

There are smaller post office branchs around the city. If you wantmail sent to you in Panama City, have people address it to:

> *your name*
> *Entregal General*
> *Zona 1, Catedral*
> *Panama, Republica de Panama*

Telecommunications
The **Intel** office *is located in the Edificio Di Lido on Calle Manuel María Icaza (tel 64-8104);* there is one in **Balboa** *(tel 62-0894);* and at the **Tocumen International Airport** *(38-4240). All are open every day of the year, 7:30 am to 10 pm.*

Immigration
The **Migracion y Naturalizacion** office *is on the corner of Calle 29 and Avenida 2 (Avenida Cuba). Open Monday through Friday, 8 am to 3 pm, (tel 27-1077).*

Foreign Embassies
- **Belize**, *Calle 50 & Calle 87 (tel 26-4498)*
- **Canada**, *Calle Manuel Maria Icaza (tel 64-7014)*
- **Colombia**, *Calle Manuel Maria Icaza, Edificio Grobman, 6th Floor (tel 64-9266)*
- **Costa Rica**, *Calle Giberto Ortega & Via Espana (tel 64-2980)*
- **Ecuador**, *Calle Manuel Maria Icaza, Edificio Grobman, 3rd Floor (tel 64-7820)*

- **El Salvador**, *Via Espana, Edificio Citibank, 4th Floor (tel 23-3020)*
- **France**, *Plaza de Francia, San Felipe district (tel 28-7835)*
- **Germany**, *Calle 50 & 53, Edificio Bank of America, 6th Floor (tel 63-7733)*
- **Guatemala**, *Calle 55, Condominio Abir, 6th Floor, El Cangrejo (tel 69-3475)*
- **Honduras**, *Avenida Justo Arosemena & Calle 31, Edificio Tapia, 2nd Floor (tel 25-8200)*
- **Mexico**, *Calle 50 &53, Edificio Bank of America, 5th Floor (tel 63-5021)*
- **Nicaragua**, *Calle 50 & Avenida Fredrico Boyd (tel 69-6721)*
- **UK**, *Calle 53, Edificio Swissbank, 4th Floor, Marbella (tel 69-0866)*
- **US**, *Avenida Balboa & Calle 40, Edificio Macondo, 3rd floor (tel 27-1777)*
- **Venezuela**, *Avenida Samuel Lewis, Edificio Banco Union (tel 69-1244)*

NEAR PANAMA CITY
THE PANAMA CANAL

Connecting the Pacific Ocean to the Caribbean Sea, the **Panama Canal** runs 50 miles (80 km) across the narrowest part of the isthmus, passing through **Lago Gatún**, an enormous artificial lake created by the damming of **Río Chagres**. Construction of the canal took ten years starting in 1904.

Plans for a canal here were long in the making. Spain originally surveyed the land for such a feat, but it wasn't until the 1880s when the French, headed by **Ferdinand de Lesseps**, took the initial steps for construction of the project. De Lesseps' company Compagnie Universelle du Canal Interoceanique unfortunately went bankrupt in 1889, leaving the United States to buy the contract and complete the canal. The cost to the United States was a staggering $352 million, but that was not all. During the construction of the canal over 25,000 workers died from yellow fever, malaria, bubonic plague, and typhoid.

When the canal was completed it hit the history books as one of the most amazing engineering accomplishments of the 20th century. The American engineers constructed a system that raises and lowers ships over the varied terrain in the canal. This was done by building 3 lock systems measuring 1,000 feet by 110 feet: **Miraflores**, **Pedro Miguel**, and, **Gatún**. The locks use gravity to transfer water in and out of the locks allowing ships to be raised or lowered. *Panamax* ships are designed to maximize cargo capacity. These ships are 106 feet wide and 950 feet long, making the most of each lock. It is an amazing sight to watch one of these cargo giants make the voyage across.

The easiest way to get to the canal is by bus. *Take the SACA bus from Plaza 5 de Mayo headed toward Gamboa or Paraiso, have the driver drop you off at the Miraflores lock (there is an observation deck there).* Another way to view the canal is by boat. This can be expensive but well worth it. **Argotours** runs a tour through the Miraflores lock every Saturday, November through May only. *Pier 18, tel 65-3549.* **Mia Travels** runs a more extensive tour all the way to Gamboa where the Río Chagres meets Lago Gatún. *Calle 59 in Obarrio district, Yasa building, tel 63-8044.*

ISLA BARRO COLORADO

The **Smithsonian Tropical Research Institute** controls **Isla Barro Colorado**. They take groups out to the island on Tuesdays and Saturdays. If you do have a chance to visit, wear long pants, socks, and waterproof shoes, because you'll be tramping through a rain forest that is home to beautiful wildlife, including beautiful bugs! These tours are booked usually 5 to 12 months in advance. If this is a spontaneous adventure call for cancellations, tel 27-6021. **Eco-Tours** (see above) is the only other environmental group allowed on the island.

PARQUE NACIONAL SOBERANIA

A nice place to spend a day or half-day. *Visitor's Center, Gamboa, tel 56-6370. Admission free, open weekdays 8 am to 4 pm.* Ranger guides are strongly recommended for a $1 per person.

ISLA TABOGA

The *Island of Flowers* is an hour's ferry ride from Panama City in the **Bahia de Panama**. The island is beautiful for those who want to snorkel or just lay around in the sun. It gets crowded on the weekend, but is practically deserted during the week.

WHERE TO STAY IN ISLA TABOGA

HOTEL TABOGA, *To the right of the pier. Expensive.*
This is a resort hotel with all the amenities.

HOTEL CHU, *To the left as you step off the pier, tel 50-2035. Moderate to Expensive.*
A nice place that has common baths and a restaurant. The deck overlooks the water.

EASTERN PANAMA
PORTOBELO

Portobelo (*beautiful port*) is truly quite beautiful and has an array of colonial ruins. It is interesting how present-day Portobelo contrasts with the old fortress ruins. The town is surrounded by the jungle and makes a nice day trip. *You can take a Panama city-Colón bus, get off at Sabanitas, and catch the Colón-Portobelo bus as it passes through.* You can take a direct bus from Colón, but it probably is one of the more dangerous places around, even during the in day. Avoid it altogether.

SAN BLAS ISLANDS

San Blas is an archipelago of nearly 400 exotic islands scattered along the Caribbean Sea. The islands are home to the **Cunas**, who also have a strong tribal body that governs the region. The Cunas are very protective of their culture but there are a few signs of modern influences. The Cunas are a peaceful group who do not believe in killing unless absolutely necessary in self-defense.

They are famous for their handicrafts, especially the molas that are hand-stitched. These can range in price from $5 to $100.

When visiting San Blas don't forget to bring your own snorkel and mask (it is difficult to rent when you are there) and bring a good amount of cash, because travelers checks are often difficult to cash. Also, if you plan on spending the night, you will be staying on Isla Nalunega or Isla Wichub-Wala, the only islands with accommodations.

ARRIVALS & DEPARTURES

Three domestic airlines serve San Blas from Paitilla Airport in Panama City to **Porvenir**, the capital of San Blas. The airlines are **ANSA**, *tel 26-7891*; **Areotaxi**, *tel 64-8644*; and **Tranpasa**, *tel 26-0932*. Unfortunately, passengers are sometimes bumped for cargo.

WHERE TO STAY

HOTEL SAN BLAS, *Located on Isla Nalunega, tel 57-9000. Moderate.*
The price of the hotel includes three meals and includes a motor launch to and from the airport and any of the other islands. The rooms are a bit unusual with sand floors, but it works.

HOTEL ANAI, *Located on Isla Witchub-Wala, tel 20-0746. Moderate.*
This hotel is not as rustic as Hotel San Blas. Rooms come with a private bath and a swimming pool is available for guests. Three meals a day are included in the price.

If you don't want to spend the night, both hotels offer day trips to the surrounding islands and will pick you up from the airport in the morning and return you to catch the afternoon flight back to Panama City.

WESTERN PANAMA

The Inter-American Highway is the only road out of Panama going west. Most of you will use this road for traveling between Panama and Cost Rica. Traveling westward, visitors will come to a nice stretch of beaches.

Some of the more notable ones are **Nueva Gorgona**, **Coronado**, **Turiscentro San Carlos**, **El Palmar**, **Río Mar**, **Corona**, **Santa Clara** and **Farallon**. All have facilities for stopovers.

Panama's westernmost province is populated by the **Guayamí** and is one of the most beautiful regions in Panama. Both the highlands and lowlands of **Chiriquí** are fertile, making the land valuable as an important agricultural region. The area produces coffee, citrus fruits, bananas, sugar cane, rum, vegetables, livestock, horses and rainbow trout.

THE AZUERO PENÍSULA

The **Azuero Penísula** is a piece of land that extends south into the Pacific west of Panama City. The area is far removed from the hustle and bustle of the city, allowing native customs and handicrafts to flourish. This is a fairly agricultural area, with lots of historical structures, patriotic events, fairs, and festivals. The coastline is dotted with beautiful beaches.

One road runs south through this peninsula, intersecting the Inter-American Highway just west of the town Divisa. If you're driving, you'll want to be heading in the direction of Chitré and Las Tablas.

CHITRÉ & LOS SANTOS

Chitré and its neighboring town Los Santos host an array of festivals and have one of the wilder *Carnavals*. Holidays are a blast here, including **Semana Santa**, **La Feria de Azuero** (late April-May), **Corpus Christi** (40 days after Easter), **San Juan Bautista** (June 24), **Chitré's anniversary** (October 19), and the **first cry of independence** (November 10). People come from all over the country to celebrate in Chitré and Los Santos, so be prepared for a wild time if visiting during these festivals.

Once you arrive in Chitré, you may want to check out the **Ministry of Commerce and Industry**, which doubles as a tourist office *(Calle Estudiante, tel 96-4331, open weekdays, 8:30 am to noon and 12:45 pm to 4:30 pm)*. Maps and other tourist information can be found here.

There a few good beaches close to Chitré: try **Playa Agallito**, **Playa Monagre**, and **Playa El Rompio** (all are served by buses in town).

WHERE TO STAY

PENSIÓN COLUMBIA, *Avenida Manuel M. Correa, 1 block from the park, tel 96-1856. Inexpensive.*

PENSIÓN LILY, *Avenida Perez in front of the INTEL building, tel 96-3134. Inexpensive.*

HOTEL EL PRADO, *3946 Avenida Herrera, tel 96-4620. Moderate.*

This is a modern, well-kept hotel that has rooms with private bath and fans. There is optional air-conditioning.

HOTEL SANTA RITA, *Avenida Herrera and Calle Manuel M. Correa, tel 96-4610. Moderate.*

Another modern hotel that offers basic rooms with overhead fans and rooms with air-conditioning and private bath.

WHERE TO EAT

EL ENCUENTO, *Avenida Manuel M. Correa, tel 96-4925.*
Great place for a basic Central American dish.
MANOLO, *Avenida Manuel M. Correa, tel 96-5668.*
This is the place to go for pizza.

LAS TABLAS

This is small, quiet community about 15 miles south of Chitré. Most people come here to enjoy *Carnaval*. Although visitors would never guess at first sight, **Las Tablas** holds the wildest of *Carnaval* parties. If you plan on staying here during the festivities, make reservations in advance.

About 40 miles from Las Tablas is a great beach, **Playa Venado**. Surfers congregate here for the breaks. You may have to spend the night at the beach depending on the bus schedule. Cabanas are available at Playa Venado for a few dollars.

ARRIVALS & DEPARTURES

By Bus

Buses have connections to Las Tablas in almost every city: Santo Domingo, Chitré, Panama City, Playa Venado, and other places.

WHERE TO STAY

HOTEL PIAMONTE, *Avenida Central, tel 93-6372. Moderate.*
This hotel offers air-conditioning, hot water, and a private bath.
PENSIÓN MARIELA, *Avenida Central in front of Hotel Piamonte, tel 94-6473. Inexpensive.*

DAVID

David is the transportation hub and the capital of the Chiriquí province. It's the third largest city in Panama and the center of a rich agricultural region. There are some nearby attractions that beckon travelers to this part of the country to stay a few extra days before heading to their final destinations in Costa Rica or Panama City.

David is a pretty big city and the temperature here is one of the hottest in the country. It may be best to limit your activities to early morning and late afternoon.

Parque Cervantes is roughly the center of town and everything you need is within a few blocks. The regional **tourist office** can provide you with a good map of the city. *It is located at Edifcio Galberna, on Avenida 3 at Parque Cervantes, tel 75-4120.*

ARRIVALS & DEPARTURES

By Air

Two domestic airlines can fly you from Panama City to David. **Malek Airport** is located just outside the city; a $2 taxi ride will drop you off at Parque Cervantes. The airlines are **Areoperlas** *(Paitilla airport in Panama City, tel 63-5363; Malek airport in David, tel 75-4362)* and **Alas Chiricanas** *(Paitilla airport, tel 64-6448; Malek airport, tel 75-0916)*. The cost is about $50 round-trip.

By Bus

David is about 7 hours from Panama City by bus. Most of the direct buses are fairly comfortable and leave regularly. *The terminal is on Avenida del Estudiante about a 10-15 minute walk from Parque Cervantes.* The same terminal can connect you with buses to all areas in and around David.

WHERE TO STAY

PENSIÓN FANITA, *Calle B Norte 2 blocks south -east of the plaza, tel 75-3718. Inexpensive.*

Here you can choose rooms with or without bath and air-conditioning. The restaurant serves inexpensive meals.

PENSIÓN IRAZU, *Avenida 5 across from Pensión Rocio. Inexpensive.* All rooms have air-conditioning. Some rooms have private bath.

PENSIÓN ROCIO, *Avenida 5 Este, in front of Romero supermarket's parking lot. Inexpensive.*

Very clean. All rooms have fans and some with private bath. The restaurant is open daily from 6:30 am to 11 pm.

Two additional hotels offering basic rooms are:

HOTEL FIESTA, *(tel 75-5454)* and **HOTEL NACIONAL**, *(tel 75-2221).*

SEEING THE SIGHTS

In David itself, the most interesting you'll want to do is take in some culture at the **Museo Jose de Obaldia**, a nice museum *located at Avenida 8, 4 blocks from Parque Cervantes, tel 75-7839, open Tuesday through Saturday 8:30 am to 4:30 pm.*

Near David
BOQUETE

Boquete sits in a valley about 20 miles outside of David. Every year Boquete hosts a flower and coffee festival that rivals those of Amsterdam.

The traditional date for this festival was in April but it's now been changed. Check with your hotel and tourist offices to find out the exact date when you're planning your trip to this area (it seems that different local groups are arguing over when it should be held).

ARRIVALS & DEPARTURES
By Bus

Buses from David drop you off at Parque Central (Parque Domingo Medica), the center of town in Boquete. Everything you need is within a few blocks of this point.

WHERE TO STAY

PENSIÓN MARILO'S, *Calle 6 Sur, across from Hotel Rebequet, tel 70-1380. Inexpensive.*
Clean with private baths available.
PENSIÓN VIRGINIA, *Parque Domingo Medica, tel 70-1260. Moderate.*
All rooms have hot water baths. The owners speak English.
HOTEL REBEQUET, *Calle 6 Sur, tel 70-1365. Inexpensive to Moderate.*
Cooking facilities are available and there's a pool table.
HOTEL PANAMONTE, *North Boquete, tel 70-1327. Moderate.*
A nice hotel with an even better restaurant.

PARQUE VOLCÁN BARU

This is Panama's only volcano and it looms over **Boquete**. This is a great place to hike and camp. **Somos Boquete Ecotours** is a good group to hook up with if you are not overflowing with volcano experience. They can arrange day trips and overnight adventures. *Their office is located on Avenida Central, near the park, tel 70-1165.*

If you're looking to stay overnight in a hotel, see Volcán immediately below.

VOLCÁN & BAMBITO

On the west side of Volcán Baru, on the way to Cerro Punta, are two towns. **Volcán** has an entrance to Parque Volcán Baru and a few lodging facilities. One in particular, **MOTEL CALIFORNIA**, *tel 71-4272*, is run by a Yugoslavian. He speaks English and Spanish and offers clean cabanas with private baths. Bambito is another small town but is home to a fancy hotel called **HOTEL BAMBITO**, *tel 71-4265*. There is a trout farm across the street that supplies the restaurant with delicious fresh fish nightly.

CERRO PUNTA

North of Volcán there is a gorgeous little town – once a thriving Swiss colony – surrounded by green mountains called **Cerro Punta**. The elevation is more than 6,000 feet and it gets a little chilly. You may be sporting a sweater most of the time. Today tourists can go horseback riding, fishing, hunting and bird watching.

Cerro Punta is also the closest point to **PILA**, the **Parque Internacional La Amistad** (International Friendship Park). The park covers parts of both Panama and Costa Rica.

ARRIVALS & DEPARTURES
By Bus

Buses can take visitors directly from David. They run every 1/2 hour stopping at Volcán and Bambito.

WHERE TO STAY

Two nice places to stay are **HOTEL CERRO PUNTA**, *Calle Principal, tel 71-2020 (expensive)* and **PENSIÓN PRIMEVERA**, *Calle Central (moderate)*.

WHERE TO EAT

Two good restaurants in town are **RESTAURANTE AIRA**, *Calle Central*, and **RESTAURANTE SANTA LIBRADA**, *Calle Central, tel 71-2109*.

Northwestern Panama
BOCAS DEL TORO

This is one of Panama's isolated provinces and is better known as banana country. It is bordered by Costa Rica to the west, the Caribbean to the north, and the Cordilla Central mountains to the south. Most people visit this area for the **Archipiélago de Bocas del Toro**, **Parque Nacional Bastimentos**.

BOCAS DEL TORO - THE CITY

Once a beautiful city , much of **Bocas del Toro** was destroyed in the 1991 earthquake. The main part of town is located on the southern tip of Isla Colón. This is a good base if you plan on visiting the marine reserve. There are also great beaches that can be explored solo or arranged through groups at Botel Thomas. *There is a tourist office in town, tel 78-9211.*

ARRIVALS & DEPARTURES
By Air

You can fly to Bocas del Toro from Panama City through two airlines: **Areoperlas** *(Paitilla, tel 69-4555)* and **Alas Chiricanas** *(Paitilla, tel 78-841)*. The airport at David also services Bocas del Toro through Alas Chiricanas.

By Boat

You can catch a boat from Chiriquí Grande direct to Bocas del Toro.

By Bus

Buses depart David for Chiriquí Grande every 1 1/2 hours from 6:30 am to 4 pm.

WHERE TO STAY

PENSIÓN PECK, *At the top of Calle Principal, tel 78-9252. Inexpensive.*
An inexpensive place to stay that is kept very clean. The owner speaks English.

BOTEL THOMAS, *Top of Calle Principal, tel 78-9248. Moderate.*
This 'botel' has been built on stilts above the water and offers guests private baths. There is a restaurant that serves breakfast, lunch, and dinner.

SEEING THE SIGHTS

Bocas del Drago offers a secluded beach. You will need to reserve the minivan at Botel Thomas to get out there, since it is quite a walk.

The main sight in the area, though, is **Parque Marino Bastimentos**. Established in 1988 as Panama's first marine park, it has become an important natural reserve for a wide variety of Caribbean wildlife. They've done a nice job on the park, and it is highly recommended. *Trips can be organized through Botel Thomas, ANCON (next to Botel Thomas, tel 78-9367) or INRENARE (Calle 1, tel 78-9244).*

7. NICARAGUA

HISTORY

The earliest traces of human habitation in Nicaragua are an archeological discovery called the *Footprints of Acahualinca*. Archaeologists estimate the age of these fossilized footprints to be over 10,000 years old. Apparently they are the last remains of the natives who were running towards Lake Managua to escape a volcanic eruption.

During the 10th century A.D., Indians migrated to Nicaragua's Pacific lowlands from Mexico and Mesoamerica. Today artifacts and ancient stone carvings remain on many islands in Lake Nicaragua. There are even traces of Aztec migration in the early 15th century A.D.

The first colonial contact was in 1502, when Columbus sailed down the Caribbean coast. In 1522, **Gil González de Avila** established the first mission on the shores of Lake Nicaragua. Gil González de Avila named the land Nicaragua after the Indian chief **Nicarao** gave the Spanish gifts of gold. Up to this point the relationship between the Spanish and Indians were peaceful. After de Avila left, other Spainards returned solely with the intent of colonizing the land and claiming the gold. The Indian population put up a fight but was no match for the Spanish. One of these Spanish conquistadors, **Francisco Hernández de Córdoba**, founded the city of Grenada and then León in 1524.

Soon the gold that originally brought the Spanish crown was gone, but Grenada, with its access to the Caribbean Sea and its productive agricultural economy, became an important trading center.

León, then the capital, was originally established on the shores of Lake Managua but was destroyed by an earthquake in 1610. It was later rebuilt farther north, becoming a center for learning and culture. León also was the base for the Liberal Party, who supported a unified Central America and who supported political reforms based on the French and Am erican Revolutions.

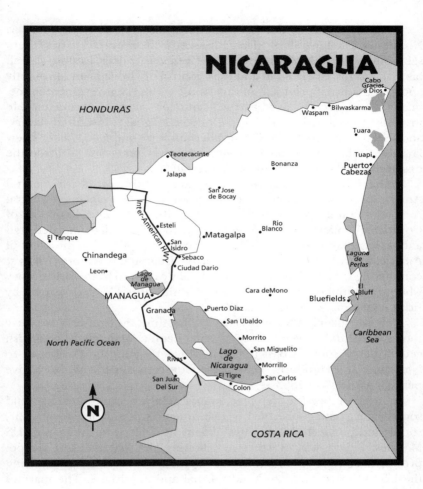

Grenada, a wealthier commercial city, became the center for the Conservative Party, favoring Spanish monarchy and Catholic authority. Over time tensions grew between the two cities as a result of the differences in political and economic philosophies.

Nicaragua gained independence from Spain in 1821, and full independence from the Central American Federation in 1838. Soon after Nicaraguan independence, the British and the US became interested in Nicaragua as a gateway between the Pacific and Atlantic Oceans. In 1848, the British seized San Juan del Norte at the mouth of the Rio San Juan, allowing Cornelius Vanderbilt, an American, to establish the **Accessory Transit Company**, which took passengers up the Rio San Juan and onto the Pacific coast by stage coach.

William Walker, another American, also became interested in Nicaragua. The Liberals of Nicaragua asked Walker in 1855 to help them seize power from the conservatives in Grenada. Walker, leading a small band of troops, marched in and took control of Grenada and promptly appointed himself president of the country. The US government immediately recognized Walker as the legitimate ruler of Nicaragua. He instantly proclaimed English as the official language, instituted slavery, and seized control over the Vanderbilt transport company. Walker's new laws would have probably been accepted over time, but he made the mistake of making an enemy of Vanderbilt.

Walker soon decided that he wanted control of all the Central American states; **five or none** became his slogan. The remaining Central American countries reacted by uniting, with the financial support of Cornelius Vanderbilt, to oppose Walker. In 1857 Walker was defeated and surrendered to the US Navy, avoiding capture by the Central American forces. Ever persistent, Walker attempted two more strikes at conquering Central America. He was finally captured by the British navy who turned him over to the Honduran authorities. He was executed by firing squad on September 12, 1860.

When Walker left Nicaragua for the first time, the Conservative Party took control and moved the capital from León to **Managua**. The British ceded the Mosquito Coast (*Costa de Miskitos*) along the Caribbean to Nicaragua and Honduras, leaving the Conservatives to rule in relative peace from 1857 to 1893.

In 1893, Liberal leader **José Santos Zelaya** became president and soon began to antagonize the US government as a result of his economic, social, and political philosophies. Finally in 1909, with the help of US Marines, Zelaya was overthrown, allowing the US to insert puppet presidents at will. In 1914, the **Bryan-Chamorro Treaty** was signed, giving the US exclusive rights to build a canal and naval base. The marines withdrew their forces in 1925, only to return in 1927.

When the US returned they were opposed by a guerrilla group led by **Augusto César Sandino**, Juan Bautista Sacasa, and José María Moncada. Sacasa and Moncada made peace with the US shortly after their arrival, but Sandino resisted American dominance in his country. Moncada and Sacasa, not surprisingly, became consecutive presidents allowing the Marines to withdraw their forces once again. This time they left behind a trained **Nicaraguan National Guard** (*Guardia Nacional*) led by **Anastasio Somoza García**.

In 1934, Somoza plotted the assassination of Augusto Sandino. He then proceeded to overthrow Sacasa and pronounced himself president. But even the power of the presidency did not appease Somoza. He created a new constitution and ruled as a ruthless dictator for 20 years, during which time he amassed wealth and land. His brutal rule led to one of Franklin D. Roosevelt's more memorable statements: *he may be a son of a bitch, but he's our son of a bitch.*

In 1956 Somoza was assassinated by a poet, López Pérez, in León. The murder was a suicide mission that escalated Pérez to the status of a national hero. Somoza's eldest son, Luis Somoza Debayle, succeeded his father until 1967. Then when Luis died, his brother, **Anastasio Somoza Debayle**, assumed the presidency.

Over time opposition to the Somoza family grew, leading to the creation of the **Sandinista National Liberation Front** (*Frente Sandinista de Liberación Nacional*) or **FSLN**. Its leaders were Carlos Fonseca Amador and Colonel Santos Lopez.

In 1972, a devastating earthquake destroyed Managua, killing thousands and leaving many more homeless. Somoza managed to pocket much of the international relief money and left thousands to die and live in poverty. In 1974, the FSLN kidnapped leading members of the Somoza regime, asking for the release of political prisoners in exchange. Somoza reacted by systematically killing FSLN supporters for 2 1/2 years, and eventually assassinating Carlos Fonseca, one of the FSLN's leaders.

Another popular political party in Nicaragua, opposing the Somoza government too, was the **Unión Democrática de Liberación (UDEL)** led by **Pedro Joaquín Chamorro**. Chamorro was owner and editor of the Managua newspaper *La Prensa*. In 1978, Chamorro was assassinated, igniting an eruption of violence and protest from the Nicaraguan public. Because of its growing national support, the FSLN forced Somoza to resign the presidency before the FSLN could march into Managua, which they did on July 19, 1979. Somoza fled the country but was eventually assassinated in Asuncion, Paraguay.

The **Sandinistas** inherited a country plagued by poverty, homelessness, illiteracy and inadequate health services. Under President Reagan, aid to the left-wing Sandinistas was suspended. The US allocated funds to organize and fund a counter-revolutionary force known as the **Contras**, consisting of many ex-soldiers from the National Guard. The Contras began operating out of both Honduras and Costa Rica, making progress difficult for the new Sandinista government.

After years of conflict, eventually the US Congress called for an end to Contra funding, but illegal assistance continued anyway (in part through arms sold to Iran with the proceeds diverted to fund the Contras). A series of government leaks led to the now-infamous **Iran-Contra Affair**.

In 1990, a new Nicaraguan election was scheduled. The **Unión Nacional Oposicion (UNO)**, a coalition of 14 opposing parties nominated **Violeta Barrios de Chamorro**, the widow of assassinated Pedro

Joaquín Chamorro, to be thier candidate. The United States supported her nomination and promised economic aid and an end to the Contra war. UNO won the presidency and the majority of the National Assembly. Today, after more than a decade of civil conflict and much greater political stability, the economic recovery of Nicaragua is slowly moving forward.

LAND & PEOPLE

Bordered by Costa Rica on the south and Honduras on the north, Nicaragua is the largest Central American republic. The Pacific Ocean forms the western border and the Caribbean Sea the eastern border. It is a land of lakes and mountains; rivers and volcanoes; and, best of all, sea and sun.

Nicaragua is divided into three distinct regions: the **Pacific Lowlands** in the West, the mountainous **Central Region**, and the **Atlantic Lowlands** in the East.

The **Pacific Lowlands** run from the Gulf of Fonesca on the Pacific border with Honduras to the border of Costa Rica south of Lake Nicaragua. This lowland strip has 25 volcanic cones that create a backdrop for Nicaragua's beautiful beaches. This is the most populated area of the country containing the capital **Managua** and many sites from Nicaragua's Spanish colonial heritage.

The **Central Highlands**, a mountainous range with lush vegetation, is filled with a great diversity of plant and animal species. Finally, the **Atlantic Lowlands** is the setting for Nicaragua's tropical ambiance. It is by far the hottest and most humid area of the country. The principle city is **Bluefields**, a typical Caribbean port. It has a strong African influence, a result of former British slavery and Jamaican immigration. The **Miskito Indians** also live in this region.

Overall the climate in Nicaragua is tropical, alternating between the dry and rainy season (summer and winter). The rainy season lasts from May through October. The dry season occurs from November through April.

The *Nicas* are a friendly people and generally speak Spanish. The majority of the population is **Mestizo**, a mix of Indian and Spanish blood. Twenty-seven percent of the population lives in and around Managua, while the rest are scattered throughout the country. Unfortunately war has left a relatively young population in Nicaragua – 60% under the age of 17.

PLANNING YOUR TRIP

Nicaragua has not developed a structured tourism center and is more concerned, at the moment, with business travelers and conferences rather than solo tourists. But it is worthwhile to stop by the tourist office and pick up a few maps, a bus schedule if available, and maybe a list of political hot spots in the country (check in with the US Embassy if in doubt). The **Instituto Nicaraguense de Turismo** (or **Inturismo**) in Managua *is located one block west of the Hotel Intercontinental, tel. 02-22498, open weekdays, 9 am -5 pm, Saturdays 9 am - noon.* There are a few Inturismo offices around the country.

If you're interested in hiking, get a topographical map of the country from **INETER** in Managua *at Complejo Civico, Edificio "O" tel. 02-50281. Open weekdays 9 am -5 pm).*

HOTEL RATES

The cost of decent accommodations in Nicaragua will run you around $3-$7 per person. Most hotels are called *hospedajes* and are characterized by concrete floors, wobbly cots, and shared bathrooms. If you are looking for luxury, you've come to the wrong place; the better hotels will run you about $20 a night.

If you planned on camping, be careful. The local populace is nervous coming off years of political turmoil, and they don't take kindly to strangers camping out on their turf. Don't forget also that the insects are like vampires here!

RESTAURANTS

The standard meal here usually consists of rice, beans, beef, pork or chicken. For the princely sum of $2-$3, you can usually fill your stomach, but there are restaurants around Managua that have a more extensive menu with higher prices. Seafood is a specialty along the coast and is quite tasty Nicaraguan-style.

HOLIDAYS & FESTIVALS

The largest celebration in the country is July 19, **Revolution Day**, celebrating the fall of Somoza. Most major towns have fairly big celebrations, but the largest is in Managua where thousands of people gather at the Plaza de la Revolución. Most cities and towns also celebrate at least one or two patron-saint festivals each year.

Festivals involve parades, fireworks, contests, and, sometimes, public drunkenness (so be alert). Popular festivals held throughout the country are in Managua, August 1-10; León, the last week in September; Grenada, the last two week of August; Masaya, the end of September; and Jinotepe, the last week in July. **El Repliegue**, a festival in the last week of June, represents the tactical retreat of the Sandinistas during the last week of the revolution and is celebrated in Managua and in Masaya. It is a wild drunken party that will wear you out.

Other national holidays include:

January 1	*New Year's Day*
March/April	*Holy Thursday and Friday*
May 1	*Labor Day*
July 19	*Revolution of 1979*
September 14	*Battle of San Jacinto*
September 15	*Independence Day*
November 2	*All Souls Day (Dia de los Muertos)*
December 8	*Immaculate Conception (Purisima)*
December 25	*Christmas Day*

GETTING TO NICARAGUA

By Air

The airline companies that provide service to the **Augusto C. Sandino International Airport** from the United States include:

- **American** *US 1-800-832-8383*
  Managua (Plaza España 02-663900)
- **Continental** *US 1-800-231-0856*
  Managua (02-661030)
- **Aviateca** *US 1-800-327-9832*
  Managua (02-668270)
- **Nica** *US 1-800-323-6422*
  Managua (02-31762)

Service from Europe is provided by:

- **Iberia** *US 1-800-772-4642*
  Managua (02- 661703)
- **Aeroflot** *US 1-800-429-4922*
  Managua (02-660565)

Service is provided for Central and South America through:

- **Copa** *US 1-800-359-2672*
  Managua (02-675438)
- **Lacsa** *US 1-800-225-2272*
  Managua (02-668270
- **Taca** *US 1-800-5353-8780*
  Managua (02-660872)

By Bus

Ticabus *(tel. 02-22-096), Barrio Martha Quezada, 2 blocks east of Cine Dorado;* and, **Sirca** *(tel. 02-75-726), in the southern part of Managua on Avenida Edurado Delgado behind Plaza de Compras,* are two bus companies that service other Central American capitals from Managua. Most buses depart before 9 am. Tickets need to be reserved and purchased two days in advance. Prices range from $15 to $40 one way depending on your destination. If you are headed towards Costa Rica, remember you need to present an onward or return ticket when entering the country. You'll save money by purchasing it in advance in Managua.

By Car

If you are leaving Nicaragua by car you must have a transit document that can be purchased for about $20 at the **Policia de Transito** in Managua (*Mercado Roberto Huembes, tel. 02-59318*) or when you enter the country. You will not be allowed to leave the country unless you have this document!

ENTERING NICARAGUA

Visitors from the United States and most European countries can get a visa when entering the country as long as they have a valid passport with at least 6 months remaining before you need to renew. Immigration officials will give you a temporary visa for 90 days (30 days for US citizens) that can be renewed twice during your stay with a charge of $1 a day.

Visitors from countries other than the US should contact their local Nicaraguan consulate to obtain a visa in advance, which can be done with two passport photos and a charge of approximately $25. Technically when entering Nicaragua proof of resources is required ($200) but it is rarely enforced. Call your local consulate to see if it is necessary to present an onward ticket, because this regulation is not consistently enforced. There is a departure tax of $10.

Custom regulations are 200 cigarettes and three liters of alcohol.

NICARAGUAN EMBASSIES & CONSULATES

• **Columbia**, *Transversal 19, Avenida 10464, Bogota, tel 215-736*
• **Costa Rica**, *Avenida Central, Calle 25 & 27, San José tel 33-3479*
• **El Salvador**, *89a Avenida Norte & 9a Calle Poniente, No 4612, San Salvador, tel 24-6662*
• **Guatemala**, *2a Calle 15-95, Zona 13, Guatemala City, tel 6-5613*
• **Honduras**, *Colonia Lomas del Tepeyac, Bloque H-1, Tegucigalpa, tel 32-4290*
• **Mexico**, *Ahumada Villagran No. 36, Izquina Juan Odonojo, Lomas Villareyes, CP 11000, Mexico DF, tel 540-5625*
• **Panama**, *Calle 50 & Avenida Federico Boyd, Panama City, tel 23-0981*
• **US**, *1627 New Hampshire Avenue, NW, Washington, DC 20009, tel (202) 939-6570*

GETTING AROUND NICARAGUA

By Air

Traveling by plane within the country is very expensive. The only commercial domestic airline is **Areonica**. It operates two domestic flights between Managua and Bluefields, and Managua and Puerto Cabezas. Charter flights are available also, but this will cost you. If you are interested in hiring a pilot you can call Nica Airlines *(tel 02-663136)* and ask them to recommend chartering companies.

By Bus

This is the most economical way to get around Nicaragua, but buses are happy hunting grounds for pickpockets. If you can avoid bringing excess baggage with you, do so. Most hotels will allow you to store your luggage for a fee.

You can get across the country on less than $5, but it's not he most comfortable way to go; if you are bringing luggage it may cost twice as much. You can catch local or express buses depending on your destination. Express buses generally cost about three times as much but there are not as many stops. Most towns are serviced by a bus. If you are unsure where a bus stop is, head for the town market; most buses stop there.

By Car

Getting around by car is convenient if you can handle the other drivers. Many roads are dilapidated so a 4x4 is generally the vehicle of choice (especially during rainy season). Gas is twice as costly as in the US, but you can find gas stations on most major roads.

Cars can be rented only in Managua. Your best bet is the American car company **Budget** (see Managua section). There are offices at the airport and the Hotel Intercontinental, who will rent you a car for around $25 a day.

By Train

There is a train that runs from León to Managua and onto Masaya and Grenada. A separate line runs from León to a few northern areas. While cheaper than the bus, this is a long uncomfortable ride.

BASIC INFORMATION

Below you'll find some basic information in alphabetical order.

BUSINESS HOURS

Government offices are open Monday through Friday, from 8 am to noon and from 2 pm to 4 pm. Some buisnesses are open on Saturday, but these hours vary. Banks usually have shorter hours, from 9 am to 1 pm.

HEALTH

Although the water tastes somewhat chlorinated, tap water is safe to drink in all areas but rural villages. Do take precautions when buying food from outdoor stands; many of these *comedores* are not sanitary.

When traveling to any country, it is wise to meet with your doctor about neccessary shots. **Malaria** is a problem in Nicaragua, so stock up on anti-malarial pills. Medication is hard to find in Nicaragua, so bring anything you may need while traveling.

MONEY

Nicaragua's monetary unit is the **cordoba**, consisting of 100 **centavos**. There are no coins, so cordoba bills are in denominations of 1 to 1,000 cordobas while centavos come in 5, 10, 25 and 1/2 cordoba (50 centavos) bills. In smaller villages the monetary unit is in **reales**, with 1 reale equivalent to 10 centavos.

There are many *casas de cambio* in Nicaragua. They give a competitive exchange rate, usually better than the government-run banks but will only exchange dollars for cordobas. Using the black market for currency exchange is illegal but widely used, and the exchange rate is often better then the state bank.

Carrying US dollars in cash is preferable (denominations under $20) in Nicaragua because there is no commission charged and, more importantly, few places outside the capital will cash travelers checks (and other currencies are not accepted).

Outside Managua the only official avenue of exchange is the state bank, **Banco Nacional de Desarrollo** (**BND**), which exchanges dollars only. **Cred-O-Matic** (*Multicentro Camino de Oriente, Managua, tel. 02-72362*) is the only place in the country where you can get a cash advance using Visa or Mastercard.

PHONES & MAIL

The national communication service is **Telcor**. It is a combined post office/telecommunications center that will allow you to contact people within and outside Nicaragua's borders. Local and interregional calls (dial the city code, then the number) are inexpensive, but collect calls to the United States are about $5 per minute. Using **AT&T USA Direct** (*dial 64 in Managua and 02-64 outside the city*) is probably your cheapest option.

Mail is slow and inefficient. Airmail can take up to three weeks and will run you about 50¢ per letter. If you want to receive mail, the post office will hold letters for approximately three weeks (you need to present a photo ID).

If people are writing you, have letters and packages addressed to:
Your Name
Listas de Correos
Telcor (town name)
Name of the department
Nicaragua, Central America

SAFETY

Violent crime is not common but pickpockets are. Keep alert, especially in Managua and while traveling on buses.

SHOPPING

Shopping is not that big in Nicaragua. There are some Nicaraguan handicrafts, the most popular being silver work that is worth investigating. The only markets in Managua are the **Mercado Oriente** *(take bus MR3 from the northern edge of Barrio Martha Quezada)* and the **Huembes market** *(take bus MR4 from the northern edge of Barrio Martha Quezada).*

Mercado Oriente is the largest market and sells everything from flatware to auto parts. For those uncomfortable in such a sizable market (and the smell is less than desirable), you may want to go to the Huembes market. It's less overwhelming and has a section devoted to Nicaraguan handicrafts.

TIME

Nicaragua is 6 hours behind Greenwich Mean Time.

TIPPING

Tipping is not expected and is usually included in the bill at the more expensive restaurants. If you are driving around the country and someone offers to watch your car, they'll expect a tip when you return.

WEIGHTS & MEASURES

The metric system is used in Nicaragua. For gasoline, US gallons are used and the **vara**, about 33 inches, is used for distance.

MANAGUA

Situated on the southern shore of Lake Managua, **Managua** is a city consisting of over 600 neighborhoods with absolutely no rhythm or reason. Most of the city's buildings were destroyed in the earthquake of 1972. The city was never rebuilt, leaving a city center in ruins. Street names are not used here, so when looking for a hotel or restaurant you will have to rely on your sense of direction and ask a lot of questions.

There are vacant overgrown lots everywhere you look and dilapidated buildings crying out for repair. Still, if you're adventurous and enjoy experiencing other cultures, you will grow to appreciate the intensity of Nicaraguans and their zeal for life.

Managua has become home to café socialists, artists, political exiles, international volunteers and those just a bit more adventurous than the average traveler. Although there are no structured tourist spots, Managua is a city filled with life and will give the curious among you an inside look at people who have survived years of dictatorship and war.

ARRIVALS & DEPARTURES
By Air

Augusto C. Sandino Airport is a few miles east of the city's center *on Carretera Norte*. Domestic charters and international flights are serviced here. There is no currency exchange at the airport but dollars are accepted. There is also an AT&T phone booth.

Take a taxi from the airport to town for approximately $5-$10 per person; it's easier. You can take a city bus, running the risk of pickpockets, or the inter-urban bus, which is much safer. Both buses stop right in front of the airport entrance so you should have no trouble finding them. All of these buses go to the **Ivan Montenegro Market**, where you can take a taxi to almost anywhere in the city for $1 or $2.

By Bus

Three markets serve as Managua's major bus depots:

Mercado Roberto Huembes serves the cities of Masaya, Grenada, Rivas, Matagalpa, Esteli, Ocotal, Somoto, and smaller towns surrounding these cities. Buses generally depart throughout the day on the half hour, starting as early as 5 am. Buses to Masaya and Grenada depart every ten minutes and buses to Ocotal leave only at 7 am, 8:45 am, and 2 pm. Take Bus 119 from Plaza Espana to get to the market.

Mercado Israel Lewities Market serves as a bus depot for the northwestern part of the country. These cities include León, Chinandega, and Corinto. Most buses here begin service at 6 am and run until 5 pm or 6 pm. If you're traveling to León, make sure you take the bus using the new highway, which will cut travel time and discomfort!) Buses to León leave every 20 minutes. Take Bus 110 from UCA to get to this market.

Mercado Ivan Montenegro serves Boaco, Juigalpa and Rama. Buses to Boaco leave hourly, 5 am -4 pm; to Juigalpa every 1/2 hour, 5 am -5:30 pm ; and, to Rama, connecting with a boat to Bluefields, at 2:30 pm every Tuesday, Thursday, Saturday and Sunday (it is advisable to show up at 10 am to get a seat on the Rama bound bus). Take bus 110 from UCA to get to the market.

By Train

Managua's train station *is located a few blocks east of the Rueben Dario Theater, tel. 02-22802*. Trains serve León, Masaya and Grenada. Trains to León depart daily at 7 am, 11 am, and 6 pm; the trip shoul take about three hours. Grenada via Masaya departs daily at 8am, 1:30 pm, and 6 pm and takes two hours. *For more information, call tel 22-802*.

ORIENTATION

Getting around Managua is not easy. In addition, street addresses are not commonly used. The best way to get around the city is to remember landmarks that will give you some sense of direction. The center, which is ruined and deserted, is on the northern lake shore. From the center of town **Avenida Bolivar** runs south past the Hotel Intercontinental (a pyramid-shaped building – you can't miss it). West of the Intercontinental is **Barrio Martha Quezada**, loaded with cheap restaurants and hotels. **Avenida William Romero** borders the western edge of Barrio Martha Quezada and runs south past **Plaza Espana**, the location of most airline offices, exchange offices, and banks. On the western side of the city, volcanoes can be seen in the distance.

GETTING AROUND MANAGUA

By Bus

Buses are the cheapest way to get around the city, but always ask where your bus is going. Bus maps and schedules are hard to find, so don't be shy about asking. Be alert! Pickpockets lurk on all buses, so guard your wallets and backpacks.

Buses start running in the early morning and stop around 10 pm, so bring extra cash for a cab if you plan on staying out until the wee hours of the morning. *For more information on intercity buses, call ENABUS, tel 44-506*.

By Car

Driving can be a bit scary. Budget usually has the best prices, but check around.
- **Budget**, *Intercontinental Hotel, tel 23–530 ext. 148*
- **Montoya**, *tel 66-6226*
- **Renta-Autos**, *Sandino Airport, tel 31-531*
- **Toyota**, *Hotel Camino Real, tel 31-411, ext 627*
- **Turi-Nica Commercial**, *500 meteres south of Plaza Espana traffic lights, tel 66-1387*

By Taxi

Taxis are a cheap and easy way to get around the city. Tipping is not expected, but you need to negotiate a fare before getting into the taxi or you'll end up paying twice as much as you should. *To phone for a taxi call 24-872.*

WHERE TO STAY

During the Sandinista years, most foreign travelers were restricted to hotels in or near Barrio Martha Quezada. This is west of the Hotel Intercontinental. Today visitors can move around the city without problems, but most decent accommodations are still in the vacinity of Barrio Martha Quezada.

Inexpensive

HOSPEDAJE SANTOS, *One block north and 1/2 block east of Cine Dorado, tel 02-23713.*

A popular place for young travelers that can get noisy at night. Rooms are concrete blocks with so-so beds; bathrooms are shared. Singles and doubles are available. There is a restaurant that serves a good filling meal.

HOSPEDAJE NORMA, *One block south and 1/2 block east of Cine Dorado, tel 02-23498.*

A friendly place that attracts foreign travelers. Bathrooms are shared and clean. There is a midnight curfew but a key is available at the front desk.

HOSPEDAJE MEZA, *A half-block west of Fabrica El Triunfo and two blocks east of Hospedaje Santos, tel 02-22046.*

A place to hang your hat for cheap. The rooms are small and the bathrooms are shared but it is quiet. There is an 11 pm curfew.

HOSPEDAJE CARLOS, *A half-block north of the Tica-Bus Terminal, 5 blocks west of the Hotel Intercontinental, House No. 735, tel 02-22554.*

This hotel is hidden behind a house and has clean comfortable rooms, all with private bath. It is family run, giving it a warmer atmosphere than other spots. Most guests are Nicaraguans. There is an 11 pm curfew.

CENTER FOR GLOBAL CHANGE, *One block east, one block south, and 1/2 block west of the Estatua Montoya, house #1405, outside of Barrio Martha Quezada, tel 02-24268 . (Inexpensive to Moderate).*

Headquarters for Augsburg College's travel seminar programs offers clean, comfortable bunk beds. It's dorm-like, but the American staff is awfully nice and can point you in the right direction if you're looking for guidance. Breakfast, lunch and dinner are available.

Moderate

CASA SAN JUAN, *Reparto San Juan, Calle Esperanza, No 560, outside of Barrio Martha Quezada near the University of Central America (UCA), tel 02-783220.*

A quiet, comfortable place filled with foreign visitors. The management is friendly and will help with car rental and airline information. All rooms have private bath. There is a midnight curfew.

Moderate to Expensive

MANAGUA'S INN, *One block south and 3 blocks east of Cine Dorado; the inn has a double arched garage, tel 02-22243.*

This is a nice place to visit. The inn is actually a ranch house with large, air-conditioned rooms and private baths. The staff is professional and very helpful. The price includes room, breakfast, and all the coffee you can drink; you can even use the kitchen. There is an 11 pm curfew.

HOTEL MORGUT, *Two blocks north and 1 block east of Hotel Intercontinental, tel 02-22166.*

If you are looking for large air-conditioned rooms, TV, and bath, then this is the place. The staff can be helpful, depending on what mood you catch them in, and will assist with car rentals and airline tickets.

Expensive

HOTEL INTERCONTINENTAL, *Avenida Bolivar Sur, tel 62-35319.*

This place has the feeling of a resort. All rooms have air-conditioning, TV, phone, and private bath. The hotel offers its guests a pool, restaurant, tennis courts, bar, gift shop, barber and car rental.

CAMINO REAL, *Km 9 1/2 Carretera Norte, tel 63-14415.*

Camino Real offers its guests the same luxuries as the Intercontinental. All in all, a very nice place to stay.

WHERE TO EAT

Although the basic meal is meat, beans, and rice, Managua recently has been exposed to a growing selection of international cuisine. **Barrio Martha Quezada** not only houses most of the hotels but also has most of the good restaurants.

VECADI, *One block north, 5 blocks west and 1/2 block north from Hotel Intercontinental. Open Monday thru Saturday, 11:30 am - 2 pm.*

A popular *comedor* that serves the basic Nicaraguan meal. The food is good and there's plenty of it.

MIRNA'S PANCAKES, *One block south and 1 block east of the Cine Dorado, (close to Hospedaje Norma), tel 02-27913. Open daily for breakfast and lunch.*

Great for some pancakes, eggs, beans, and rice.

SARA'S, *Seven blocks west, 1 block south from the Hotel Intercontinental (next to Tica-Bus). Open Monday thru Saturday for breakfast and lunch. Dinner only on Sundays.*

If you want a relaxed atmosphere and would like to meet some fellow travelers, you're in luck at Sara's. The menu has a nice selection, including some tasty vegetarian dishes.

EL CIPITIO, *Two and a half blocks from Cine Cabrera or from Hotel Continental 1 block north, 4 blocks west, and 1 1/2 blocks south, tel 02-24929. Closed Sunday.*

The food here is delicious, without the crowds.

MAGICA ROMA, *One half block west of the south side of Hotel Intercontinental, tel 02-27560. Open daily noon-midnight.*

If you are longing for some good ol' Italian food, this is the spot, with everything from elaborate pasta dishes to some old fashioned pizza.

ANANADA, *Across from Estatua Montoya. Open Monday thru Saturday, 7 am - 2 pm.*

Ananada is a little café that serves good vegetarian food and refreshing fruit juices.

PASTA FRESCA, *One block east and 2 blocks south of UCA's main entrance, tel 02-74849. Open Tuesday thru Saturday 10 am - 8 pm.*

Another establishment offering fresh pasta dishes. Great place for a fun midday lunch.

SEEING THE SIGHTS

Most sights within the city are close to each other and can be seen during the day.

A good place to start is the **Plaza de Revolución**. The plaza is similar to a large concrete parking lot, but try to picture it filled with wild crowds at the Sandinistas' victory celebration on July 19, 1979, just days after Somoza left the country. Every year, on July 19, the plaza is filled with patriots and reckless partyers alike, while speeches and music can be heard in the background. *To get there, take Bus 109 (catch it at the corner of Avenida Bolivar and Calle Julio Buitrago, a few blocks north of the Intercontinental) up Avenida Bolivar.*

Nearby, *on the east side of the Plaza de Revolución*, is the **Metropolitan Cathedral**, a beautiful building that was mostly destroyed in the 1972 earthquake. On the south side of the Plaza, the once-grand **Palacio Nacional** (National Palace) now is used as a tax office. The facade displays the portraits of Augusto Sandino and Carlos Fonseca, while the inside walls depict the Nicaraguan and Mexican revolutions.

The **tomb of Carlos Fonseca** can be found *on the east side of the Plaza*. Carlos Fonseca, leader and founder of the FSLN, was killed in 1976 by the National Guard. In 1991, the tomb was bombed, resulting in riots led by outraged Sandinista supporters. Situated *on the north side of the Plaza* is the **Teatro Rubén Darío**, with its memorable performances, plays, and concerts.

If you're like to view a fine collection of modern Latin American art, visit the **Casa Julio Cortazar**, *located two blocks west of the Plaza de Revolución across from Telcor (tel 02-27272, open Monday thru Saturday 9 am - noon, 2 pm -4 pm; donation requested).* The gallery is named after the famous Argentinean writer. Cortazar wrote a favorable critique of Sandanista art work, pleasing the Sandinista government so much they nam ed the museum after him.

Managua boasts two interesting – well, semi-interesting – museums. The **Museo Huellas de Acahualinca** is a small museum that houses a few archaeological artifacts. The main exhibit includes ancient footprints made over 10,00 years ago. The footprints were preserved by volcanic ash from Volcano Momotombo. *From Plaza de la Revolución take Bus 112 to Barrio Acahualinca and walk north 1 block past railroad tracks, tel 02-25291. Open weekdays 8 am - noon, 1 pm -3 pm. Donations requested.* The other museum is the **Museo Nacional de Nicaragua**, which houses pre-Colombian jewelry and ceramics from Ometepe Island in Lake Managua. Unfortunately, many pieces were destroyed in the 1972 earthquake. *From Plaza de la Revolución, take Bus 112 about 13 blocks east to Colonia Dambach, tel 02-25291. Open weekdays 8 am - noon, 1 pm -3 pm. Admission is $1.*

FESTIVALS

El Repliegue occurs during the last week of June, and begins as an all-night march to Masaya from Huembes Market. This festival commemorates the tactical Sandinista retreat that saved thousands of lives. It turns into an all-night fiesta, so bring your party shoes.

Revolution Day is July 19. It is the anniversary of the FSLN's victory over Somoza. Thousands gather at the Plaza de la Revolución to hear speeches and music.

The **Santo Domingo** festival celebrates Managua's patron saint. This festival runs the first 10 days of August and can get a little crazy. There are often casualties when the music dies down. Don't venture out in this crowd alone; there are a lot of drunks who are liable to do something crazy.

NIGHTLIFE

Entertaining yourself at night in Manauga usually revolves around finding the right bars or clubs. There are a fair number of them to find. Some of the better bars are listed below.

Pina Colada, *Centro de Diversiones El Carnaval, in front of UCA, tel 02-74140* and **Bar Chaplin**, *Km 5 Carretera Masaya, tel 02-74375* both feature more of a North American atmosphere. **Sara's** and **El Cipitio** also double as an evening hangout for many visitors to Managua and locals alike.

Centro Cultural El Cipres, *one block east of UCA, and* **El Latinoamericano,** *La Pinata, across from UCA*, offer occasional music on Wednesday and Thursday nights.

Videoteca, *one block northeast of Estatua Montoya, tel 02-27092*, shows foreign films in English or with English subtitles.

Music and dancing can be found at the following popular clubs:

Rancho Bambi, *Km 3 1/2 Carretera Norte*; **Reggae Mansion**, *Km 6 Carrtera Norte, tel 02-94804*; **Bar Munich**, *5 blocks south of the Linda Vista stoplights, tel 02-668132*; **El Quelite**, *five blocks west of Telcor Villa Fontana, tel 02-701671*; **La Pinata**, *across from UCA, tel 02-678216*.

PRACTICAL INFORMATION

Money

There is no American Express office in Managua. Travelers will see little difference in rates offered by the banks and the *casas de cambio* in town; a few will charge a commission, unless you want to change travelers checks into dollars. Most *casas de cambio* are open weekdays, 8 am - noon and 2 pm -6 pm, and some are open on Saturday mornings as well.

Hotel Intercontinental will exchange dollars at any time. **Multicam bios** *(tel 02-22576)* and **Banco Mercantil** *(02-668228) are both located at Plaza Espana*. **Intercam bios** *(02-73471) is located at Plaza de Compras*.

Embassies

• **Australia**, *Barrio Bolonia (1 block west and 1/2 block north) tel 02-22056. Open weekdays 9 am -4 pm.*

• **Canada**, *in front of Telcor Central, tel 02-24541. Open weekdays 9 am -noon and 2 pm - 4 pm.*

• **United Kingdom**, *main entrance on Los Robules, 4th house on the right tel 02-70034. Open weekdays 9 am - noon and 2 pm -4 pm.*

• **United States**, *Barrio Batahola Sur, Km 4 1/2 Carretera Sur, tel. 02-666010* US citizens should register with the embassy in case of an emergency.

Emergency Numbers

• **Police**, *tel 11*
• **Fire,** *tel 23184*
• **Red Cross**, *tel 51761* (offers names of English speaking doctors and an ambulance).

Health

For travelers in need of a hospital in Managua, the public hospital won't charge you a cent. **Hospital Lenin Fonseca** *is located in Las Brisas, tel 02-666544*. The biggest private hospital is **Hospital Bautista**, *tel 02-26913*, where you will probably find English speaking doctors and a better equipped hospital. This will cost you some bucks, but it also has a dental clinic and a 24 hour pharmacy.

Laundry

Almost all *hospedaje* will offer laundry services for a small price, but there is a **Lavamatic** in Managua that will wash your clothes for around $6 per pound *(tel 02-660837, open Monday through Saturday 7 am -7 pm).*

Phones & Mail

The **Telcor** building in Managua *is located just west of the Plaza de la Revolución near the lake. The post office is open weekdays 8 am -5 pm* and offers airmail, telex, telegraph, fax, and express-package service. You can also rent a mail box at this location if you plan on staying for awhile. Local and international phone calls can be made here, open 8 am -10 pm daily. The AT&T USA Direct is not available at this location, but there are other Telcor offices around town.

Tourist Information

Inturismo is the government's tourist office, but it is not well equipped to handle independent travelers. Maps, however, are available. *It's located one block west of the Hotel Intercontinental, tel 02-22498.*

Tur-Nica, Inturismo's travel agency, can be helpful and will call ahead to *hospedajes* to make reservations. *Their office is located at Plaza Espana, tel 02-661387.*

NEAR MANAGUA

There are no lifeguards or safety equipment on Nicaraguan beaches, so consider yourself warned. The undertow and tide changes can be deadly.

POCHOMIL

Pochomil is the closest beach to Managua *(37 miles southwest of Managua).* It is most popular in the dry season and during Easter week (coincides with a 7-day beach party). *Buses leave Israel Lewites every 40 minutes.*

MONTELLMAR

A modern beach resort, *about an hour outside the capital.*

LAGUNA DE XILOA

Laguna de Xiloa is a volcanic lagoon that attracts weekend travelers and can get quite crowded during the dry season. An extensive tourist complex has been built here, making it a popular recreation area. Unfortunately, transportation is difficult. *Buses leave from Las Piedrecitas park only on Sundays.* But taxis can get you there for about $5 per person any day of the week.

NORTHWESTERN NICARAGUA

Northwestern Nicaragua is home to a number of nice destinations, worth a few days' visit from the Managua area if you have the time. León is the main town in this part of the country, but there are other charms here as well.

LEÓN

Once one of Nicaragua's most important towns, **León** was the home to some of the region's greatest writers and politicians. One of the more famous poets who lived here was **Ruben Dario**. The city was the capital of Nicaragua for over 300 years before and after independence (the capital was moved to Managua in 1857). Although no longer the capital city, León is home to the largest cathedral in the country and the main campus of the national university.

León was founded in 1524 and originally sat 15 miles west of its present location. It was moved after the **Momotombo** volcano erupted, which some say caused the earthquake of 1610. The construction of León's great cathedral began in 1746 and was not completed until 1815. The structure was well built and survived civil conflict between 1821 and 1842, and survived more recent conflict again many years later during the Sandinista insurrection in the 1970s.

ARRIVALS & DEPARTURES
By Bus

The bus depot *is located next to the market, one block north and 8 blocks west of the train station.* Buses leave regularly for Managua from 4:30 am - 6 pm. Take the bus using the new highway for speed and comfort! This bus depot also services Chinandega, Corinto and other close-by towns. A taxi or horse-drawn carriage can take you to town from here for a small fee.

By Train

León has a train station *located on Avenida 14 de Julio at 5a Calle Norte.* There are no tourist facilities here, but you can catch a taxi for a short ride downtown. Trains leave for Managua 3 times a day: an express at 6 am, and, two regular trains at 5 am and noon.

GETTING AROUND TOWN

León is an easy city to get around. The *calles* run east to west and the *avenidas* run north to south. The center of town is **Parque Central**, with roads beginning at **Calle Central Ruben Dario** and **Avenida Central** on the northeast corner of Parque Central. Most sights are an easy walk from here, and a cab can take you anywhere in the city for about $1.

WHERE TO STAY

HOTEL AMERICA, *Two blocks east from the southeast corner of Parque Central, tel 03-115533. Inexpensive.*

Not a bad place to hang your hat for the night. The management is friendly and all rooms have a private bath. The front door is locked at 10 pm, so make arrangements if you will be out late.

HOTEL EUROPA, *Two blocks south and one block east from the train station, tel 03-112596. Reservations are recommended here. Moderate.*

Clean rooms and a professional staff await you here. Rooms come with or without private bath and a few with air-conditioning, priced accordingly. There is a restaurant on the premises.

WHERE TO EAT

LA CUEVA DEL LEÓN, *Two and a half blocks north from the northwest corner of Parque Central, tel 03-116562.*

Good food set in a beautiful old building.

RESTAURANTE SACUANJOCHE, *In front of Museo Ruben Dario, 3 blocks west of the northwest corner of Parque Central, tel 03-115429.*

This is probably the fanciest restaurant in town and the most expensive – but the food is worth the trip.

LAS RUINAS, One *and a half block* west of the northwest corner of Parque Central, tel 03-114767.

This restaurant doubles as a fun night spot, serving a decent dinner.

SEEING THE SIGHTS

The 18th century **cathedral** *in the middle of town*, which contains the tomb of Ruben Dario, underwent extensive renovations in 1992 and is worth checking out. The **Museo Ruben Dario** *is three blocks west from the northwest corner of Parque Central.* The museum is housed in Rueben Dario's childhood house. Donations are strongly encouraged. *Open Tuesday through Saturday 9 am - noon and 2 pm - 5 pm, Sunday 9 am -11 am.*

El Fortin is an abandoned 19th century fortress once used as a prison by the National Guard. It sits on a hill *a mile south of town,* offering spectacular views of León and nearby volcanoes.

Near León

PONELOYA

Visitors can come to **Poneloya** for a relaxing day at the beach. It is about 12 miles from León. A hotel is available for food and drinks, but most people do not spend the night. There is a strong surf here, so watch out.

CHINANDEGA

Chinandega is one of the hottest places around and so is not often frequented by tourists. But if you're looking for a quiet escape, a day or two here will allow you to soak up the colonial charm of the town.

WHERE TO STAY

HOTEL CHINANDEGA, *Four blocks east and 1 1/2 blocks south from southeast corner of Parque Central. Moderate.*

A nice family run place with large beds and a shared bath.

HOTEL GLOMAR, *One block south of Mercado Central, tel 03-412562. Moderate to Expensive.*

This hotel offers rooms with or without private baths and air-conditioning. There is a restaurant on-site.

TO THE SOUTHWEST

MASAYA

Masaya (*City of Flowers*) is 11 miles from Managua and is considered to be the center of Nicaraguan folklore and handicrafts. It also happens to be the most densely populated department. The town has colorful markets featuring woven hammocks, woodcarvings, hemp tapestries, embroidered blouses, and pottery.

Although many come here to buy indigenous crafts, **Volcan Masaya** is not far away. This is the only volcano in Nicaragua where you can drive up to its crater on a paved road for a close look. The view is fantastic. Before reaching the top, stop in at the **Centro de Interpretation Ambiental**, one of Nicaragua's best museums. There's an excellent exhibit on the geological and cultural history of the volcano. The museum also traces other volcanic activities throughout the country and informs visitors of the area's exotic animal and bird life.

Laguna de Apoyo, whose waters supposedly have magical healing powers, is a short distance southeast of town

If you are here between late September and the end of October you can enjoy the **Torovendo carnaval**, a series of parades that portrays the cultural heritage and history of the Masaya people.

ARRIVALS & DEPARTURES

By Bus

Buses to and from Grenada and Managua use the bus depot at the old market, *one block behind La Asuncion Cathedral*. Buses leave to both cities about every 1/2 hour. Buses also stop on the highway north of the town center.

By Train

Masaya is a stop on the Managua-Grenada line. *The train station is 8 blocks north of the back of La Asuncion Cathedral.*

WHERE TO STAY

HOTEL REGIS, *Three and a half blocks north behind La Asuncion cathedral, tel 05-22300. Moderate.*

Accommodations are not luxurious but the shared bathrooms are clean.

HOTEL CAILAGUA, *A half mile south of town road and highway intersection, tel 05-244356. Moderate to Expensive.*

This hotel offers rooms with private bath and has a parking lot that is locked up at night – good for those with a vehicle. Air-conditioning is optional. A decent restaurant is on-site.

WHERE TO EAT

TIP TOP, *Km 27 1/2 Carretera Masaya.*

Great Nicaraguan food.

RESTAURANT SANDALO and **RESTAURANT BAHIA**, *both located at the southwest corner of Parque 17 de Octobre.*

The food is OK but the prices are inflated. The market *comedores* may be the best place to get your money's worth.

GRENADA

Founded in 1524 by Spanaird Hernández de Córdoba and once the grandest and most important cities in the Americas, **Grenada** is now a sleepy town. Situated on the eastern shore of Lake Nicaragua, Grenada carried Latin America's commercial and trading industry for many years. It became a powerful city and was home to the Conservative political party. Although not as glamorous as it once was, Grenada still retains its colonial charm.

If you're looking for historical architecture, this is a great place to visit. Today restoration and revitalization is much discussed, but a lot of work lies ahead.

ARRIVALS & DEPARTURES

By Boat

If traveling to Isla de Ometepe and San Carlos you can catch a boat every Monday and Thursday. *The lakeside dock is 6 blocks east of Parque Central at the end of Calle La Calzada.*

By Bus

Buses leave every 20 minutes for Masaya and Managua. Buses also service Rivas and other southern destinations. *The bus depot is located 7 blocks west and 1 block north of Parque Central.*

By Train

Trains leave daily at 4:55 am and 10 am to Masaya and Managua. *The Grenada train station is 6 blocks north of the northwest corner of Parque Central.*

WHERE TO STAY

HOTEL GRENADA, *East down Calle La Calzada, tel 05-52974. Expensive.*

A colonial-style hotel with nice, airy rooms.

HOSPEDAJE VARGAS, *1/2 block east of Parque Central, tel 05-52897. Inexpensive.*

Clean rooms with shared bath.

HOSPEDAJE CABRERA, *Across the street from Hospedaje Vargas, tel 05-52781. Inexpensive.*

Offers the same accommodations as Hospedaje Vargas but looks a little neater.

WHERE TO EAT

EL LIMONCITO, *near the cemetery.*

Another seafood resturant, the specialty is a local fish called *Guappote*.

EL OTRO, *located on the main square in the Palacio de Cultura.*

Typical Nicaraguan food.

ASESE.

A fish resturant with a nice view. Boat trips to the isletas can be arranged from here.

SOUTHERN PACIFIC

SAN JUAN DEL SUR

This is one of Nicaragua's most popular and pleasant beach towns. Divers especially love this place. The clear waters, coral reefs, and the great variety of marine life make it ideal for scuba diving and underwater photography.

WHERE TO STAY

CASA INTERNACIONAL JOXI, *One and a half blocks east of the market, tel 04-66348. Moderate.*

Looking for a little comfort? Come to this lovely place with private baths and air-conditioned rooms. The hotel gets crowded on the weekend, so you probably should call ahead.

HOTEL ESTRELLA, *Two blocks east of the market/bus stop, tel 04-66210. Moderate.*

Hotel Estrella is right across from the beach and is clean, attractive and has a friendly, helpful staff.

LAGO DE NICARAGUA

Lago de Nicaragua is the world's 10th largest fresh water lake. With over 300 islands, it offers some incredible sights. The Spanish *conquistadors* named it the *Fresh Water Sea*. The lake is so large that salt water marine life have adapted to its environment, including the world's only fresh water sharks. Scientists speculate that it was once part of the Pacific and then was cut off by volcanic eruptions. The slow decline of the water salinity allowed marine life to adapt naturally.

The largest island in the lake is **Ometepe**, with a population of 28,385 and featuring two volcanoes.

ISLA DE OMETEPE

This is an island worth exploring for its cultural history, archaeological finds, and natural wildlife that prospers in its thick vegetation. The people are warm and friendly, making this a nice place to visit.

ARRIVALS & DEPARTURES

By Boat

Boats go to Isla de Ometepe from Grenada and San Jorge (near Rivas). Boats from Grenada leave on Mondays and Thursdays at 3 pm, docking first at Altagracia and then at Moyogalpa, with return to Grenada on Tuesdays, Fridays, and Sundays. Boats from San Jorge service Moyogalpa Monday through Friday, returning to San Jorge on the same day.

WHERE TO STAY & EAT

In Altagracia

HOSPEDAJE Y RESTAURANT CASTILLO, *One block south and 1/2 block west of the main church.*

Senor Castillo is a friendly gentleman who can give you the oral history of the island and tips on what to see. He offers decent rooms and a pleasant atmosphere.

In Moyogalpa

Bar y Restaurant Moyogalpa, *less than a block up from the dock on the main street. Inexpensive.*

Hospedaje Aly, *less than a block up from Bar y Restaurant Moyogalpa. Inexpensive.*

A basic *hospedaje*, nothing fancy.

RIO SAN JUAN

Rio San Juan is one of the best places to go for nature lovers. The Channel between Lake Nicaragua and the Atlantic Ocean served as a lifeline for the Spanish and today is a main throughway for trading. The river is surrounded by jungles filled with alligators, birds, monkeys and other wildlife. The trip upriver can also give you a glimpse of **Castillo Viejo**, the fort that survived a fierce attack by English pirates in 1762.

If you want to see this treasure you'll need to hop a boat from San Carlos. It is best to travel by boat from Grenada to San Carlos, spend the night at one of the local *hospedajes*, and take the river journey the next day from San Carlos.

8. EL SALVADOR

HISTORY

If you're into pre-Columbian and colonial history, you'll want to visit El Salvador. The Olmec people, whose culture was established in Mexico, migrated to and established settlements in El Salvador at least as early as 2000 B.C. Evidence of this culture is shown in the much-visited giant stone sculpture, the **Olmec Boulder**, located near the western city of **Chalchuapa**. Other archaeological wonders, the pyramid ruins at **Tazumal** and **San Andres** in western El Salvador, give scientists proof of the Mayans' presence in Central America's smallest country. The Mayan Empire, a civilization that ranged from Mexico to Panama and survived well over a thousand years, continues to puzzle archaeologists despite the presence of many elaborate ruins throughout the region.

In the 11th century the **Pipils**, descendants of the Nahuatl-speaking Toltecs and Aztecs, settled in present-day El Salvador. Their culture was similar to the Aztecs, but with heavy Mayan influences. Their culture was based on an agricultural economy, hieroglyphic writing, astronomy and mathematics – and a little human scarifice now and then. Their language, *Nahua*, is still heard in some of the more remote Indian villages. The Pipil's neighbors included the tribes of the **Lempas**, the **Pokomans**, and **Matagalpas**.

The first European contact with El Salvador came in 1524. The conquistador, **Pedro de Alvarado**, who had ravaged Mexico and Guatemala, was soundly rebuffed by the native Pipils on this first military exploit. But in 1540, with revenge and conquest in his heart, de Alvarado returned and thoroughly vanquished the native Pipil. Despite his conquest, El Salvador became only a secondary acquisition in the Spanish Empire.

From 1540 until 1811 the Spanish ruled, and were ruthless overlords. As in other countries absorbed by Spanish conquest, brutal atrocities

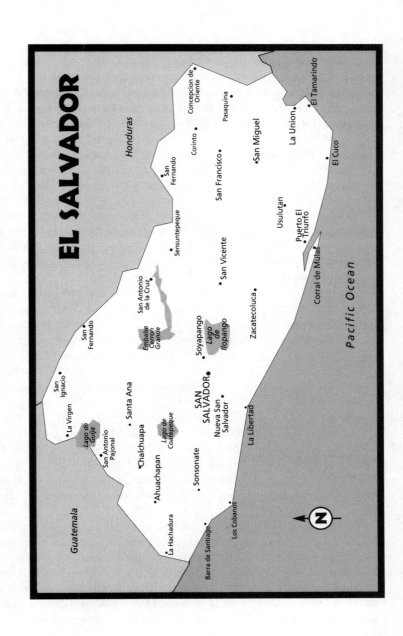

were a way of life. Not until 1811 did **Father Jose Matias Delgado** dare speak out against Spanish rule and so began the process of independence. It was a long and bloody struggle, but finally, on September 15, 1821, El Slavador gained its independence from Spain.

In 1823 the new nation joined Honduras, Guatemala, Nicaragua and Costa Rica in an economic and military confederacy called the **Provincias Unidas del Centro de America** (**United Provinces of Central America**, more commonly known as the Central American Federation). But the union was riddled with regional and ideological conflict and lasted only until 1838. Soon thereafter, El Salvador adopted a constitution as a sovereign nation and began its journey of true independence.

Independence was not for the native Pipil but for the local European aristocracy. During this time the Indians were pushed off their lands and forced to work on large Spanish plantations as virtual slaves. In 1833, an Indian rebellion – given life though the slogan *land for those who work it* – foreshadowed the troubled political future of El Salvador. Although the uprising was unsuccessful, the slogan still rings true for much of the indigenous population today. Even now, the Indian rebellion's leader, **Anastasion Aquino**, is regarded as a national hero.

For most of the 19th century, El Salvador suffered from frequent border penetrations from neighboring states and a string of internal political squabbling. Finally, with the stability from large-scale coffee cultivation, there was a short-lived period of peace. By the early part of the 20th century, 95% of El Salvador's income came from coffee exports. With the stock market crash of 1929, conditions in El Salvador grew extremely harsh, and in 1931, **Augustin Farabundo Marti**, one of the founders of the Central American Socialist Party, led a popular uprising of peasants and Indians. The government responded swiftly and brutally, leaving over 30,000 people dead. This bloody atrocity soon became known as *La Matanza* – the massacre. Although Marti was arrested and killed by a firing squad, his name lives on in the left-wing political party **FMLN** (**Frente Marti Liberacion Nacional**), which represents the labor movement and whose political philosphy calls for a more equitable distribution of wealth.

Increasing political and economic turmoil in the 1970s led to a complete breakdown in political, economic, and social relationships. Poverty, unemployment, and overpopulation exacerbated long-simmering tensions. Popular demonstrations led to acts of civil disobedience and generated labor strikes. Again these activities were vigorously repressed, but this time by the right-wing **National Republican Alliance** (**ARENA**) party, with the use of their now notorious *esquadrones de muerte* (death squads).

Inspired by Nicaragua's socialist revolution in 1979, many Salvadorans felt an armed conflict was the only way to create change. This, combined with fraudulent elections and the assassinations of priests who preached equality among all men, led El Salvador into one of the bloodiest civil wars in Central America **(and that's saying a lot)**. In 1989 Alfredo Christiana, a leader in the ARENA party was elected President. Within the year FMLN launched an all out attack on strategic sites (government building , radio towers, etc.) in an attempt to force the government to make equitable changes in the country. ARENA's death squads retaliated leaving a final death toll of over 4,000.

In 1990, after almost two decades of armed conflict the UN intervened to facilitate peace negotiations. Debates included human rights, economic, judicial, electoral and constitutional reform and the elimination of the death squads **(and a return to human sacrifices?)**. Presently, peace negotiations are still under way and a cease-fire agreement has been signed. Even so, there still are areas of the country where rebels and government forces meet in some not so amicable situations. But, these locations are generally confined to the northeastern regions of the country, leaving the majority of the country open for exploration.

LAND & PEOPLE
Land

El Salvador is situated east of Guatemala; Honduras borders the north and east, while the Pacific Ocean runs along the southern border. El Salvador has 320 kilometers of coastline and some of the most beatiful beaches in the region. Perfect for any vacation!

El Salvador is the tiniest of the Central American countries. It is only 124 miles (200 kilometers) long and takes a mere 5 hours for any bus ride in the country. The countryside is marked by several volcanoes – some still active – and a few good-sized lakes. Resulting from volcanic eruptions, El Salvador is blessed with a rich soil that produces large quantites of coffee, sugar, cotton and fruit – all money-making exports.

Savadorans also raise cattle and sheep in the northwest giving the country a true argricultural feeling. The largest volacanos are the **San Salvador**, the **San Vicente**, the **Santa Anna**, and the **San Miguel**, each with a city or town at its foot. Although potentially dangerous locations, these are good farming places due to the rich volcanic soil (volcano San Salvador erupted last erupted in 1917 and volcano **Ilopango** in 1879). Although hurricanes are not a direct threat to El Salvador, strong Carribbean storms can generate heavy, damaging winds and rains as occurred in 1974 with Hurricane Fifi.

WET & DRY SEASONS IN EL SALVADOR

The weather in this delightful country can be quite hot and usually humid. Relief can be found in elevated areas, but these are much closer to volcano openings. So to gain a respite from the heat you could end up taking a lava bath! Two ranges divide the country into three regions, each with its own distinct climates. The **Plains**, *which lay along the Pacific, is at sea level and is very hot and tropical, averaging 80° F. The* **Central Plateau**, *2000 feet above sea level and where San Salvador is located, has a temperature range from 50° F to 90° F year-round (it can get quite chilly at night). The* **Northern Highlands** *rise an additional 1000 feet and have the coolest tempatures in the country.*

El Salvador has two seasons – the **wet** *– el invierno – and the* **dry** *– el verano. The wet season runs from May to November, and produces beautiful clear days with a daily rain storm. Usually they come in the late afternoon, but on occaision it can rain for a few days in a row (it is best not to travel during these wet spells). The dry season runs from December to April and brings the hottest months of the year.*

El Salvador boasts 350 rivers. The largest is **Rio Lempa**, flowing 150 miles from northern to central El Salvador and is one of the most important Pacific watersheds in Latin America. It is also the only navigable river in El Salvador. Traveling by boat, then, is not a viable means of transport.

Earthquakes and volcanic eruptions have been consistent over the centuries. Earthquakes ranging from 6.5 to 7.9 on the Richter scale have struck San Salvador 13 times since 1700. The most recent earthquake occurred on October 10, 1986, causing considerable damage. Although the smallest in historical record (5.4 on the Richter scale), the quake left an estimated 1,400 peoople dead, approximately 20,000 injured, and over 300,000 persons homeless.

People

El Salvador is the second most densely populated country in the Americas, next to Haiti, with about 5.3 million inhabitants and an annual growth rate of 2.5%. The population is remarkably homogeneous, with no significant minority. The breakdown is **89% Mestizo** (a mixture of Spanish and Indian); **10% Indian**, and **1% Caucasian**. The majority of the indigenous population has adopted the Spanish language and culture, leaving only a few local Indian customs and dialects surviving in remote areas of the country.

There is a continual migration from rural areas to El Salvador's cities, causing overcrowding. This situation, plus refugees from the civil war, has left many people displaced and living in poor economic condirtions.

PLANNING YOUR TRIP

Tourism has not been a priority for the El Salvadoran government but neither has it been a prime spot for many vacationers. This situation obviously developed from the civil war that has plagued the country for so many years and the widely publicized human rights violations. Although there are still areas where outbreaks of fighting occurs, it is mostly isolated, allowing citizens and tourists to continue with everyday life. It is important to check with the **Instituto Salvadoreno de Turismo (ISTU)** to get updated safety lists for travelers. *The office is located at 619 Calle Rueben Dario, betweeen 9a and 11a Avenida Sur (tel. 22-8000). It is open Monday through Friday, 8 am to 4 pm.*

The lack of a concerted tourism policy within the government has made traveling unpredicatble at times. Travelers should be patient and flexible because undoubtedly your itinerary will change. So smile and roll with the punches and soak up as much of the cultural life, archaeological sites, and exotic beaches as possible – as well as the good *cerveza*.

RESTAURANTS & HOTELS

The cost of living and travel witin the country is very reasonable. A good meal will usually cost less than $5; meals at the better resturants will cost anywhere from $6 to $10. Tipping is not common, but if your service is exceptional it won't hurt to give a 10% tip. Sometimes the more expensive restaurants will add a service charge to your bill (remember to check your bill for such an arrangement so you don't overpay). Comfortable lodging for a double occupancy can be less than $15, and bus travel is still the cheapest way to get around the country.

NATIONAL HOLIDAYS

New Year's	*January 1*
Holy Thursday	*Thursday before Easter*
Good Friday	*Friday before Easter*
Salvadoran Labor Day	*May 1*
Feasts of San Salvador	*August 3, 5-6*
Salvvadoran Independence	*September 15*
Columbus Day	*October 12*
All Souls' Day	*November 2*
Day of First Cry of Independence	*November 5*
Christmas Holiday	*December 25*

GETTING TO EL SALVADOR

By Air

There are regular flights to San Salvador from the US. The international airport, **Ilopongo**, is about 44 km south of San Salvador near **Comalapa**. The airport has a post office, a bank, and a tourist office that does not hold regular hours. Here are sthe main airlines that service El Salvador, with their US toll-free phone numbers:

- **American**   1-800-832-8383
- **Continental**   1-800-231-0856
- **United**   1-800-241-6522
- **Iberia** 1-800-772-4642
- **Aeroflot**   1-800-429-4922
- **Aviateca**   1-800-327-9832
- **Copa**   1-800-359-2672
- **Lacsa** 1-800-225-2272
- **Taca**   1-800-535-8780
- **Mexicana**   1-800-531-7921

The international airport is about 45 minutes away from downtown. Private taxis are expensive but there are microbuses (*colectivo service*) offered by **Acacya**, available for about $3 per person. *Acacya has an office in San Salvador (71-4937) and at the airport (39-9271).*

When leaving the country by air, the departure tax is aproximately $10.

By Bus

From Guatemala City, San Salvador is only a 6 hour ride along the Interamerican Highway. From El Poy, Honduras, San Salvador is about nine hours. Usually travelers will stop for the night at the eastern El Salvadoran city of Santa Rosa de Lima, which is only about a 5 1/2 hour ride from El Poy.

By Car

If you plan on driving to El Salvador, plan on taking your time and paying some substantial border transit fees. The Mexican/Guatemalan border could run you about $100. When crossing the border into El Salvador, the government requires a valid US or international driver's license, proof of ownership of the vehicle, and usually insurance papers. At the border you will need to fill out a number of forms and you may be asked for an entrance fee.

You'll need a sound automobile to make the trip, although the main roads through Mexico, Guatemala, and El Salvador are in good shape.

The local drivers, however, can be more than you bargained for. Hints: mind your own business, let the speed demons pass, and watch out for animals and people, because they sometimes pop out of nowhere. Basically, don't try to become Mario Andretti, but also don't drive like his grandmother. Be patient and alert.

There are many border crossings on the map, but because of political conflict many of them are closed. The principal crossings are at **Las Chinamas** (Guatemala) and **El Amatillo** (Honduras).

And on your way out, don't forget the departure tax, usually under $5.

Visas & Documents

Check with the Salvadoran consulate in Washington, D.C. on regulations concerning **visas**. Currently most foreigners need a visa to enter El Salvador, obtained from a Salvadoran consulate prior to arriving at the El Salvadoran border, but the immigration office advises all travelers to check shortly before entering the country because visa requirement can change at any time. – welcome to Central America! North Americans and Europeans may be asked to supply the consulate with a fee of approximately $10, a passport photo, a police-clearance letter (stating you have not committed a felony), and a letter from your employer testisfying to your employment. Always call the consulate and find out what you need exactly before arriving to obtain a visa. This will save you a few trips and much aggrevation.

The visa stamp is good for a single entry within 90 days of being issued. The maximum stay in El Salvador is limited to 30 days, but officials may decide to give you less time. Acutally, officials may deny you entry to the country (visas have a disclaimer allowing officials to deny you entry at the border. This could be based on a number of reasons, so be well dressed and polite.). Once in El Salvador, you can have your visa extended twice allowing a total stay of three months. Visa extensions cost less thasn $3 dollars, and you'll also need two passport-size photos. Anything more than a three-month stay requires a **temporary resident's permit**, good for one year, which can be obtained at the El Salvador immigration office (see below).

Visas can be extended at the **Office of Immigration** *in San Salvador (21-2111), located in the federal building in the Centro Gobierno. The office is open Monday to Friday, 8 am to noon and 1:30 to 4 pm.*

To get a visa you must contact an El Salvadoran embassy or consulate. In the United States, El Salvador has consulates in Houston, Los Angelos,Miami, New Orleans, New York, and San Fransico, in addition to its embassy at *3308 California Street, NW, Washington DC 20008 (202) 265-3480.*

Other El Salvadoran consulates are located in:
- **Belize**, *120 New Road, Belize City (44-318)*
- **Canada**, *150 Kent Street, Suitew 302, Ottawa, Ontario KEP5P4 (613) 239-2938)*
- **Colombia**, *Carrea 9, No 80-15, Oficina 503, Bogota (212-5932-0012)*
- **Costa Rica**, *Avenida 10, Calle 33 &35, Los Yoses, San Jose (24-9034)*
- **Guatemala**, *12 Calle 5-43, Zona 9 , Guatem,ala City, (32-5848, 36-2421)*
- **Honduras**, *Colonia San Carlos, No 205, 1 block from Blvd Morazan (32–5045)*
- **Mexico**, *Paseo de las Palmas 1930, Lomas de Chapultepoec, Mexico DFg 1100 (596-3390)*
- **New Zealand**, *24 Seccombes Rd, Epsom,Auckland 3 (549-376)*
- **Nicaragua**, *Pasaje Los Cerros, Avenida del Campo, No 142, Las Colinas (71-734)*
- **Panama**, *Via Espana, Edfificio Citibank, 4th Floor, Panama City (23-3020)*
- **UK**, *5 Great James St, London WCI 3DA (071-4320-2141)*

Currently, there are no vaccination requirements, but it doesn't hurt to get a booster shot. Consult with your phisician about this.

Customs

Customs is generally not a problem, especially when arriving by plane. Arriving by car or bus you might be scrutinized more, but if you keep well dressed and remain polite everything should be fine. Since custom officials have a great deal of discretionary power here's a few tips for dealing with them: present yourself as a clean, respectable person. Do not wear dark, camouflage-type clothing or any other military-stlye clothing. Do not bring in anything that could be construed as 'communist.' For example, take care of the books you bring, T-shirts and visa stamps from countries with leftist tendencies (particularly Nicaragua and Cuba). You can ask the immigration officials to stamp a seperate piece of paper when entering and leaving one of these countries if you wish to enter El Salvador.

Generally visitors are sent through customs without a problem. The importation of fruits, vegetables, plants and other agricultural products are restricted and questionable materials can be confiscated. You are allowed to bring in two cartons of cigarettes and two bottles of liquor duty free.

GETTING AROUND EL SALVADOR

El Salvador is such a small country that it is relatively easy to get around. The most economical way to travel is by bus; they will get you to almost any destination. Renting a car is also convenient but is much more expensive.

By Air

The national domestic airline is **Transportes Aereos de El Salvador** (**TAES**), which flies to the country's major cities – but the cost is more than its worth. The country is so small that you can take a bus or drive to any part of the country in under 5 hours. If you do want to fly, you will need to get to the domestic airport, **Areopuerto Ilopango**, *about 13 km east of San Salvador.* TAES's main office *is in the Edificio Plaza (27-0314).* Again, getting to the airport, waiting for your plane, and flying to your destination often takes almost as much time as going by bus or car.

By Bus

Buses are the cheapest way to get around the country. The shorter bus rides (30 minutes or so) will run you about 15¢. The 1-2 hour trips are about 25-50¢ and the most expensive are 60¢. Two dollars will basically take you anywhere in El Salvador. Remember, on the weekend these rates go up. Although the buses run frequently it would be wise to check the schedule (these change quite frequently). Also, there are a few destinations that run only a few buses per day. If you are going on a relatively long journey try to get on the first bus out of town, since it is not advisable to travel after dark. Buses rarely travel at night and final departures are anywhere between 4 pm and 6 pm.

Don't be shocked when the buses start picking up passengers on the roadside. Drivers will pack as many people as possible onto the bus. Another bit of in-country info: at times you will have to change buses at a highway junction (*desvio*) to get to your final destination.

By Car

The highways in El Salvador are in good shape and the **Inter-American Highway** runs right through the center of the country. There are smaller roads which are passable but it is best to stay on those roads that are paved unless you have a 4-wheel drive vehicle.

Carry proof you own the car or are renting it along with a drivers license (US licenses and international licenses are valid) and proof of insurance is recommended. There are car rental agencies at the airport but are pretty expensive. In the city, a popular rental company is **Sure Rent** *(25-1810).*

BASIC INFORMATION

Some basic information that should prove useful to you follows:

BUSINESS HOURS

Normal hours of business are Monday through Friday, 8 am to noon and 2 pm until 4 or 5 pm. Shopping hours are usually longer, but Saturday's hours are usually only in the morning.

ELECTRICITY

Electricity in El Salvador is tricky. It never stays on for long periods of time, so bring a flashlight with extra batteries. The water supply is just as unpredictable, so fill up a bowl of water before showering in case the water is turned off while shampooing.

HEALTH

Talk to your physician about any shots you may need before traveling to El Salvador. Although vaccinations are not required, some doctors recommend a tetanus and gamma globulin shot before venturing to Central America. Water in the country is not purified so it's best to drink sodas or bottled water, which is safest. When eating out in the country, be conservative unless you have a cast-iron stomach. Rice, beans and eggs are always available and usually filling.

Even though the meat is of good quality, make sure it is thoroughly cooked. Also ensure that your vegetables are thoroughly washed before eating. If there is any doubt in your mind leave it on your plate. Seafood is a specialty item in many areas and is generally safe to eat. In case you do get dysentery, ask your doctor to prescribe some appropriate medication. Dehydration from such a situation can be deadly.

MONEY

The monetary unit in El Salvador is the **colon**. Like the US dollar, the colon is based on the decimal system. Bills are issued in units of 100 (the highest), 50, 25, 10, and 5 colones, and coin denominations are 1 colon, and 50, 25, 10, 5, and 2 centavos.

As of April 1995, the exchange rate is 8.7 colones = $1.

El Salvador welcomes US dollars; you can change them most anywhere. If you have travelers checks, make sure they are American Express. Be prepared to present the original receipt. Try to get most checks in denominations of $20. The larger hotels and banks can cash $50 and $100, but smaller denominations are better for smaller hotels. You don't want to waste precious travel time looking for a bank that is capable of cashing a large traveler's check. Your best bet is to change money at the local banks or the *casas de cambio* (exchange houses).

There is a bank at the **central post office** in the Centro Gobierno, at the airport, and, on the west side of the Parque Infantil, there are *casas de cambio*. There are black market exchangers all over the place where you can get a reasonable exchange rate, but it's always safer going to the bank (the *casa de cambio* at the airport generally has a higher exchange rate).

MAIL & PHONE

The mail (*correos*) is unreliable and can take forever. Do not send valuables or money through the mail because it most certainly will never arrive at its final destination. Don't even think about sending anything politically controversial unless you want to be harassed by thye local police. A letter costs around 10¢ to the United States and 15¢ to Europe, but if you want to be sure your mail arrives, use either the international courier services (like **DHL**) or the express services that charge you approximately $1.50 per letter. The two largest express companies are **Gigante Express** and **Urgente Express**, which are safe, reliable (mail arrives within 10 days), and are practically in every town in the country. If you want to receive mail have it addressed to: *your name, Lista de Correos, name of the city, name of department, El Salvador, Centro America.*

To telephone anyone, travelers will use the national phone company **Antel**, which has an office in virtually every town. Operators can connect your international and domestic calls. To connect with an **AT&T Direct USA operator**, *dial 190*. Public telephones are available but often it's better to use the Antel offices.

SAFETY

Personal safety is always a concern for travelers. Tourists will always be a logical target, so try to blend in and don't flaunt wealthy possessions. Don't travel after dark and certainly don't walk around alone after dark – especially women. Due to the shortage of electricity there are no street lights, which leaves you vunerable to petty crime. Keep items out of backpack side pockets; it's an easy mark for an experienced pick pocketer.

If you like the fanny packs, make sure you keep it on your stomach and tie the cord to your belt. I had a friend who lost all her money, even though she was wearing her pack properly. Some clever thief managed to unzip the pouch and take her money without her even realizing it (this was in a market place). So be aware, and go with the money belt. In this pouch, hidden under your garments, hold your passport, credit cards, travelers checks and extra cash. Wear this at all times! Do not leave valuables and identification in the hotel – always carry identification with you and never leave your money behind.

SHOPPING

Your hotel or the **Instituto Salvadoreno de Tourismo (ISTU)** can give you information on local shopping areas. El Salvador has a number of distinct local crafts including textile arts, ceramics, and woodwork. A favorite memento of those visiting El Salvador are the *sorpresas* (surprises) made in the town close to San Salvador called **Ilobasco**. They are tiny ceramic pieces about the size of a walnut with little carvings on the inside. Other favorites are the textiles made in San Sebastian and brightly painted wooden artwork from Las Palmas and traditional basketry made by the Pipil Indian population. All of these crafts can be found in their towns and cities of origin, in the **Mercado Ex-Cuartel**, or the **Mercado Nacional de Artesanias** in San Salvador.

The most expensive items are imported products. This includes camera eqipment, film, tape recorders, radios, western-style clothing, food, and gasoline. It's best to purchase these items (except for gas, which is kind of tough to carry with you!) before going to El Salvador. Also stock up on film, because it is difficult to find outside San Salvador. If you're driving and in need of repairs, expect a long wait and a big draw on your spending money.

TIME

El Salvador is 6 hours behind Greenwich Mean Time.

WEIGHTS & MEASURES

The metric system is generally used in El Salvador. The main exception is gasoline, which is often sold by the gallon. There are also some local non-metric measurements, but ask the seller to translate it into their metric equivalents.

SAN SALVADOR

El Salvador is a developing country without a strong economy. This has led to urban migration that has resulted in a new urban poor. With unemployment at almost 50%, poverty is apparent everywhere you turn, as well as desperate street vendors who are prepared to sell anything. There is of course a small, elite wealthly population, but they have managed to section themselves off into nicer enclaves.

The capital city of **San Salvador** lies in the *Valle de las Hamacas*, the valley of the hammocks, at the foot of the San Salvador volcano, which was called the mountain of *queztaltepec* (quetzal birds) in the *Nahua* language. Although the weather is generally mild, the air pollution generated by the city hovers above the city, and it can often be quite uncomfortable.

San Salvador was originally the capital of the colonial province of Cuscatlin. Between 1834-1839, it was the capital of the United Provinces of Central America. In 1839, it finally became the capital of El Salvador. Although San Salavador has an extensive history, earthquakes in 1854, 1873, and 1986 devastated many buildings. Today there are only a few remaining structures that will give you a glimpse of the city's earlier history.

ORIENTATION

San Salvador is an easy city to get around. You just need to remember that *avenidas* (avenues) run north to south; *calles* (streets) run east to west. In the center of the city there is an intersection from which all roads begin to number out, with **Avenida Espana** to the north; **Avenida Cuscatlin** to the south; **Calle Delgado** to the east; and **Calle Arce** to the west. On the west, *avenidas* have sequential odd numbers, increasing as they go out, while east *avenidas* have the even numbers, again increasing as they go out. The *calles* are numbered similarly, with the north *calles* odd, and the south *calles* even.

The *avenidas* running north to south are *norte* on the north side of **Calle Arce/Calle Delgado**, and *sur* on the south side of it. *Calles* on the west side are *poniente*; on the east side all *calles* are *oriente*.

Other major roads include **Boulevard de los Heroes**, **Paseo General Escalon** and **Alameda Juan Pope II** (formerly *7a calle*), renamed because Pope John Paul II walked down it during a visit in 1983.

For general tourist information, the **Instituto Salvadoreno de Tourismo (ISTU)** *is on 619 Calle Ruben Dario, between 9a and 11aAvenida Sur, tel. 22-8000. Its hours are Monday through Friday, 8 am to 4 pm.* Travelers can find free maps (although the best maps are found at ESSO service stations) and tourist information, including literature in Spanish and English. The staff is also very helpful. It would be a good idea to get a list of political hot spots in the country in order to avoid these areas. This information can also be obtained at the **airport** *(39-9454) open daily from 8 am to 5 pm.*

The **post office** in San Slavdor is *in the Centro Gobierno, and is open Monday through Friday 8 am to 5 pm, Saturdays from 8 am to noon.* At this location there is also the **Banco Cuscatlan** where money can be exchanged. If you are adventurous, black market exchangers are always lurking outside – but take only cash. Money can be exchanged at *casas de cambio*, which can be found in many locations around the city and at the airport. But it is best to change the bulk of your money in town.

WHERE TO STAY

For each listing, the first number you'll see in parentheses is the telephone number. In some instances, the address is not given, because of poor or non-existent street markings and/or addresses. Most of the hotels below are in the budget category.

In El Centro

This is smack in the middle of the city, so it can get pretty noisy, crowded, and congested. It also unsafe to walk around at night, especially alone, so please exercise common sense and caution here.

HOTEL RITZ CONTINENTAL, *(22-0033) 219 7a Avenida Sur*
This is probably one of the nicest hotels in the city. Rooms have all amenities like TV, telephone, and private bath.

HOTEL CENTRO, *(71-5045) 410 9a Avenida Sur*
This is a modern hotel and always kept clean. All rooms have a TV, telephone, and private bath.

HOTEL CUSTODIO, *(22-5603)*
This is a large impersonal hotel but it is kept clean. Single/double rooms are available along with a private bath at an extra cost.

HOTEL NUEVO PANAMERICANO, *(22-2959) 113 8a Avenida Sur, 1/2 block from Mercado Ex-Cuartel*
Dark rooms, each with a private bath concealed by a half partition.

HOTEL SAN CARLOS, *(22-8975)*
This hotel is set back from the noisy street and has small, clean, comfortable rooms. All have private baths.

Near the Terminal de Oriente

This group of hotels is located on *Calle Concepcion*, about a ten minute walk from the **Terminal de Oriente** bus station.

HOTEL IMPERIAL, *(22-4920)*
This is a three story hotel with meals served in the quaint central courtyard. These rooms are available with or without private bath.

HOTEL IZALCO, *(22-2613)*
This is another large hotel with clean rooms that come with private baths and ceiling fan.

Near Terminal de Occidente

Near the **Terminal de Occidente** (western) bus station you'll find a number of very basic guesthouses, all in the same block as the bus station on *Boulevard Venezula*.

HOTEL OCCIDENTAL, *(24-3648)*
This hotel is opposite the bus station. It's open 24 hours and uses a common bath.

HOTEL PASADENA, *(23-6627)*
This hotel is a few doors down to the west of the bus station. It has simple accommodations, all with a private bath.

HOTEL ROMA, *(24-0256)*

This is very close to the Hotel Pasedena, offering rooms with or without bathrooms.

Suburban Guest Houses

These guest houses are approximately a five minute walk from the center of town, but are located in a residential area.

THE AMERICAN GUEST HOUSE, *(71-0224)*

This is a clean, comfortable place to hang your hat, built in Spanish style. Hot water baths are available with these rooms. There are some larger rooms.

THE AMERICAN GUSET HOUSE ANNEX, *(71-5613)*

This annex is directly across the street from the American Guset House. Prices are similar and there is a small restaurant.

FAMILY GUEST HOME, *(21-2349)*

This guest home sits on a side street and offers single/double rooms with a private hot bath. There are also several larger rooms that sleep 4 to 12 persons. Meals are served in a courtyard resturant.

XIMENA'S GUEST HOUSE, *(26-9268)*

This is a small, clean and quiet place that is close to the *Boulevard de los Hereos*, with all its resturants and nightlife. This is a relatively safe area that has a nice ambiance supplied by local street musicians (*mariachis*). Single/double rooms are available with private bath, but they also offer weekly rates for single/double occupancy with a shared bath.

FLORIDA GUEST HOUSE, *(26-1858)*

This also is a small and clean place close to Ximena's. It offers single/double rooms with private bath.

WHERE TO EAT

In the Centro

RESTAURANTE ENTREMESES DE FREDERICO, *a few blocks to the west of the centro. It is only open at lunch time, Monday to Saturday from noon to 2 pm.*

This is a good place for lunch that offers patio dining.

TEATRO CAFE, *in the Teatro Nacional building towards the back. It's open every day, usually from 8 am to 6:30 pm and on Friday and Saturday nights.*

A pleasant place. During the week there is a guitarist who plays during lunch and in the early evening.

Boulevard de los Heroes

In this area there are many inexpensive resturants and a lively nightlife.

MANOLO RESTAURANT has a great atmosphere, with the street musicians playing in the background. The food is pretty good, and there is a bar if you want to just sit down for a drink.

KORDI, *open weekdays from 8 am to 5 pm, Saturday from 8 am to 3 pm.* For you vegetarians there is hope! Kordi is a tiny vegetarian resturant and health food store with a good reputation. And there's also **LA ZANAHORIA**, *open weekdays from 8am to 6pm, Saturday from 8am to 2pm,* which is a large, popular open-air restaurant and cafe. Rounding out the vegetarian scene is **ARBOLDE VIDA**, *within walking distance of La Zanahoria.*

NIGHTLIFE & ENTERTAINMENT

There are three areas within the city that cater to nightlife: **Zona Rosa**, **Colonia Escalon**, and **Boulevard de los Heroes**. All are safe for walking around at night.

Teatro Nacional is always a good place to start when looking for some fun. Offerings include musical performances, dance, theater and other performing arts. **Teatro Café** has a musician on hand during the week from 12:30 pm to 2 pm and from 4:30 pm to 6 pm. On Fridays from 6:30 pm to 11:00pm there's an open mike, and on Saturdays there are literary readings from 6:30 pm to 8 pm. This is a popular hangout for students

Boulevard de los Heroes is popular among the street musicians. Their most popular hangout is the **Manola Restaurante**, *open from noon to 11 pm Sunday through Thursday and noon to midnight Friday and Saturday.* The musicians also flock to **Plaza Masfrerrer**. All around the plaza there are cafés, usually staying open until the wee hours of the morning.

Zona Rosa is probably the most well-known and most expensive place to spend an evening in San Salvador. Some of the hots clubs are **Club M**, **Faces on the Top** and **Mario's**. You can also find entertainment within the more expensive hotels.

Colonia Escalon is another of the ritzier areas that have good restaurants, cinemas, and nightclubs.

EAST OF SAN SALVADOR
LAGO DE ILOPANGO

Lago de Ilopango is the largest lake in El Salvador, about 15 km long and 248 meters deep. The lake was formed from a gigantic volcano crater and has become a popular spot for swimming, boating, and fishing, The best place to visit on the lake is **Apulo**. Here there is a government *Turicentro* that will charge you a small fee for the use of good swimming lots, picnic tables, and restaurants. Boat rides are also available for an additional fee. The restaurants serve the local specialty of fresh water fish and crayfish. There are a few simple hotels in Apulo including **Hotel Colonial** and **Hotel Las Malvinas**.

If you are coming from the city, take bus No 15 from the stop at Avenida Espana and 3a Calle Poniente.

COJUTEPEQUE

Cojutepeque is located east of San Salvador and is best known for *Cerro de las Pavas* (Hill of the Turkeys), a park that overlooks Lake Ilopango and has a spectacular view of the surrounding volcanoes. In the park stands a shrine of the **Virgin de Fatima**. The statue was brought here in 1949 from Fatima, Portugal. The site was already holy due to the many visions that have reportedly been seen at that spot. Sundays get very crowded and at times you can run into groups and individuals who have traveled far just to pay tribute. May 13 is Virgin Day.

If you are coming from the city, take bus No 113 which comes from Terminal de Oriente - the trip takes around an hour.

ILOBASCO

Ilobasco in *Nahua* means 'the place tortillas made from young corn,' but this place is not famous for its tortillas but for its traditional crafts. The famous ceramics of Ilobasco, the tiny *sorprosas*, can be purchased in the village or in the capital city at the **Mercado Ex-Cuartel** and the **Mercado Nacional Artesanias**. Tours are given to show visitors the making of clay to the painting of the delicate figures. **Centro Artessanal de Ceremica Banafi**, *open Monday to Friday from 8 am to noon and 1pm to 5pm*, and at the **Taller Escuela de CeramicasKiko**, *open from 8 am to 5pm Monday through Saturday*. Ilobasco is about 1 1/2 hours away from San Salvador.

Take bus No. 111 from Terminal de Oriente or from Cojutepeque.

SAN SEBASTIAN

San Sebastian is about an hour away from the city and is another town rich in traditional handicrafts. This is a textile town, making elaborate goods on large wooden looms. The annual fair is January 20 with a festival the week preceding it.

Bus No. 110 departs from Terminal de Oriente in the city, but you can also travel directly from Cojutepeque.

SAN VINCENTE

San Vincente is a town to the southeast of San Salvador and is most commonly known for **El Pilar**, a colonial church built in the 1760s. It sits at the base of the volcano **Chinchontepec** in the Valle Jiboa. The local festival is November 1. Just outside of San Vincente lies **Amapulapa**, a wonderful park with restaurants and recreational swimming pools. Also close by you'll find **Lake Apastapeque**.

Bus No. 116 runs regularly from Terminal de Oriente to San Vincente and from there Bus No. 171 can shuttle you to Amapulapa.

ZACATECOLUCA

Zacatecoluca is home to **Ichanmichen** (about 1 km outside of town; buses are available), the largest tourist attraction in the area. It is a wooded area of many acres with natural springs, pools, flowers, fish, and trails. The natural springs are dedicated to ancient folklore characters, some with statues overlooking their pool of water. The park does not close at night so cabanas are available.

Bus No. 133 can take travelers from Terminal de Occidente in San Salvador; buses are also available from San Vincente.

WEST OF SAN SALVADOR
BOQUERON

Boqueron, *Big Mouth*, the smaller of the two peaks on the San Salvador volcano, towers over the capital city and the Valley of the Hammocks. This is a great place for hiking and grabbing a spectacular view of not only the city but the surrounding mountaintops, including **Volcano Chinchontepes** that looms over **San Vincent**e. On a clear day hikers can even see the coast.

Those of you with hiking boots can enjoy a 1 1/2 km hike around the perimeter of the volcano's crater, and you can even hike down 543 meters into the crater itself.

Those interested in hiking the volcano should take bus No. 101 to Santa Tecla, departing regularly from the bus stop at 3a Avenida Norte near Ruben Dario. From Santa Tecla, bus No. 103 departs hourly near the second (western) plaza to the village of Boqueron. From there it's a 1 1/2 km walk up to the crater (make sure to ask the bus driver if he is going all the way to the top). Note the time the last bus departs from the village.

LOS CHORROS

Los Chorros is a popular spot for residents and foreign visitors alike. It is not far from San Salvador and can relax even the most stressed-out person. Three pools of natural volcanic springs provide a cool refreshing respite from the chaotic city. There is an abundance of flowers and ferns that provide a backdrop for the pretty waterfalls, which welcome those who wish to stand underneath them.

Los Chorros is open daily, 8 am to 5 pm. Go during the week if you can, otherwise you may run into the crowds. A small entrance fee is charged.

Lunch is available at the restaurant at the **Hotel Monteverde** (*28-1903*), a clean pleasant place to spend the night. Reservations are suggested.

Los Chorros is right off the Inter-American Highway. Bus No 79 leaves regularly from the stop at 13a Avenida Sur and Calle Ruben Dario.

RUINAS DE SAN ANDRES

If you came to see the ruins of an ancient civilization, go to the Ruinas de San Andres. These ruins were first discovered in 1977 and there are still a number of areas that need to be excavated. This site also goes by the name of *Ruinas de la Campana de San Andres* and is the home of the **Museo Nacional David J. Guzman**, which houses many of the artifacts found at the site. *The ruins are open Tuesday through Sunday (9 am to noon and 2 pm to 5 pm. Admission is free.*

Take any bus heading west of San Salvador at the Terminal de Occidente, get off at 33km just past Rio Sucio where there is a sign for the ruins, and walk north (to the right) a few meters to the ruins.

LAGO DE COATEPEQUE & CERRO VERDE

These two lakes are closer to Santa Ana and Sonsonate than they are to San Salvador, but they can be visited from the capital by car.

SOUTH OF SAN SALVADOR
PARQUE BALBOA

This is a wonderful park to visit, just a short 12 km away from downtown San Salvador. Situated in the *Planes de Rendoes* district, it is a 28-hectare woodland with gardens and trails; a skating rink; shady picnic areas; and, plenty of cafés. There is a small admission fee.

From the city take bus No 12 'Mil Cumbres' from the eastern side of Mercado Central, at 12 Poniente.

PUERTA DE DIABLO

The Deveil's Door is formed by two huge boulders (a single stone split in two) resting atop *Cerro Chulo*. This is a great place to view the surrounding region.

Not far past Parque Balboa, visitors can take bus No 12 'Mil Cumbres' right to Puerta de Diablo.

LA LIBERTAD

For a relaxing day at the beach, this is the closest one to San Salvador. La Libertad is a coastal village with popular black sand beaches. You can spend the night or just make a day of it.

Bus No 102 departs regularly from 4a calle Poniente and 17a Avenida Sur.

COSTA DEL SOL

This is another beach, but a bit farther away and with white sand. Costa de Sol is much hotter than La Libertad. There are several luxury resorts here that cater to those who wish to spend the extra cash.

Bus No. 495 goes to Costa Del Sol from Terminal de Occidente.

WESTERN EL SALVADOR

LA COSTA DEL BALSAMO

Between La Libertad and Acajutla is **La Costa del Balsamo**, the *Balsam Coast*. This area once supplied much of the world with balsam, but now there are few trees left. The trip to the Balsam Coast is quite lovely. The highway cuts into the cliffs, which allows for some fantastic views. **Zunzal** is the most famous beach in this area, but there are plenty others for you to discover.

WHERE TO STAY

HOTEL LOS ARCOS, *(35-3490). Mastercard and Visa accepted.*

This is a fancy hotel complete with fountain and swimming pool. All rooms have air conditioning, TV, telephone and private bath. Singles/doubles are available.

LA CABANA DE DON CHEPE, *(71-1313)*

This place is set back from the beach, with a swimming pool in the courtyard. Holidays and weekends see these rooms filled up with Salvadoran families, so think twice if you don't want the child bonus. Hammocks are available to take to the beach and meals are served for an additional cost. Rooms are available with or without private bath.

ATAMI BEACH CLUB, *(23-9000)*

This is a private beach club that can be visited by day with rooms available. The club is populated mostly on the weekends and holidays (the restaurant is open at these times only) so if you plan to spend the day or a few weeknights, pack some food. Atami has swimming pools, tennis clubs and good beaches.

EL BOSQUE

Near La Libertad, **El Bosque** is a family-style park with swimming pools, a small lake for canoeing, and lots of areas for the kids to play. It is visited mostly in the daytime but there are a few inexpensive rooms available. Camping is an option here too.

Bus No 287 from La Libertad runs west along the Costa Del Balsamo and then heads toward Sonsontate.

LAGO DE COATEPEQUE

Lago de Coatepeque is a beautiful sparkling lake at the base of **Cerro Verde**. Swimming, fishing, and boating are all popular activities at this holiday and weekend getaway. There are many private homes along the lake, so access is difficult if you don't enter through the *balnearios* or the hotels.

If traveling from San Salvador take any bus heading west towards Santa Ana. Get off at El Congo. At El Congo you hop bus No 220 coming from Santa Ana. If you are traveling from Santa Ana just take bus No 220 to Lago de Coatepeque.

WHERE TO STAY

BALNEARIOS LOS OBREROS. If you ask the Ministerio de Trabajo in San Salvador, with written permission, you may be able to stay here for free. It is a popular place for government workers on the weekends so you may just get lucky. Accommodations are cabins with beds, showers, and private kitchens.

HOTEL TORREMOLINOS, *(41-1859)*

This is a relatively expensive hotel with clean rooms and a private bath. There is a swimming pool and a nice restaurant to serve you meals with a waterfront view.

HOTEL DEL LAGO, *(78-2873)*

This Spanish-style hotel has a romantic terrace overlooking the lake. There is a swimming pool and a beautiful beach.

WHERE TO EAT

There are many small restaurants around the lake that serve good food at more reasonable prices than the area hotels.

CERRO VERDE NATIONAL PARK

Above **Lago de Coatepeque** is a national park atop an old volcano. There is plenty of wildlife, camping sites, and a magnificent hotel. From this vantage point visitors can view the lake below and get a look at the **Volcano Izalco**.

Volcano Izalco is still considered active but has not erupted since 1966. For over 187 years, Volcano Izalco was continuously erupting, giving those on land and at sea a marker glowing from lava. For many sailors this was the 'Lighthouse of the Pacific.'

Buses travel from Santa Ana to Cerro Verde twice a day (10:30 am and 3:30 pm). If coming from San Salvador you can get off at El Congo and catch the Santa Ana bus from there.

WHERE TO STAY

HOTEL DE MONTANA, *(28-1903)*

This hotel sits atop Cerro Verde and has twenty large rooms, all complete with a fireplace, TV, sitting area and a private hot bath with tub. Ten of the rooms have a view of the surrounding forests and the other 10 have a view of the volcano. The hotel has a bar, cafeteria, and a restaurant. Reservations for the weekend and holidays must be made at least 15 days in advance, while weekday reservations must be made at least 8 days in advance. Some rooms sleep up to 4.

SANTA ANA

Santa Ana is the second largest city in El Salvador and the main hub for western El Salvador. The atmosphere is more laid-back than San Salvador and, because of the close attractions, it is a good base for day trips. Santa Ana has a few interesting sights, including the city's gothic **Cathedral** and the **Teatro de Santa Ana**.

Buses run from Santa Ana to: San Salvador; Las Chinamas (border crossing); Ahuachapan; Sonsonate; the ruins of Tazumal, Chalchuapa; Lago de Coatepeque; Cerro Verde; Metapan; and, direct buses to Guatemala City.

WHERE TO STAY

HOTEL LA LIBERTAD, *(41-2358)*

This is a small clean place to stay. All rooms have a fan and a private bath.

INTERNACIONAL INN, *(40-0804)*

This is a more modern hotel but is situated on a noisy road (try to get a room away from the street). All rooms have a fan, TV, and private bath with the availability of one double, two beds, and/or three beds all priced accordingly.

HOSPEDAJE SAN MIGUEL, *(41-3465), 126 Avenida Jose Sur.*
Shared and private bath.

HOTEL LIVINGSTON, *(41-1801), 10a Avenida Sur, No 17-A .*
Shared and private bath.

HOTEL NUEVO ROSEVELT, *(41-1702), 8a Avenida Sur and 5a Calle Poniente*
Private baths and overhead fan.

MONTECRISTO CLOUD FOREST

The cloud forest is approximately 14 km northeast of **Metepan** (north of Santa Ana). The forest is an international nature reserve that sits on the borders of El Salvador, Guatemala and Honduras. Only 2100 meters above sea level, this is the most humid place in the region (a wet 100%

humidity)! This is a habitat for exotic and rare wildlife and can be visited only during the months of October through March. It is closed the rest of the year due to the mating season of its inhabitants.

To visit the forest travelers must get permission from the **Department of National Parks** *at the Ministry of Agriculture in San Salvador (77-0622).* This is not usually a problem but getting to the forest is (see below). You can camp in the forest; usually a ranger will ask you for your permission slip.

Buses from Santa Ana can take you to Metepan, but after that the only way to get to the forest is by a 4-wheel drive vehicle or, if you're feeling hardy, you can walk the 14 km route. It is possible to hire a driver to bring you there and back.

CHALCHUAPA & TAZUMAL RUINS

The Mayan ruins of **Tazumal** are the most important ruins in El Salvador. Tazumal means *pyramid where victims were burned* in the Quiche language. Archaeologists believe this area to have been inhabited since 1200 BC, with some estimates placing the first settlements about 5000 BC. Currently the town of **Chalchuapa** sits atop most of the ancient city.

Tazumal has great importance because artifacts recovered are signs of active trade between the ancient civilizations from Panama to Mexico. At the site is a restored ancient pyramid and a playing field.

Tazumal is open from 9 am to noon and 1 pm to 5:30 pm, and admission is free. Bus No 218 from Santa Ana will get you there in about 20 minutes.

If crossing the border at Las Chinamas to Guatemala, you may want to stay in the town of **Ahuachapan**. It is a small quiet town and is a good place to rest before continuing on with your journey.

Bus No 202 and 210 run between Ahuachapan and Santa Ana. Bus No 263 comes from the border Las Chinamas.

WHERE TO STAY
HOSPEDAJE CASA BLANCA, *102 Calle Gerado Barrios (43-1505)*
HOSPEDAJE GRANADA, *8a Calle Poniente (family run)*

ACAJUTLA

This is El Salvador's principal port and happens to have a nice beach that attracts lots of tourists and surfers in the summer.

Buses run from Acajutla to Sonsonate frequently.

WHERE TO STAY
MOTEL MIRAMAR, *(532-3183)*
Simple rooms with a private bath. During the holidays the swimming pool is filled with water.

EASTERN EL SALVADOR

Check out the political situation before traveling to this region. There are a few spots that are of interest, especially **San Miguel** and **La Union**, but be aware of the current political climate. The only advisable border crossing to Honduras is at El Amatillo.

SAN MIGUEL

San Miguel is El Salvador's third largest city and was founded in 1530. There are lively markets here where people from all over the region come to buy and sell. The town sits at the base of the **San Miguel Volcano**, also called **Chaparrarique**, which is still active. The last eruption was in 1976.

San Miguel is on the Inter-American Highway, about 3 hours east of San Salvador and a little more than 2 hours from the Honduras border at El Amatillo.

For information, stop off at the **Office of Immigration** *on 1a Avenida Norte between 2a and 4a Calle Poniente.*

Buses run routinely from San Miguel to San Salvador, departing from San Salvador at Terminal Oriente, the last bus leaving the capital at 4:30 pm. Bus No. 324 goes to La Union, on the Golfo de Fonesca, and bus no. 330 goes to El Amatillo. On the way the bus stops at the village of Santa Rosa Lima (a small village with a marketplace where many border crossers stop to shop).

The few sites in town include the **Cathedral of San Miguel**, dating back to the 18th century; the **Antiguo Teatro Nacional**; **Las Ruinas de Quelepa**, *a half hour ride from San Miguel, local bus No 90*; and, for you sun-worshipers, a volcanic beach with black sand, **Playa El Cuco**, *a two hour ride on bus no. 320.*

WHERE TO STAY

HOSPEDAJE MODELO, *(61-3122), 17a Calle Poniente, No 208.* Large, clean rooms with fans, all with private bath.

BOARDING HOUSE DIANA, *(61-3314), close to the bus station.* Another clean, pleasant place with air-conditioning and private bath.

Two more decent places to stay in town are **HOTEL SAN RAFAEL**, *(61-4113), 6a Calle Oriente, No. 704*, and **EL MOTELITO**, *(61-3748), 10a Avenida Sur, No. 104.*

WHERE TO EAT

COMEDOR PATY, *three blocks behind the cathedral at 4a Calle Oriente.* One of the few places that stays open at night. You choose your meal straight from the kitchen. *Open every day from 6:30 am to 9:30 pm.*

A. FOOD & DRINK IN CENTRAL AMERICA

If you haven't yet sampled the many culinary delights of Central America, you're in for a treat! Below you'll find descriptions of national cuisines for four of the countries in the region: Costa Rica, Belize, Honduras, and Guatemala. There is much overlap, but there are also differences between countries. Let us know what you think.

COSTA RICA

Costa Rica's food holds few surprises. Most restaurants in San José serve what they call "international cuisine," which is a combination of standard North American and European fare. *Bistec* (beef), *pollo* (chicken) and *pescado* (fish) are most often encountered on the menu, usually in forms that need little explanation. They're generally accompanied by rice and cabbage. You might as well call this Tico-style food, rather than Tico specialties.

COMIDA TÍPICA

Genuine Costa Rican specialties are generally enjoyed at home, in a very rare city restaurant that advertises its *comida típica* (native food), in simple country eateries, and as snacks. One of the most common plates in the countryside is *casado* - fish, meat or chicken married (*casado*) to rice, beans, and chopped cabbage. *Gallo pinto*, rice and beans with herbs and spices, is the staple of poor people's diets, usually served with tortillas, flat cakes made of ground, lime-soaked corn.

But you don't have to be poor to enjoy the taste of black beans and tortillas, or of *olla de carne* (a stew of beef, yucca and plantain), *chiles rellenos* (stuffed peppers), *maduros*, or *plátanos fritos* (fried plantains), *chilasquiles* (meat-filled tortillas), *pozol* (corn soup), *tamales* (corn dough with a filling of meat, rice and raisins, steamed in a banana leaf, and served at holiday times) or *tayuyas* (tortillas stuffed with cheese or beans, a Guanacastecan regional specialty). You merely have to search these dishes out, if you're not part of a Costa Rican household.

The **Cocina de Leña** is one San José restaurant that challenges the prejudice against eating Costa Rica's soul food in public.

SNACKS

Traditional snack foods are easier to find. Vendors sell *pan de yuca* (yucca bread), *gallos* (tortillas with fillings), *arreglados* (bread filled with meat and vegetables), *empanadas* (stuffed pastry), and various other starchy items at markets, on trains, and at bus terminals. Other favorite snacks are tropical fruits (papayas, bananas, passionfruit, pineapple and many others) sold from carts everywhere in the country, and pipas, young juice coconuts, as well as the juice of fruits and sugarcane (*agua dulce*).

Pejivalle, a pasty palm fruit, and palmito, heart of palm, are enjoyed as hor d'oeuvres or in salad. *Cajeta*, a heavy milk fudge, is served sometimes as dessert, as it is in other Latin countries. Hot sauces and peppers — chiles — are condiments to be added as desired, and are rarely included in a dish before serving.

THOSE ODD FRUITS & VEGETABLES

Some of Costa Rica's vegetables and fruits will be only sketchily familiar. Rice is served at almost all meals, but a common vegetable is *chayote* (chay-YO-teh), known as *huisquil* in Guatemala, *batata* in the Dominican Republic, *chocho* in Jamaica, *christophee* in other parts, and vegetable pear in the dictionary. It's terrific when baked with butter or mashed like a potato, but when just boiled and plopped in front of you it can be, as a reader complains, "horrible in taste and texture." *Yuca* (manioc, or yucca) sometimes draws similar reactions.

Fruits can draw more pleased reactions. *Cas* and *granadilla*, full of seeds, are used to flavor fruit ices, and in preserves. The delicious *zapote* (the same as the Mexican *mamey*), brown on the outside, with a large pit and blood-red flesh, may be consumed directly, as can large mangos, but not cashew fruit (*marañón*).

When in doubt about whether you can peel and eat an unfamiliar fruit, or whether you'll be stuck with a squishy, seedy, tart-tasting mess, buy your fruit from a sidewalk stall in San José, or at least take a good look at one, to see what's in season and what the locals do with it.

MANY CUISINES

Gourmet restaurants in San José and nearby cook tender meats to order and serve them in delicate sauces along with crisp vegetables. Chinese, German, French, Italian, Swiss and even the better "international" restaurants produce superb results with foods that are fresh and abundant throughout the year. At the less expensive eateries in San José, and in the countryside, culinary arts and sciences are, unfortunately, not widely diffused.

What you'll find can most generously be described as home-style cooking — wholesome, reasonably priced, but not finely prepared — comparable to the fare at Joe's Diner. A *bistec* (steak) will generally be a tough, nondescript slab of meat, served with some of the grease in which it was cooked. The fate of fresh seafood is often similar. Vegetables, other than rice, beans and cabbage, when they are served, will have been in the pot for too long. None of this will do you any harm, especially when you pay only three to four dollars for your meal.

Not that you won't find some pleasant surprises. At one anonymous roadside eatery near Cañas, I had the most exquisite gallo pinto, seasoned with fresh coriander and a hint of garlic, accompanied by a thin *bistec* smothered with onions. There, as elsewhere, the presence of truckers was a good sign. And at a few coastal resorts, standards are as high as in San José. But generally, when you leave the capital, lower your expectations.

Fortunately, almost every small town in Costa Rica has a Chinese restaurant, if not two or three, where *chao mein* (chow mein), chop suey and more elaborate plates tease bored palates. These restaurants are not gourmet-class, but they work interesting and edible combinations from Costa Rica's fresh vegetables and meats.

Service in Costa Rican restaurants is relaxed. You'll never be presented with a bill and ushered toward the cash register in order to make way for the next customer. The pleasures of lingering over nothing more than a pastry and a cup of coffee can still be enjoyed. If leisurely dining isn't what you have in mind, you'll have to call the waiter over to place your order, and to ask for the bill (*la cuenta*). A 13% tax and a 10% service charge will be added on. No additional tip is required.

MMMM . . . ¡CAFÉ!

Costa Rica's excellent coffee, of course, is enjoyed with all meals, and is often prepared by pouring hot water through grounds held in a sock-like device. Costa Ricans claim all kinds of special properties for their brew — it won't keep you up at night, nor jangle your nerves, but will stimulate you to overall better functioning. This is only understandable chauvinism. Sometimes coffee is served with sugar already added —

specify without (*sin azúcar*) if you prefer it that way. *Café con leche* (coffee with milk) is at least half milk. The concept of coffee with cream is understood only in hotels and restaurants that have a foreign clientele.

WHISKEY & EGGS

Costa Rican eating and drinking habits in restaurants can be disorienting. As you have your morning coffee and bacon and eggs, the Tico to the left of you will be starting the day with a whiskey and a chicken sandwich. The Tico to the right of you will be cutting into a steak, accompanied by a beer. The Tico in front of you enjoys a rum and Coke while he ponders the menu. You are too polite (or dumbfounded) to turn to the Tico behind you.

I have no explanations for these customs, except to state that restaurant food is not necessarily derived from what is traditionally eaten at home. *You* were taught that eggs are eaten at breakfast. Maybe they were not. Explaining an affection for liquor is a touchy thing, but there is no doubt that Costa Ricans enjoy their booze in large quantities and at varied hours.

HOOTCH & BEER

Much of what is consumed is *guaro*, which can be roughly translated as "hootch." Guaro is the cheapest liquor, distilled from sugarcane, and sold in bars by the shot. Sugarcane is also the base for rums of various qualities and maturities, some of them quite good. Most guaros and rums are distilled by a government-owned company, but other companies make quite drinkable vodkas and gins. Local whiskeys and liqueurs are also available, but their quality is not as high. The exception is Café Rica, a coffee liqueur, which costs more than other Costa Rican drinks. Imported alcoholic drinks are quite expensive (with the exception of whiskey, which is only moderately expensive), so if you have a favorite brand, bring a bottle or two or three with you, or shop at the duty-free store in the airport before you pass through customs. Rum and Coke (*Cuba Libre*) is Costa Rica's most popular mixed drink.

Local fruit wines are interesting for amusement, but are not taken seriously by anyone who has enjoyed wine elsewhere. Imported wines are quite a luxury. Wine drinkers will have to fork out the money (a few duty-free bottles won't go very far), or else switch to another drink for the duration.

An excellent alternative to wine is beer. Pilsen is a superb brand of beer (in my opinion), and Tropical and Bavaria (*rubia* in local slang) are almost as good. There are various others, such as Imperial (*águila*) to suit different tastes, including a local version of Heineken, that is a ringer for the real thing, but for the health warning — *tomar licor es nocivo para la salud (drinking liquor endangers health)* — which all alcoholic beverages must carry. Beer is inexpensive — as little as 50¢ in some eateries, rarely more than $1. The alcohol content is 4%.

Bars are generally the cheapest places to drink, and they serve a dividend: *bocas.* These are hor d'oeuvres that range from cheese and crackers to little sandwiches that, over enough rounds, will constitute a meal in themselves. In classier joints, you pay for the bocas.

The easiest place to buy liquor, beer or wine is at a supermarket. In small towns with no supermarkets, try the bars themselves or small general stores (*pulperías*), though the selection will be more limited. The deposit on a beer or soda bottle is usually as much as the price of what's inside.

BELIZE

Lower your sights. The food in Belize is usually none too elegant and none too cheap, the service is none too good. An expanding hospitality industry is sorely pressed to come up with the kind of food visitors appreciate. The few notably good cooks are hired away every few months.

Some of the makings of memorable eating experiences are available in Belize. Fish, lobster, shrimp and many other forms of seafood are fresh, abundant, and relatively cheap. Beef is plentiful, and a number of tropical fruits and vegetables are available. But preparation and presentation can be down at the heels, or at least inconsistent. In one of the better restaurants in Belize City, a succulent, inch-thick steak might be served with greasy fried potatoes, and nothing else. A delicious boiled lobster may be married to lukewarm spinach fresh from the can, and paper-textured white bread.

One problem is that Belizeans themselves have no tradition of dining out for pleasure. Belize's ethnic groups have a variety of staple foods and cuisines, but they enjoy them at home. Eating out is a relatively recent phenomenon. The demand for creative cooking comes almost exclusively from visitors, foreign residents, and from the small but growing class of bourgeois Belizeans.

TRADITIONAL & LOCAL CUISINES

This doesn't mean you can't eat well in Belize. Some marvelous food is available, if you look for it.

Creole cuisine dominates, of course. The most typically Belizean dish is rice and beans, a holdover from the times when these foods, in dry form, were carried to logging camps in the interior. Rice and beans can be prepared with vegetables, coconut milk, and spices, with lobster, chicken, or beef, ending up as a tasty melding of flavors. But in a small-town eatery, they might be nothing more than what the name says. Ask before you order.

Game meat — gibnut (paca), armadillo and brocket deer — is traditionally stewed in pots over open fires. You can occasionally find game meat on the menu at hotels in Belize City, to please curious visitors, and at country lodges. But most Belizeans no longer hunt their own food, and what gets distributed commercially is beef, chicken, and imported ham. On small-town menus, you'll generally find fried chicken and steak (a thin, somewhat tough piece of meat), usually served with rice, sometimes with French fries, almost never with a green vegetable. This isn't typically Creole, it's just what is served to hungry stomachs until they can get home.

More traditional is "stew chicken" and "stew beans," exactly what they sound like, slow-cooked in dark sauce, and tasty. Conch fritters, meat pies, cow foot soup, and fruit pastries are also Creole staples that are available in some Belize City eateries.

For breakfast, you may find fry jacks (corn cakes), Johnny cakes (biscuits), and, in genuinely Belizean homes, fried fish and Creole bread.

A hamburger is often the best choice on the menu in Belize, if you're not familiar with an eatery — it's likely to be large and tasty. But specify what you want on it — you'll sometimes find the most unpredictable dressings pre-applied.

If you want something other than a bottled soft drink or beer to go with your meal, you're generally out of luck. Canned fruit juices and fruit drinks from Mexico, of all places, are sometimes available. Places with good taste offer fresh-squeezed orange juice, or limeade ("lime water").

FOREIGN CUISINE

Other cuisines carry better to restaurants. Hispanic food — tamales, salbutes (something like the tostadas of central and northern Mexico), beef seared over the coals or cooked in sauces, and eggs with tortillas and beans are served in restaurants everywhere in Belize, and not just to Hispanics. Where else but in Belize would you find Gilhooly's tortilla factory?

Most noticeable, though, are Belize's Chinese restaurants, many founded in the last ten years by new immigrants. In a small town where not long ago you couldn't find a place to eat, there are now two or three Chinese diners.

But even if you like Chinese food, be warned that the version in Belize is not *haute cuisine*, and you could overdose quickly. Almost all Chinese restaurants have the same menu: chow mein, chop suey, egg foo young, and one or two house specialties, along with rice and beans, steak, and sandwiches. You can usually have a meal for $6 or less, though sometimes the tab is surprisingly high. Decor is limited or non-existent, you get a paper napkin, your special house chicken comes on big pieces of bone, and the sweet-and-sour sauce is mostly sugar. A couple of hotels and restaurants in Belize City serve something more elegantly Chinese.

FOOD AROUND THE COUNTRY

In Belize City, the food scene is generally better than elsewhere in the country, though there are still rough spots. The curried shrimp surrounded by condiments, attractively served, turns out to be mushy. Nevertheless, it's obvious that people are making an effort. In hotels here and there, on the cayes, in Placencia, and around Cayo, there are some pleasant surprises, and standards are getting higher. If you limit your expectations, ask about what you're getting, and choose carefully, you won't be disappointed. Just don't trust that the food is good unless some reliable recent visitor has reported it to be so. And even then, the cook could well have gone off.

The fact that so much food is imported to Belize in dry or preserved form makes it easy for backpackers and budget travelers to picnic. Even in the smallest settlements, stores offer tinned powdered milk, Australian butter, and Dutch cheese, all at reasonable prices. (There are also cans of peas and carrots for $3, but you can pass these up.) Don't forget your can opener. Fresh oranges and grapefruits as well as tomatoes, onions, and a few other vegetables are available everywhere on the mainland.

RUM, BEER, & WINE

Belize produces a number of brands of rum, all of them quite good, as well as Belikin and Crown beers, which come in a small bottle, and may or may not agree with your tastes. Dutch, German and American brands of beer are also widely available, at about double the price of domestic brew, hence the Belikin slogan, "the only beer worth drinking."

A premium version of Belikin tastes something like American beer, comes in a larger bottle, and carries an American price. There is also Belikin stout, which I prefer to all of the above. Wines made from cashew fruit and berries are a traditional product of Belize, though they're getting hard to find, as American and French wines take over the market.

HONDURAS

As a tourist, you'll probably run across "international food," American cuisine adapted to local tastes and cooking abilities; and food served in the local *style*, without showing off too many local specialties. Your grilled steak (*bistec a la parrilla*), pork chop (*chuleta*) or chicken (*pollo*) might be accompanied by fried plantains (*plátanos fritos*), beans (*frijoles*) and/or rice (*arroz*). Garlic and onion are part of any sauce, and vegetables may include the less-than-familiar *chayote*, or vegetable pear, or *yuca* in place of potatoes. Sometimes you'll get *tortillas*, flat cakes of corn, used in place of bread.

At home, Hondurans enjoy *tapado* (vegetable-meat soup), *mondongo* (tripe soup), *enchiladas* and *tamales* (meat and sauce in tortillas or corn dough), and black beans. You can partake, too, if you get friendly with the locals, or if you take a meal or two at the bare tables and benches in a local market, where food shops cook up filling, cheap repasts for people of modest means.

On the streets, you can snack on fruits to your heart's content. Peeled oranges and bananas are sold for a few cents each, with or without salt and nutmeg, according to your taste. You'll also find *mermelada de papaya* (papaya marmalade) and other local fruit preserves at every breakfast table.

Along the highways, you'll see food stands everywhere. Field corn, cooked in the husk over open fires, is especially popular. It's not the sweet corn you might know — it's chewy, and usually quite pale — but it's fresh and delicious.

In the Bay Islands, and among the Black Caribs, or Garífuna, of the northern coast, there are some variations. Seafood of all kinds is eaten more than elsewhere, and coconut invades many a menu item: mixed with rice, or, more usually, in coconut bread.

Soft drinks are sold everywhere in Honduras, probably more than are healthy for the population. On the other hand, carbonated beverages are always safe to drink, while the local water supply may be suspect. Coke, Fanta, Stripe and Canada Dry ginger ale and soda water are major brands, sold for from 25¢ to 60¢, depending on whether you're consuming at a street stand or in a hotel restaurant. The price is for the contents only. The bottle costs as much as what's in it, or more. If you intend to walk away as you drink, ask for your soda in a plastic bag (*en una bolsa*) with a straw (*con pajilla*).

There *are* local wines in Honduras, made from fruits and imported grape concentrate, but having said this, I'll say no more — they're not worth further mention. And you can find imported California, French and Chilean wines, though by the time they reach your table, with hefty import duties, taxes and markups added on, they'll generally cost at least double what they would in the United States, and sometimes much, much more.

If you're a drinker, moderate or otherwise, this leaves you to choose between hard liquor and beer. Imported liquors, like wines, are pricey.

Local rum (*ron*) is generally quite good, while gin (*ginebra*) and vodka are just so-so, though their defects can be well hidden in a mixed drink.

If you're so inclined, I can recommend that you try the beer. Salva Vida, Imperial, Nacional and Port Royal are all light beers, and to me, they all taste the same, which is good enough. Port Royal comes in a fancy bottle, suitable for taking home as a souvenir.

GUATEMALA

Unless the visitor makes an effort, he or she will probably encounter few distinctively Guatemalan dishes. Many restaurants serve what is locally known as international cuisine, which is a combination of standard North American and European food. Most items on the menu will be familiar to visitors: *bistec* (beef), *pollo* (chicken), *mixtos* (ham and cheese sandwiches), *hamburguesas* (hamburgers) and *chuletas* (pork chops). Some of this nomenclature can be deceiving in the native environment, however.

For example, except at a McDonald's or a similar franchise, your *hamburguesa* will consist of a speck of meat in a bath of mayonnaise and wilted lettuce. Be tolerant at modest eateries, or ask in detail about what you'll be getting.

COMIDA TÍPICA

Genuinely Guatemalan dishes are usually eaten at home, in the more inexpensive restaurants, at eateries in markets, and in a rare better restaurant advertising its *comida típica* (native food). In such places, the bistec is likely to be a strip of beef, grilled over coals and served with chirmol, a sauce of fresh tomatoes, onions and spices. The hot sauce — *salsa picante* or *salsa de chile* — is usually placed in a separate dish for the diner to add as he chooses. Those who want a tender piece of meat ask for *carne guisada*, stewed beef served in a tasty sauce. Most beef in Guatemala is on the tough side, since it's fed on grass and isn't aged or chemically tenderized. But the better restaurants manage to soften it, sometimes by pounding a steak into a large wafer.

Vegetables on the side may include *güisquil* (chayote, or vegetable pear), a vine vegetable cooked in much the same way as potatoes, and there might also be some guacamole, mashed avocados served with onions and tomatoes. Instead of bread, a native-style meal is served with tortillas, flat cakes made from corn soaked in lime water (which softens the outer layer of the kernel) and then ground. *Tortillas* are used to scoop up bits of food and to make little fold-over sandwiches. Ideally, the meal should be taken in a small eatery, with a charcoal or smoky wood fire in the corner, and the food washed down with beer or steaming cups of coffee to fight the chill of the evening air.

A standard breakfast in a small town will probably include oatmeal (*mosh*) flavored with sticks of cinnamon, or corn flakes served with hot milk, eggs, black beans with white, crumbly cheese, tortillas, and steaming cups of weak coffee. The ideal setting is the same.

Other local specialties include *plátanos fritos* (fried plantains, or green bananas); *chiles rellenos* (stuffed peppers); breaded and fried native vegetables, such as *pacaya*, which has long, finger-like appendages and a slightly bitter taste; and *chuchitos* (corn dough stuffed with spicy meat and wrapped in a corn husk). An occasional appearance will be made by the Mexican *enchilada*, a tortilla rolled around a chicken or cheese filling.

These items are often sold as snack food by roadside vendors who stand at highway junctions and scurry aboard buses that stop for a few minutes. You'll also have a good chance of finding native food at a place that advertises itself as a *comedor* (diner), rather than at a *restaurante*.

HOLIDAY FARE

A few items appear only on holidays. *Tamales*, the big brothers of chuchitos, may have a spicy turkey filling in the corn dough, and are wrapped in banana leaves. *Fiambre* is a sort of salad prepared from vegetables and bits of meat and fish. *Pepián* is a dish of meat served in a dark, spicy sauce that includes squash seeds.

COFFEE

Coffee is one of the disappointments in many a smaller Guatemalan restaurant. Guatemala produces some of the finest mild coffee in the world. But most of the good stuff goes for export. Cheaper restaurants will usually serve a weak brew made from second-rate beans, often with the sugar already added. You'll get used to it, maybe, as a part of standard native cuisine.

When the coffee's good, however, it's superb. In better restaurants, coffee is served either black, or half and half with hot milk. You'll sometimes be brought small pots of hot coffee and milk to mix in the proportions that please you.

The concept of coffee with cream is understood only in hotels and restaurants that have a foreign clientele.

MANY CUISINES

Variety in food is provided by restaurants serving foreign cuisines, usually Spanish, Italian, German, or Chinese. Most of these are in Guatemala City, but there are Chinese restaurants in many large towns, and Chinese dishes may be served in any eatery. These days, chow mein (or *chao mein*, as it's known locally) is as Guatemalan as a good *hamburguesa*.

SERVICE IN RESTAURANTS

Quality of service in restaurants varies considerably. In general, things will be a bit slower than what you're used to, and you'll have to call the waiter when you want the bill (*la cuenta*). There's no need to tip in small, family-run eateries, though it's a nice gesture. In larger restaurants, ten percent of the bill is usually an adequate tip.

For reassurance about whether the food's safe to eat, see "Health Concerns" in Chapter 6.

ALCOHOL

Guatemala produces excellent beer. Popular brands include **Gallo** (Rooster) and **Cabro** (Goat). Higher-priced brands are **Medalla de Oro** and **Marzen**. **Moza** is a good dark beer. Most beers come in the bottle, though draft beer is available in Guatemala City and some of the larger towns. Beer has a relatively light alcoholic content, but if you are not used to the altitude, it will wallop you.

The most popular local liquors are rum (*ron*) and *aguardiente*, which, like rum, is distilled from sugar cane. Most rums are quite good. Decent vodka is also distilled locally. Guatemala produces whiskey, anisette and a variety of other spirits. Like rum and aguardiente, they're low-priced, but quality is not high.

Liquor is sold in bottles ranging from an *octavo* (an eighth of a liter, or about four ounces) to a *botella* (three-quarters of a liter, or about a fifth). Imported liquor is quite expensive.

Local wines are made from grape concentrates, oranges, and cashew fruit. They're hardly award winners. One brand of grape wine, **Viña Real**, is better than others, while **Santa Vittoria** can be tolerated by the unfussy. Local vermouths are also a fair bet. The cheaper wines are quite sweet, and are best mixed with soda water or avoided. Look for a wine made from *mosto de uva* or *pasas*, rather than an orange or cashew-fruit wine.

The cheapest places for drinking are ordinary bars without licenses to serve mixed drinks. At these places, you can order a small bottle of liquor for about the price you would pay in a grocery store, along with some juice or bottled sodas, and mix your own drinks at your table. Cheap bars are best frequented in small towns. Bars serving mixed drinks are more expensive. You can often bring your own bottle to better restaurants, but you may have to pay a bottle fee, called the descorche. Most bars serve snacks (*boquitas*) with drinks.

All supermarkets in Guatemala City have large selections of liquor, wine and beer. In smaller towns, you can purchase liquor by the bottle at bars and small grocery stores (*tiendas*), though the selection may not be large. The deposit on a beer or soda bottle may be higher than the cost of the contents.

B. WHAT TO PACK

Before you pack, consider what your trip will be like. You don't want to carry items that you'll never unpack. On the other hand, you don't want to leave behind any essentials. If you'll be at one hotel, take as many changes of clothes as you feel you'll need (as long as it all fits in a couple of suitcases), and do the laundry when you get home.

The other extreme is incessant travel, a single change of clothes in a carry-on bag, and laundry in the hotel sink every night.

A compromise is to leave a large bag at your hotel, and carry a smaller bag as you travel around the country. At the very least, this leaves you less vulnerable to having all your possessions stolen.

COSMETICS, TOILETRIES, & PERSONAL ITEMS

Bring your cosmetics, toiletries, and small personal items, including:
• sunglasses
• your favorite personal kit of aspirin or substitute, sunscreen, sunburn cream, malaria pills, spare prescription glasses, mosquito repellent (most convenient in stick form), etc.

HABITS, HOBBIES, & VICES

According to your habits, hobbies and vices, take your:
• camera and waterproof bag, film (more than you think you'll need), batteries
• camping equipment and flashlight
• personal stereo
• duty-free cigarettes and liquor.

OTHER BASICS

If you'll be traveling by bus and train, a travel alarm will come in handy for early departures. Hotel wake-up calls are unreliable.

PACKING CHECKLIST

Essentials include:
- *passport*
- *travelers checks*
- *tickets*
- *some U.S. cash in small-denomination bills*

Money Belt

Protection against pickpockets and robbery is an increasing concern in Costa Rica. Take a money belt or some other concealment device if you feel comfortable wearing it.

Which Clothes?

Take lightweight all-cotton clothing, or loose-fitting, easy-care cotton blends.

Include:
- *hat with ample brim. Cheap straw and cotton hats are widely available in Costa Rica, but the fit is often tight on gringos.*
- *a bathing suit*
- *a few shirts or blouses*
- *shorts*
- *comfortable walking shoes. Running shoes will suffice for most purposes. Boots can often be rented when really needed.*
- *socks, underclothes*
- *sandals or surf shoes*
- *at least one lightweight, long-sleeved top and slacks, in case you overexpose yourself to the sun, and for evenings, when mosquitoes might lurk.*
- *a light sweater or jacket for cool mornings and evenings, though a heavier one or a jacket will do at higher altitudes, such as at the peaks of volcanoes.*
- *a raincoat or umbrella if you travel during the rainy months (May through mid-December in San José), or along the Caribbean side of the country. Taking shelter from the rain for a few hours, however, is no special inconvenience.*
- *a dress-up outfit, if you think you might need it – a jacket and tie, or dress, or formal blouse and skirt.*
- *for forest reserves, slippery jungle walks, and back-road travel, take one set of expendable lightweight clothing, preferably with long sleeves.*

Reading Material

Bring a moderate amount if your visit will center on San José, where you can trade your used books, or a pile of books for a beach holiday.

Keep your luggage as light as practical, tag your bags inside and out, and pack your indispensable items in your carry-on. Remember: if you don't take it, you might not find it, or you might not want to pay the price.

FISHING & DIVING

Fishing and diving equipment are available, but the selection is sometimes limited, so you're often better off with your own gear. If you have them, take:
• mask, snorkel and fins
• regulator, buoyancy compensator, certification card, wet suit (optional)
• preferred fishing equipment (unless assured of availability)

PACKING FOR OTHER SPORTS

Take equipment for other sports that you practice, as it is unlikely to be found easily in Costa Rica.
• a day bag for carrying purchases, sunscreen, whatever. I prefer a see-through mesh bag — it shows that you have nothing worth stealing. Fanny packs are insecure and undesirable in towns, but fine for the countryside.
• A pen or two, including a felt-tip pen (ballpoints clog up) and paper.

GENERAL INDEX

COUNTRY INDEX

FROM THE PUBLISHER

Our goal is to provide you with a guide book that is second to none. Please remember, however, that things do change: phone numbers, prices, addresses, quality of food served, value, etc. Should you come across any new information, we'd appreciate hearing from you. No item is too small, so if you have any recommendations or suggested changes, please write to us.

Have a great trip!

Open Road Publishing
P.O. Box 20226
Columbus Circle Station
New York, NY 10023

TRAVEL NOTES

TRAVEL NOTES

TRAVEL NOTES

TRAVEL NOTES

TRAVEL NOTES

YOUR PASSPORT TO GREAT TRAVEL! FROM OPEN ROAD PUBLISHING

THE CLASSIC CENTRAL AMERICA GUIDES - ALL NEW!

COSTA RICA GUIDE by Paul Glassman, 6th Ed. This classic travel guide to Costa Rica remains the standard against which all others are judged. Discover great accommodations, reliable restaurants, pristine beaches, and incredible diving, fishing, and other water sports. Revised and updated. **$16.95**

BELIZE GUIDE by Paul Glassman, 7th Ed. This guide has quickly become the book of choice for Belize travelers. Perhaps the finest spot for Caribbean scuba diving and sport fishing, Belize's picture-perfect palm trees, Mayan ruins, tropical forests, uncrowded beaches, and fantastic water sports have made it one of the most popular Caribbean travel destinations. Revised and updated. **$14.95**

HONDURAS & BAY ISLANDS GUIDE by J.P. Panet with Leah Hart and Paul Glassman, 3rd Ed. Open Road's superior series of Central America travel guides continues with the revised look at this beautiful land. **$14.95**

GUATEMALA GUIDE by Paul Glassman, 9th Ed. Glassman's treatment of colorful Guatemala remains the single best source in print. **$16.95**

OTHER TITLES OF INTEREST

AMERICA'S MOST CHARMING TOWNS & VILLAGES by Larry Brown. The book everyone's talking about! Larry Brown shows you the 200 most charming and quaint towns in America - all 50 states included. Great coverage of each town includes local sights, interesting historical notes, and up-to-date information on where to stay and eat. **$14.95**

WALT DISNEY WORLD AND ORLANDO THEME PARKS by Jay Fenster. *The* complete guide to Disney World and all of Orlando's great theme parks (including Sea World, MGM Studios, Busch Gardens, Church Street Station, Spaceport USA, and more), shows you every attraction, ride, show, shop, and nightclub they contain. Includes 64 money-savings tips for hotel, airfare, restaurant, attractions, and ride discounts. **$12.95**

SOUTHERN MEXICO & YUCATAN GUIDE by Eric Hamovitch. Complete coverage of beautiful southern Mexico and the Yucatan peninsula. Discover terrific beaches, majestic Mayan ruins, great water sports, and the latest on hotels, restaurants, activities, nightlife, sports and more! **$14.95**

PLEASE USE ORDER FORM ON NEXT PAGE

ORDER FORM

Name and Address: _____
_____
_____
_____ Zip Code: _____

Quantity	Title	Price

Total Before Shipping _____

Shipping/Handling _____

TOTAL _____

Orders must include price of book <u>plus</u> shipping and handling. For shipping and handling, please add $3.00 for the first book, and $1.00 for each book thereafter.

Ask about our discounts for special order bulk purchases.

ORDER FROM: **OPEN ROAD PUBLISHING**
P.O. Box 20226, Columbus Circle Station, New York, NY 10023